PEACEKEEPERS AND CONQUERORS

MODERN WAR STUDIES

Theodore A. Wilson
General Editor

Raymond A. Callahan
J. Garry Clifford
Jacob W. Kipp
Allan R. Millett
Carol Reardon
Dennis Showalter
David R. Stone
Series Editors

PEACEKEEPERS AND CONQUERORS
THE ARMY OFFICER CORPS ON THE AMERICAN FRONTIER, 1821–1846

SAMUEL J. WATSON

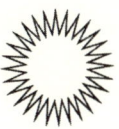

UNIVERSITY PRESS OF KANSAS

© 2013 by the University Press of Kansas
All rights reserved

Published by the University Press of Kansas (Lawrence, Kansas 66045), which was organized by the Kansas Board of Regents and is operated and funded by Emporia State University, Fort Hays State University, Kansas State University, Pittsburg State University, the University of Kansas, and Wichita State University

Library of Congress Cataloging-in-Publication Data

Watson, Samuel J.
Peacekeepers and conquerors : the Army Officer Corps on the American frontier, 1821–1846 / Samuel J. Watson.
pages cm. — (Modern war studies)
Includes bibliographical references and index.
ISBN 978-0-7006-1915-3 (cloth : alk. paper)
1. United States. Army—Officers—History—19th century. 2. Southern States—History, Military—19th century. 3. United States—Territorial expansion—History—19th century. 4. Civil-military relations—United States—History—19th century. 5. Indians of North America—Wars—1815–1875.
I. Title.
UB413.W39 2013
355.00975'09034—dc23
                              2012049027

British Library Cataloguing in Publication Data is available.

Printed in the United States of America

10 9 8 7 6 5 4 3 2 1

The paper used in this publication is recycled and contains 30 percent postconsumer waste. It is acid free and meets the minimum requirements of the American National Standard for Permanence of Paper for Printed Library Materials Z39.48-1992.

CONTENTS

Preface and Acknowledgments . . . vii

1. National Military Expansion on the Western Frontier: Contexts, Comparisons, and Outcomes . . . 1

2. Subordination and Discretion: The Dilemmas of Expansion, Peacekeeping, and Civil-Military Relations on the Northwestern Frontier . . . 35

3. Federal Authority under Attack: The Army, Southern States, and Citizens during the Adams Administration . . . 77

4. The Army and the Jacksonians Tangle on the Southern Frontier: Indian Removal and Civil-Military Relations, 1831–1834 . . . 105

5. The Army and the Cherokee Removal: Coercive Diplomacy, Peacekeeping, and Preventing Mass Atrocities amid Civil-Military Tensions, 1836–1838 . . . 141

6. "This Thankless . . . Unholy War": The Crisis of Military Reactions to Removal in the Second Seminole War . . . 179

7. "The Duty of a Soldier to Obey": Disenchantment, Dissent, and the Crucible of Professional Accountability in the Second Seminole War . . . 209

8. Changing Military Attitudes toward Foreign Relations: The Dilemmas of Discipline and International Order along the Canadian Border, 1815–1838 . . . 239

9. Maintaining National Sovereignty and Keeping International Peace: Operations to Suppress American Filibusters against Canada, 1838–1841 . . . 271

10. The Dilemmas of Sovereignty and Expansion:
    Peacekeeping and Law Enforcement along
    the Texas Border, 1821–1838   317

11. Cautious Interventions and Power Projection:
    Southern Plains Diplomacy, Dragoon Expeditions,
    and the Initial Move into Texas   345

12. Manifest Destiny Meets Military Professionalism:
    The Army Faces Britain and Mexico, 1844–1846   379

Conclusion. Army, State, and Profession in
Nineteenth-Century American History   416

Appendices   443

Notes   465

Selected Bibliography   579

Index   619

PREFACE AND ACKNOWLEDGMENTS

During the last decade there has been considerable debate over the American experience in warfare. The U.S. Army has been condemned as a Cold War dinosaur, celebrated for its rapid conventional victory in seizing Baghdad, again condemned as a blunt instrument fighting wars long past, and most recently celebrated for transforming itself in the midst of war, becoming the adaptive force for counterinsurgency and nation building many think it should have become two decades ago. These reactions have often been more political than historical in character. They have fostered greater attention to the "small wars" of America's past, for which I have to be grateful. But the polemical ebb and flow have led to caricatures and straw men, an exaggerated dichotomy between conventional and unconventional, kinetic operations and counterinsurgency (hardly a monolithic phenomenon itself). Through their histories, the United States and its army have engaged in a wide spectrum of military missions and operations, often conventional and unconventional at the same time, which cannot be reduced to catchphrases like "small wars," "Indian wars," or "nation building."

Peacekeepers and Conquerors continues where my previous volume, entitled *Jackson's Sword*, left off, telling the tale of those "constabulary" roles and their effects in the years between the War of 1812 and the war with Mexico, years American historians label the age of Jackson or sometimes, more recently, the age of Indian removal. *Jackson's Sword* examines the first big part of the story—the "problem" of institutional instability, multiple loyalties, and insubordination. The present volume explores the second part—the "solution" of greater professional commitment, experience (as much political and diplomatic as specifically military) developed during extended careers, and accountability to civilian authority, tempered in the forge of frustrating, politically complex constabulary operations along the nation's frontiers. If there has ever been an American way of war—a debatable construct, given its inherent oversimplification—these two volumes show that it was highly variable and adaptive.

On the one hand, American military strategy and operations have been contingent on specific situations and objectives, rather than archetypal military developments (whether from Napoleonic example or technological change) or comprehensive American social phenomena (political ideologies of republicanism and Jacksonian democracy, the citizen-soldier ideal, or antagonism to standing armies). On the other hand, there have been critical elements of continuity in the development of American military institutions and culture, particularly in civil-military relations and the enduring character of American military professionalism. More important than their adaptation to any specific mission, threat, or skill set, the career officers of the national standing army—the army's enduring core—developed quantitatively greater and qualitatively different commitment and cohesion, practical experience (in administration and logistics as well as combat operations), and subordination to civilian authority. Congress and the executive rewarded their effectiveness and accountability with insulation from partisan political attack and substantial autonomy in their implementation of national policy, a monopoly of strategic and operational command they have retained ever since. Hence, this story is as much about American civil-military relations—both on the scene of operations and in the nation's capital—as it is about coercive diplomacy and conquest against Native Americans, Spain, and Mexico.

Jackson's Sword examines the army on the frontier, particularly that in the Gulf South, during the years 1810–1821, concentrating on the actions of Andrew Jackson and his subordinates in the army's Southern Division from 1814 forward. Though the army conducted a number of peacekeeping and law enforcement operations against brigands, marauders, corsairs, and smugglers on the Louisiana-Texas frontier, the Louisiana coast, and Amelia Island off the northeast coast of Florida, and though it frequently used the threat of force to remove whites intruding on Indian lands, most of its attention was directed against Native Americans—Seminoles and Red Stick Creeks—and Spanish rule in Florida. Relentlessly working to drive Spain from Florida, to eliminate possible bases for future British intervention, to repress Indian resistance, and to destroy refuges for fugitives from American slavery, Jackson and his subordinates seized the initiative and repeatedly launched incursions into Florida, commonly without civilian authorization and sometimes in direct contradiction of War Department orders. They usurped congressional war-making authority and cabinet direction over policy, but they got away with doing so and felt justified by their success, as Britain backed away from confrontation, Spain ceded Florida, the Creek and Seminole Indians surrendered most of the land they had lived on, and refugees from slavery were killed, reenslaved, or forced to flee deep into the wilds of Florida. Jackson calculated the odds correctly, but could an army of loose cannons serve the nation's interests effectively in the long term?

The last third of *Jackson's Sword* turns to the army in the arc between the Mississippi and Missouri Rivers during the decade after the War of 1812 and provides context for the changes in military conduct that flowered during the period covered by *Peacekeepers and Conquerors*. Readers should note that much of the deeper social, political, cultural, and institutional context for *Peacekeepers and Conquerors* is laid out in the extended introduction and conclusion to *Jackson's Sword*. (These two volumes were originally a single book.) Between 1810 and 1821 the officers of the national standing army were often motivated by highly subjective emotions of regionalism, sectionalism, and antagonism toward Indians, Spaniards, and Britons, born from sympathy for frontiersmen and experiences in the War of 1812. Many of these men felt as much loyalty to section (the South) or region (the frontier) as to the nation as a whole. Andrew Jackson set an example of repeated insubordination against civilian authority, and the officer corps remained as unstable, and often dysfunctional, as it had been since the end of the Revolution. The resulting belligerence encouraged junior and field-grade officers to support Jackson in his usurpations of constitutional civilian authority and repeated invasions or threats to invade Spanish Florida without authorization, to pursue primarily military solutions to complex intercultural and international dilemmas.

Chapter 7 of *Jackson's Sword* shows that many of the belligerently confident War of 1812 veterans in the Southern Division left the army around 1820, when they felt their work had been done, and sought new opportunities in civil life; Congress agreed and reduced the army and officer corps. The conclusion to *Jackson's Sword* examines the reform of the Military Academy at West Point during the decade after 1817, when virtually all entrants into the officer corps were Academy graduates, producing a more consistent socialization in nationalism, subordination, and accountability. At the same time, the decline of international threats allowed the army to concentrate on continental expansion and pacification through the peacekeeping, largely aimed at white citizens, and conquest, largely aimed at Native Americans, explored in the present volume.

These developments—the beginning of an institutional stability that enabled and encouraged the growth of professional cohesion, responsibility, and expertise—are explored in chapter 7 and the conclusion to *Jackson's Sword*, which examine officer socialization, commissioning, resignations, and assignments in the context of social, political, economic, technological, military, and cultural changes during the age of Jackson (the 1820s through 1840s). (These sections also suggest significant limits to change and substantial sources of continuity.) Thus, although chapter 1 and the conclusion to *Peacekeepers and Conquerors* contain extensive contextual analysis, readers who want a full assessment of officer personnel patterns, the significance of the Military Academy to officer professionalization, and contexts external to the army should look to the last third of *Jackson's Sword*. The introduction to *Jackson's Sword* is where I examine interpretations of military professionalism and the nineteenth-century American nation-state, providing extended critiques of the "weak state" and "state of courts and parties" theses, which scholars studying the late nineteenth century have projected, without archival evidence, backward onto the first half of the century.

The present volume focuses on the quarter century after the reduction in force in 1821, when the United States was much less concerned with British threats or the possibility of expansion across international territorial boundaries than during the preceding generation. Instead, the nation and its standing army concentrated on internal development, though this development took extensive as well as intensive forms. The army continued to move west, into modern Arkansas and Oklahoma (then known as the "Indian Territory") and the region between the Mississippi and Missouri Rivers. Chapter 1 provides context for this extension of U.S. sovereignty and power and serves as something of an introduction to the volume as a whole, emphasizing the significance of the national standing army rather than citizen-soldier volunteers, militia, or the ecological or economic impact of the settlers.

Chapter 2 focuses on the range of peacekeeping and peace enforcement operations in the arc between the Missouri and the Mississippi over the course of this quarter century. Though these rarely involved overt war, they were intended to quell substantial or sustained Indian resistance to U.S. hegemony and succeeded in doing so by the mid-1830s. Continuities—the inefficacy of the militia, the government's reliance on the standing army, and that army's efforts to restrain atrocity by citizen-soldiers—rather than discontinuity most characterized the spectrum of U.S. government and American citizen expansion and violence in the northwestern forests and prairies. From this chapter forward, we see that the processes of peacekeeping (on U.S. terms), peace enforcement, coercive diplomacy, and domination and conquest were intricately and inextricably woven together. (For a brief elaboration, see appendix A, which outlines a spectrum of coercive diplomacy and deterrence from passivity to violence, from indirection to direction, from implication to action, from generally small scale to larger scale, from lesser to greater demands on the targeted populace.)

The minuscule national standing army also tried to maintain peace and order—on American terms—on the thinly settled frontiers between the United States and Mexican Texas, where nonstate actors[1] were less organized but perhaps more common than during the decade of the first Mexican Revolution (1810–1821, the era of *Jackson's Sword*). After a controversial but indecisive intervention in Texas in the autumn of 1836, in which President Jackson reprimanded his former protégé Edmund Gaines for exceeding instructions, the U.S. Army continued to try to keep peace on that border, which involved guarding against Texan incursions on U.S. territory as much as fending off the Indians of the southern Plains. This peacekeeping became one of the principal missions of the First Dragoon Regiment, which engaged in diplomacy with Plains Indians from its formation in 1833. I delay sustained attention to these operations until chapter 10 in order to provide context for the army's move into Texas after its annexation in 1845 and the move toward war with Mexico during the following year, the subjects of chapters 11 and 12.

The core of this volume, not unlike the first, explores the conquest and dispossession of the southeastern Indians, potentially the most powerful resistance to U.S. expansion after the defeat of the northwestern Indian confederations during the 1790s and the War of 1812 and the rapprochement between the United States and Britain between 1815 and 1823. *Jackson's Sword* concludes with the Seminoles, Mikasukis, and Red Stick Creeks driven into central Florida by Andrew Jackson's invasion in 1818 and the Spanish cession of Florida three years later. Chapter 3 of the present volume examines the dispossession of the Creeks remaining in Georgia and Alabama during the decade between 1825 and 1834, although I do not address the "Second Creek War" of 1836, the subject of a superb book by John Ellisor. This process often involved operations to remove whites intruding on Creek land contrary to the federal trade and intercourse acts, operations that frequently led to clashes between federal and state governments as well as soldiers and local settlers. Indeed, Georgia threatened civil war to resist federal authority in 1825, and junior as well as senior army officers (Edmund Gaines and Jacob Brown) played crucial roles as diplomats and peacekeepers, showing the national flag as representatives of federal military power, communicating with Georgia leaders on the spot, and mobilizing nationalist sentiment within the state.

Chapters 4 and 5 explore similar federal-state tensions, military peacekeeping roles, and ultimately unity in federal and state goals toward Native Americans in the expropriation of the Cherokee between 1836 and 1838, operations that spurred significant tension between John Wool, the military commander on the scene, and the Jackson administration. Indeed, Wool requested a court of inquiry into his conduct, in which his successor in command, Winfield Scott, exonerated him while permitting Wool to excoriate Jackson's understanding of constitutionalism. By this time, however, Martin Van Buren was president and proved much more friendly to the army (and much less stringent in demanding policies, like Indian removal, without being willing to suffer their political consequences) than his predecessor. While Cherokee nonviolence was certainly the most important reason there was no war, the national standing army provided a much less violent instrument of expropriation and ethnic cleansing than the Georgia militia, probably preventing atrocities. Indeed, many of the army's roles in the Cherokee country would seem familiar to officers engaged in overseeing the transfer of ethnic populations in Bosnia during the 1990s or ethnic group interactions in Kosovo after 1999.[2]

Chapters 6 and 7 explore the Second Seminole War, not through operations but as a nexus of army-Indian, civil-military, and army-militia attitudes and interactions, presenting further evidence of the military's disenchantment with but ultimate execution of Indian removal. Sadly, much of the army's subordination to civilian authority developed in that crucible at the expense of Native Americans, with whom officers often sympathized due to their friction with white frontiersmen. From the Native American standpoint, the most important thing about the army was that it was white. From the perspective of American politics and society, however, the army's autonomy from Jacksonian values and dynamics—particularly populism, decentralization, and partisanship—stands out.

Chapters 8 and 9 explore the army's role keeping peace with British Canada by restraining American citizens. They follow the chronological trajectory of the army's operational focus by shifting to the Canadian border, which exploded in rebellion and filibustering against British rule at the end of 1837. Though the vast majority of the army remained in Florida, and far more troops were deployed to force the Cherokee west, half a decade of instability produced the greatest crisis in Anglo-American relations during the half century between 1814 and 1862, perhaps the most dangerous crisis the two nations have endured since the War of 1812. Initially deployed to deter or oppose possible British incursions, the army soon began to cooperate with the British to preserve national sovereignty and international peace by enforcing U.S. neutrality laws. Though no more than a thousand soldiers were deployed, British officials applauded the U.S. Army for calming tensions and demonstrating its government's support for the international state system and the rule of law. Officers expressed much the same attitudes toward frontier citizens, local civil officials, and citizen-soldiers as they had during the Seminole conflict, but the Canadian border crises provided an experience of national-level civil-military harmony that helped soothe the wounds of Indian removal.

The final three chapters explore the gradual, intermittent but ultimately effective extension of U.S. sovereignty and power in the Southwest, along the borders with Texas and Mexico. The filibustering of the generation before 1821 was replaced by the colonization of Texas under Mexican auspices during the 1820s and by rebellion and independence in 1836. Anglo-Texans then proved more antagonistic toward U.S. sovereignty than Mexico had been, attacking Indians and Mexican merchants in U.S. territory until they were restrained by the U.S. Army. Nevertheless, the key political and diplomatic factor was ultimately the Texans' whiteness, and in 1845 the army was sent into Texas to defend it against Mexico, precipitating the war with Mexico. Chapter 10 explores the trajectory of U.S. military operations west and southwest of the Missouri River and along the Louisiana-Texas border between 1821 and 1838. Chapter 11 examines the dragoon expeditions and frontier diplomacy in the central and southern Plains as far as the Rocky Mountains between 1834 and 1845, as well as Zachary Taylor's selection to command the Army of Occupation in Texas in 1845. Chapter 12 explores officer attitudes toward Britain, Oregon, and Texas and the likelihood, desirability, and probable outcomes of war with Mexico, assessing their values and priorities on the eve of the first conventional war the United States had fought in more than three decades, the sort of war the national standing army was putatively designed for.

American military professionalism did not develop independent of civilian society, nor was it simply a matter of growing expertise in the art of warfare. The career officers of the U.S. Army served as federal, international, and interethnic mediators; national law enforcers; and de facto intercultural and international peacekeepers, effectively advancing national objectives and power with remarkably little overt violence—"warfare" in the traditional sense—by extending and enhancing the authority and cohesion of the American nation-state along its borders and frontiers. The federal government and its army were almost continually challenged by nonstate actors—citizen, Indian, or foreign—while constrained by republican and liberal ideology, representative but racialist (white supremacist) democracy, adherence to due process and the constitutional separation of powers, and federalism and decentralization in sectional, regional, and localist forms. The officer corps' claim to professional status and a role in its definition depended on civilian acceptance of its claim to authority over a distinct role in society's division of labor, especially the power to select, promote, and exclude aspirants to that role. This claim was continually contested by the anti–standing army and militia ideals, private and volunteer military units, and frontier constituencies who acclaimed those ideals and created such units when they believed the regular army was acting contrary to their interests, as often seemed the case in the confused welter of borderlands diplomacy and settler expansion.

Nevertheless, despite widespread public criticism as aristocrats, martinets, dandies, and Indian sympathizers, the officers of the regular army secured a fundamental acceptance of their professional role and institutional autonomy in the federal government and among the middle classes and elites who served in and identified with it. This acceptance permitted extraordinarily secure employment, making possible careers that lasted an average of more than two decades, and it meant that the regulars ordinarily exercised senior-level command over volunteer and militia forces during wartime. The officer corps gained this acceptance through fiscally accountable administration; genteel interaction with local and national civilian elites; the exercise, through military command, of an authority most civilian elites could only dream of; and the politically reliable performance of their duties negotiating, mediating, intimidating, and coercing along the borders and frontiers. Officers made cogent arguments for the value of experience and specialization in military tasks—arguments accepted by most nationalist Republicans, National Republicans, and Whigs—and they clearly proved their capability advancing U.S. territorial expansion during the war with Mexico.

Most previous accounts have suggested that the army was subordinated to partisan politics—essentially patronage regardless of education or experience—in officer commissioning and promotion, or that it was physically isolated and mentally alienated from civilian society. These assertions are inaccurate, individually and collectively. Crucially, and unlike most other institutions of Jacksonian government, the army was able to secure substantial insulation, even autonomy, from partisan politics and sectional or civilian economic interests in its internal administration and field operations. The army officer corps became increasingly accountable to civilian authority in its internal institutional processes; in representative, constitutional, and federalist civil-military relations; and in the execution of foreign policy. Indeed, it struck a more diplomatic—a more just and less violent—balance among varying social, political, and interest groups than most civilian frontiersmen or its European counterparts, which were thoroughly linked to civilian politics through commissioning and civilian officeholding, serving elite class power at home while launching imperial and colonial adventures abroad.

Army operations in the Jacksonian borderlands restrained entropy, enhanced national security, and advanced orderly national territorial expansion. The efforts of the army's frontier diplomats, including their exercise of restraint, discipline, or command over citizens and citizen-soldiers, helped prevent the establishment of competing polities (nations, states, or other political entities) that might have constrained U.S. growth, limited settler and citizen-soldier atrocities against Native Americans, and played a crucial, perhaps decisive role in averting a devastating war with Britain circa 1840. Their logistical expertise proved equally crucial to successfully projecting U.S. national power, first to drive Indians from land sought by white citizens, then to do so against Mexico, and finally to reunite the nation during the Civil War.

Although the army was certainly authoritarian in its internal discipline and officer attitudes toward Indians and frontier civilians, and although it was certainly oriented far more toward national government, centralized authority, and social and political hierarchy than the decentralization acclaimed by the majority of Americans, its growing and (in Jacksonian America) unique professional autonomy did not come at the expense of political accountability. Indeed, autonomy, and the insulation that sustained it, enhanced accountability and subordination to civilian authority, to due process and the rule of law, and to the processes—however frustrating officers sometimes found them—of representative constitutional government. If one is looking for themes and keywords to the civil-military relations in *Peacekeepers and Conquerors*, mine are responsibility, accountability, and subordination, institutional insulation and operational autonomy rather than isolation or alienation.

During the quarter century after 1821 the officer corps became decisively more professional—more committed to extended careers of subordination, responsiveness, and accountability to national civilian authority rather than local, regional, or sectional interests, despite endemic tensions between these sources of authority. U.S. Army professionalism developed in great part because most junior officers were socialized in nationalism and statism, in subordination to constitutional civilian control, at the national Military Academy. These foundations, so thoroughly explored in William Skelton's pathbreaking book *An American Profession of Arms*, were reinforced and confirmed during officers' frustrating experiences trying to keep peace between white frontiersmen and Indians, between the United States and Britain, while forwarding the territorial expansion American citizens demanded of their government. That expansion is the conquest side of *Peacekeepers and Conquerors*, but the two dimensions could not, cannot, and should not be separated. Their interplay was the interplay of American civil-military relations, their nuances the complexity of the American frontier.

Jackson's Sword contains a very extensive and specific set of acknowledgments; here I can no more than touch the surface of my debts to others. I thank the Department of History at the United States Military Academy; Rich Stevenson, our department's computer officed; my colleagues, family, and friends; and the dozens, probably hundreds, of librarians and archivists who have helped me over the years. In particular, I must always thank Bill Skelton and Jim Bradford and my mother and father for inspiration and support. Mike Briggs, Fred Woodward, and all the staff at the University Press of Kansas deserve unending thanks for their patience; knowing them better now, I can cite Larisa Martin, Susan Schott, Kelly Chrisman Jacques, and my copyeditor for their indispensable assistance. Elizabeth Boyles cleaned up a rather convoluted index for *Jackson's Sword*, and Jana Mansoor prepared the index for the present volume. I dedicated the first volume to my mom; I don't think my dad will mind if I dedicate this volume to the cadets who follow the officers I study in the service of our nation.

PEACEKEEPERS AND CONQUERORS

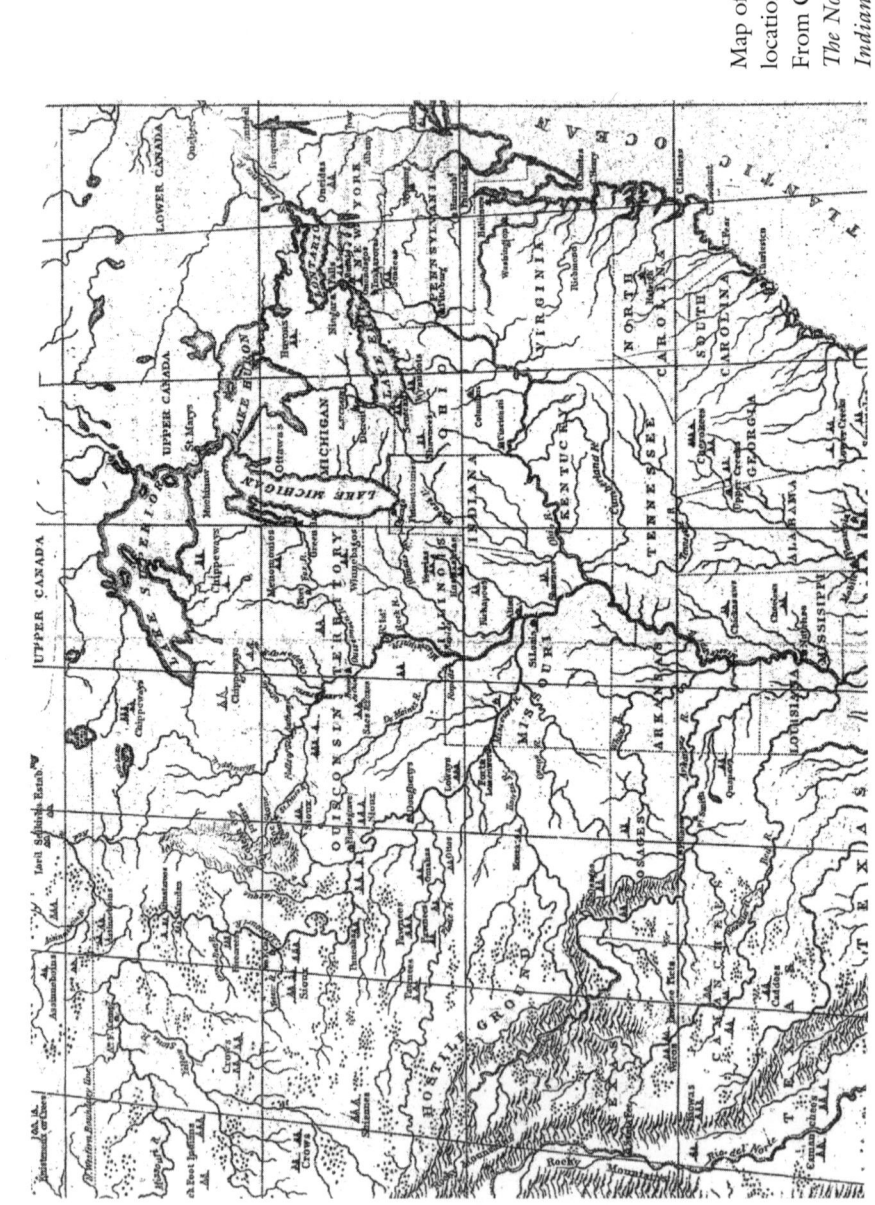

Map of Indian tribal locations, c. 1833. From George Catlin, *The North American Indians*

1

NATIONAL MILITARY EXPANSION ON THE WESTERN FRONTIER

Contexts, Comparisons, and Outcomes

Military attitudes toward American territorial expansion were profoundly shaped by officers' experiences—usually frustrating if not antagonistic after 1821—with civilian borderers. Due to democratic federalism, civilian control was far stronger on the contiguous American settlement frontiers than in the French, British, or Russian empires; federal military commanders did not have the extreme autonomy of their French, Russian, and often British counterparts to "deliberately exclude civilian colonists [and often civilian governors] from any effective participation" in diplomatic and military decision making.[1] Because they were bound to execute controversial national policies, involving the restraint of white citizens as well as Indians, officers frequently became embroiled in conflicts with local civilians and civil authorities and had to worry about their representatives and allies in Congress. (One of the weaknesses of this book is its inattention to that congressional oversight; I have not attempted to assess the frequency or intensity of congressional complaint about army operations in the borderlands.) Indeed, everyday "civilian control" of the military meant officers mediating between local interests and national objectives and coping with the prejudices and subjectivities of majoritarian populism—disdain for institutions and disregard for law, especially Indian treaty rights—as much as protecting due process and the rule of law against the encroachments of military authoritarianism.[2]

Intolerant of abstractions and constraint, Jacksonian populism often proved a source of civil-military confusion, pitting impatient majoritarian sentiment against the legal forms and procedures career government officials (elected and appointed) identified with accountability to republican government under the checks and balances of the Constitution. (The Jacksonians preferred to ignore these when they got in the way.) The ambiguity of these conflicts led many career professional officers to hope for dual policies of domestic and international restraint for fear that "disorderly" borderers would get out of hand; this reflected a conservative preference, common to Federalists, National Republicans, and Whigs, for the ultimately hierarchical order and stability imposed by the nation-state through the disciplines of domestic and international law. The political tensions and dilemmas posed by the army's law enforcement duties along the nation's borders and frontiers contributed significantly to the decline of aggressively expansionist sentiment among career military officers during the 1820s and 1830s.

The growing professional cohesion of the officer corps owed much to its quest for hierarchical order and predictability in all its critical relationships: within its units of working-class enlisted men, in the decentralized civilian social order of the frontier, and in the national sovereignty and professional jurisdiction over the direction of violence that ultimately provided officers with careers and authority. Like other Americans among the nation's elites and aspirants to that status, professional soldiers sought prestige and legitimacy by identifying their values with those of the Old World and its elites. In American domestic society, this meant a growing emphasis on refinement and gentility; in foreign relations and the borderlands, professional soldiers sought respectability in the eyes of their European and civilian counterparts by adhering to the forms and disciplines of national and international law. Enforcing these norms along the nation's borders provided the sanction of European precedent and practical utility for the army's monopoly over the direction of organized armed force in the eyes of its employers in Congress and the executive branch. Class, state, and professional formation were closely linked phenomena in the army officer corps' behavior in the borderlands, a pattern that encouraged military accountability to the authority of national civilian political structures centered in Congress and the cabinet.

Officers' increasingly unenthusiastic responses to the opportunities presented by internal colonialism and frontier expansion demonstrate the close links among institutional maturity, occupational monopoly, elite class and nation-state formation, and professional accountability in the development of the commissioned officer corps between 1815 and 1846. Under the federal territorial system, the process of geographic expansion involved forming states as well as extending the existing pattern of local self-government; expansion therefore contained the potential both for social reproduction, in the decentralized agrarian mode envisioned by Jeffersonians and their Jacksonian legatees, and for the institutional elaboration and political consolidation of a more powerful nation-state sometimes capable of restraining its citizens. Put on the spot between whites and Indians and often between center and periphery, Washington and the frontier, unable to take refuge in the abstractions civilian policy makers could easily espouse, the professional soldier's zeal for order had surprisingly similar consequences for military attitudes toward white and native frontiersmen.

Added atop Euro-American images of native barbarity, the military thirst for order meant that soldiers ultimately saw Native Americans as savages, childlike captives to impulse and passion who had to be restrained by threat or force. Toward white frontiersmen, genteel military professional values of order and integrity meant distaste and antipathy for the apparently insatiable materialism, rapacious lack of self-restraint, and thoughtless belligerence of individuals grasping at native lands while demanding military protection. Proud military commanders felt their profession, their nation, and their civilization degraded and disgraced by predatory frontier citizens, who often took soldiers to court if they attempted to enforce laws intended to protect the Indians and keep the peace. Indeed, career officers faced greater threats from white democracy than from Native Americans: the Seminole War aside, the chance of death or injury at Indian hands was far less than the likelihood of legal and political harassment, perhaps leading to reassignment and personal disruption, by individualistic frontier citizens antagonistic toward the authoritarianism of "military despots" from the national center.

Though that harassment rarely affected officers' promotion, which was almost universally determined by strict rules of seniority, historian Francis Paul Prucha observes that officers were "ill-supported" by the War Department in such disputes, adding another layer of uncertainty to the jumbled mix of values, attitudes, and perceptions that influenced their decision making. Constrained by due process and federalism, loyal to the rule of law that undergirded the nation-state that gave them authority, they did not attempt to punish white citizens as they did Indians; even intimidation—coercive federal diplomacy aimed at restraining citizens without overt violence—was risky, even if apparently sanctioned, or explicitly directed, by the executive branch. Convenience and careerism gradually led many wearied professional soldiers to accept, and sometimes to more directly espouse, white expansion, but this did not resolve their moral and emotional dilemmas in the face of boundless citizen demands. This dynamic of frustration with white citizens, anger that could not be expressed in action, and the pursuit of catharsis through violence against legally and ideologically permissible antagonists—Native Americans—increasingly encouraged military atrocities against Indians after the Civil War, and chapter 7 suggests a similar trajectory in many officers' thinking during the Second Seminole War.[3]

Vilified and sometimes punished for doing their duty to uphold the laws under the Constitution, even the most experienced professional commanders had difficulty grappling with the dissonance between legal precept and political practice. In 1835, his twenty-seventh year of national military service, plain-spoken Colonel Zachary Taylor reviled the employees of the American Fur Company as "the greatest scoundrels the world ever knew." Two years later, after a quarter century of military service, dragoon colonel Stephen Watts Kearny condemned the Indians' "shameful" treatment by white frontiersmen; chapters 3–7 provide numerous examples from officers engaged in the removal process and the Second Seminole War. Under these circumstances, professional soldiers usually blamed land-hungry citizens for stirring up frontier conflicts, vowed that the government had "pledged its faith" to protect the natives, and tried to restrain citizens unwilling to restrain themselves. Their antipathy for the chaotic excesses of white individualism, combined with values of good faith, equity, and justice, meant a skepticism toward white claims and demands, toward the actual process of everyday American expansion, which commonly made the career professional officer the most objective actor on a frontier torn by the passions of cultural prejudice and greed.[4]

This comparatively objective understanding of white-Indian relations, however limited or flawed from modern perspectives, was widely shared in the army and exerted substantial influence on its operations in the field. That objectivity tended to reinforce the very skepticism, antipathy, and desire for equity in which it was rooted, and the national military officer could easily find courageous native patriots a more fitting object of empathy than the poorly educated, rough-and-tumble frontier citizens who sought to dispossess the Indians, usually by spilling soldiers' blood rather than their own. Prior to the 1850s, this empathy encouraged a much less overtly brutal approach to pacification than in European empires or among most American frontiersmen. During the period of this book, with the exception of the "battle" of Bad Axe (the destruction of Black Hawk's band of Sauk and Fox Indians trying to cross the Mississippi River in 1832), the U.S. Army did not commit massacres of the sort common among their European counterparts in Algeria, India, or the Caucasus. It did engage in the "food fights," resulting in the destruction of crops and villages, that had characterized Anglo-Indian warfare since the seventeenth century, but officers did the same, perhaps just as often, against white citizens settling on Indian lands without the permission required by the federal trade and intercourse acts, when the War Department authorized them to do so.

Military skepticism toward white frontiersmen was derived not from romantic sentiment or unadulterated admiration for Native Americans but from the distaste genteel national officers felt for the excesses of white democracy and individualism, intensified on the frontier, and the consequent aggression against the Indians that drew the army into complex, essentially no-win situations fraught with political ambiguity and danger. The broad contours and objectives of Indian policy were determined in Washington, primarily in response to white citizen demands, not by the motives of military commanders on the frontier. Career officers could not turn their empathy for Indians into overt anger against whites, for such anger could not be publicly sustained in the political and legal arenas. In contrast, European governments often felt less sympathy for white settlers than the Jacksonians did, and in Algeria (France's principal imperial venture during this era), this led to military mistreatment of both natives and settlers.

The balance of power and the degree of tension between European governments and their colonial military forces and settlers varied significantly. In France, efforts by the civilian government in the metropole to restrain colonial military autonomy were often unsuccessful; in Russia, this was attempted less often because there were fewer civilian colonists to question military demands, and the tsar usually supported his generals as long as they were successful. Civil-military relations in the British Empire varied, from a general civilian desire to hold down costs, which the military appears to have followed outside of India, to the "militarization of Britain's ruling elite" (and English civilians in India) during the French Revolutionary and Napoleonic Wars, which blurred "the boundary between civil and military spheres of authority." British government relations with settlers fluctuated over the course of the century, becoming increasingly supportive and open to settler autonomy as the costs of containing conflicts between settlers and natives increased. Greater settler autonomy commonly led to greater violence against the indigenous inhabitants, particularly when volunteers, militia, and vigilantes replaced the army, as in Australia and to some extent New Zealand.[5]

Limits to power do not mean powerlessness, nor were the limits of American military power filled effectively by civilian agents. Historians often confuse the U.S. Army's role and impact on the nineteenth-century frontier; with a few cursory exceptions, political scientists and students of American political development have not addressed the subject at all. Indeed, some senior western military historians have contributed to this neglect by downplaying the army's impact, perhaps hoping to win greater acceptance among the majority of historians, who increasingly prefer to study social forces, language, and culture rather than government. The assumption that the army's mission was little more than conquest, combined with the well-known tactical difficulties it faced, leads many scholars, including leading military historians, to assume that the army was ineffective. Thus Robert M. Utley, the dean of military historians of the trans-Mississippi West, maintains that "if the Indians in the end lost the Indian Wars, it was not because the army defeated them." Yet if we fail to recognize the army's diplomatic and peacekeeping roles, or its actual efficacy, however gradual, in defeating Native American resistance, the army in the West becomes known primarily as an instrument of racism and atrocity, of conquest in the crudest and most reductionist sense, or perhaps as a market for farmers and entrepreneurs—either way, a dependent variable of limited significance.[6]

That misperception encourages a misunderstanding of state and army autonomy and the significance of these institutions in nineteenth-century America, and that misinterpretation fosters an oversimplified notion of American politics and political culture. Contrary to crude notions of racial conquest, the nation's Indian relations were militarized by restraints on whites as well as aggression against Indians. Until agrarian settlement caught up with the national military presence, a large portion of the army's everyday energies was spent enforcing the trade and intercourse laws intended to limit friction between white and native by restraining white encroachment in areas as yet unceded by the Indians. Violence was common among the Indians themselves, between tribes (or "nations") and factions within tribes competing for resources or revenging past aggressions.[7] The army's peacekeeping task was multiplied and complicated as the removal policy concentrated larger, more diverse Indian populations within smaller spaces, placing once-stable ecosystems under growing pressure.[8] Increasingly dependent on white trade goods and supplies, Indian populations were diminished by epidemic diseases brought by white contact. Native tribes and factions recognized and often tried to draw support from the increasingly hegemonic military and economic power of the United States in their disputes, creating another set of diplomatic dilemmas—civil-military as well as interethnic—for national military officers.[9]

National officials feared that tensions among the Indians would spill over into depredations against white citizens, but they worried that intervention by citizen-soldier militias or volunteers loyal to local interests might turn into vigilante actions and escalate into full-fledged racial warfare that would be costly in revenue, public opinion, and international reputation. Thus, the army's most common mission along the nation's inland frontiers between 1821 and 1846 was to uphold the sovereign *Pax Americana* asserted by treaty and national law (the trade and intercourse acts) against all comers, to intimidate those on all sides who might break the peace, and to coerce them if they did. Given the potential for incident, atrocity, and political embarrassment if white militias were employed to compel emigration, federal troops were often called on to step between natives and citizen-soldiers, to push the Indians west while limiting the risks created by harassment by whites. Yet in practice, given the ability of white citizens to draw on representative political processes to prevent, restrict, or punish military intervention, these peacekeeping duties were largely directed at Indians, especially when they struck back against white intruders and committed acts defined as assaults or robberies by white law, as in the Arikara and Winnebago "wars" and associated turmoil between 1826 and 1828. Though removal was supposed to be voluntary, national military power was commonly used to encourage and enforce the unequal treaties by which tribes supposedly agreed to move west and to prevent them from returning to their former homes, as in the Black Hawk War or the expulsion of the Potawatomi and Winnebago later in the 1830s and 1840s.[10]

Peacekeeping required diplomatic and political (or civil-military) as well as tactical military competence and discipline. Given their prejudices and indiscipline, state and territorial volunteers and militia usually proved diplomatically and militarily incompetent for the missions citizens demanded, unless they were able to operate with genocidal freedom against fragments of Native American societies. In contrast, the national standing army—so often maligned by frontiersmen—provided protection at a cost in both lives and taxes that ultimately proved acceptable to most citizens, East and West. Most of the army's enlisted soldiers were men with limited resources and prospects in civilian economic life. Increasingly, they were recently arrived immigrants, especially Catholic Irishmen or Germans, who were denigrated by much of native-born civil society; their unskilled labor could easily be replaced, and their deaths in the army would be little mourned by the middle class or elites. Financially, civilian War Department officials and army leaders agreed that per soldier, regular troops were less expensive to sustain than volunteers or militia; once Jacksonian expansionism led Congress to pay for regular mounted troops, citizen-soldiers lost their principal military advantage. Thus, as leading western military historian Robert Wooster recently observed, the national standing army "became the driving force behind national military policy in the West."[11]

Indeed, though citizen-soldiers still served as the equivalent of colonial or early national "rangers" in mountainous regions, they only became a significant military force on the central and northern Plains in the massacres at Bear River and Sand Creek. (Texas, with its strong tradition of state military forces rooted in the republic, remained something of an exception with its Rangers and associated vigilantes.) And citizen-soldiers never proved willing to serve over sustained periods (more than a few months): though they were sometimes—if organized, and if advance intelligence of an Indian attack was available—able to spring to action for local defense, they rarely went far from their families and businesses. They could sometimes launch raiding expeditions but rarely attempted seasonal campaigns, particularly during winter, when Indian bands were more vulnerable. Thus, despite their self-proclaimed skill at unconventional warfare, the effectiveness of citizen-soldier forces depended almost entirely on destroying Indian villages, a tactic particularly likely to produce atrocity and public and international condemnation (however limited compared to the twenty-first century), given their indiscipline and racism. A similar dynamic operated among volunteer units in the war against Mexico.[12]

Regular troops did not lack racist attitudes and emotions, and army commanders sought to attack Indian villages on the same military grounds—compelling surrender by destroying food and shelter, rather than trying to chase down more agile Indian horsemen—as citizen-soldiers. With larger cavalry forces available after the Civil War, more hardened commanders were able to lead surprise attacks in winter, when warriors and their families would be intermixed within villages. This led to atrocities—at the Washita in 1868 and on the Marias River against the Piegans two years later (both incidents encouraged and defended by the army's senior commanders)—on a scale committed by regular troops on only one occasion prior to 1861 (against the Brule Sioux at Ash Hollow in 1855). The ultimate example was Wounded Knee, but we should note that the trajectory was by no means assured: the outcome might have been different had George Crook rather than Nelson Miles been in command. We might also compare the outcome—racial segregation and impoverishment—with the genocides in California, conducted almost entirely by citizen-soldiers, and the Australian outback, where British officials turned security responsibilities over to volunteers and militia.[13]

Military restraint toward expropriating the Indians was most evident in the ambivalence expressed by career professional officers during the Second Seminole War, discussed in chapters 6 and 7. It is also evident, and most significant in terms of the conduct and human impact of federal Indian relations, in the history, or lack thereof, of atrocities against Native Americans by the national standing army during this era. Neither Sand Creek nor Wounded Knee was characteristic of the decades between 1783 and 1846. During these years, massacres were almost entirely the province of citizen-soldiers, such as the Georgia, Kentucky, and Tennessee militias and volunteers, and of individuals who killed natives out of hatred, greed, or revenge. (The "battle" at Bad Axe, the virtual massacre of a band of Sauk and Fox Indians trying to escape across the Mississippi River during the Black Hawk War in 1832, was something of an exception to this rule, involving regular troops as well as militia, volunteers, and Indians allied with the United States.) Indeed, one of the many elements of crisis spurred by the Second Seminole War within the army was the brutal-

Frontier diplomacy: Stephen H. Long negotiates with the Oto and Pawnee Indians, 1819. Engraving by John H. Clark, after a painting by Samuel Seymour. (Courtesy Library of Congress, LC-USZ62-7778)

ization that developed over the years of war, culminating in the hanging of several Indians by Lieutenant Colonel William Harney in 1839.

Yet atrocities like these remained rare prior to the war with Mexico, perhaps surprisingly so given the seven years' corrosion of the fighting in Florida—the longest continuous war by the national military forces of the United States against the indigenous peoples of North America. One reason for the lack of atrocities was the threat they posed to social, cultural, institutional, and professional hierarchies and the debate they occasioned among career officers, who generally considered them contrary to genteel professional norms; such behavior threatened to reduce the army to the level of the unrestrained frontiersmen so many professional soldiers detested. Experienced federal military officers worried about the effect such excesses would have on the discipline of enlisted soldiers and the army's image as a disciplined, accountable instrument of national policy. They rejected atrocities and indiscipline as characteristic evils of their volunteer competitors. They knew that loosening the bonds of discipline would not win them converts among the devotees of white democracy, who would always find the volunteers more attractive, in image and rhetoric if not in practice, as purer expressions of their radically egalitarian, anti-institutional values. Thus, as in so many other relationships, civil-military interactions, and the predispositions and expectations both sides brought to these relationships, pressed career military officers toward a Whiggish (though nonpartisan) affinity with the national state and the values of stability and cohesion they associated with it.[14]

Exploring the army's operations provides opportunities to understand large-scale geopolitical outcomes in the clash between ethnically based polities—the sources, trajectories, and extent of growing U.S. domination versus native power and decline. Chapter 2 evaluates the sources of U.S. hegemony, clear in political breadth if not cultural depth, over the watershed of the upper Mississippi. This hegemony was confirmed by the Black Hawk War and culminated in the expulsion of Native Americans from Illinois and southern Wisconsin during the 1830s. Compared with some later chapters, chapter 2 focuses more on military coercion of the Indians and less on civil-military tensions among whites. In doing so, it provides the important caution that white solidarity, and military subordination to democratic control by the constitutionally elected civilian officials who represented the nation's citizens, ultimately trumped military distaste for white frontiersmen or whatever sympathies career officers felt for the Native Americans they dispossessed (attitudes explored at some length in chapters 3–7). In the broad view, professional army officers certainly remained "agents of empire," the sword of a republic increasingly defined by whiteness, carrying out the final stage in the process of ethnic cleansing that historians commonly label Indian removal.[15]

Nevertheless, the desire for expansion at minimal financial cost presented military commanders with complex dilemmas, fostering uncertainty, friction, and ambivalence. The government's demand that officers further expansion while limiting the costs incurred by white citizens—indeed, the expectation among civilian as well as military policy makers that some temporary restraint on white citizens would further future expansion—implied the use of force against all parties. Yet large-scale bloodshed was remarkably, indeed surprisingly, rare: intimidation and deterrence rather than physical violence, coercive diplomacy rather than out-and-out war, characterized the vast majority of army operations on the inland frontier. All these operations were intended to avoid escalation and allow unimpeded white settlement; the army served as much as a facilitator of population growth and economic power as a weapon of direct, violent conquest. Nevertheless, modern interpretations in which the trans-Mississippi West is conquered by vast impersonal forces of demography and ecology, with military force functioning primarily as the embodiment of white racism, present far too simple a caricature, particularly for the era before the U.S.-Mexican War. Without specialist caveats to encourage correction, most college-level U.S. history textbooks now portray the American conquest of the

West in reductionist and determinist tones historians normally reject, with the appearance of railroads and settlers signaling inevitable native retreat. Indeed, the teleology and determinism of the "population, bison, and epidemics" school of interpretation standard in twenty-first-century college textbooks inadvertently replicate the triumphalism and Social Darwinism of ethnocentric nineteenth-century spokesmen for expansion. Despite the devoted efforts of ethnohistorians, the claims of demographic and ecological interpretations often leave the impression that Native Americans were fundamentally helpless, unable to adapt in the face of a white agrarian onslaught that substituted its own resource base for that of the Indians.[16]

Even outstanding western military historians have done their share to foster these ahistorical assumptions: Robert Utley asserts that "in the large picture the tribes succumbed to forces . . . more devastating than military force clumsily applied," forces that "flowed from an irresistible tide of westering Americans—irresistible to the Indians militarily, irresistible to their own leaders politically." Yet this hardly seems probable if the Indians resisted white aggrandizement as tenaciously as our stories of their agency suggest: as William Tecumseh Sherman observed of the southern secessionists in 1861, "no man surrenders from conviction, but from Superior Force." Nor does any modern scholar claim that settlers en masse possessed the field skill or warcraft of a Kit Carson. Why, then, would hardy warriors, so superior to most whites in individual fighting skill, so skillful in the fieldcraft that enabled them to seize settlers' horses and cattle, have found sedentary settlers militarily irresistible?[17] Nor should we make the emotional leap, whether in the old mode of American triumphalism or the modern critical one, to an interpretation that privileges private nonstate actors—white frontiersmen acting as vigilantes or citizen-soldiers (a distinct but related embodiment of American racism)—as the primary source of native dispossession. With the exception of California, trans-Mississippi settler societies lacked the numbers and concentration to quell substantial Native American resistance through citizen-soldier mobilizations or the impact of daily aggression by individual bullies and vigilante groups—as occurred in Alabama, Georgia, and Indiana during the 1830s—until quite late in the period of white expansion. There is little in the historical record to suggest that the citizenry made or wanted to make the sustained sacrifice of livelihood and personal independence necessary to defeat the Indians or coerce them onto reservations.

Thus, in most instances during the period of this book, racist violence by nonstate actors became a precipitant for national military action, producing an unjust enforcement of peace on white terms but consisting of expulsion rather than massacre or extermination. The army was not an independent causal factor, nor was it independent of subordination to civilian political authority constituted through the racially delimited processes of white man's democracy. The army's actions alone were not sufficient to enable the white settlement of the West, but they did influence the shape of that settlement both geographically, with forts as nodes of security and economic activity, and morally, through the restraint of genocidal violence against Indians. One can point out that white civilians destroyed most of the very loosely organized Indians of central and southern California with little national military assistance during the 1850s, and that citizen-soldier volunteers and militias proved capable of repressing Native Americans in California, Colorado, and the Pacific Northwest during the Civil War. Yet the pursuit of the Nez Perce, Sioux, Cheyenne, and Apache, and the defeat of the Modoc and the Comanche in battle, was accomplished by national military forces. The army, rather than the poorly trained, temporary militia or vigilantes, provided the rapid reaction (compared with that involved in mobilizing citizen-soldiers) and the consistent pressure—impossible for part-time soldiers to exert—that forced these Indians onto reservations and repressed their efforts to escape.

Nor, given the combat effectiveness of these tribes against disciplined regulars, were untrained, poorly coordinated citizen-soldier forces likely to defeat Indians consistently in battle: volunteers and militia proved most effective against Indian villages, in massacres like Sand Creek and Bear River. With the exception of the Texans fighting the Comanche early in the 1840s, citizen-soldiers usually fled from cohesive Indian combat forces, as at Stillman's Run in 1832 or from the Paiute in 1860. Indeed, the defeat of the Shoshone during the Civil War stands as perhaps the only offensive battlefield victory by volunteers without substantial regular army—or Native American—assistance (as Andrew Jackson had in his battles) over a sizable, organized Indian force. The defensive victories of the Wagon Box Fight and Adobe Walls notwithstanding, the postbellum Comanche barrier to white settlement in West Texas was broken by a strategically, operationally, and tactically effective offensive by converging columns of the national standing army.

There is certainly much to be said in favor of ecologically focused interpretations that emphasize the decline of the Plains Indians' resource base with the destruction of the buffalo, but these interpretations do not explain the defeat of the Apache, the Navajo, the Nez Perce, or the Indians of the Pacific Northwest, who relied on different food sources. Those societies were defeated militarily, usually by the persistent force of the national standing army. (Much of the American war against the Navajo was conducted by volunteers during the 1850s and the Civil War.) Moreover, we face an explanatory chasm between historical interpretations of the pre– and post–Civil War eras: students of the postbellum West should remember that the Cherokee, Creek, Seminole, and Ohioan Indians had to be defeated in war before the territories between the Appalachians and the Mississippi could be settled by whites. In Florida and the Old Northwest, to say nothing of the trans-Mississippi West after the Civil War, this was done almost entirely through the agency of the regular army, *not* by citizen-soldier volunteers, vigilantes, or militia, who commonly ran away when they encountered Indians who fought back. This was true in Ohio in 1790 and 1791 and in the opening skirmishes of the Black Hawk and Snake wars in 1832 and 1864, to name only a few examples. Nor did the eastern Indians lack for food, so long as they retained control of the land on which they hunted and farmed.

The Sioux were not driven from the Black Hills by the inhabitants of Deadwood: political pressure from the white intruders led the War Department to order the army into the Black Hills, where it ultimately defeated, through persistence as well as cumulative battlefield attrition, the previously hegemonic Sioux. Indeed, this was the case in virtually every conflict between whites and Indians during the period of American nationality, from the Ohio wars of the 1790s through the Seminole Wars to the final conquest and pacification of the western Indians a century later. Utley does recognize that "the standing army . . . proved indispensable to the advance of the frontier" *east* of the Mississippi. Indeed, he begins his 1984 book with Stephen W. Kearny's Army of the West departing Fort Leavenworth for Santa Fe, referring to it as an "instrument of decision" that "marked the end of one era and the beginning of another" for the Cheyenne observing the march. What, if anything, changed that equation in the trans-Mississippi West after 1846 or 1865? Railroads did not suddenly produce population concentrations greater than those in the early years of the Old Northwest or the Old Southwest. The scale of white settlement in the Plains and beyond probably approximated that in early national Ohio and Jacksonian Florida, but it was far less, in any one spatially equivalent area, than it had been in Jacksonian Alabama or Georgia during the dispossession of the Creek and Cherokee, where citizen-soldiers and vigilantes played more significant roles than on the Plains. Neither the Apache, the Navajo, nor the Indians of the Pacific Northwest were driven or removed to reservations by ecological, cultural, or economic processes of resource decline or by the adoption of white practices or dependence on white goods, as may be argued, however incompletely, for the southeastern tribes. The belief that nonstate actors—private economic enterprise in the form of railroads or buffalo hunters, or private military enterprise in the form of citizen-soldiers—drove the Indians onto reservations and kept them there is yet another version of the American exceptionalism of statelessness.[18]

Intercultural peacekeeping led the army into inescapably political situations: as William Skelton has observed, "even more than the pursuit of [institutional] service interests . . . the army's constabulary role . . . drew officers into civil affairs," intensifying the authoritarianism rooted in their professional culture. Yet, unlike many of their European counterparts, American military officers had no comprehensive "imperial" vision for the borderlands, beyond their support for American national expansion in general, tempered by their desire that expansion proceed in an orderly manner through national processes. Though they shared many features of the essentially authoritarian "ethos of Imperial service," the fundamentally aristocratic "call to discipline and respectability" that historian C. A. Bayly has delineated among contemporary British imperial agents, American officers did not expect, or consciously set out, to shape postfrontier or postcolonial civil society. Sociologist Anthony Giddens observes that "a final characteristic of internal pacification [of intrasocial, intracultural, or intrastate violence] . . . is the withdrawal of the military from direct participation in internal affairs of state." As borderlands became frontiers, frontiers became borders, and territories became states, American military officers expected to move on (generally westward to new frontiers) or to assume purely international, interstate functions as defenders of national sovereignty against foreign aggression. They showed no interest in becoming civil policemen or administrators within states, and little desire to do so within the federal territories; they sought to carve out an international security role and to avoid domestic missions requiring intervention in disputes among citizens.[19]

The American officer corps was unusual, perhaps exceptional, in this preference for a primarily international rather than domestic or colonial security role, for the latter was common in every major European army, even the British. Giddens notes that "the differentiation [between domestic and international security or policing roles] is usually full of tension," as the people of France, Russia, Spain, the German states, and even Britain (for example, the Chartists, to say nothing of the Irish) could attest with regard to their nations' armies during the mid-nineteenth century. This difference merits far more exploration and explanation than it is normally given, particularly when we observe the military interventions, or threats of intervention, in politics during the American Civil War and the substantial increase in the use of military force, national and state, against labor unrest after Reconstruction. The difference may lie solely in American political, ideological, or constitutional traditions external to the army, but it is surely worth considering whether the army's own experiences, attitudes, and traditions played some role in its antebellum restraint toward white citizens or its wartime and postbellum willingness to serve as an instrument of repression.[20]

There were also substantial differences between American and European frontiers. The American frontier, like European overseas colonial and imperial frontiers, presented a contrast between two very different cultures (or culture groupings), a contrast aggravated by an extreme chauvinism, amounting to racism, on at least one side. Yet on the American frontier, driven by a rapid, ultimately tremendous influx of families and individuals (far too many for the imperial state to halt without resorting to extreme violence against its own nationals) rather than a few businesses or military policy enforced by a few temporary residents, there was little crossover or sustained mixing in settlement. The modern historiographical concept of "middle grounds" notwithstanding, white Americans expelled Native Americans whenever they could, rather than settling permanently among them, whether as equals or masters. Few whites felt any desire for the sort of accommodation required to sustain middle grounds; where white populations grew, native dispossession soon followed.[21]

Furthermore, most Indian frontiers encountered by the United States were within the international territorial borders it claimed. After the British withdrew their support for the northwestern Indians in the decade after the War of 1812, only the Caddo on the Louisiana-Texas border could claim refuge across an international boundary, and this did them little good during the white expansion of the 1830s that led to the Texan Revolution and raids by Texans into the United States against the Caddo. The Sioux, the Nez Perce, and other northwestern Indians would attempt to use the Canadian border for refuge later in the century, with mixed success, particularly as British and Canadian authorities began to pursue a pacification policy not fundamentally dissimilar from that in the United States. As *Jackson's Sword* demonstrates, the Seminole, the Mikasuki, and the maroons of the Negro Fort found that the Spanish border offered little refuge from Andrew Jackson and his protégés.

Finally, and perhaps most important, the government of the American frontier was politically distinctive, far more representative and far less dependent on military officers than those of most European colonies and empires. After some experimentation and tension during the Federalist era before 1800, the combination of American federalism, legal due process, and representative democracy meant that nearly all the officials governing states along the borders and national territories along the frontier were civilians, elected or appointed through civilian influence—increasingly, the influence of local frontier citizens. The laws of the United States applied in territories as well as states, although states also had their own laws and courts and territories had their own ordinances and federal courts; military officers were subject to all of them. In contrast, most French and British imperial officials (to say nothing of Russians in the Caucasus, central Asia, or Siberia) were military commanders or civilians imbued with militarist examples and an imperial ethos of authoritarian hierarchy operating far from parliament, usually without civilian courts, and often applying martial law with little restraint from civilians in either colony or metropole. The officers of the American national standing army shared much of their counterparts' authoritarian ethos but faced much stronger pressure from civilian officials and their constituents, and they remained subordinate and accountable to the civilian representatives of the borderland regions where they were stationed. (European systems of "indirect rule" bear instructive comparison to U.S., and U.S. Army, relations with the Indians, but they are beyond the scope of this book.)[22]

Despite the nonintercourse laws passed by Congress to minimize friction between white and Indian, the combination of formal legal neutrality—the supposed monopoly of legitimate violence by the nation-state and its federated elements, and its denial to individuals, whether white or native—with white supremacist politics enabled whites to flood native territory. When the Indians lashed out or resisted white encroachment, white citizens used the democratic process to deny native claims of self-defense and call on white political authorities for assistance, which the army was then obligated to provide. Yet rumors of Indian attack often proved as illusory, as rooted in white visions of native savagery, as those of slave unrest in the South, leaving the army to handle the costs of overreaction. Opposition politicians would criticize the army and administration, the president and secretary of war would be irritated by the criticism, and Congress and the Treasury would complain about the expense. If military commanders actually used violence, they might be criticized for civilian casualties if they were unable to contain the Indians and the natives struck out against white frontiersmen, or for Indian deaths that might impugn the nation's reputation for paternal humanity and fair dealing toward childlike "savages."

While professional military officers had little *formal* or legal insulation or autonomy from political pressure, they were expected to exert substantial operational initiative and discretion so long as they could balance its exercise with the demands of subordination. The *practical* autonomy of the national standing army was enhanced but also complicated by institutional, social, political, technological, and cultural factors (see chapter 7 and the conclusion of *Jackson's Sword*). Most important, politicians virtually never interfered successfully with the basic system of promotion by seniority. Nor were military courts-martial or courts of inquiry initiated by civilian officials, by the army hierarchy at civilian instigation, or for overtly political reasons. Even more fundamentally, communications and transportation technology on the landward frontier changed very little between 1820 and the Civil War. Steamboats began to increase the speed of mail delivery and transportation up navigable rivers, but railroads and the telegraph did not become significant factors on the trans-Mississippi frontier until the 1850s, and they were not extended past the edge of the Plains before 1861.

Nor did military commanders have formal legal training or designated legal or political advisers, whether from the State Department (responsible for administration of the federal territories), the civilian Bureau of Indian Affairs, or state or territorial governments. Under these circumstances, responsible career officers were expected to exercise a great deal of discretion—a term repeated over and over again in their instructions—but they had to be discreet, taking care not to exceed the restraints, real or perceived, of subordination to civil authority, whether local (the demands of legal due process) or national (executive policy and congressional statute). Like policemen in tough neighborhoods, career professional officers had to judge the political situation, both on the ground ("in the street") and "at headquarters" in national, state, and territorial capitals, assessing how far they could go using intimidation and force against the contending parties, acting as diplomats to the Indians while mediating between local demands and national priorities. Although they would not be dismissed from the army for erring—I have not found a single officer who was—they surely knew that the army, and they as individuals, might suffer, through reduced appropriations or less desirable postings, if their actions led to controversy and embarrassment for their political masters. Their decisions were hardly permanent, but they certainly influenced the extent, shape, and limits of U.S. hegemony, while minimizing financial costs and human bloodshed, if not Indian suffering.[23]

Though they continued to share civilian convictions of the superiority of white civilization and engaged in land speculation like other Americans, the career professional officers of the nation's standing army felt more economic and emotional autonomy from sectional or sectoral attachments in the West than their counterparts and predecessors in Jackson's Division of the South during the strife on the Florida frontier in the 1810s. Historian Thomas Hietala demonstrates that "many Democratic expansionists viewed the acquisition of land and markets as essential to their program for sustaining the unique character of American social and political life" during the 1840s. While neither insensible to these desiderata nor incapable of profiting from their pursuit, army officers no longer lived in the agrarian Jeffersonian milieu that civilian expansionists were attempting to preserve and restore. Their service within increasingly formalized bureaucratic institutions led them to a Whiggish yet institutionally nonpartisan perspective that valued order, restraint, and stability in all aspects of personal and national life. By proclaiming themselves the neutral servants of the nation-state, army officers were usually able to avoid taking a direct stance on what Hietala calls the central cultural conflict of the decade. The officer corps had led the American conquest of Spanish Florida during the 1810s, in general agreement with the southern and western civilians who took a strong interest in the subject, but it proved content to follow the gradual trajectory of American public opinion in coming to imagine and accept the seizure of the Mexican Southwest during the 1840s.[24]

Given the limited population of the western states and territories and West Point's monopoly on new commissions during the 1820s, military commanders were rarely westerners themselves, though Tennesseans, Kentuckians, and Ohioans doubtlessly shared some of the antagonism toward Native Americans felt on frontiers farther west. This antipathy was surely aggravated by the experience of the War of 1812, but few officers of the postwar army had served in the West during that conflict. Hence, the desire to exterminate Indians common among contemporary civilian frontiersmen, and not uncommon among army officers prior to the War of 1812, depended largely on circumstance and the attitudes of their postwar counterparts: how violently did the Indians resist, and how easily were they overcome? U.S. power overawed most overt native opposition during the generation between the wars against the Seminoles, and military commanders rarely felt enough of a threat to discuss annihilation or extermination as a policy option. Indeed, the army's ranking westerners, Brigadier General Edmund Gaines (from Tennessee) and Zachary Taylor, who was retained in 1815 because of a frontier victory and was one of the few Kentuckians who wanted to remain in the army, displayed little of the extreme ethnocentricity and racism of many civilian frontiersmen. Gaines showed as much empathy for Indians as any white nineteenth-century American not involved in humanitarian reform (though his second wife was a famous peace advocate) and ultimately came to oppose his former patron's policy of removal. (However, this never altered Gaines's fundamentally coercive and paternalistic approach to dealing with the Indians.)[25] Despite his defense of Fort Stephenson against Indians in 1812 and his image as "Old Rough and Ready" in the 1840s, Taylor had worked earnestly to fashion himself into a gentleman whose Whiggishness was a compound of experienced caution, genteel moderation, and a subdued authoritarianism directed at white, Indian, and slave alike.

Nor were career military officers closely associated with any major sectors of the western economy: while many engaged in localized land speculation, at the cost of civilian envy and criticism, there is little if any evidence that they invested in fur companies, lead mining, or the Indian trade or were financially dependent on these or other primarily western economic sectors. Gaines did have plantation holdings and became an advocate for southern economic development, but his expansionism appears to have been more national than sectional or economic in motivation. Nor, unlike British colonial commanders, were army victories rewarded with large cash bonuses and peerages.[26] Taylor owned a plantation in Louisiana; the other senior officers (colonels and brevet brigadier generals) who became identified with the West by commanding there for extended periods—Henry Atkinson, Hugh Brady, Matthew Arbuckle, and Stephen W. Kearny—consistently advocated moderation and diplomacy toward the Indians whenever they thought it possible. Indeed, some company-grade officers believed that Arbuckle's Arkansas plantation distracted him from enforcing peace more vigorously among Cherokee emigrants, but Arbuckle could claim twenty years of local knowledge and experience to justify his moderation and restraint.[27]

Personal and institutional security, and a personal and institutional reputation for the values of order and good faith officers held dear, proved more powerful motives in the officer corps' worldview than white supremacism or the urgent drive for territorial expansion that had permeated Jackson's Division of the South. Most career officers preferred to imagine themselves commanding large-scale conventional operations, gaining reputation, fame, and glory leading soldiers in linear battles against their European counterparts. The army officer corps devoted little attention to the actual practice of warfare with Native Americans prior to the Second Seminole War, and little beyond debates in the *Army and Navy Chronicle* even then. The combination of this Eurocentric focus with the army's cautious, nonpartisan execution of the removal policy and frequent friction between officers and white frontiersmen hints at the officer corps' mental orientation and loyalty toward the nation-state that paid and employed it. Indeed, service in the West engendered at least as much disdain for white frontiersmen as for Native Americans, resentment that turned to disenchantment and outright disgust as the army became bogged down executing the removal policy in Florida during the Second Seminole War. Officers' distaste for this seemingly thankless work fostered ambivalence toward territorial expansion, especially as social and cultural distinctions grew between West Pointers socialized in the allied values of nationalism and gentility—expressed in disinterested service and hierarchical order—and rough-hewn frontiersmen pursuing material self-interest at the expense of national sovereignty and social hierarchy. By the late 1830s, many officers saw themselves as national policemen, their role as much to preserve law and order among unruly white citizens as to facilitate the westward movement.

Whatever diplomatic skills military commanders developed at the strategic level, whether through experience or their comparatively more objective position as representatives of national central authority, the nation's reliance on the standing army often proved counterproductive at the tactical and operational levels. Cost rather than desired capability drove force structure, and the regular army had never had a substantial mounted component in peacetime. In twenty-first-century terms, the constraints of the army's force structure meant that strategy was neither threat nor objective based; fiscal constraints drove force structure, limiting the missions the army could perform and the objectives it could pursue. The initial northwestern advance was conducted by infantry, which was unable to catch mounted Indians and was tethered to rivers for supply. It proved difficult to project or sustain military power—strategic, operational, or tactical, for whatever purpose—without greater mobility. Expense permitting, infantry commanders sometimes mounted small units (a company or two at most) for temporary patrols or pursuit, but this was playing the Indians' game, surrendering the cohesion and firepower of the army's linear discipline and exposing small, isolated contingents to defeat by more experienced Indian horsemen.

This was much more than simply a tactical dilemma for the army, which would ultimately rely on taking the offensive to destroy native food stocks and shelter in case of extended war. Developing mounted mobility was a critical factor in frontier civil-military relations and the army's aspiring professional monopoly. White frontiersmen used the army's inability to catch small parties of marauders to demand and sometimes secure funding for a variety of state and local citizen-soldier organizations, from the militia to expeditionary mounted volunteers ("rangers"), threatening the officer corps' hegemony over the direction of organized American military force. The army could not ensure its control, and thus an effective national direction, unless it could develop the mobility to catch Indians who dispersed to avoid its firepower. Indeed, given frontier citizen-soldiers' tendencies toward atrocity and ethnic cleansing, experienced professional soldiers considered them more likely to start wars than end them. Tactical capability was essential to executing national strategy, and even more important to maintaining national control over security strategy. On the western frontier, mounted mobility was ultimately a prerequisite for national sovereignty and geopolitical efficacy.

Army leaders therefore demanded greater mobility as the focus of national policy began to turn toward the central and southwestern Plains during the 1820s and 1830s. Following congressional demands to protect the Santa Fe trade during the 1820s, the Black Hawk War (the most serious outbreak of frontier hostilities since the First Seminole War) led to the creation of the Battalion of Mounted Rangers later in 1832 and the First Dragoon Regiment the following spring, the army's first permanent mounted units since the War of 1812. With that ice broken, the quest for mobility dominated War Department planning during the mid and late 1830s in reaction to the concentration of Indians driven from the Southeast. Following the apparent success of significant dragoon expeditions in the Southwest between 1834 and 1836 and the redeployment of most infantry regiments to Florida against the Seminoles in 1836 and 1837, mobile units assumed the dominant role in western military strategy and operations. Indeed, the single dragoon regiment deployed on the western frontier between 1833 and 1842 demonstrated the greatest economy of force in the national military strategy of that era.[28]

Despite this limited mobility, the national standing army did deter or quell Indian resistance to white expansion in the Upper Mississippi Valley, a task at which state and territorial volunteers and militia proved consistently inadequate and often dangerously incompetent. White frontiersmen and settlers were emphatically *not* irresistible: apart from the Civil War years, it was the national standing army—not the temporary, locally organized militia, volunteers, or vigilantes—that provided the consistent pressure required to force the Indians onto reservations and repressed their efforts to escape (certainly not without great difficulty and several tactical defeats) within a single generation after 1865. (Citizen-soldiers did commit most of the genocide against the California Indians in the 1850s.) Apart from the Texas Revolution and the years of the Civil War, regular forces directed by career officers dominated the U.S. force structure in virtually every large-scale conflict between whites and Indians from the Ohio wars of the 1790s through the final conquest of the western Indians. With the significant but intermittent exceptions of the Tennessee war against the Chickamauga Cherokee (roughly 1786–1795), the "First Creek War" (1813–1814), the Indian wars of the Texas Republic, the Civil War, and the genocides of the 1850s, volunteers were never more than auxiliaries, however important their service as scouts. In two of these cases, the federal government had bigger issues to deal with; in two, it did not seek war; and it had no sovereignty over the Texas Republic.

The army also became a significant, though hardly complete, restraint on intertribal warfare, at least between native and immigrant Indians in the region immediately west of Arkansas and Missouri, where U.S. policy needed peace most. Indeed, in its role as the enforcer of U.S. assertions to a monopoly on the legitimate use of force within the nation's boundaries, the army acted as the principal stimulus (or goad) to Indian pacification and the gradual development of a rational-legal social order among the native polities. Some Indian nations, particularly those with long experience adjusting to white pressure in the Southeast, like the Cherokee, developed impersonal or "objective" legal systems; they outlawed customs of individual and clan retaliation and revenge, largely on their own initiative, as defensive or preclusive responses akin to the "defensive modernization" of developing nations during the age of European imperialism. But for most tribes on the western frontier of white settlement, their adoption of a more centralized political system of relatively impersonal written law was first mediated through the U.S. Army. The army intervened to halt or prevent violence between individual whites and Indians and between Indian factions or tribes, limiting the unrestrained violence of massacre and turning native suspects over to white civil authorities per the principle of due process and civilian supremacy. Meanwhile, federal courts rarely met or accepted jurisdiction on the frontier, and state legislatures extended their jurisdiction largely as a means of ruling the Indians more directly, without federal mediation. Given the prejudice of white courts and juries and Indians' frequent inability to testify under state law, each tribe or nation gradually moved to create a formal legal system and police force of its own, if only to ward off white intervention.[29]

Though some historians have criticized the army for failing to sustain a presence on the upper Missouri between 1825 and the war with Mexico, the Missouri and Yellowstone expeditions of 1818–1825 were exceptional in scale, distance, and duration among western military operations prior to 1846. The army eventually succeeded in projecting U.S. power wherever civilian interest was sufficient to pay for doing so. In other words, while the army was insulated in personnel matters and autonomous in its routine operations and administration, it could not sustain policy independent of funding authorized by Congress. Apart from the First Seminole War and that with Mexico, the army was more the shield than the sword, as Francis Paul Prucha terms it, of the republic; it usually provided protective cover for settlement, albeit somewhat (and sometimes significantly) forward of most white farmers, rather than launching offensive wars against native polities prior to the arrival of numerous settlers and the growth of popular demand. Apart from the Missouri expeditions, this shield normally operated along a contiguous frontier, not far beyond the Mississippi or far up its tributaries (particularly the Red and the Missouri), until the 1840s. Indeed, by the mid-1840s, the national military presence lagged behind settlement in Minnesota, leading to popular demand for forward posts to encourage further settlement. The War Department learned a lesson from this disparity between military supply and political demand, and during the 1850s, new lines of forts were dispersed across the northern, central, and southern Plains to guard emigrant trails and settlement while intimidating the regional Indian hegemons, the Comanche and Sioux. Indeed, with the expansion of white settlement in California, the Pacific Northwest, and the Great Basin during the decade after the war with Mexico, the army was compelled to deploy posts across the now-continental United States in a scattershot pattern that had far more to do with civilian demand than any cohesive vision of military strategy.[30]

The result, whether of military action or its absence, was ultimately a more secure and more cohesive nation. By the mid-1820s, international competitors like Britain were excluded from significant authority among the Indians of the Old Northwest and the upper Mississippi, though this was accomplished at least as much by cabinet-level diplomacy and changes in the internal business dynamics of the fur trade as by military presence. (Of course, we might question how great that influence really was, or to what extent it was a projection of white inability to credit native agency.) White frontiersmen did not feel so neglected by the federal government that they attempted to mobilize a more locally responsive armed force by establishing independent republics within the boundaries or along the peripheries of the United States; nor did they appeal for international patronage or intervention, as some of their predecessors in the southern borderlands had done before 1820. Though armed settlement on other people's land certainly qualifies as a form or variant of filibustering on the spectrum of illegal group violence, white encroachment on Indian territory was not accompanied by political separatism or other fundamental, sustained challenges to U.S. national sovereignty. Texas was distinctive in its retention of an active state military force under the guise of the Rangers, and dissatisfaction with federal military protection proved a substantial factor in the state's secession in 1861, but these were southern political and cultural phenomena as much as western ones.

Most important for the future course of American development, western interests were never so dissatisfied that they united in sectional political form as a third major competitor for national power with the North and South. This was no small achievement, given the fluidity, even chaos, scholars usually associate with borderlands, and the value of the trans-Mississippi states to Union victory in the Civil War. With lower population densities, and without the desire to protect and extend plantation slavery, the western territories and states posed few of the challenges to national sovereignty seen in Georgia (discussed in chapter 3) and exhibited little of the alienation from national military policy that began in the southern states (especially Georgia) during the 1780s. Indeed, the unusual combination of relatively dense white settlement with federal reluctance to deploy military power against the Indians in Georgia is the exception that proves the rule of federal initiative in the pacing of expansion.[31]

Few organized nonstate actors, whether political or economic, seriously challenged U.S. sovereignty over relations with the Indians, and further white expansion ultimately depended on the contingencies of securing political support within the institutions of the nation-state through the constitutional processes of election and representation. To repeat, the ultimate physical pace and contours of citizen expansion ultimately depended on the nation-state, particularly its deployment of military forces to deter, defend against, or expel Indians. The American fur companies retreated, along with the United States, from Arikara and Blackfoot attack in the mid-1820s, and by the 1830s, most American trapping and trading were done by individuals—either mountain men or Indians who sold furs to American traders—rather than the "brigades" organized by the fur companies to penetrate Indian country in the early 1820s. Without national military assistance, the Indian trade on the central and southern Plains, like that at Bent's Fort in Colorado, remained dependent on native, particularly Comanche, cooperation, although dragoon expeditions hinted at the proximity of American power after the mid-1830s. More successful in their negotiations with the federal nation-state, the St. Louis merchants engaged in trade with Santa Fe secured U.S. military protection for their convoys as early as 1829. Despite some calls for military support of U.S. claims in Oregon, Congress and the executive were content to defer national intervention and military power projection into the Pacific Northwest until the 1840s, after white settlement had reached a politically significant level with the opening of the Oregon Trail and the migration of farmers. Even then, American military commanders did little detailed planning, unlike their British counterparts.[32]

Ultimately, civilian demands, rather than a military thirst for glory or hatred for Indians, drove westward expansion, yet this expansion usually required a permanent, and thus national, military presence to persist and succeed at an acceptable cost. To repeat, sustained white settlement on a substantial scale, by farmers rather than individual trappers or traders, rarely occurred prior to the deployment of national military forces—a pattern repeated across the continent from the Ohio Valley in the 1780s to the closing of the frontier a century later. (Georgia and Tennessee in the 1780s, when the nation-state was almost nonexistent, provide the best examples to the contrary.) Consequently, constraints on national military powers due to expense and political antagonism—usually from Old Republicans and Democrats, but potentially from Whigs and National Republicans if the rationale for larger forces was extermination of the Indians—limited the actual pace and extent of white expansion. (See appendix E for a schematic illustration of these dynamics.)

This constraint, however unintentional, contributed to a degree of conservation of national energy—economic, political, and social, as well as military and diplomatic—and thus to greater national cohesion and more intensive, powerful national growth—the commercialization, urbanization, and industrialization in eastern centers that historians now label the Market Revolution. Scholars should ponder whether that transformation would have taken the same shape if territorial expansion, and the replication of the Jeffersonian agrarian vision, had been as unrestrained as many contemporaries hoped, or as helter-skelter as many accounts have implied. Historians have commonly portrayed the decentralized character of politics between the Constitution and the Civil War as a source of expansive energy. They should also contemplate the extent to which democratic, liberal, and republican antipathy toward centralized power—particularly national military power and the taxation necessary to sustain it—actually operated to constrain the expansion that liberal populists sought, and ask what impact this unintended restraint had on the form and character of the American social and political order. Would the North have developed so differently from the South? Would there have been a Civil War, and would the greater dispersal of population and resources have prepared the North for subjugating the South?[33]

EXPLORING THE TRANS-MISSISSIPPI WEST: OFFICIAL RECONNAISSANCES, JUNIOR OFFICER INITIATIVES, AND THE CORPS OF TOPOGRAPHICAL ENGINEERS

Fiscal constraints limited the frequency of government-sponsored exploration, but career military officers were some of the leading actors in the "Great Reconnaissance" of the North American West. Such forays tended to correspond with new opportunities for imperial expansion, so they remained ad hoc and intermittent, rather than part of a concerted plan of continuing scientific inquiry, until the 1850s.[34] Nevertheless, they demonstrate both the fundamental expansionism of American military strategy and operations and the contingencies of bureaucratic structure and individual agency that so often limited the army's expansionist efforts. The expeditions led by Lewis and Clark and Zebulon Montgomery Pike between 1804 and 1807 were initiated to examine newly acquired and prospective territories as much to gather general strategic intelligence and to serve diplomatic purposes, like intimidating the Indians and arguing the boundaries with Spain, as to gain scientific knowledge per se. Once the flag had been shown, the Indians had been instructed in the identity of the new claimants to sovereignty, and general geographic information had been collected, the quest for scientific knowledge provided too little justification for more detailed exploration of regions so distant from the frontiers of significant white settlement. By 1808, Thomas Jefferson was about to leave office, James Wilkinson was busy defending himself against inquiries into his expansionist intrigues, and it was clear that the next president would have his hands full with Britain and the Floridas.

Another decade passed before the next major exploratory forays sponsored by the federal government in the West, under the direction of topographical engineer Stephen H. Long between 1819 and 1824. Long conducted two extended reconnaissances in the Plains and the Upper Mississippi Valley, in 1819–1820 and 1823 respectively. These followed three shorter trips to inspect the Illinois, Mississippi, Wisconsin, and Arkansas Rivers for potential sites for military posts between 1816 and 1818. In the process, Long chose the site for Fort Smith, reported on the resources and Indians of Illinois, and advised department commander Thomas A. Smith on the positioning of posts across the arc from the upper Mississippi to the Red River, providing an outline for strategic planning as the United States redeveloped its northwestern outposts and began to reach toward the Plains. Like Wilkinson, who had proposed the last strategic plan for western posts a full decade before, Long recommended a post at the mouth of the Platte; responding to Smith's suggestion, he advocated placing a post at the head of the Yellowstone and advised locating an intermediate post at the Mandan bend. Long thereby expanded routine efforts to site forts into more extensive reports on the Illinois and Oklahoma regions, leading his superiors to request similar reports to buttress their plan to launch a reconnaissance up the Missouri to the Yellowstone. This was virtually established policy by mid-1818, but Long's work provided useful ammunition to support requests for appropriations, and his forays to the Red, Washita, and Kiamachi Rivers laid the groundwork for the establishment of Fort Gibson on the Arkansas and Fort Towson on the Red in 1824. These efforts encouraged Secretary of War Calhoun to send Long onto the Plains for an exploratory expedition far beyond the existing boundaries of settlement.[35]

Like the Jeffersonian reconnaissances, Long's 1819 and 1823 expeditions were as much diplomatic as scientific, intended to show the flag among Indian populations distant from the centers of American power. Much like Zebulon Pike in 1806, Long referred to his 1819 foray across the Plains as a "military survey," seeking information that would be useful in future campaigns. His 1823 foray followed and then passed Pike's footsteps, exploring the region granted to the United States west of the Lake of the Woods by the Convention of 1818, where Long raised the flag and placed a boundary marker at Pembina. Carrying a letter of introduction from the British foreign minister, Lord Canning, Long went a hundred miles into Canada and then returned to the United States along the northern shore of Lake Superior. Both forays were accompanied by company-sized escorts of federal troops, and both led to tense encounters with local Indians. Indeed, Long fired Congreve-style rockets to intimidate the Kansa Indians, who had spent the winter of 1818–1819 harassing the advance guard of the Missouri River expedition at Cow Island.[36]

The army also contributed to a civilian expedition, led by scientist Henry Schoolcraft, in the upper Mississippi region in 1820. Schoolcraft was an ethnologist as well as a physical scientist, and Michigan territorial governor Lewis Cass accompanied him in order to confer and negotiate with the Indians, taking a company of soldiers for escort. One might have expected the Adams administration to continue or even expand these exploratory efforts, but the army's advance into the Upper Mississippi Valley and its retreat from the upper Missouri after the Arikara War made these expeditions less imperative by the mid-1820s. More generally, Long's condemnation of the Plains as the "Great American Desert" discouraged further exploration on the entire arc of the Plains and prairie frontier. (Long's record at assessing economic potential was not very good: he also misjudged the timber and mining potential of the northern woods he explored in 1823–1824.) A decade later, with Jackson as president and Cass as secretary of war, Schoolcraft, now U.S. agent to the Sioux, led an expedition to study the fur trade, report on British influence among the Indians, and try to discourage conflict between the Ojibway and the woodlands Sioux. Escorted by a company-sized force, he performed some vaccinations and took a census of the natives he was able to contact. But by the 1830s, the upper Mississippi was becoming too well known to require further government exploration, and the scene of reconnaissance, like the fur trade during the age of the mountain men, began to shift west.[37]

Indeed, the next significant exploratory venture undertaken by an officer was only quasi-official and was initiated by the officer himself, illustrating the dilemmas involved in permitting government agents to undertake official duties in private capacities. In 1831, sixteen-year veteran Benjamin L. E. Bonneville, a captain in the Seventh Infantry, sought and gained permission to travel to and beyond the Rockies, receiving leave of absence to do so. Although Bonneville intended to engage in the fur trade for his own profit, commanding general Alexander Macomb saw an opportunity to gather strategic and tactical intelligence and gave Bonneville instructions to that effect:

> Note particularly the number of Warriors that may belong to each tribe or nation that you may meet with: their alliances with other tribes and their relative position as to a state of peace or war, and whether their friendly or warlike dispositions towards each other are recent or of long standing. You will gratify us by describing the manner of their making War, of the

mode of subsisting themselves during a state of war . . . their Arms [and their effects], whether they act on foot or on horse back, detailing the discipline and maneuvers of the war parties, the power of their horses.[38]

After two years of silence, Bonneville reported from the Wind River country in present-day Wyoming, requesting an extension of his furlough to expand the range of his investigations (and his mercantile efforts). He regarded the local Indians as "extremely peaceable, and honest." Though very thorough, his report was much more concerned with the fur trade than Indian warfare; his principal diplomatic advice was to occupy Oregon to forestall British economic competition, "the sooner . . . the better." Indeed, Bonneville believed that a single infantry company, usually about forty soldiers, would be sufficient "to enforce all the views of our Government" there, particularly against the aggressive but dispersed trappers of the Hudson's Bay Company. Unfortunately for Bonneville, the War Department was undertaking an effort to compel officers to serve with their units, and he was denied an extension of his leave. Yet the orders seem to have missed him in the wilderness, and the intrepid captain overstayed his leave by a full two years, returning in 1835 to find he had been dropped from the rolls of the army. His reaction demonstrates some of the effects of socialization at the Military Academy after the War of 1812:

> Judge then . . . what must have been my mortification, when instead [of] the approbation I had expected for my exertions and enterprise [I lost the commission] I held dearer than life. Trained at the Military Academy, I became as it were identified with the Army; 'twas my soul, my existence, my only happiness . . . 'tis mortifying indeed. My character as a soldier has been fair too long to believe that my superiors will hesitate one moment, to restore me my character, and my rank.[39]

The ensuing controversy illustrates the internal fractures created by promotion by seniority and disparities in leaves and postings, but it also spotlights the army hierarchy's judicious evaluation of officers' future potential. Bonneville overstated his misfortune. Although he had gained some familiarity with the West during his regimental service on the edge of the Plains, he had already held a privileged, autonomous post as a recruiter in New York City. His ability to secure another such opportunity that was even more profitable, unsupervised, and exciting, while avoiding the responsibilities of troop duty at unhealthy Fort Gibson, irritated many of his fellow officers stuck on routine peacekeeping and company duty. Indeed, about half of those in the Seventh Infantry Regiment petitioned against his reinstatement, which would have cost them the increments of seniority (and for several, the promotion) his dismissal had produced. Macomb recognized Bonneville's ability, however, and the case ultimately went to the Senate, which consented to the administration's recommendation to restore the adventurer's rank. Macomb's faith in Bonneville's initiative and enterprise was rewarded six years after the general's death, when Bonneville commanded the Sixth Infantry at Mexico City, earning a brevet promotion to lieutenant colonel for gallant and meritorious conduct at the battles of Contreras and Churubusco, where he was wounded in action.[40]

Army exploration returned to official channels after Bonneville's expedition. The Corps of Topographical Engineers, autonomous since 1831, was augmented nearly 300 percent and became fully independent of the Corps of Engineers in 1838, after Congress passed legislation to expand the army. Most historians have followed William Goetzmann in viewing the topographical engineers as passionate proponents of territorial expansionism, attributing the 1838 increase to the growing pressure for expansion after a generation's hiatus. Missouri senators Lewis Linn and Thomas Hart Benton, for example, were ardent advocates of the Santa Fe trade and the settlement of Oregon, and Benton would soon become the political patron of John C. Frémont, commissioned as the second-lowest-ranking topographical engineer directly from civilian life in 1838. Frémont woud marry Benton's daughter Jessie three years later.

Yet promoting westward territorial expansion was not the statutory mission of the topographical engineers (aka "topogs"), nor was it their commanders' intention: the corps sought augmentation largely to meet the prosaic demands of military roads, river and harbor improvements, and the Seminole War in Florida (where commanders needed the topogs as mapmakers). In other words, executive branch intent and congressional support for the 1838 law were complex; the law was not simply a means by which expansionist Democrats could redirect national surveying expertise westward or a set of restrictions imposed on army engineers by egalitarian Democrats, as several scholars have recently suggested. Since the 1838 statute sharply restricted the assignment of army engineers to civil engineering projects, the enlarged corps had the personnel necessary to resume the exploration that western politicians demanded, but there is no evidence that the senior topogs saw this as their principal mission or envisioned it leading to the aggressive incursions Frémont undertook in Mexican California.[41]

Investigating the papers of these commanders, Vincent Ponko and Vernon Volpe recently demonstrated that the initial thrust of the Corps of Topographical Engineers, as led in 1838 by twenty-seven-year veteran Colonel John J. Abert, was scientific rather than expansionist. (This was also the case in 1839 and 1840 with the United States Exploring Expedition under navy lieutenant

Charles Wilkes, who was instructed to continue his scientific work even if the United States became engaged in war with Britain during the Canadian border crises of those years.) Indeed, Volpe found that Frémont, one of the most junior topogs, was initially subordinated to a civilian engineer, Joseph Nicollet; Frémont gained command of the 1842 expedition that made his reputation as the "Pathfinder" only because Nicollet died shortly before the journey was scheduled to begin.[42] Though Abert placed strict limits on Frémont's freedom of action, the junior engineer conspired with his father-in-law to go beyond his commander's instructions, ultimately to the point of aiding American rebels in California in 1846. Frémont's third expedition was intended to clarify the sources of the Red and Canadian Rivers, but he detached Lieutenant James W. Abert, son of the chief topographical engineer, to do so while he proceeded to California. Though Abert recommended a location for a new post, showed off his percussion rifles to the Indians, and observed that Americans would invest in the mines of New Mexico if the United States gained control there, his party was composed mostly of civilians, without a significant military escort. The junior Abert's report included a number of caustic aspersions directed at various Indians but was notably free of expansionist sentiment.[43]

Frémont's disobedience and belligerence were exceptions to the midcentury officer corps' pattern of subordination to civilian authority, and relying on Frémont as an archetype of the midcentury army officer presents a badly distorted picture of military sentiment regarding territorial expansion. Indeed, Frémont's political connections—which helped him secure assignment to the exploratory missions—and aggressiveness were unusual even in the Corps of Topographical Engineers, where officers' support for expansion was certainly increased by Frémont's example and the romantic vision of national potential fostered by their experiences as explorers. Frémont was also distinctive in that he was one of only six topographical engineers out of seventy-two commissioned without some socialization at West Point. (All six were commissioned in 1838; the corps was eliminated in 1863, and the experiment was not repeated.) Indeed, just as many of the new topographical engineers commissioned in 1838 were former officers and West Point graduates, including George Gordon Meade and Andrew A. Humphreys, who had resigned during the boom times of the mid-1830s; their professional socialization and commitment reemerged amid the instability of civilian life following the Panic of 1837.

The culmination of Frémont's first term in uniform provided a potent demonstration of both the army's political subordination and its institutional autonomy from civilian control—the fate that lay in wait for junior officers motivated more by politics and ideology than by institutional rank and discipline. Ultimately, professional military roles and routines triumphed over the

John C. Frémont, expansionist icon expelled from the army, in an 1856 presidential campaign lithograph. (Courtesy Library of Congress, LC-DIG-ppmsca-03212)

politicized self-assertion of the romantic rebel. Frémont was court-martialed after he refused to turn over the military governorship of California to thirty-six-year veteran Brigadier General Stephen W. Kearny, the genteel, authoritarian dragoon commander designated governor by President Polk, the Democratic expansionist. Kearny had his own connections to match the Benton-Frémont ties: born to a wealthy New Jersey family and married to the stepdaughter of William Clark, the former explorer, Missouri governor, and superintendent of western Indian affairs.

Polk sought to avoid court-martialing Frémont, but he went ahead after Senator Benton threatened to mount a congressional investigation to vindicate his son-in-law. Nor did the junior topographical engineer get the sympathetic court of peers and former subordinates that General Macomb had arranged for Inspector General John Wool in the Cherokee country a decade before. Benton provided the legal defense, which was surely intended to intimidate the court's members, accusing the army of prejudice against an officer who had not graduated the Military Academy. Although the court sentenced Frémont to dismissal, it did compromise by recommending leniency (reinstatement with sanctions like suspension of pay or seniority). Senior topographical engineers Stephen H. Long (the explorer from the 1810s and 1820s) and James D. Graham joined in that verdict and recommendation. Still hoping to smoothe things over, the president invalidated the most severe conviction (for mutiny), remitted the sentence, and ordered Frémont back on duty without further penalty, but the arrogant Pathfinder demanded full exoneration, an annulment of the conviction on all charges.

Polk then acknowledged the autonomy of the army as a professional institution and accepted the court's sentence, costing him the support of Benton, a former ally in the cause of territorial expansion. Frémont demonstrated his limited commitment to the army and its professional ethic by departing its ranks to enter politics. His partisan efforts would lead to his appointment as a major general of volunteers in 1861 and to his resignation amid friction with President Lincoln in 1862. Career army officers were not discharged in peacetime reductions in force after 1821: if they were dismissed it was for ethical deficiency or indiscipline; if they resigned it was to pursue civilian economic opportunities or because they could not adjust to military subordination. Politically focused officers were much more likely to leave the army than to suffer political sanction—a remarkable demonstration of the army's autonomy from the partisanship of Jacksonian civil government.[44]

Stephen W. Kearny: genteel dragoon, stern peacekeeper, frontier diplomat. From *Graham's Magazine*, reprinted in Zoeth Eldredge, *The Beginnings of San Francisco* (1912)

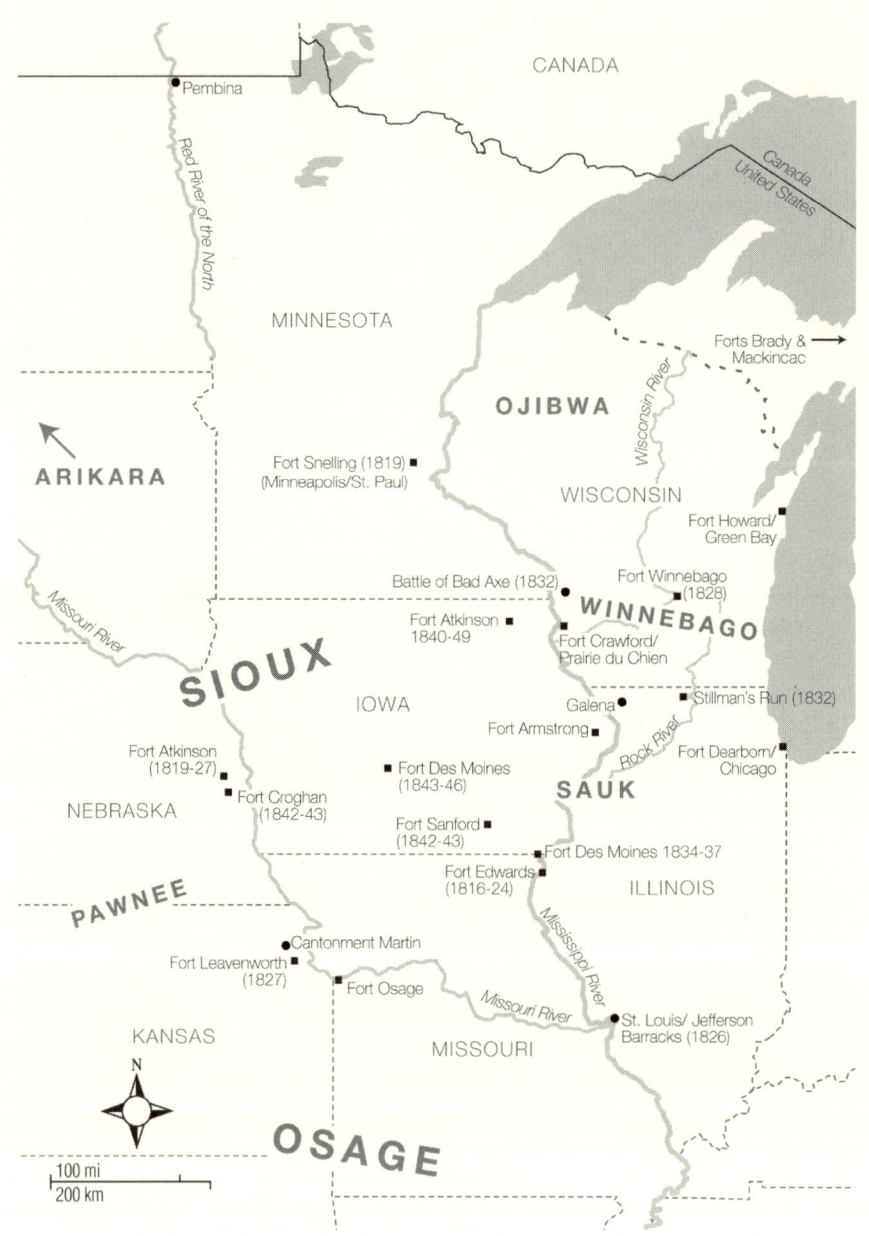

The western frontier (map by Tracy Ellen Smith)

2
SUBORDINATION AND DISCRETION
The Dilemmas of Expansion, Peacekeeping, and Civil-Military Relations on the Northwestern Frontier

Professional soldiers shared civilian faith in the superiority of white culture over Indian. Following the general Enlightenment concept of social progress through stages of civilization, they routinely labeled the Native Americans savages and expected their physical extinction, or at best their assimilation and cultural extinction in the face of white expansion. Apart from that deep-rooted ethnocentrism, the career officer's most significant values, and those most important or distinctive to him as a professional soldier, were stability, personal integrity, and service to the polity. When they reflected on the character of their society as a whole, career officers shared the general civilian belief in a liberal republican social and political order and majoritarian democracy, but in their daily institutional practice, order meant authoritarian discipline and hierarchy rather than republican liberty or independence. Combined with the value of service (responsibility and obligation), stability (cohesion and order) ultimately meant subordination and accountability to constitutional civil authority, to protect, preserve, and advance the objectives established by elected civilian representatives to foster and maintain a liberal republican society. Although the professional military ethic was distinctive, it was neither isolated nor alienated from the most fundamental values of its parent society: the formal legal and political equality of white men and their superiority over non-whites.[1]

Beyond personal ethics, military integrity meant "honor," in the form of good faith, equity, and some sense or vision of justice. Good faith, equity, and justice came from a sense of fair dealing and fair play rooted in genteel moderation and *noblesse oblige*, the American military officer's heritage from his

35

European, and particularly his British, predecessors. The obligation to serve, or at least to protect, those less powerful (not so much in the sense of less armed, but less organized, less trained, and less experienced) gave the professional soldier his claim to honor and provided the ethical justification for departing from the liberal, relatively democratic norms of American civilian society in favor of the authoritarian order of military hierarchy and discipline. Maintaining the existing social order through relatively impartial national service meant something akin to a strict paternalism, the professional officer's dominant approach to Indians, enlisted soldiers, and ordinary white citizens alike. Thus, though they often felt empathy, even sympathy, for Native Americans and their plight amid white expansion, in practice, military commanders ultimately viewed relations between Native Americans and whites, like international relations and relations within military institutions, through the lens of authoritarian hierarchy. As Thomas Jefferson vowed three decades before, "the principles on which our conduct toward the Indians should be founded are justice and fear." In practice, authoritarian paternalism meant that officers often saw fear as a means to achieve justice and short-term violence as a means to secure long-term peace, security, and survival, for Indians as well as whites. Power would serve liberty; officers believed the larger liberty of citizens could not be preserved without infringing on the individual liberties of those temporarily subjected to the army's authority, itself subordinate to the legitimate decisions of constitutionally elected civilians.[2]

The professional officer's vision of Indian relations was neither simple nor united in an integrated whole. When the nation's objective was expansion, career soldiers pursued expansion, but they were not fervent, ideological, or missionary expansionists. Unlike many civilians, even conservative ones, veteran officers did not sing hymns to the future of the frontier or the West or ardently seek opportunities to dispossess the Indians before the 1850s. Indeed, from Zebulon Montgomery Pike to Stephen H. Long's "Great American Desert" to General William Hazen after the Civil War, nineteenth-century army officers denigrated the potential of the West as often as they praised it. Facing Jacksonian populism, anti-institutionalism, and contempt for the abstract rule of law, conservative military commanders hoped to maintain social and political order while advancing national expansion, to minimize disruption through discipline, to maximize national growth and enhance national cohesion through the accumulation and employment of nation-state authority and nation-state power.[3]

This dynamic might have produced an authoritarian desire to restrain fellow citizens regardless of circumstances, but the reality of white greed and aggression multiplied military ambivalence toward their imperial mission. Officers looked forward to national greatness and accepted the objective of national, ethnically white expansion, but they found it difficult to blame Native Americans for resistance and strained to justify the greed, deceit, and disorder of expansion to themselves. In contrast, while civilian policy makers, drawn from the same class and culture, shared the professional military officer's values of integrity, equity, and justice, they did not have to apply them in practice amid tension and conflict or confront the dissonance between values and reality on the frontier. Civilian policy makers, congressional or executive, had little direct contact with the damage frontier whites did to native culture, the degradation and disintegration military commanders saw in the borderlands every day. The Revolution encouraged the faith of cosmopolitan civilian elites in the possibility of transforming native culture and society without the use of massive resources or power; like critical historians writing in the twentieth century, professional soldiers implicitly recognized "the hollowness and uncritical naiveté of the[ir] optimistic rhetoric."[4]

Wars against European powers were certainly more attractive to officers than those against Indians, because deterring foreign aggression was thought to require military preparation by trained career professionals organized at the national level, which posed significantly less danger of conflict between officers and their civilian employers. Surprising as it may seem, however, career self-interest—in effect, a stake in a bureaucratic social order—made the professional officers of the Jacksonian era significantly less likely to seek expansion and war or to willfully violate American neutrality and foreign borders than their Jeffersonian predecessors, for fear of the disorder, and perhaps the competition for military command, such adventures might foster. The army's officers were much less enthusiastic about war and expansion than many historians have suggested; the average officer certainly did not sing the slogans of Manifest Destiny and Young America with the fervor or frequency their professional interests might lead one to expect. The army was the first major public-sector employer on a national scale in the United States. Its officers espoused centralist, indeed statist, values that served but were also shaped by their interests and roles, values that fit their assumptions about the way American society was and ought to be. Their professional role as the principal defenders of American national sovereignty fostered a strong personal and institutional interest in augmenting the federal government's power and legitimacy, and their ongoing search for personal and organizational security bred a yearning for order and stability that they expressed in the stern idioms of legalism and national sovereignty. Their vocation challenged by the American fondness for locally controlled militia, volunteer citizen-soldiers, and extralegal filibustering, professional military commanders increasingly responded by proclaiming the need for centralized national control over the organized use of armed force.

Changing social, political, and institutional dynamics decisively influenced military responses to the law enforcement and foreign policy problems they confronted in the nation's internal and external borderlands. As officers became more sensitive to the fragility of social order and their place within it, they increasingly came to believe that American national honor and security were endangered less by patchwork collections of Indian polities than by restless whites whose aggression repeatedly led to war. Constantly on the move, without effective regulation by the government or national social and economic elites, frontier settlers were a threat to the existing social order and a glaring demonstration of the limited value the government held for its citizens. Nevertheless, the officer corps proved willing to serve these settlers' interests if ordered to do so by a government that allowed them to remain in service despite disputes with frontier citizens. Nor did career officers have much choice if they wanted to remain in service, given all that meant in terms of personal economic security, self-image, authority, and prestige among whites of the genteel upper middle class and elites. Empathy for Native Americans, combined with devotion to order, might mean efforts at paternalistic restraint toward white citizens but rarely the physical violence directed at Indians, since the professional soldiers' dedication to service, and their legal and ideological subordination to the constitutional authorities who represented civilian society, normally precluded the coercion they otherwise tended to advocate. Whatever their distaste for the effects of racialized majoritarianism, career military officers normally accepted the constraints of representative democracy and the constitutional separation of powers and adhered to civilian legal procedure; there are very few examples of that distaste actually overwhelming officers' subordination in operations and diplomacy on the frontier.

Much as historian Thomas Leonard has shown for the post–Civil War army, this combination of empathy and anger meant that officers' anger toward Indians was actually aggravated by the anger they felt toward whites. Indeed, commanders accustomed to obedience could easily shift from empathy to anger when frustrated, when the subjects of their empathy refused their paternal direction. Unable to lash out at white citizens, officers could only dissipate their anger against bad Indian "children," who were, after all, the obstacles to successful national expansion. When Native Americans resisted white customs and norms, or when white customs were harmful but the Indians did not adapt or reject them, professional soldiers as well as civilian reformers and policy makers blamed the childlike native savage, who was apparently unable to overcome his environment as enlightened philosophers had hoped. No longer considered a likely candidate for incorporation in American society, he became an obstacle to be driven from the path of progress. Whatever regret officers professed to feel, they were loath to spare the rod because they saw few, even diminishing prospects of sustained progress toward white standards of civilization among most Indians. With the Indians out of the way, career soldiers might hope to redirect their attention to more pleasant professional pursuits, like commanding large units in splendid drill to prepare for wars with European foes in which they could win fame and glory without the moral ambiguities and political dilemmas of peacekeeping and conquest.[5]

The qualms Leonard identifies occurred more at the level of daily practice than in general attitudes and policy between the 1820s and 1840s; senior officers' attitudes toward Native American cultures and their future status within the United States usually took overtly humanitarian but ultimately coercive forms quite similar to those found by scholars investigating the attitudes of contemporary civilian officials. In 1816 future commanding general Alexander Macomb summed up his vision of Indian relations in orders to several subordinates in the Fifth Military Department along the northern border:

> A respectful distance, avoiding all kinds of familiarity . . . and protecting them from injury and insult have always had a happy effect. In cases where the Indians themselves are insolent and wicked prompt punishment will go a great way towards commanding their respect and bringing them to order. Above all to be prepared for every contingency, to punish or protect them cannot fail to insure that harmony and good understanding which result from a knowledge that the power & disposition are ever ready to protect the innocent and punish the guilty.[6]

Macomb's language was more forceful than that of civilian policy makers, who were insulated from the reality of frontier violence and the threat of its escalation, but the difference was in degree rather than kind. Despite the many differences between European and American colonial practice, the indispensability of force, predicated on assumptions of native savagery shared by career soldiers and most white civilians, always remained at the core of American official thinking, both civil and military, about Indian relations. The denial of tribal sovereignty or U.S. citizenship allowed commanders to apply these fundamentally authoritarian values far more extensively, and coercively, toward the Indians than toward disorderly white frontiersmen, who were assured the protection of citizenship in the polity—increasingly democratic among white men—to which professional officers were held accountable. Andrew Jackson's disdain for any notion of Indian sovereignty, expressed six months before he left the army, accurately reflected the attitude of most white Americans, civilian and military alike:

> There can be no question but congress has the right to Legislate on this subject—The policy of treating with Indian tribes within the Jurisdiction of the united States and acknowledging its sovereignty, could only have arisen at a time when the arm of Government was too weak to execute any law passed for the regulation of the Indian tribes within our Territorial limits—To treat with the Indians acknowledging our sovereignty, and situate[d] within our declared Territorial limits as a nation has always appeared very absurd to me. . . . It appears to me that it is high time to do away the farce of treating with Indian tribes.

Writing the same year, Colonel Joseph Smith of the Third Infantry demonstrated what this would mean in practice, warning of "great evils" from the Indians "unless kept in constant check by a display of force, suitable to their complete control." Smith did not attempt to understand the particular reasons behind Indian attacks; to him, they were simply "evidence of the mischievous character of savages generally."[7]

Yet American military officers were much less belligerent or ruthless against Arikara, Winnebago, Sauk, and Seminole than their British, French, and Russian counterparts were in India, Africa, and Asia. Indeed, the civil-military, or at least center-periphery, dynamic of European imperialism—whereby military commanders in the colonies seized the initiative to launch adventures to win personal fame and brutally punish natives, often to the dismay of metropolitan government and public opinion—was ordinarily reversed on the North American frontier. U.S. Army officers normally restrained expansion and mass violence rather than accelerating or intensifying them; indeed, they saw moderation as the norm, even when constraining others with threats and violence. Senior American military commanders were suspicious of all potential troublemakers, including Indian haters on the frontier, and they were usually far more skeptical of rumors of native unrest and violence than civilians (federal or local, official or private) or their counterparts among British officers in India.[8] Indeed, Smith had hinted at the depth and extent of the officer corps' authoritarianism a year before, remarking that several courts-martial against enlisted men accused of robbing Indians had failed for lack of admissible evidence: confessions were "drawn from the soldiers in such a manner as to forbid them to be used as evidence before any court." Nevertheless, Smith saw to it that "a portion of the men were summarily & severely punished"—effectively a second round of brutality—and ordered the soldiers to repay the Indians' losses. Indeed, though few enlisted soldiers were killed, their routine subjection to casual blows and elaborate punishments meant that they, rather than Native Americans, suffered the most frequent violence at the army's hands.[9]

Macomb, Smith's superior, dismissed rumors of native hostility even as the regiments under his command moved to establish the northwestern posts and extend U.S. sovereignty over the Indians. An engineer and staff officer for most of his career, Macomb was always a moderate and a peacemaker, commanding in only one battle (Plattsburgh in 1814) as he rose to the army's top post of commanding general, which he held between 1828 and 1841. Preparing to establish Fort Howard at Green Bay in May 1816, he advised division commander Jacob Brown that he would sound out the Indians to see whether they would oppose his advance. "It will be most prudent to avoid irritating those numerous tribes, and it will comport better with the interest, and I trust with the views of the U. States, to arrange amicably, our business with them." Macomb was working to forge good relationships with his British counterparts opposite Detroit and had the vision to see Indian relations as a problem for both nations. That August he assured Brown that guns the British had given the Indians were "nothing more than a customary present," like those given by the United States, necessary for Native Americans to hunt and subsist at a time when neither government could supply them with food.[10]

Like Macomb—and most officers of all ranks stationed on the frontiers—brevet General Henry Atkinson normally doubted that Indian unrest and violence were as great as civilian frontiersmen suggested. Practical concerns—limited resources, demands for economy in spending, and possible political repercussions—encouraged institutional caution and restraint in reacting to endemic rumors of native violence raised by white frontier citizens. But for many soldiers, the most emotionally powerful source of skepticism about alleged native violence was their growing antagonism toward, rooted in repeated friction with, disorderly frontier citizens, whose rapacity and lack of self-restraint were so clearly the source of Indian rage, however "savage" that response. Reacting to an 1829 incident (the "Big Neck War") in Missouri, Atkinson expressed both a responsible caution and the professional officer's desire for equity, integrity, and honor: "as some doubts exist who were the aggressors . . . it is necessary to a fair understanding of the matter that the whites as well as the Indians should be prosecuted. Justice as well as policy demands this course."[11]

Edmund Gaines went even further; his blend of anger and empathy toward natives and citizens is perhaps the best example of military paternalism on the inland frontier. As a son of the Tennessee frontier, the brigadier always envisioned himself as the protector of white settlement. He certainly did not doubt the superiority of white culture and civilization and frequently called out expensive citizen-soldier volunteers at the first rumor of Indian unrest, to the point that he was sidelined from operational command for the last decade of his career. Excitable as he was when action seemed to loom, Gaines was a thoughtful, critical, and articulate advocate for his causes. Preparing to invade Florida in pursuit of the Seminoles in 1817, he advised new secretary of war John C. Calhoun that "the savage must be taught and compelled to do that which is right, and to abstain from that which is wrong. The poisonous cup of barbarism cannot be taken from the lips of the savage by the mild voice of reason alone; the strong mandate of justice must be resorted to, and enforced." Yet, while ever ready to crush native threats to the progress of white civilization, Gaines also felt a moral obligation to shield the Indians from illegal aggression and the corruption of dissolute frontiersmen. "We must cultivate the friendship of these savages, be just to them, feed the hungry, clothe the naked, visit and heal the sick, and do unto them as we would that our strong civilized neighbors should do unto us. Otherwise we *must annihilate them*. This we cannot do without forgetting what is due to our own interests, and our own self-respect."[12]

The trade and intercourse acts appeared to present unequivocal declarations of national sovereignty over Indian relations. They delineated specific geographic boundaries "between the United States and various Indian tribes," authorizing the president to have these marked, and deemed that no cessions or sales of land by Indians were valid unless confirmed by treaties made by the United States. Whites (whether U.S. citizens or not, such as British traders) could enter and do business in Indian lands only with licenses granted by federal officials. Crimes against Indians and their intended punishments, which were mostly equivalent to those for similar crimes against whites, were laid out in great detail. The president was authorized to employ military force to remove intruders, and the 1796 law declared "that it shall be lawful for the military force of the United States, to apprehend every person, who shall, or may be found in the Indian country, over and beyond said boundary line . . . in violation of any of the provisions or regulations of this act," though they had to be remanded to the civil authorities of adjoining states or territories within ten days. Indeed, the act pronounced it "the duty of the military forces of the United States, when called upon by civil magistrates," to aid the latter.

Whites within the states and territories were to receive compensation for Indian crimes committed against them, so long as they did not seek "private satisfaction or revenge." The ascension of the Jeffersonian Republicans did not change these provisions, save to intone that the army should treat violators "with all the humanity which the circumstances will possibly permit" and turn them over to civilian custody within five days of arrest. These laws remained fundamentally similar throughout the period; only one statute was added between 1802 and 1834, and the 1834 law added little except an emphasis on keeping liquor out of Indian territory.[13]

Despite the outward clarity of these laws, enforcing them entangled military commanders in a web of greed, politics, and legal ambiguity for which their army experience provided little preparation; whether rough-hewn, authoritarian, or genteel, professional soldiers rarely found aggressive frontier businessmen very congenial. In 1822 Colonel Talbot Chambers and Major Willoughby Morgan (son of Revolutionary War general Daniel Morgan) were assessed a fine of $5,000—several years' pay and compensation—for arresting two American Fur Company traders because they considered the licenses issued by a civilian Indian agent inadequate. Returning from an expedition to seize liquor from dealers in the Caddo villages along the Texas-Louisiana frontier the same year (1817), brevet Major David Riddle fumed that "those Damned villains will get their property again" through the civil courts; "three of them have already." Riddle was pleased that his commander (William Trimble) approved of his performance, but the favor of military superiors could only salve so much: as historian Francis Paul Prucha has observed, federal military commanders "had little hope of a sympathetic court" on the frontier and were "ill-supported" by Washington. Similar harassment by well-connected local businessmen afflicted Majors Stephen W. Kearny, David Twiggs, and Enos Cutler at northwestern posts during Jackson's first administration.[14]

This "uneven match" with frontier civilians, who could readily draw on egalitarian values to secure representation, fostered ill will and civil-military tensions when career soldiers accustomed to command realized the practical political limits to federal executive (or nation-state) autonomy. The Treasury appears to have paid officers' court costs and fines during the 1810s and 1820s, but in 1832 Jacksonian populism and the tensions of southeastern squatter removal led Congress to warn that it would no longer appropriate funds to do so. Subject to costly sanction for enforcing the law, commanders naturally felt embittered. Zachary Taylor provides an example: after more than a quarter century of national military service, disillusioned by half a decade of indefinite, often contradictory instructions from the Jackson administration,

Taylor raged that Secretary of War Lewis Cass had "acted a mean & contemptible part" in his "timid" response to the colonel's expulsion of miners trespassing on Indian land in Illinois.[15]

Experienced military commanders recommended a number of alternatives to facilitate enforcement of the intercourse laws. In 1819 Atkinson blamed the competitive character of the Indian trade for the "underhanded, backbiting policy" of private-sector merchants, who fostered "jealousy & distrust . . . toward Gover[n]ment" among the Indians; he recommended the federal government take over all trade with the Indians, though it seems unlikely this could have been attempted without the support of military government or martial law. Five years later, Major Daniel Baker advised Edmund Gaines that each tribe should be concentrated geographically because the courts interpreted the laws to apply only within lands unceded to the United States rather than to Indians themselves, wherever they actually lived or traveled. Without such a reservation policy, merchants could "violate the laws with impunity, and to render abortive the benevolent views of the Government in relation to their welfare and improvement." In 1845, following another generation of friction and frustration, First Dragoon Regiment commander Stephen W. Kearny contended that "the good of the Indians would be much advanced and the peace of the country much more effectively secured if Congress would pass a law declaring the whole of the Indian country under martial law." Commanding general Winfield Scott agreed with Kearny's rationale, but it was as politically unacceptable to Americans in 1845 as it had been seventy or eighty years before, in the Proclamation of 1763 and the Quebec Act.[16]

Military antipathy toward frontier citizens also extended to the federal executive branch officials charged with overseeing relations with each tribe or subgroup—the so-called Indian agents. Given their socialization as the most nationally minded, overtly disinterested government officials, professional soldiers often disdained these civilian agents because they seemed so susceptible to partisanship and grasping local interests. Like most federal civil officials, including surveyors, land office registrars, customs collectors, district attorneys, and marshals, Indian agents were appointed on the basis of local and political connections, even those being rewarded for national service, often as former army officers. (This accounted for a substantial proportion of Indian agents during the decade following the War of 1812; see appendix C.) Andrew Jackson brought the "rotation in office" concept of partisan patronage to Indian agents along with other civilian officials (but *not* army officers) in the executive branch, replacing half the agents, many of whom had a decade or more of experience, within thirty months of his inauguration.[17]

Indian agents increasingly acted as party electoral operatives among nearby whites; historian Ronald Satz observes that "political factionalism . . . turned the Indian service into a sordid battleground." During the 1830s this politicization drew agents into the web of financial patronage and collusion by which networks of Jacksonian "new men" took advantage of Indian removal. Commissioner of Indian Affairs C. A. Harris appears to have embezzled federal funds and secured land for himself in Indian treaties, something no army officer had done since Jackson, in the surveys he had overseen as a general (though some individual officers certainly profited from lands ceded by Indians due to their pressure). Harris resigned under a cloud in 1838. Several years later, Major Ethan Allen Hitchcock's report on Indian affairs west of Arkansas demonstrated that some agents were employed by businesses with contracts to supply the same Indians the agents were supposed to protect. Striving to preserve peace, and at least the appearance of objectivity and integrity in Indian relations, professional commanders sought greater military influence over the conduct of Indian relations, and they showed no more faith in the objectivity of former officers, now loosed from the institutional priorities and disciplines of the army, than in agents without military experience.[18]

Reservations about the civilian Indian agents could come from either side of military paternalism: whether Native Americans needed more paternal care and protection, which officers thought agents were too greedy to provide, or further reminders of U.S. power, career professional officers believed they had the disinterested integrity to balance the competing demands of nation, natives, and citizens. Indeed, the assignment of agents to specific tribes encouraged the agents to identify with their Indian charges, complicating and confusing the government's efforts at supervising intertribal relations. Thus, anticipating debates later in the century, Alexander Macomb advised a subordinate that he considered the agents "inferior to the military" and repeatedly avowed that the army should replace the civilian agents altogether: "the natives would be both better satisfied and better treated. . . . our relations with the Indians would be both more honourable and profitable to the government and nation." On the eve of the "Winnebago War" in 1827, Colonel Josiah Snelling, commander of the Fifth Infantry stationed in Minnesota and Wisconsin, complained that the army had too little authority to control Indian relations: "The Military on this frontier are useless for want of discretionary power . . . if it is not intrusted to the Commander, Men of Straw with Wooden Guns and Swords will answer the purpose [just] as well."[19]

Some veteran commanders believed that this division of authority—or, more specifically, their lack of authority—threatened national objectives. When the Wisconsin tribes went at each other seven years later, Henry Atkinson asserted that the confusion of authority and jurisdiction was so great that the

Indians should be allowed to settle their differences among themselves. This concession would have essentially voided both the pacification policy, critical to the advance of white settlement, and the "civilization" policy. Indeed, Atkinson blamed civilian judicial authorities for violence among the Indians because they tended to claim lack of jurisdiction and release natives who had committed violence against other Indians. The brigadier reacted by holding Indian prisoners under military control, but he lacked the authority to do so routinely or for the long term. In 1827 Edmund Gaines advised that the army should take over the agents' role, and a decade later he summed up military attitudes and objectives toward Indians and the government's civilian agents while explaining the value of a cordon of posts along the frontier: "This line . . . will enable us to afford complete protection to the emigrating . . . Indians, and [to the] frontier inhabitants . . . provided always, that the commandants of these posts are amply supplied with means and authority to act as general superintendents of Indian affairs, to settle promptly, all their disputes; to restrain the irritated parties by timely admonition, and, if necessary, by force."[20]

Spurred by their sense of responsibility for peace and national security, senior military commanders often communicated with Indian agents as if they were subordinates subject to army hierarchy. This was particularly true when officers wanted to ensure that Indians were supplied with food and clothing (or cloth), a basic condition in most treaties and a starting point for sustained diplomacy. In 1816 Andrew Jackson's adjutant lectured the veteran Indian agents of the Southeast that "the major general commanding expects your attendance" to receive goods for distribution to the Indians; a generation later Henry Atkinson admonished the Potawatomi subagent that he was obligated to provide rations to fulfill that tribe's treaty. Yet, unlike some British officers who sought posts as "politicals" in India, American professional soldiers disliked being tasked as agents themselves, as happened to Zachary Taylor and other officers at Forts Crawford and Winnebago when the government was pushing to expropriate the Winnebago during the mid-1830s. Professional soldiers socialized in disinterestedness and accustomed to hierarchical command invariably worried about the extent of their authority as agents; the usual problems of distance were aggravated by local and commercial expectations of favor and the lack of bureaucratic regulations that had become increasingly familiar to career military officers, especially in matters of supply and accountability. (Unlike the army staff bureaus, neither the Bureau of Indian Affairs nor its predecessors had comprehensive written regulations prior to 1850.)[21]

Officers' reactions to the impact of white traders and settlers on the enlisted soldiers under their command neatly illustrate the confluence of class and ethnic biases and their desire for military discipline and order. Despite a series of laws restricting its sale or trade within Indian country, alcohol was a leading source of trouble for enlisted men as well as Indians. Colonel William Whistler hoped that moving military posts from Arkansas to Indian country would have a steadying effect on his soldiers, reducing local civil-military conflict while enhancing discipline. "One strong reason why the troops should be placed in the Indian country . . . is, that the government of the civil and military is so different that the two cannot well exist in the same vicinity. . . . The influence exercised . . . by the civilians over the soldiery often tends to produce acts of insubordination." An enlisted man's son made genteel by his epaulets, the colonel claimed this malign influence was only "exerted by the lower order of citizens." Whistler thought these degraded citizens were as much in need of control as the Indians; indeed, he hoped that insecurity would instill a sense of anxiety, dependence, and order among them: if troops were placed inside Arkansas, "the people would consider themselves safe and secure from the Indians. The abandoned and disorderly portion of them would at once commence their lawless aggressions on the persons and property of the Indians." The thrust of Whistler's discipline was reversed by dragoon lieutenant Richard Stoddard Ewell, who considered the Cherokee "very well disposed . . . towards the whites" and believed "it would be much better to have the post in Arkansas where the people are cutting each others throats ad libitum." Whether the army policed whites or Indians, these professional soldiers felt that it was better to keep whites and Indians separated and dependent on the army's aid, subject to the sovereign power of the nation-state that gave career officers employment.[22]

Historian Francis Paul Prucha suggests that the ambiguities of enforcing the intercourse laws may have fostered "trepidation" among career officers, but concludes that "the disputes and controversies between agents and officers were more than balanced by the energy and zeal with which most of the frontier commanders undertook to carry out the federal government's Indian policy. . . . army officers [proved] able and devoted" executors of national policy. However disenchanted they became, officers' execution of policies they found frustrating and disagreeable, in the face of constant provocation and harassment from whites they found distasteful, is a testament to their subordination to civilian direction, prefiguring the patterns of responsiveness to civilian values and accountability to civilian control apparent throughout the remainder of this work.[23]

The frequency of civil-military friction did not alter the fundamental ethnocentrism that constrained military visions of relations between Native Americans and whites. The intricate confluence of operational considerations and ethnocentrism is evident in Edmund Gaines's view of the corrosive impact whites had on Indians and the need for force to restrain the latter. Warning against the withdrawal of Atkinson's regiment from the upper Missouri in 1826, he suggested that redeployment would produce "the most unfavorable impressions on the minds of the Indians . . . they may suppose us . . . unable to sustain . . . the requisite force to keep them in check." The Indians would then "become more licentious from the entire removal of all restraints than if they had never existed, for those Indians like most others in the incipient stages of civilization have learned many of the vices but few of the virtues of their white neighbours."[24]

The army faced remarkably little native opposition as it occupied a series of positions in the Upper Mississippi River Valley between 1815 and 1820. Ethnohistorian John Hall suggests that the Indians of the region expected the United States to assume much the same role Britain and France had played, as a supplier of trade goods and potential diplomatic patron, though Britain's withdrawal from official sponsorship gradually obviated the need for the United States to seek alliance partners among the Indians. Thus, Hall believes that by 1822, "most of the Indians of the Upper Mississippi River Valley and the officers of the American government had reached an accommodation," neither threatening the other as long as violence among Indians did not extend to whites. Farther to the north, Fort Brady, named for the colonel of the Second Infantry, was built in 1822 at the outlet of Lake Superior near Sault Ste. Marie; that year a small post was established to observe the still-powerful Ojibwa near Saginaw Bay in northern Michigan, but it proved unhealthy and was abandoned a year later. Detroit, the center of British and American security planning along the Great Lakes west of Ohio since Pontiac's Rebellion and the end of the Seven Years' War, was left ungarrisoned after 1825, although Hugh Brady often made his headquarters as commander of the Seventh Military Department in that bustling town, the most mature social center northwest of Pittsburgh and Cincinnati.[25]

This apparent calm soon ebbed, as intertribal rivalries and factionalism within tribes, already deeply rooted in highly decentralized settlement patterns and political systems, increased with the defeat of political and religious Pan-Indianism (embodied in Tecumseh and his brother Tenskwatawa) and the growth of white settlement and ecological pressures after 1815. Dependence on white material goods seems to have deterred large-scale violence against whites, but conflicts over hunting territories intensified (whether for subsistence or for access to skins for trade to whites), aggravating the potential for conflict among Indians. Like policemen dealing with domestic disputes, responsible professional officers had to walk a fine line to appear objective but forceful in conflicts between Native American nations or among factions within them. To the south, Gaines admonished the warring Osage and Cherokee in 1826 that the United States could not apply force against "supposed offenders" "unless it should be first clearly proven . . . that the complainant . . . had been faithful in its observance of the Treaty" seeking to establish peace between them. Gaines was fully prepared to use force to *prevent* war between the Indians if it proved necessary, "a precaution which (to say nothing of what is due from the United States upon principles of natural law towards our untutored neighbours . . .) appeared to me absolutely essential to the security of our slender frontier settlements." But the decision had to be an American one if U.S. sovereignty was to be upheld: tribes seeking U.S. aid had to wait for an American decision on the merits of their claim, rather than taking justice into their own, presumed savage, hands. Thus, Native Americans who fought back against attack were perhaps even more likely to face U.S. sanction, particularly when they struck out against white encroachment.[26]

Clashes with the Sioux and Ho-chunk (Winnebago) provide examples of this dynamic in U.S.-Indian relations. Though the Sioux were divided into plains and woodland societies and were no more politically united than any other Indian people, they were numerically the most powerful nation the United States faced in the region between the Great Lakes and the Missouri. Historian Gary Anderson has observed that early U.S. relations with the woodland Sioux were generally peaceful, if only because American military power was so obviously limited that the Sioux felt little threat, and generally remained neutral during the War of 1812. Afterward, U.S. influence slowly increased as British traders withdrew, the Sioux became dependent on Americans for guns and other necessities, and overhunting began to deplete the deer the Indians relied on. U.S. objectives in the upper Wisconsin and Minnesota woodlands then centered on encouraging peace between the Sioux and the Ojibwa, who had pressed the Sioux west from the Great Lakes during the eighteenth century; ending intertribal hostilities would ease future white settlement while minimizing the need for troops and the expense to the government. Since these polities lacked the sense of unity developed by earlier Indians during sustained conflict with the United States and white settlers in Ohio and Indiana, the negotiations conducted by Henry Leavenworth, lieutenant colonel commanding the Fifth Infantry Regiment, in 1820 failed to prevent a reescalation of intertribal tensions after 1823. Eventually, two de facto alliances formed: the Sauk, Fox, and Ojibwa on one side, and the Sioux and Menominee on the other. The Kickapoo and some of the widely dispersed Potawatomis often joined the Sauk and the Fox, who proved just as aggres-

Hoo-Wan-Ne-Ka, a Ho-chunk (Winnebago) war chief. (Courtesy Library of Congress, LC-USZC4-3416)

sive as the Sioux; bands of Ho-chunks, perhaps the most decentralized of all these tribes, ranged on either side.[27]

In 1825 the United States held a council of northwestern leaders—principally Sioux, Sauk, Fox, and Ojibwa, but also Ho-chunk, Menominee, Potawatomi, and Ioway—at Fort Crawford (Prairie du Chien) to try to apportion hunting grounds and end their wars. So "remote and dispersed" were the Ojibwa, or so reluctant to accept U.S. intervention, that the United States had to pursue a second treaty with them the following year, to ratify that of 1825. Nor did the Ojibwa acknowledge American "supremacy"—only U.S. "authority." These efforts had little real effect, and in May 1827 U.S. troops seized a dozen Sioux at Fort Snelling after their warriors challenged the sovereignty of American law by murdering two Ojibwa camped near the fort. Colonel Josiah Snelling, a nineteen-year veteran and as hard a man as there was in the army, threatened to execute the prisoners out of hand unless the Sioux surrendered the killers; when they did so, he turned the prisoners over to the Ojibwa, who killed and scalped them just outside of the fort. Always careful to calculate the costs and benefits of using force, Henry Atkinson approved of Snelling's decision as "proper and just and in accordance with the spirit" of the peace; dependence on or desire for white supplies appears to have kept the Sioux from joining the Ho-chunk uprising that summer.[28]

The growth of white settlement, however temporary or legally dubious, spurred more active operations by the army. Its campaign during the "Winnebago War" of 1827, like that against Ho-chunk unrest the previous year, was really an armed sweep to arrest individual criminals (the killers of white settlers) and deter further violence; the army would conduct a third significant deployment in 1831 to intimidate the Sauk and Fox into withdrawing across the Mississippi. The Ho-chunk resistance, like that in the Black Hawk War of 1832—the army's only extended combat between the First and Second Seminole Wars—was rooted in the onslaught of whites, primarily lead miners, during the 1820s. Drawn by news of native success as miners, whites began entering the Fever River district of northwestern Illinois (in the area of modern Galena), populated largely by the Sauk and Fox. Military commanders questioned the legality of the intrusions, but their opposition was outweighed by the political connections of the leading trespasser, James Johnson of Kentucky, brother of Senator Richard M. Johnson (the contractor who had failed the army's Missouri expedition in 1818). The area was theoretically organized as the United States Lead Mining District in 1824, and the army ordnance officer assigned as superintendent began granting leases to the white miners, with little regard for treaties acknowledging Indian title to the land, in return for a federal tax of 10 percent on their earnings. The Sauk and Fox, who did not pay such a fee, were told that they had to accept the white miners because they had ceded the region in an 1804 treaty, although they had long disputed that cession. Like most U.S. treaties with Indians, that document had been signed by a handful of leaders of limited status who either did not understand or, under pressure from those they did not or had failed to represent, could not accept the interpretations the United States later attached to its provisions.[29]

National economic policy then aggravated the situation: in 1824 Congress doubled the lead tariff, which raised U.S. prices for the commodity by approximately 20 percent. Between 1825 and 1827, the white population of the lead district appears to have increased twentyfold, but little provision was made for civil government, and the Sauk and Fox often resorted to intimidation and harassment to prevent further encroachment. Nevertheless, the Ordnance Bureau superintendent, Lieutenant Martin Thomas, began leasing lands guaranteed to the Ho-chunks in the 1825 treaty, and Ho-chunk warriors murdered a family of five settlers in March 1826. Now colonel of the Third Infantry, Henry Leavenworth marched through the Ho-chunk country, and Major Willoughby Morgan demanded the killers' surrender. Whatever the Ho-chunks may have heard about Leavenworth's Arikara campaign (discussed in *Jackson's Sword*), they remembered his violence against them years before and complied, although Morgan released four of the six prisoners because of insufficient evidence. U.S. justice and peacekeeping appeared to be working; that October, Morgan's garrison at Fort Crawford was redeployed to Fort Snelling to save money and reinforce Josiah Snelling's efforts to prevent a war between the Sioux and Ojibwa.[30]

Commanding general Jacob Brown lauded Leavenworth's efforts at intimidation in forceful language that illustrates the psychic violence beneath U.S. claims to an evenhanded sovereignty that would protect all parties: "By a prompt and imposing display of military force in the very heart of their country, those savages have been awed into perfect subjection"—rendered childlike by the threat of death. Yet the redeployment from Fort Crawford, combined with that from Fort Dearborn (Chicago) earlier in 1826, may have dispelled some of that awe, as did rumors of Sioux or even British assistance. The Ho-chunks' willingness to listen to such unlikely rumors suggests their anger and their persistent hope for an alternative white presence to play against the United States. Meanwhile, Lieutenant Thomas had begun hinting that the army would protect white lessees on lands claimed by the Indians. This constituted a virtual invitation to intruders, who occupied the principal Sauk village, Saukenuk, while the Indians were away hunting in the spring of 1827. (Thomas was a significant exception to the usual pattern of military restraint against whites trespassing on native land: because his assignment brought him into such intimate contact with the civilian economy, he saw the miners as his clients.) In June 1827 the Ho-chunks heard a rumor, based on the events at Fort Snelling, that U.S. agents had slain the last two prisoners from 1826 or acquiesced in their death at the hands of the Ojibwa; several warriors sought retaliation by killing two homesteaders and scalping a child. Almost simultaneously, white miners kidnapped half a dozen Ho-chunk women; thirty-five or forty warriors then ambushed their boats as they returned from Fort Snelling, killing several.[31]

In 1827 the Ho-chunks in question had no more than 400 warriors. Henry Atkinson took 580 infantrymen northeast from Jefferson Barracks; another 650 infantry, mounted militia, and allied Indians, including some northern Ho-chunks, deployed from Forts Howard and Snelling to the northeast and northwest. Fearing threats from Potawatomis near Chicago and Peoria, militia mobilized in Illinois as well as the mining district. Perhaps remembering Leavenworth's hesitance against the Arikara, General Gaines promptly assured Atkinson that he would sustain him in inflicting "exemplary punishment" unless the Indians "promptly and unconditionally surrendered" the Ho-chunk killers. The expansionist Gaines also saw an opportunity for further land cessions as a condition of peace, but Atkinson now shared Leavenworth's belief that less punishment made better peace, and responded that he "did not feel authorized" to demand a cession. (Nor was Gaines authorized to do so, though that rarely held him back.) Trying to avoid precipitate action that might lead to a bloodbath, and probably confident that the overwhelming forces converging on the Ho-chunks would be more than adequate unless other Indians joined in, Atkinson moved cautiously, taking five days to depart St. Louis and then stopping at Fort Armstrong for another week to talk with Sauk and Fox leaders. Though he worried that the Sauk and Fox might join the Ho-chunks, these nations felt old enmities and were competitors for the same resources, leading some Sauk to offer Atkinson their aid, which he declined. Though he sent out two large patrols early in August, the brigadier spent most of that month at Prairie du Chien waiting for news of diplomatic efforts by Michigan territorial governor Lewis Cass and superintendent of Indian affairs Thomas McKenney; he did not advance up the Wisconsin until August 29. Several days later the Ho-chunks surrendered to Major William Whistler, whose troops had advanced down the Fox River from Fort Howard at Green Bay.[32]

On September 22 Atkinson proclaimed victory: "having surrendered up all the offenders . . . and showing an entire submission to the authority of the United States, I have granted [the Ho-chunks] peace." The balance had shifted even further against the Indians. Tribal leaders disclaimed responsibility for the murders, and the leader of the killers (Red Bird) died in prison at Fort Crawford, which was reestablished along with a new post, Fort Winnebago, halfway between Crawford and Fort Howard on the Wisconsin River, north of present-day Madison. Fort Dearborn, evacuated in 1823, was regarrisoned, leading commanding general Macomb to avow that "there is a complete cordon from Green Bay to the Mississippi," restraining the Winnebago and other opponents of white expansion, such as the Sauk and Fox. Two other Ho-chunks were convicted by white courts but pardoned by John Quincy Adams after the tribe promised to cede land in the mining district: there is little better evidence of the fundamental continuity between Adams and Jackson in Indian policy. Officials at the national center rallied in support of the outcome: despite criticism from local civilians that he had moved too slowly, Atkinson was praised by both civil and military hierarchies, including Brown, Gaines, Cass, McKenney, and Winfield Scott. Unlike Leavenworth, Atkinson also gained his subordinates' approval; Major Stephen W. Kearny, a less impetuous, more genteel officer than Atkinson's critic Bennet Riley, lauded the general's combination of "good [diplomatic] judgment" and "military firmness . . . in the management of this affair." Kearny and Atkinson would continue to appreciate each other's diplomacy, working closely together during the next decade.[33]

White intrusions continued while the military response varied, depending on personalities and circumstances. In February 1828 Fort Crawford's commander refused an Indian agent's request for troops to remove squatters; several small-scale patrols drove trespassers from Ho-chunk land in June and December 1828, but the Ho-chunks ceded a large tract that August. The most aggressive miners, led by War of 1812 militia general Henry Dodge, refused demands by army officers and Indian agents that they depart, and the commanders at Fort Crawford considered their forces inadequate to compel Dodge to do so. Atkinson's moderation toward the Indians did nothing to reverse the white tide that disturbed them; the 1827 campaign demonstrated that the United States had the Ho-chunks at its mercy, encouraging further encroachment. The election of Andrew Jackson brought the government's full weight to bear in support of white expansion, and in 1829 the Ho-chunks, Ojibwa, Ottawa, and Potawatomis were compelled to sign away much of their Wisconsin land at a council where brevet Brigadier General John McNeil, colonel of the First Infantry Regiment, served as a U.S. commissioner.[34] The administration also ordered the Sauk and Fox to give up their claims in the lead district and move west of the Mississippi. This was another recipe for trouble: the Sauk already hunted across the river on ground normally used by

Henry Leavenworth, by Samuel Sartain. (Courtesy Frontier Army Museum, Fort Leavenworth)

the Sioux, with whom they clashed in 1829 and 1830, as well as by several smaller tribes (the Oto, Ioway, and Omaha), some of which asked the United States to establish a hunting ground they could share free of Sauk aggression. During the summer of 1829, just as Atkinson moved his headquarters to Louisville during Gaines's absence, Sauk warriors robbed some white settlers on the Grand River, leading Leavenworth, now in command at St. Louis and perhaps trying to regain his hard-line reputation, to advance up the Missouri.

Atkinson quickly halted him, ordering that he rely on diplomacy unless military action proved "imperative." None was taken.³⁵

The limits to U.S. power over warring Indians were clearly demonstrated the following May, when Sioux and Menominee warriors murdered some twenty Fox who had been invited to Prairie du Chien by an American agent. The commander at Fort Crawford failed to prevent the killers from parading through the town, showing off the dismembered bodies of their victims; he persuaded them to depart only after they had publicly cooked and eaten the heart of a Fox chief. Nor was Josiah Snelling around to avenge American military honor, having died eighteen months before. Responding to the massacre, Colonel Willoughby Morgan, an eighteen-year veteran commanding the First Infantry Regiment, oversaw a council at Prairie du Chien in July 1830. The subsequent agreement claimed to establish a demilitarized zone, often labeled the "Neutral Ground," between the Sioux and their Sauk and Fox enemies, while taking land from the defenseless Missouri, Oto, and Omaha as a reservation for Indians hounded from the East. Yet few Sioux leaders appeared at the council or signed the treaty, and the army lacked the manpower or speed to react effectively to repress incidents between Indians. Indeed, some career officers apparently tried to avoid catching or punishing those who broke the peace, claiming that the treaty lacked a provision for punishing violence among the Indians. In 1833, for example, Morgan's successor Zachary Taylor (a veteran of more than twenty years' service) protested an order to interpose 150 soldiers between the Ojibwa and Sioux, fearing that it would produce "a contemptible opinion of our power"; he was able to beg off when cholera struck the area. The 1830 treaty *did* include a provision for the punishment of peace breakers, so it seems that Taylor feared embroiling the United States in another round of endemic tribal warfare without sufficient force to repress the violence. In contrast, hard-nosed officers like Snelling and Leavenworth had shown little hesitation demanding that Indians surrender tribesmen accused of crimes against whites or other Indians.³⁶

A SLOWLY SPREADING HEGEMONY: THE BLACK HAWK WAR AND MILITARY PEACE ENFORCEMENT IN THE NORTHWESTERN PRAIRIES AND FORESTS, 1830–1845

Taylor was not usually so reluctant: in 1830 and again in the winters of 1831–1832 and 1832–1833, he led or dispatched forces that expelled white squatters from unceded Fox mines at Dubuque, west of the Mississippi, and then remained to guard them. (The Fox had fled the mines in 1830 not due to white encroachment but from fear of attack by the Menominee and Sioux.) But his effort was far too little—too rarely repeated—to prevent tensions from exploding. The Jackson administration intermittently ordered the army to evict trespassers from Native American lands, but its policies of land preemption and expropriation, affirmed by Congress in the preemption and removal laws passed almost simultaneously in 1830, made it clear that squatter removal was no more than a temporary measure to mollify the Indians and facilitate their expulsion. (Squatter removal ended in the South after 1833 but continued in the federal territories, now concentrated in the Northwest, where state sovereignty was not an issue. The dynamics of these removals deserve more scholarly attention.) Despite the administration's demands, the "British Band" of Sauk and Fox, led by Black Hawk, refused to move west of the Mississippi until pressure from Illinois led the federal government to employ coercion. This time Edmund Gaines, the highest ranking soldier in the West, was sent to direct operations, taking six companies from Jefferson Barracks to Rock Island, opposite Black Hawk's villages at Saukenuk, in June 1831. Brevet Brigadier General Hugh Brady, a sixty-three-year-old who had first entered the army in 1792, reinforced Gaines with four companies of the Second Infantry from Detroit that were "prepared to defend the interest of the Government," though he did not say against whom.[37]

Gaines was known to oppose Jackson's removal policy, at least for the "Civilized Nations" of the Southeast, but in this instance, perhaps because Black Hawk had supported Britain during the War of 1812, he seems to have managed a professionally accountable balance between the extremes of overzealousness and dissent that precluded his assignment to significant operational commands after this campaign. Like Leavenworth and Atkinson, Gaines used harsh language but limited force, hoping to minimize or avoid bloodshed, recriminations, and future hostility through displays of overwhelming power. Facing 1,200 to 1,600 Indians, including some Potawatomis and Ho-chunks, Gaines was worried that more Ho-chunks might join the British Band and that he would be able to drive them across the Mississippi but not prevent depredations against white settlers without a mounted force. Gaines therefore tried to stall and divide the Indians by calling a council and denigrating Black Hawk, while awaiting the arrival of mounted volunteers. A third of the Indians had already departed when 1,500 militiamen arrived and Gaines launched a converging advance on the Sauk villages, with artillery mounted on steamboats for support. Fearing massacre by the undisciplined militia, the British Band had fled across the Mississippi the night before; Gaines then gave the Indians 3,000 bushels of corn and Black Hawk signed a treaty reaffirming the cession.[38]

Facing stiff hunting competition from other Indians, Black Hawk's people were near starvation, angry, and confused by their separation from their native land. His band of 1,100 (including about 200 Kickapoo, 100 Potawatomis, and 50 Ho-chunks), with approximately 500 warriors, returned east of the Mississippi in April 1832. Henry Atkinson had already planned another show of force to keep peace between the Fox and the Menominee, who had exchanged blows in 1830 and 1831; even before Black Hawk crossed the river, 220 soldiers had begun moving north from Jefferson Barracks to arrest Fox warriors who had murdered some Menominee at Prairie du Chien the previous summer. At first, the British Band committed no depredations; hoping for peace and worried that his force would be insufficient in the event of war, Atkinson called for militia but delayed any pursuit until a militia unit attacked the Sauk and was routed at Stillman's Run (named as much for the militia's precipitate flight as for the watercourse at the site) on May 14. Though the militia in question promptly deserted, the popular and political outcry stirred by its casualties made a more aggressive pursuit unavoidable: Atkinson's cautious policy—to diplomatically wait on events while preparing for the worst case—angered many frontiersmen. Embarrassed, the administration dispatched Winfield Scott from the Artillery School at Fortress Monroe, where a full regiment was concentrated, to take command with 950 reinforcements, but they were struck by a cholera epidemic and arrived too late to engage in operations. After Black Hawk's attempts to surrender were frustrated by language barriers, the army caught up with his starving band crossing the Mississippi at Bad Axe on August 2, where soldiers and militiamen slew more than 250 Indians, including women and children, at a cost of 14 dead.[39]

The conflict demonstrated the limits of native unity, the growing speed and impact of communications, and the power of racist democracy in Jacksonian politics, despite the ineffective performance of the militia. The British Band never comprised more than a sixth of the Sauk and Fox; more than 750 Sioux, Menominee, and Potawatomi warriors joined U.S. forces at various points in the hunt, while thousands of Ho-chunks and Potawatomis gathered at Forts Dearborn (Chicago), Crawford, and Winnebago to draw army rations and avoid the militia. Black Hawk was ultimately captured by Ho-chunks, who also served as guides to the Americans, and was conveyed to Washington by Lieutenant Jefferson Davis. The Sauk and Fox leadership signed yet another treaty accepting expropriation in return for a reservation west of the Mississippi; Black Hawk and ten other Sauk were held hostage, and the British Band was to be divided and parceled out among the other Sauk to prevent future resistance. Despite the Ho-chunks' valuable assistance and general neutrality, the United States used their presence in Black Hawk's band to coerce another land cession from them, much as Andrew Jackson had done to his Creek, Cherokee, Choctaw, and Chickasaw allies during the 1810s. The troops from Fortress Monroe helped spread cholera to Detroit and Chicago, and one company traveled in part by railroad, the first recorded military use of this technology in the United States. Henry Dodge, former militia general and leader of miners trespassing on Indian lands, understood Jacksonian politics best and benefited most. His belligerence won him the authority to hunt Black Hawk as leader of the volunteer Battalion of Mounted Rangers; his initiative and aggressiveness then earned him national status as colonel of the First Dragoon Regiment, the first cavalry in the standing army since 1815. Dodge was commissioned over the heads of a dozen serving veterans in 1833; three years later, Dodge traded up to territorial governor of Wisconsin, twenty-four-year veteran Stephen Watts Kearny took command of the First Dragoons, and that regiment slowly became an efficient professional unit.[40]

The Black Hawk War also provides a rare wartime case study in the range of officer attitudes toward Indian policy and force structure at an interim point between the short Arikara engagement and the far longer Seminole War. Remarkably, war aggravated rather than diluted the irritation professional soldiers expressed toward frontier citizens, which at least equaled that toward Black Hawk's band. Indeed, professional soldiers could easily understand native resistance as brave if desperate patriotism, while the disorder of civilian life was only magnified in the indiscipline and inefficiency of volunteers and militia, at a time when professional commanders expected citizen-soldiers to recognize the danger of their ways and accept temporary subordination. Zachary Taylor tried to appeal to both civil and military qualities when he lectured a battalion of mounted scouts, shouting that they would never gain the political offices they desired "unless you do your duty." The militia commander had the temerity to respond by accusing Taylor of cowardice, perhaps the only person ever to do so. (Taylor had been brevetted to major for leading the defense of Fort Stephenson against some of the same Indians in 1812 and had fought the Sauk near the Rock River in 1814.) Commanding a division of volunteers, Hugh Brady, whose experience against Indians dated to Anthony Wayne's campaign against the Ohioans nearly forty years before, demonstrated how frustration could turn empathy into anger, displacing his irritation with the citizen-soldiers onto the Sauk and Fox, whom the army could punish for their transgressions. "No one can form an idea of the difficulties & disappointments that have been thrown in [Atkinson's] way by the ridiculous conduct of the volunteers . . . for his sake as much as anything else I hope to see those Indians cut to pieces."[41]

Among more junior officers, Lieutenant Philip St. George Cooke later stated that "the militia (that prosopopoeia of weakness, waste, and confusion)" precipitated the war when it "came upon a few quiet and inoffensive Indians, and murdered several of them in cold blood." "The organization of the volunteers was painfully slow," Cooke observed, "a fine harvest for the humorist," "notwithstanding daily information of Indian ravages." Indeed, Cooke was so put off that he claimed the militiamen deliberately got up a scare in order to discard their rations (about thirty pounds worth), sneering that "some ill-natured persons" considered the citizen-soldiers "more dangerous to their friends than to their enemies." Nor did he feel much more respect for the civilian frontiersmen; those in Galena "were in a state of complete panic, and the most unbridled disorder; martial law was declared by the notorious Col. S [a militiaman] . . . but it may be presumed that martial law entered as little as the civil, into their crude conceptions of order." Lieutenant Reuben Holmes, also of Atkinson's Sixth Infantry, doubted that the Sauk wanted anything more than to win an additional annuity in return for peace, and he understood the roots of Atkinson's caution, worrying that "I do not believe this country will sustain any man who suffers defeat from indians no matter what . . . the disparity in numbers." Indeed, Holmes, who served as chief quartermaster for the Illinois volunteers during the war, preferred Indian allies to the militia. "They certainly would be *cheaper* & economy or *parsimony* is the present order of the day, besides there is too much already said on the *merits* of the militia, which, as indians could be easily obtained for a ration of corn, pork & whiskey, & as they would be the best partisans, would, by employing them, be obviated for the future." Holmes's sympathy was reserved for fellow professionals, however: five months later, the lieutenant sent his friend, commissary officer J. H. Hook, an Indian scalp taken by one of those citizen-soldiers.[42]

The delays in Atkinson's campaign frustrated some subordinates, like Taylor, who considered the brigadier too hesitant. (Atkinson may have been developing more sympathy for Leavenworth.) Taylor thought the fundamental problem was uncertainty over whether the brigadier had the authority to pursue the Sauk but argued that he should have reinforced Fort Armstrong on the Rock River as soon as the ice broke in late March: "there would have been no Indian war, & consequently the reputation of the nation would have been saved." Once Atkinson failed to prevent the Sauk from ascending the Rock River, Taylor believed the militia's recklessness at Stillman's Run "brought on the war, for there is little doubt . . . had the regular troops overtaken them . . . before blood had been shed, they would have been removed back to the West side of the Mississippi, without there being a gun fired." The colonel agreed with Hugh Brady that Atkinson had then been beset by "new, greater difficulties," meaning the need to feed the masses of militia, who were almost universally "unfit for service," while mollifying state and local politicians and their constituents. Nevertheless, Taylor believed the brigadier "had too high an idea of the prowess of the enemy, & too little confidence in his own command," foibles never attributed to Old Rough and Ready.[43]

Writing as lieutenant colonel of the Second Dragoons a quarter century later, Philip St. George Cooke was more forgiving of Atkinson: "A prudent General and an able staff were evidently blameless." Cooke then summed up the officer corps' frustration with the politics of Indian warfare: "How unenviable is rank and power thus (in our Indian wars). . . . The exalting consciousness of well-used power, warming and ennobling the mind, is denied" the commander; "he knows his government and his fellow-citizens will not, and cannot, appreciate" his efforts. "Fame, glory, are not accorded to the conqueror of Indians!" Fusing the attitudes developed over a thirty-year career, the colonel took aim at civilians, politicians (whom he quickly dismissed as "humbugs"), citizen-soldiers, and Indians alike. Though the volunteers' attack at Wisconsin Heights caused Black Hawk significant casualties, the veteran dragoon emphasized that the Sauk had broken contact and got away without pursuit; "doubtless had regulars been opposed to them . . . a fatal blow would have been struck." Indeed, Cooke made the striking assertion that the professional army would have done a better job than the Sauk in their own role as irregulars. "Very incapable would I have pronounced that captain of our army, who with a hundred men, could not have repeatedly thrown our army [the one pursuing Black Hawk] into great confusion, and have disputed for weeks the passage of [those] fifty miles."[44]

Yet this range of reactions was ultimately no more than a matter of degree, a difference of opinion over the means to be employed. Cooke recognized that "the usual one-sided treaty" had alienated the Sauk land "for a mess of pottage," but romanticized that "they were destined to atone in blood for their only fault or misfortune, that they loved not wisely but too well." These attitudes were certainly characteristic of professional soldiers during the Seminole War. If anything, twenty-five years of intermittent disenchantment must have aggravated Cooke's uncertainty and skepticism about U.S. Indian policy, yet he continued to serve the cause of white expansion, shrugging aside his ambivalence with a tone of genteel irony. (Cooke repeatedly resorted to fanciful "dreams," escapist literary devices officers also employed in the army's professional journal during the Seminole War, to discuss and romanticize Indian life and culture.) Indian submission was the paramount goal of white soldiers trained in hierarchy and inured to subordination to the sovereignty

Black Hawk. (Courtesy Library of Congress, LC-USZCN4-27)

of the nation-state, and paternalism was the best their victims could expect. The following January, Lieutenant George McCall, Gaines's aide-de-camp, followed Taylor in faulting the Illinois militia for precipitating full-scale war at Stillman's Run: if the army had made first contact, "the difference would have been arranged without bloodshed & at little expense to the Government." Nevertheless, he expected Illinois would "be sustained at the Palace" (the White House), and anticipated that the state would "seize the first occasion to pick a quarrel with the Potawatomis." McCall recognized the relationship between frontier and national politics: "if the grand scheme is to remove all the Indians to the west of the Mississippi . . . in that grand dance the minor fiddles [state and territorial governors] will certainly sound in unison with the leading one."[45]

To the south, the arc between the Mississippi and Missouri Rivers and the frontier west of the state of Missouri presented comparatively little concern for military leaders between the end of the Missouri expeditions in 1825 and the beginning of the expropriation of the Mississippi Valley Indians circa 1835. There, in northern Missouri, southern Iowa, and immediately west of Fort Leavenworth, in the northeastern corner of modern-day Kansas, the army faced smaller, less powerful tribes: the Ioway, Missouri, Omaha, Oto, and Ponca. The Kansa, active opponents of military expeditions in the 1810s, had been weakened by growing dependence on white food supplies and trade goods, factional divisions (largely over how to distribute American treaty annuities), and epidemics, yet an 1828 council of Pawnee, Oto, Missouri, Ioway, Omaha, Sauk, and Shawnee leaders did little to calm hostilities between Kansa and Pawnee. With the army focused on Wisconsin and the Ho-chunks and, after 1828, on tribes (Pawnee and Comanche) ranging farther down the Santa Fe Trail, most of the friction between white settlers and natives was handled by Missouri authorities, who proved much quicker on the trigger than their counterparts in the nation's army. In 1829 Governor John Miller of Missouri, an army brigadier during the War of 1812, mobilized militia in response to a clash between newly arrived settlers and Ioway Indians returning to an old hunting ground. The whites, Kentucky veterans predisposed to expect Indian hostilities, precipitated the crisis when they killed the wife, brother, and child of the Indian leader during a parley. The Ioway then routed the militia, suggesting the limited cohesion and military effectiveness even of frontier veterans who claimed to be defending their homes. Rumor quickly numbered the Ioway at 1,500 warriors, at least ten and perhaps thirty times their real force. Miller realized that the crisis known as the "Big Neck War," after the Ioway leader, was greatly exaggerated and demobilized the militia. Indeed, a jury found the Indians innocent.[46]

Atkinson agreed, advising commanding general Macomb that the militia should merely protect settlers against further attack rather than pursuing the Ioway, which might spark the war the Missourians professed to fear. The commanding general agreed that Henry Leavenworth's rapid advance with six companies from Jefferson Barracks to Fort Leavenworth would "supersede the necessity of employing the volunteer and Militia forces." Yet Jacksonian parsimony clashed with Jacksonian expansionism: "It is a great object to avoid all unnecessary expense," Macomb counseled Atkinson, "and while the individual Indians . . . may be made to suffer for their conduct by a firm and judicious course, it is hoped that the matter may be adjusted without carrying the affair to extremities." Driving the Indians west would take time, if spending and taxes were to be minimized. Yet removal would open a great deal of land for sale to the public, providing the revenue necessary to fund further removal operations, despite the loss of revenue to preemption and the reduction of the tariff after the Nullification Crisis.[47]

By the mid-1830s, the weight of white intrusion began to stir further conflict along the Missouri frontier, leading to half a decade of military peacekeeping efforts. Smaller tribes like the Ioway often cooperated with U.S. military authorities in the hope of avoiding settler or militia violence. In 1833 Ioway warriors became impatient when the United States failed to secure justice against the Omahas, who had slain an Ioway leader; after they slew six Omahas, the principal Ioway chief turned eight of his warriors over to brevet Major Bennet Riley for trial at Fort Leavenworth, even though the Ioway normally handled punishment for murder within the tribe through traditional methods. Reversing his past roles, Colonel Henry Dodge tried to scare squatters off Ioway lands in February 1836 but quickly moved on after being appointed first territorial governor of Wisconsin. Unconvinced of federal support, the Ioway felt unable to resist the pressure of white settlement and ceded their land in a council with Dodge's successor, Stephen W. Kearny, that September, after a clash between white horse thieves and Potawatomi warriors (the "Heatherly War") led to another militia mobilization.[48]

Fed by the revolution in Texas, the Seminole uprising, and the Creek rebellion in Alabama, rumors of war wafted across the western frontier throughout 1836. These rumors appeared more credible because the southward advance of the Sioux had led to wars among the Indians; Kearny warned that the nations of the Mississippi-Missouri bend might combine against the Sioux. The colonel therefore recommended delaying the expulsion of the Potawatomi from Illinois to Iowa, which he expected to precipitate such a conflict. Like most American frontier commanders, and unlike their British, French, or Russian counterparts in Africa and Asia, Kearny seemed much more concerned with maintaining peace—and thus protecting existing settlement—than advancing further expropriation. The colonel believed western citizens created more trouble than they could handle and worried that their "shameful" treatment of the Indians would lead the tribes to "wipe out the militia." Still, Kearny remained a zealous government official and an authoritarian military commander, in one case threatening to whip four Ioway braves as punishment for theft until a missionary persuaded him otherwise. Whether as peacekeeper or intimidator, Kearny gradually became the nation's leading military diplomat on the inland frontier, effectively replacing Atkinson when the latter died in 1842.[49]

Despite health problems that prevented him from commanding field forces after the mid-1830s, Atkinson served as the federal government's primary military liaison and diplomat on the western frontier during the 1820s and 1830s, writing multiple letters about every rumor and incident to clarify the situation for the War Department, the commanding general, and state, local, and territorial civil officials. As a veteran with nearly twenty years' experience on the landward frontier, and as the government's most important information clearinghouse on that frontier, Atkinson provided the "local knowledge" national policy makers otherwise would have had to seek from traders and civil officials, without the self-interested, parochial political and economic filters the latter brought to bear. Whether the Indians were Osage, Oto, Kickapoo, Potawatomi, Ho-chunk, Menominee, or emigrant Creeks, the experienced brigadier consistently remained skeptical of rumors of hostility but worked responsibly to ascertain and communicate the truth, to minimize misunderstanding and tension and preclude bloodshed. Like John Wool in the Cherokee country claimed by Georgia in chapter 5, Thomas Sidney Jesup in Florida in chapters 6 and 7, or Winfield Scott, William Worth, and other experienced officers along the Canadian border in chapters 8 and 9, Atkinson's communications amounted to federal diplomacy and what today's military labels "information operations," attempting to shape relations between the national center and frontier periphery, as well as between whites and Indians. Despite, or perhaps in part because of, their lack of partisan credentials, these national military officers were able to reassure edgy civilian governors subject to popular electoral pressure that their citizens would be protected, without mobilizing those citizens in expensive militias prone to pillaging and atrocity.

Local connections undoubtedly helped: Atkinson had spent nearly two decades on the Missouri frontier, and Scott earned his epaulets as a hero of the War of 1812 in the Canadian theater, while Wool and Jesup were new to Georgia and Florida in 1836. Atkinson feared, or recognized, that the western Indians heard news of the Florida war as quickly as white frontiersmen did, "and exult[ed] at the success of their red brethren," but he "apprehend[ed] little danger" and repeatedly called Indian leaders together to resolve disputes diplomatically. While Edmund Gaines rushed off to Florida and spent most of 1836 on the Texas border, Atkinson carefully managed the entire 800-plus-mile western arc from southern Missouri to the Great Lakes, shuffling infantry around the upper lakes and upper Mississippi while dispatching patrols by the First Dragoons to potential trouble areas west of the Mississippi. His troops and funds severely limited by operational demands farther south, the brigadier deployed forces large enough to remind the Indians of American power but not so large as to provoke native (and perhaps more importantly, white) fears and rumors that might lead to further friction and violence. Like other experienced officers, Atkinson knew that "a timely restraint is the prudent course" to prevent escalation.[50]

Much like Winfield Scott along the Canadian border several years later, this veteran military diplomat astutely varied the language of his communications according to the interests and expectations of his audiences, especially in moments of crisis. Communicating with a wide range of subordinates like Colonel Kearny (his principal deputy and operational commander west of the Mississippi), and upward to Adjutant General Roger Jones (who often served as a liaison between the commanding general and the secretary of war) in Washington, Atkinson urged "the greatest vigilance" but tended to downplay rumors of Indian aggression along the Missouri frontier. Thus, writing to the skeptical Kearny and the cost-conscious Jones in July 1836, the brigadier dismissed the killing of two white horse thieves by Potawatomi warriors on the Grand River (in what became the extreme northwest corner of Missouri) as "a drunken brawl at some whiskey house on the border." As in the Big Neck War seven years before, the whites initiated the violence and then fled when resisted. Frontiersmen claimed the Sauk, Fox, and Ioway were involved, and the incident rapidly flowered into the so-called Heatherly War, named after the leader of the horse thieves. Atkinson assured Jones that the character of the citizens in question was "so notoriously bad that they received no countenance from any Quarter," but he must have recognized that unscrupulous frontiersmen were using the incident as a pretext to try to drive the Potawatomi out of the fertile "Platte Country," which the state sought to incorporate within its borders. Writing to Missouri governor Daniel Dunklin the same day, Atkinson left out the dismissive reference to a drunken brawl and underscored his subordination to civil authority and his sensitivity to the governor's political needs, emphasizing that he would keep Dunklin informed while coordinating a response to protect the citizenry.[51]

The brigadier then deployed two companies of dragoons to prevent violence; rather than searching for marauding Indians, the patrol shadowed a force of 600 militia and persuaded them to return home. When "some straggling parties of Osages" entered southwestern Missouri and stole cattle a year later, Atkinson cautioned Macomb that "the alarm was groundless," but he dispatched a dragoon patrol under Captain Edward Vose Sumner that released Osage women seized by the militia, while formally assuring Dunklin's successor that "no serious danger existed." If such danger did appear, Atkinson vowed that the governor could rely on Colonel Kearny's "zeal and promptness" to protect the people of the state; a series of patrols returned to reassert peace after another clash between the Osage and whites the following spring. During 1839 hysteria shifted to the Oto, a very small tribe that posed little threat. Nevertheless, Kearny took 200 dragoons to Iowa to hold a council with the Oto in September, threatening to whip three warriors who had robbed whites, and Captain Nathan Boone led two companies to investigate rumors of Oto and Ioway depredations in Missouri the following spring. (Boone then drove a dissident fragment of the Ioway from Iowa to Kansas.) Kearny presented the Oto with a classic good-cop, bad-cop routine, threatening an unspecific but public punishment until the civilian agent ("their peace-father") interceded; Kearny then asserted that he had intended to do no more than whip the three offenders, but would ignore the agent's pleas for mercy if he had to return. The dragoon's performance was topped off by a Pawnee leader accompanying the expedition, who reportedly "reproached the Otoes for their conduct, for their turbulence and internal discord, and for the murder of the only man [a former chief] among them," concluding that the Oto leaders were unworthy if they could not control their own warriors.[52]

Given that white violence equaled, and white fears far exceeded, actual Indian violence, and that whites commonly used "Indian panics" as pretexts to seize native land and demand federal pay, the unrestrained violence of frontier citizens quickly emerged as the most likely cause of war and Atkinson's most pressing concern. It might have appeared that peacekeeping was aimed at defending settlers from Indians, and Indians certainly suffered more at the army's hands, since Indians who were arrested remained in custody, whereas the few whites the army was able to arrest (given the need for warrants served by civil officials) were usually freed. Yet the real objective was to mollify the frontiersmen so they would not take matters into their own atrocious hands. Given the weakness of civilian policing (sheriffs' dependence on volunteer posses) and the populist Jacksonian vigilantism of frontiersmen (exercised

Henry Dodge gains a promotion. From Stevens, *Black Hawk War* (1903)

toward whites as well as Indians), the army was compelled to play a role more akin to policing crime than conducting war. Under the circumstances, local security measures were as likely to create violence as to forestall it. For example, the Missouri legislature tried to enhance the militia's responsiveness to Indian threats by requiring county-level commanders to call out their troops, without waiting for orders from the governor, in case of any reported depredation or attack. Atkinson complained to Kearny that the legislation had produced "much indiscretion," and he tried to induce the governors to limit these local mobilizations, lecturing Macomb that "if the authorities of the State raise Troops . . . and take the management of Indian difficulties into their own hands, I cannot be [held] accountable for the results."[53]

Atkinson's correspondence, combined with that of officers relating to the Second Seminole War, also hints at a shift toward trying to control the financial expense of large-scale militia mobilizations by limiting their initiation to experienced military commanders rather than politically appointed territorial governors, even those with national military experience, during the military crisis of Jackson's last year in office. While there was no chance that Congress would attempt to assert active federal control over state militias, Jackson's War Department denied the Missouri militia pay for its "service" in the Heatherly affair, an effective restraint that soon became common in Florida. Yet the most immediate restraint in these time-sensitive situations, with war and peace at stake, was still the restraint imposed on the spot by experienced military diplomats like Atkinson, Scott, and Kearny, who could calm the anxieties of the insecure Jacksonian frontiersmen. This skill was not universal among senior military leaders: John Wool never quite learned it, and Thomas Jesup, a superb logistician and administrator as quartermaster general, suffered from his lack of diplomatic experience representing federal interests when he commanded in Florida.

Scattered from Indiana to Missouri, the Potawatomis proved second only to the Ho-chunks in the ability to resist U.S. compulsion short of war, a characteristic example of the diaspora that resulted amid the "drawn out, piecemeal" reality of removal in the Northwest. Two 1833 treaties gave up Potawatomi territory in Michigan, Illinois, and Wisconsin in return for land in western Iowa and Missouri, and the administration repeatedly ordered military commanders to convoy the Potawatomis west from Wisconsin, Illinois, Michigan, and Indiana between 1833 and 1835. Yet the fertile land they were assigned between the western Missouri border and the Missouri River (the "Platte Country") in 1833 was claimed by Missouri; responding to those claims, the United States promptly compelled Potawatomi leaders to sign a new treaty in 1835, trading that region for territory in northwestern Iowa near Council Bluffs. The focus of military action changed repeatedly amid this flux. As colonel of the First Dragoons, former Missouri militia general Henry Dodge ejected citizens from land still occupied by the Potawatomis early in 1836, but the state of Missouri secured legal control of the Platte Country (now the northwest corner of the state) after Stephen Kearny oversaw a council that led the Ioway to cede their claim to the region. When the Potawatomis refused to leave, U.S. officials stopped supplying the rations on which the Indians had come to depend during their hegira. Atkinson tried to ensure that federal Indian agents provided rations per the Potawatomi treaties, but Macomb ordered Atkinson to remove the Indians by force. Edmund Gaines stepped in to resume the issue of rations—a much more common solution among experienced military commanders than cutting them off—and the Indians accepted a second eviction to avoid starvation.[54]

Duplicitous or not, the inconsistencies discouraged further emigration from the East, and the Indiana militia was mobilized to compel removal in 1838. In 1839 Kearny's expedition to the Oto stopped at a Potawatomi village to press for an exchange of land; the following year Kearny led dragoons to intimidate the Potawatomis at a council called to encourage their emigration. Nevertheless, a letter to the *Army and Navy Chronicle*, probably from Kearny or one of his subordinates, warned that the United States would have to provide the rations and annuities stipulated by treaty before the Potawatomis would be willing to make another cession. Hugh Brady was then given temporary command of the Fourth Infantry, in addition to his own Second, and was authorized to use "all necessary measures" to complete the expropriation. Brady's letters do not provide any evidence that he undertook active operations (he did distribute rations to the Indians), and at least 2,000 of the 7,000 Potawatomi were able to avoid expulsion westward before 1842. In the end, many remained in or returned to the northern forests of Michigan and Wisconsin; others were pressed first to western Iowa, then to the southeast of what became Kansas; and about a third fled to Canada, a common Indian response to U.S. aggression throughout the nineteenth century.[55]

Atkinson could rely on his subordinates to share his relative objectivity, patience, and moderation in the face of Potawatomi and Ho-chunk resistance. Despite his criticism of Atkinson after the Black Hawk War, Zachary Taylor followed his superior's cautious precepts when he took temporary command while Atkinson sat at the court of inquiry into the Florida operations of Gaines and Scott early in 1837, and Taylor's adjutant counseled a subordinate that rumors of Indian depredations were "generally *vastly exaggerated*." In keeping with his concerns about Atkinson's hesitation, Taylor warned Kearny to "take the most prompt and decisive measures . . . without waiting for orders" to keep the peace among the Sauk, Ho-chunk, and Sioux with a patrol from Fort Des Moines, but he advised an officer east of the Mississippi that he expected peace would be maintained without using force. Farther north, Hugh Brady had followed a similar path to a similar assessment in 1836, making "every exertion to ascertain the temper of the Indians," advising preemptive action if necessary, but quickly concluding that rumors of war lacked foundation. Most notably, none of these commanders tried to use Indian depredations or intertribal conflict as pretexts for war, national expansion, or personal or professional aggrandizement. The American frontier was far from Washington, but not as far as Africa, India, or central Asia. Nor was there much chance that state or territorial governors and ambitious militia leaders would refrain from interfering in military operations, as those of Missouri and Illinois so often did, giving career military commanders much less room for the belligerent exercise of ambition than their European counterparts.[56]

Victory in the Black Hawk War established U.S. domination but not hegemony in the Northwest, and the army continued to conduct peacekeeping operations against a variety of white and Indian challengers to national sovereignty until the war with Mexico. White military power notwithstanding, the Sauk, Fox, Potawatomi, and Ho-chunk remained on or returned to lands they had ceded by treaty to grow corn and hunt, sometimes into the 1840s. No decisive step was taken to expel them between 1833 and 1835, and by 1836, the demands of the Second Seminole War precluded the concentration of forces necessary to do so. Yet these nations were clearly caught between two fires, threatened by the growing power of the Sioux from the northern forests across the northern and into the central Plains. In January 1833 Macomb informed Atkinson (who probably already knew) that Sioux warriors had scalped nineteen Pawnee on the central Plains; that May he ordered the brigadier to end Sioux depredations against the Ojibwa in the Wisconsin forests.[57]

The Sioux warred constantly with the tribes in Iowa and west of the Missouri, but by the mid-1830s U.S. attention was focused on consolidating the eastern Indians in the future "Indian Territory," well south of the Sioux range. Though the army dispatched dragoon patrols in 1835 and 1836 and established a series of forts in Iowa during the early 1840s, it did not consistently engage the Sioux in diplomacy or make any serious attempt to punish them for depredations against their Ojibwa enemies or the Potawatomi, Sauk, and Ho-chunk. Neither of the regional powers—the United States and the Sioux—needed or demanded significant resources from the other, and the costs of asserting hegemony would have been far higher than the United States was willing to pay, particularly in the midst of the Second Seminole War. The growing number of wagon trains to Oregon and California did not alter this informal equilibrium until the 1850s, when the white emigrants began to put pressure on resources already depleted by drought and commercial buffalo hunting by competing groups of Indians. With neither side clearly hegemonic in the other's eyes, the attempted formalization of U.S. relations with the Plains Sioux in the 1851 Treaty of Fort Laramie heralded the growth of open friction, conflict, and war.

In the interim, military policy makers focused their attention closer to the frontier of white settlement. In 1833 Macomb directed Atkinson to evict miners from the land the Sauk and Fox had ceded to the United States and warned him against "combinations to resist the Government" among the Potawatomi and Ho-chunk, suggesting that the brigadier deploy some of the Mounted Rangers to intimidate the Indians and keep peace. Whether this "evidence of discontent and hostility," reported by Illinois governor John

Reynolds to the War Department, was real or not, Macomb left no doubt that all the troops from St. Louis to Green Bay were at Atkinson's disposal. The brigadier was given complete discretion to act, being told only that the federal troops should be "sufficient to control" the Indians "without the employment of the militia," which had disrupted operations at considerable expense the previous year. All the interminable Jacksonian criticism of the army notwithstanding, national professional forces furthered Jacksonian expansionism at a price that tax-averse egalitarians preferred to the militia.

Responding to the popular pressure conveyed by Governor Reynolds, the commanding general ordered Atkinson to drive the Ho-chunks out of Illinois in 1833; homesick, assailed by the Sauk and the Sioux in Iowa, the Ho-chunks returned east of the Mississippi whenever possible. Indeed, despite a U.S.-sponsored peace treaty with the Sauk, dragoon patrols in 1836, a revised treaty of cession and expropriation in 1837, and a visit by Winfield Scott two years later, the Ho-chunks were not "finally" compelled to leave Illinois until 1840, when the Eighth Infantry was deployed to do so before continuing south to Florida. Its commander, Colonel William Worth, embodied the officer corps' authoritarian search for order. A stern disciplinarian, Worth had been the first official commandant of cadets at West Point and had refused to protect American citizens against Canadian raids if they would not forswear support for filibusters in 1839. Worth would go on to conduct intensive operations in the summer heat of Florida to compel the Seminoles to accept peace in 1842. Nevertheless, Worth wrote to Winfield Scott that he "regret[ted] the necessity or policy" of Atkinson's seizure of Ho-chunk leaders during a council at Prairie du Chien, "which greatly increases our chances of a bootless contest."[58]

The United States ultimately concentrated more than 1,100 troops from four different regiments to effect the "final" expulsion of the Ho-chunks, the largest federal military force employed in the region between the War of 1812 and the Civil War. By 1840 the United States had attained hegemony over the contested ground of northwestern Illinois and southern Wisconsin. Yet none of these efforts proved sufficient to establish U.S. hegemony, much less pacification or true peace, in the forests and prairies of eastern Iowa, just across the Mississippi, until several years later. Until then, the Sauk and Sioux continued to war against each other, the Sauk continued to resist U.S. expansion, and the First Dragoon Regiment spent as much effort showing the flag on peacekeeping patrols in Iowa as it did in Missouri and Kansas or in Arkansas and the "Indian Territory," for which it is better known.

This effort began soon after the Black Hawk War. At the end of 1834 Stephen W. Kearny led three companies of dragoons to establish a temporary fort at the mouth of the Des Moines River (present-day Keokuk). The following spring, he moved to select a site for a new post farther up that river, then advanced up the Mississippi into present-day Minnesota, visiting Sauk and Sioux villages before returning. The aggressive colonel marched his soldiers through the Sioux villages, "convincing them," he felt certain, that "they are not inaccessible to us, and that we can reach them when we think proper to do so." Kearny reaffirmed the fundamental role of force in U.S. policy toward the Indians, rooted in stereotypes of savagery and barbarism: "mild measures will not restrain an Indian, from gratifying his passions, when provoked," but "if a permanent peace" was desired, the dragoon felt confident that he could "easily effect it" through threats and punishment. Consequently, he advised that the location suggested by the War Department, at the Raccoon Fork of the Des Moines, was too far from either the neutral ground between the Sauk and the Sioux or the Missouri frontier, adding that the Sauk opposed such a post for fear that it would draw whites who would compete for game.[59]

Dragoon peacekeeping operations alternated between forcing Indians onto reservations and removing white intruders from them. In 1840 a dragoon company was deployed to protect Ho-chunk emigrants from the Sauk, building a new Fort Atkinson near the northern boundary of modern Iowa in the Neutral Ground west of Fort Crawford. Two years later, a dragoon company moved to Iowa City to help the territorial governor intimidate the Sauk and Fox into ceding their reservation in Iowa in return for land west of Missouri. That same year, Fort Sanford was established near the site of modern Ottumwa to protect the Sauk from white squatters, while the company at Fort Atkinson deployed twice to expel these intruders; Fort Croghan (originally Camp Fenwick) was built near Council Bluffs to protect the Potawatomi and Ojibwa emigrants from the Sioux. Forts Croghan and Sanford lasted only a year before the War Department decided to shorten the western defense perimeter by shifting their garrisons to a new Fort Des Moines at the mouth of the Raccoon Fork (the site of present-day Des Moines) to protect the Sauk from the more immediate threat of squatters. Early in 1846 the dragoons rounded up the last 180 or 200 Sauk and Fox and drove them from Iowa. (Note that removals on the western frontier were commonly conducted under military guard, unlike those of the Cherokee, Choctaw, and Chickasaw in the Southeast.)[60]

Yet none of these operations resolved the growing competition for shrinking resources or stopped white squatters, alcohol, and disorder from following the Indians west. Indeed, many Winnebago continued to return to the Wisconsin woods, where troops were repeatedly deployed to drive them back west. During the autumn of 1842, more than a thousand Ho-chunks remained outside the land supposedly reserved for them, and a year later Captain Edwin Vose Sumner took a dragoon company from Fort Atkinson to capture those still hunting in Wisconsin. The United States then tried to curtail these expenditures through a second removal, attempting to persuade the Ho-chunks to depart the neutral ground established between the Sauk and the Sioux in 1830 for new lands farther south; it should come as no surprise that the Indians rejected the ploy or that portions of the tribe were ultimately forced from Iowa to Kansas. A band of Fox Indians returned to the Iowa River early in 1844 and was driven west by dragoons from Fort Des Moines under Captain James Allen; that scene was repeated a year later, just months before the United States annexed Texas.[61]

Farther north, Fort Wilkins was built at Copper Harbor on Lake Superior four years later to protect the mines in case of renewed tensions with Britain, but it was not garrisoned after 1845, and most of the northern posts were abandoned as the frontier moved out onto the Plains and the army redeployed against Mexico. Forts Des Moines and Wilkins were closed in 1846 and Fort Atkinson in 1849, along with the Wisconsin and Fox River line established to intimidate the Sauk and Ho-chunks in the 1810s and 1820s. (Wilkins reopened in 1867 due to Anglo-American tensions during the Fenian filibusters against Canada, but it closed permanently three years later.) Fort Winnebago was shut down in 1845, followed by Fort Crawford four years later. Howard was closed in 1841, reopened in 1848, and closed for good in 1852. Of all the posts established in the fourth phase of westward military expansion, only Washita, far to the south, survived until the Civil War.[62]

Two final dragoon expeditions in 1844 and 1845 suggest U.S. pretensions, as well as U.S. military capability and its limits, in the Upper Mississippi Valley. In 1844 Captains Allen and Sumner each led their companies to the Minnesota River as part of what commanding general Scott labeled the "standing policy, to prevent Indian hostilities by the exhibition of military force on *and beyond* our frontiers." Allen saw very few Indians (doubtlessly because they were avoiding him) but felt that his force was having "a great moral effect upon these wild Indians, as showing them conclusively that we can easily throw cavalry enough into the heart of their country to chastise them for any wrong they may do to our people and government." (Note the captain's mention of the U.S. government in the same breath as, yet distinct from, the people of the nation, another indication of the state-centered mentality that pervaded the officer corps.) Allen returned along the Big Sioux River in the eastern part of modern South Dakota, farther north than any U.S. military foray since Stephen H. Long's journey in 1823 and farther northwest than any since the Yellowstone expedition.[63]

The following year the captains combined to revisit the woodland Sioux before advancing through the western half of Minnesota to the Red River of the North and Devil's Lake (in the northeastern quadrant of modern North Dakota), warning the nomadic métis (hunters, trappers, and traders of Franco-Indian origin) in that area against entering the United States without permission. Both captains asserted the army's power to punish Sioux depredations, although Sumner claimed that the métis were far more likely to become American citizens than to resist. In 1845 the hard-nosed captain seized four Sioux accused of crimes against whites and defiantly marched them through several Sioux villages without resistance. He turned "three of the murderers of Watson and party, that escaped last fall from Col. Wilson's detach. of the 1st Infantry," over to civil authorities; Sumner had no witness to testify against the fourth, who was accused of stealing a horse from Allen's expedition in 1844, so he vowed to keep the Indian in jail at Fort Snelling until ordered otherwise.[64]

Sumner's confidence suggests the advance of American power. Notwithstanding Indians returning to hunt, the army had essentially conquered the Indians of Illinois and southern Wisconsin between 1827 and 1832, encouraging a large-scale influx of white farmers, who then destroyed the Indians' remaining resource base. Thus the fundamental threat to peace, and Indian acceptance of expropriation, remained resource scarcity, aggravated by the influx of eastern tribes into the unfamiliar (to them) and increasingly arid lands west of the Mississippi and intensified by the advance of whites, regardless of the land or region in question. This competition, combined with the loss of farming seasons during the physical process of expulsion and emigration, often left Indians dependent on rations issued by the army or civilian agents. In 1836 Wisconsin became a territory, amplifying the political pressure for expropriation, and in 1837 the Ho-chunk, Sioux, and Ojibwa ceded most of the native land remaining within the present boundaries of the state.[65]

The following summer, as the local woodland Sioux starved in the aftermath of a smallpox epidemic, Major John Plympton handed out army rations but felt compelled to call for reinforcements in case of trouble. Henry Atkinson responded by advising Plympton to arrest "lawless [white] vagabonds" who were "exciting discontent" among the Ojibwa and to eject the vagabonds from the military reservation around Fort Snelling, where the Indians had gathered for trade and rations. Atkinson was hardly the only military leader to blame white citizens for tensions: a year later, Inspector General John Wool visited the fort and recommended evicting white squatters from the military reservation, both to improve discipline in the garrison and to reduce the likelihood of friction with the Indians. Nevertheless, acting through civil due process took time; not until 1840 did soldiers under the supervision of a deputy U.S. marshal destroy squatter cabins around the fort. Nor did the United States commit the forces necessary to truly pacify the Minnesota woodlands Indians until compelled to do so by the great Sioux uprising of 1862. Yet the Upper Mississippi Valley had been forced open to white settlement, as the Upper Missouri Valley had not, and there would be no middle ground to succeed the native ground once dominated by Ojibwa and Sioux.[66]

3
FEDERAL AUTHORITY UNDER ATTACK
The Army, Southern States, and Citizens during the Adams Administration

Military commanders ultimately agreed with civilians that Indians in contact with whites were doomed, whether to absorption or extinction. They had seen too much to believe that the government truly wanted to stop white settlement. Like virtually every national civilian policy maker from Knox through Jefferson to Jackson, they believed the Indians should make some sort of deal to salvage whatever they could, whether that meant tools and techniques for acculturation or some distant refuge from white irritation and corruption. With the exception of treaties at the conclusion of the wars for Ohio and the War of 1812, the United States normally forwent the "conquest theory" of sovereignty as a justification for expropriation, yet the spectrum of options U.S. officials presented to the Indians varied little in practice. Nor did eastern location, "civilized" status, or the relative political centralization of Indian nations with written constitutions, like the Cherokee, fundamentally alter their standing in white eyes. Few policy makers, even those who saw themselves as humanitarians or have been labeled reformers, truly envisioned native integration with whites in the East, much less native autonomy there. Indeed, the very concept of a distinct "Indian country" suggested emigration, exclusion, and segregation from political, social, and economic spaces white citizens sought for themselves. Secretary of War Calhoun's "policy of moderation," as some historians have termed it, shared Andrew Jackson's assumptions of U.S. sovereignty—and, under American federalism, the probable assertion of state sovereignty—and the choice of emigration or eventual extinction; Calhoun's "patience" and moderation were matters of tone and timing, relative to Jackson and the frontiersmen, rather than objective or trajectory.

John Quincy Adams. Engraving by Asher B. Durand, after Thomas Sully. (Courtesy Library of Congress, LC-DIG-ppmsca-15717)

The second section of this chapter demonstrates that John Quincy Adams ultimately proved little different in practice, initially resisting but gradually surrendering to the demands of the most aggressive frontier state, Georgia. Despite northeastern and Whig opposition to their removal during the 1830s, the Indians could not find firm ground to justify remaining: the most politically centralized and most socially, economically, and culturally "advanced" Indian nation, the Cherokee, appealed to American legal and constitutional processes, but that only provided Chief Justice John Marshall the opportunity to declare the Indians "domestic dependent nations" subject to American will. Whatever form the incentive, whatever form the pressure, the implication was emigration or removal west.[1] Nevertheless, although the army did not resist national removal policies, its position as the intermediary charged with their implementation continued to spur civil-military friction. Southern and western frontiersmen demanded everything they wanted, immediately, while the army tried to execute Jackson's policies at the low cost, both financially and in terms of domestic and international public opinion, demanded by the administration. Presumably, until the date set by treaty for removal, federal executive officials were obligated to enforce the trade and intercourse acts against white intrusion. National civilian officials continually sent signals that officers could use their discretion to ignore such infractions, but military commanders on the scene felt ethically, morally, and professionally responsible for upholding the Constitution and the laws of the land, despite all the hints to the contrary. Jacksonians local and national wanted to have their cake and eat it too, but since the subsidiary (tactical and operational, so to speak) objectives and necessary means of execution contradicted the overarching (strategic) goal of a cost-free removal, conflict was inevitable. This clash between letter and spirit presents perhaps the strongest evidence of Jacksonian disregard, indeed contempt, for the rule of law.[2]

The question still at issue was really the distribution of power among whites, the autonomy or lack of autonomy of the federal nation-state and its executive agents—particularly those in the military—to mediate between the land hunger of white citizens and the costs and qualms of taking native lands. The United States claimed sovereignty over the Indians, who were culturally distinct from white Americans and thus excluded from citizenship yet subject to U.S. rule, to the extend that its power permitted. The growing influence and rigidity of racialized categories, along with the decline of environmental theories of culture and development associated with the shift from Enlightenment to cultural romanticism and the expansion of democracy for ordinary whites during the 1820s and 1830s, increased this exclusion and intensified white claims to relations of supremacy and subordination. Surrounded by democratically elected civilian officials antagonistic to the Indians, the military officers of the executive branch were caught in a temporal dilemma—whether to enforce protective laws, increasingly out of touch with majority opinion, that the majority was embarrassed to repeal—as well as the federal dilemma of national law (which included treaties with Native Americans, per the Constitution) versus local majorities. Indeed, shifting congressional coalitions, based more on the desire to reduce the costs and qualms associated with expansion than actual changes in policy objectives, passed a comprehensive trade and intercourse act, supposedly to protect the Indians more effectively than ever before, in 1834, only four years after Congress passed the Indian Removal Act. The army paid for these qualms, and for Jacksonian hypocrisy, with decades of friction and frustration.[3]

Enforcing the laws against unauthorized white trade and settlement on Indian lands was one of the most difficult missions faced by federal military commanders. Despite the seeming clarity of the laws, contemporaries and historians alike have deemed the legislation passed in 1790 and 1802 mere window dressing. Critics' language may be overdrawn, given the army's repeated efforts to enforce the laws, but federal policy toward white intruders on native land was fundamentally disingenuous. Federal officials—civil as well as military, Democrat as well as Whig—recognized that some short-term effort to control white intrusion was essential to convince the Indians to cede land without constant warfare. Thus, in return for cessions, the government promised the Indians security from white encroachment in their remaining territory, imagining that they might rationalize and accept their defeat in the hope that the pattern would not be repeated. Protecting the Indians against intruders might also reduce injustice, hardship, and violence; prevent incidents that could otherwise lead to war; tranquilize white consciences; save lives, money, and national reputation; and avoid embarrassment that political opponents could exploit. Although they may have been soothing their own consciences, most career military officers truly believed that upholding national treaties—national law, national sovereignty, and the Constitution itself—by restraining the aggression of individual white citizens was a national moral responsibility, a matter of national faith and justice that reflected on the army's professional reputation and the officer's personal honor.

For reasons both practical and principled, military commanders conducted dozens of operations to eject white citizens squatting—settling without title—on native land between 1815 and 1830. Such operations were far more common than those expelling squatters from federal public lands; the latter were usually treated as matters of civil process to be executed by marshals and civilian posses. Indeed, the pressure to democratize land policy gradually led to a de facto acceptance of squatting on public lands as "preemption," legitimized—as only the Jacksonians had the capriciousness or indifference toward law to do—by an 1830 statute. (Remove the Indians, and whites could squat on their former lands without fear of ejection.) While Indian land remained distinct from public land open to sale, ejecting intruders from Indian land was generally thought to require the sanction of civil officials, and the federal government faced ever-growing pressure to accept citizen claims to unceded native land as if it were public land subject to preemption. The populist dynamics of white man's democracy rapidly infiltrated and soon pervaded the structures of civil government at all levels, often undermining some of the constitutional restraints of federalism and the separation of powers. In the borderlands, career military officers repeatedly found themselves stuck in the middle representing unpopular national policies.[4]

The 1834 trade and intercourse law had little chance of serious or sustained enforcement, given the attitudes of frontiersmen and their Democratic allies. The real meaning of sovereignty had to be negotiated, and the balance of power was shifting against national authority and executive autonomy. As the United States became a racialized democracy, the need to attain the support of citizens whose votes represented consent to sovereignty ultimately compelled the government to accede to their demands, which were increasingly mediated and promoted by well-organized political parties eager to distribute benefits to their constituents, whatever the motives or objectives of federal executive officers. As historians widely recognize, the nation-state's insulation from popular pressure decreased during the Jacksonian era. Concerns about financial and political costs, personal and national integrity and reputation, and humanity still held officials back from the violent extremes of overt ethnic cleansing, but the political legitimacy of coercing obedience from white citizens declined even as that of coercing nonwhites increased, and federal authorities gradually gave in to citizen demands. Ultimately accountable to laws passed by elected politicians in a democracy defined by race, the army's most important effect was inevitably to facilitate the seizure of Indian lands. "In the long run," as army historian Francis Paul Prucha admits, "the settlers nearly always won."[5]

If this balance of power made expropriation inevitable, did its implementation by federal rather than state or local authority ameliorate its horrors? What were the responsibilities of the executive branch, as its agents understood them, and to what standards can we hold them under the circumstances? With the basic question of intent and objective decided by Congress, the practical issue became the speed, humanity, and cost of execution. Speed and humanity cost tax money. Most white frontiersmen would have been happy to wave a wand and have the Indians instantaneously disappear, but dispossessing them—whether "peacefully" moving them west or defeating them militarily—involved real costs that few tax-averse citizens wanted to pay. Indeed, the citizens most eager to dispossess the Indians were reputedly the most tax averse. Thus, despite all the rhetoric about saving the Indians, removal inevitably became a mean, sordid, degrading process that soiled everyone involved. Doing the dirty work of removal, how could military officers and civil officials maintain the appearance of humanity; their personal, institutional, and national reputations for good faith and honor; and their personal psychological integrity and moral and professional self-image, without exceeding their limited budgets and irritating the public they served?[6]

The rapacious individualism of white citizens and the small scale of the national army made it almost impossible to effectively restrain encroachment on Indian land, and the claims of state and popular sovereignty so common in pre–Civil War America meant that attempting to restrain intruders embroiled federal military commanders and the national government in crises that threatened civil war. The civilian executive branch, including the War Department, normally responded by pressing military officers to accelerate the process of expulsion while holding down costs and somehow minimizing actions that might result in public outcry from opponents of removal. Fiscal and legal accountability, humanity, and efforts to avoid political liability constantly clashed; it proved virtually impossible for officers to attain all three objectives. Ironically, civilian politicians even pressured commanders to avoid aggressive measures to accelerate expulsion because they might spur panic about Indian resistance among white frontiersmen. Amid all this confusion, military officers faithfully carried out the forcible ejection of white squatters upon demand by the civil authorities, and their efforts had some effect, however limited or difficult to measure, in restraining the pace and extent of white aggression and depredation. Indeed, many genteel career commanders, irritated, frustrated, and angered by the individualism and disorder of the frontier citizens they served, appeared to take personal pleasure in ejecting white intruders from Indian land whenever authorized to do so.

The ejection of whites squatting on native lands was never more than intermittent, driven much more by the immediate exigencies of diplomacy—the desire to reassure the Indians that the government would protect them in their remaining lands while pressing for cessions—than by law or a sense of moral responsibility. Indeed, it can reasonably be argued that the federal government gave up on squatter removal—regardless of repeated legislation to the contrary—as national *policy* after its failure north of the Ohio River in the 1780s. Never again would the government attempt anything like a consistent enforcement of the laws and treaties forbidding encroachment on Indian lands. To do so would have been prohibitively expensive, both financially and politically, for any administration that attempted it; it probably would have hastened the southern and western reaction against Federalism that eventuated in the "Revolution in 1800," perhaps placing Thomas Jefferson in the presidency four years earlier. Extensive operations to eject squatters were undertaken in the Cherokee lands during the late 1790s and on several occasions during the next three decades, but their very repetition testifies to their ineffectiveness. Squatter removals in the Choctaw, Chickasaw, and Creek lands were much less frequent, and the defeat of the Federalists meant that the tug-of-war with Georgia during the mid-1790s would be the last successful effort by national policy makers to actively resist state, quasi-state (filibuster), or vigilante forces warring on the Indians within the boundaries of the United States. Jefferson's election meant a far more harmonious relationship between federal and state Indian policy, with the United States facilitating state initiatives rather than restraining them. Meanwhile, the Indians were too weakened by the wars of the Federalist era to mount concerted opposition until Tecumseh rose to power through the antagonism created by Jeffersonian aggression. Whether in 1789, 1795 (with the Treaty of Greenville), or 1801, the era of removal began long before Andrew Jackson was elected president.[7]

Squatter ejection resumed after the War of 1812 but remained inconsistent. The focus of such operations conducted in the southern borderlands during 1815 was surveying the boundaries of the public lands ceded by the Creeks in the Treaty of Fort Jackson, expelling white intruders, and maintaining land values both for the Treasury and, it was rumored, for large-scale speculators preparing to buy them up. Army attitudes toward these missions were ambivalent: faced with the threat of citizen pressure, even lawsuits, the opportunity to exercise command and discretionary authority often fostered as much uncertainty, confusion, and trepidation as decisiveness. Even the most decisive commander could provide little guidance amid such ambiguity. Jackson's example provided little clarity for his subordinates: though he continually pressed for Indian removal and successfully resisted Secretary of War Crawford's effort to return land to the Cherokee in 1816, he espoused the supremacy of federal authority with more ardor than most civilian leaders, moving aggressively to expel squatters when called on to do so that summer. These efforts did not prevent new waves of settlers from invading the Creek and Cherokee lands in northwestern Georgia while Jackson was busy in Florida, and in 1819 squatters were ejected from Creek territory on the upper

Chattahoochee, but they soon returned. The following May the general toured East Tennessee, warning intruders they would be forced to depart Cherokee territory. Indeed, Jackson unilaterally extended squatter removal operations to Georgians encroaching on Creek lands to the south.[8]

The general dispatched his protégé Captain Richard K. Call (who would later follow in his mentor's footsteps, pursuing Indian removal as territorial governor of Florida) to conduct those ejections in lieu of a less experienced officer. Call zealously carried out his commander's intent, warning the "infatuated people" (as Jackson labeled them) who spoke of resistance that they would face "speedy and exemplary punishment" from federal forces. The captain reported that "the border citizens there, are of the worst characters," but he devised a plan to limit the administration's exposure to public opprobrium, employing the Cherokee "light horse" police to undertake the removal while keeping his contingent of regulars in the background, emerging only when violence threatened. The appearance of federal troops cowed such resistance, leading armed squatters to disperse, but the army had to do more than drive them off and burn their farms to prevent their return. Indeed, Jackson explained to the War Department that the settlers had salted the ground to encourage their stock to return after being driven off, so he had been compelled to seize the cattle: "Three times I had the stock of intruders driven from the Cherokee land North of [the] Tennessee river, their houses and improvements [fences and the like] destroyed. But this availed nothing, the Troops would no sooner leave the country, than the Intruders would return."[9]

Most professional officers shared these authoritarian tendencies, but Sharp Knife (as the Indians called Jackson) expressed them so idiosyncratically, so overbearingly, that they provided little practical guidance for junior officers with less weight to throw around. Perhaps the best example of Jackson's muddled approach to federal authority over Indian relations was the aftermath of the Chehaw massacre, in which Georgia militiamen murdered the women and children of a Creek village allied to the United States while the general was campaigning in Florida in 1818. Jackson saw no parallels between his actions and the Georgians'; he relied on some dubious but technically correct distinctions between federal and state authority to damn the Georgians, civil as well as military, for their arbitrary action—something the Tennessee tornado could not stand in anyone else. Indeed, Jackson hectored the governor of Georgia that had the militia commander followed the proper trail, "it would have led him to the Mickasooky," whose villages the general had burned. Jackson's response to the Chehaw massacre focused on the command of the state militia, to which he felt entitled as the national government's military theater commander; that is, once the militia had been mustered into federal service and Jackson had assumed command, the governor's authority ceased. Fearing their individual, national, and institutional reputations would be sullied by such atrocities, professional officers distinguished between Indian warriors and noncombatants: after the skirmish at the Fowl Towns the previous fall, Edmund Gaines had taken care to report that civilian casualties were minimal and accidental, and Jackson's subordinates doubtlessly agreed that the Chehaw massacre was "base" and "cowardly." Yet their humanitarian and reputational motives were equaled by practical concerns that the Georgian atrocity infringed on federal sovereignty over Indian relations and might drive more Creeks to hostility.[10]

Subordinate officers may not have felt Jackson's anger at the writ of habeas corpus issued for the Georgia militia commander, which he termed an "illegal interference of the civil with the military authority," but they surely agreed that "the mode of trial recommended by the [Creek] agent [David B. Mitchell, with whom Gaines had quarreled] is truly farcical & . . . ought to be spurned." Former captain Christopher Vandeventer, who had become chief clerk of the War Department, was probably representative of these views, concurring with Jackson's recommendation that a court-martial would be "decidedly preferable to a civil prosecution in the federal court," where a trial by jury "would be a mockery," since the court had already refused to take jurisdiction over similar cases. Belief in federal sovereignty and professional direction of military force probably led most career officers to support Jackson's dictum that "it is absolutely necessary for the safety of our frontier . . . that governors of states may be Taught to know it is Treason against our government to levy war against any tribe under the protection of the u states, over which the sovereignty of the union extends." None but Jackson would put such provocative language in a public letter, though.[11]

Jackson was certainly representative of the professional officer corps in his advocacy of national control over the borders between white and Indian lands, approving a plan from Henry Atkinson to prevent white intrusions in the arc between the Red and Mississippi Rivers. By 1820, after two years of congressional criticism, Old Hickory had learned to speak more softly about the relative weight of civil and military authority, cautioning Atkinson that "in all cases the civil authority ought to be treated with respect by the military." Jackson added the caveat "that as far as our [military] rights and duties will permit[,] harmony [with civilians] may prevail." Though not truly professional subordination, this was progress for Sharp Knife. Junior officers, now pressed into service as Indian agents in the new territory Jackson had conquered, acted to support the separation Atkinson envisioned. In April 1822 Captain John

Bell advised Secretary of War Calhoun that "it should be the object of the Agents of Government in Florida to protect the Indians in the little property they now possess." Bell therefore directed that "no sale of negroes, horses, or cattle should be made by the Indians to the [white] inhabitants or traders before . . . they [are] informed . . . [of] their true interests"—that is, whether they would remain in Florida.[12]

Former major Gad Humphreys, for whom Bell was standing in, later earned a reputation for supporting the Seminoles' claims against those of white Floridians, but such neutrality proved difficult to sustain. Enforcing the ethnic separation of the nonintercourse laws in the face of local citizen opinion required commanders who shared Jackson's self-assurance, but their gentility and authoritarianism often clashed in execution: ejecting squatters from Creek territory in November 1820, Captain George Birch reported that "burning and destroying property . . . [is] a disagreeable business for a man that has any feeling." The uncertainty expressed by two field-grade veterans, as the army tried to craft a balance between white and Indian in areas newly opened to white settlement, was more characteristic than any extreme. The first officer, Lieutenant Colonel Abraham Eustis, was a moderate, dutiful subordinate commander whose past experience, primarily in the War of 1812 and along the Atlantic coast rather than the southern frontier, was characteristic of the post-1821 officer corps. Reporting from Florida in 1822, Eustis noted "considerable anxiety" among whites and Seminoles and complained that he lacked specific instructions about mediating between them. Like most career professional officers, Eustis hoped to minimize friction—federal-local and civil-military, as well as ethnic—by controlling and limiting interaction. Thus, he advocated that traders be licensed to go to the Seminoles so the Indians could avoid trading at white settlements, where access to liquor would spur tension. The territorial authorities had already sought military aid to arrest liquor sellers, but this threatened to embroil commanders in lawsuits from angry retailers, leading Eustis to hesitate. Under pressure from local citizens, Eustis backed away from Bell's restrictive approach, while he awaited more detailed instructions.[13]

To the west, at Fort Smith in Arkansas, public opinion led the second officer, Seminole War veteran Matthew Arbuckle, commanding the Seventh Infantry Regiment, to hesitate over ejecting intruders from Indian land; he emphasized the settlers' fear of native attack instead. Washington sent no instructions for Eustis to halt trade or for Arbuckle to expel squatters, aggravating the two colonels' hesitation and reinforcing their willingness to bend before local public opinion. This compromise of native lands and federal sovereignty was probably the best that most commanders could achieve, given the faith in popular sovereignty—and thus white supremacy—underlying the Jeffersonian regime. Although it is common for American historians to view the Republicans of 1815 to 1828 as more nationalistic and statist, and perhaps less harshly racist, than those before or after, the impact of the Madison, Monroe, and Adams administrations was largely to advance and accelerate the policy trajectory toward Indian removal. Though Jeffersonian expropriation lacked the dramatic speed and crude excess of that under Jackson, continual pressure, usually intensified by whatever opportunity developed, was the thrust of U.S. Indian policy from 1801 (if not 1789 or 1776) forward. Jackson's withdrawal from federal office in 1821 ended the Southern Division's insistence on native land cessions and emigration during his command, but the vast majority of officers continued to share Sharp Knife's assumptions about the Indians' future. Eustis soon received his answer from Calhoun and hastened to assure Florida territorial governor William Duval that he saw no reason to interfere with white activity "unless some grave act of misconduct . . . should render my interposition absolutely necessary."[14]

In the meantime, the Panic of 1819 intensified the usual demands for economy, leading Calhoun to attempt to shift the burden of ejecting white squatters from the army to the Indians. Yet doing so could only spur anger among white citizens, and quite possibly resistance and bloodshed, exposing once again the dilemmas of the Indians' status as "domestic dependents" under the weight of white supremacy, amid the competition of two or perhaps three sovereignties (federal, state, and tribal or "national" among the Indians themselves). How could American law permit men who were not entitled to citizenship to coerce those who were? Would the political consequences for the federal government be better, or worse? Thus, within a year (in 1820), even Jackson was employing contingents of federal troops against white Georgians on Cherokee lands. In 1823 Calhoun mustered the Tennessee militia to secure the Cherokee boundary against encroachment, but the most appropriate and most effective approach remained federal. As veteran Cherokee agent Return Meigs (father of Montgomery Meigs, an 1836 Military Academy graduate and the nation's quartermaster general during the Civil War) advised in 1822, "twenty regular troops . . . commanded by a Good subaltern officer would be respected by the intruders [however temporarily] when two hundred indians would be driven home with loss [casualties]." Regardless of the forces employed, the dominant factor in policy making remained white public opinion. Calhoun ordered Meigs to allow squatters to stay to complete their harvest; having made this concession, it was unlikely the federal government would then compel the white farmers to leave their settlements just before the onset of winter. As Francis Paul Prucha, otherwise

George M. Troup, governor of Georgia. From Edward J. Harden, *The Life of George M. Troup* (1859)

sympathetic to federal efforts, observes, the executive branch "readily acquiesced in illegal settlements when they had gone so far as to be irremediable" without a politically unacceptable use of military force. Making Indian removal national law in 1830 did not reconcile principle and practice or diminish the hypocrisy, nor did it resolve the dilemmas posed for the military agents of the executive.[15]

WHO WAS THE ARMY SUPPOSED TO REMOVE? GEORGIA, THE CREEKS, AND THE ARMY, 1825–1827

The potential for collision between federal policy and popular sentiment escalated dramatically in 1825, when Georgia took advantage of John Quincy Adams's weak political position to demand control over the Indian lands remaining within the state. The United States had promised to extinguish Indian titles within Georgia when the state ceded its western land claims to the federal government in 1802, and Georgians wanted the federal government to pay for not keeping its promise. Monroe had maintained that the legitimacy of Indian titles was not affected by the so-called compact with Georgia, that the United States was only obligated to seek Indian land through peaceful means, but in January 1825 he recommended that all Indians east of the Mississippi move west to escape "inevitable . . . extermination." In Georgia, Crawfordite governor George Troup needed an issue to ward off former governor John Clark's populist challenge in the 1825 election, so he used thefts by hungry, resentful Creeks as an excuse to assert the state's sovereignty over the Indians within its boundaries. Rather than rely on federal promises, unfulfilled for a generation, Troup planned to take matters into Georgian hands by subjecting the natives to state law, nullifying their land titles regardless of federal treaties, and denying them citizenship or recourse under state law. Legally defenseless, the Indians would either make the best deal they could and leave, or resist and give the Georgia militia the excuse to drive them out.[16]

Monroe recognized this dynamic and sought to avoid bloodshed through diplomacy. The problem was to find Creeks willing to give up their land. The Treaty of Indian Springs, signed by a small minority of well-off Creeks early in 1825, promised to meet Georgia's demands by claiming to cede all the tribe's land in Georgia to the federal government, which could then turn the land over to Georgia. Reflecting majority opinion, the Creek National Council responding by ordering the execution of one of its own—William McIntosh, leader of the treaty faction and cousin of Governor Troup, who had received $25,000 as part of the treaty—for ceding national lands without its authorization. This was the first time the council had ordered the execution of a Creek for violating Creek rather than white law, indicating that resistance to white provocation was stiffening. The execution was led by Menawa, commander of the Red Sticks at Horseshoe Bend a decade before, and another Creek civil war seemed imminent. White Georgians remembered that the Creek War of 1813–1814 had begun with strife among the Indians over how to respond to white pressure, and Troup took advantage of the ensuing panic to mobilize the militia and threaten the Creek majority. But he undoubtedly would have preferred the federal government to intimidate the Creeks into leaving, rather than risking civilian deaths in Indian raids against scattered farms should he have to employ the militia.[17]

Adams was hardly a humanitarian at this stage of his career, but these proceedings struck him as too much Georgia for the federal system to bear. The president sought to restrain Troup and prevent a costly conflict but remained obligated to enforce the treaty, which the Senate had ratified, without much knowledge of the circumstances or thought about their implications, the day before his inauguration. Hence military attention was initially directed at restraining the Creeks rather than the Georgians, a clear indication of the core assumptions about federal Indian policy that Adams inherited from the Virginia Dynasty. The critical issue was means—capability and cost—rather than ends: "My principal solicitude," commanding general Jacob Brown informed Eastern Department commander Winfield Scott, "has been that no militia should be called into service, so that whatever military [force] . . . may be called to act . . . may be purely of the regular establishment." A former militiaman himself early in the War of 1812, Brown doubtlessly worried that the militia would prove unreliable in enforcing federal sovereignty; the militia would certainly be too expensive, and probably too poorly disciplined to be effective, if employed against the Creeks. Whoever the opponent, the army wanted credit as the effective instrument of federal policy, and the administration sought the faster, more comprehensive resolution professional soldiers promised. Ultimately, the use of federal military forces would provide the basis for agreement between nation and state—the Georgians, like so many Americans claiming to seek a more decentralized government over the course of the nation's history, actually wanted the rest of the states to share the cost of their demands through federal action. But first Troup had to score his point with the voters, and state and national authorities had to sort out appearances—fictions for political consumption—and reality. While Adams may have preferred the status quo, Georgia forced his hand and made the federal government take military action to secure the state's "rights" under the compact of 1802.[18]

Meanwhile, Edmund Gaines and paymaster Major Timothy Andrews, the scion of a well-connected family in Washington, were dispatched to Georgia. Andrews, an accountant, was sent to investigate criticism of federal Creek agent John Crowell; Gaines was instructed to protect the Georgians while keeping peace among the Creeks and pressuring them to accept the treaty. Adams suggested that Georgia delay the treaty's implementation—the survey of Creek lands for white settlement, which was sure to provoke conflict and was not mandated until September 1826—while Gaines shaped the situation to minimize violence. This conciliatory policy failed to calm the Georgians, hinting at the political limits to any "policy of moderation" toward the Indians. In 1820s Georgia, the politics of white supremacy was as much about dispossessing Indians as about slavery: expanding the plantation system, and citizen opportunity more generally, depended on expanding the physical territory available to white citizens. Patience was no virtue to the Georgians, and Troup refused to subordinate himself or the state to federal restraint—which might have cost him the election—by waiting a year to distribute the benefits of the fraudulent treaty to the voters. Accepting his constituents' rumors and panic at face value, the governor continued to exaggerate the Creek threat, convening the state legislature in June for a special session to pass a law attaching the ceded lands to adjacent Georgia counties, thus bringing them under state law.[19]

Gaines arrived in Milledgeville four days after the state passed this law. During this crisis, we see the hard-bitten Gaines—Andrew Jackson's principal lieutenant in the Division of the South, second only to Sharp Knife in pressing U.S. expansion along the Florida frontier between 1815 and 1820—turning down a new path that was just as representative of the views of the career officer corps after 1820 as Jackson's had been before. Old Hickory did not extend his animosity toward nullification to assertions of state sovereignty over Native Americans: he may have criticized the Crawfordite Troup, but as president he would soon accept Georgia's claims against the Cherokee, essentially nullifying the verdict of the Supreme Court. Yet after international conditions settled down in 1820, a growing proportion of professional officers, dependent on the power of the nation-state for their livelihood and authority, felt empathy for the Indians and antagonism toward aggressive state governments representing white frontiersmen. Gaines's career spanned the decade of Jeffersonian expansionism before the War of 1812 and ran through the principal period of Indian expropriation to the war with Mexico. Thus, despite his many idiosyncrasies and his ongoing sympathy for frontiersmen as American citizens, the junior Tennessean provides one of the best examples of the officer corps' changing attitudes toward Native Americans and removal, views dramatically reshaped by the endemic federal-state friction over the pace and form of expropriation that burst into the open in 1825.

Entering office through election by the House of Representatives, John Quincy Adams probably feared that Jackson's principal military subordinate, a grizzled veteran of a quarter century on the frontier, would prove too sympathetic to the Georgians. Yet Gaines commanded the Eastern Department and Winfield Scott, the only other general officer available for assignment outside Washington, had no Indian experience, no friends or connections in Georgia to smooth civil-military relations and federal-state diplomacy. Adams need not have worried: Gaines's bitter struggle in 1817 and 1818 with Crawfordite David Mitchell, federal agent to the Creeks, predisposed him in a direction very different from the one he normally would have taken against the Creeks, and Troup's confrontational attitude alienated the intemperate general almost immediately. On May 31 Gaines advised Secretary of War James Barbour that a Creek war was unlikely "unless . . . some evil disposed white man should attack" the Indians. The brigadier repeated this opinion to his friend Thomas Cadwalader, a civic leader and militia commander, the following day, regretting that his assignment was "particularly objectionable" due to the humidity. "Above all, [the mission] will probably bring me in collision with our red neighbours, under circumstances of a disagreeable character . . . in which I may find it to be my duty to differ in opinion from some of my old *friends* of the south[:] those who have often contributed to involve the Indians in trouble with the frontier inhabitants, but who have not manifested so much talent, or disposition, to restore harmony between them." Gaines's friendship with the Cadwalader family, one of the most elite in Philadelphia (one of the nation's top five metropolitan social centers), had developed during his service on the northern border in the War of 1812 and demonstrates his gentility and social status. Though the tidewater Virginian Winfield Scott looked down on him, the junior Tennessean probably had more social connections outside the South and the West than Andrew Jackson.[20]

Gaines, who praised citizen-soldiers throughout his career, probably wanted to give the Georgians a sense of participation and responsibility, so he called on Troup for two regiments of militia, to be paid for by the federal Treasury, two days after his arrival. But the Georgia leader had already expressed his anger toward "your Government," and matters would only go downhill from there. Gaines remained quiet, at least in writing, for another month, but his subordinates gave up on the Georgians more quickly. Major Andrews, who had had more time to investigate, anticipated the brigadier's later views on June 2 when he exonerated the Creek agent, Crowell (whom the Georgians considered too sympathetic toward the Creek majority), of charges of financial impropriety while declaring to Secretary of War Barbour that "every principle of good faith and humanity calls for forbearance" in surveying the Creek lands. Andrews's role is worth noting as another example of executive branch trust in the insulation, autonomy, and objectivity of military professionals. President Adams sent a military finance officer with only three years' service, rather than a more experienced civilian War Department or Treasury agent, to investigate Crowell's fiscal accountability, and the paymaster vindicated Crowell, a fellow War Department employee whom Secretary of War Calhoun had reprimanded. Within a week Andrews faulted the Georgians for the trouble, ridiculing the alarm as a matter of "idle rumor." He went on to denounce Troup's message to the legislature as "inflammatory," though he regretted, "exceedingly, that my duty to the Government compels me to differ . . . from the Governor of an important member of the Union."[21]

Discussions soon began with representatives of the Creek majority, and at the end of the month, the paymaster warned that "in fairness to the Indians," the Georgia commissioners should be required to send written questions to the Creek chiefs, rather than speaking with individuals in private—a common means of intimidating, bribing, and dividing native leaders. Vilified by the Georgians after he submitted his report, the major responded to defend his personal integrity and reputation, manifested by his role in sustaining the nation's good faith and honor toward the Creeks; he used his Washington connections to good advantage to condemn the character and integrity of the state commissioners in a signed letter to the *National Journal*.[22] Yet Georgian anger had little impact on his subsequent career. Andrews had probably needed some political influence to gain his commission as paymaster, since the lowest grade in that department was major, and paymasters secured their appointments without graduating from West Point, unlike virtually every other officer commissioned during the 1820s. (Presumably this was because they, like medical officers, lacked any command authority.) In other words, if Andrews had gone to Georgia as a civil servant and then sought military appointment, he might not have been commissioned as a paymaster (and was too old to enter the Military Academy), but once he had been appointed, there was little the Georgians could do to him so long as he adhered to the ethical norms of his profession.

The Andrews family did very well in the army, suggesting just how insulated the professional officer corps could be. Timothy Andrews served two relatively uneventful decades before his connections enabled him to gain promotion into the line to command the newly raised Regiment of Voltigeurs (light infantry) in Mexico, where he distinguished himself at the storm of Molino del Rey and was brevetted to brigadier general for gallantry in the

Edmund Pendleton Gaines, passionate frontiersman and nationalist, later in life. (Courtesy U.S. Army Military History Institute)

assault on Chapultepec. He then gave up his lineal rank (since the regiment was disbanded at the end of the war) and returned to the Pay Department, where he rose to become paymaster general of the entire U.S. Army—nearly a million soldiers—in 1862, retiring two years later. Timothy's brother George entered the Sixth Infantry from West Point in 1823, was wounded and brevetted for gallantry at Okeechobee during the Second Seminole War (when few brevets were awarded), and ultimately became lieutenant colonel (one of only nineteen in the line of the army) of the Sixth in 1855, retiring early in 1862. Jacksonian connections helped brother Christopher secure the same appointment as Timothy—as a paymaster with the rank of major—directly from civil life in 1836; he served thirteen years. Christopher's son, George T. Andrews, served from 1847 to 1856 as a lieutenant in the Third Artillery.

Clearly, Andrews had more influence than the usual officer, but he performed his duties with professional accountability and objective impartiality. The paymaster's language toward the Georgians was subdued compared with that of Gaines's aide-de-camp and fellow Tennessean Lieutenant Edward G. W. Butler, cousin of Jackson's adjutant general Robert Butler (who had left the army in 1821 to serve as surveyor of public lands in Florida, where he advanced white expansion for a quarter century). In a private letter dated July 1, the young Butler remarked that "such a mass of corruption and bribery as has been elicited in the course of this investigation . . . has never been presented to the world. The Indians have proven themselves superior to Americans, in virtue & magnanimity." Butler echoed Andrews's strictures on the Georgians' attempts to negotiate with the Creeks, emphasizing the "pride and satisfaction I experience in being afforded an opportunity of offering my feeble testimony to the independence, frankness, and astonishing natural abilities, which so eminently distinguish[ed]" Creek leaders. Going a step further than Andrews, Butler made his loyalties clear to fellow southerners: "I spurn your insinuations against the General Government, under which I have the honor to hold a commission." As far as this junior Jackson was concerned, "the only enemies we shall have to contend with, will be the crazy governor and his corrupt and designing politicians."[23]

Gaines took longer to break with the Georgians, but he rapidly came to doubt the legitimacy of the Treaty of Indian Springs. After meeting Troup and leaders of the McIntosh faction, he concluded that "near forty-nine fiftieths" of the Creeks "are, and have uniformly been, opposed to the treaty," while the treaty supporters included "the worst men, *white* and *red*." Although Gaines warned the Creek majority that the government would implement the treaty, this was not enough for Troup, who continued to insist on Georgia's sovereignty, despite and above the federal sovereignty of the treaty, the law of the land under the Constitution. Indeed, the governor claimed the authority to survey the land ceded in the treaty as soon as possible, though this contradicted its stipulation of "protection against the encroachments, hostilities, and impositions of the whites" prior to September 1, 1826. Reaffirming his support for this provision, President Adams attempted to forbid the Georgia survey, actually authorizing Gaines to use force to prevent it. This could have meant shooting state officials, but the general responded that he would implement Adams's "just, enlightened, and moderate views," reminding the president that he had done similar service to the nation when capturing Aaron Burr a generation before. Troup enjoyed a firmer base of support than Burr, however, and Gaines could not use the violence necessary to compel the surveyors to withdraw without risking civil war with Georgia. The Creeks might have done so, but Gaines's troops probably intimidated the Creeks more than they did the Georgians, permitting the state's survey to proceed unhindered.[24]

The army deployed an entire regiment in the Flint and Chattahoochee Valleys, and overt peace was temporarily preserved, but the Creeks still refused to accept the treaty as valid, and even Andrew Jackson recognized that it had been negotiated with a tiny fraction of the nation. Gaines urged canceling or renegotiating the treaty, arguing that "no principle of justice" could "sanction a demand" that it be enforced. Wanting to avoid another Creek civil war, Adams agreed, authorizing Gaines—rather than a civil official—to lead the negotiations that produced a new agreement aptly named the Treaty of Washington, the place where it was signed the following January. In the meantime, the state governor and the federal military commander exchanged increasingly bitter barbs, assuming the honor and integrity of their agents and allies, both white and Creek, as their own. Thus a minister later reported that Gaines had declared the treaty "was founded in the deepest fraud and treachery," that "I tell these Indians the white people will cheat them out of their lands, get all their money and then kick them to hell!" Responding to condemnation from Troup, the imaginative brigadier demonstrated the truculence that would ultimately make him persona non grata for missions of borderlands diplomacy, equating Georgian rhetoric to that of the Holy Alliance of European monarchs, "the angry vapouring paper squibs of the little and great demagogues."[25]

None of the American officials—federal or state, military or civilian—came out looking good. Indeed, Gaines went much too far, both in engaging the governor and in the language he used to do so. Professional military officers often labeled politicians demagogues, but most did so in letters to like-minded comrades rather than the media. Gaines's temperament did not allow him to keep quiet, and Troup secured affidavits that the brigadier had repeatedly and publicly labeled him "unprincipled," an "intriguing demagogue," and "guilty of treason," threatening that Troup "would be tried for treason and hung" if he attempted to survey the lands in question. Andrew Jackson could say such things, but no one else. Worst of all, Gaines reportedly referred to "the little demagogue state of Georgia" and said that "the people of Georgia were a set of demagogues." This was not fundamentally inaccurate, but it was certainly impolitic and disrespectful of the citizens Gaines was sworn to serve. Sadly, the general may well have said such things in his fury. He was certainly right about Troup's demagoguery, but the governor used Gaines's excess to his advantage, winning reelection as a defender of Georgia's honor and integrity. Meanwhile, *Niles' Weekly Register*, which supported the administration's course, censured the brigadier for airing the nation's dirty laundry in view of the European monarchs he so detested. Winfield Scott took the opportunity to mock his rival's "puerility, egotism, & vulgarity"; Jacob Brown probably just shook his head. Adams forbade Gaines to write for publication (actually a reminder of existing army regulations) but refused to reprimand or arrest him, as Troup demanded.[26]

Jackson lamented that "my friend . . . permitted himself to be drawn into a political newspaper controversy" that could do general, army, and nation no good, "however Justifiable his conduct." Ironically, Old Hickory feared that "it is to be tested how far the Executive will sustain him, should his own popularity be endangered in the least thereby . . . [Gaines and I] have had sufficient experience to know, unless shielded by positive instructions, the executive will shield itself from responsibility if it can, and throw it upon its subordinates." Yet Gaines would suffer far more from his old commander's irresponsibility than from that of John Quincy Adams, when Jackson feared political hot water after ordering Gaines to secure the Texas border in 1836. Nor would Jacksonian Democrat John Wool, the army's inspector general, fare any better as Sharp Knife's emissary to intimidate the Cherokee into leaving Georgia that autumn: perhaps Jackson learned more about the crucial political skill of evading responsibility than any of those directly involved in the 1825 crisis. Gaines looked as intemperate and partisan as those he denounced, and 1825 was the first time he demonstrated the irascibility that transformed his former zeal and energy into the eccentricity for which he later became known. Fundamentally antipolitical in values and outlook, the brigadier failed—indeed was unwilling—to take the delicate political situation into account. Yet Gaines made an important point about the balance between moderation and firmness. "By speaking out," he declared, "I opened the eyes of many virtuous citizens . . . and I am rather inclined to think that I checked the Governor in his course of folly, that would otherwise have ended in an *overt* act of *Treason*." Gaines went beyond rhetorically espousing the nationalism he had developed during a quarter century of military service. As a federal diplomat ordered to investigate a disputed situation in a discontented state, his sense of duty compelled him to assume the unpleasant responsibility of offering his professional evaluation, inescapably political as well as military.[27]

The general was echoed by his aide, Butler, whose loyalty to his commander hints at the growing divergence between state and local civilian leaders and the national military officers charged with maintaining peace between white and Indian. After examining the new treaty, the lieutenant warned Andrew Jackson that "had not the Senate interposed its strong arm, a procedure even more corrupt than that which gave birth to [the] ill fated and infamous Treaty [of Indian Springs], would have received the *concurrence*, if not the *sanction*, of our pure administration." If so, "the Creek nation—a brave, patient, and injured people—rising in their majesty, and perceiving how basely their interests were betrayed, would have rushed, with the violence of a torrent, on their former favorite" leaders. Butler's words are a testament to the ambiguous, even ambivalent views, as well as the institutional interests, of career professional officers grappling with the complex dilemmas of borderlands diplomacy: he praised the Creeks but appeared to blame their leaders for the unfair treaties, while positioning himself and his commander as the defenders of injured virtue. Gaines, "like myself, was deeply interested in the fate of these poor Indians; and if ever an honest man labored for other[s'] good, regardless of the consequences to himself, he did for theirs."

The army's officers were certainly much more objective, much more morally upright than the frontiersmen and elected state officials with whom they clashed, but this was not the kind of language Jackson would have much patience for as president, despite the old comrades from whom it came.[28] Nor did the controversy fundamentally alter administration policy. Entering office under Adams, Secretary of War Barbour had proposed the creation of an Indian refuge, with true territorial status—meaning a delegate to Congress—somewhere west of the Mississippi. Meanwhile, Native Americans in the East were not to be dispossessed by violence or intimidation. Based on Barbour's proposal, and on the reputation of superintendent of Indian affairs Thomas McKenney for reform, some historians have implied that Adams's policy was one of "patience and moderation" (like that they attribute to Calhoun), in contrast to Jackson's drive for expropriation. Yet Adams had long recognized the determination of American frontiersmen: in 1814 he argued that all the government's force, "and all that of Britain combined with it, would not suffice" to prevent white expansion. As the summer of 1825 turned to autumn, Georgia had been restrained from seizing the Creek lands and outright ethnic cleansing, and there had been no violence between state and federal forces. Adams could have read the uproar as evidence of Georgian extremism, perhaps of a need for stronger federal control over Indian relations on the frontier. Instead, whether from principle or fear of civil war, he remained committed to resolving Georgian demands for the cession of Creek lands.[29]

Given the accurate information military officers communicated to the president, this persistence demonstrates that Adams's policy was neither moderate nor fundamentally pacific, except that he interposed federal authority to precipitate and ease expropriation without the disorder, violence, and bad publicity state action would provoke. In December 1825 Secretary Barbour, as much a Jeffersonian Republican as a national one, argued that the Creeks should be compelled to accept Georgia law, which would make any treaty meaningless. The president rejected such complete abdication of federal authority as unconstitutional, but his fundamental objective remained constant: harmony among white citizens and between state and nation, which could come only at Indian expense. Adams wanted to claim that good faith had been maintained, so no overt bribes would be employed. He hoped to secure Creek acquiescence by limiting the proposed cession of their land to that in Georgia—all of it, if possible; they would be allowed to keep their territory within Alabama, presumably until that state became influential enough to follow Georgia's example. Indeed, the "Second Creek War" of 1836 and beyond began after Alabama did so, and Jackson's administration crafted another fundamentally fraudulent treaty, pressing the Creeks in Alabama to move west of the Mississippi. When they were forced to do so, the McIntosh faction Creeks who were already in the West panicked, and brevet Brigadier Matthew Arbuckle felt compelled to mobilize troops to calm the anticipated tensions. Because of the army's involvement in Florida (where the units freed from Alabama were sent) and the movement of most of his Seventh Infantry to the border with Texas, Arbuckle had to call on the Arkansas militia. Perhaps more fearful of the latter than of each other, the two factions came to a tenuous agreement; the Creeks driven from Alabama were in such want that Arbuckle was able to compel them to accept Roley McIntosh, half brother of the assassinated William, as their "chief."[30]

Gaines and Crowell conducted the renegotiation that led to the Treaty of Washington during the autumn of 1825, excluding most Georgians from the proceedings. The Creeks were probably not reassured. Though both Americans had publicly disparaged the Treaty of Indian Springs and the Creeks retained some land claimed by Georgia, the long-range purpose and outcome of the new negotiation were no different than before. The new treaty's language appeared to recognize Creek sovereignty—the right to refuse the Treaty of Indian Springs—but compelled the Creeks to accept the same essential demand for removal. Indeed, the Creeks were to surrender the land in question by the beginning of 1827, though the treaty granted them until early 1828 to remove west; the discrepancy was blatant and unexplained, fostering further uncertainty and anxiety among the Creeks. The self-serving duplicity of Adams's vision, both moral and political, became even more transparent a month later, when David Brearley, the former colonel who had served as a Crawfordite tool against Gaines earlier in the decade, was appointed to recruit Creeks for "voluntary" emigration west. Nor was any treaty ever sacred: within two months of signing the agreement, Secretary Barbour secured a "supplementary article" intended to ensure that the Creeks gave up all their land within Georgia.[31]

Georgians were not satisfied even then; no longer restrained by presidential ambitions, William H. Crawford wrote to Senator Samuel Smith of Maryland that November, threatening "civil war" to resist the new treaty. The range and currency of southern expansionism were reaffirmed in January 1827, when Alabama extended its sovereignty over the Creek lands within its borders. Ironically, the Creeks' only hope seemed to be in playing the states against one another: despite Barbour's "supplement" to the Treaty of Washington, confusion over the border between Georgia and Alabama—still incompletely surveyed in 1826 because of Creek opposition—left as much as 200,000 acres in Creek hands within the boundaries claimed by Georgia. Eager to reap the political benefits of racialized democracy, Georgia officials continued to refuse federal direction over the pace of expansion, responding to the continued native presence by establishing a lottery to dispose of the disputed lands without resorting to any further negotiations. Desperately hoping to preserve a veneer of national honor, Adams seems to have been unwilling to accept the implications of his decisions, and federal-state tensions escalated in 1827—another election year in Georgia—when the War Department ordered the U.S. attorney and marshal to arrest state officials surveying the "lottery lands." Troup responded by mobilizing two divisions of militia, and Adams warned that he would employ "the arm of military force" to uphold the supremacy of federal law.[32]

Again hoping to avoid civil war while sustaining the forms of federal authority, the president dispatched Lieutenant John R. Vinton, Jacob Brown's aide-de-camp, to Georgia with instructions for Creek agent Crowell to negotiate a cession of the land in question. Indeed, Vinton, only eight years out of West Point, was to open a separate channel of communication with the Georgia authorities. With Gaines now commanding the army's Western Department, Brown laid out the situation for Winfield Scott: "The faith of the United States is pledged. The treaty [of Washington, which did not include the lands in question] having received the constitutional sanction it becomes one of the supreme laws of the land[;] its obligations are sacred and its conditions as binding upon the United States as those of any treaty with a sovereign and independent people." The executive branch would attempt to proceed through civil process, with the district attorney and marshal taking the lead, and the Creeks would have to trust the government to protect them from imminent expulsion. Counseling Scott that February, Brown doubted that "any very serious disturbance will ensue," but the army's commanding general soon disregarded his delicate health and set out on a southern "tour of inspection" intended primarily to remind the Georgians of their membership in the national fraternity. The Virginia presidents might have made this trip themselves, but with a centralizing New Englander as president, military heroes took the lead as federal diplomats showing the national flag in disaffected southern states. The commanding general was close to Adams, and the president consistently employed professional military officers, rather than State Department officials or private friends, on these diplomatic missions to Georgia. This may have been because he wanted to hint at national military force, or because he felt he lacked influence himself; he may have believed that the office of the presidency meant less than his personal unpopularity, and that military heroes from the War of 1812 would better remind the Georgians of their nationality and its value.[33]

Vinton felt less sanguine than his patron. Traveling in advance of the general with the president's dispatches for Crowell and Troup, Vinton feared that the state "puts herself in array against the U.S. Since the formation of the Federal compact, I doubt if ever the federal & state Governments have ever met at such serious issue." The governor disingenuously pointed to Vinton's military status in his call for the militia to prepare resistance, and the lieutenant noted in his diary: "This looks like civil war!! But the Govr. reaps popularity . . . and *therefore* he chooses to pursue it. . . . Since the formation of our Government we have never had a conjuncture so pregnant with threatened evil." Yet Vinton felt sure a compromise would be reached, and the Treaty of Fort Mitchell did so that fall, ceding the last Creek lands in Georgia. Thus a struggle older than the federal government under the Constitution ended in victory for the most aggressive state in the Union. Nowhere does the history of federal Indian relations show more clearly that the squeaky wheel got the grease, that federal law, policy, and constitutional interpretation were ultimately subordinate to the populist politics of white supremacy.[34]

Given these dynamics, the army was ultimately no more than a façade for Adams's dissimulating policy of form and delay. Surely the president was engaged in a remarkable feat of compartmentalization, or legal-bureaucratic obfuscation, to elude the cognitive dissonance so deeply embedded in his policy and practice. Indeed, his final State of the Union message—after he had been defeated by the Jacksonian electoral mobilization of the South and the West—truckled to decentralizing frontier opinion by condemning Indians who resisted state sovereignty and hinting at the desirability of removal. Meanwhile, Winfield Scott asked Brown whether he should move to Washington from his usual headquarters in New York City. Though a National Republican and a nationalist like Adams and Brown, the brigadier expressed little enthusiasm for a clash: "I am most happy to find that the difficulty . . . has been referred . . . to the *civil* authorities . . . & sincerely hope that these will be sufficient to maintain peace, & to do justice." Scott hoped that civil conflict ("God forbid") could be avoided, although he was "ready to do my duty." Brown responded that the president had placed the question in the hands of Congress, that "we must keep *ourselves* entirely out of sight until we are called upon to Act," a contingency that "every lover of his country would deplore." Doubting that this would prove necessary, the commanding general counseled Scott that "every thing which might tend to increase the excitement should be carefully avoided." This Brown did, enjoying a conciliatory, patriotic tour through Charleston, Savannah, Augusta, Milledgeville, Montgomery, and New Orleans before swinging north. Unable to use his right arm due to the effects of a stroke he had suffered in 1821, the general did not attend the public dinners given in his honor; the tour was Brown's last significant national service before his death the following winter.[35]

Jacob Jennings Brown, commanding general and federal diplomat. Engraving after Alonzo Chappel. (Courtesy Library of Congress, LC-USZ62-121124)

Andrew Jackson in 1833. (Courtesy Library of Congress, LC-DIG-pga-02360)

4

THE ARMY AND THE JACKSONIANS TANGLE ON THE SOUTHERN FRONTIER

Indian Removal and Civil-Military Relations, 1831–1834

Historian Mary Hargreaves observes that for all his nationalist rhetoric, the Indian policy of John Quincy Adams proffered "little more . . . alternative than a holding action in defense of federal jurisdiction."[1] Jacob Brown's tour prefigured those Winfield Scott would undertake during the Nullification Crisis and the Canadian border crises five and ten years later, suggesting the value of military heroes in the federal-state diplomacy of union. Likewise, national military power remained one of the principal instruments of U.S. Indian policy, though that policy was supposedly predicated on voluntary negotiation and compromise. Duty in the southern borderlands should have become less complex for the army during the years following Adams's electoral defeat, for U.S. policy toward the southeastern tribes was quickly recast in a direction that promised to minimize federal-state conflict and maximize clarity, as Andrew Jackson actively promoted the extension of state sovereignty. Within two years of Jackson's election, Congress passed laws authorizing settlers to preempt the sale of public lands and the executive branch to exchange public land west of the Mississippi for Indian land to its east. Sharp Knife's thrust was never subtle; soldiers, states, and citizens knew its direction and read their cues. Yet several years of discord and confusion would pass before Indian removal by federal military forces actually got under way, and a decade of civil-military tension, frustration, and dissension followed.

Part of the delay between Jackson's election and the passage of the Removal Act lay in the administration's need to assess the balance of political, military, and budgetary forces. In 1829 John Crowell advised the War Department that "a strong military force" would be required to compel complete removal by the Creeks, but the new administration's economy drive precluded the expenditures necessary to do so. The need for political compromise, particularly between northern and southern Democrats within the Jacksonian coalition, also slowed the process of decision, and in 1829 Jackson probably feared that precipitate action would embarrass his efforts to secure comprehensive removal legislation, which was opposed by many northern Democrats as well as National Republicans. A sectionally divided Congress, not yet accustomed to partisan voting discipline, was unlikely to enact legislation that would authorize overt national coercion to dispossess Indians largely for the benefit of southerners. Hence the Removal Act of 1830 authorized Indian expropriation as voluntary emigration in return for land west of the Mississippi and an opportunity to escape the pressure of white intrusion, necessitating the negotiation of treaties despite Jackson's often-stated belief that they were unnecessary due to U.S. sovereignty. It then took several years to pressure the southeastern tribes into negotiating agreements to exchange their land for that west of the Mississippi, employing time-honored American methods of deception, corruption, and disingenuous negotiations with unrepresentative tribal minorities.[2]

By 1834, the administration gained a series of cessions and treaties requiring emigration by set dates, but the physical impetus for removal still depended on indirect coercion, through encroachment, bullying, and intimidation by white intruders or the extension of state laws, from whose protection most Indians were excluded. In the southern context, the imposition of state laws without grant of citizenship threatened slavery, and more than a few Indians were enslaved amid the chaos of the removal years. Given the continuing, indeed growing, political opposition to the sordid realities of expropriation, fueled by the excesses and corruption evident even in the earliest stages of the policy's execution, Jackson hesitated to accept the costs of employing national military power unless the Indians became desperate enough to provide a pretext through violent resistance. The Cherokee, Chickasaw, and Choctaw realized this and restrained their anger to escape greater evils.

THE DILEMMAS OF EXECUTING A DISINGENUOUS POLICY: SQUATTER REMOVAL AND CIVIL-MILITARY FRICTION DURING JACKSON'S FIRST ADMINISTRATION, 1830–1833

Meanwhile, the discovery of gold in western North Carolina and northwestern Georgia drew new waves of intruders onto Cherokee land shortly after Jackson's election. Military officers on the scene proved slow to perceive the thrust of the coming changes, despite a good deal of private support from senior officers for Jackson in 1828. To many of them, from Henry Atkinson in Missouri to company-grade officers in Georgia, the president's quest to dispossess the Indians seemed far less urgent than restraining white citizens, whose aggression violated national faith and law, damaged the nation's reputation, and might stir the Indians to costly war. Keeping the peace remained difficult and often impossible, and the attempt to do so drew every senior military leader on the southern Indian frontier into differences of opinion with citizens and civil officials, from county sheriffs to the national executive. The army obeyed, and military subordination to civilian authority was maintained, but War Department directives were often so vague, even disingenuous, that honest, experienced soldiers felt compelled to uphold the existing laws and treaties in the relatively objective, impartial spirit of peacekeeping to which they had become accustomed, despite constantly growing evidence that the administration preferred more leniency toward white aggressors.

Like their counterparts in the Georgia-Creek dispute, these military commanders tended to blame local whites for most of the trouble with the Cherokee, dismissing the frontiersmen in language shot through with markers of class and gentility. Reporting from the Georgia mining country in June 1830, Captain Francis W. Brady (no known relation to Colonel Hugh Brady of the Second Infantry) maintained that "the most numerous body of those engaged in digging gold are of the most abandoned part of the community," who worked the mines "without any kind of system or skill." Georgia governor George Gilmer had forbidden mining by whites and Indians alike, on the grounds that the Cherokee land had become state public land, and he eventually created a "Georgia Guard" (aka the "home guard") of volunteers to enforce his proclamation. Over the next eight years, the Guard's principal function would be to intimidate the Cherokee. In the meantime, Gilmer first demanded the army's departure, then asked for its return until he could gain legislative authorization to raise a state force. Local law enforcement had no more impact than motivation: white intruders arrested by sheriffs were granted writs of habeas corpus by local magistrates, and Brady concluded that "the idea of removing them peaceably will be delusive." The captain warned his civilian superiors that the white miners' depredations would lead to Indian retaliation and war "unless the government should interfere more effectually . . . and put a stop to the proceedings of the lawless multitude." Indeed, this national military officer advised shooting white citizens: "a few cartridges spent upon them, I think would teach them to respect the laws and treaties of their country." Unfortunately for Brady, state law and federal treaties—supposedly the supreme law of the land under the Constitution—no longer coincided.[3]

Perhaps the sixteen-year veteran was politically naïve, but Brady probably believed he had the authority to use force against the citizenry. The War Department's initial (February) order instructed the army to "stay any acts of hostility that may be contemplated on either side" in the gold region. A second order three weeks later mandated the ejection of white intruders from Indian lands there, instructing the army to keep a detachment along the Cherokee boundary to prevent further encroachment. Three months later, as the captain imagined his whiff of grapeshot, commanding general Alexander Macomb followed Governor Gilmer's lead by instructing Brady "to prevent all persons whatsoever from working the mines in the Cherokee Nation." Brady was to rely on "pacific methods . . . in the first instance," but Macomb delegated him executive discretion to use force if necessary, a determination Brady would have to make in conjunction with the federal marshal and district attorney, with the advice of whatever local officials he might trust.[4]

Tensions between state and federal forces rapidly threatened to come to a head as the Georgians targeted Cherokee miners for expulsion. Indeed, on June 17 Gilmer asked President Jackson to order the army to keep the Indians out of the mine regions, cleverly blaming "wealthy half breeds," Jackson's favorite frontier scapegoats, for violating Georgia's sovereignty. Yet communications were too slow to prevent soldiers of the national standing army from arresting and disarming a group of Georgia militia, led by a colonel, as well as a sheriff's posse a week later, after the Georgians had detained a number of Cherokee miners in accordance with the governor's proclamation. The thrust of Jacksonian policy quickly became apparent when civilian officials learned of these developments. Following Jackson's view that Indians were subject to state sovereignty, Secretary of War John Eaton had already proclaimed that squatter removal was a state responsibility, and he advised Brady that "your suggestion [to shoot squatters] . . . would entail consequences which you would probably be the first to feel." Unable to perform his duty without compromising his ethics or his sense of accountability to law, the frustrated captain resigned a year later. Subordinate to the end, he left no statement of protest.[5]

Valuing the security and prestige of their careers, few other officers would express such authoritarianism toward white citizens to their civilian superiors, much less resign—a flight from the duty they so ardently espoused as a virtue—to escape the dilemmas they faced. Yet any operation to eject squatters had the potential to lead to civil-military violence. In most cases squatters put up a bold front but left peaceably, returning and rebuilding their cabins—usually burned, per orders, by the soldiers—after the troops departed. But between 1831 and 1833 the contradictions of Jacksonian nationalism and expansion led to a series of incidents in Alabama, as several enlisted soldiers used deadly force to defend themselves and compel squatters to depart. Following half a decade of federal-state tensions over Creek expropriation, and coinciding with the Nullification Crisis, these incidents point to the more general crisis of federal authority in the borderlands during the 1830s. (Although there is little evidence of serious civil-military friction related to Indian removal in the Northwest, it seems probable that southern Democrats expected, and perhaps received, some sympathy for their states' rights positions from western frontiersmen impatient with federal efforts in their region.) The majoritarian demand for Indian removal came together with egalitarian individualism, states' rights ideology, and populist anti-institutionalism to pit national military officers against fellow white citizens rather than the Indians and foreigners they had generally combated during the 1810s. This development—first in the southern borderlands, but later along the Canadian border—would accelerate the officer corps' shift from racial and sectional identifications with white, often southern, farmers toward more cohesive, unified professional identities as servants of the national central—though still inescapably white—power.

Brevet Major Philip Wager, a nineteen-year veteran from Virginia, was at the center of the first set of incidents in Alabama. Wager had first been deployed to that state in 1828 to protect the Creeks who wanted to move west from intimidation by their more resistant counterparts. Even the Jackson administration recognized that white encroachment angered the Indians and obstructed removal, so peacekeeping between Indians soon extended to peacekeeping between whites and Indians, with the temporary ejection of white intruders preceding and facilitating that of the Indians. Nevertheless, political considerations delayed squatter removal operations until early 1830, when contingents from Fort Mitchell were dispatched to the Creek and Cherokee lands. Six companies, drawn from posts across the South, were deployed during the spring, and three more reinforced them during the summer, ejecting white intruders from the goldfields on Cherokee land in northwestern Georgia. This contingent, nearly a tenth of the entire army, engaged in a campaign of hide-and-seek, carried out largely by detachments of about a dozen soldiers led by noncommissioned officers, unaccompanied by civil officials, to arrest trespassers. When the intruders began to raid the goldfields at night to carry off bags of gravel for sifting at their new bases across the Tennessee line, the soldiers started to patrol at night and for several days at a time. Despite surveillance by the miners, Wager's troops captured and arrested nearly 200 intruders in a single nighttime raid, and a total of at least 500, while routinely burning the buildings constructed by the trespassers. Nevertheless, Wager did not have the legal authority to detain or charge the miners once he had escorted them off Cherokee land, and he does not appear to have been assisted by a federal marshal or U.S. attorney, much less state or local officers. Released as soon as they left Indian territory, the miners could easily evade Wager's patrols and return, much like white intruders on Indian land everywhere else.[6]

Wager's success without the use of violence won no more applause from the War Department than Brady's threat to use it—a paradox that would recur repeatedly over the next decade as professional military officers attempted to mediate among federal, state, and local imperatives while negotiating the rocks and shoals of Jacksonian Indian policy in the South. Wager had already clashed with Creek agent David Brearley (the former colonel driven from service by Jackson and Gaines due to his support of then-agent David B. Mitchell in 1820, who President Adams appointed to replace John Crowell and placate the Georgians) when he refused Brearley's demand for the arrest of the Creek National Council in the autumn of 1828. (Creek leaders had accused Brearley of profiteering at their expense the previous year.[7]) In other words, Adams gave in to Georgian pressure for a more amenable agent, but his military commander on the ground continued to exercise restraint in relations with the Creeks, effectively curbing the belligerence of the civilian agent. This de facto compromise, maneuvering through the interstices of federalism and what is now called the interagency process, was a workable option during the Adams administration but would be far less viable under Jackson.

When Wager moved to the goldfields in the spring of 1830, Secretary of War Eaton warned him that "the President would have you practice forbearance" and "discretion . . . in performing this unpleasant duty." It was unusual enough for the secretary of war to bypass the army chain of command to instruct a mere major. But how does one uphold the laws and constitution— as Wager had sworn to do when commissioned an officer of the United States—while exercising forbearance and discretion in their execution? That November the secretary wrote to Wager with pointed praise for Lieutenant F. D. Newcomb's decision not to halt Alabaman road construction in Creek territory, essentially recognizing state sovereignty over those lands. Did "discretion" still mean an experienced officer—usually a gentleman socialized in years of national service, with his career and integrity, his public and private autonomy, insulated from local, state, and sectional pressure and partisan manipulation by his federal commission—using his professional judgment to interpret and prioritize? Or did it mean going easy on those violating the trade and intercourse acts, breaking national treaties, and otherwise undermining the national sovereignty enunciated in the Constitution?[8]

Like Brady, Wager refused to fully accept the implications of Jacksonian

Indian relations. These national officers were not partisan or sectional in their appointment, values, or source of authority, and perhaps they had difficulty recognizing and resisted accepting the implications of partisan and sectional politics, but they were not political innocents. Rather, they were subordinates in the largest, the most hierarchical organization in the American nation-state, and they owed their employment, status, and authority to Congress and the executive. Perhaps their insulation once commissioned—their promotion by seniority, the channeling of orders through like-minded military superiors like Macomb, and the lack of effective civilian sanction apart from locally instituted lawsuits—encouraged an exaggerated sense of autonomy from sectional and partisan politics during the 1830s. The War Department recognized the customary "rights" of fellow government officers and gentlemen and could not seriously penalize them without military court proceedings conducted by their peers; it could withhold some debatable financial allowances requested by individual officers, like brevet pay for commanding posts of a certain size, and it might transfer officers from the Indian country, but that probably proved a welcome relief. Like promotions, postings and assignments were largely matters of rank and seniority, with remarkably little War Department intervention (far less than in the navy or some European armies).[9]

Brady's language suggests an increasingly common reaction to the officer's dilemma in nationalist authoritarianism, but Wager appears to have felt torn between objective formal accountability to law and Constitution and subjective responsiveness to clamorous citizen demands and obvious executive intent. In effect, he was being asked—not ordered, but certainly under pressure—not to enforce the law he had putatively been sent to enforce. If he did enforce the law, he would become subject to civil and possibly criminal lawsuits for damage to property or even assault, with no assurance of aid or defense from the civilian superiors who had ordered him to act. The War Department's hints—oblique and insincere, if not intentionally duplicitous—did little to clarify Wager's understanding of his duty. Nor did matters improve when Jackson withdrew the army from the goldfields at Governor Gilmer's request in November 1830. Responding to citizen complaints against his operations to eject squatters in Alabama early in 1831, Wager maintained that some severity was "impossible to prevent." The previous September, the Fort Mitchell commander had blamed enlisted soldiers for some of the harsh treatment—probably beatings in the course of effecting squatters' capture—meted out to intruders fleeing arrest in the Georgia woods. Wager now justified his actions by observing that the squatters were contemptuous of the government and army, so he would rather have "went too far than have been compelled

Alexander Macomb, commanding general, by Thomas Sully. (Courtesy West Point Museum)

to stop short of fulfilling the orders of the government" and undermining respect for federal authority.[10]

Stationed in Washington far from the scene of tension, commanding general Macomb contentedly approved the major's severity and repeatedly ordered him to station detachments to protect the Creeks against "the encroachments and depredations of the Whites." Indeed, Macomb probably confused his subordinate, and reinforced his obstinacy, by forwarding critical letters published in the *Montgomery Planters' Gazette* to give Wager an opportunity to explain his severity: "I do this on your own account, not doubting but that your conduct has always been correct, and that the good of the service has been your constant aim." Yet the general's instructions were so vague as to make the major almost entirely dependent on his own experience and judgment for guidance: "it is left to your judgment to adopt such measures as may seem calculated to effect the objects in view, having a due regard to the interests and economy of the service." Presumably, however, the interests of the army included avoiding criticism in the Jacksonian press. Faced with rules of engagement like these, it is little wonder that some officers became tentative or hesitant in the face of citizen defiance: the wonder is that they acted as energetically as they did.[11]

Officers like Wager often acted contrary to pressure from states, localities, and the executive because their personal, institutional, and professional loyalties united in the concept of national faith and honor. They felt an obligation of duty to the nation, represented by the democratically elected federal civil officials acting on the constitutional supremacy of federal law. Even when incumbent civil officials counseled forbearance, career military officers felt a sense of personal honor—integrity and good faith, obligation embodied in action as duty—as individuals sworn to uphold the laws enacted by previous officials, and they believed their personal honor was closely connected to professional, institutional, and national honor, that of the officer corps, army, and nation. Each of these values and allegiances reinforced the others. Professional and institutional honor depended on the performance of national duty, carrying out the nation's obligations with good faith and integrity. Though the Indians were not legally regarded as American citizens, and officers did not regard them as citizens or equals, many commanders felt an empathy for the natives founded largely in the contrast with the rapacious disorder of white frontiersmen, who were actually violating the nation's laws and Constitution. Federal military officers would use their autonomy to enforce the law unless explicitly ordered not to do so; more important, they would execute orders with limited tolerance for the flagrant defiance of rabidly individualistic frontiersmen.

The institutional interests of career professional officers encouraged subordination and accountability to civilian authority, so their empathy for the Indians did not lead to radical social or policy critiques, much less resignations to protest national policy. Nor was the officer likely to forsake his career and profession by resigning to protest state or local pressure. Instead, military commanders often proposed compromises intended to mollify the Indians and facilitate their departure west, like that Wager sent the commanding general in September 1832. That March the Creeks were subjected to another unequal treaty encouraging emigration. The treaty presented the usual disingenuous compromises and ambiguities, ceding all Creek land but granting the Indians use of individual allotments (termed "selections" in the treaty) for no more than five years, with a right to sell those lands; in addition, the treaty mandated that intruders be removed from the allotments during that period. Many Creeks objected to allotment, if only because it was clearly intended to spur them to move west. Wager advised them "in the most friendly manner not to be rash, but to wait a little longer," but since this was unlikely to resolve the deeper problems occasioned by white greed, he proposed that the federal Treasury purchase the allotments outright. This would save the government money, and payment could be made conditional on emigration west. The implication was obvious—those who did not go west would be cheated out of their land altogether—but the major's experience in Alabama led him to doubt the realism of any other alternative. "Under the present arrangement the Indian will, in most cases, be cheated out of his reserve, before he gets it. Companies of speculators are now forming, ready to take every advantage of these ignorant people, and there is hardly a white man to be found in this section . . . that is not looking out . . . for the time when he expects to be able to swindle an Indian out of a good tract of land." Wager doubted that any entity besides the federal government would ever pay the Creeks anything; only "honest, disinterested persons" like career federal military officers could or would make the best of a bad situation for the Indians.[12]

The Jackson administration had no desire to spend white taxpayer money to buy the Creek allotments. With Jackson focused on nullification, reelection, and his war against the Bank of the United States, Secretary of War Lewis Cass was left to mediate between the demands of state sovereignty and the violent anarchy of white intrusion on Indian lands. Though the 1832 treaty with the Creeks required the expulsion of squatters once their crops were harvested, Cass was a former Indian fighter and territorial governor, a believer in state sovereignty, who was always sympathetic to frontiersmen. He quickly promised Alabama congressmen that the "settlers" could remain until January 1833, and every effort was made to secure the approval of individual Creeks for specific squatters to remain. Yet army operations to remove white citizens illegally intruding on Indian land continued to slip through the fissures of Jacksonian politics, particularly when local public opinion was less rabidly in favor of Indian expulsion, as in North Carolina and Tennessee, which lacked both large Indian populations and the populist political dynamic of Georgia's legal claims against the federal government for removal. That summer (1832), troops were deployed at the state's request to eject white miners from Cherokee lands in North Carolina; finding the intruders had already fled, the federal Cherokee agent and the military commander, brevet Brigadier General Walker Armistead, took the initiative, apparently with the acquiescence of state authorities, to do so in Tennessee as well. In March 1833 Alexander Macomb advised the governor of North Carolina that two companies would return to the Cherokee "Valley Towns" to evict miners who had reappeared while the army was absent during the Nullification Crisis. Nor was Macomb's initiative against American citizens and potential Jacksonian voters limited to the South: he also ordered the commander at Fort Dearborn, Illinois, to expel intruders on Potawatomi land, and Zachary Taylor to remove prospectors from diggings in Fox territory in Wisconsin.[13]

The crisis in Alabama only escalated, however, as confrontations between federal troops and armed intruders increased. In July 1832 a company from Fort Mitchell burned the town of Irwinton, built on the site of the Creek town of Eufala, which had been seized by whites and incorporated by the Alabama legislature two years before. As such, Irwinton was legally much more than a squatter settlement, and state officials attempted to arrest the U.S. marshal and the captain in command of the removal operation. A soldier bayoneted a sheriff in the arm while resisting what his commander regarded as an illegal arrest, though nothing seems to have come of these incidents. That November threats of violent resistance to squatter removal led Macomb to order two additional companies to Fort Mitchell, but a more dangerous crisis intervened, and the contingent was redirected to Charleston to help Winfield Scott tamp down the threat of nullification. Meanwhile, Alabama took advantage of the pause in military law enforcement to establish counties within the territory ceded in the treaty, essentially placing the Creeks under Alabama law, their allotments to be determined by Alabama surveyors.[14]

The rapid compromise reached in the Nullification Crisis enabled Macomb to order the resumption of squatter removal in Alabama early the following spring (1833). Escalating tensions soon led the War Department to dispatch still another company to Fort Mitchell, where the new commander, brevet Major James S. McIntosh, a twenty-one-year veteran who had been wounded at Fort Erie in 1814, was drawn into an increasingly obstinate struggle with local citizens and state officials. As always in sensitive situations, McIntosh had been instructed to act only upon the requisition of civil officials, usually meaning the federal district attorney, Indian agent, or marshal. That August, while executing a civil writ under the direction of a federal deputy marshal, soldiers shot and killed a squatter, Hardeman Owens—also a county road commissioner—who had fired on the troops after attempting to lure them into his house, which he apparently planned to blow up once they were inside. Warned by the Indians Owens had bullied, the soldiers remained outside and escaped the explosion.[15]

Major McIntosh, a Georgian from one of the families that had led the filibuster against Spanish East Florida in 1812, gave no ground to local critics, telling one lawyer that he had not been ordered to cooperate in an investigation and did not expect to be, because "the soldier who shot [Owens] was in the lawful execution of his duty." Following this logic, the major refused to surrender his subordinate to the local sheriff, but he preferred conciliation to the use of force. Simultaneously faced with another request for troops to aid the federal marshal, and certain that the intruders would resist more violently than before, McIntosh counseled caution lest local tensions become sectional and national: "Should more blood be shed in the ejectment of these [intruders] it may eventuate in a general rupture between the State and the General Government." (In addition to the Nullification Crisis, we can assume that most officers remembered Gaines's travails in Georgia during the mid-1820s.) Hearing rumors that the squatters were forming armed companies, he sent for more ammunition from the Augusta arsenal but asked the marshal to meet for consultation before requesting further military action against the squatters.[16]

Following a county grand jury indictment for murder, the Superior Court of Alabama charged McIntosh with contempt when he refused to turn over the detachment of soldiers present during Owens's killing. The major refused to appear before the state judiciary, essentially rejecting the state's claim to jurisdiction over national officers, and the court called on the governor for militia to compel McIntosh's appearance. Major McIntosh now requested guidance from his superiors, justifying himself on the grounds that "it is scarcely necessary for me to say that I ever would disregard the *proper legal civil mandates* of my country," yet his soldiers "had unquestionably only been engaged in the legal Constitutional performance of their duty" under federal statutes. Like many commanders caught in civil-military and local-federal controversy, McIntosh blamed the local civil authorities, narrow-minded, self-interested men elected by and responsible only to the greedy frontiersmen who seized the Indians' land, for the clash: "I believe this is only the commencement of a determined opposition" to the supposed federal policy of ejecting intruders from Indian lands. Concerned that the military power of the state would be deployed against him, the major advised Macomb that "it will take a much larger command to execute your orders than the present garrison."[17]

Just three years out of West Point, Lieutenant David Manning had worse to worry about. Though he had "done [naught] but my duty" while leading the operation in which Owens was killed, the state of Alabama indicted him for murder. Apart from "the odium" of the charge, the lieutenant found his "steps dogged by a set of men, who, influenced by interest or political fanaticism, would be willing to risk their lives to make me prisoner." "Such is the state of excitement, and so inveterate is the feeling against the troops," that Manning feared being lynched. "I am always willing to do my duty—I am willing to meet all the vicissitudes of a military life in my country's service," but Manning preferred to do "some other duty, out of the limits of this state" and its vigilante justice. He was protected and rewarded by reassignment to Key West in the federal territory of Florida, but sickened and died there two years later.[18]

McIntosh was an unelected national executive officer who openly rejected state jurisdiction within a region Jackson had already surrendered to state sovereignty. In the wake of the Nullification Crisis, Jacksonian civil officials had to balance the legalism McIntosh expressed with attention to populist sentiment, his nationalism with attention to the states' rights they had already acknowledged as supreme over land occupied by Indians in the South. Even Winfield Scott advised caution, lest the threat of national military power in Alabama "excite the sympathies and inflame the passions of Virginia, North Carolina, South Carolina, Georgia, and Mississippi . . . [for] the heresies of nullification and secession." Secretary of War Cass, an experienced mediator between federal and local concerns from his long tenure as governor of Michigan Territory, responded immediately that the major would "oppose no obstacle to the service of legal process upon any officer or soldier under your command," regardless of its origin or presumed intent. Cass warned that the president wanted to avoid a clash and reminded McIntosh that "in all questions of jurisdiction, it is the duty of the [military] to submit to the [civil authority], and no considerations [whatsoever] must interfere with that duty." Cass appears to have promised the governor that the accused soldiers would be turned over to the state courts, but the secretary reassured his military subordinate that the federal district attorney, along with "a legal gentleman, of high standing"—Francis Scott Key—would be sent to secure the discharge of military personnel subjected to state process.[19]

In effect, Cass recognized that in the operations of a federal system, law, like politics, would run along multiple lines simultaneously. Alabama would charge McIntosh and his men, the United States would charge intruders, and each political entity would defend its agents in the other's courts. In effect, the two systems would probably cancel each other out, with state and local juries letting off those charged by federal officials, and federal lawyers finding ways to remand federal officers from state and local prosecution. The squatters would ultimately remain, and the land occupied by the Creeks would be incorporated into Alabama, while the federal military presence discouraged white bullying and prevented Indian uprising or war. Army officers apparently never served jail time in such disputes; their fines were commonly, though not always, paid by the Treasury, though often after several years' delay and frustration. Those whose fines were not paid were outraged by the absence of support from their civilian superiors, and the entire process was difficult to stomach for federal military commanders schooled in national supremacy and obedience to executive authority, aggravating the ulcer of their antipathy to frontiersmen. Yet in the end, the officer corps preserved enough institutional autonomy that Wager and McIntosh could serve long careers as national military officers. The soldier charged with shooting Owens must have felt less confident of protection, and took matters into his own hands by deserting.[20]

Cass reiterated the major's original instructions: to act only under the direction of the U.S. marshal. The secretary's letter took longer to reach McIntosh than the major's had taken to reach Cass, for on November 8 McIntosh urged "the necessity of removing the intruders without further delay." He had received the ammunition requested from Augusta but worried that the Alabamians "have gained confidence . . . from the belief that the troops and the marshal are afraid to execute their orders. This state of things must not, shall not exist if I can prevent it. Let me repeat the absolute necessity of an immediate removal of these lawless people." McIntosh believed that the nation's sovereign authority—ultimately sustained against dissenting minorities, as in European monarchies, by its willingness to threaten violence—was at stake. Yet military commanders were compelled to balance that abstract sovereign authority, and its practical physical exercise, with the effect of active law enforcement operations, and the violence that would undoubtedly ensue, on public opinion and a national administration that normally favored decentralization. McIntosh's letter was transmitted to Washington from the Alabama frontier in eight days: before the War of 1812, delivering such letters had taken at least a month. As historian Richard John points out, the bonds of union were capable of strengthening—if Jacksonian politicians had been willing to tighten the cords.[21]

The commanding general now backed federal authority with an entire regiment. In total, fourteen companies were deployed at Fort Mitchell, almost exactly one-eighth of the entire army and its largest troop concentration in the field, apart from the Black Hawk War, since Jackson's invasion of Florida sixteen years before. Indeed, this force equaled all those deployed throughout the Nullification Crisis. Macomb took care to balance firmness with politesse, putting the slightly more conciliatory Philip Wager back in charge, soon followed by the more senior Lieutenant Colonel David Twiggs, a Georgian with more than twenty years' service who had been engaged in situations of similar delicacy while commanding at Augusta during nullification. Macomb instructed Twiggs that although squatter removal would continue under the direction of federal civil officials, it "is of a very peculiar nature, and while you will be firm . . . let me recommend as little violence and injury to the persons and property of individuals as possible." Ideally, perhaps ultimately, the commanding general wanted federal sovereignty upheld: "if you should be opposed by force, you must, as a matter of course, put it down by all the means you possess"—implicitly including lethal force. Yet strict accountability to legal process and civil authority would be maintained: Twiggs was to turn over soldiers accused of civil offenses to the civil authorities, in accordance with the Thirty-third Article of War (which was reaffirmed in Cass's instructions to McIntosh). What the use of force might mean for the colonel and his career was left unstated, but Twiggs—like most officers other than McIntosh, which accounts for the latter's removal from command—could read the tea leaves, and there were no further incidents of deadly force.[22]

The die had long been cast. Less than a year later, the War Department adopted Wager's 1832 plan for the government to purchase the allotments itself, sending brevet Lieutenant Colonel John J. Abert, chief of the topographical engineers, as one of the commissioners to negotiate the purchases. Abert took care to soothe the settlers, and Alabama dropped its prosecution of McIntosh; meanwhile, the United States agreed to halt the ejection of intruders pending the allotment surveys. In practice, this meant that Alabamians would seize the Creek lands by fraud, economic coercion, or physical intimidation and violence. Indeed, many of the allotment titles had already been secured by white speculators. Already cynical after supervising the Shawnee removal from Ohio the previous autumn, Abert explained the situation in pragmatic terms: the government had "a choice of two evils, between a small fraud and [the] uninterrupted prosecution of its declared policy [of removal], or a large fraud, [and] embarrassments to its policy at every step" as whites claimed Creek debts. The outcome would not change.[23]

The federal-state crisis quieted, but federal military officers could never be sure of the extent of their discretion. Nor was this possible in the American federal system: senior federal officials had to sustain both national sovereignty and the representative processes of federalism, however much they worked at odds. Edmund Gaines tried to clarify matters for one subordinate:

Lewis Cass, populist secretary of war, by Daniel Huntington. (Courtesy Army Art Collection)

You are placed in a position where conflicting laws, with adverse authorities and interests, operating powerfully upon the worst of the bad passions of man, white as well as red, combine to render your command . . . delicate and difficult. . . . When we recollect that we are *solemnly sworn to bear true faith and allegiance to the United States of America, and to serve them honestly and faithfully against their enemies or opposers whomsoever* . . . we [see] the strong outline by which we are to pass through the labyrinths of conflicting legislation and opinion.[24]

Gaines believed that duty to the nation, and specifically to orders from the executive branch, provided a compass to guide the professional officer, but the Jacksonian political compass rarely pointed true north. In reality, national sovereignty, certainly in the form of the supremacy of federal law per the Constitution, was often a legal fiction during the Jacksonian era, repeatedly asserted but rarely pressed to a conclusion in the face of local resistance backed by growing claims of popular democracy embodied in state sovereignty. Recognizing this, the Creeks and other Indians lost whatever faith they may have had in federal protection and increasingly resorted to violence to resist violence. Unfortunately, the trump card in swaying Jacksonian public opinion on borderlands issues was the white citizen's ability to point to Indian violence, however provoked (or merely rumored), to justify his own. Denied recognition as citizens of any state, the obverse strategy never worked for the Creeks, and in 1836 their violent resistance enabled Georgia and Alabama to secure federal assistance for the final expulsion of the Creek Nation across the Mississippi. Back in command at Fort Mitchell following Philip Wager's death from illness, James McIntosh was one of the officers who executed the orders for their removal.[25]

THE DIRTY DUTY OF REMOVAL: CONTEXTS, POLICY, AND INITIAL OPERATIONS AGAINST THE CHOCTAWS AND CREEKS, 1830–1834

No sooner did Philip Wager escape the perils of squatter eviction than he was engaged removing Creek Indians from Alabama. Racialized Jacksonian populism and sectional threats to the unity of the Jacksonian coalition each played a part in the policy transformation that led to Wager's redeployment. In 1830 the passage of the first Preemption Act, granting squatters first rights to purchase public (though not Indian) lands they occupied, signaled an end to the nuances and ambiguities of federal Indian policy during the previous decade.

Squatting gained statutory sanction, and popular and partisan politics, rather than ethical vision or the trade and intercourse acts—still in effect, and actually renewed in 1834—would determine whether intruders would be expelled from Indian land. Thus, although the first Jackson administration sometimes ordered localized squatter removal to reassure the Indians it wanted to move west, the sectional tensions that burst to the forefront of national politics in the Nullification Crisis (in which Wager had also been deployed) effectively put an end to sustained federal efforts to prevent encroachment or remove intruders on Indian land in the South. Winfield Scott observed that continuing to do so would "inflame the passions of Virginia, North Carolina, South Carolina, Georgia, and Mississippi, and thus give wider spread to the heresies of nullification and secession." Whatever Whiggish or National Republican sympathy Scott felt for the Indians, whatever disdain he felt for the Jacksonians, the national union of white men certainly meant far more to him than justice for Native Americans.[26]

Old Hickory must have appreciated his former antagonist's political judgment: the implied (dare we say corrupt?) bargain was even more obvious for Jackson, a southerner who had never considered Indian polities sovereign nations with standing to make treaties. Historians sometimes view the president as a nationalist because of his characteristically violent threats to crush the nullifiers in South Carolina, when a small group of white citizens threatened majority rule and national security (and, perhaps most important, Sharp Knife's own authority) by directly challenging laws passed by the representatives of other white citizens, but there is little other evidence that he supported policies of domestic centralization (such as the national bank, a stronger tariff, or more coordinated internal improvements). Though Jackson pioneered a new height of executive authority in the Oval Office, he did so to decentralize opportunity among whites, and the contradiction is probably best explained by personal authoritarianism. The president was willing to assert federal sovereignty and threaten war against nullifiers, but not to protect Indians, and he knew that doing the former depended on state militiamen, who would resent the latter.

This choice should hardly surprise us, for few white leaders, federal or state, truly regarded Indians as citizens (or even potential citizens) meriting equal protection; even when a few isolated Indians were able to secure citizenship, its meaning was primarily state determined rather than national prior to passage of the Fourteenth Amendment. Jackson was a southerner as well as a nationalist; the Indian Removal Act of 1830 preceded the Nullification Crisis, the Bank War and Specie Circular, and the Maysville veto and the muddled campaign against federally funded internal improvements, among the policy battles and achievements of his presidency. Jackson would fight for union because he believed it was the will of, perhaps a precondition for, the white man's democracy he embodied, but Indians were no more likely than African Americans to secure the protection of white majorities in Jacksonian America. Thus, while operations to remove intruders from Indian lands tell us a great deal about officers' attitudes toward whites on the frontier and their social attitudes and political values more generally, we should not forget that the army's most significant role in American social, political, and economic development prior to the Civil War was to help drive the Indians from the path of white settlement. After a single experiment in removal under civilian supervision (the first wave of Choctaw emigration in 1832), Jackson called on the army, an authoritarian hierarchy on whose subordination and violence he knew he could rely.

The process of "Indian removal" began with the first European conquests, and every treaty took place in a context of violence, whether threatened or actual, not unlike the ultimatums presented to the Chinese, Japanese, and others compelled to accept "open trade" through unequal treaties with the West. Some commentators still distinguish "removal" from conquest per se, largely based on the distinction white policy makers made: that removal was voluntary emigration, negotiated as an exchange of native land east of the Mississippi for U.S. land to its west, rather than the armed invasion, conquest, and expropriation embodied in the treaties of Greenville and Fort Jackson. Others might be tempted to assert a continuum, with many Indians moving westward to minimize or escape white contact, particularly the Cherokee in the 1790s, 1809, and 1819 (the first example of what became the pattern for Jacksonian removal, when the Cherokee Nation exchanged some of its territory for land in Arkansas). But most historians have recognized the central role played by white population pressure, its malign cultural influences (especially the relentless supply of alcohol), and the monetary debt (for alcohol and other supplies, or simply invented amid the tumult of threatened expropriation) and physical coercion that steadily circumscribed native autonomy. As Stuart Banner observes, "the actual land transactions that constituted removal were indistinguishable from earlier Indian land purchases," except that land was exchanged as well as goods or money. (The latter were still given as annuities to win tribal support and as bribes to win the endorsement of individual leaders.) Facing ambiguous decisions from the Supreme Court, with his proposal to employ eminent domain rejected by Congress back in 1818, Jackson continued to resort to the deceptive, unequal treaties, unrepresentative of any native political consensus, that had characterized U.S. policy since 1801, and he continued to back Georgia, Alabama, and Mississippi laws asserting state sovereignty over the Indians. Ultimately, the most important distinction was the pace of change, not its source or direction.[27]

Any protection the national army might afford Native Americans was the result of individual ambivalence and the complexities of policy implementation, rather than presidential, congressional, or judicial intent. From a narrowly focused institutional or policy standpoint, it may appear significant that the army played no overt role in the first formal land exchanges and "removals" westward by the Cherokee, who hoped to escape white intrusion in 1809 and (along with some Choctaw and Chickasaw) 1819. Yet in a larger sense, so focused a perspective obscures more about the process of conquest and dispossession than it reveals, for the army's absence from these movements was primarily a consequence of national frugality and congressional parsimony resulting in inadequate military forces, rather than principled policy. In 1809 the army was concentrated at New Orleans against possible British aggression, and in 1819 it was divided between occupying the Florida borderlands and making expeditions high up the Mississippi and Missouri during the early days of an economic depression.

The scale of these early Cherokee emigrations was small enough, the cohesion of the Indians still strong enough, that the Indians and civilian agents could handle logistical problems and ensure peaceful movement west with little military assistance. Nevertheless, though both migrations were overtly uncoerced, their pace largely under native control, they were certainly initiated in reaction to white pressure, embodied in Jackson's belligerence during treaty negotiations with the southern tribes between 1816 and 1818, and in anticipation of future coercion. Indeed, these movements, and the land cessions made to facilitate them between 1817 and 1819, produced enough internal conflict that the eastern Cherokee rallied together and refused to make any further cessions of land to the United States between 1819 and 1835. White aggression encouraged Cherokee nationalism, and the 1827 Cherokee constitution declared the nation independent, a belated challenge to U.S. and state sovereignty that no elected white authorities accepted. (Indeed, the Supreme Court's initial reaction was to declare the Cherokee a "domestic dependant nation," distinct from the United States but still subject to its sovereignty.) In this cycle of escalation, Cherokee nationalism spurred a more rapid, aggressive imposition of white sovereignty, embodied in the victory of the Jacksonian movement.[28]

Nor had the trajectory of U.S. policy changed when John Quincy Adams replaced the Virginia Dynasty in Washington. Despite his anger with the Georgians in 1825, Adams gradually acquiesced in their dispossession of the Creeks, ultimately deploying the army to conduct the first overtly forcible federal

Indian expropriation on U.S. soil since Jackson and Gaines swept through the Treaty of Fort Jackson cession in 1816. Yet the pressure for confiscation and expulsion increased dramatically when Jackson arrived in the White House. Indeed, historian Alfred Cave has shown the degree to which Jacksonian Indian removal was an abuse of constitutional and statutory power, executed with little regard, and often contempt, for the moderate parameters—essentially little different from those embedded in earlier policy—set forth in the authorizing legislation, the Indian Removal Act of 1830. Cave observes that, as a compromise measure written to secure the support of moderates and northern Democrats, the act "neither authorized the unilateral abrogation of [existing] treaties guaranteeing Native American land rights . . . nor the forced relocation of the eastern Indians." Layer upon layer of deception, fraud, bullying, and intimidation would be necessary to compel the Indians to accept offers most of them wanted to refuse.[29]

Yet Cave's focus on the dissonance between legislation and reality exaggerates the discontinuity between Jacksonian policy and its antecedents, for Jackson relied on much the same techniques as all his predecessors, including John Quincy Adams, since Thomas Jefferson. Recognizing the slim margin of national public support for expropriation and facing mixed messages from the Supreme Court, Jackson preferred to seek cover through unequal "treaties" that were often conducted out of public view, involved small minorities unrepresentative of their tribes, and relied on bribery, trickery, and negotiations, rather than dispatching the army to round up the Indians by force. These fraudulent arrangements enabled the president to argue, however disingenuously, that he had *not* unilaterally abrogated existing treaties or deprived the natives of land without compensation, and this mollified enough consciences, particularly those striving for white unity and sectional harmony, to permit dispossession to go forward with little check. Cave states that there was no constitutional precedent for abandoning federal authority over Indian relations, but Adams had moved toward acceding to demands for state sovereignty over the Indians in 1828, and selective enforcement of the trade and intercourse acts had been the norm since their inception. This is not to deny that Jackson's policy was an abuse of power, but he was following a long-standing pattern of presidential negligence and dereliction of legal duty. Jefferson's policy of luring Indians into debt so they would sell their land was hardly less deceitful than Jackson's, and Adams's conduct as both secretary of state and president was actuated primarily by his desire to expand or maintain federal power, rather than any intention to employ that authority with full faith and integrity to enforce treaties and the law.

Both Cave and Donald Cole, author of the standard text on Jackson's presidency, suggest that he could have compelled the states to accept national sovereignty over Indian relations, implying that wholesale expulsion was not inevitable. Maybe this is so in theory, had Sharp Knife wanted to protect Indians against the white citizens and voters who composed the nation. Yet while Cave marshals impressive evidence of northern Democratic hesitation over voting for the Indian Removal Act and makes the important point that the president was obliged to make concessions to secure its passage, it is just as important to recognize that Jackson was a *southern* Democrat who really believed in national sovereignty only as a tool of expansion that would benefit individual whites. Historiographically, Cave's thesis of presidential dishonesty and abuse should be extended to encompass the thoroughgoing partisanship, endemic corruption, dereliction of legal duty, and culpable negligence that characterized every step of the removal process—and Jacksonian politics and the Jackson administration more generally, notwithstanding the electoral democracy still commonly celebrated (albeit with genuflections toward its damage to Native and African Americans) in textbooks today. Removal, whether of Native Americans, federal executive officers, or federal bank deposits, was a representative example of the sordid reality of Jacksonian politics that is so often passed over by historians still enamored of its egalitarian rhetoric.[30]

Though the evidence is not conclusive, removal seems to have had a significant effect on civil-military relations and officers' attitudes toward Jacksonian politics. Some recent political historians have argued that the debate over expropriation was one of the four principal sources of the Whig Party, finding that Indian policy united National Republicans and future Whigs in nearly 85 percent of congressional roll-call votes between 1830 and 1842. Though officers, like most Americans, favored national growth and territorial expansion in the abstract, we have seen that personal and professional honor encouraged officers to seek insulation or autonomy from racial, sectional, and sectoral pressures on the frontier during the 1820s and 1830s, and conflicts over Indian and squatter removal provide some of the most powerful examples of how the ethical dilemmas presented by borderlands service influenced their professional worldview. Although a substantial proportion of the army's field-grade and general officers backed or applauded Jackson's election in 1828, and although a slight majority (proportionate to that in the voting population as a whole) of those few officers whose partisan views are known expressed support for the Democrats, the officer corps' growing professional affinity for order, hierarchy, institutions, and interdependence increasingly predisposed career soldiers toward National Republicanism and its Whig successors. Friction between the Jackson administration and its military commanders over removal accelerated their movement toward Whiggery, whether partisan, nonpartisan, or antipartisan.[31]

Officers wrote too little about their political views for us to trace cause and effect with any certainty during the decade between 1828—when a number of senior commanders, colonels as well as generals, left records of their support for Jackson—and the development of the mature Second Party System circa 1838. In 1828 officers supported Jackson because of their personal ties to him as their former commander, because they believed he best represented the will of the American electorate, or because he was a military man and might be expected to understand their dilemmas. Only four years later, during the 1832 campaign, most army leaders remained silent. Alexander Macomb may have gone silent because he had become commanding general and felt his involvement in politics was inappropriate, though that had not stopped Jacob Brown from supporting Adams in 1824. Winfield Scott may have been quieter in 1832 than in 1824, when he had actively supported his civilian superior, Secretary of War Calhoun, because he was charged with directing preparations to resist the nullifiers. (In 1828 Scott held grudges against both candidates: Jackson because of an earlier personal dispute and Adams because he had refused Scott the position of commanding general after Brown's death.) John Wool remained a Jackson man in 1832, and Thomas Sidney Jesup had begun to express Democratic proclivities, but the 1832 and 1836 elections present a much more passive senior officer corps than those in 1824 or 1828. (Even then, support was expressed in private letters, personal conversations, and occasional pseudonymous letters to newspapers.) Is the sample size small enough that we can account for each of these commanders as individuals? Did the Democratic critique of the army and the Military Academy silence them? Or must we combine these factors with the tensions—federal-state, civil-military, and ultimately over the role and authority of the nation-state—aroused by the resurgence of populist expansionism that produced Jackson's policy of removal?[32]

Whig politicians were often no more ethical than Jacksonians, but hierarchical Whig and National Republican values of order, stability, and authority certainly proved more likely to protect most minorities and were far more congenial to the career professional officers of the national armed forces. Combined with the constitutional requirement of subordination and accountability to civil authority, these attitudes affected the officer corps' response to the removal policy in contradictory and often paradoxical ways. As a group, professional soldiers believed that whites and Indians should be separated, that this would be best for both in the long run. More immediately, they worried about the disorder that would attend wholesale ethnic cleansing, which they would have to police. This would inevitably draw further condemnation from local whites impatient with the pace of federal action, angered by authoritarian military commanders, or eager to profit in ways that federal military officers had difficulty reconciling with the removal mission as a whole.

The genesis of the removal policy was wholly civilian. Until the army was sent to defeat the Seminole and Creek uprisings in 1836, the pressure for Indians to move west came mostly from bullying by white intruders and the threat of state laws and courts, in which Indians had little or no standing. In the South, the national army spent Jackson's first administration focused on restraining white belligerence, providing cover for the United States in the courts of international and public opinion, and deterring slave unrest, rather than threatening the Indians. Indeed, at the beginning of 1832, Edmund Gaines, now the Western Department commander and in charge of most of the frontier, privately rejected the president's policy, writing to a subordinate that he believed the United States should interfere in Indian affairs only so far as was necessary to protect its own citizens. This generation of American military professionals normally thought first in terms of deterrence, and in 1836 junior as well as senior officers complained that the troops allotted to Florida had proved insufficient to intimidate the Seminoles and prevent war. In effect, and increasingly on paper, officers blamed the Jackson administration for failing to prepare for the trouble, so obviously rooted in white aggression, that anyone could have anticipated unless blinded by greed, prejudice, or party. Military officers were certainly ethnocentric, and the army ultimately served as the mailed fist inside the glove of emigration, but professional military commanders recognized that pressure for expropriation would probably cause a native backlash, and they found it hard to understand why the Jacksonians seemed so willfully obtuse about the possibility of resistance and war. Things would only get worse later in the decade, when the Jacksonians blamed the army—that is, the civilian executive branch blamed senior military commanders—for failing to prevent the wars fomented by Jacksonian policy. The demands of partisanship—to deny that anything in one's actions might possibly be contradictory or counterproductive—often trumped those of policy itself, making Jackson's own removal policy more difficult to execute. For most professional military officers, this was a fundamentally irrational, if not morally corrupt, approach to governance.[33]

Gaines articulated his mature view of Indian relations most thoroughly less than a decade after he served as Jackson's right-hand man in Florida, in an 1826 memorial embedded in an extended report on the western posts. His words bear extended quotation, both for their comprehensiveness and for the extent to which his views were shared among career officers. The brigadier began by professing his subordination to civilian authority but observed that "the most important duties that ever occur in our Indian relations necessarily devolve, either directly or indirectly, on the army." The Western Department commander then asserted a paternalistic humanitarianism, vowing that "acknowledged principles of natural law . . . make it the duty of civilized communities to lend a helping hand" to suffering tribes. National reputation and honor would be well served if they did so: "The faithful discharge of this duty [would] elevate [the American] character for *justice* and *humanity*" in the court of international opinion, while there would be little hope for enduring peace, pacification, and acculturation or assimilation "without such a system." Gaines considered it "the duty of every citizen . . . to raise his voice . . . against [the Indians] being driven from their *homes*." Instead, like the senior military leaders in chapter 2, the brigadier advised turning the everyday conduct of Indian relations over to military authority. Gaines believed the Indians trusted the army's humanitarianism and accountability; the army was accustomed to "feeding the hungry and clothing the naked" Indian "*according to law and orders*." He therefore recommended that Indian agents be clothed with military rank to command mounted companies to keep the peace. Structure would replace entropy, and paternalism would replace greed; the nation would benefit, not just a few frontiersmen.[34]

The administration's principal criteria for successful removal were to get the Indians out of their homelands as soon as possible and at the least possible cost to tax-averse citizens. Jacksonian social and political values combined with lack of concern for the Indians to decentralize direction over their initial move west. Given pervasive racism among white frontiersmen, state officials, and federal civil officials, the pressure for speed combined with limited oversight to produce lawlessness, oppression, chaos, and starvation, embarrassing the administration and damaging the nation's reputation abroad. Lack of oversight encouraged redundancy and corruption, multiplying fiscal and thence political costs. The obvious contradiction between cost-efficiency and effectiveness—whether humanitarian, international, or within the Democratic coalition, by ameliorating northern concerns—quickly suggested the necessity of on-the-spot oversight, if only to minimize later investigations by Congress. Who could provide that oversight? After a single experiment in removal under civilian supervision (the first wave of Choctaw emigration in 1832), Jackson called on the army—at the same time he and his supporters were damning the Military Academy and army monopoly and privilege—to serve as the disinterested, accountable, "trusted agent" that civilian administrators had failed to provide.

Essentially an organization of accountants in Washington, the Treasury had no deployable agents to conduct emigration. The federal marshals relied on citizen posses or the army to execute their writs; the State Department was equally lacking in personnel. Indeed, since the Jacksonians accepted state sovereignty over the Indians, the State Department could play little role in U.S.-Indian relations; military commanders presented a much more potent threat to back up expulsionist diplomacy, without the excesses and expense of frontier posses or citizen-soldiers. Indian affairs were the responsibility of the War Department, but its "Indian agents" were individual civilians whose experience was primarily in mediation rather than administration, who had to rely on Indians, citizen posses, or the army for manpower. As civilian appointees, the agents were increasingly subject to Jackson's principle of rotation in office, leading to an influx of men motivated more by greed than service, more conspicuous for their political connections and partisanship than the experience or empathy necessary to cajole the Indians to move west with limited disruption to whites en route. Indeed, more than half the veteran Indian agents, who had often held their positions for a decade or more, spanning the transitions between the Jeffersonian and National Republican eras, were dismissed during Jackson's first administration.

The army was the only existing organization with the size—sufficient salaried officers available for deployment—discipline, and administrative experience necessary to carry out the government's policy with any degree of expertise and fiscal accountability. Thus, Jackson's experience as a general in the standing army, his personal desire for obedience in the execution of his policies, and his public persona as a man of rigid honor and integrity encouraged him to employ professional military commanders in removal, much as he continued to rely on West Point for most of the army's new officers despite criticizing the institution's governance. Citizen-soldier rhetoric notwithstanding, Jackson felt little faith in the undisciplined, unreliable Georgia militia, which had failed to seize East Florida in 1812, mutinied at a critical point in his offensive in the Creek War, and threatened to disrupt his tenuous Creek alliance with the Chehaw massacre. The contrast could not be more clear, in both operation and effect, between the Jacksonian patronage system of rotation—replacing civil officials before or after elections to reward one's supporters, ultimately (by the 1850s) requiring financial payments if they wanted to remain in office—and the continued insulation of army commissioning and promotion from partisan influence. Lacking a cadre of experienced civilian administrators capable of disbursing federal funds without arousing charges of embezzlement and fraud, Jackson quickly resorted to career military officers in the hope of restraining costs, minimizing scandal, and avoiding political embarrassment. Nor was he wrong. On the whole, these career soldiers proved far more honest and accountable than many of the civilian businessmen contracted to supply the Indians, reducing the fiscal and political costs incurred by partisan favoritism and corruption. They also proved more responsible toward their native charges than the Jacksonians expected, increasing some expenses and reporting frauds perpetrated by partisan contractors and civilian officials. Nevertheless, though most historians have labeled these efforts conscientious under the circumstances,[35] the army was ultimately an instrument of coercion, and when the Creeks and Seminoles refused to remove, the army went to war—America's longest between the Revolution and Vietnam.

Fear of criticism and political embarrassment pervaded Jacksonian Indian policy, so in the South, the War Department turned first to the Choctaw, the tribe considered least powerful and most likely to accept expropriation quickly and quietly. The Choctaw went west under the threat of incorporation into Mississippi and violence from state militia and vigilantes, rather than coercion by federal troops. Indeed, the administration displayed its distrust of the national standing army, probably aggravated by the army's faithful execution of squatter evictions, when Secretary of War John Eaton deployed volunteer state cavalry rather than national professional infantry to intimidate the Choctaw in 1830. The administration was pressing hard for fiscal economy, yet volunteers cost significantly more than professionals, and cavalry far more than infantry. Nor was the army especially busy at the time. Eaton's choice suggests that the administration's initial focus was on expulsion—compelling cessions and removal, which could be done by state volunteers, militia, or the groups of rowdies common on the frontier—rather than the emigration to follow, which tax-averse Jacksonians hoped would somehow take care of itself. The emigrating parties were to be supplied by private contractors submitting bids for the lowest cost, a system abandoned by the army a decade before, after a generation of frauds, delays, defaults, and disasters when cost-cutting contractors proved unable to supply large troop concentrations with edible food during the War of 1812 and the Missouri expedition. These perils were well known to Jackson, who had often complained of them himself.[36]

The confusion, disorder, and political embarrassment that resulted during the initial phase of Choctaw removal in 1831 led to some recentralization under more direct national oversight for the second round of expropriation the following year.[37] Given the insufficiency of federal civilian agents in number, ethical socialization, and logistical expertise, doing so required the employment of army officers to direct and oversee movement and supply with a semblance of integrity. At least ten such officers, all captains or lieutenants, were involved as contracting, disbursing, and "conducting" agents, most of them in more than one of the annual waves of emigration between 1831 and 1833. (Conducting agents, usually lieutenants, accompanied the emigrant parties, disbursing payments to contractors and making emergency contracts, when necessary, en route.) Though responsible through a military chain of command, these officers were effectively federal civil officials, chosen for their availability as salaried employees without more urgent duties. Half had experience as quartermasters or commissaries of subsistence—the three captains averaged nearly eleven years of such experience each—but the presence of officers without this preparation suggests that even young junior officers were considered better administrators than civilian businessmen. Whether they were actually more capable is open to question, but they certainly were more accountable, under army regulations and the Articles of War, as men dependent on a government salary and potentially vulnerable to dismissal. Their exposure to sanction was apparently not a primary consideration, however—an act of 1820 provided authority to hold civil as well as military agents liable, if it was enforced.[38] But these professional soldiers were socialized in accountability, through endless inspections of and by others, through reams of record keeping, and through their employment by the nation for its defense. All seven of the lieutenants involved in the removal were West Point graduates, whose youthful inexperience was buttressed by four years of thoroughgoing habituation to accountability at the Academy.

Historians have credited military officers with ameliorating the Choctaw's plight even before the army received oversight authority for the second year of removal. Francis Paul Prucha maintains that Choctaw emigration was "carefully planned," that these officers "exerted extraordinary efforts to meet [the Indians'] needs." Choctaw historian Arthur DeRosier, usually more critical than Prucha, insists that "the removal agents . . . did their jobs meticulously, overlooking no detail." Working on extremely short notice from his civilian superiors just before the first wave of expropriation, the army's commissary general, George Gibson, ordered subordinates to take a census of the Choctaw to plan supply needs early in 1831. Officers then fanned out to survey the availability of drinking water; to widen, surface, and grade roads and build additional bridges; to advertise for corn and cattle; and to establish supply depots—the same things supply officers would do to support the army on campaign. Western Department commander Edmund Gaines encouraged Arkansas farmers to plant corn rather than cotton; Gibson placed substantial orders for corn with merchants in New Orleans and St. Louis and used his purchasing power to pressure local suppliers to maintain prices at ordinary levels. Army logistical operations during Indian removal were much like those during war and probably had similar effects, enhancing local infrastructure and stimulating local and regional commodity markets. Indeed, these duties probably had as much impact on furthering the economic "Market Revolution" of the Jacksonian era as the railroad and canal surveys (increasingly narrow in focus) undertaken by officers per the General Survey Act of 1824.[39]

Gibson's actions suggest one of the principal operational concerns among these military officers: fraud or price gouging by civilian suppliers. Contracting from multiple sources helped hold down prices, but fraud was a more dangerous threat to Choctaw food supplies because it was more difficult to detect in time to remedy, given the range and complexity of the transactions involved. Nor was accountability simply a matter of oversight: partisan ties played an influential, often decisive role in the appointment of civilians temporarily engaged in removal, and military officers suspected these positions would be employed for profit at the government's expense. Secretary of War Eaton first promised the office of superintendent of Choctaw emigration to George S. Gaines, Edmund Gaines's brother; he had been an Indian trader for more than a generation, was trusted by the Choctaw, and had extensive connections throughout the southern borderlands. Though General Gaines had supported Jackson for president in 1828, he may have planted seeds of doubt in the president's mind by defending the Creeks against Georgian aggression during the 1820s, and in 1830 he appealed to Jackson in favor of the Cherokee. Whatever the reason, the superintendency of Choctaw removal went instead to Francis W. Armstrong, an army lieutenant between 1812 and 1817 and a federal marshal in Alabama between 1823 and 1827; Armstrong's brother had provided Jackson with valuable support in 1828. Choctaw protests quickly led to Armstrong's transfer to the position of Western Choctaw agent (for the elements of the tribe already west of the Mississippi), and he was replaced by George Gaines as superintendent for removal operations east of the Mississippi. Nevertheless, Armstrong's appointment, combined with partisan dismissals of Indian agents, the clamor against the army by state and congressional Jacksonians, and rumors of Jackson's discontent with the administration of West Point, led military officers to question whether the administration would back them in disputes with partisan favorites.[40]

Military concerns for the autonomy, integrity, and effectiveness of the removal process—that some minimal justice be done to the emigrants, that national, personal, and institutional reputations not be sullied by partisanship, greed, and corruption—were intensified by the hurried pace of execution and the ambiguities of fiscal accountability. Apart from designating land for the eastern Indians west of Arkansas, no long-range or strategic planning had been done by civilian leaders (in, for example, the Treasury Department), leaving military leaders to piece plans together for each operation. Since the Indian Removal Act was passed in 1830 and the Treaty of Dancing Rabbit Creek was signed that September, the first of these requirements came to Commissary General Gibson with only a few months' notice. One might ask whether military leaders should have anticipated and planned for this mission themselves, given the known proclivities of Jackson and his followers and the long-standing tendency of the government to employ military officers to execute any Indian policy. Yet the Commissary and Quartermaster Departments could hardly have begun inquiring about Indian needs, or the supplies potentially available en route, without alerting the Choctaw as well as white farmers and speculators, spurring who knows what reaction among the former and hoarding or price gouging among the latter. Either way, the uproar and political embarrassment that would probably result were not the attention army leaders were looking for at a time when congressional Jacksonians were condemning West Point and the officer corps, making pointed budgetary inquiries, and proposing pay cuts and reductions in force. Initially, rather than providing an opportunity for the army to demonstrate its value by claiming a new mission, the political dilemmas of expropriation combined with increasingly antagonistic civil-military relations (largely the product of Jacksonian ideology and practice) to further complicate policy execution.

Following the standard precept that officers on the scene should be vested with the autonomy to adapt to changing circumstances, the War Department allowed Captain John B. Clark, appointed superintendent of Choctaw emigration west of the Mississippi, "discretion as to all matters that may incidentally arise." But discretion also meant accountability: Clark was to be "strictly responsible" for the performance of disbursing officers (whom he nominated) and for choosing the points at which rations and other supplies were to be issued. That level of responsibility implied a degree of supervision, potential partisan intrusion, and financial liability that would go beyond the oversight and accountability (Gaines's "*law and orders*") to which officers were accustomed: the captain was to report "every thing that concerns your duties." Clark shied away from these demands, responding that he did not want the responsibility—which might ultimately mean financial liability or criminal charges, should he fail to prevent fraud among his civilian subordinates or contractors—of selecting "agents from persons [probably nominated through partisan connections] with whose integrity or qualifications I am entirely unacquainted, to be placed on duty beyond my immediate control." The army hierarchy tried to protect its officers from assignments that might imperil their integrity as gentlemen: unable to get a clear answer about the limits of his responsibility for the actions of others, Clark requested and received a transfer back to purely military duties. Logistical efficiency required accountability, which required insulation; compromising the latter could easily compromise the former, while hazarding an officer's personal sense of integrity and his reputation among his peers.[41]

The other officers tasked with facilitating Choctaw removal proved more dutiful, but their mission entangled them in much the same tensions and ambiguities as squatter eviction. Once again, their professional accountability was tested by pitting subordination to the subjective intent of their partisan civilian superiors against their sense of impartial personal, institutional, and national integrity, which they expressed as good faith and honor. Like other career soldiers dealing with Indian relations, several blamed white civilians (wealthy businessmen as well as poor frontiersmen) for placing individual profit over national policy: Lieutenant Gabriel Rains, who served throughout the Choctaw emigration, grumbled about "the worthless population" of whites squatting on Choctaw lands, impeding the execution of national removal policy with their demands for the payment of Indian debts. Similar patterns developed west of the Mississippi, where Captain Jacob Brown (no relation to the former commanding general) discerned a "sordid and avaricious combination [to defraud] the Government." Other commanders blamed the Choctaw, who felt little motivation to share the precise time sense that pervaded the military culture of system and regularity, for making their unpleasant task more difficult: Lieutenant Isaac Simonton maintained that "nothing can exceed the tardiness with which an Indian performs . . . manual labor. He forms no estimate of the value of time, and has no idea of what is to be gained by dispatch." Career ordnance officers like Simonton also pressed this quest for discipline, order, and efficiency upon soldiers and civilian workers in the national armories; combat commanders would find ample reason to dispute his assessment of Indian speed and motivation when they tried to drive the Seminoles from Florida several years later.[42]

Like army logistics, the emigration process was more effectively conducted by career military officers than civilian contractors, many of whom entered the "removal business" as a speculative venture, with little or no experience supplying large moving populations. Arthur DeRosier estimates that "at least half of the emigrating Choctaws would have perished en route had it not been for the attention and resourcefulness exhibited by these agents." The professional officers engaged in removal operations learned lessons from the confusion of

1831, vaccinating the second and third years' emigrants against smallpox and pushing to start movement earlier to avoid winter. In May 1832 the War Department issued a set of guidelines giving the commissary general control over the purchase and positioning of supplies and placing all disbursement of funds in the hands of army officers. Yet the intractable dilemma of trying to accomplish a rapid, cheap, yet humane expulsion proved impossible to resolve. The 1831 migration had cost two to three times what the parsimonious administration had hoped to pay. Under political pressure, the War Department pushed more and more strongly for economy; it reduced the prices it was willing to pay for rations, which reduced the incentive for farmers to supply the Indians or to do so with edible food.

Like army logistics in the era of civilian contracting before 1820, the incentive was to offer the lowest prices to win a contract, then provide rations at the lowest cost by using those of the lowest quality. Army commissary officers were then compelled to choose between distributing stale, putrid, or otherwise deficient rations and trying to secure better ones at an additional cost in time and Indian health, as well as public money. Under pressure from an economizing administration and the expensive civilian marketplace, officers sometimes resorted to unethical practices themselves. In the fall of 1831 Gabriel Rains attempted to issue spoiled salt pork—four or five years old and rejected by a board of officers as unfit for the soldiers at Fort Gibson—to the Choctaw, assuring the commissary general that it was "not putrid or spoiled, except by age." General Gibson accepted Rains's rationale, although it was several years before the Choctaw became desperate enough to consume the pork, apparently "scraped" free of its spoilage.[43]

Historian Ronald Satz states that "most agents placed the welfare of their charges as their first priority." Though fair, this judgment goes too far to be accurate: executing policy rapidly, in obedience to the national civil authority, ultimately took precedence over more time-consuming but humanitarian approaches like greater planning, putting off the first wave of emigration until the following spring, or delaying the second and third waves until the end of the cholera epidemic that erupted in 1832. The experience of conducting removal could certainly be chastening for officials accustomed to privilege and authority: Lieutenant Simonton concluded his discourse on Indian time-consciousness with the admonition that "whoever finds himself in the situation of an Indian agent must treat them with paternal care." Conducting agent William S. Colquohoun, a former lieutenant and commissary officer dismissed for striking his superior while drunk in 1829, repeated that offense against Francis Armstrong, whom he considered too harsh toward the Indians. Despite being dismissed from government service a second time, Colquohoun would return in a similar capacity during the war with Mexico, testimony to his Democratic connections as well as the need for logistical experience (or perhaps simple fiscal accountability). Apparently, these qualities were still in short supply among civilian businessmen, notwithstanding the "Market Revolution" so vaunted by historians.[44]

Military direction did limit the corruption and mismanagement of removal. Rains's example (scraping putrid meat) is the only case of mistreatment by an army officer cited by the principal historians of the Choctaw expropriation, and one would expect them to list more cases if they could be found. Instead, most of the problems developed with the civilian contractors, who felt little sense of personal, national, or professional integrity, whether that meant the good faith and justice of "paternal care" or merely budgetary accountability. Indeed, DeRosier concludes by quoting Commissary General Gibson's report to Secretary of War Lewis Cass: military officers "acted with praiseworthy . . . interestedness toward the Indians." Officers were required by their subordination to civilian authority to place the interests of the government over those of the Choctaw, but they remained disinterested enough "to protect the Indians in their rights," limited though these were, and to place the interests of the Choctaw over personal gain or popularity with other whites. Ultimately, a decade later, Major Ethan Allen Hitchcock would cause a bipartisan political uproar by reporting objectively on the frauds practiced against the Indians removed from the South; as with Timothy Andrews in 1825, the government entrusted the investigation to a military officer rather than a Treasury agent.[45]

Such relative objectivity should not be taken for granted. As junior staff (commissary, quartermaster, and ordnance) officers, the young West Pointers conducting the removal were much more subject to partisan censure and career obstruction (primarily the loss of desirable future postings) than the veteran field-grade commanders directing peacekeeping on the western frontier. Gibson's willingness to assert military interest in favor of Native Americans may have been intended to shield the army from National Republican, Whig, or humanitarian criticism, but it was also likely to draw fire from rabid southern Democrats. As such, it is indicative of the autonomy, complexity, and ambiguity, even ambivalence, of military attitudes toward the execution of Indian removal, of the dilemmas and tensions in which national military commanders were placed by a duplicitous policy predicated on exploiting the intricacy and confusion of federalism to individual, partisan, and sectional advantage. Facing politically connected civilian contractors able to shrug off repeated defalcations, junior army officers performed a remarkable balancing act, treating the Indians under their charge with surprising sympathy. Their impartiality in comparison to the civilians around them and in government, as well as their European counterparts in Asia and Africa, came from their professional culture, not from the racialized democracy and liberal individualism of Jacksonian America.

The death, corruption, and expense associated with Choctaw emigration—greater than that initially estimated for the removal of all the southeastern Indians put together—embarrassed the administration and compelled Jackson to slow the pace of expropriation. After 1833, the tempo of expropriation slowed almost to a halt as the Cherokee and Seminoles continued to balk at demands for treaties surrendering their land. When the United States foisted fraudulent agreements on them at Payne's Landing in 1834 and New Echota in 1835, the Seminoles began preparing for war, while the Cherokee kept up a peaceful resistance through legal processes for two more years, until military success in Florida allowed President Van Buren to divert several regiments to round them up for expulsion. The Chickasaw proved perhaps the most adept of the southeastern Indians at evading removal, negotiating the rocks and shoals of federalism by maneuvering between state, section, and nation to escape cession and expulsion until 1837; many remained in Mississippi well into the 1840s. Yet with the army thoroughly preoccupied in Florida and Georgia, less than half a dozen officers were involved in Chickasaw removal; only one—Lieutenant Gouverneur Morris—was an actual conducting agent during the first removal season in 1837.[46]

Significant military efforts to remove intruders from Creek land ceased after 1833; land invasions multiplied, and in 1836 a substantial portion of the remaining Creeks launched an uprising that bled into the Second Seminole War. Historians remain uncertain whether this was an essentially spontaneous outbreak of frustration and anger at white intrusion and cultural breakdown, exaggerated and aggravated by white panic and overreaction, or a more extensively coordinated effort by Creek militants, perhaps along the lines of the Seminole offensive, which sought to compel the Florida Indians to unite in resistance to emigration. Indeed, historian Michael Green notes that many contemporary observers considered the "Second Creek War" a "humbug . . . devised by interested men" to conceal the pervasive fraud perpetrated against the Creeks, who had been promised individual land allotments in their most recent treaty several years before.[47]

That view underestimated Creek discontent, however. The uprising was defeated by overwhelming force, directed by Eastern Department commander Winfield Scott and Quartermaster General Thomas Sidney Jesup, early that summer. The removal operation, begun with the transportation of prisoners of war even before the conflict came to an end, was more hurried than the first Choctaw removal in 1831. The officers who conducted the 1836 movement were an ad hoc group detailed from the more urgent duties of war, including three Marine Corps lieutenants available because the marines had deployed a battalion to Florida to fight the Seminoles; only one of these officers, Captain John Page, had participated in previous removal operations, with the Choctaw in 1832 and 1833 and an early contingent of Creeks in 1834. Only a single officer above the rank of lieutenant, the experienced Captain Francis Belton, was actually assigned to accompany the Creeks on their move west; his lieutenants, half of them marines, had a grand total of three years' quartermaster or commissary service to supplement his four years as a paymaster and inspector general during the War of 1812.

Despite their limited administrative experience, the paternalistic attitudes of the soldiers charged with conducting the Creeks west were similar to those engaged in Choctaw removal. The Creeks no longer resembled the fearsome warriors they had been two decades before; the social and cultural disintegration that accompanied their loss of political and economic independence led officers, like civilians, to belittle their motives and cohesion. Like Lieutenant Simonton with the Choctaw, Colonel John J. Abert, chief of the topographical engineers, warned Secretary of War Cass that the Creeks were "a people who appear never to think of tomorrow," a people "incapable of such an effort and of the arrangements and foresight which it requires." Recognizing the extent of the social dislocation that white pressure—debt, alcohol, violence, and land seizures—had produced, Abert lamented that "their helpless ignorance, their generally good character (for they are a well disposed people) . . . renders them more liable to wrongs." Like most officers at this stage of the expropriation, Abert advised that "emigration is the only hope of self-preservation left," recommending "the unceasing exertions of a vigilant and intelligent agent, to urge them forward, and to supply their wants, to protect and encourage them."[48]

Lieutenant John T. Sprague, a marine who would transfer to the army and become friendly with many Seminoles while writing his *History of the Florida War*, used virtually identical language about the Creeks: "It is an absurdity to say that the Indians must take care of themselves; they are men it is true, but it is well known that they are totally incapable." (Sprague became less patronizing after a decade of combat and negotiation with the Seminoles.) Like Rains and Brown, Lieutenant John W. Barry, son of Jackson's faithful postmaster general (the only original cabinet officer to remain after the Peggy Eaton affair), identified disorderly whites as the root of Indian anger: "we have experienced more trouble and difficulty from the white men [hanging about the emigrant camps] . . . than from all the Indians; they [the whites] are the most depraved, lying, cut-throat scoundrels I ever met with." Sprague agreed, showing his budding sympathy for the southeastern Indians, along with the imperative to execute government policy: "however indignant their feelings, or however great the sacrifice, it was but justice to get them out of the country as soon as possible" to escape white depredations.[49]

These views often led emigration officers into conflict with white civilians and local civil officials. Charged with protecting the Creeks' health, Sprague halted the column he was conducting to give the Indians a rest, despite complaints by civilian supply contractors that the delay would cost them their profit margin. When the contractors failed to provide rations in a timely manner or to take steps to deny the emigrants access to liquor, Sprague threatened to dismiss them. This was unlikely—and dangerous to Sprague's future prospects—given the political connections that had gained them their contracts in the first place. Most important, with neither federal troops nor confidence in their legal authority to back them up, marine lieutenants T. T. Sloan and J. G. Reynolds found it impossible to stop the robbery, rape, and murder committed almost nightly by bands of Georgians and Alabamians who pursued the Creek emigrants. At this point, federal military officers had few options besides moving the Creeks west as fast as possible, stopping only for short attempts at rest and recuperation, which were disrupted by the pursuing whites. Indeed, the Creeks would have been safer with a substantial army escort, but Jacksonian politics would not permit this expense, nor the civil-military violence that might follow. Creek removal, far more than that of the Choctaw or the Cherokee, physically resembled the European ethnic cleansings of the 1940s and the 1990s; the law enforcement officers of America's racist democracy proved helpless at best.[50]

5

THE ARMY AND THE CHEROKEE REMOVAL

Coercive Diplomacy, Peacekeeping, and Preventing Mass Atrocities amid Civil-Military Tensions, 1836–1838

The most extensive effort at Indian expropriation apart from the Second Seminole War was directed at the Cherokee. The largest of the southern tribes, the Cherokee held areas claimed by four states, essentially the juncture of Tennessee, North Carolina, Alabama, and Georgia. Besides providing land to sustain the exploding population of yeoman farmers unable to compete with slaveholding planters in lowland regions that were more easily accessible to markets, this mountainous region contained deposits of gold, which had set off a land rush as early as 1827. As the first step in southeastern expropriation, the Jackson administration secured treaties with the smaller, less resistant tribes—the Choctaw and Chickasaw—who already lived in a single state bordering the Mississippi River. The administration then turned to the Creek, concentrated in Alabama. By 1834, the Creeks who were most susceptible to pressure had already departed, and at the end of 1835, the Seminoles set an example of resistance that revived hope among those who remained; however, the social disintegration that followed the seizure of sovereignty by Georgia and Alabama prevented the remaining Creeks from organizing a more effective resistance in 1836. That year was crucial for Jackson's removal effort: federal and state officials feared that the Seminole uprising would spread throughout the southern backcountry, a situation the standing army would be unable to handle on its own, leading to great financial expense and political and diplomatic embarrassment even as Jackson's handpicked successor ran for election. The years from 1836 to 1838 were even more crucial for the Cherokee: some scholars estimate that their population was reduced by a quarter due to disease and privation on the "Trail of Tears" and in the camps

141

John Ellis Wool, the embodiment of duty, later in life. Photograph by Mathew Brady. (Courtesy Library of Congress, LC-DIG-ppmsca-08354)

where they were concentrated for removal. The alternative—"removal" by Georgia citizen-soldiers without federal military restraint—might have produced genocidal massacres similar to other scenes of ethnic cleansing, such as the example of the Creek emigrant party discussed in chapter 4. Indeed, many of the army's roles in the Cherokee country would be familiar to American officers engaged in overseeing ethnic group interactions and population transfers in Bosnia and Kosovo since 1995.[1]

Decisive action by Quartermaster General Jesup quashed the Creek uprising during the summer of 1836, leaving the Cherokee as the most powerful native force still in the balance. Despite their long-standing peacefulness, the Cherokee's numbers, cohesiveness, and mountainous terrain might have made them as formidable as the Seminoles, against whom the United States was on the strategic defensive throughout most of the year. (Although the army launched a series of counteroffensives against the Seminole heartland on the Withlacoochee, the Indians clearly retained sufficient freedom of action to raid as far north as St. Augustine, while holding off U.S. thrusts until late in the year.) Though bullied by Georgia surveyors, militia (often not in uniform and visually indistinct from settlers or vigilantes), land lotteries, and intruders since 1830, and as riven as any other Indian society over how to deal with white pressure, the mountain-dwelling Cherokee had not been completely inundated by whites and remained relatively free from the alcoholism and indebtedness that had crippled Creek cohesion and resistance. On December 21, 1835, Georgia legislated that the winners of its land lottery could occupy Cherokee land beginning in November 1836. Operating along the usual lines of divide and conquer—or perhaps as a result of the frequent confusion and disarray of Jacksonian-era policy and administration—federal commissioners gained the signatures of a minority of Georgia Cherokee for the Treaty of New Echota, mandating emigration two years after its ratification, which occurred a week later. Only a couple hundred of the more than 16,000 Cherokee were present at New Echota, a town the commissioners had chosen precisely for its isolation, and a majority of Cherokee leaders, headed by John Ross, immediately rejected the treaty's legitimacy. The treaty included a provision for the Cherokee to remain in the East as citizens of the states, with limited preemption rights to the land they occupied, but even this was too much for Jackson, who compelled the Cherokee to strike that provision three months later.[2]

AN INSUBORDINATE GENERAL CLASHES WITH SORDID POLITICIANS OVER AN AMBIGUOUS MISSION: JOHN WOOL AND THE FIRST ATTEMPT AT CHEROKEE REMOVAL, 1836

The Cherokee remained peaceful in their resistance. The Seminole example was soon countered by that of the army's rapid repression of the Creeks, and Cherokee leaders could take comfort that the army was too busy in Florida to be deployed against them. (The force employed against the Creeks in Alabama was almost entirely volunteers and militia, though under regular army command.) Lacking any compelling reason to change his approach, John Ross continued to pursue the diplomatic strategy he had crafted during the previous decade, traveling repeatedly to Washington to meet with congressmen and executive branch officials. His success in arousing public sympathy nearly prevented the treaty's ratification by the Senate in May 1836, but brevet Brigadier General John Wool, ordinarily the army's inspector general (overseeing soldier training and discipline), was dispatched to begin preparations for removal the following month. Faced with Creek and Seminole wars and a possible conflict on the Texas border, the War Department instructed the brigadier to discover whether the Cherokee were "meditating hostilities," to calm them if possible, and to crush them if they struck out against whites. No federal military forces were available, but Jackson had issued a call to the states for volunteers, and Wool was to direct these troops in hunting down fugitive Creeks and reminding the Cherokee of the government's determination that they be removed. Although the treaty did not require the Cherokee to depart until May 1838, the administration wanted to minimize complaints from local whites by pressuring the Indians to leave before the deadline, but it was unable to begin physically rounding them up unless they turned to violence, which their leaders were too canny to permit.[3]

What, then, was Wool's mission? Most important, he was to ring the Cherokee with enough force to prevent them from joining the Creek and Seminole uprisings and to keep the Creeks from finding refuge in the Cherokee country. Though he succeeded in this principal mission, this was probably due more to the Cherokee's choice of diplomacy and delay than the presence of his volunteer troops. The Cherokee may have feared the troops' potential for genocidal violence, but they might have been even more intimidated if Wool had been backed by well-drilled regulars. Since there was no substantial effort among the Cherokee to prepare armed resistance, the brigadier quickly found that most of his problems were with whites. A capable tactician and drillmaster, imbued with the strictest sense of accountability from nearly two decades as inspector general, Wool was new to the South and to the civil-military diplomacy of the borderlands; he proved unable to negotiate a harmonious path between the political quandaries he faced and failed in his tacit mission to accelerate removal at minimal political embarrassment to the administration. Indeed, Wool, a New Yorker without significant southern ties, was also the least experienced general officer sent to deal with such a situation during this era. The administration had few alternatives, however. Edmund Gaines had plenty of hard-won experience but had long since declared his sympathy for the Cherokee and was stationed on the Texas border, where he would get in trouble with the Jackson administration soon enough. Winfield Scott had two trips to Europe and successful peacekeeping during the Nullification Crisis under his belt but was assigned to suppress the Creek uprising; he had failed to defeat the Seminoles earlier in the year and was engaged in an acrimonious controversy with Gaines over responsibility for this setback. Indeed, Scott's apparent sluggishness in Florida and Alabama kept him in the doghouse until his friend Martin Van Buren assumed the presidency.

The army's ability to detach two of its three most important administrative officers, Wool and Jesup, for operational commands during the same year is some of the best evidence of its professionalization. (The third officer, Adjutant General Roger Jones, remained in Washington throughout his long career, serving as a clearinghouse for communications from the field as well as the chief personnel officer.) Apart from a few months spent reporting on the Hartford Convention to James Monroe, and perhaps his plotting to invade Cuba in 1816, Jesup had only bureaucratic experience (though plenty of it) in civil-military relations when he was dispatched against the Creeks in Alabama. Yet Jesup was the most senior officer without an operational command, he was a known Democrat, and he had professionalized quartermaster procedures to the point that his subordinates could conduct removals and supply the army in Florida, where his success against the Creeks garnered him command that autumn. (Indeed, Jesup's subordinates ran the Quartermaster Department for fully two years before he returned from Florida.) Commanding general Alexander Macomb, the only general besides Wool without significant southern connections, seems to have had little interest in frontier diplomacy or operational command and was busy coordinating affairs and fighting turf battles with the adjutant general in Washington. These kept him from serving in any borderlands crisis apart from brief visits to Florida and the Canadian border in 1838 and 1839.[4]

A soldier since 1812, Wool did have substantial administrative and some logistical expertise as inspector general, and he was a known Democrat. Like Gaines, he found that this was not enough to forestall the furies of frontier avarice; like the Tennessean, Wool would end 1836 alienated from Jackson and his War Department. The general's problems began when he arrived in East Tennessee and found that 2,500 volunteers had responded to meet a quota of 1,000. Wool had no authority to muster the excess men into service or pay them, but he recognized that sending them home would be impolitic, particularly in a presidential election year. Indeed, Tennessee governor Newton Cannon, an opponent of the Jackson administration, rode to the camp and warned Wool that the volunteers might resort to plunder to feed themselves if discharged, so the brigadier told them to wait in case they were needed; the men were fed with army rations but received no pay. The administration came under attack even for paying for these rations, so Wool was ordered to discharge the volunteers, and Secretary of War Cass, his longtime personal friend, inferred that the brigadier was wasting public funds. Always scrupulously accountable, with a sense of personal and professional reputation second to none, Wool deeply resented these imprecations and justified his actions on the grounds that Gaines had asked Cannon to provide a brigade to help police the Texas frontier, and that Cannon had promised Tennessee would pay the volunteers if the United States did not. Thrown off balance by the ambiguous intersections of federalism and partisan politics, Wool explained that he had refused to excite antagonism "against the administration and myself" by rejecting "the pledge of the chief of a sovereign State, which no officer could well refuse without giving offence to the State." National security and unity, as well as the immediate practical need to secure Tennessee's cooperation, seemed to dictate some compromise to federal authority, even the president's.[5]

Wool repeatedly warned the War Department that the greatest danger to peace was white aggression. He hoped to encourage the Cherokee to depart early for the West, thus removing the potential for conflict, but he could not overcome the determination of the antitreaty faction led by John Ross, which continued its lobbying efforts in Washington. To preserve peace in the interim, before the treaty mandated removal, the brigadier tried to secure a monopoly of armed force in the Cherokee country. Unable to coerce the Cherokee directly, Wool initially concentrated active operations on the search for fugitive Creeks, who might rouse the Cherokee to rebellion. Yet he lacked professional subordinates to supervise these patrols, and depredations against the Indians by undisciplined citizen-soldiers, particularly the Georgians, soon seemed an equal threat to peace. Wool therefore forbade "collisions" and "encroachments" on Cherokee persons and property, demanding that all soldiers in the Cherokee country act under national control and instructing the Tennessee volunteers that "you will prevent any interference [by] the [unfederalized] Georgia troops with the Cherokees." If the Georgians turned out to be rowdies without legal authority from their state, the Tennesseans were to "order them to disband or leave the country. If authorized by the authorities of Georgia, they will immediately report to me and receive my orders." Yet Wool had to strike a balance between firmness and moderation along several axes: between whites and Indians, between military and civilian, between state and nation. Hence, the volunteers were ordered to "prevent every improper exercise of military control over the Indians or the white inhabitants. The whole subject is left to your discretion, taking care to do nothing which will bring you into conflict with the authorities of Georgia. The sovereignty of the State and its laws must be respected."[6]

The Tennesseans soon seized a group of Cherokee prisoners from Georgia militiamen who were operating independent of Wool's control. The incident occurred without the general's orders or knowledge, but the governor of Georgia, Wilson Lumpkin, blamed him and protested the presence of Tennessee troops on Georgia soil as an infringement of state sovereignty and honor. When Wool discharged most of the Tennesseans involved in the incident, including the commander, R. G. Dunlap, they turned on him; Dunlap complained directly to President Jackson. The Tennesseans' antagonism was multiplied because the hierarchical vision of the federal executive officer and professional military commander clashed with the representative expectations of citizen-soldiers, who have elected Dunlap. To Wool, the discharge was the equivalent of reassigning a subordinate, but the volunteers felt that the general from Washington was disapproving of their choice for military self-government. Nor did the brigadier regain any support from Georgia, for he had refused to pay an excess battalion of Georgians that Thomas Jesup had sent to his aid from the Creek campaign.[7]

Scholars have commonly viewed Wool as sympathetic to the Cherokee, to the point of arguing that his qualms led to requests for reassignment. But as historian Laurence Hauptman points out, this mistakes sympathy for the general's desire to secure Cherokee compliance at the least cost to the Treasury—without war. Yet Hauptman takes us only so far in portraying Wool as a stern agent of federal policy, for the general's devotion to duty always faced more severe challenges from whites than from the Cherokee. Given the context in which he operated and army officers' historic response to these dilemmas, it seems most likely that Wool arrived in the Cherokee country with a predisposition to blame whites for unrest, and that this inclination was quickly confirmed and then intensified by his contact with federal and state civil officials. Thus, only two weeks after his arrival, we find the brigadier remarking that he had "little doubt [that] there are many white men advising [the Cherokee] not to move." This in itself is no indication of antagonism toward white frontiersmen, for Andrew Jackson often explained native resistance in similar terms, and these tropes would often be repeated by officers during the Second Seminole War. Indeed, the tendency to blame whites or mixed-blood Indians for Indian agency was common, whether because whites could not comprehend native agency or because they did not want to acknowledge native opposition to white aggrandizement and had to find some outside force to blame. By arguing that full-blooded Indians wanted separation from whites, aggressors like Jackson could justify dispossession as protection for endangered cultures. Though few career professional soldiers went as far as Jackson in blaming mixed-blood Indians for resistance to expropriation, most shared his belief that Indians could not survive extended contact with whites and that white expansion was inevitable, necessitating removal if any Indians were to be preserved.[8]

Yet commanders like Wool had real cause to blame whites for delaying removal because so many had taken advantage of Indian desperation by selling them alcohol or making them loans. White individualism then clashed with collective ethnic aggrandizement when white creditors sought payment through the courts, which required the Indians to remain until they paid their debts. Since the effort to profit from native misery never ended, the courts were compelled to press native debtors to remain within the creditors' reach, despite the national policy of removal. (Wool expected whites would siphon off all the money owed to the Cherokee under the treaty before they were compelled to depart.)[9] State and local politicians sought Indian land for the majority of their constituents but could not ignore the debts Indians owed to this unscrupulous minority, many of whom had important political connections stretching to Congress and the federal executive. Nor would the federal government cut the Gordian knot of native debt. This was not just a matter of federalism and the separation of powers; the Jackson administration prided itself on its responsiveness to pressure from below, and the creditors were some of the squeakiest wheels on the road. Political and ideological considerations were reinforced by ethical and financial ones: Congress understood that any blanket federal payment of Cherokee debts would encourage and reward fraud, while reducing the budget surplus being redistributed to the states. Together, partisanship, federalism, and the separation of powers enabled the most opportunistic and grasping of whites to confuse and obstruct the national removal policy cherished by Democratic majorities. Long accustomed to unquestioned military obedience from the military subordinates he evaluated as inspector general, John Wool must have been unnerved to discover that he had virtually no influence, let alone control, over the many moving parts he was now supposed to coordinate.

Unable to exert much control over whites, and recognizing that most Cherokee opposed the treaty, Wool turned to coercing the latter more directly, pressing them to openly avow support for the treaty and begin preparing for an early removal, which would reduce the opportunity for white aggression and Cherokee retaliation. At an August 3 council, the brigadier became concerned that the antitreaty faction among the Cherokee would use the opportunity to gain a declaration against the treaty; when they suddenly left the council grounds he feared a move toward uprising and had troops seize several leaders, including Ross. After holding them overnight, Wool dispatched soldiers accompanied by Baptist minister Evan Jones, whom the general had arrested the previous day, to seize Cherokee arms. The Jackson administration cared little for pious troublemakers from the North—and in September Jackson ordered Wool to arrest and expel them—but the brigadier had given critics of Jacksonian policy an opening by taking preemptive action. Fearful that coercion would cause a Cherokee war on top of the Creek and Seminole ones, and trying to minimize criticism from either set of whites, the acting secretary of war, Commissioner of Indian Affairs C. A. Harris, cautioned Wool against using "intimidation or coercion," whether against the Cherokee or white intruders. With the fugitive Creeks rounded up, it turned out that the brigadier's task was simply to quash the Cherokee should they turn to violence. He was not to attempt to secure Cherokee acquiescence to the Treaty of New Echota; the administration worried that further discussion could only disclose the depth of Cherokee opposition, bolstering its critics in the North. More likely to spur tension than resolve it, Wool and the volunteers should have been withdrawn from the Cherokee country entirely, but they were not; one can only assume that the administration wanted them to remain as a sop to white fears, or lest the Cherokee view their withdrawal as a retreat from the removal policy.[10]

Political constraints prevented Wool from cutting the Gordian knot, whether that meant arresting white trespassers or Cherokee leaders. He was there to glower at the Indians, nothing more. Knowing that few Cherokee wanted to leave, Wool wondered how the administration expected to get the nation as a whole to do so. Until this was done, white intrusion and aggression would certainly continue. Indeed, comprehensive expropriation would be delayed further as the Cherokee became more deeply indebted to whites, who employed legal process to hold them in the East until their claims could be settled, presumably by the sale of individual land allotments or livestock or in cash from the Cherokee annuity or some other federal claims settlement. There was no sign this cycle would end, and Wool feared the desperate Indians would finally erupt in rebellion: the trajectory of inattention, racist and partisan pandering, and wishful thinking that had permitted or provoked the Black Hawk War, the Second Seminole War, and the (second) Creek War would be repeated in the Cherokee country. Or perhaps individuals and small groups of Cherokee would flee (maybe to join the Seminoles in Florida), stealing or demanding food from whites along the way, and he would be charged with hunting them down. Wool therefore wrote directly to Jackson, arguing that "the time for decision and action" had come, reminding the former general that "no commander will be respected without some discretionary power." Without that power, Wool believed it "utterly impossible for him to do his duty either towards the government, the Indians, or the white men residing in the Cherokee country." The brigadier also warned Harris against temporizing and self-deception, and repeated this advice to Joel Poinsett when the latter became secretary of war in the new Van Buren administration the following spring. More frustrated than chastened by Harris's reproach, the brigadier promptly asked Secretary of War Cass for reassignment, a prerogative normally granted to military officers in deference to their integrity as gentlemen. Unwilling to create an opening for Whig critics, Cass refused.[11]

The Jackson administration feared a Cherokee uprising, with good reason given its treatment of the Cherokee and the deployment of most regular army units against the Seminoles and Creeks. But the Cherokee as a whole had long since chosen a political path of resistance rather than a military one. The surprise of the Creek uprising, after at least a decade during which Creek military resistance had seemed unlikely, if not impossible to coordinate, surely contributed to the administration's worries. Its most influential concern, however, remained the avoidance of white criticism, particularly in this election year, and particularly in the face of a southern opposition candidate, Hugh Lawson White. Both military and political factors would have come together if Wool's use of force had spurred an uprising; southern and Democratic critics of military unpreparedness (a product of the Jacksonian combination of aggressive expansion and fiscal economy) would have added to the clamor already coming from northerners and Whigs. In a policy environment dominated by the Jacksonians' desire to achieve controversial objectives while minimizing actual controversy, generals were wise to keep low profiles while trying to satisfy everyone, but few could walk so narrow a tightrope. The tortured logic of removal now came home to roost, as Wool's ethical qualms and professional concerns began to merge. A September letter lamented his "dirty assignment" and the "heart rending" scene in the Cherokee country: facing white "vultures . . . ready to pounce on their prey and strip them of everything they have or expect." The general declared that his "firm and decided" course had been intended to protect the Cherokee by speeding emigration. "I could not do them a greater kindness" than to "remove every Indian tomorrow beyond the reach of the white men." The brigadier believed he had to remove the Cherokee as soon as possible if he was to save them (and perhaps himself); in contrast, the Jackson administration wanted to wait for the Indians to move on their own, presumably in desperation, so it could declare the removal voluntary, in accordance with the terms of the Indian Removal Act.[12]

The administration cared little about what happened to the Cherokee in the interim; its principal objective was to secure their expulsion at the least political cost, by keeping things quiet until the Indians either left or provided justification for coercion by refusing to abide by the treaty's deadline (as ultimately occurred). Ever wary of incurring criticism and losing votes by taking a firm stand on the ethically dubious mechanics of a policy already under moral and political assault, the administration's instructions provided little concrete guidance, and Wool had proved too dutiful, too energetic, and too zealous in carrying out the responsibilities he assumed the president intended. Instead, Jackson now confirmed that the general was on his own, claiming that "I do not see that I can add anything" to the slender guidance provided by the treaty and Harris.[13] At least Wool heard directly from the president that autumn: Jackson left communications with his former favorite Edmund Gaines entirely to the War Department, now administered by a temporary secretary like those Sharp Knife had ignored two decades before. Effective military diplomacy on the frontier had always depended on grants of executive discretion; in 1836 "King Andrew" demanded subordination and responsibility to implicit—indeed, contradictory—goals and procedures, a situation far too complex for ambivalent officers to avoid friction, embarrassment, and damnation. Refused relief; driven by his sense of national, personal, and professional responsibility and honor; or at least hoping to escape the quagmire with his reputation intact, Wool continued to struggle to balance firmness and justice amid censure from all sides, allowing the Cherokee to hold another council in September in the hope they would somehow accept expropriation as inevitable.

Alienated by the general's dismissal (authorized by a Federalist statute from 1796) of their claims to participate in the council, Wilson Lumpkin and the Georgians saw this as a sign of Wool's sympathy for the antitreaty Cherokee; more likely, it was the Democratic general's self-deluded effort to employ democratic methods to secure Cherokee adherence to U.S. policy. But Wool

Wilson Lumpkin, another Georgia governor. Painting photographed by Edwin Jackson. (Courtesy Georgia Archives, Georgia Capitol Museum Collection)

understood the essence of Jacksonian democracy much less than he thought—the brigadier was attempting to apply democratic forms in a democracy defined by skin color. True to form, the administration hinted that such councils were undesirable but did not explicitly forbid the Cherokee to hold them, and it had already tied the general's hands against using coercion to prevent them. Though Wool stationed troops nearby and warned the antitreaty faction against using the council to stir up or declare opposition, the Cherokee—a significantly larger number than had been present at the treaty signing—voted to repudiate the treaty, pulling the rug out from his feet. Hoping to mollify the Indians, and perhaps no longer willing to stonewall them in defense of a fraudulent policy, Wool then aggravated his own situation by forwarding an address to the War Department from Cherokee leaders disputing the treaty's legitimacy.[14]

Accurately or not, this was received as a direct challenge to administration policy, and in mid-October Harris ordered the general to act only when authorized by the civilian commissioners appointed to negotiate with the Cherokee—Lumpkin, now finished with his term as Georgia governor, and newly elected Governor William Carroll of Tennessee. (It is worth noting that Wool was not appointed as one of the commissioners, as Jackson and James Wilkinson had been a generation before.) Now that its general had broken the code of silence, Jacksonian reservations about the army's loyalty resurfaced: Wool was ordered to arrest any military officers who "countenance resistance or opposition to the treaty"; Harris promised that Jackson would dismiss them from the army, though this would have been contrary to all the forms and procedures of military justice. From the administration's perspective, such arrest and dismissal could have applied to the general himself. Wool felt a "humiliating" mortification; even Lumpkin recognized the general's "fear that he might lower his dignity as a military man." All autonomy lost, Wool again requested and was refused relief.[15]

Gentlemen who made their careers as army officers were predisposed to reject so degrading a subordination, but they hardly wanted to give up their salaries and status by resigning, particularly when they believed they were right. Wool's principal subordinates reacted by publishing pseudonymous letters vindicating him in the *Athens (Georgia) Republican*. They implied that the fault lay with the War Department, provoking further recriminations from the civilian superintendent for Cherokee emigration, Benjamin Currey, who complained to Harris and published the secretary's reprimand to Wool in the *Republican*. Interim secretary of war Benjamin Butler (not to be confused with the Civil War general) allowed the brigadier to publish the letters necessary to defend himself but cautioned the general on the propriety of anonymous military letters to the press, which were already forbidden by army regulations. By November, facing censure from all directions, Wool's subordination started to slip, and he began to express his frustration by writing more aggressively—though still privately—to condemn the constraints he considered public slights against his reputation. To Mrs. Nathaniel Warren, the general proclaimed that his assignment was "only made tolerable under the hope that I may stay cruelty and injustice, and protect those [miserable] beings called Cherokees, who are the prey of the Whitemen who reside among them." To fellow Democrat and long-term friend Nathaniel Tallmadge, U.S. senator from New York, Wool belittled Currey as "detested by all classes, white, red, and black," stating that "a greater rascal never went unhung." Despite some civilian sympathy, this was a game that federal military commanders could not win in the Jacksonian South, and the general's position continued to deteriorate.[16]

Although Wool initially promised to follow the commissioners' instructions, he was particularly suspicious of Lumpkin, whom the brigadier considered part of a more general plot to soak up the federal funds to be paid (in scarce specie) to the Cherokee under the treaty. (There were only two commissioners, and Governor Carroll was rarely present.) In October, Lumpkin ordered food distributed to a group of Cherokee awaiting emigration at New Echota, requesting reimbursement from the War Department. Military commanders often issued military rations to relieve suffering among Indians and white civilians, but Lumpkin's action smacked of conflict of interest. Well aware of existing native debt and the unscrupulousness of most southern whites dealing with the federal government and the Indians, Wool protested the order and asked for a detailed cost accounting. At the end of November the brigadier openly rejected his subordination by returning an order from Lumpkin without response. Apparently, the general and the commissioner came to a temporary understanding, with a division of labor Wool could accept, and he seized the Cherokee national archives at Lumpkin's request. Nevertheless, the brigadier felt he had won a victory, and he irresponsibly communicated this to his quartermaster, a mere lieutenant: "I gave them strictly to understand, that I would receive no orders from them." Even less professionally, he vowed to Senator Tallmadge that "I will receive no orders or dictation from the Commissioners." The general bragged that "I shall keep cool and do my duty most thoroughly. I am always cool but never careless . . . when I have enemies about me. You may rest assured I will never be taken by surprise [by enemies] in the field, although I may be surprised at the acts and conduct of individuals in Washington."[17]

Wool kept his cool, but was certainly surprised, and had to endure further reprimand and denunciation, something he had never experienced before his assignment in the Cherokee country. (As inspector general, Wool was especially insulated from civilian attention, since he dealt mostly with subordinates and the discipline of their soldiers, and little with finances or civilian officials.)

Feeling that the Indians would keep the peace only if they believed they had a disinterested official to resort to, the general was certain he held the moral and practical high ground. But the ground that mattered most was political. Wool's inability to balance so many conflicting interests led him ever deeper into a partisan swamp, and as president, Andrew Jackson proved much less forgiving of self-righteous military transgressions than he had been as a general invading Florida, pressing for Cherokee land cessions, and challenging the War Department's right to issue orders to his subordinates a generation before. Wool received a blunt lecture on subordination to civilian authority from interim secretary of war Butler at the beginning of January: "In our Government, civil authorities . . . determine the cases in which . . . resort is [made] to military force." Even then, despite his supposed accommodation with Lumpkin, the general continued to give the impression that he rejected civil control: three weeks *after* Butler's rebuke, the commissioners told Harris that "we have found ourselves repulsed, if not insulted, in every attempt" to gain the general's cooperation.[18]

Wool was predisposed against such cooperation. His primary mission was to prevent a Cherokee uprising; since the Indians seemed peaceful, his principal concern was that white bullying would goad the Cherokee to rebellion. As he observed to Tallmadge, "all those now in civil stations [the commissioners] . . . were engaged in making the treaty, consequently, [they are] hated and detested by the whole Nation. The Indians will not go to the Commissioners when they can avoid it." Because he was "constantly annoyed by [Cherokee] complaints," the brigadier received a more threatening picture of native anger than the situation warranted, and he warned commanding general Macomb that war was imminent. To forestall it, Wool tried to reduce sources of provocation, ordering soldiers to destroy whiskey shops and advising them that their pay would be withheld if they committed depredations against the Indians. Unfortunately for the general, each of his actions, intended to smooth the way for removal, intensified the pressure against him. When Tennessee volunteers became restless with inactivity and showed signs of indiscipline in camp, he discharged all save a single company. Acting on the basis of the 1834 Trade and Intercourse Act, which forbade any introduction of liquor onto Indian land, the brigadier banned the sale of liquor in Cherokee territory, but the governor of Alabama immediately protested that Wool had no authority over the purchase of alcohol by white citizens. After a futile dispute over the legal status of the Cherokee country, the general finally accepted the political reality that state sovereignty superseded national sovereignty in this arena, and he restricted his order to the sale or purchase of alcohol by soldiers and Cherokee.[19]

An initial group of Cherokee emigrants went west in March 1837, encouraging Wool to return to sternness in the hope of speeding removal. Ample evidence of Cherokee acculturation proved insufficient to alter the paternalist assumptions the general shared with most whites. On March 22 he proclaimed that "your fate is decided. . . . Hitherto I have been able in some degree to protect you from intrusions; in a short time it will no longer be in my power. [Even if,] however, I could protect you, you could not live among [whites]. Your habits, your manners, and your customs are unlike, and unsuited to theirs. They have no feelings, no sympathies in common with yourselves." Trying to preempt resistance by a show of force, Wool ordered a new search for Creek fugitives among the Cherokee, who were to be arrested if they refused to cooperate. Yet it had been forty years since the Cherokee had used violence against the United States, and the 150 Creeks taken prisoner and deported west really were fugitives, or Creeks who had settled among the Cherokee years before, not insurgents or agents coordinating resistance.[20]

Wool's limited cooperation with the civilian commissioners had not halted the scorn and censure he received from state and local politicians and newspapers, and the arrival of a new administration gave him the opportunity to renew his application for relief from command. With most of the army committed against the Seminoles and Creeks, the Jackson administration had been compelled to rely on state volunteers and militia, a choice the general consistently found unsatisfactory. Facing renewed pressure to muster volunteers, who would be paid in scarce specie and fed at federal expense, Wool laid out his concerns to Secretary of War Joel Poinsett:

> All those who have expressed a desire to enter the service of the United States as Volunteers from North Carolina and Alabama reside in the Cherokee Country and are generally of that description of men who have no character to lose. The love of gain alone has prompted them to offer their services. They live upon the Indians. If they cannot procure it one way they will [do so] in another. Most of them would delight in war for no other object than to plunder the Cherokees. . . . They are not to be controlled. . . . [When given the choice I] received those who resided farthest from the Cherokee Country.
>
> I have thus far been able to preserve an ascendency over the Volunteers as well as the Cherokees. To secure a quiet and peaceable removal of the latter that ascendency must be preserved. I need not tell you that Indians never respect civil Agents, and many of those in this country are particularly obnoxious to the Cherokees, especially all those

[such as Lumpkin] who have had anything to do with making the late treaty. They look to the military and the military alone for justice.... They complain to me only, and their complaints are ... often heart rending.

Wool was no longer a democrat (as he had been in the early 1830s) or a stooge for sectional advantage or white supremacy. Repeating the language of his unofficial letters the previous fall, he concluded that "this command is one that no man of honor or feeling can desire and to me it would be intolerable but for the hope that I may stay cruelty, and in some degree injustice."[21]

The general received some relief in May, when Colonel William Lindsay of the Second Artillery replaced him, but his troubles were not over. That June, the Alabama legislature formally condemned him for intervening in a dispute over the disposition of a Cherokee estate that had been partly claimed by a white man. Wool's attempt to protect Indian property, authorized by Articles 6 and 16 of the Treaty of New Echota, backfired as the quarrel escalated and two whites were killed by the Cherokee, though no soldiers were present at the time. President Van Buren, who was usually more sympathetic to the army than his predecessor, felt compelled to order a court of inquiry into the incident. His frustration overflowing, Wool lost his cool and demanded that the court investigate his entire tenure in the Cherokee assignment, but the administration had no intention of allowing the general to embroil it in an extended controversy, particularly when Scott and Gaines had just finished going at each other in an embarrassing court of inquiry over their conduct of the Seminole War. Instead, Van Buren and Poinsett overlooked the insubordinate tenor of Wool's rage against the "degrading orders of the President of the United States"—meaning Jackson's reprimands—and arranged matters to exculpate the general while minimizing public embarrassment.[22]

The composition of the court—Wool's friend Winfield Scott (also a good friend of Van Buren and Poinsett), recovering from two trying courts of inquiry earlier in the year into his operations against the Creeks and Seminoles; Wool's successor, Colonel Lindsay; and Wool's own adjutant during the Cherokee mission, Major Matthew M. Payne (who lacked the rank normally required to serve on the court)—virtually guaranteed the brigadier's vindication. Though Wool initially protested Lindsay's inclusion, he must have realized that his replacement would experience the same harassment and persecution. The government of Alabama proved unwilling or unable to produce any evidence, and five days' testimony by friendly witnesses showed no evidence that the general had usurped civilian authority as charged. Responding to a series of leading questions by Wool and members of the court, the general's principal subordinates, volunteer as well as professional, repeatedly praised his mild and conciliatory attitude, while faulting local whites and civil officials for their "oppression" of the Cherokee. However, the sheriff of the Alabama county where the incident had occurred echoed military testimony by declaring Wool prudent and discreet, opining that "respectable" whites had hoped the general would remain in command. (This language of social respectability allied with national military command would recur during Wool's service on the Canadian border the following year.) According to his volunteer aide-de-camp Thomas Lyon, the brigadier "acted . . . with great caution, as far as the rights of States or of individuals were involved"; if there was "any error," it lay in "an excess of caution on these points." Despite all the travails outlined above, Wool actually seems to have balanced respect for states' rights and due process with effective interethnic diplomacy, for Lyon affirmed that the general's "course tended much to allay the excitement of the Indians against the whites," tempering any Cherokee disposition to retaliation or resistance.[23]

The issues raised in the testimony went far beyond Wool's conduct or the independence of white Alabamians. Freed from Jackson's overbearing glare, the army leadership seems to have used the Wool inquiry to voice its longstanding frustration, irritation, and ambivalence toward its unpleasant missions on the southern Indian frontier. (Jackson had rejected the findings of both courts of inquiry into Winfield Scott's performance against the Creeks and Seminoles in 1836; each court absolved Scott, and one criticized Democrat Thomas Jesup for undermining Scott. The result was a stalemate; the army was unvindicated but unharmed.)[24] At home among a friendly court of fellow veterans and long-term colleagues, the general defended himself by taking the high ground, asserting that he had been hounded simply for executing "the sacred trust reposed in me" by attempting to protect "the weak as well as the strong" against the "daily encroachments of the whites." With all the witnesses supporting his contention that the civil courts provided a "miserable mockery" of justice to the Indians, the brigadier proclaimed that "my crime [was] listening to [Indian] complaints and redressing [Indian] wrongs. . . . The path of justice being clear, I but obeyed the still small voice of conscience."[25]

Indeed, Wool took the moral and political offensive, advancing his own rather Whiggish interpretation of national sovereignty, federalism, and the Constitution, rejected by Jacksonians a decade before, arguing that "the laws of Alabama, extending her jurisdiction over the Indians and their country, are contrary to treaties . . . of the Union, and therefore void." Though he claimed "much embarrassment" in raising the issue, the erstwhile Jacksonian cited the opinion of "that pure-hearted man and most eminent jurist," John Marshall, to remind his fellow commanders and civilian observers that the Constitution declares treaties part of the supreme law of the land, while asserting that, despite Marshall's opinion in *Cherokee Nation v. Georgia*, Indians had "always [been] recognized as independent communities capable of making treaties." Wool then delivered his own dictum on Congress's constitutional authority to regulate commerce with the Indians, finding "the laws of Alabama . . . void, [because] repugnant to" the trade and intercourse acts of 1802 and 1834, and concluding that the states had implicitly accepted the supremacy of federal treaties as a condition of entrance into the Union. The general had moved a long way from his respect for "sovereign States" the previous summer.[26]

The crux of Wool's dilemma lay in a conflict of obligation. His sense of institutional and professional accountability—objective subordination to constitutionally authorized, but partisan and often unscrupulous civilian officials and their policies—clashed with his subjective sense of moral responsibility, or obligation, to protect the lives and property of citizens and, he clearly felt, Indians, regardless of the policies of the administration in office. The root of the general's problem—much like that Edmund Gaines faced on the Texas border the same autumn—was an unusually restrictive subordination imposed on a proud commander who felt a professional duty to secure the objectives of national policy while anticipating and countering future threats to that policy, regardless of parochial local interests and individual greed. Recent experience told the generals that these politically driven constraints were ultimately dangerous to the citizenry they were sworn to protect. In November 1836, following a line senior officers had already laid out regarding the Black Hawk and Ho-chunk (Winnebago) uprisings, which brevet General Duncan Clinch was arguing in defense of his conduct in Florida earlier in the year, Wool advised the War Department that "by timely and decided measures the Florida and Creek wars might have been prevented." If so, it logically, and perhaps morally, followed that he should use his professional judgment to deter a similar outbreak of violence among the Cherokee: "if I am to do nothing until hostilities are commenced, I can only say that I cannot be recalled too soon from this command. I will never consent to risk my reputation as an officer with the restrictions embraced in the Acting Secretary's letter."[27]

Wool was not resigning from the army, but he was asserting a division of labor and a level of professional autonomy the Jackson administration was unwilling to accept. Frustrated by the administration's tendency to demand national security on the cheap and then blame military commanders for failing to quash Indian resistance to removal with minimal force, publicity, and expense, Wool asked for the operational discretion genteel officers expected, as befit their status—a discretion that had usually been accorded them in similar situations in the preceding generation. During the 1820s and early 1830s, career army officers both junior and senior criticized one another, officially as well as privately, for failing to anticipate and react quickly to unrest among the Arikara, Ho-chunk, Sauk, and Fox, but neither Monroe, Adams, nor Jackson (initially) reprimanded them. Instead, Indian diplomacy had been treated as a matter for military professionals, who sometimes fell short when it came to diagnosing and responding to emerging threats but used their extensive experience in the national interest. The complaints of fur trappers may have influenced the abandonment of the Missouri expeditions, but they did not lead to embarrassing reprimands from national civilian authorities.

That changed, across the southern borderlands from the Cherokee country to Florida and the Texas border, in 1836. Whether because Jackson had become impatient with his generals' operational caution, was angered by the uprisings among the Creeks and Seminoles, or feared setbacks to his cherished policy, or perhaps because his handpicked successor (Martin Van Buren) was running for election, professional military autonomy suddenly took a backseat to ideological and partisan imperatives, with enduring consequences for civil-military relations. Clinch resigned from the army, Wool left the Democratic fold, and Jackson's enmity combined with Scott's to bar Gaines from future operational command. The army's senior leadership, which apart from Scott had been largely favorable or at least neutral toward the Jacksonians before 1836, became skeptical not just of populist frontiersmen and a few radical congressmen but of the Democratic Party as a source of reasoned national security policy.

Without autonomy, Wool did not believe he could serve effectively. Indeed, like Captain Clark in the prelude to Choctaw emigration, the proud general feared that loss of autonomy would imperil his integrity, reputation, and honor: he was being assigned responsibility to implement a complex, often confusing, and ultimately contradictory policy without the necessary authority; he might be held accountable for wrongs committed against his will and judgment. Writing to his wife in January 1837, the brigadier condemned "the imbecility and weakness of the administration" and observed, "I was determined not to be put down by General Jackson."[28] Yet for all his pride and obstinacy, the problem was not with Wool as an individual. The brigadier was thrown into the same sort of situation that Clinch encountered when he tried to warn the government of Seminole unrest in 1835, and that Gaines faced when he tried to ascertain the Jackson administration's true intentions on the

Texas border, at the same time Wool was attempting to keep the peace in the Cherokee country. Whether because of Jackson's imperiousness or the administration's eagerness to douse the political fires aroused by its confrontational, duplicitous policies, professional military discretion and calls for preparedness were given very short shrift during the southern borderlands crises of 1836.

The Van Buren administration eased civil-military relations and encouraged effective frontier diplomacy by permitting far greater military autonomy in peacekeeping operations directed at preventing war with Britain along the Canadian border in 1838 and 1839. Still, Wool's successor would find that professional discretion had to be balanced with consideration for state and local sensitivities in southern Indian removal. Wool was fortunate that Van Buren had replaced Jackson; he was cleared of all charges and would be promoted to the permanent rank of brigadier general when a vacancy occurred during the administration of John Tyler four years later. He remained in service until 1863—a career of fifty-one years, second only to Winfield Scott—leading a campaign in Mexico and several operations in the Pacific Northwest during the 1850s, where he again ran into trouble with Democratic administrations unwilling to restrain the violence of white democracy (filibusters, the San Francisco vigilante conflict, and white attacks on California Indians). His leading antagonist in the federal bureaucracy, C. A. Harris, resigned under a cloud in October 1838, having apparently used his position to financial advantage.[29]

As president of Wool's court, Scott had properly refused to address the inspector general's constitutional arguments, but he did make sure to remark that he had "naturally considered" treaties—implicitly including those with Native Americans—part of "the supreme law of the land" per the Constitution. The army protected its own, and under Van Buren the national government allowed its military agents to continue their careers, with greater operational autonomy than before, within their self-insulating institution. Indeed, it is remarkable, almost dumbfounding, that the president tolerated the way Wool turned his court into an attack on Jacksonian policy, constitutional interpretation, and Democratic state leaders, particularly when the record would be published in congressional documents. Yet with an interminable war in Florida and a financial panic erupting, Van Buren had good reason to allow the army to dispense with the general's case, and he could afford to ignore Wool's constitutional commentary (which was certainly not inaccurate according to the letter of the Constitution). This tolerance did not extend to Jacksonians in the southern states: William Lindsay was soon subjected to much the same sort of vilification from the rabid advocates of states' rights and white supremacy, and Scott would face similar irritants when he took the colonel's place for the final removal operations a year later. Yet Wool's trial must have helped prepare them for the tribulations to come, and it reassured them of Van Buren's support.[30]

The executive did learn from Wool's sour experiences with state volunteers, ordering contingents from all four artillery regiments, the Fourth Infantry, and the Second Dragoons to the Cherokee country in April 1837, when it seemed that Thomas Jesup had gained Seminole acquiescence in removal from Florida. Colonel Lindsay, a twenty-five-year veteran and longtime Alabama planter involved in land deals at the fledgling town of Chattanooga (previously called Ross's Landing, home of the leader of the Cherokee antitreaty faction), initially considered Cherokee resistance his most likely problem, boasting to his wife that "we shall have force enough to boil pepper & eat the Cherokees." He was not alone: army surgeon John Reynolds observed that "most intelligent officers" in the expeditionary force expected "a bit of a Cherokee war" and worried that the mountains would prove as difficult as Florida swamps, but hostilities with local citizens proved much more real. Civilians and enlisted men exchanged shots across the Hiwassee River, and Reynolds observed that "our lives have been threatened by these outlaws and most officers go armed." Yet Lindsay did not permit such outlawry, or any impressions he might have developed at Wool's court of inquiry, to distract him from the need for civil-military cooperation. Hoping to accelerate the settlement of claims by and against the Indians—the treaty commission was supposed to compensate the Cherokee for losses to whites, using funds set aside under the treaty—the colonel advised the appointment of a third commissioner to ensure majority votes.[31]

Despite these efforts, Lindsay quickly became embroiled in the same sort of difficulties that had plagued Wool, following a similar trajectory toward disillusionment with state and local officials. Recognizing that virtually every Cherokee had civil claims to settle and that the settlement process had been delayed by Governor Carroll's absence from the commission, the colonel advised extending the deadline for emigration. Lindsay continued to believe that the Cherokee "must necessarily remove at a certain period, whether ready or not," but he soon began to lament "outrageous violations of laws, vainly ordained for the protection of a weak and dependent people." As his disillusionment grew, the Alabamian asserted that Georgia was different from any other state in its utter absence of sympathy for the Indians: "he is the most popular man, who oppresses them most." As this friction reemerged, civil-military relations with state and local officials proved little better than before: Lindsay soon felt the same suspicions as Wool and reacted with a similar disdain and insubordination toward civil officials. Convinced that the civilian removal commissioners—who were essentially state and local politicians, despite their appointment by the federal government—were "pursuing a deep underhanded game toward the military," he decided not to call on them unless they called on him first.[32]

The year 1838 found Lindsay glad to escape the "importunate crowd of Rowdies & Vagabonds" hanging about his headquarters, but he remained "engaged in an open squabble with the Commissioners." (It no longer mattered who the individual commissioners were; Lumpkin had been elected U.S. senator and resigned as commissioner.) Though nearly 20 percent of the army had been deployed to the Cherokee country, state volunteers—"a very expensive & worthless military force," in Lindsay's eyes—were once again mobilized to help intimidate the Cherokee, aggravating civil-military friction. The Indians remained "friendly & quiet, but resolutely determined not to remove"; the colonel believed he could "manage them without difficulty" through a show of force with his professional troops. When Winfield Scott took over the command in May, Lindsay claimed a place for himself among those "who are friends of the [Cherokee] Nation," rejoicing that John Ross had been given permission to direct the logistics of emigration. Though one Cherokee had been slain, "no doubt wantonly by the militia," Lindsay felt there was "not the slightest possibility of hostilities." Instead, his principal worry, soon amply confirmed, was the insufficient resources devoted to supplying the Cherokee during their journey west. Taken ill with fever, Lindsay relished the news that his regiment would be transferred to the Canadian border, where his children would be better educated, his soldiers would avoid the sickness and swamps of Florida, and he could shake off the miasma of removal. But Lindsay never escaped that cloud, dying of "bilious fever" (a generic nineteenth-century term for fever accompanied by vomiting) on September 15.[33]

INTENTIONS, CONTINGENCIES, AND CONSEQUENCES: WINFIELD SCOTT AND THE FINAL CHEROKEE REMOVAL, 1838

Fresh from calming tensions on the Canadian border, Winfield Scott took command from Lindsay in May 1838. The two years' grace permitted the Cherokee under the Treaty of New Echota were now up, and the executive branch prepared for war in case the Cherokee refused to leave. John Ross had roused significant support in Congress, and the Van Buren administration had queried the southern state governors about delaying removal, leading the Cherokee to hope that expropriation could be avoided. Encouraged by this prospect, the Cherokee remained dispersed across millions of acres of moun-

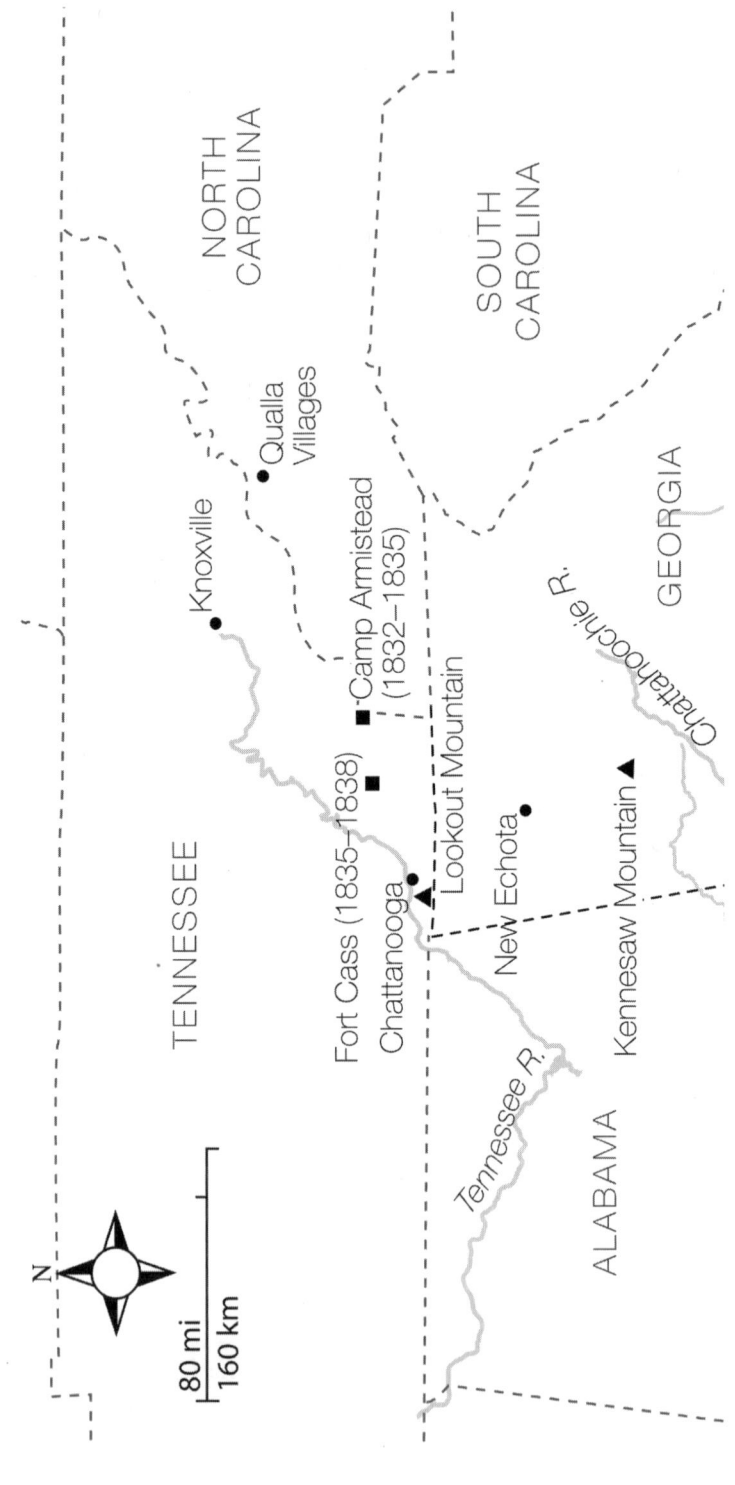

Posts established to concentrate the Cherokee for removal (map by Tracy Ellen Smith)

tainous terrain, and few outside the small "Treaty Party" (those who accepted the Treaty of New Echota and hoped for a better life if they moved west, particularly the Ridge family) had made serious preparations for emigration. The army was ordered to round up the Cherokee and bring them to camps where they would be issued supplies prior to their departure. Thus, the Cherokee emigration would be the first major removal operation conducted at a point on the spectrum midway between the "voluntary" emigration of the Choctaw, directed by military officers but without direct coercion by soldiers, and the wartime expulsion of the Creeks and Seminoles, in which removal proceeded directly from capture in the course of active operations.

Scott's selection for this command—like his deployments by Democratic presidents along the Canadian border, in Charleston during the Nullification Crisis, and in Mexico in 1847—indicates the essentially nonpartisan character of senior officer assignments. As usual, his selection also depended on the limited number of alternatives available in so small an army, along with the political dilemmas or liabilities other commanders would have brought to the mission. Of the army's general officers, Thomas Jesup was just coming off a year and a half of arduous and controversial command in Florida; Edmund Gaines had incurred such criticism in Florida and along the Texas border in 1836 that he never held another operational command; and commanding general Alexander Macomb was as busy as ever tending to army administration in Washington. None of the army's brevet brigadier generals had the name recognition or the personal authority required for such a sensitive mission. Nor could the president give the command to a state governor, since the area of operations encompassed several states, and doing so would spur controversy among them.

This was all quite fortunate, for Scott was much more experienced in the nuances of civil-military relations in the borderlands than his predecessors; this was his third major exercise in federal diplomacy during the 1830s. He also had personal advantages that Wool and Lindsay lacked: the general counted both President Van Buren and Secretary of War Poinsett—a principal Unionist leader and one of Scott's allies in South Carolina during the Nullification Crisis—among his personal friends. At the beginning of 1838 Van Buren sent the general to the northern border to calm the international crisis created by Americans aiding rebellions in Canada. Usually an ideologically motivated states' rights advocate, the president demonstrated that he had a great deal in common with his Unionist secretary and his chief military diplomat when it came to maintaining national sovereignty over international relations and moderating the tensions international crises aggravated within the federal system. Scott's advantages in his Cherokee assignment were multiplied because Poinsett remained at his post throughout the general's tenure, whereas Wool had faced three secretaries of war (Lewis Cass, Benjamin Butler, and C. A. Harris), all essentially partisan politicians, in less than six months. Smooth civil-military relations ensued. Though an avowed Whig, the proud general approached the operation as a stern and essentially straightforward duty to execute the law, including that created by the Treaty of New Echota, whatever doubts he may have felt. Thus, Scott's relations with the Van Buren administration were far better than Wool's or Gaines's with the Jackson administration, and there were none of the controversies that had dogged Lindsay or Wool. Indeed, Poinsett and Scott took care to conciliate the Georgians, seeking out Senator Lumpkin for advice before the general's departure south. Not surprisingly, Lumpkin counseled "the use of military officers not heretofore employed in the Cherokee country," because he believed most officers found Ross persuasive and sympathized with the antitreaty party.[34]

Lumpkin's understanding of causation was probably overblown, given career soldiers' irritations in their dealings with white frontiersmen; most of the regimental officers deployed to the Cherokee country had already experienced ample frustration with frontier disorder in Florida or the trans-Mississippi West. Nor, despite their partisan differences and Wool's earlier egalitarianism, were Scott's values much different from his predecessor's: both were determined to implement removal but hoped to do so as humanely as possible. Unlike Wool, however, Scott had both the reliable military force and the administrative capacity to do so, unless conditions changed significantly: with two and a half regiments of federal troops, the general possessed the largest contingent of the national standing army assembled outside Florida since the Black Hawk War. He would need few citizen volunteers unless war broke out, and the use of professional soldiers made that less likely by preventing the sort of incidents that were common when undisciplined citizen-soldiers came in contact with the Indians they despised. Scott was accompanied by one of the largest and most functionally articulated American field staffs in the era between the War of 1812 and the war with Mexico: he had at least eight experienced officers, including William Worth, his favorite protégé and a fellow veteran of the Canadian border strife, as de facto chief of staff. Other staff officers included Assistant Adjutant General Robert Anderson, of future Fort Sumter fame; Wool's former adjutant, Matthew Payne, as acting inspector general; and experienced quartermaster and commissary officers like John Page. There were also several volunteer and professional aides, at least one of whom had accompanied Scott along the Canadian frontier. These men averaged nearly fifteen years' national military service apiece. Scott also had a far more solid operational foundation for both concentrating and supplying the Cherokee prior to removal: Lindsay had paved the way, establishing twenty-three military posts and supply depots blanketing the Cherokee country.[35]

Most important for maintaining calm civil-military relations, Scott had the clear mission Wool had lacked. The deadline was up, and the Cherokee would be compelled to move west. Few professional officers expected the Cherokee to fight, but none expected the Indians to dispossess themselves. Indeed, the financial morass of white and Cherokee claims had deepened with the economic panic, and the consequent shortage of specie and credit, that began the previous fall; this led to increased pressure to keep individual Cherokee in the East so the whites they owed could pursue payment. Despite extensive Cherokee agriculture and acculturation, Scott's subordinates saw little distinction between the Cherokee and other Indians. Army officers asserted that, though the Cherokee were idle and "ignorant of economy of time, or money," during peace they were "mild, unassuming and seldom or never disposed to resent even an affront offered by a white man unless when roused to fury by spirituous liquors." Their "feelings of superstitious veneration" for the graves of their ancestors encouraged the "natural sympathy" of their "love of home"; "good tempered or sullen according to the treatment [they] received," "the great mass" of the Cherokee were "decidedly hostile to emigration." Captain William Williams believed that poverty and privation might have tempted the Cherokee to look beyond the horizons of their homeland, but like many Jacksonians, he blamed their persistent desire to avoid removal on selfish whites and Indian leaders "stimulated by sordid views," who encouraged "every proposition adverse to their own true interest and the wishes of the U.S. Government." Army commanders expected passive resistance and wanted to ensure it did not become active through military error or irritation.[36]

Scott proved just the diplomat for the situation. The future "Fuss 'n' Feathers" had learned from his own Creek and Seminole campaigns two years before, and he made none of the overly elaborate plans that had failed in 1836. He also, it should be reiterated, had a functioning operational infrastructure in the depots and posts Lindsay had established, which Scott had lacked during his earlier campaigns. "Considering the number and temper of the mass to be removed, together with the extent and fastnesses of the country to be occupied," the general's first objective was to minimize violence and prevent an uprising like those among the Indians farther south. Using similar language in both the orders to his troops and an address to the Cherokee—"the address of a warrior to warriors," as he told them—Scott advised coolness and moderation. He told his soldiers, "It will readily occur that simple indiscretions, acts of harshness and cruelty on the part of our troops may lead, step by step, to delays, to impatience and exasperation and, in the end, to a general war and carnage—a result, *in the case of these particular Indians, utterly abhorrent to the generous sympathies of the whole American people.*"[37]

Following his lecture on the sensitivity of American public opinion, Scott ordered that "it is . . . the special duty of the nearest good officer or [enlisted] man instantly to interpose" to prevent or halt "wanton injury or insult," appealing to their regard for personal and national honor. Having thrown down the gauntlet with threats of "general war and carnage" and "the destruction of the Cherokees" should they resist, he expressed the hope that "by early and persevering acts of kindness and humanity . . . the Indians may soon be induced to confide in the army, and . . . flock to us for food and clothing." He then promised the Cherokee that they would not be fired on unless they actively resisted, that families would not be separated, and that no guards would be placed on the men if their families were also present to act as their security. Trying to maintain his sense of personal, professional, and national honor—a compound of justice and equity—he assured the Cherokee, and reassured himself, that "soldiers are as kind-hearted as [they are] brave, and the desire of every one . . . is to execute our painful duty in mercy," a formulation he repeated several times. Officers were enjoined that injury or insult to the Cherokee must be punished by "the severest penalty of the laws."[38]

Field-grade commanders echoed these admonitions in their instructions to subordinates who were rounding up the Cherokee and guarding the camps where they awaited removal. Their language indicates the genteel conjunction of personal, national, and professional honor with sentiments of sympathy and humanity and even a legalist rights consciousness. "Your own feelings will cause you to respect those of the Indian People, and to afford them all the indulgence compatible with the great objects of the Government—rights of persons especially," Major Reynolds Kirby advised Captain Lucien Webster on June 11. (Kirby's emphasis may have derived from the officer's legal status as a representative of the government; just as probably, he was concerned about protecting Cherokee women from rape, the most likely violation.) Lieutenant Colonel William Foster ordered Lieutenant Charles Larnard to institute patrols around the camps, both to keep whites out and to keep the Cherokee in. Following Scott's move to provide physicians and vaccinations, Foster directed that "you will observe and report on the health, cleanliness and general good or bad condition of all the Indian Camps . . . your conduct will be marked with the utmost humanity, affording them all the protection and assistance in your power." These instructions were not new or unusual among military leaders attempting to relieve suffering populations, whether white, Indian, or the Afro-Seminoles they conveyed west during these years.

Nevertheless, Scott's explicit stricture against firing on unresisting Indians marked a change, however minimal it appears by twenty-first-century standards, in the development of military rules of engagement during stability and support operations. Viewed from the standpoint of Georgian attitudes toward the Cherokee, we can recognize that the army was engaged in preventing mass atrocities as much as keeping the peace, enforcing a treaty, or deterring a Cherokee uprising.[39]

Captain Webster observed that most Cherokee "remain[ed] quietly at home at work . . . as though no evil was intended them" that spring, refusing to prepare for the expropriation they sought to avoid. Nevertheless, the weather proved the most significant factor complicating efficient and humane removal. Only three emigrating parties, totaling several hundred Cherokee, were able to depart before drought closed the Tennessee and Arkansas River route west from mid-June until October. Even if the Cherokee were forced or chose to walk, the necessary supplies could be conveyed at acceptable expense only by water; there were too few wagons, and hiring more would be too costly amid the scarcity. Stockpiling food would have been similarly expensive, probably aggravating, and aggravated by, hoarding among whites threatened by the drought. Confidence in Scott and fear of further embarrassment encouraged Van Buren to authorize a delay until autumn. In the interim, Scott had to push the Cherokee into encampments and then hold and feed them for several months, while trying to minimize the sickness that inevitably occurred in the crowded temporary camps. Whatever the limits of the medical care provided to the Cherokee, these problems proved endemic among any large, concentrated population in the nineteenth century, as demonstrated in the Crimean War and the military and refugee camps of the Civil War.[40]

Some Cherokee, especially men, and some of the Creeks still living among the Cherokee, responded by fleeing deeper into the mountains, leading experienced commanders like Major Sylvester Churchill (soon to become one of the army's inspector generals) to march Cherokee warriors to the camps in chains. Indeed, the major noted that he "yoked, or harnessed" women suspected of aiding men who had escaped the camps. Nevertheless, there was no violent resistance to speak of until most of the Cherokee had been concentrated or had begun the trek west. On November 1 a group of five refugee warriors, led by Charley Tsali, killed two soldiers of the Fourth Infantry Regiment and wounded a third in the vicinity of the Qualla (or Oconaluftee) Cherokee villages in North Carolina, possibly in response to soldiers prodding a woman (their mother and grandmother) with bayonets. Suddenly worried that Cherokee reactions might take a "most unexpected" turn, Scott's priority shifted from removal—already well under way and perhaps irreversible—to peace enforcement and retribution.[41]

The balance between Scott's fear and anger is not clear. He must have feared a repetition of the quagmire in Florida, where thousands of troops were hunting several hundred warriors, but he probably considered the Cherokee country more open to invasion; he knew there were far fewer fugitive warriors than in Florida, and his language was that of murder and satisfying national honor through law enforcement, not war. Either way, the general's response was overwhelming. He dispatched Lieutenant Colonel Foster (wounded under Scott's command at Lundy's Lane a quarter century before) with at least five companies—several hundred soldiers—of the Fourth Infantry to the Qualla area, primarily to punish the "outlaws." (Protecting "white families" repeatedly appeared as an afterthought in Scott's letters, as well as Foster's.) Scott's anger, and perhaps his anxiety and even a bit of repressed guilt, boiled forth in his order that "the individuals guilty of this unprovoked outrage must be shot down." Though the general tried to anticipate criticism by claiming there was nothing "vindictive" about his orders, they were forceful; the colonel was now authorized to "fire upon any warrior who may disobey you, or run from the troops under your command."[42]

Scott carefully distinguished the "outlaws" from the rest of the Cherokee, declaring that the killers had "obstinately separated themselves from their tribe, and refused all obedience to the orders and entreaties of its chiefs." He assured the War Department that "every Cherokee . . . who has heard of the recent outrage has expressed the utmost indignation and regret" and claimed that "it would be very easy to obtain from the emigrants . . . any number of warriors to march with the troops against the outlaws." The general may have been deceiving himself about the Cherokee's sense of obligation to enforce U.S. law, but he was not going to admit any need for Indian aid or chance any defections, asserting that he would "only accept . . . the services of a few runners, to bear invitations of kindness" to the fugitives, "deeming it against the honor of the United States to employ, in hostilities, one part of the tribe against another." This may have been the "fuss and feathers" or Scott's favorite wine talking, since he certainly intended no "kindness" to the killers, nor had the United States ever hesitated to use one group of Indians against another.[43]

Still, Scott continued to advise restraint toward the Cherokee as a people, taking a page from long-standing U.S. efforts to encourage Indians to police their own crimes against whites by implying that Foster could offer exemption from removal in return for assistance in catching the killers. "The

Oconeelufty Indians, in Haywood county," who had taken individual allotments and U.S. citizenship under the U.S.-Cherokee treaty of 1819, were "not to be considered fugitives, or to be interrupted, if they continue . . . peaceable & orderly." The colonel was to do only "enough to satisfy national honor in respect to the murders & murderers," to assure "the safety of our citizens," and to bring "away for emigration to the west as many of the fugitive Indians . . . as practicable"—in that order of priority—before returning to his previous route toward Arkansas. These instructions may have meant that Cherokee fugitives who did not aid the killers would be exempted from expulsion, or that Foster was tacitly granted the authority to narrow the definition of "fugitives" solely to the killers and Cherokee who gave them aid. Indeed, some accounts assert that "Scott eagerly seized the incident as an opportunity for compromise" with a band of fugitive Cherokee led by a man named Euchella or Utsala, whom the army had been unable to catch, to hunt down the killers in exchange for exemption from expropriation.[44]

Though some of the Qualla leaders hesitated, others hoped to preserve or enhance their status and remain in the East by working with Foster. With their aid, the killers were captured within three weeks; after identification by a board of inquiry, with no opportunity for appeal, three of them were tied to trees and "executed by the Cherokees themselves, in [the] presence of the Fourth Regiment of Infantry [drawn up] in line of Battle" alongside a river. Owing to "his youth," the colonel spared a fourth, Tsali's son—ironically named Washington. Foster lectured the local Cherokee leaders on the army's power but released captives unrelated to the killers and promised to end removal operations in the vicinity. The fifth fugitive, Tsali himself, was soon caught and executed by the Qualla after the army had departed. Employing tribal referents peculiar to the regular army, Foster remarked that "the honor of the [Cherokee] Nation has been fully cared for, as well as the honor of the Regiment to which I belong." Indeed, the colonel advised Scott that Euchella's band had "behaved *nobly*"; "their friendship, indefatigable & untiring industry, in the late pursuit" spurred him to request permission for them to remain in North Carolina.[45]

Foster's diplomacy with the Indians and local whites demonstrates the blurring of boundaries so common in the borderlands, the contrast career soldiers often saw between white frontiersmen and Indians, and the peculiar blend of empathy and condescension characteristic of nationally oriented officers who had spent extended periods on the frontier. The colonel covered his flank against civilian criticism by reporting that he had reassured (he wrote "pacified") the "poor and ignorant population"—white citizens who would "long regard the presence of the Troops . . . as a great blessing"—as soon as he arrived in the area. Yet he dismissed the need to protect them from Cherokee attack: "I hear nothing [further] of *fugitives* . . . I do not believe there are sixty [such] souls . . . perhaps fifteen or twenty grown men, poor, needy, naked, and destitute, entirely harmless, and wholly inoffensive, and even useful, to this sparsely settled Country."[46] When he left, he forwarded a petition from local whites that the Indians be allowed to remain, confidently asserting his authority with a proclamation to the inhabitants:

> I, William Stanhope Foster, a Colonel in the Army of the United States, in command of the Troops now in North Carolina do, in consideration of the general good character, & peaceable, inoffensive, and useful conduct of Euchella and his band . . . combined with his . . . solemn pledges to me given of good and peaceable conduct, and obedience, to the Laws . . . as well as their promise to apprehend, and deliver, any offender, of their tribe against such Laws to the Civil Authority of the State . . . grant to him my permission to live in this country, as associates and Brothers, of the O co ne lufty Indians until a final decision shall be made . . . by the Government at Washington.[47]

This grotesque incident, the sole case of death incurred by U.S. troops at the hands of the Cherokee throughout the removal process, became the basis of a Cherokee legend in which Charley Tsali sacrificed himself so that his people could remain in the eastern hills. To term the incident grotesque is not to label it bizarre, however, for it unfolded very much according to the logic of the U.S. assertion of sovereignty over the "domestic dependent nations" of Native America since 1789: the United States would permit the Cherokee to police themselves, on white terms. Scott praised Foster's "intelligence and judgment"; perhaps a hundred more Cherokee were ultimately permitted to remain in the East; local whites, who employed some of the Qualla as farmworkers, seem to have been placated by their accommodating reaction and Foster's balance of targeted retribution with general moderation. Indeed, the colonel's reference to the Indians' usefulness precisely echoed that of the civilian petitioners. Pro-removal extremists apparently did not protest, or perhaps they did not get wind of the story in time to do so effectively, and everyone on the scene was satisfied, except for Charley Tsali and his patriotic sons.[48]

Given the extent of Cherokee acculturation to white practices and norms, the greatest threat to "peaceful" expropriation still seemed to come, as Wool and Lindsay might have warned, from the Georgians, whom Major Churchill accused of planning a general massacre. Federal troops had used some force to compel the Cherokee to move from their homes to the camps; trying to avoid civil-military friction, they had done little or nothing to prevent white civilians from looting and burning the abandoned homesteads. Hence, this rumor afforded Churchill the opportunity to draw a sharper distinction between professionals and militia, between nation and state. The rumored plan for massacre "was abandoned in consequence of the employment of *regulars* to guard the Indians—the patriotic party of Georgians wisely concluding that they would be sorely resisted in their wicked attempt. . . . Had the guard consisted of militia, they calculated on their acquiescence, and perhaps aid." Fearing the racism and indiscipline of the state troops, and downplaying the likelihood of Cherokee resistance, Scott soon discharged all but one company, of "respectable" Tennessee volunteers; he employed them as police to deter resistance to federal authority from white frontiersmen.[49]

The general aside, career officers left no record of satisfaction, much less pleasure, with their work in the final Cherokee removal. Few left much record one way or the other, probably preferring to submerge any sense of personal responsibility and avoid any ethical or emotional conflicts between their duty and livelihood and their sense of honor through subordination to the dictates of civilian authority and the Constitution. Those who did comment found the work distasteful: "for a moment I regarded myself as a trespasser, as one of a gang of robbers," as Scott's aide-de-camp and assistant adjutant general Erasmus Keyes later put it. Lucien Webster's words to his wife Frances are probably representative: "These are the innocent and simple people, into whose houses we are to obtrude ourselves, and take off by force. . . . If there is anything that goes against my conscience it is this work, and I would not do it, whatever might be the consequences, did I not know that there are thousands that would, and probably with much less feeling towards the poor creatures." Perhaps Webster felt morally superior to his fellow officers; more likely, his reference to thousands of others meant the armed citizens of Georgia and Alabama. In that sense he was certainly correct, and a temperate, subordinate execution of national policy was the least brutal outcome one could expect once the United States set out on the path of ethnic cleansing. For better or worse, the army followed orders.[50]

This empathy appeared, along with a tinge of paternalism and primitivism, in Captain George McCall's description of a phrenological examination of Charley Tsali's oldest son, Nantayalee Jake, before he was executed. (Phrenology, a pseudoscientific practice common during that era, was supposed to identify a person's intellectual and psychological tendencies based on the physical contours of the head.) Though phrenology lent itself to the rampant biological racism emerging during the 1830s, McCall stressed environment rather than heredity and positive rather than negative qualities, claiming that "the most fully developed organs were . . . '*firmness*,' or perseverance and steadiness of purpose; '*self-esteem*,' or love of independence and personal dignity; [and] '*veneration*,' or love of worthless objects consecrated by time, or of antiquated customs. . . . His '*destructiveness*,' or propensity to kill and to murder, was moderate or rather weak." Thus, although the captain denigrated the fugitives as being "of very low order," with "less intellect" than other Cherokee, and noted their "very dark . . . complexion," he blamed their "degraded" state on their "low . . . circumstances," meaning poverty. McCall, a socially well-connected Philadelphian, may have intended the distinction between the killers' intellectual qualities and those of the Cherokee as a whole, to differentiate between Indians who resisted the United States and those who accepted its authority, but he concluded that Nantayalee Jake had been motivated by "an all-absorbing love for the country of his birth . . . his willingness to destroy his guard was simply to enable the women and children of his party to escape." Courage and selflessness: what more could a soldier ask?[51]

The tenuous balance between officers' professional sense of national duty and their personal ideas of justice was most evident in a dispute between Scott and Captain John R. Vinton, Jacob Brown's aide-de-camp and emissary to Georgia during the Creek controversy a decade before. Distinguished in action against the Seminoles, Vinton converted to evangelical Christianity in 1837 and became opposed to that war but continued to serve in Florida. The following May, ordered to Tennessee along with his regiment to round up the Cherokee, the captain noted in his diary "that my ostensible purpose is to drive them from their soil & dispossess them from their homes." A week later, observing a steamboat race on the Mississippi at New Orleans, Vinton pondered his profession: "My feelings are too catholic—scarcely less interested for the welfare of one people than for another, since we are all children of one God." He contrasted these sentiments with chauvinistic "*Patriotism!*" but reflected that he had "adopted the profession of a warrior." Displaying a growing capacity for self-deception, the captain expected "not to wage war against [the Cherokee], but to recreate my constitution [threatened by previous bouts with dysentery and malaria] by breathing the pure air of their mountains."[52]

The mountain air proved less pure than Vinton had hoped, and he applied to Scott for leave, citing his health and that of family members in Rhode Island. The general refused, upset that Vinton had taken an indirect route to meet his company in Tennessee. More seriously, Scott had "heard that, whilst in Florida, you had avowed a determination to avoid, if possible, serving in the expected campaign against the Cherokee Indians—on grounds, I suppose, of a more enlightened conscience, or a higher sense of justice than belongs to officers who have expressed no such scruple." Vinton was shocked by Scott's tone and immediately wrote to deny the allegations and allay the general's anger. Yet he had to explain the rumor, and in doing so, he laid out the ethical principles by which he tried to balance public duty with his "private sentiments as to the moral right or wrong of our Indian policy":

> Every citizen, I presume, Officer or otherwise, can entertain such [sentiments] as may seem fitting to himself, without being called into question for them. I have made it my inflexible rule, however, as I think every Officer should do, to avoid any publication of such sentiments, especially when adverse to the measures of the Government, or to suffer them in any respect to impair his usefulness as a faithful and efficient public agent while he consents to remain in the public service. This rule as a general one I presume we would all subscribe to.[53]

Vinton appealed to Scott's sense of honor and integrity by protesting the general's denial of his request for leave on the basis of rumor, "a principle so injurious to military pride and so hostile to the essential attributes of equal justice." Hard-pressed by unscrupulous Jacksonians, military officers, normally presumed to be gentlemen, would constantly be vulnerable to political slander. "Should such a principle as this prevail," Vinton asked, "what more would be wanting to consummate [the army's] downfall?" Vinton left the matter in Scott's hands: trusting the general's professional judgment and discretion, his "high martial spirit and . . . pure patriotism," the captain tendered his resignation for Scott to accept or reject, depending on whether he agreed with his subordinate's distinction between public duty and private conscience. Indeed, Vinton reminded the general of "a gentleman who had himself felt the pangs of injured innocence"—referring to a statement Scott had made to Vinton over dinner in 1828, after being passed over for the position of commanding general of the army.[54]

Vinton did not miscalculate: his independent yet subordinate integrity proved the perfect way to approach the high-spirited general. Old Fuss and Feathers responded that "I am as much pleased with [your] tone of manhood, as with the courteous terms in which it is expressed." The general explained that he had intended his letter to prompt a vindication by Vinton; having received "an explanation [so] entirely satisfactory," he refused the captain's resignation and approved his leave. Vinton returned to active duty against the Seminoles in Florida; four years later, after he became the commanding general, Scott recommended Vinton for a brevet promotion to honor his service there. Trying to restrain the growth of brevet ranks, which enabled officers to claim higher pay and allowances and often fueled disputes over command, the War Department refused. The conscientious captain gained his brevet for gallantry in the assault on Monterrey in 1846 but was killed in action during the siege of Veracruz the following March. The principles of private conscience and public subordination he laid out in 1838 are substantially those that army officers profess today.[55]

The responsibility for conveying the Cherokee westward was taken out of the army's hands when John Ross won the right to oversee the movement and its supply. Though Scott became petulant at losing control, criticizing the Cherokee's estimates of cost and transportation and their employment of Ross's brother as lead contracting agent, the decision was ultimately a relief for him and the army. Scott followed the Cherokee columns at least as far west as Nashville, but federal troops, much in demand by commanders in Florida and along the Canadian border, did not escort the Cherokee parties much beyond the initial concentration camps. (Three parties left with troop escorts before the responsibility was transferred to the Cherokee; several officers accompanied later parties as disbursing and receipting agents, and they may have had small, squad-size escorts—ten men or fewer.) Pictures of the Cherokee driven west at bayonet point convey the spirit of removal rather than its execution (although the army did drive the Cherokee to the emigration camps at bayonet point). The principal responsibility for the mass hardship and death on the Trail of Tears the following winter lay with the priorities of removal policy rather than the means employed to execute it—a significant distinction both morally and epistemologically. Nevertheless, this ethnic cleansing took the lives of perhaps 4,000 Cherokee, a fifth of the Cherokee people.[56]

Regardless of who is most to blame, Lieutenant William Tecumseh Sherman left an ironic testament to the dynamics and consequences of ethnic cleansing—indeed, of federal Indian policy since 1789—as well as a strong statement characteristic of the career officers who left records of their views. Passing through northwestern Georgia in 1844, he lamented that "if ever a curse could fall upon a people or nation for pure and unalloyed villainy towards a part of God's creatures we deserve it for not protecting the Cherokees that lately lived and hunted in peace and plenty through the hills and valleys that stretch from the base of Kennesaw Mountain. All I can say [in praise] of their successors [the white settlers] the Indians might with perfect safety challenge [by] a comparison in honesty, charity, and good faith." Sherman and his nation would reap that curse in full bloody force twenty years later, on the very spot where he stood.[57]

The army's professional subordination and autonomy were sorely tested

John Ross. (Courtesy Library of Congress, LC-USZ62-12857)

during Cherokee removal. Indeed, civil-military relations on the frontiers, often fraught with friction during the decades since 1815, approached a point of crisis between career military commanders and their civilian superiors in 1836. Nor was the crisis in civil-military relations and military professionalism at an end when Scott's court vindicated Wool. The army now faced its first real war in a generation, a conflict that many officers detested, a quagmire that would leach the army's blood and threaten its tenuous professional development for years to come.

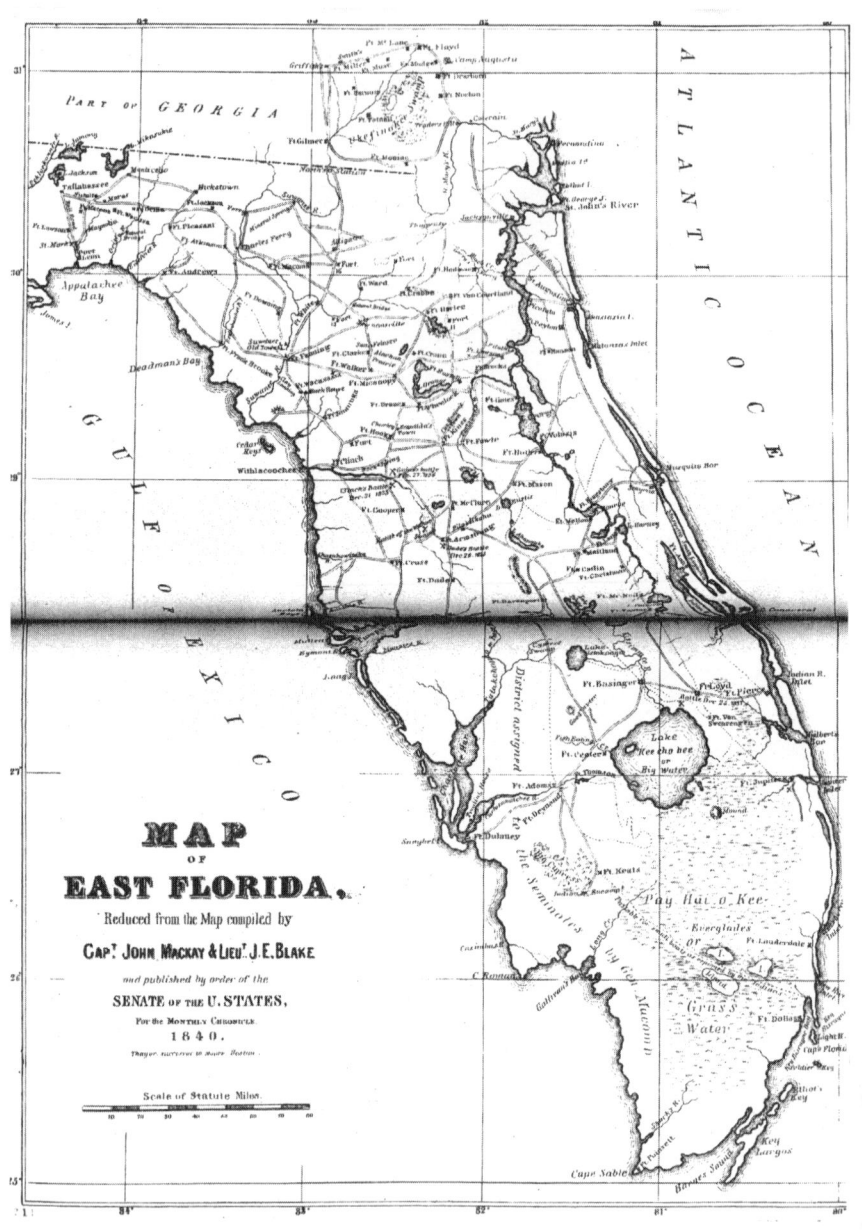

Army map of Florida. From the *Monthly Review* (1840)

6

"THIS THANKLESS... UNHOLY WAR"

The Crisis of Military Reactions to Removal in the Second Seminole War

The scene was Florida, the year 1838, the author a career army officer, his medium the army's only professional journal. The army had just won the largest battle of the war, but something continued to trouble this veteran, and he did not hesitate to express it: "The present state of affairs cannot exist much longer; the army is becoming daily more dissatisfied, and justly so; and if some hope of receiving justice . . . is not shortly held out to them, the country will find . . . that it must look elsewhere for the courage, energy, and devotion, heretofore so repeatedly displayed in contending against a foe, whose defeat brings with it neither honor nor reward."[1]

The army's law enforcement duties along the nation's borders and frontiers contributed to the decline of military bellicosity during the 1820s and 1830s, an aversion that increased during the Jacksonian era of removal. Although the officer corps generally shared civilian assumptions that white culture was superior to the Indian, many commanders felt qualms while executing removal, particularly amid an influx of disorderly, rapacious whites; for such officers, two decades of service along the frontiers had engendered as much disdain for white settlers as for Indians. Officers' distaste for this dangerous yet thankless work multiplied their distrust for the short-term consequences of territorial expansion, particularly as distinctions grew between West Pointers socialized in the allied values of nationalism and gentility, embodied in disinterested service, and rough-hewn local frontiersmen pursuing material self-interest at the expense of political and social hierarchy. Indeed, by the late 1830s, many officers had come to see themselves as the nation's policemen, and they believed their duties to the government, to say

179

nothing of good faith, integrity, and justice, required enforcing law and order among unruly whites as much as facilitating westward expansion. Yet a number of factors combined to temper the loyalties of the officer corps in the forge of adversity: resignations by officers who entered the burgeoning field of civil engineering during the boom of the mid-1830s, the difficult experiences of the Seminole War, and the economic depression of the late 1830s and early 1840s. These crises—first civilian opportunity, then its evaporation—left behind a group that offered faithful professional accountability to constitutional civilian political authority, almost regardless of the nature of the service. Although some officers resigned when they were sent to Texas in the mid-1840s, their numbers were far fewer than a decade before, and resignations during the prosperous 1850s never approached those occurring during the crisis in 1836.

Long-standing resentment toward frontier citizens turned to open disgust and potential alienation as the army became bogged down executing the removal policy in Florida after 1835. This chapter explores the sources of officers' discontent during the Second Seminole War, the forms and circumstances in which it was expressed, and the meanings of this dynamic for American civil-military relations and a more nuanced understanding of the contested terrain of U.S. policy toward the southeastern Indians during the eras of Jacksonian democracy and Manifest Destiny. Many career officers questioned the war's motivation, and virtually all who wrote on the subject questioned its desirability and the effectiveness of the methods used to fight it. Indeed, the onset of hostilities accelerated an unprecedented wave of resignations from the army that had begun during the economic boom in 1835. More than 200 officers resigned between 1835 and 1837, 117 in 1836 alone—nearly 18 percent of the entire regular army officer corps in an era when an average of only 20 officers (less than 4 percent of the corps) resigned each year. (The number of resignations exceeded 40, or 5 percent of the officer corps, in only one other year between 1820 and 1860—the peaceful boom year 1833.) Throughout the conflict, officers repeatedly maneuvered to procure leaves of absence to avoid or escape service in Florida. While in Florida they constantly quarreled with civilians, politicians, and citizen-soldiers, often to the point that, as one scholar recently suggested, many officers seemed to prefer the Seminoles to the white citizens they were assigned to defend.[2]

The distaste officers felt for this sordid, dangerous, seemingly thankless work aggravated their growing misgivings about expansion. Yet there were political, institutional, and professional limits to the disenchantment and alienation, as well as the successful socialization, of the career officer corps. Thus, professional military officers served the cause of sectional and national aggrandizement in Florida, Texas, and Mexico, but they did so as members of a bureaucratically structured and constitutionally accountable organization under national control, not as individuals or representatives of a single sectional or economic interest like slaveholding southern planters or land-hungry frontier settlers. Moreover, they did so without the ardent Indian- or Mexican-hating enthusiasm that characterized the officers of the 1810s or the civilian expansionists of the 1840s. In the final analysis, the personal material security guaranteed by stable careers in a large-scale organization led professional commanders to a dual restraint: neither avid belligerence nor countercultural alienation in their attitudes toward territorial expansion and Indian removal. Despite the dissent expressed during the Second Seminole War and along the Rio Grande, it would be grossly inaccurate to portray the officer corps as a countercultural force resisting or hindering American territorial expansion. Officers professed a wide variety of reasons for their unhappiness with the Seminole conflict, but it is clear that personal inconvenience rather than political allegiance or ideology was their primary source of aggravation. The war was not a simple matter of meeting and defeating an enemy army in a set-piece battle. Indeed, the government's policy throughout the conflict was to seek peaceful, presumably inexpensive removal by "voluntary" emigration, so the fighting and negotiating proceeded simultaneously, punctuated by a series of short-lived truces that repeatedly raised hopes of resolution only to be dashed, often by unyielding civilian demands contrary to military advice.

Guerrilla warfare in a humid, disease-ridden climate did not fit the scientific, Enlightenment ideal of conventional European warfare that military officers imbibed at West Point, nor did it fit the romantic Napoleonic ideal of glorious battle they shared with civilians. Service in the Florida swamps was much lonelier than that at established posts on the western frontier or the northern border: because of the climate, few officers brought their families with them, and there were no standardized provisions for rotating exhausted veterans out of the territory. Under these circumstances, the conflict soon came to seem "arduous, irksome, and thankless," a duty "inglorious and disagreeable" to men who sought public acclaim for risking their lives.[3] The dilemmas of removal and the frustrations of military failure were further aggravated as military commanders charged with the disposition of Afro-Seminoles and African American maroons became targets in the debate over slavery; criticism mounted from northern reformers and southern slaveholders alike, while hard-bitten veteran officers grew increasingly contemptuous of the "silly wailings" of their detractors, whatever their motive and origin. The impasse led many regulars to advocate harsher measures to achieve a decision, but this only intensified Seminole resistance and civilian condemnation, magnifying disenchantment among soldiers who felt unappreciated and misunderstood. Few officers were eager to commit genocide: tactics based on treachery and atrocity stirred moral qualms among some of their practitioners, while the rapacious greed of white frontiersmen spurred many veterans to question the value of their sacrifices to the nation as a whole.

This dialectic of estrangement ultimately led the majority of officers at all ranks to advocate peace short of the government's announced goal of total Seminole removal—the clearest alternative to an unending cycle of frustrated escalation. A remarkable number of these career officers—including several of the army's theater commanders and highly respected officers with strong Democratic ties, like Quartermaster General Jesup—recommended that the United States simply quit and leave Florida, or some substantial part of it, to the Indians, whom many had come to respect and admire as patriots. Some lesser-ranking officers advocated that the federal government withdraw from Florida altogether and even declare martial law to compel white settlers to leave—the utter antithesis of the government's removal policy and of their predecessors in the officer corps examined in *Jackson's Sword*.[4] Despite their apparent material interests as career officers, these soldiers were hardly the amoral automatons feared by Jacksonian critics of the standing army and abolitionist critics of the Seminole War. Indeed, some readers might be tempted to imagine a morally principled group roused to oppose the dominant Jacksonian ideology of racist chauvinism and expansion. This was surely the case among some soldiers, and it is certainly true that many thought the nation's honor had been tarnished by the faithlessness of Jacksonian Indian policies, but the officer corps' interest in peace was complex and ambiguous in both motive and expression. Officers' antagonism toward white frontiersmen preceded and usually outweighed any sympathy they developed for the Seminoles, and the former sentiment was present among many soldiers who felt nothing but hatred and rage for the "savage" Indian foe. The officer corps' response to white frontiersmen was much more uniform than that toward its designated opponents.

The point is not that professional soldiers were moral paragons ahead of their time but that their specific situation produced a remarkable degree of estrangement from the government and society they normally felt so accountable to. This alienation was exceptional in both degree and incidence; it was an exception to the normal pattern of civil-military relations caused by the potential inherent in a particular set of circumstances rather than a harbinger of things to come. The Seminole conflict brought previously suppressed grievances to the forefront of American civil-military relations by casting a spotlight on the contested meanings of public service and the officer corps' distinctive values as a professionalizing group, but the experience ultimately strengthened officers' commitment to serving the national government and, through it, the nation. American professional soldiers would not face another test of such intensity until 1861, when they had to choose between two nation-states, both claiming the allegiance of, and an affinity with, the professional values espoused by career officers.

In the long run, the army officer corps became a force—probably *the* crucial contingent force—for an end to the war, though by that time it was too late for the hundreds of dead Indians and soldiers and the thousands who had been deported from their homes. Faced with the unyielding determination and stubborn battlefield resistance of the Seminoles, by 1838 few officers believed the conflict was worth its cost in lives, political capital, or, perhaps most important for individuals, personal inconvenience. The collision between the corps' professional ethos of social order and the frustrating circumstances of its service in Florida led a remarkably large number of commanders to question where their duties and responsibilities as public servants lay—to ask to whom they were primarily accountable. These complaints continued throughout the conflict, and the army's semiofficial professional journal faithfully mirrored this disenchantment in the most extensive debates ever published in its pages. In the end, the war was halted before a complete victory had been won, in large part because military commanders were in charge of the negotiations and had convinced the president and the secretary of war that the value of complete removal had passed the point of diminishing returns.

Until that point was reached, a compound of political neutrality—the product of an ethos of disinterested professional subordination to the civilian political authority that represented the national interest—group cohesion, and self-interested careerism sustained the officer corps' allegiance to the policy and practice of Seminole removal. The men who resigned in 1836 and 1837—when the army was on the offensive and fighting some substantial engagements, before the conflict had clearly reached a stalemate—did so for essentially personal rather than political reasons, including health, distance from wives and family, and more attractive opportunities outside the army. (After two fruitless campaign seasons and multiple battles in 1836, they may have realized that stalemate was likely and glory unlikely, but most of those who resigned did so before the autumn offensive bogged down.) The onset of the Second Seminole War gave added impetus to all these traditional reasons for resignation, for the conflict began amidst an economic boom and a sustained political assault (however ineffectual in practice) on West Point and the army. Yet despite these attacks, despite officers' distaste for dispossessing the Indians, no officer stated that he was resigning for political or ideological

Osceola, by George Catlin. (Courtesy Library of Congress, LC-USZC4-4564)

reasons or cited them as factors in his personal or official correspondence. Thus, although officers became increasingly disenchanted with, even alienated by, the dubious justifications for the war as their tactical and operational frustration mounted, the wave of resignations crested late in 1836 and receded to all-time lows within two years, as economic opportunities dried up amidst the Panic of 1837. Indeed, the decline in resignations occurred even as the stalemate became clear and the officer corps grew more sympathetic toward the Seminoles—a phenomenon that probably peaked during the first half of 1838, two years after resignations peaked—and more disdainful of white Floridians, an attitude that reached a high in 1837 or 1838 and did not decrease significantly during the remainder of the war.[5]

What were the sources and limitations of officers' disillusionment? What sort of conflicts fostered officers' antagonism toward civilian settlers and citizen-soldiers, in contrast to their admiration for the Seminoles? How much of their discontent was with the circumstances, how much with the methods, and how much with the ends for which the war was fought? Most important, how did embittered officers, aspiring to careers and professional status, balance their feelings of disenchantment against their ethos of responsibility and their subordination to civilian political authority, and why was this unrest virtually absent during the Mexican War several years later? In other words, what did the increasingly cohesive officer corps learn from the Seminole conflict, not in the realm of tactics or strategy but in that of civil-military relations: what role did their experience play in the development of the corps' sense of accountability to civilian authority? On the whole, we shall see that the corps learned patience and remained a dutiful servant of representative government, but the road was long and frustrating, full of tensions and dilemmas.

The Second Seminole War was the longest sustained "Indian war" in U.S. history. Over nearly seven years, the army suffered 1,466 deaths, 328 of them in combat—a 14 percent mortality rate among the regular troops stationed in the theater. Of these, 107 men were killed in the "Dade Massacre," the ambush that opened the conflict in December 1835, but it was the long years of disappointment that wore the army and its officers down. The situation was all the more maddening because the army's commanders knew from the outset that the conflict would be difficult. Two months before the outbreak of hostilities, then–theater commander Duncan Clinch, colonel of the Fourth Infantry, lamented that his duties were "arduous, disagreeable, & perplexing, & without the least prospect of reaping any honor" through success. When Winfield Scott failed to catch the Seminoles the following spring, he warned that "it [will] continue . . . to be the policy of the enemy to remain scattered in small parties and to avoid a general battle—thereby protracting the war almost indefinitely."[6]

This pattern was clear to officers of all ranks and experience. Indeed, in February 1836 Lieutenant George McCall warned his father that the conflict "will prove to be a *seven years' war*," a reference to the worldwide conflict of that name that took place between 1756 and 1763. Nor could momentum easily be sustained when the army succeeded, as smaller, decentralized Seminole bands became more difficult to find and catch: three years later, another veteran expressed the consensus that chasing the Indians "to capture or give them battle [is] useless and absurd." During the war's seventh February, amid what became its final campaign, theater commander William Worth advised Scott that "every diminution of [Indian] numbers adds to the difficulty of taking the remainder." McCall, a captain since the autumn of 1836 leading troops in southern Florida six years later, labeled "*catching* Indians . . . perfectly ridiculous," asserting that Worth's policy of aggressive "pursuit" (in which McCall was cited for distinguished efforts) was "worse than useless" because the Indians became more difficult to communicate and negotiate with.[7]

Experienced veterans of all ranks repeatedly warned that it would take anywhere from 20,000 to 100,000 troops to bring the conflict to a successful conclusion. Most realized that the nation had no intention of raising such forces. Scott understood this but seriously underestimated the problem when advocating a moderate buildup in mid-1836, after his own campaign against the Seminoles had failed: "although I believe that 800 or fewer regulars might easily beat the whole of the Seminole warriors, *if they would but stand*, yet at least 3000 of the best troops are required to finish this war." A year later, longtime theater commander and quartermaster general Thomas Jesup estimated that he needed 6,000 soldiers; the entire army's authorized strength was then about 8,000. Congress and President Van Buren agreed that more troops were required, and the 1838 army law authorized filling companies to their wartime strength of 100, more than doubling the army's size. However, the number of regular troops in Florida did not peak, reaching about 5,000, until early in 1841.[8]

The logical corollary to these conclusions was a pervasive doubt that the government would ever be able to accomplish its objectives. "Should they [stand and] fight the result cannot be doubted," army surgeon Thomas Henderson asserted early in 1838, shortly after the war's largest battle had been fought at Lake Okeechobee. But the Seminoles dispersed into small bands and were usually able to avoid pitched battles. Indeed, as early as February

1836, less than three months after the war began, George McCall had predicted the Seminoles would retreat to the Big Cypress Swamp (by which he also meant the Everglades) when pressed. Moreover, no one actually knew how many Indians were in Florida at any one time, either before, during, or after the war. In February 1838 only 200 hostile warriors were said to remain; this figure would be cited like a mantra, despite the subsequent capture or surrender of several hundred warriors, until the final armistice in 1842. Less than a week after his first letter, Henderson concluded that the Seminoles remained unbeaten, lamenting that "no human mind can discern the probable termination of this war." Thomas Jesup thought similarly and had declared a truce during that week while he asked the War Department to allow the Indians to remain in southern Florida. Eighteen months later another surgeon advised readers of the *National Intelligencer*, one of the nation's principal political newspapers, that the war would take five to ten more years to finish, even with more troops and better tactics.[9]

Amid a seasonal cycle of fruitless advances and pursuits, occasionally catching an Indian or two while seizing their cattle and burning their increasingly makeshift villages and crops, every patrol and operation came to seem much the same to field commanders, fostering a continual resurgence of frustration, disillusionment, and discontent. In May 1841 Captain John Clark asserted that the conflict would go on "so long as there [are] one hundred warriors in this country"; the following February, Captain Michael Clark feared that "there appears to be no end to it." Despite the efforts of at least seven different theater commanders, including such army luminaries as Jesup, Worth, and Zachary Taylor, and despite adaptation and innovation through a series of strategic and operational approaches, the war did not end until the Tyler administration allowed the army to cease its operations, with several hundred Indians still unremoved, in June 1842. Several theater commanders had sought such an armistice since early in 1838, when a frustrated veteran concluded that "we are . . . really 'licked' and that's the long and short of it. . . . God and nature have interposed such obstacles as man cannot surmount. I for one feel humiliated at this confession and would rather have perished than live to make it—but it is true—we *cannot* [beat] these Indians."[10]

One of the most frequently mentioned reasons for officers' dissatisfaction was the humid climate and the pervasiveness of disease, which killed and incapacitated far more men than the Indians did. In July 1841, for example, 2,428 of the 5,000 regular troops in Florida were on the sick list. The following January, when Captain George McCall led patrols in the Big Cypress Swamp (where, almost six years before, he had warned the Seminoles would flee), only 200 of his regiment's 800 soldiers were physically capable of duty. McCall noted that "as the officers were broken down pretty much in the same ratio as the men," only eight officers were available for the four consolidated companies, out of twenty-four who held rank in the eight companies from which they came. Some of the established posts in the South were equally if not more deadly, in proportional terms, but the sheer scale of sickness in Florida, made more obvious by the large concentrations of troops, lent an epidemic atmosphere to army camps that triggered lassitude, demoralization, and despair among officers and enlisted men alike. The army had made some significant progress in improving the health of its soldiers during the preceding decade, and the struggle against malaria and dysentery in Florida came as a shocking setback that left officers feeling helpless. The Seminoles were well aware of the debilitating effects of the climate: Thomas Jesup reported in December 1837 that "it is extremely doubtful whether the Indians will fight—their policy is to fly, knowing as they do that on the approach of summer the climate will fight their battles for them, and drive us from the country."[11]

Jesup was not entirely correct: ten days later, 400 to 500 Indians and maroons joined together in a rearguard action against Zachary Taylor's column at Okeechobee. Jesup received his fifth war wound when a bullet shattered his glasses and tore open his cheek at Lockahatchee the following February. (The first four had come in a single battle, against the British at Lundy's Lane a generation before, when his right hand was crippled.) Nevertheless, every summer the war came to a virtual halt as toiling soldiers collapsed from heatstroke while officers fled "the inglorious field" on leaves of absence to their homes and families in the East. Many of those who could not escape became demoralized as well as debilitated: after a five-month bout of sickness, dragoon lieutenant Nathaniel Wyche Hunter considered himself "a wreck in both mind and body." Soldier-satirists whose work was published in the *Army and Navy Chronicle* mocked "the absurd idea of removing an army from pestilence," using Seminole and Mikasuki characters like "Sam Jones" to voice their bemusement at the policy that kept the army in Florida during the summer, supposedly to secure the gains made the previous winter. Parody aside, the war's duration combined with the malarial climate caused Captain George Pegram to joke uneasily with staff officer Robert Anderson (the future hero of Fort Sumter): "Think not, my dear Capt., that we shall leave nothing undone for you. There will be plenty of *game* left to hunt up, for years yet to come . . . and the bones of many [officers] will yet bleach upon these unhealthy shores, before it is ended."[12]

The danger and discomfort these soldiers experienced were not ameliorated by the consolations of family, to which many had become accustomed in their static posts before the war, even on the frontier in the trans-Mississippi West.

Between the Seminoles, the heat, and the malaria, few officers brought their wives and children to Florida, and many regarded service in the territory as "banishment." Temporary visits failed to make much difference: some wives came to St. Augustine to visit their husbands only to find that they were out of reach on duty in the field. One soldier-editorialist, realizing that the war was not going to end soon, suggested that officers bring their families south, which he claimed would make service there "comparatively easy, pleasant, and agreeable," but this was not done on any significant scale until after the war. Instead, Pegram advised Anderson to "put off your thoughts of love or marriage until this Florida war is ended," and Pegram's wife later persuaded him to resign (though doing so was rare) when he was not given a leave of absence to visit her. Unmarried officers also felt this sense of isolation in the Florida wilderness: even before the conflict, Lieutenant Morris Smith Miller, a well-connected New Yorker, lamented to his sister Sarah that "I would prefer any other post, as far as society is concerned." Like many young officers, he considered Florida "entirely out of the world." Nathaniel Hunter sounded the doleful refrain of the soldier far from home: "Here we are on Christmas night 26 miles from Tampa with the eternal forest around us and nothing but Indians and wolves . . . what a holiday it has been. I doubt that I will ever forget it."[13]

Postings to and furloughs from Florida became an arena of constant conflict between junior officers and their civil and military superiors. Here, officers in the field often had the upper hand because of the presumed shortage of men willing and qualified to take their places if they resigned. Indeed, the total size of the commissioned officer corps actually declined some 10 percent in 1836 due to resignations—an unprecedented event for the first year of a war— even though Congress increased the army by another regiment. But regiments sent to Florida remained for several years, with no relief, and transfers between regiments occurred only when both officers agreed, so field commanders routinely tried to avoid summer duty by securing leaves of absence and threatening to resign if their leaves were denied. This aggressive pursuit of self-interest, so far removed from the professional officer's avowed ethic of duty and public service, compelled the government to adjust its personnel policies by both accommodation and innovation. In an instance of the former, Lieutenant Joseph R. Smith appealed directly to the commanding general, received leave, and was then posted to recruiting duty in New York State, for a total of almost twenty months of recuperation before being sent back to Florida. In effect, personal leaves and detached duty (often in eastern population centers) provided individual officers something akin to the "dwell time" accorded to entire units today. (Enlisted soldiers served in Florida until their units left or their three- to five-year enlistments expired—usually about the same amount of time—or until they died.) Already, infantry officers who had served for years in the West, far from their families, and artillerymen who had had limited family contact as they shuttled between squatter removal, the Creek uprising, and Cherokee removal, sought leaves lasting several months to take care of personal financial business, much of which had to be done face-to-face, or because they expected not to see their families for years afterward. (Death and disability pensions were granted on a war-by-war if not case-by-case basis during the nineteenth century; no official provision was ever made for the casualties of the Second Seminole War as a group.)[14]

Dwell time aside, officers on detached service were performing essential staff duties like recruiting, administering the army supply system, supervising arsenals (the 1832 law creating an Ordnance Department allotted only fourteen officers for that duty and specifically authorized the use of artillery officers to supplement them), designing and constructing fortifications, and teaching, drilling, and socializing cadets in professional norms at West Point; regimental officers had to be assigned for these essential tasks even after Congress augmented the army staff in 1838. None of these were civil duties; the army organization, established at John C. Calhoun's initiative in 1821, consisting of five officers for each artillery company when no more than two or three were needed, was predicated on company officers doing detached duty to maintain the army as an institution. Yet individual efforts to secure leaves and detachment worked against the political interests of the officer corps as a professional body, particularly one rooted in the West Point monopoly on commissions. Officers' reluctance to serve in Florida, combined with the Academy's inability to graduate enough cadets to supply the vacancies created by resignations and the army's increase by approximately ninety officers in 1838, angered civilian policy makers and forced them to commission large numbers of lieutenants directly from civilian life for the first time in a generation. Indeed, the 117 resignations of 1836 (mostly by West Pointers, given the makeup of the officer corps as a whole) were nearly matched by 102 commissions from civilian life between 1837 and 1839, accounting for 43 percent of the commissions issued in those years. By 1840, about one in six officers had been commissioned directly from civil life during the preceding decade.[15]

Even more portentously for a corps of men pursuing the social status accorded gentility, the demonstrated ability of noncommissioned officers to lead independent detachments probably encouraged the short-lived experiment in commissioning a few of them in 1838. The exigencies of war accomplished what a decade of Jacksonian rhetoric had not, a significant indicator of the contestation of public service and professional responsibility fostered by the removal policy and the Seminole conflict. However, while most of the army's field-grade officers, and even the majority of captains, had been commissioned from civilian life between 1808 and 1818, they had developed plenty of experience and habituation to professional norms, which they supported by advocating Military Academy socialization for their subordinates and successors. Even when the demand for officers was most urgent, the majority of new commissions went to West Point graduates—Congress and the executive still considered every graduate entitled to a commission.

Neither of the innovations in commissioning was openly employed for partisan purposes, and neither altered the social or political character of the officer corps as a whole. Both were temporary expedients; by 1840, the vacant commissioned ranks had been filled, and the Van Buren administration returned to relying on Academy graduates to replace losses even before the Whig victory that fall. Neither practice was resumed by the Democrats when they regained the presidency in 1845. Virtually every succeeding case in which officers were commissioned directly from civilian life—for the permanent Regiment of Mounted Rifles (today's Third Armored Cavalry Regiment) in 1846, for the regular regiments (the Third Dragoons and the Tenth through Sixteenth Infantries) raised for the duration of the war with Mexico, or the four permanent regiments raised in 1855—was necessitated by West Point's lack of funds, faculty, and facilities to rapidly multiply its production of graduates. Yet after the war with Mexico, Academy graduates remained in the prewar regiments, forging careers through the Civil War and beyond, while the wartime regiments and their officers were disbanded. Indeed, despite numerous commissions from civilian life in 1855, the proportion of West Pointers reached its historic peak in 1860, at 75 percent of the officer corps.[16]

The most important spur to officers' disenchantment was potentially more political: the "ignominy" of a conflict that several publicly branded "this inglorious war." Such discontent proceeded from two sources: the officer corps' distaste for the "drudgery," as one lieutenant branded it, of chasing Indians, and a growing realization that they would win little public acclaim for their sacrifices, even if they succeeded. During the first six months of the war, popular fear combined with cultural romanticism to induce a wave of volunteering and glorification among newspapermen and the public, particularly in the South, but this soon died down as it became apparent that the struggle in the swamps would not come to an easy end. Jungle skirmishes did not fit the romantic image of Napoleonic battle that permeated officers' socialization and American ideals of warfare; daily patrols and convoy escorts were hardly likely to provide opportunities to win reputation and fame. Most veterans soon came to respect the Seminoles as determined fighters, but they remained disenchanted with their work because ethnocentric public opinion was quick to dismiss the Indians' valor, while many northerners and Whigs questioned the morality of the removal policy and war. The territory of Florida seemed the embodiment of "a howling wilderness, the proper abode of Owls and bats and Snakes . . . savage things all, in a savage land"—not a place worth the sacrifices of a gentleman. As a result, many officers with Napoleonic visions of grandeur reacted by belittling their assigned task: "Very little [glory] could have been gained in the best possible issue of the war, against so small and miserable a race of Indians," a disillusioned veteran remarked in the autumn of 1837. Another, watching as sweating troops swung picks and shovels to build roads and fortifications sixteen months later, anticipated tending the sick come summer and sarcastically observed that "this is warfare! glorious, noble, chivalrous warfare!"[17]

Glory and reputation were rewards that came from civilian society. Officers extolled one another's gallantry at every turn, but it was public recognition they were looking for, and this was hard to come by amid a guerrilla war against Indians in Jacksonian America. The officer corps already faced constant denunciation from critics of West Point and advocates of the volunteers and militia. In addition to necessitating appointments from civilian life, the rash of resignations in 1836 reinforced the Jacksonian belief that officers and West Point graduates were effete dandies or lazy place-seekers. Meanwhile, the cycle of friction observed elsewhere along the frontier was repeated: the army's duties in Florida brought it into frequent conflict with frontier citizens, who sought military protection without accepting the need for any sort of self-discipline or external constraint. As a result, many career soldiers considered white Floridians greedy cowards unworthy of the army's sacrifices. This attitude had developed long before the conflict, and it quickly became evident at the very top of the army hierarchy. Angered by civilian criticism after the panic that followed the Dade Massacre at the outbreak of war, Winfield Scott excoriated the planters of Florida for their "infinitely humiliating" exodus to the towns and neighboring states. "The inhabitants could see nothing but an Indian under every bush," he asserted in Order No. 48, where he contrasted their behavior with that of the army. No longer the diplomat of the Nullification Crisis, Scott warned that "no General . . . can cure a disease in the public mind, so general and so degrading, without some little effort on the part of the people themselves." Instead of adopting "the simple and manly course" of self-defense, the Floridians had thrown "execrations upon the general [Scott] who has the misfortune to command a handful of brave troops in the midst of such a population." Scott never returned to command in Florida.[18]

Civil-military strife had always been common in frontier regions, where soldiers often had to restrain white squatters and enforce regulations against liquor sales to Indians and soldiers, and historian James Denham has demonstrated that friction between soldiers and settlers in Florida antedated the war by at least a decade. Enforcing the trade and intercourse acts, which became more stringent in 1834, was particularly important to everyday peacekeeping during the year of tension just prior to the outbreak of the war (though Duncan Clinch felt compelled to permit a local judge to employ Seminoles in what was probably an exploitative relationship). Regardless of their economic interests, middle-class civilians considered army enlisted men the scum of the cities, while working-class civilians considered army officers effete aristocrats or petty tyrants. Both soldiers and officers returned the civilians' contempt in full measure, and the prolonged duration of the war intensified their acrimony. There were several brawls between enlisted soldiers and armed civilians when one group felt threatened by the other or sought revenge for earlier injuries, and regular troops were actually withdrawn from southern Georgia early in 1841 after a civilian was killed in such an incident. Indeed, Lieutenant Robert A. Wainwright told a friend that he felt compelled to take "the law into my own hands by arming two of my men, and going in pursuit" of an Alabamian who had murdered one of his soldiers: "Unless I push this matter nothing will be done. . . . So much for the laws of Alabama."[19]

Civilian malfeasance ultimately provided frustrated officers with an alternative explanation for the prolongation of the war. As early as 1837, officers up to and including Thomas Jesup—the theater commander and most prominent Democrat in the army—began to complain that whites were actually supplying the Indians and fomenting or taking advantage of the chaos to enrich themselves. Trying to understand why the war went on after two-thirds of the Seminoles had surrendered for removal to the West, Captain John Clark asserted in May 1841 that white frontiersmen "are doing more to keep [the war] up than the Indians . . . I believe that two-thirds of the recent murders have [been] committed by the whites themselves." Another disenchanted veteran wrote to the *Army and Navy Chronicle* in August 1840 with an astonishingly impolitic remedy, demonstrating the danger these clashes (like those over squatter removal in the preceding decade) posed to democratic civil-military relations: "The war can never be ended until the savages are cut off from supplies; they will be joined by whites, and I only wonder that more do not join the marauders. There never was a better theatre for land piracy than Florida is now. . . . I would advise that an appropriation be made for hemp, to hang a squad of pale-faces, who infest the country much more to its detriment than [any] troop of red-skins." He concluded with a telling reference to Andrew Jackson's drumhead court-martials in Florida nearly twenty years before: "It would have a good effect to *Ambristerize* a few of them." Indeed, this anonymous soldier's perspective was in some respects much more irresponsible, or insubordinate, than Jackson's: in 1840 the perceived traitors were American citizens the army was charged with protecting, not supposed British infiltrators stirring up resistance to U.S. expansion. But he did suggest some of the dilemmas of white man's democracy: what was the balance between majority rule and individual liberty, and who was to determine it— the individual, or the executive agents of his representatives in government?[20]

Some junior commanders took matters into their own hands and had civilians confined or whipped, while others looked on with tacit approval when soldiers under their command retaliated against civilian attackers. At least one officer who did so was able to avoid a grand jury indictment issued against him, while another successfully disclaimed responsibility for his soldiers' retaliation against a brutal sheriff. Nor did such friction end with the armistice: Major George Wright was accused of ordering a deputy federal marshal to expel the local civil officials from the environs of Tampa Bay late in 1842, apparently in execution of William Worth's order that civilians "who have made themselves obnoxious to the military" be removed from the military reservation at Fort Brooke. Worth was theater commander for the Military Department of Florida at the time he ordered the "obnoxious" civilians expelled, but it is not clear whether he instructed his subordinate to include the magistrates; Wright probably exceeded his instructions. Orders to expel civilians from military reservations (public property legally reserved for military uses, usually around forts) were not unusual but were normally limited to unlicensed liquor salesmen and petty troublemakers, not civil magistrates. Outside Florida, military violence, particularly abuse and oppression committed or sanctioned by officers, had declined precipitously after 1820, despite continual frontier tensions, suggesting the positive impact of Military Academy socialization on military subordination and accountability, as well as its limits amid the exasperation in Florida. Perhaps Worth had finally tired of civil-military diplomacy; before arriving in Florida, he had served as the principal field commander along the Niagara frontier of the Canadian border, where he tried to suppress filibustering despite the opposition of local civil officials and civilians (a clash explored in chapter 9).[21]

From the civilian side, county grand juries constantly brought in "findings" of military incompetence and abuse, and theater commanders Jesup and Taylor both sought, but were refused, relief from their posts due to civilian crit-

Duncan Clinch, Florida empire builder, older and wiser. (Courtesy Library of Congress, LC-DIG-cwpb-06860)

icism. So did Lieutenant Colonel William Davenport, who referred to the "evil" influence of territorial governor Richard Keith Call, a leading Jackson protégé who had left the army in 1822. Such antagonism came to a perversely logical conclusion in September 1842, when Lieutenant Colonel Josiah Vose, the acting theater commander, explicitly refused to execute War Department orders to resume operations against the Seminoles, blaming "vagabond classes" among the whites for any ongoing unrest. (Vose was not alone in his skepticism: at the same time, Zachary Taylor and Ethan Allen Hitchcock were displaying similar doubts about civilian rumors of a Cherokee confederation and war west of Arkansas.) The federal executive branch ultimately sympathized with the army in such conflicts, probably because it had to perform the same sort of delicate balancing act between local and national considerations, and discrediting the army would have brought discredit to the national government as a whole. Nor was the administration truly keen on reviving an interminable conflict: the War Department not only agreed with Vose—who had warned four years earlier that whites were always the aggressors in conflicts with Indians—but ordered him to protect the Seminoles against unprovoked violence by white citizens. That a lieutenant colonel prevented war testifies to the authority of comparatively junior (but highly experienced) officers, the skepticism toward white frontiersmen that Whigs shared with military commanders, and, above all, the army's autonomy—the trust executive branch officials placed in the oft-maligned standing army.[22]

As in other Indian wars, large numbers of volunteers and militia were called into service to supplement the limited contingents of regular soldiers available in the theater, and there was constant conflict between them. Floridians continually sought to mobilize additional militia and volunteers, whether out of fear or their desire for employment, for the federal government paid in increasingly scarce specie, a motive professional officers were quick to point out (and, of course, to share themselves). Federal military officers argued that the undisciplined amateurs were a hindrance to operations and an unjustifiable expense to the Treasury—Lieutenant Andrew A. Humphreys labeled them a "swarm of locusts"—and controversies over their conduct arose after every campaign as each side pilloried the other for indecisiveness or cowardice.[23]

Florida appeared free from this friction before the war. Brevet Brigadier General Duncan Clinch, who had destroyed the Negro Fort in 1816 and purchased plantations near St. Augustine and the Alachua Prairie, served in Florida for twenty years and was the senior army commander in the territory at the outbreak of the conflict. He seems to have absorbed some of the attitudes of the local settlers, sometimes disparaging their motives but responding to their concerns and repeatedly proclaiming that removal was humane and inevitable. Fearing that "the whole frontier may be laid waste by a combination of the Indians, Indian negroes," and slaves, and increasingly sure that "force will have to be used to compel" removal, Clinch sought additional troops more than a year before the war broke out. When it did, he initially praised the "gallant volunteers," reporting that Jackson's old protégé Richard Call, then a territorial militia general, had fought an engagement on December 20.[24] Nevertheless, Clinch soon became embroiled in a dispute with Call and the administration over the citizen-soldiers' performance at the Withlacoochee River on December 31, 1835, the first large-scale engagement after the Dade Massacre.

Clinch's initial report of the battle, made to the adjutant general on January 4, 1836, lauded Call's "coolness and judgment" and the conduct of the volunteer officers, as did a letter on January 8. On January 15 the brigadier advised artillery colonel Ichabod Crane that Call and his officers were "Gentlemen & good soldiers," but trouble securing local troops seemed to chill the general's empathy for his neighbors: writing to Brigadier General Joseph Hernandez of the Florida militia on January 23, Clinch deplored militia officers who chose to remain at home. (Presumably, they did so to defend their homes, a telling example of the militia's limited ability to perform any sort of coordinated action in a conflict where whites feared Indians could strike anywhere.) Politics added to Clinch's worries, as newspaper reports led him to suspect that the administration was trying to pin the responsibility for early Seminole victories on him, rather than accept their consequences during the upcoming elections. Trying to shift that blame, the brigadier soon asserted that the volunteers had shirked battle by refusing to cross the Withlacoochee, labeling them "mutinous and insubordinate" in a letter to the War Department.[25]

Call responded that Clinch had exercised insufficient caution by placing his troops in an isolated position, but this made little difference to the professionals when fifty-two of the fifty-nine wounded and all four of the dead soldiers had been regulars. The government's preparation for and response to the Seminole resistance then became an issue in the extended court of inquiry into the performances of Edmund Gaines and Winfield Scott, who commanded the second and third significant American offensives in Florida early in 1836. Scott tried to shift the spotlight from himself to the administration; former secretary of war Lewis Cass, a prominent Democrat now serving as minister to France, defended himself in the newspapers, and Clinch responded, keeping the issue in the public eye into mid-1837.[26]

Commanding general Macomb was left to try to smooth over the harsh feelings, writing to Call that August that the censure published in the War Department's annual report at the end of 1836 had been based on limited information (from Clinch). Assuring Call that there was no intention "to do injustice to the patriotic volunteers who so promptly rallied under your standard," Macomb promised to send the governor's letter explaining the volunteers' role to the newspapers so the public would understand why they were unable to cross the river. Yet career officers continued to disparage citizen-soldiers publicly and privately. Rehashing the 1836 Battle of Wahoo Swamp, Lieutenant John W. Phelps told his father that General Armstrong of the volunteers had "refused to charge the hummock [where the Seminoles were positioned] with his command because it embraced a large number of young men of the choicest families of Tennessee." The greatest of these controversies came when Zachary Taylor, exasperated by a generation of frontier diplomacy and much more opinionated than historians tend to recognize, drew the ire of Missouri senators Thomas Hart Benton and Lewis Linn for his public letter damning the inaction of that state's volunteers in a similar situation at the Battle of Okeechobee in December 1837. Their response led Taylor to demand a court of inquiry, but Secretary of War Joel Poinsett refused. Surely both men had John Wool's recent vindication in mind.[27]

Beginning with Clinch, professional officers worried that citizen-soldiers would be given what little credit could be gained in the conflict. This debate masked much harsher realities. Career officers conditioned by a generation of frontier friction believed—with good reason, given the casualty statistics—that the popularly vaunted volunteers had left the professionals to do the fighting and dying, showing "a decided preference [for] the post of safety, rather than the path of honor." Writing for sympathetic readers of the *Army and Navy Chronicle*, "Sheer Justice" contrasted the "manful" advance of the professional troops at Okeechobee with the "base" hesitation and purported flight of the volunteers. Another angry veteran told a friend that "it is said that the Genl [Taylor] put his pistol to the head of an officer of the Missipians [*sic*] and told him he would blow his brains out if he did not force his men over" a creek in support of the professionals. Surgeon Thomas Henderson summed up this critique to his comrade Benjamin King: "in *all* [the battles] the regulars have done the fighting—in *all* the irregulars have been false—leaving the honor and the loss chiefly to the army." Still another veteran proclaimed that Jesup faced more resistance from the volunteers and militia than from the Seminoles.[28]

The political dimensions of professional irritation with citizen-soldiers were evident in officers' repeated calls for an enlargement of the army in order to dispense with the volunteers and militia altogether; a bigger army would also mean faster promotions. Like most so-called Indian wars, the Seminole conflict was conducted without explicit constitutional authorization from Congress, which exercised an oversight role through the appropriations process and held special hearings on specific issues. The duration of the war enabled antislavery forces to mobilize around the issue at the same time that radical

Jacksonian Democrats were condemning West Point, the regular army, and its officer corps, and there were numerous efforts to cut military appropriations during the war years. "Sheer Justice" went further than most officers and blamed Congress's failure to expand the army for the dire consequences produced by mixing volunteers with professionals, maintaining that "the blood that has flowed so freely is to be charged to their account." Another junior correspondent to the *Army and Navy Chronicle* sneered that the Seminoles could never be subdued by "volunteers, whose lives are so valuable," reaffirming the career officer's national allegiance and utility by vilifying citizen-soldiers as "fit subjects to take up arms for political effect, at the expense of the nation."[29]

Winfield Scott proved more politic toward citizen-soldiers—many of whom were volunteers, with pretensions to gentility, from Georgia, South Carolina, Alabama, Louisiana, and Tennessee—than toward the civilian citizens of Florida. His initial order to the Army of Florida contained both praise and constraint, reminding the volunteers that "valor and patriotism alone, are not sufficient. . . . Some tactical instruction and an exact obedience to commands, are also necessary." Scott attempted to ease the bad blood by establishing a clear principle of command based on rank, rather than defaulting to professional superiority over amateurs. His "Order No. 1" emphasized that "every junior will obey any senior . . . whether the parties belong to the militia, or to the Marines and Regular Army," but many career professionals rejected this temporary insertion of men commissioned to high ranks on the basis of recruiting ability or political popularity rather than experience. They not infrequently refused orders from higher-ranking volunteers, and hard-bitten William Foster, lieutenant colonel of the Fourth Infantry, threatened to resign if compelled to serve a second time under volunteer Leigh Read.[30]

In several cases this resistance led to extended controversies and causes célèbre. Duncan Clinch serves as an example of the dangers of becoming too closely identified with a region and too closely engaged in its politics, particularly when war provided opportunities for controversy. Smarting over his clash with Governor Call during the spring of 1836, the brigadier failed to act on an order from Scott to relieve a besieged blockhouse containing fifty Florida militiamen, later citing insufficient troops as justification. Clinch may well have believed that the "siege" was a figment of jumpy civilian imaginations, or that they could break it on their own with a little initiative and aggressiveness rather than wearing down his soldiers with a difficult march. Yet the siege lasted for forty-eight days before Leigh Read led a volunteer contingent to its relief; meanwhile, Clinch had established his headquarters on his own plantation. Jackson then made Call the territorial governor and theater commander, hoping to improve coordination between citizen-soldiers and regulars. Clinch responded by resigning, one of only two field-grade officers among the 117 who did so that year (the other being former militiaman Henry Dodge, a regular for only three years, who became governor of Wisconsin), and only the fifth to resign from the combat arms regiments since 1821 (see appendix D). Clinch's economic interests then combined with resentment against Jackson to make him a Whig. He served briefly as a congressman from southeastern Georgia during the 1840s and was defeated in the 1847 gubernatorial election, virtually the only senior officer to resign and engage in electoral politics—albeit fully eight years after resigning—after 1821.[31]

Governor Call won the battle to avoid the blame for failure, but he lost the war for command. An anonymous group proclaiming themselves "Many Officers of the Army" appealed to the attorney general in opposition to Call's appointment as theater commander in November 1836, on the legal grounds that Call was a civilian with neither army nor militia rank. These career soldiers, whose petition quickly appeared—in effect, was leaked—in the *National Intelligencer*, questioned whether Call's appointment by the president without Senate confirmation was "a *lawful* order" and asked whether the governor could "be held amenable to any military tribunal" (i.e., court-martial) if accused of misconduct. With Van Buren safely elected, Jackson relieved Call from his military post within the month and replaced him with Quartermaster General Jesup. Call had offered Jesup the command in September, while the general was in Alabama leading troops against the Creeks, but Jesup, a Democrat, had chosen to serve under Call until the governor had had a chance to prove himself. Like so many of those abandoned or betrayed by the Jacksonians, Call soon became a Whig and was dismissed from the governor's office in 1839, after complaints from William Davenport and Zachary Taylor (also a Whig) provided a pretext. The army command then tried to diminish the new governor's influence by requesting that he route all his communications to its officers through the War Department, which would have been extraordinarily cumbersome.[32]

Much of the antagonism among professionals, volunteers, and civilians originated in the stereotypes they held about one another and the proper character of American soldiers. Career officers found volunteers, like the frontier population they came from, "mercenary" and self-centered, "rapacious men who come for plunder [and] negroes, and run as soon as an Indian fires a rifle at them." These officers were certain that citizen-soldiers lacked the discipline, cohesion, and moral stamina necessary for either attritional guerrilla warfare or decisive battlefield victories. Writing in the *Army and Navy Chronicle*, "Mentor" agreed with civilian critics that "from the facility with which every

The price of empire: Edmund Gaines discovers skeletons from the Dade ambush, 1836. (Courtesy Florida State Library and Archives)

industrious man in America can get a living, and become independent, the material of the ranks of the army is vastly inferior to that which compose the militia." Yet he also reminded readers of militia defeats during the War of 1812 and warned that "in time of war we should suspend the song" of militia superiority. In this representative view, volunteers lacked "military discipline and subordination"; despite their recruitment among friends and neighbors, they had "no confidence in each other or in themselves," in stark contrast to the esprit de corps and stability that professional soldiers developed over long periods of mutual service under strict discipline. "If the Missouri men had done their duty" at Okeechobee, Thomas Henderson concluded, "that battle . . . would have produced results. As it is it shews the difference between volunteers and regulars."[33]

Another disenchanted veteran lamented the nation's romance with citizen-soldiers because he thought it bred "disappointment and despair in the ranks of our own ill-fated troops." Though Scott was careful to praise the volunteers, the professional soldier's division of military labor was implicit in his disclaimer that "it would be unreasonable to call on the gallant and patriotic to volunteer . . . where nothing but hardship and suffering can be expected, unrelieved by the hope of battle and the glory consequent upon victory."

(This letter was basically a political covering action, written after his criticism of the Floridians became public.) "Quasi-Major" proposed a compromise, similar to a number of other proposals from officers at the time, to enlist native-born backwoodsmen as riflemen and light infantrymen under professional command; the frontiersmen could provide the speed, stealth, and hunting skills foreign-born enlisted men from the cities were said to lack, and the officers could inculcate the discipline necessary for sustained warfare. Indeed, this hard-bitten veteran proposed a new level of adaptation to the exigencies of Indian warfare, not only to abandon "all formal 'plans of campaign'" but to dress the new corps like the Seminoles. Nothing substantial of the sort was ever done. Ultimately, only 55 of the 30,000 volunteers and militiamen who served in the war were killed in action, versus 328 of 10,000 regulars. These numbers suggest both the power of the professional monopoly and the volunteers' willingness to forgo "hardship and suffering" to grant the officers their wish.[34]

Professional soldiers showed little inclination toward cultural primitivism and rarely referred to "noble savages," but they appreciated and acknowledged the Seminoles' patriotism, bravery, and self-sacrifice—qualities the soldiers thought they exemplified in their own society. It is not clear to what degree the officer corps' admiration for the Seminoles predated the conflict, but no evidence has been found that the officers who led the seizure of Florida during the First Seminole War in 1817 and 1818 felt anything remotely akin to empathy for the Indians. Between the wars, officers seem to have found the Seminoles quaint, the women and children becoming objects of sentiment. It was the wartime contrast between the Seminoles' persistence, patriotism, and fighting qualities and the greed, carping, and (according to officers) cowardice of white Floridians that engendered military admiration for the army's native opponents. Lauding the Seminoles' abilities also served the self-interested purpose of explaining away the army's failure to defeat the resistance. Though many professional military commanders condemned the Indians as treacherous savages, many also contrasted their opponents' "spirit of freedom and daring" with the greed and self-interest of "the vampyre-like pioneers of civilization who have been fast crowding upon them." Going a bit further than most, "Agricola" included among the Seminole's advantages "the justice of his cause, and his abiding consciousness of moral right," while "Subaltern" exemplified the value officers ascribed to patriotism by denouncing the relentless pursuit of men who would "live on roots rather than . . . desert the home of their fathers."[35]

Professional soldiers found Seminole determination both admirable and daunting. Lieutenant William Warren Chapman, a commissary officer initially ardent in his pursuit of combat, reported to his fiancée Helen Blair that he had met the captured Seminole chiefs Jumper and Powell (Osceola) in the autumn of 1837. Chapman commended Jumper, a former Red Stick Creek, as "a brave, devoted patriot, and an injured, unhappy Indian," and he exalted Osceola (also a former Creek, though too young to fight in the 1810s) as "a brave warrior and a patriot," concluding that "future generations will honor his memory." Unknown to Chapman, by 1837, the duration of Jumper's devotion exceeded the lieutenant's own life span: the chief had begun his career of resistance to American expansion as a leader in the charge at Fort Mims in 1813. Readers might discern undertones of romanticism here, but it was a military romanticism, rooted in officers' faith in the martial virtues of patriotism, courage, and duty, that encouraged conclusions with practical military implications. Firsthand experience led Chapman to believe that "anyone who has ever visited their beautiful villages . . . would not be surprised at [the Seminoles'] . . . reluctance to exchange Florida for the cold country of Arkansas," while another veteran felt certain that "they will never leave this land while there is a swamp or a palmetto in Florida. They are as devoted to die on the soil that gave them birth as ever a martyr was to die for his religion." Though probably exaggerated for effect, this sort of praise bolstered the image of the Seminoles as worthy opponents, both for officers and for the civilians they hoped to convince, and thus served to excuse the length and inconclusiveness of the war. Yet it also reflected a more accurate assessment of Seminole motives and determination than that made by the Jackson administration and civilian advocates of removal and war.[36]

Professional soldiers commonly blamed white frontiersmen and their allies and representatives among local and federal civil officials for the causes—land hunger and greed—as well as the duration of the conflict. "The source of all the failures that have happened, is to be attributed to the misrepresentations of the [local] Governmental agents," asserted Vermont-born Lieutenant John Phelps, a principled critic of the removal policy who recognized that the Seminoles had been tricked into signing the treaty of emigration "by the fawning machinations of unprincipled agents." The lieutenant was echoed by his conservative counterpart George McCall, an experienced Florida hand, as well as humanitarian Captain Ethan Allen Hitchcock. Indeed, Phelps's only error was in thinking that the government might have cared about the probity of its civilian diplomats and agents: at this point (July 1837), he continued to distinguish between the president and the War Department and their agents, perhaps unable to see or accept that those agents faithfully pursued their masters' objectives. Nor could professional military leaders do much to stop the fraudulent claims commonly put forward by frontier citizens, given military subordination to civilian control and the diffusion of political authority under federalism. Echoing decades of officer correspondence, one commander lamented to Captain Samuel P. Heintzelman in August 1840 that "the iniquity of the people in this country is a frightful thing and indeed their code of morals is sunk [extremely] low." As close to alienation as any officer ever came, Nathaniel Wyche Hunter privately reviled the removal treaty as "a compact begot in fraud" by "a government that incites you to the commission of a crime."[37]

Nor did these conclusions take long to form. Less than a year after the conflict began, Connecticut-born Lieutenant J. K. F. Mansfield, nephew of former West Point professor Jared Mansfield, echoed Hunter's disenchantment in a letter to his brother Edward, a Military Academy graduate and professor of constitutional law at the College of Cincinnati: "I hope they will require no engineers . . . it would be a satisfaction to risk my life where honor is to be gained [but] not in an unjust war on a few miserable savages, goaded to the fighting point with a view to drive them from soil no rational man would live upon. Alas! my country, I blush for your principles of freedom, your justice and your honor! Heaven will reward thee according to thy deserts." Mansfield went on to condemn "this money making, money loving, hypocritical community"—the United States—envisaging the consequences of its moral degeneracy in a nightmare of civil war, "the glitter of thousands of bayonets in deadly strife [—] Father against son & brother against brother." If we shift the picture from Florida to Texas and the spoils of the war with Mexico, we recognize the accuracy of his critique of racialist territorial expansion. Mansfield served as chief engineer for Zachary Taylor in northern Mexico and as inspector general of the army in the 1850s; he was mortally wounded in his first field command, as a major general leading the U.S. Twelfth Corps into the East Woods at Antietam twenty-six years later.[38]

Writing to the *Charleston Courier* early in 1838, "An Officer of the 4th Artillery," possibly Phelps, extolled the Seminoles' "integrity" and adherence to the treaties made in the 1820s. The artillerist damned the war as "our great injustice," ominously invoking Christianity and republicanism against it: "Can any Christian in this Republic . . . still pray for the continuance of blessings[?] . . . Can a *people* who boast the freest institutions, so far forget themselves as to assume the blackest attributes of tyranny[?] . . . Not with impunity. An equilibrium will ever be maintained in the moral world as well as in the physical—retribution will inevitably follow dereliction." He then denounced the removal policy in general, comparing its "crowding and condensing [of] disaffected Indian tribes" in the West to "congesting thunderous clouds" that would "[lavish] their fury on the earth" and bring desolation to "our now happy country." Phelps denied penning this letter, but he shared its sentiments: after the Mexican War he refused an honorary promotion to captain for gallantry at Contreras and Churubusco, and he later became an abolitionist, resigning the day John Brown was sentenced to death in 1859. Recommissioned as a brigadier general of volunteers early in the Civil War, he resigned a second time in August 1862, after being refused permission to enlist escaped slaves in Louisiana.[39]

Phelps was an unusually reflective commander, and such apocalyptic imagery was rare, regardless of sectional origin, among the pragmatic, conservative public servants of the career officer corps. Apart from socially and economically focused stereotypes about genteel southerners and greedy Yankees, between the time of the Nullification Crisis and the annexation of Texas, their sectionally related political comments were limited to occasionally deploring abolitionism as a threat to the Union. Products of extensive socialization in a personal style modeled on the image of the English gentleman, most career officers were unreflective, unimaginative, and nonideological in temperament. Exemplifying the values of disinterestedness, honor, and order explored in previous chapters, Lieutenant William Wall agreed with the war's detractors that the dispossession of the Seminoles "will be injustice in our view of it, and will result from selfishness and depravity." Nevertheless, like many officers, he placed the origins of the removal policy in the context of a cultural determinism that assumed the ultimate outcome of Indian-white conflict was inevitable. "Who will call to account the majestic oak because his lofty and extended limbs prevent the mature growth of other trees in the forest," Wall asked, illustrating the ease with which many officers could reconcile doubts and duty without worrying deeply about their moral implications.[40]

Northern origins seem to account for much of the unease (however rare among officers) felt by men like Phelps and Ethan Allen Hitchcock, both born in Vermont; Mansfield of Connecticut; and New Yorker John Wool. In keeping with the officer corps' general lack of religiosity, evangelical religion does not seem to have been a prominent source of unease or dissent among these men, much less the corps as a whole, although it was a potent influence on some individuals, like Phelps. Southern officers were not united in favor of the war, however. Nathaniel Hunter was a Georgian, and Thomas Jesup and Zachary Taylor were Virginia-born Kentuckians and substantial planters and slaveholders, men for whom inner moral qualms were apparently less influential than their sense of mission, duty, and honor (personal and professional) as military commanders representing the nation in the midst of complex, often exasperating circumstances. After several years, qualms about the war began to have an effect among officers at both the individual and the policy-making levels. A soldier of the Fourth Artillery called on "the people" to "crush" the war by instructing their representatives "not to make the necessary appropriation" to pay for military operations, while other writers urged Congress to investigate and compel negotiations. Other officers made individual moral decisions to reject elements of the conduct of the war: Nathaniel Hunter observed in his diary that he had decided to ignore an order to stop taking prisoners, which he termed "wringing [my] hands in innocent blood." (The origins and scope of this order are unclear from Hunter's entry; there was no theater-wide policy to this effect, but his regimental commander, William S. Harney, advocated such measures and may have given such an order informally.)[41]

Nor was this sort of moral unease confined to company commanders in the field. Army Surgeon General Thomas Lawson, a medical doctor who had commanded volunteer soldiers against the Seminoles in the field during Scott's 1836 campaign, wrote to subordinate Benjamin King a year later to advocate "acknowledging their independence, and yielding up to them the country for which they have so gallantly and so successfully fought, and so nobly won. It will be manifest then that the Almighty is in their favor, and God's will should be done." Frustrated by his difficult mission and civilian criticism, Thomas Jesup asked to be relieved from command in June 1837, concluding that only extermination (which he implicitly rejected) would displace the Seminoles from their homeland. His request was refused on the grounds that the administration wanted to retain his energy and experience and, no doubt, to avoid a new occasion for attacks on its policy and competence. At the opposite end of the spectrum from the officer of the Fourth Artillery, William Tecumseh Sherman supported William Henry Harrison in the 1840 election in the hope that he would do "something decisive." Sherman believed that "a war of extermination" was "the most certain and economical method." But even the "white Tecumseh" could change his views: remember his lament for the fate of the Cherokee at Kennesaw Mountain four years later.[42]

Military commanders at all ranks began recommending peace after less than two years of war, and their proposals often involved restraining whites as much as Indians. When Congress debated a strategy of colonization by armed settlers in 1839, "Mentor" acknowledged the "respectability" of Middle Florida planters, whom he considered "most anxious for the termination of this war," but he advised readers of the *Army and Navy Chronicle* that the conflict would end much sooner if all whites left East Florida. Unable and perhaps unwilling to overcome Seminole "detestation" and "contempt" for settlers, either as soldiers or citizens, "Mentor" preferred to withdraw from a large portion of Florida, most of it outside the land reserved to the Seminoles in the Treaty of Moultrie Creek in 1823, rather than defend the citizens he supposedly served. Whether he was playing divide and conquer or making a rare positive distinction among white Floridians, this professional soldier's praise for the elites of Middle Florida (the region from the Suwannee River west to Pensacola) demonstrates how career officers identified social and moral status ("respectability") with the policy outcomes they preferred.[43]

More often, disillusioned veterans simply recommended an armistice and abandonment of removal from Florida: "drop that feature in the arrangement that requires their emigration; that done they will instantly make a treaty, and abide by it," one accurately observed five years before that action was taken. But officers had half a century of experience as evidence that treaties alone would not halt white immigration or pressure on the Seminoles. Thus, some actually proposed to reverse the targets of national coercion by seeking martial law to remove white frontiersmen and their property from areas that could not be defended from Indian attack. Indeed, the professional soldier's desire for social discipline led some to expect that this extreme, probably unconstitutional version of squatter removal would cause the Indians to stop providing refuge to "the vagabond white man," whom they increasingly blamed for aggravating the conflict. Thomas Jesup took a step in that direction, probably not authorized by the president, by warning whites that he would declare martial law and deport them from the territory if they usurped federal authority by seizing Seminoles as criminals or debtors. In April 1837 his Order No. 79 actually forbade white civilians to enter Florida south of the Hillsborough River, but their outrage compelled him to modify and effectively rescind the order. Presumably, Jesup would have justified both measures as emergency war powers employed in a federal territory, even though Florida had a civilian governor and legislature. Given Jesup's Democratic affiliations, these statements are powerful testaments to his frustration and anger at the stalemate in Florida.[44]

Convinced that immediate removal had no purpose worth its cost, Jesup first sought a truce and negotiations at the request of his senior subordinates, Abraham Eustis and David Twiggs, early in February 1837, but the tenuous peace agreement he fashioned fell through because of the resistance of Seminole hard-liners, including the Afro-Indians and maroons, who feared reenslavement if they surrendered. A year later, pressed by his senior officers after the major battles of Okeechobee and Lockahatchee—in which the Seminole force was about equally divided between Indians and blacks—the general declared another truce and wrote directly to the president, bypassing the secretary of war, through whom communications were normally routed. Jesup advised permitting the Seminoles to remain in Florida for the time being: "we exhibit in our present contest, the first instance, perhaps since the commencement of authentic history, of a nation employing an army to explore a country (for we can do little more than explore it), or attempting to remove a band of savages from one unexplored wilderness to another."[45]

This was also commanding general Macomb's plan, undertaken at the recommendation of theater field commander Zachary Taylor and his council of officers, when he was dispatched to Florida two years later to seek a peace treaty at congressional request. Brevet Brigadier General Walker Armistead, the least experienced of the theater commanders, deviated from Taylor's de facto de-escalation by pressing a more aggressive campaign in 1841, but his senior field commander, the normally forceful William Worth, seems to have avoided acting in earnest and reportedly "could not tolerate the idea." Early the following year, Major Ethan Allen Hitchcock, who served intermittently as a special agent under the commissioner of Indian affairs from 1837 to 1842, wrote directly to Secretary of War Spencer counseling peace, certain that "sooner or later the government would be compelled" to take that step. Hitchcock claimed that "several officers rejoiced in the prospect of my being able to convince the Secretary . . . that a pacific policy was the only one that could succeed in Florida."[46]

Worth switched to a policy of aggressive patrolling and relentless pursuit after he assumed the theater command, before finally returning to negotiations and declaring victory a year later. Though veteran commanders like Thomas Childs and George McCall pushed hard enough to convince many Seminoles to surrender for removal, other company officers were much less keen. Less than a year out of West Point, Lieutenant Alfred Sully was proud that the Second Infantry had driven Seminole war leader Halleck Tustenugee to surrender, but he told his father that he had torn up a letter about Creek depredations in West Florida, "fearing that Col. Worth might think it necessary for us to scout again." Veteran Captain William McClintock had long since lost patience for delicate strategies of coercive diplomacy. Looking forward to Worth's offensive in the early summer of 1841, McClintock completely inverted the nation's objectives and the army's purpose, warning influential Captain Robert Anderson that "the white flag" was the army's "most successful . . . commander." McCall agreed: rejoicing at peace the following spring, he concluded that negotiations "have really done more to bring [the war] to a close than by all the battles fought." Sadly, former secretary of war Poinsett came to much the same conclusion, only months after he left office.[47]

7
"THE DUTY OF A SOLDIER TO OBEY"
Disenchantment, Dissent, and the Crucible of Professional Accountability in the Second Seminole War

The army's reactions to the Seminole War proceeded from a pervasive, unusually intense feeling of unappreciated sacrifice and isolation. "How little the country knows of the army when they prate about the danger of increasing our force. The intelligence, patriotism, and valour of our officers is not exceeded by any class of citizens in the republic—and this war tries those qualities severely," surgeon Thomas Henderson remarked in February 1838. Lack of civilian appreciation for the army's hardships combined with racism toward Indians and maroons (armed fugitives from slavery) to sour officers even further, fostering disillusionment toward their antagonists and cynicism toward national policy and the war. "When they gain a victory it is over a gang of negroes and savages, the whole of whom are not worth a finger of such a man as Thompson" (lieutenant colonel of the Sixth Infantry, killed in the battle at Okeechobee), Henderson lamented. Fellow surgeon Jacob Rhett Motte ridiculed "the abusive comments of some civilians, who reclining on cushioned chairs in their comfortable and secure homes vomited forth reproaches, sneers, and condemnation, wantonly assailing the characters of those who, alienated from home and kindred and all the comforts of life, were compelled to remain in this inglorious war." "They give us but little credit at the north for our sufferings and privations here; no one, out of Florida, knows what they are," asserted another bitter veteran, calling for the removal of his regiment in August 1840: "We are worn out and disheartened . . . a regiment of victims." A third surgeon publicly rebuked "citizens who sit at home and smoke their cigars in the quiet enjoyment of ease and luxury, who have never *seen* the Territory of Florida, and are *perfectly* ignorant of the difficulties which embarrass

Thomas Sidney Jesup, strategist, tactician, and logistician, later in life. (Courtesy Army Quartermaster Museum, Fort Lee)

our military operations on every side." His broadside, published in the *National Intelligencer* for all politically attuned readers to see, proclaimed that "the army does not need the *advice of citizens* to teach it *how* to do this duty."[1]

This vitriol, eventually focused on motives and goals as well as methods and experience, was directed at superior officers and national politicians as well as local and northern civilians. Nathaniel Hunter thought chasing the Indians in large bodies was "damned foolishness" and worried that his immediate superior was recklessly exposing the troops to ambush, confiding in his diary that "General Armistead assumes command . . . to the surprise of all, the mortification of many, and the distrust of not a few. What does the grey-bearded and imbecile dotard imagine he can do?" (Armistead was one of the first graduates of West Point, class of 1803, and had not held an independent frontier or field command since the War of 1812. His selection was probably a matter of seniority and an absence of volunteers—essentially the product of inertia when Taylor left command.) Hunter, a Georgian who felt great qualms over the removal policy, considered the army's work "the vilest machinations man or demon could invent" and compared its executors to Lady Macbeth. Indeed, the captain was later suspected of authoring an antiwar petition circulated in his home state, though like other dissenters, he remained in uniform.[2]

As Hunter's words suggest, military officers ultimately blamed civilian politicians, their superiors under the Constitution, for the war. Doing so was not inaccurate: the civilian national security strategy of coerced, often duplicitous Indian removal had placed a conventionally oriented army, whose constabulary expertise was in diplomacy rather than guerrilla warfare, in a difficult tactical and operational situation without substantial reinforcement. Civilian political leaders then condemned the army at every turn. Hence, far higher up the military chain of command, and only months after the war began, theater commander Duncan Clinch moved toward a war of words and resignation with a letter to Florida territorial governor and former secretary of war John Eaton, one of President Jackson's favorites, vowing that "I will not permit the political aspirants of the day to use my case for their own aggrandizement, without making some little struggle." But how much could the officer corps struggle without imperiling its professional subordination and the monopoly on command civilian society gave in return?[3]

Elsewhere, an anonymous missive to the *Army and Navy Chronicle* scorned Senator Linn of Missouri as "an intoxicated man or a falsifier" for his speeches against Zachary Taylor in 1838, while "Sheer Justice" pilloried "those [meaning Floridians and militiamen] who have not possessed the courage to face boldly and openly the enemies of their common country." Writing from Fort Brooke in July 1840, "Canard" faulted the government as a whole, which "followed on, step by step, its own views until lives after lives have been lost, and the country disgraced." This bitter veteran concluded that the army was being "sacrificed by bad management. . . . This war has, with all its tragic scenes, been a farce from the beginning." Yet senior commanders like Clinch, trying to defend their individual reputations as much as that of the army, did not necessarily win much sympathy among their subordinates, who probably felt the generals' disputes muddied the army's reputation and threatened its political insulation. This was especially true when the egotistical generals quarreled among themselves. In the autumn of 1836, with all the army's senior generals embroiled in one public controversy or another, Lieutenant J. K. F. Mansfield wrote that "Scott & Jesup are pretty lightly spoken of & in justice too. Jesup by his letter to Blair [referring to an attack on Scott published in Francis Preston Blair's *Washington Globe*, in which Jesup reproached his superior for delays during the Creek War that summer] has made himself odious as a man." Mansfield may have been politically biased; in 1852 his brother Edward wrote a promotional biography for Scott's presidential campaign. Yet the lieutenant also condemned Edmund Gaines and a third, unidentified general, probably Armistead.[4]

Unable, and probably unwilling, to firmly ally with any one sector of civilian opinion to change policy, disenchanted professional soldiers identified their sullied honor with that of the nation as a whole in their appeals for peace. One supporter of commanding general Macomb's peace plan asked readers of the *Army and Navy Chronicle* "what honor is there to be gained by the extermination of a nation of aboriginal inhabitants, a brave but simple people, who, if they had been treated with less cruelty and injustice by their immediate neighbors, might before this, have ceased to be their deadly foes, and would probably have left the country of their forefathers . . . peaceably yielding [it] to the harpies?" While that officer certainly underestimated Seminole attachment to Florida, he reflected the values of the officer corps by tacitly appealing to the unity of national honor against the selfish materialism of frontier civilians. Another bitter veteran complained that the conflict had led his comrades to feel "alienated from home, kindred, and friends . . . compelled to remain in this inglorious war, defending a domain which can never be densely populated, and protecting some . . . who would suffer much in comparison with the savages." "A Subaltern" exemplified this sentiment by proclaiming, "The war is a humbug . . . there is but one thing in which it at all resembles a war, and that is, in its loathsomeness. In a regular war, there is something noble, something inspiring. . . . It makes me sick to read the accounts of [this war]. . . . No wonder the army should have become disgusted with this thankless . . . unholy war."[5]

It should come as no surprise that many officers sought to avoid service in Florida. Lacking any regular system for rotating units in and out of Florida, many frustrated veterans wrote to the *Army and Navy Chronicle* to decry favoritism and press their regiments' case for relief. Refused relief himself, Thomas Jesup provoked cries of outrage when he censured the junior officer corps during the summer of 1837, growling that "the spirit of the service is gone . . . when officers of respectable standing can be found ready to abandon the high and honorable duties of their profession to become *schoolmasters* at West Point." (Jesup's words suggest the exasperation the Seminoles had caused, since he relied heavily on the Academy for trained subordinates in his permanent post as quartermaster general.) William Wall expressed a sentiment more common among the army's company officers: "How happy I would be to surrender the command of Company D 3d Artillery to some friend on such a glorious campaign," he vowed. Wall had missed the Creek War—where Jesup proved such an outstanding success—in the summer of 1836 and remarked that an alert was "the nearest approximation that I have made towards being involved in an Indian battle—may I never be more near!" During the spring of 1838, Lieutenant Joseph Smith looked forward to promotion and a transfer "anywhere, so [long as] I get out of Florida this summer."[6]

Individual desire spurred collective eagerness for an end to the conflict. "I trust that the war will soon be closed, for I am heartily sick of this country," grumbled Lieutenant Robert Wainwright, who was embroiled in a civil-military dispute over the murder of one of his men in Alabama during the spring of 1837. (Wainwright was detailed to teach at the Military Academy shortly thereafter, defusing the controversy; his reassignment was the case that aroused Jesup's ire.) Like many of his comrades, Major Sylvester Churchill was "cheered with the favorable prospects of speedy peace" during Jesup's negotiations in early 1837; once they failed, he could only give thanks for "life, health and for *exit* from Florida" when granted leave in 1839. After two years of service commanding several expeditions in Florida, sometimes clashing with volunteers under his command, brevet Brigadier General Abraham Eustis vowed that "I shall feel devoutly thankful, when I can be permitted to turn my back upon this hateful territory." Eustis had temporarily acted as theater commander in 1836, but he was getting on in age and warned the adjutant general that he did not want the post any longer than was necessary; he secured a transfer to the Canadian border early in 1839.[7]

None of these men were green lieutenants or career malcontents: Eustis entered the army in 1808 and had commanded the Artillery School for most of its decade-long existence, while Churchill was appointed inspector general for the entire army in 1841. That spring, George Pegram inferred that most of his fellow veterans would "calculate on getting out in the summer. There will be [much] scrambling for leaves of absence." The army command reacted by prohibiting furloughs from Florida, a measure that filled William McClintock with foreboding: "This prohibition . . . seems to squint at a summer campaign. . . . The experience of the last five years is lost with the old Administration . . . much use is made of the words *vigour* and *energy*, in a manner that convinces me they don't know the meaning of those words as applied to Florida.... Our sick list next fall, will be sure to furnish them a definition."[8]

Another focal point for officers' qualms and frustration—one specific to the Seminole Wars rather than Indian relations in general or conflicts after the Civil War—was the army's struggle with white settlers and Creek Indian allies over slaves, former slaves, and their descendants captured from among the Seminoles. Slaveholding was so central to plantation agriculture and white expectations for prosperity in Florida that a committee of prominent local whites warned Jesup and the War Department that reenslaving escapees was "an object of scarcely less moment than that of peace in the country." No war had been declared in Florida, nor did white racial attitudes provide any protection to Seminole prisoners, much less black ones. White speculators scrambled to purchase as many captured maroons and Afro-Seminoles as possible, along with any other African Americans who could be swept up in the wide net these labels provided. The Creeks who served under the Americans in Florida in 1836 and 1837, like those who did so against the Negro Fort, Bowlegs Town, and other maroon communities a generation before, received quasi-official promises that they could seize and enslave Seminole blacks or maroons taken captive, supposedly because they had once been slaves of the Creeks. Yet, while the army had long provided a buttress to southern slavery, the physical repression of slave rebellions, rumored or real, was normally carried out by local volunteers and militia, and most national military officers viewed this role as incidental or a last resort, rather than an integral part of their responsibility for national security. They shared the racial prejudices of most white Americans but did not go to great lengths to expound an ideology of racial control, much less a national military mission to do so.[9]

The struggle for possession of the former slaves captured in Florida became one of the least noted but most profound tests of the army's professional autonomy. In this case, officers' professional discretion supported accountability to the core goals of national policy (removing the Seminoles), contrary to specific War Department orders supporting individual property claims. Much like Gaines and Jackson twenty years before, commanders like Jesup soon realized that the Afro-Seminoles were among "the most active and determined" of their opponents, and in March 1837 the general declared that the conflict was actually "a negro, not an Indian war." This assessment led to a variety of policy recommendations, however. Several officers, including Jesup, drew analogies between the Seminole conflict and maroon wars in the Caribbean in letters to the *Army and Navy Chronicle*, citing the difficulty of earlier conflicts in Jamaica as justification for the duration of the American war. In the mouths of men like Jackson or Gaines, these words had expressed the interest of the planter class in obliterating maroon resistance from the southern borderlands. Yet Jesup, a substantial slaveholder with several plantations in Kentucky, gradually shifted his emphasis from warning his civilian peers, in order to secure further support for the war, to accomplishing his assigned task (Seminole removal) by neutralizing the focal points of Seminole opposition, ultimately without regard for the property rights of southern civilians. Reflecting the professional officer's objectivity and subordination to national policy, he sacrificed the interests of individual slaveholders in order to excise the maroon threat to the sectional system of slavery and defeat the Seminoles, whose emigration would eliminate a tempting refuge for slaves from Florida, Georgia, and Alabama. Jesup manipulated the theme of maroonage to secure more volunteers from southern governors, but he had no desire to launch a slave hunt through Florida. "I will not make negro-catchers of the army," the Kentucky planter told Secretary of War Poinsett in May 1837.[10]

Disenchanted veterans felt little sympathy for the selfish demands of planters and speculators amidst the more pressing exigencies of war, and the army hierarchy pursued a de facto policy of refusing these supposed "property rights," conveying any blacks found among the Seminoles to the West along with the Indians as de facto prisoners of war. Jesup's initial agreement with the Seminoles in March 1837 allowed blacks to emigrate with them, and his General Order No. 79, forbidding civilian movement south of the Hillsborough River, was largely intended to end the "interference of unprincipled white men with the Negroe property of the Seminoles." This language may indicate that Jesup still had difficulty envisioning the maroons as individuals distinct from their supposed masters; more probably, he realized that phrasing the issue in this manner would be the easiest way to deflect white criticism. Though Jesup doubted whites' legal authority to demand the return of escapees living among the Seminoles, criticism from Florida whites—who saw recently escaped slaves and those seized or rescued by the Indians slipping away under cover of an assumed ethnicity—quickly pressured the general into revising the truce to restrict this provision to blacks present among the Seminoles before the war. Jesup was immediately rebuked by antislavery forces in the North; more important, Osceola and a large proportion of the Seminoles who had turned themselves in for removal returned to the wilds and resumed the war. This defeat led Jesup to warn the War Department that the blacks and Indians were "rapidly approximating—they are identified in interests and feelings."[11]

That summer, Jesup offered captured blacks to his troops—both volunteer and regular—as booty, but he quickly abandoned that initiative when it became clear he was alienating Afro-Seminoles who might otherwise surrender themselves for emigration to escape white demands. Frustrated and stung by criticism from all sides, the Kentuckian's distaste for the slavers returned to the fore. Jesup later wrote that "I was apprised of the [War Department's] order to surrender the negroes, but protested against the measure and probably had some influence in preventing it from being carried out." This distaste certainly did not distract Jesup from his duty to carry out the removal policy, and he suggested several measures to divide the African and Indian elements of the Seminole resistance, including colonizing the Afro-Seminoles in Africa. Indeed, Jesup wanted to ship the Afro-Seminoles west even if the Indians remained in Florida, hoping to end black support for the Indians and remove the magnet for further flight, maroonage, and civilian criticism of the army. In his truce proposal of February 1838, Jesup offered the African Indians freedom so long as they turned themselves in for deportation westward, a tactic that successfully divided the Seminoles along ethnoracial lines and secured the surrender and emigration of most of the blacks among them during the following year.[12]

Indeed, black Seminoles routinely sought "freedom papers" based on Jesup's promises and agreements, and they used these as evidence of their free status after arriving in the Oklahoma region. Though he was originally motivated by self-interest, Jesup's sense of honor would not allow him to sanction the maroons' reenslavement once they were out of sight in the West. Years after he left Florida, the general continued to follow the fortunes of those he had deported, writing in 1844 to President Tyler and Secretary of War William Wilkins that he had pledged that the blacks would not be sold to whites: "I cannot remain passive and witness the illegal interference with the rights of these people. . . . I earnestly hope that the Executive will not permit the national faith . . . to be violated . . . and that measures [will] be taken to recover all who have been separated from their families and sold." Jesup's language, and that of so many of the junior officers discussed in this and the preceding chapters, was remarkably like that of William Worth, Winfield Scott, and their subordinates on the Canadian border (see chapters 8 and 9). National honor and the rule of national law were their central values, obligations they identified with military duty and tried to embody in their conduct. Like John Wool in the Cherokee country or commanders like Henry Atkinson and Stephen W. Kearny along the western frontier, Jesup was neither a humanitarian reformer nor a crypto-abolitionist; he was a genteel but hardheaded pragmatist who valued a stable hierarchical order and upheld a distinctive professional conception of personal, institutional, and national honor. Given the perceived class origins and brutal reputations of slave catchers and the opprobrium of northern elites, hunting escaped slaves was even less glorious than chasing Indians; if giving blacks their freedom from thankless, grasping civilians meant shortening the war, achieving the government's objectives, and reducing the army's sacrifices, Jesup would not hesitate to do so.[13]

Jesup's successors—a fellow Kentuckian, a Virginian, and a New Yorker—along with many of their subordinates, seemed to share these attitudes, although they are evident only in passing references outside the correspondence of senior commanders. Like other officers, Major Sylvester Churchill—who, as acting inspector general, was extensively involved in providing logistical support for prisoners and emigrant Indians—consistently referred to captured African Americans as "negro prisoners" (their military, though racially tinged, status) rather than "escaped slaves" (their civil status). Upon taking Jesup's place, Zachary Taylor, a slaveholder with plantations in Louisiana, declared to the adjutant general that he would do nothing to reduce the Afro-Seminoles "from a comparative state of freedom to that of slavery." Taylor refused to separate Indians and blacks and effectively left the handling of policy toward them in the hands of a junior subordinate, who refused to turn over seventy black captives despite a lawsuit by their putative owner. The War Department supported the civilian plaintiff, but generals Edmund Gaines and Matthew Arbuckle—who, like Jesup and Taylor, were planters and slaveholders themselves—avoided executing the order to return the blacks to the claimants, and that group arrived safely in Arkansas. Indeed, Gaines felt so certain that the claim was fraudulent that he made an unsuccessful motion to formally declare the Afro-Seminoles legal prisoners of war under army jurisdiction in a civilian court. (Readers of *Jackson's Sword* will remember Gaines's eagerness to destroy the "Negro Fort" in Florida a generation before.) Faced with consistent military recalcitrance extending to the highest levels of the army, the civilian executive branch effectively backed down from its pro-slavery policy. When the Whigs took office in March 1841, the new secretary of war ordered the Seminole emigrants and their military captors to surrender all runaways to the civil authorities for return to claimants, *unless* doing so would inhibit the successful prosecution of the removal policy. This is precisely how army officers continued to interpret the situation, rendering the order void. Given the previous four years, it is difficult to see how the War Department could have expected anything else.[14]

Apart from Jesup, Gaines, and perhaps Taylor—three slaveholding sons of the Upper South—a bureaucratic desire to avoid responsibility for the disposition of blacks captured among the Seminoles appears to have been the most common response among senior officers. Not until August 1841 did new theater commander William Worth, a New Yorker and a Whig known for taking the most direct approach to problem solving, finally establish a formal mili-

"Soldiers in Field Dress, Florida, 1839," by H. Charles McBarron (Courtesy Army Art Collection)

tary policy for handling the Afro-Seminoles, among whom he included prewar maroons and slaves who had fled or been seized during the war. Anticipating Abraham Lincoln, Worth explicitly identified the blacks as prisoners of war subject to military jurisdiction, while he cut the Gordian knot of conflicting claims by announcing that he would guarantee the Indians possession of all blacks found among them, regardless of the "mode or time" of their joining the Seminoles. White claimants would be compensated after a board of officers determined the value of their losses, placing the officer corps at the heart of this mediated emancipation, but the extent to which this occurred remains unclear. Meanwhile, officers charged with settling the Seminoles in Oklahoma continued the policies of Jesup and his successors. In 1840 Matthew Arbuckle pressured the Creeks not to act as slave catchers for white claimants; three years later Taylor ordered a subordinate not to surrender one of the blacks to Creek claimants, on the grounds that Jesup's promises remained binding, presumably as de facto treaties made by wartime executive authority. The following year Taylor warned a prominent Creek that the army would arrest and detain him if he seized blacks from among the Seminoles, and he pressured the Creek leader into releasing those he had already seized.[15]

The army incrementally crafted an independent policy of de facto emancipation, a nearly unique exception to federal government support for slavery prior to the Civil War. Ironically, doing so removed, and was intended to remove, a larger threat to the system of slavery. Officers did not do so out of humanitarian or abolitionist sympathies. They emancipated hundreds of former slaves to achieve the objective set for them by the president, who proved content to allow them to do so in the way they thought best. In the most contentious issue in American politics, a president elected largely by the slaveholding states, and a slaveholding president from Virginia, allowed slaveholding military commanders to free slaves, contrary to the orders of the secretary of war. No greater example of the army's professional autonomy and insulation from external pressure exists—and none was more portentous.

The wartime estrangement of the officer corps and its symbiotic, even parasitical relationship with the Indians were most obvious in the occasional, but by no means rare, use or advocacy of what scholars today might call appropriation or inversion—assuming Seminole dress or personae to more effectively attack opponents, be they Indian or white. Before the conflict, officers had sometimes joined the Seminoles in dancing and other festivities, albeit as de facto diplomats, and they continued to do so during wartime truces. Some of this was human emotion and functioned as a form of escapism: Lieutenant

Morris Miller was one of a number of soldiers who wrote about the affection he developed for a Seminole child, and he found at least one Seminole woman "fascinating." Sympathy soon became empathy and open admiration for valiant warriors defending their homeland. This respect extended not only to Osceola but to Jumper, who had led the Dade ambush. An anonymous *Army and Navy Chronicle* obituary labeled him a "distinguished Seminole chief," noting that he had been buried "with all the honors of war" after dying of illness in New Orleans. One might speculate that Jumper's surrender mitigated his leadership of the ambush, but the burial and obituary were for an Indian who had directed the deaths of more than a hundred soldiers and officers. In a similar vein, Lieutenant John Sprague's 1848 history of the war, the single most comprehensive contemporary source, is packed with paeans to courageous Seminole patriots. While the Massachusetts-born Sprague had become personally sympathetic to the Indians since his escort of the Creek emigrants as a marine lieutenant in 1834, and may have hoped for a northern readership, he was hardly likely to publish a history his fellow officers would roundly condemn.[16]

More significantly, several critics and satirists signed their letters to the *Army and Navy Chronicle* with the names of Seminole leaders or used Indian characters to express their amusement or disgust with the army's methods, the removal policy, or the course of the war. In a seven-part series published during the spring and summer of 1840, "Junius" pretended to visit the camp of "Sam Jones," a white nickname for Arpeika or Abeika, one of the most persistent of the Indian leaders. The fanciful soldier made more cultural than diplomatic progress, learning that the chief's speech was "as long as a white President's message, except mine . . . has some sense in it." Unable to foresee a sensible end to the conflict, "Junius" turned to more emotionally profitable matters, daydreaming about a native "Miss Jones (the General's Daughter by a former wife), between whom and myself there had sprung up a sort of sentimental friendship." Yet "Junius" found his most ingenious use for imaginary Indian friends in political form, when he dispatched "Jones" from Florida to defend the Military Academy against Jacksonian critics, who had pressed removal while denouncing the professional army. Presumably, too few politicians read the *Chronicle* to make an issue of this startling alliance between the army and those it fought.[17]

A small but growing number of officers combined admiration for Seminole patriotism with a tactical willingness to adopt "savage" methods. Adaptation to reduce asymmetry, via the appropriation or emulation of Seminole methods, was an obvious tactical option as the war ground on, since the principal military problem was catching the Seminoles. Recognition of the Indians' effective adaptation to their environment underlay repeated proposals that soldiers dress like Seminoles, which would also ease the tortures of saw grass, heat, and damp. Some *Army and Navy Chronicle* letter writers went further, arguing that only "when the whites will consent to live as the Indians do . . . may these ruthless bands of savages be [defeated] . . . and not before." The appropriation of Indian dress by whites dated back to the colonial period; besides the Boston Tea Party, examples include the "White Indians" of postrevolutionary Maine and the Anti-Rent forces in New York during the early 1840s. The practice also bears some resemblance to the appropriation of the passion and proximity to nature associated with African Americans through the blackface minstrelsy common during the nineteenth century. The case of these career soldiers is significantly different, however, in that a privileged national elite was using Indian symbols to express antagonism toward white frontiersmen, as well as disenchantment with national policy, an inversion of the usual relationship in such instances.[18]

Representatives of the national center, stationed on its periphery, were mocking and condemning center (national policy) and periphery (frontiersmen) alike. Sentimental feelings toward Seminole women and children did not preclude the adoption of Indian dress to deceive and more effectively ambush and pursue refugees, and correspondence to the *Army and Navy Chronicle* on the subject contained equal parts empathy and irony. The professional soldier's use of Indian tactics did not hint at or reflect a moral or ethical "counterculture" in formation; it was a practical adaptation to circumstances, with an inkling of regret overlaid, and perhaps ultimately repressed, by the employment of irony to critique government policy and objectives. Psychologically, it seems reasonable to conclude that, quoting historian Alan Taylor, "by donning Indian costumes, [officers] doffed their inhibitions; as Indians they could engage in violence [savagism] inappropriate to white men; taking off their costumes, [officers] became [civilized gentlemen] once again, shorn, in their minds, of responsibility for what they had done as Indians."[19]

From a different angle, and looking at a different relationship—that with the government that employed them and the citizens whose interests they "represented"—this phenomenon allowed soldiers to extend the anonymity of the *Army and Navy Chronicle* by adopting a disguise, affording them the ironic pose they often assumed in personal communications. "There was more than a little ironic hypocrisy in this mock identity," as Taylor observes of white settlers donning Indian dress in Maine, since professional soldiers took the physical lead in dispossessing the Seminoles. Nevertheless, the psychological tensions inherent in this self-reinvention illustrate the nuances of the national military officer's role and the complex dilemmas of his relationships with different "clients" and antagonists in the borderlands. Taylor suggests a similar dualism in "the tension between the two faces" presented by the Maine frontiersmen: "as 'white men' negotiating with outside authorities, they presented an alternative face: quiet, humble, obedient, and industrious citizens burdened . . . and deserving legislative redress." By 1840, this had become the norm for the career officer corps dealing with its civilian paymasters: soldiers were politically neutral, institutionally subordinate instruments of the national government, concerned primarily with preserving organizational jurisdiction and augmenting appropriations, rather than advancing national destiny or the expansion of the plantation South. They could publicly criticize government policy only if they wore a disguise.[20]

Emulation and inversion soon shaded into escalation and atrocity. Desperate to cut the Gordian knot the Seminole stalemate presented, officers hardly needed to adopt the disguise of inversion to carry out practices they otherwise would have condemned. These deceitful methods were sanctioned by the widespread and growing assumption that "savage" Indians—whose presumed racial and cultural inferiority and putative statelessness denied them the protection of the laws of war that European nations applied to combatants—deserved no better. (However, soldiers rarely labeled the Seminoles "banditti," in contrast to the First Seminole War.) Military departures from the norms of civilized conventional warfare began as early as the spring of 1836, when Major Francis S. Belton had pits lined with stakes dug and concealed outside Fort Brooke to trap attacking warriors, and a militia commander timed the explosion of Fort Alabama to kill Indians scavenging for supplies when the post was abandoned that April. These tactical innovations by field officers were soon emulated at higher levels. Exasperated by the stout Indian resistance to their offensive during the winter of 1836–1837, the army's senior leaders also began turning to harsher measures, and Thomas Jesup allegedly threatened to hang Seminole prisoners en masse if Osceola refused to surrender. When the Seminoles fled the emigration camp at Tampa early in June, the enraged general told dragoon William Harney that he would sanction whatever means the brutal colonel deemed necessary, and Jesup ordered blacks hung if they were captured in battle. The normally genteel Kentucky slaveholder soon rescinded that order, which apparently was not carried out, but he still threatened to hang prisoners if they refused to give him information.[21]

Most important, the frustrated Jesup soon made seizing Indians under flags of truce an unofficial policy. Since the Seminoles often relied on negotiations during truces to replenish their food and even gunpowder (supposedly for hunting) with gifts from the army, this policy proved the most successful method of taking them prisoner throughout the war. Recognizing that both sides were fighting and talking simultaneously, officers accepted the expediency of doing so even as they applauded Seminole virtues. Thus Lieutenant John Hatheway agreed with his sister that Osceola "was a Patriot, a deep & devoted lover of his oppressed Country" and remarked that "we buried him as we would have buried an Officer," but called his seizure during a truce "perfectly correct." Despite the uproar Osceola's seizure stirred among officers as well as civilian opponents of the war, Jesup soon created another public furor by proposing, or accepting civilian proposals, to employ bloodhounds to catch the Seminoles. In 1837 the general sought War Department advice about the probable public reaction, doubting that it would be favorable due to the obvious parallels with the techniques of slave catchers. However, both he and Zachary Taylor suggested the use of hounds after the Indians dispersed and refused further battle the following year. Neither Congress nor the executive branch was willing to take responsibility for such a measure, so Florida territorial officials imported thirty-three bloodhounds from Cuba in 1839. Trying to mollify congressional critics, the War Department ordered the animals leashed and muzzled when used. Only two dogs saw active service, and only two Indians were captured with them before the army gave up the experiment. Not surprisingly, dispensing with the hounds won more condemnation from white Floridians than commendation from opponents of the war.[22]

Efforts to adapt to the wilderness environment would threaten the army's discipline and self-restraint, and senior officers knew it. Thus, and perhaps because of his reputation for brutality, William Harney of the Second Dragoons was refused when he first requested permission to dress his troops in Seminole-style shirts. When Harney finally gained that authorization late in 1840, he promptly hunted down an Indian band in the Everglades that had humiliated him in a night attack, causing him to flee in his underclothes. Harney hanged five members of that band on the spot, after shooting one who tried to surrender. The colonel also tortured "a Spaniard [a Cuban fisherman] who came in with a white flag . . . almost [hanging him] to death" in an attempt to discover Arpeika's location. These hangings brought the army its only sustained applause from white Floridians, but northern civilians condemned the action. Harney's brutality toward the Seminoles seems to have been the act of a cruel man and a true Indian hater, though a tough and effective fighter, and other officers were split in their opinions, depending on whether they emphasized decorum or decisiveness. The majority of soldiers who put their thoughts on paper found his actions expedient, but it is a telling sign of their disenchantment that they could suppress their normal values of good faith and gentility to do so. Others continued to think atrocity counterproductive: Lieutenant John W. Phelps worried that the Cuban Harney had tortured would confirm rumors, spread by Indian leaders, "that we are hanging all that we can catch," deterring Seminoles from surrender.[23]

Meanwhile, Jesup began taking Indian hostages and threatening them with death if other Seminoles did not surrender. William Worth tried the same tactic on several occasions in 1841 and 1842, just as he and his predecessor, Walker Armistead, returned to the effective policy of seizing Indians under truce flags, despite Worth's complaint about Henry Atkinson doing so in the West a year before. (Worth also extended a bounty for Seminoles captured or killed to his enlisted soldiers.) There is no evidence that these threats were carried out; Harney's atrocities appear to have been unique, rooted in the combination of personal humiliation and an exceptionally violent personality untempered by West Point socialization. (Harney narrowly escaped conviction in St. Louis for the murder of a slave woman in 1834, forced enlisted soldiers to fight one another in public to resolve disputes, and refused to take male prisoners among the Brulé Sioux in 1855, allowing his troops to kill their women and children.) On the whole, the officer corps' sympathy for the Seminoles had a clear humanitarian effect; Harney aside, there is no record that the army resorted to the physical torture soldiers sometimes employed during the war for independence in the Philippines, the army's next experience in tropical guerrilla warfare. Nor, apart from Harney, did the army refuse to accept Seminole surrender: a genteel professional self-image trumped race in the dynamic of atrocity.[24]

However much officers wanted to resolve the psychic tensions of their duty by projecting their anger on the Indians, by punishing or eliminating the intractable enemy whose persistence brought civilian censure against the army,[25] they continued to fight the war in a remarkably Europeanized way, illustrating their personal and professional commitment to ideals of gentility, discipline, and order. Indeed, the use of such harsh measures would only raise further qualms among the disenchanted by undermining their carefully cultivated sense of identity as self-disciplined career leaders practicing a genteel profession. Faced with such a quandary, they ultimately found it necessary to stay the course in order to retain the security and status they sought. In an extreme instance of inversion, Nathaniel Hunter asked himself whether "every act [meaning ambush, plunder, and deception] of the Indians [is not] sanctioned by the practice of civilized nations"— a moral conflation that might undermine every basis for the army's role and the officer corps' status. If the army's commanders truly believed the Seminoles were in the right, they would have resigned or been replaced by citizen-soldiers, less self-critical and more eager to assert superior Indian-fighting abilities, and the officer corps would have lost its otherwise growing dominance over the direction of national military force. If Americans became convinced that either white or Seminole frontiersmen were completely in the right, the army would be unnecessary: citizen-soldiers could commit genocide, or the United States would end its aggression. An army loyal to the national policy of removal (rather than genocide) was needed only if the conflict presented complex costs and trade-offs that precluded total war.[26]

Thus, while historians might expect exasperated officers to sanction or commit atrocities, whether from frustration or desperation or because they shared the racism of other Anglo-Americans, doing so underestimates the sway of their institutional socialization in professional and class-based norms of gentility, decorum, and honor. As elsewhere on the frontier, officers' sense of their position in the hierarchy of white society trumped their racism toward the Seminoles. "Omicron's" 1838 letter to the *Army and Navy Chronicle* illustrates the social and cultural roots of professional soldiers' unease in the Enlightenment heritage of limited war, focused around the Eurocentric juxtaposition of savagism and civility officers used to privilege their genteel claims to authority over Indians, frontiersmen, and enlisted soldiers. The author maintained that "it is impossible that the army can improve [whether ethically or professionally] while officers can employ themselves in introducing such novel and barbarian methods of warfare." He vowed that "the old-fashioned and civilized . . . forms of intercourse, which should obtain [even] with a savage foe, are the only ones which can be upheld by good policy, propriety, or the voice of the people"—by pragmatism, gentility and honor, and accountability to national public opinion, especially that of the gentlemen officers, whom he considered peers.[27]

Indeed, Jesup himself provides the best example of the dangers the conflict posed for the carefully cultivated image, both self and public, of the professional military commander. Lauded for his initiative, speed, and decisiveness rounding up the Creeks in Alabama during the summer of 1836, the quartermaster general was dispatched to bring order and terminate hostilities in Florida that autumn, but he found the enemy, the terrain, and the climate far more difficult there. Beginning in mid-1837, after Seminole hard-liners led by Osceola and Coacoochee broke his armistice with less stubborn Indian leaders, Jesup regularly seized Seminoles who accepted his offers to negotiate under flags of truce. After attempting to justify his conduct and ultimately securing relief from command, Jesup sought to mend his reputation for good faith and integrity by pressing the government to honor the promises he had made to Indians who had supported the removal effort, particularly the Creeks who served with the army in 1836 and 1837. He later extended this plea to

Two faces of duty: William S. Harney (courtesy Library of Congress, LC-DIG-cwpb-04404) and—on the facing page—a young Robert Anderson (from Stevens, *The Black Hawk War*).

the Seminoles he had sent west, maintaining in 1844 that "as the Commander of the Army in Florida I assured them in good faith that the country [in the Oklahoma region] set apart by the treaty was ready for their reception. I consider it due to my honour, as well as that of the Country . . . to urge upon the government the prompt fulfillment of the treaty." Acting simultaneously as a government official, a military commander, and a gentleman, Jesup conflated a paternal sense of personal and national faith and honor in the execution of

his duties to the nation-state, simultaneously embodying the closely allied processes of occupation, state, and class formation in his own values and behavior.[28]

The army drove forward despite these irritants and controversies. Indeed, resignations declined precipitously during the same years (1838 and 1839) that demoralization and discontent became pervasive in Florida. Conversely, support for harsher measures, which gained strength among officers in 1839, signaled a plateau or decline in the officer corps' admiration for its opponents, as the Seminoles proved recalcitrant, and in military eyes faithless, when armistices collapsed each summer. Soldiers continued to serve for three basic reasons: the security of their careers; their comparatively neutral attitude toward ideology, politics, and policy; and their cohesion and commitment as a professional group, tempered by the collective misery of an "unpleasant and horrendous service." These factors came together in the same sense of nonpartisan accountability to the national government simultaneously evident along the Canadian border and on that with Mexico half a decade later. In each instance, officers expressed this ethos in a common idiom of obligation and service, duty and honor. Pondering his future early in 1838, William Warren Chapman resented the "cold ingratitude" of the government but grudgingly assured his fiancée that "I remain in Florida because it is my duty to do so." Another bitter veteran informed the *Army and Navy Chronicle* that only "the consciousness [that] 'I have done my duty'" had allayed "the stigma of *ingratitude*." Pondering policies he considered atrocious, even Nathaniel Hunter recurred to the "duty of a soldier to obey." The majority of the officer corps wanted to carry matters to a clear conclusion, whether that meant removal or peace, to demonstrate its faithful performance of the duties it had been assigned, however onerous or distasteful its members found them.[29]

Whatever their motives, many soldiers believed that duty meant sharing sacrifice. William Tecumseh Sherman, George H. Thomas, and Stewart Van Vliet all volunteered for service in Florida. Robert Anderson, one of the army's most professionally minded officers and the translator of French cavalry and artillery tactics, could have chosen any post he wanted when he was promoted to captain in his regiment after five years' service as West Point artillery instructor, Winfield Scott's aide, and assistant adjutant general (where he already ranked as a captain). The 1838 army law allowed some officers to retain their regimental ("lineal") rank while serving on the army staff; staff duty usually paid better, due to a variety of supplemental allowances, and often meant comfortable postings in sociable coastal cities. Yet Anderson rejected advice from Scott, Abraham Eustis, and his peers and relinquished his staff job for combat command in the swamps. Anderson's sense of duty and responsibility went hand in hand with his ambition. He had not served in Florida, he believed (like most officers) that lineal rank was inherently senior to staff rank, and he was certain that "an officer holding two commissions should serve under the highest."

> I believe that however good and perfect may be the organization of the staff of an Army, unless the character, pride, and esprit de corps of the company officers have been elevated and maintained, that that army cannot be depended upon either in peace or in War. . . . The best means . . . of securing good discipline and perfect order in the companies is to keep the captains of the line with their companies—as experience has shown that none but the captain feels that interest and pride in the welfare and condition of the company which are essential [to] make the soldiers contented and efficient.[30]

The army's leaders considered Anderson too valuable to waste in a line command, warning him that his regiment was leaving Florida and offering him another position at West Point. Scott's current aide, who, like Anderson, had spent much of his career (eight of eleven years) in that role or at West Point, pressed the captain to return to the Military Academy; however, he followed Anderson's example by joining his own company when promoted to captain a year later. Scott ensured that Anderson received a brevet for gallantry for his service in Florida, and he earned another commanding a battalion (as a brevet major) in the assault on Molino del Rey in Mexico, where he was severely wounded. Even before the Seminole War, the versatile Kentuckian was a leading advocate for a "Soldiers' Asylum" for aged and infirm enlisted men (for whom there were no retirement provisions), and he ran the first of these between 1853 and 1855. Scott's other aide, Bradford Alden, served for six years as commandant of cadets and the principal instructor in infantry tactics at West Point; he resigned after being severely wounded fighting Indians in 1853.[31]

Another veteran sought institutional vindication through military victory, assuming the pseudonym of Mikasuki chief Sam Jones to demand a new campaign in the autumn of 1839. He felt that "it is due the army, to Florida, and the United States generally, that this protracted war should be closed! It is due the army because it has already spent too much of its time here for its own comfort and advantage." "Jones" was eager to move on to better times. Nathaniel Hunter, who had resigned soon after receiving his commission in 1833 but accepted reappointment three years later, knowing he might go to Florida, accepted promotion to captain in 1841, the same year he was accused of authoring a pamphlet condemning the army and the war. (He does not appear to have served in Mexico, however.) Nor did the federal government attempt to stifle the anonymous dissent among its officers. They returned the favor by limiting their dissent to rhetorical outbursts, usually tucked away in the *Army and Navy Chronicle*, where few outside Washington, and probably few outside the army, would read them. In doing so, they preserved both their individual careers and the army's monopoly over the direction of national military force.[32]

The availability of the *Army and Navy Chronicle* as a public but usually anonymous forum for the career soldier's pride and frustration encouraged but also moderated dissent. This weekly paper, founded in 1835, was partially dependent on federal subsidies in the form of payments for relaying official news and orders, but it had no set editorial policy regarding the war; it was the army's platform, open to any officer's opinions. By 1835, the career officer corps had developed significant group cohesion, and its members' self-image as expert and personally disinterested national servants encouraged them to speak out on policies related to their duties. The *Chronicle* served as their primary sounding board at a crucial moment in the development of the army's professional culture, a semipublic space that provided a vehicle for rebuilding much of the cohesion that otherwise would have been lost because of the resignation crisis of 1835–1837. Indeed, even the most critical letters were phrased in language suggesting that the authors remained in the army and intended to continue to serve.[33]

Although it published many analyses of military tactics and operations, the *Chronicle*'s most significant effect was to buttress the officer corps' collective identity as a professional body and to provide a safe forum to express the frustrations engendered by the Seminole War and partisan criticism. In the end, this role became either unnecessary or insufficient, because the *Chronicle* folded for lack of readers in 1844, after several years of near insolvency. (Indeed, it had ceased publication for several months early in 1841 before finding new sponsorship.) Until the 1840s, soldiers' letters and articles in the civilian press were usually polemics aimed at fellow commanders rather than expositions on the nation's military needs and policy; the latter were published in various reports by senior officers to Congress and the War Department. A few junior officers, mostly instructors at West Point, began to write anonymously for the civilian press during the 1840s, usually to defend the Military Academy and the army in periodicals friendly to military preparation. Articles like these were intended primarily to convince the public of the necessity of a strong army and Military Academy in the face of congressional attacks and resolutions by state legislatures and militia conventions. As such, they demonstrated a more public sense of professional identity than had been the case in the 1820s or 1830s, a development attributable to the intersection of officers' disenchantment and dissent over their Seminole War experience and the postwar wave of congressional attacks on the army's size and compensation.

From an institutional perspective, dissent was possible among career soldiers because the seniority system of promotion meant that they could not be held directly accountable for their statements without using the cumbersome formal instrument of courts-martial for "unofficerlike conduct" or other vague charges. Doing so would have been an obvious political move that senior commanders, attempting to keep the army apolitical, would have resisted. In addition, such measures would have been countered by congressional inquiries from friends of the accused, particularly if they were northerners with ties to opponents of the removal policy. The court-martial of John Wool for his conduct in Cherokee country provided a clear warning of the limits of that instrument, and a similar commitment to maintaining the cohesion of the professional officer corps was evident in how senior commanders handled personal disputes among their subordinates. Though a common means of pursuing personal vendettas or disputes over perquisites, charges of disrespect to fellow officers were commonly skirted or dismissed because of technicalities related to the language and regulations involved. Ultimately, the army's personnel policies toward officers were still based on the model of the independent gentleman asserting his rights in an eighteenth-century language of personal honor rather than that of an officeholder in a routinized bureaucratic hierarchy. Thus, apart from extreme and extraordinary cases of drunkenness, oppression, or dereliction of duty, the great majority of courts-martial and courts of inquiry were initiated by officers engaged in vendettas against personal enemies within the corps. Despite aggravating personal friction, this "independence" and the opportunity to dissent did much to ameliorate civil-military tensions in the larger political arena, for officers were able to sustain their morale by letting off steam, providing the psychological breathing space necessary for them to move forward with policies they found distasteful.[34]

Officers also reacted by showering one another, or the officer corps and the army in general, with acclaim, while developing internal rituals to cope with the losses they suffered. Foremost among these was the custom of group memorials in the *Army and Navy Chronicle*, paying tribute to slain comrades. Besides a brief and usually stylized (though varying) epitaph, these memorials normally included a promise to "wear the usual badge of mourning for thirty days, as a memento of respect for our brother officer." More permanently, officers of the regiments involved in the Dade Massacre formed a committee to collect subscriptions for a monument "in gratitude to the memories of men who have done such honor to their corps [meaning their regiments] and profession." Lieutenant Benjamin Alvord's address to the cadets' Dialectic Society at West Point commemorated Dade's "gallant band" and its determination "to defend their unfortunate comrades until the last drop of blood [was] shed upon that consecrated ground. . . . How solemn, religious and impressive was that scene!" Alvord exclaimed. Despite all the backbiting between individuals, he easily could have been speaking for the officer corps as a whole in his admiration for the self-sacrifice that "so faithfully preserved the integrity of its members, adhering to each other up to their dying gasp."[35]

This mythic image stands as an apt metaphor for the soldier's sense of solidarity—moral, ethical, and professional, as well as physical—with his fellows. The officer corps was satisfied with its own performance, and that had to suffice. "The army has done well what was given it to do, and is unwilling to take any of the responsibility of failure," proclaimed "An Officer of the Line." These words demonstrate a neutral dedication to performing the tasks assigned by the nation-state, as much as an unwillingness to be held responsible for their consequences. In this way, a sense of martyrdom and alienation paradoxically served to shore up rather than undermine soldiers' support for

This is how many civilians viewed the army: "A Bivouack in Safety or Florida Troops Preventing a Surprise," lithograph by H. R. Robinson, 1840. (Courtesy Library of Congress, LC-USZ62-49595)

the war they were charged with prosecuting. The potential for strains in civil-military relations, never greater before the Civil War, was eased by officers' ability to express their dissent in public forums without fear of reprisal: refusing the full burden of responsibility for their beliefs, they received a hearing without being compelled to choose between fighting in Florida and leaving the army. Nor, ultimately, did Congress hold them responsible for the sluggish progress in Florida by replacing them with citizen-soldiers. Although the army's enlisted strength was reduced after the conflict (when tensions along the Canadian border had also diminished), only a handful of officers were dismissed during the war or after its end. The officer corps maintained its monopoly over the operational direction of national military force and was in position to win the glory it sought, in the drier climes of Mexico.[36]

The friction and antagonism that characterized civil-military relations during the Second Seminole War were ultimately deceptive and exceptional. Military frustration and disillusionment grew exponentially between 1837 and 1839, by which time a strong overtone of weariness, cynicism, and inertia had set in, but the resignation crisis of the mid-1830s ended with the Panic of 1837 and the depression. Indeed, the wave of resignations peaked in 1836, after a single season of campaigning in Florida, and then dropped to an all-time low, with absolute numbers in the single digits annually, within two years. The decline in resignations between 1836 and 1837 may have been due to the hopefulness induced by clarification of the command structure under Thomas Jesup, by Jesup's victories during the 1836–1837 campaign, and by the possibility that his armistice would end the conflict, but this does not explain why resignations did not increase again when the war continued. Clearly, officers' disenchantment with war must have been less potent than the decline in alternative economic opportunities after 1837. In any case, the combination of economic depression and tolerance from the army's civilian masters enhanced the attractiveness of career security, hinting at both the rewards for dutiful service and the practical limits of individual dissent in an increasingly professional army.

Officers received no pensions for delaying retirement, so the pecuniary deterrents to resignation were minimal, especially for staff officers who could readily put their experience to use building railroads or managing businesses. Career soldiers were constrained by a highly structured bureaucratic hierarchy, probably the most rigid in the United States at the time, and junior officers had few opportunities to pursue independent success within their profession. (Some found success—but limited autonomy—serving as staff officers, aides to generals, or instructors at West Point, or by developing ordnance or working on tactical or administrative regulations.) Yet the army offered a fixed salary, and it never went out of business: barring dismissal for misconduct, officers of the national standing army—supposedly so feared by republicans, liberals, and democrats of all stripes—did not lose their jobs during the quarter century between the reductions of 1821 and 1848 (and very few were dismissed in 1848). Promotion was certainly slow—superiors had to resign or die—but soldiers above the rank of captain had a great deal to lose—in prestige and authority over others, if not financially—by quitting the army. Indeed, there was no resignation crisis among field-grade officers, only two of whom resigned in 1836: Duncan Clinch, angered by Jacksonian criticism of his failure to defeat the Seminoles, and Henry Dodge, commander of the First Dragoons, who had been commissioned colonel of the Battalion of Mounted Rangers directly from civilian life after demonstrating his leadership as a vigilante ruffian in the Illinois lead mining district. Dodge was using his political connections to trade up and become governor of Wisconsin. Soldiers who sought greater opportunities for upward mobility resigned to participate in the flourishing market economy, until it collapsed in 1837; those who remained in the service often considered themselves unsuited to the uncertain prospects of a life in business.[37]

Besides the security of a structured career path, the primary psychological stimulus for soldiers' service was the promise of glory and public acclaim. Because this support was denied to officers in the Seminole conflict, many of them felt disenchanted and turned to complaint and dissent; some assumed masks of martyrdom and alienation. But most officers—the silent majority who wrote nothing of their views and cannot be cited in quotations—simply carried on with their jobs, doing their duty, drawing their secure salaries amid a turbulent economy, and waiting for promotion and an end to the war. For some, this was too slow. One veteran with more than thirty years' service was still a captain in April 1838, when he asked, "Will Congress do anything to improve our condition? If not, I think this campaign will nearly use us up, and when it shall have terminated, the army (at least the Florida portion of it) will disband itself; for it cannot much longer endure the privations to which it is subjected here, and the neglect of our country at home." He then pleaded for promotion: "I have been waiting for it *thirty-one years*, and if it do[es] not come shortly, I shall die outright, either of poverty or despair."[38]

Few officers died of either; nor did many die during the Second Seminole War as a whole. Only eleven commissioned officers of the national standing army were actually mortally wounded or killed in action during the seven campaign seasons that followed the Dade Massacre. Professional military commanders had secure careers and incomes; they enjoyed social respectability and usually prestige as gentlemen in the eyes of national elites and the local and regional middle classes, outside the rawest frontier areas; and they had the power to command working-class enlisted soldiers. The friction and dilemmas of civil-military relations on the frontiers aside, the cultural prestige enjoyed by European officers and embodied in aristocratic concepts like glory was the only benefice American soldiers truly lacked. Professional officers felt unappreciated and put upon in 1840, but they were already used to enduring censure and frustration, and they had been deliberately socialized in an ethos of service, sacrifice, and duty to the nation that upheld cohesion, service, and disinterestedness as the most important of values. These norms were highly functional for career soldiers as individuals and as members of an institution and profession under frequent political attack, for they enabled the officer corps to turn criticism on its head by proclaiming themselves the most disinterested, self-sacrificing servants of the national government. Military commanders could privately view themselves as the truest of republicans, nonpartisan agents of the public will mediated through elective representative government. From this perspective, distance from public influence was held to be the measure of disinterestedness and thus of an ability to act "independently" to serve the interests of the nation as a whole.[39]

The professional rhetoric of disinterested and politically neutral duty, service, and responsibility proved materially and psychologically attractive for men in this situation. Officers were socialized in genteel values of social distance and hierarchy, personal decorum, and honor; they were taught to aspire to reputation and glory rather than great material wealth, at a time when all these ideals seemed under constant attack. Aspiring military professionals felt a growing threat to their livelihood and their ability to command respect as American society became more unsettled and democratic. They continually compared their opportunities to the burgeoning possibilities available in the rapidly commercializing civilian world, but apart from the boom times of the mid-1830s (which coincided with the advent of the Seminole conflict), remarkably few resigned their commissions to pursue the economic boundlessness promised by Jacksonian America. Instead, these career soldiers reacted to rampant individualism, egalitarianism, and anti-institutionalism with a growing distaste for chaos and a quest for orderly self-advancement through the structure of a bureaucratic hierarchy—in short, through institutionalized careers. The key was the availability of a fledgling bureaucracy that could fuse their concrete material aspirations for security at a "respectable" level with their psychosocial pretensions to altruistic public service, authority, and honor. And, although scholars could stress careerism as the predominant individual dynamic at work in this development, institutional and experiential socialization in professional values was at least equally central to officers' growing commitment to and accountability in those careers.

Psychologically, these attitudes were highly functional for aspiring career officers, for they developed a professional community and a professional culture based on shared values and the daily experience of their duties. They longed for the opportunity to distinguish themselves in combat, and courage and decisiveness were two of their core values, but the competitiveness and individualism, so significant to Jacksonian culture, that might seem to go hand in hand with these values were restrained by the same battlefield imperatives of command, discipline, and cohesion that encouraged them in the first place. The American officer's sense of himself as a gentleman in the English mode meant that command was ideally exercised through the display of dispassionate rationality: a cool, decorous touch providing calm, steady reassurance to the supposedly unreliable working-class soldiers under his command. Officers despised rabble-rousers and disorder; they had to overcome disruptive impulses toward ideological fervor and excessive sentiment if they were to maintain the stable order and predictability necessary for a functioning organization and success in battle. This meant not only that military commanders felt a strong distaste for the anarchic individualism of white frontiersmen but that this distaste was moderated by a temperamental commitment to political neutrality, an attitude buttressed by the institutional structures of the nation-state and embodied in the army regulations and the Articles of War. Professional military officers were not isolated from their society as a whole, though its values commonly irritated, frequently disillusioned, and occasionally alienated them. Their sense of accountability to civilian political processes was enhanced not by partisan or ideological faith in the glories of republicanism and democracy but by their position as members of an organization dependent on those processes for its survival—by the implicit threat of sanction and the desire for security rather than overt ideological allegiance or emotional enthusiasm. Professional soldiers had a good thing going, and the material, social, and psychological benefits clearly outweighed their frustrations.

Perhaps the officer corps' political behavior and its ethic of responsibility, subordination, and accountability to civilian control might best be encapsulated in the phrase "professional neutrality" or "professional objectivity." This implies not political isolation—hardly possible when the army's funding was determined by elected representatives—much less alienation or disaffection or simple self-interestedness, but a quest for political insulation and professional autonomy, the better both to defend one's career and authority and to exercise the expertise and discretion necessary to perform one's duties with impartial integrity. This assertion of insulation and autonomy from the partisan and ideological pressures that so strongly influenced the rest of mid-nineteenth-century American government took the form of a putatively objective, non- or antipartisan nationalism, embodied in officers' identification with the national state and their nationalist understanding of the Constitution.[40] In practical terms, career soldiers won a tacit exchange with mutual benefits: instead of attempting to intervene in electoral politics, as republican ideologues feared, officers concentrated on the relatively narrow institutional politics of promotions, postings, and the allocation of resources and power among different branches of the army. They certainly hoped for, and increasingly sought, greater appropriations for the army as a whole, but they did so in a highly deferential manner, appealing to national unity against potential European threats while downplaying or passing over divisive issues of Indian removal and territorial expansion. In return (and perhaps because aversion to taxation kept the army so small), they secured de facto insulation from the concrete effects—above all, "rotation in office"—of partisan politics. This insulation enabled officers to commit themselves to careers developing expertise in professional skill sets, primarily in troop training (drill) and logistics, that were lacking elsewhere in American society, rather than scrambling for political favor or continually training new political appointees.[41]

Equally important for their actual mission effectiveness and for sustaining the public support that undergirded this tacit bargain, insulation permitted military commanders a necessary but not excessive autonomy in the execution of their diplomatic and peacekeeping duties on the borders and frontiers. Despite persistent qualms and perpetual irritation, they would forward white expansion without the political and financial costs incurred by undisciplined, genocidal citizen-soldiers who lacked the training, cohesion, and commitment to defeat persistent native adversaries like the Seminoles, or the Sioux and Apache in the trans-Mississippi West. Buttressed by its implicit bargain with Congress and the civilian executive, the national standing army and its officers developed a staying power—and an effectiveness in policy execution, however gradual—unusual in the anti-institutional Jacksonian milieu. Under these circumstances, the standing army's demands on civilian society were usually limited to increases in military spending and compensation, faster promotions due to expansion of the army, operational command over the militia and volunteers, and control over entry into and the values of the officer corps by requiring specialized training and socialization at West Point. The most important of these, both to the officer corps as an occupational group and to its development as a profession, was a monopoly over the direction of national military force, which was the boon most amenable to control by the executive branch. Despite frequent congressional pressure, the Military Academy's monopoly on officer entry and socialization (second in significance for professional development) was easily maintained by the executive unless compelled to commission civilians or enlisted men due to shortages of West Pointers. Indeed, the Military Academy's monopoly was effectively codified in 1843, when Congress mandated that nominations to the Academy be allocated in proportion to a state's or territory's representation in Congress. This law gave every senator and representative a personal patronage stake in the professional socialization of the officer corps.[42]

Career soldiers did not lack ties to political elites, and they longed for public recognition and acclaim, but they rarely expressed republican or other ideological sentiments in any detail or form save that of antipartisanship. This suited their sense of nationalism and complemented their desire for career security through identification with the national government, representative of a national community regardless of electoral change. Given officers' education and political connections, we must account for their ideological inarticulateness. This should probably be attributed to their nascent professional ethic, which stressed national service in the politically and ideologically neutral form of duty rather than missionary impulse. American officers aspired to a putatively objective responsibility to the nation-state that employed them,

Dade Monument, U.S. Military Academy. Photograph by the author

rather than a subjective one to expansive ideals about "free institutions" and the egalitarian community of white men. Their hopes for national greatness were not expressed in the triumphal ideological rhetoric of Manifest Destiny. The specific circumstances of the Second Seminole War aggravated soldiers' individual dilemmas and civil-military friction, but the war was not the underlying source of these phenomena, which manifested deeper tensions of gentility and federalism. Nevertheless, the Seminole conflict proved a sore trial of professional commitment and responsibility, a testing ground where aspiring professional commanders gained valuable experience dealing with political, military, and cultural frustration. "Unhappy Florida! Thy soil has drunk the heart's blood of the army!" one lamented, but the experience provided the career officer corps with hard-won lessons in patience and accountability to civilian direction, a crucible that left a tested professional body willing to lead the nation's armies wherever they were sent, as long as the national government did the sending.[43]

8

CHANGING MILITARY ATTITUDES TOWARD FOREIGN RELATIONS

The Dilemmas of Discipline and International Order along the Canadian Border, 1815–1838

American military responses to international affairs changed significantly between the wars with Britain and Mexico. Aside from the engineers' attention to coastal fortifications, career army officers as well as civilians turned their attention inward, to the North American continent, after 1820. Many army leaders privately applauded democratic revolutions in Europe and Latin America during the years before 1823, but like most Americans, they quickly came to see the United States as a republican example to the world rather than an aggressive agent of international republicanism or democratic revolution. Like civilians, professional soldiers came to use the language of revolution as a rhetorical trope for application to distant lands; on the rare occasions when they applied it to areas contiguous to the United States, it served as a cover for American expansionism or became a threat to international stability, rather than a promise of liberation. After advocating and initiating campaigns that secured Florida for the United States, the army officer corps had fairly little to do or say about international territorial expansion during the next two decades, as the nation concentrated on rearranging or consolidating its internal affairs in the absence of immediate foreign threats or politically viable opportunities for aggrandizement.

Territorial expansion across international boundaries was a much more complex, ambiguous, and contested issue for professional military commanders than many scholars might expect. National military officers policing the borderlands were compelled to play multifaceted diplomatic roles that often seemed to pit their responsibilities for national defense, or their more subjective desire for national growth and aggrandizement, against their accountability to the constitutional procedures of the federal nation-state. This tension created ethical, political, and professional dilemmas as well as opportunities. Constrained by the often paradoxical, even contradictory, demands of representative politics, federalism, and the separation of powers, military responses to the possibilities of territorial expansion were far more nuanced than historians' usual explanatory models of self-interest and romantic nationalism imply. No single factor can explain the diverse military reactions to the dynamics of territorial expansion and war; military enthusiasm for expansion varied from crisis to crisis and officer to officer, depending on the specific circumstances and individuals.

Beginning with this chapter, *Peacekeepers and Conquerors* pursues the often complex, sometimes paradoxical motives, trends, and meanings of army officers' responses to the dynamic opportunities and dilemmas presented by the various foreign policy crises they encountered along the international borders of the United States, specifically those with Canada and Mexico. This analysis uncovers a growing sense of remarkably objective professional accountability to the national government—much like that demonstrated by career soldiers on the Indian frontiers in the preceding chapters—that increasingly restrained the subjective emotions of nationalist expansion and self-interested belligerence many soldiers otherwise shared with civilians. Most important, then and for the nation's future, the army's efforts had the practical value of inhibiting filibusters whose actions might have drawn the United States into a devastating war with Britain. The remaining chapters explain how and why this accountability developed and what it suggests about the trajectory of the officer corps' professionalism, its responsiveness to and autonomy from the values of civil society, and its subordination to representative democracy embodied in constitutional civilian authority. Though often conventionally liberal in their attitudes toward economic growth and development, career army officers redefined republicanism, emphasizing elements of its classical and aristocratic traditions to forge a duty-bound, nationalist authoritarianism that was materially and psychologically conducive to men whose livelihoods, status, and legitimacy depended on the institutions of the national state.

MILITARY ATTITUDES TOWARD FOREIGN AFFAIRS AND NATIONAL SECURITY POLICY: A SUMMARY OF SOURCES AND CHANGE, 1821–1846

In the past generation, historians of American foreign relations have begun to emphasize that a nation's foreign policy is not the creation of the state alone, especially under highly decentralized (contemporary European officials, usually aristocrats, often said chaotic) social and political conditions like those in the early American republic. Thus, with or without Andrew Jackson at the helm, the fledgling central government and its agents were forced to reckon with the expansive and potentially explosive actions and demands of a mushrooming frontier population whose movements were virtually unregulated—and almost impossible to regulate, given democratic, liberal, and republican political and ideological constraints—by civil institutions and authority. Whether acting as settlers or filibusters, American citizens—nonstate actors—proved capable of withholding their sanction and support from national policies or reshaping those policies in pursuit of local objectives. Under these circumstances, peaceful behavior from international neighbors could not preclude international crises.[1]

Indeed, a passive or laissez-faire border policy, otherwise so agreeable to American ideologies of limited government, was more likely to enable trouble than avoid it. As the most visible and potent agents of nation-state authority and power in the early republic, military commanders were repeatedly assigned to confront private initiatives along the nation's international boundaries, often without the physical numbers or political backing to effectively enforce unpopular national laws and policy. Nor did tasking by the president provide officers undisputed sanction in the court of public opinion: they usually patrolled the borders in the face of resistance or criticism from local, state, or federal civil officials who owed their positions to partisan patronage and support for local interests. Viewed from the centralist and often openly authoritarian perspective of federal military officers charged with enforcing national sovereignty over citizens, the most immediate product of expansionism usually seemed to be lawlessness and social disorder. Without restraint, expansionists would become filibusters, and filibusters would draw the nation into war or seize territories and establish competing polities. Whatever the outcome, the choice between restraint and entropy seemed clear.

Moreover, the soldiers of the national standing army faced potential competition from locally based militia and volunteer commanders who did not share their centralism. This constant struggle for professional jurisdiction over the direction of military force gave urgency and concrete focus to the officer corps' growing sense of professional mission and identity, internal cohesion, autonomy from and resistance to local pressures, and objective accountability to its patrons and paymasters—that is, the civilian authorities of the national central government, particularly the executive branch. As such, career military officers preferred an indirect, representative version of democracy and a process of government focused at and through the nation's geographic center in Washington, rather than in state capitals or among the turbulent, individualistic settlers along the borders and frontiers. Much as James Madison suggested in *Federalist Number Ten*, referring complex, contested political issues to the top first concentrated but then diluted the confusing, sometimes contradictory streams of interest, influence, and complaint from the nation's many regions, sections, and economic sectors. Doing so joined liberalism with classical republicanism, permitting those multifaceted interests to express their wishes through representatives in Congress before being balanced and shorn of excess by the clash and compromise of interests therein. Though professional officers worried (albeit, on the whole, unnecessarily) about congressional influence on their careers and the army as an institution, they ultimately preferred this nationalist, or National Republican, process of governance, in which their status as executive branch officials provided a substantial degree of insulation and autonomy, to a more decentralized, directly democratic one that promised social entropy and threats of war.

As demonstrated in earlier chapters, professional military attitudes toward territorial expansion were profoundly shaped by officers' experiences—usually antagonistic—with civilian borderers. Because they were bound to execute contested national policies, military commanders frequently became embroiled in conflicts with local civilian authorities. (It bears repeating that little evidence of congressional intervention trickled down into officers' correspondence, public or private.) These experiences led many professional soldiers to hope for dual policies of international restraint and domestic constraint (of citizens), for fear that the disorderly borderers would get out of hand. Such responses reflected a quasi-Hamiltonian preference for the order and stability imposed by the nation-state through rules of international law structuring an otherwise competitive, potentially entropic, interstate system. Contrary to stereotypes of belligerence, and in contrast to the real belligerence shown by Andrew Jackson and his subordinates before 1821, the officer corps' long-term interests as an occupation and a profession—in secure employment and social status through a legal monopoly over the legitimate direction of national military force—increasingly dictated caution, accountability to national civilian authority, and adherence to the rule of law in the pace and process of territorial aggrandizement. As a result, the officer corps was substantially less enthusiastic about American territorial expansion in 1846 than it had been thirty years before.[2]

Occupation, class, and culture were all linked in the trajectory of officers' attitudes toward territorial expansion, whether against Indians or internationally. Military commanders were directly accountable to the central government for their jobs and budgets, and they generally considered the frontiersmen and filibusters who challenged national sovereignty over foreign policy and military force disruptive criminals who posed a greater threat to domestic and international order and stability, and hence national security, than the weak forces of America's southern neighbors. Much the same was true along the Canadian border, where professional officers felt certain that the dramatic growth of the American population and communications links would sustain successful offensives in any future war without requiring extensive peacetime preparations. A similar process shaped commanders' conceptions of national honor, which Andrew Jackson had viewed largely as an extension of his own will. Thus, in 1838 Winfield Scott and his leading subordinates on the Canadian frontier saw faithfulness to the rule of international law as a matter of personal and professional honor, which they attempted to affirm by securing the nation's border against all comers in support of federal sovereignty and the government's treaty obligations. These men often cooperated closely with their British counterparts during the crises between 1838 and 1842, acting as strenuously as possible to maintain national sovereignty and neutrality by securing the borders against the private aggression of American citizens, as well as British or Canadian retaliation.

Army officers were tasked with acting as the nation's leading "agents of empire" in an era of exuberant nationalism and territorial expansion, and historians have naturally assumed that they were ardent expansionists. Regardless of the influence of their society's boisterous chauvinism, expansionist wars provided army officers with rare chances for significant command responsibilities and martial glory in combat against "civilized" opponents—one of their primary psychological compensations for the boredom of peacetime routine on distant frontier posts. Materially, the casualties of war promised promotion (and thus higher pay) and command for ambitious military professionals. (The added compensation came with the promotion itself; there was no "combat pay.") Despite these attractions, the army officer corps was far from united in support of expansion, and the overall tenor of its reactions changed significantly, in some respects even dramatically, over the three decades of this study. Like the Jacksonian Democrats of the 1840s examined by historian Thomas Hietala, the officers of the 1810s (treated in *Jackson's Sword*) "expressed their sense of boundlessness primarily through their advocacy of territorial expansion." Twenty years later, the officer corps had lost much of this enthusiasm, just as it was reemerging in full force among Jackson's civilian supporters.[3]

The remainder of *Peacekeepers and Conquerors* explores the officer corps' experiences along the nation's international borders to show how professional soldiers came to serve the nation-state not as loose cannons or agents of sectional interests like Jackson in the 1810s, nor simply as ad hoc law enforcement officers and federal diplomats like Scott and his subordinates along the Canadian border in 1838. Instead, they ultimately did so as the politically accountable military agents of an empire that many of them, like Zachary Taylor, commander of the Army of Occupation in Texas in 1846, were privately reluctant to see absorbed into the United States. In exploring this transition, chapters 10 and 11 survey Edmund Gaines's career on the borders of Texas between 1823 and 1846, where he attempted to practice the bellicose expansionism he had learned at Old Hickory's knee but was repeatedly disavowed by the national government, including expansionist presidents Jackson and Polk. By moving from Jackson through Scott to Gaines and Taylor and the junior career officers who served under them, we can follow the officer corps' gradual evolution into a socially, politically, and professionally accountable instrument of American foreign and national security policy. By 1846, career army officers served the cause of national expansion as members of a bureaucratic institution accountable to a variety of institutional and internalized controls, not as individuals or as representatives of a particular sectional or sectoral interest like slaveholding southern farmers. Moreover, they did so without the ardent enthusiasm of their predecessors during the 1810s and without much of the racialized rhetoric of Manifest Destiny espoused by civilian expansionists during the 1840s. In the final analysis, the personal material security guaranteed by stable careers in large-scale organizations encouraged restraint rather than belligerence in national military responses to foreign policy crises.

The most fundamental issue officers addressed in their thoughts about foreign affairs was the desirability of war. In the immediate aftermath of the War of 1812, there appears to have been little hesitation by any substantial segment of the officer corps to advocate war in pursuit of the nation's interest or honor. The willingness of an Andrew Jackson, a James Wilkinson, or an Eleazar Ripley to use the army or recruit from it for ventures independent of government sanction was the greatest practical threat to military subordination and accountability to civilian authority among the generation of senior military commanders before 1821. This belligerence, combined with a confused situation and somewhat credible pretexts, made it easy for Jackson to launch the army into Florida again and again until Spain capitulated. Yet the danger of a European alliance against American republicanism virtually disappeared after the proclamation of the Monroe Doctrine and—much more immediately important—its British analogue and after France's recognition of British opposition via the Polignac memorandum. Aside from operations connected with Indian removal within the supposed boundaries of the United States, American expansionism proceeded largely through the private paths of commerce and settlement during the 1820s and 1830s, and the thinking of military commanders followed suit. Of all the senior army leaders asked to submit reports on the 1821 reduction—the army's only comprehensive effort at strategic planning between the War of 1812 and the late 1830s—only Winfield Scott referred directly to the potential for "another offensive war against Canada."[4]

During those years, the frustrating, often distasteful experience of Indian removal and the Second Seminole War pushed many officers toward a less aggressive stance than their predecessors, and expansionist sentiments are difficult to find in officers' papers from the generation between 1821 and 1836. Indeed, military enthusiasm for expansion ebbed and flowed in time with, but slightly behind, civilian aggressiveness, not ahead of it; during the 1830s, it was largely filibustering's immediate threat to American neutrality and peace, rather than latent hopes for expansion or war, that drew the officer corps' attention to relations with Britain and Mexico. Professional military commanders along the borders of Texas and Canada took much less belligerent and expansionist stances during the late 1830s than their predecessors on the Florida frontier two decades before, while Oregon and California went virtually unmentioned in military diaries and correspondence before the mid-1840s. Whatever his own intentions might have been, Edmund Gaines was as clearly Andrew Jackson's subordinate on the Texas frontier in 1836 as he had been in Florida in 1818, and he obeyed the president's demand for restraint just as he had obeyed the general's demand for action. Two years later, Winfield Scott and his subordinates were instrumental in breaking up private efforts to invade Canada and plunge the United States into war with Britain. Though Scott and some of his subordinates initially welcomed the "Patriot" risings against British rule in Canada, they quickly reverted to a dutiful stance that stressed the sovereignty of the nation-state and the inviolability of international borders by private parties, rather than American expansion. A decade later, the most bellicose officers were young lieutenants and West Point cadets eager for glory and promotion, while more experienced commanders' interest in war over Texas and Oregon varied significantly. Indeed, prior to the war, more officers counseled against the annexation of Texas than in favor of the conquest of California or central or southern Mexico, prominent objectives among civilian expansionists that were virtually invisible in the papers of career soldiers.

The most fundamental problem for anyone attempting to plan or predict the American future in the nineteenth century was the growing space over which U.S. citizens settled and traded. The wide expanses of North America and the Atlantic, the desire to conquer the former and the virtually free security provided by the latter, inescapably conditioned the army officer corps' perspectives on foreign relations and national strategy. On the one hand, military officers had ample functional (professional) and organizational (careerist) imperatives to remind the nation of the continuing possibility of war—by which they fundamentally meant conflict with European-style forces rather than the American Indians—and the need to prepare for it, however remote the actual probability of war with a European power. On the other hand, the pacific implications of American geopolitical isolation from Europe were widely understood among men of affairs in both civil and military life. A realistic assessment of the nation's limited military capabilities, founded on its fiscal and ideological aversion to large peacetime forces in an era when general warfare seemed a declining possibility, led the majority of experienced commanders to be cautious in advocating war or territorial expansion against opponents, like Britain, that were much more powerful than Spain. Consequently, very few officers composed general analyses of the American geostrategic situation apart from the reports of the Fortifications Board on coastal defense, and planning for war with European powers received little attention after 1821 aside from that board and a set of reports during the Maine boundary crisis.[5]

This restraint was possible because of officers' confidence in the latent power and future prospects of the United States. Though they repeatedly lamented their budgets and routinely called for measures to improve the nation's military capability, experienced military commanders ultimately shared the optimism of civilian policy makers that the nation would be able to defend itself if attacked and expand if the opportunity arose. Socially and culturally, the growing fissures between boisterous Jacksonian populism, rabid materialism, and the gentility and order to which soldiers aspired, continually demonstrated in officers' frustrating experiences with civilian frontiersmen, had a similar practical effect, discouraging them from associating themselves with the belligerent egalitarian chauvinism of civilian expansionists. Instead, the career military officer could keep his composure in international crises, demonstrating the poise and self-possession appropriate to a professional seeking to control the application of national military force.

The officer corps as a whole grew more patient and less bellicose—though no less self-interested—as a result of these social and occupational developments, and a spirit of conservative legalism gradually replaced the aggressive republican internationalism of the 1810s as the basis of the officer corps' approach to foreign policy issues. Commanders seeking order, authority, and stability constantly reaffirmed the principles of international law, the inviolability of national borders, and the sovereignty of the federal nation-state over the application of organized violence, and their activities on the frontiers gave these abstractions a concrete reality that had been lacking in the turbulent southern borderlands before 1820. This process of attitudinal and behavioral change accelerated with experience, as the dangers of a decentralized foreign policy and the demands and consequences of adherence to international law became increasingly real to military commanders during the frontier and border crises of the 1830s and 1840s. Indeed, experienced career officers became as interested in stability along the borders as in military preparedness per se, because both were equally essential to their ongoing employment, authority, and prestige as individual gentlemen, as professionals, and as members of an internally self-governing organization facing potent political competition from the militia and volunteers. In this sense, the officer corps' quest for military preparedness was only the specifically military manifestation of a more general search for individual, organizational, and social security and stability, which encompassed personal, professional, and class concerns to encourage a quest for subordination as well as autonomy.

This chapter explores officers' attitudes toward international relations during the generation after the War of 1812. Together with the following chapter, it ties together civil-military relations and military diplomacy along the nation's northern border, culminating in the army's efforts to restrain American filibusters and prevent war with Britain during the crises between 1837 and 1842. These chapters illustrate the intimate connections among the officer corps' class values, professional interests, and worldview; its growing sense of accountability to the nation-state; and the elaboration of American national sovereignty (and indeed, of the international state system) through the hierarchies of military discipline in the borderlands of the early republic. The analysis of operations intended to maintain national sovereignty and international peace provides apt case studies of the army officer corps' growing sense of objective procedural accountability to national civilian political authority, while illustrating the subtle distinctions between accountability and responsibility and the complex dilemmas these ideals posed for military professionals trying to mediate among national, regional, and international considerations.

Career soldiers trying to preserve the personal and institutional security of their state-sponsored monopoly over the direction of organized military force responded with growing caution to the rabid demands of aggressive frontier settlers, preferring the stability, authority, and order fostered by adherence to national and international law to the potential for self-aggrandizement and social disruption posed by territorial expansion. In doing so, professional officers remained accountable to the dictates of the democratically elected government and thus to the values of their society, even the egalitarian segments many commanders felt distaste for, while faithfully upholding that government's policies even when they were unpopular with expansionist frontiersmen and their partisans. Career professional officers led the operations designed to effect Indian removal and the expulsion of Mexico from the Southwest, but only when ordered to do so through constitutional processes, and they ardently suppressed filibustering by private forces—both in significant contrast to the years before 1820. In contests between locality and nation, military commanders could be relied on to serve the nation-state that employed them, substantially diminishing the potential for constitutional conflict presented by earlier military usurpations of authority like Jackson's invasion of Florida, while helping to keep the nation out of potentially disastrous wars against the superior military power of Britain, for which American coastal defenses were wholly unprepared.

A BIT OF A MUDDLE: MILITARY ATTITUDES TOWARD RELATIONS WITH EUROPEAN NATIONS DURING THE 1820S AND 1830S

Officers continued to raise the banner of international republicanism and its defense during the 1820s, but the vehemence and frequency of this rhetoric declined quickly as European threats receded and the nation turned inward amid whirlpools of economic panic and sectional division. The reports presented by general officers and staff chiefs in anticipation of the force reduction of 1821 included numerous expositions about the continuing need for military preparedness, but most of their recommendations were couched in defensive terms that suited the country's isolationist temper as the wave of postwar nationalism dissipated. Despite some fears of the Holy Alliance of the Continental monarchies during the early 1820s, the tensions that had drawn the United States into conflicts along its borders before 1821 declined into relative insignificance after the annexation of Florida. European concern with American events eased with the forcible repression of organized revolutionary activity on the Continent, particularly the Austrian intervention in Naples in 1820 and the French intervention in Spain three years later. The latter spurred Britain to warn against Continental efforts to recolonize Latin America, and significant European threats to the territorial integrity of the Western Hemisphere evaporated as the Royal Navy barred the Atlantic and France declared (in the Polignac memorandum of October 1823, repeated in July

1825) that it would not actively support recolonization. Spain invaded Mexico at Tampico in 1829 but was defeated by yellow fever, and France would bombard Veracruz in a claims dispute in 1839, but there was no permanent recolonization and little American outrage at these incidents.[6]

Whether from generals or cadets, republican internationalism became increasingly defensive, indeed isolationist, in focus and implication after 1820. In particular, although most officers surely agreed with its precepts, the Monroe Doctrine had little impact on their lives and little presence in their letters before the 1840s. Early in 1824 Zachary Taylor addressed an extensive commentary on the subject to Thomas Jesup, flatly asserting that "the nation will be prepared to go [to] any lengths" to prevent the reimposition of Spanish rule in Latin America, but Taylor also believed the United States should avoid entanglement in European conflicts, specifically the Greek revolt. Taylor's changing perspective provides an individual example of the transition reflected in the Monroe Doctrine—from the expansive revolutionary ideology and internationalism of early republican soldiers and politicians like Scott and Jefferson to the more narrowly defined realism and national self-interest of Jacksonian-era foreign relations. Though he later became a Whig, the colonel's views aligned him with the Jacksonians, who stressed the defense of national interests rather than hemispheric cooperation between republican governments. (Jackson favored a Pan-American coalition only in response to an aggressive European one, and only for the purpose of defending Cuba and Mexico.) The isolationist dimensions of Jefferson's "doctrine of the hemispheres" were echoed by soldiers' silence concerning the internal squabbles of Europe, while its expansionist implications received little comment among military commanders during the quiet of the late 1820s and the Indian fighting of the 1830s.[7]

Though officers' values remained more republican than liberal, the nation's general ideological shift from eighteenth-century republicanism to nineteenth-century liberalism was quietly reflected in the way articulate professional soldiers envisioned potential European threats, particularly those from Britain. By the 1840s, military fears of British encirclement and containment, largely forgotten or suppressed during the 1820s but revived with the Canadian border crises, were increasingly expressed (like those of civilian commentators) in the language of zero-sum commercial competition and a fear of worldwide British trade monopolies, rather than a millennial conflict between monarchy and republicanism. The beginnings of this shift were first apparent in the reports of the Fortifications Board, particularly when Joseph Totten took over principal responsibility for their formulation from French émigré Simon Bernard during the 1820s, and in the quest for economic development stressed by Edmund Gaines in his memorials to Congress on coastal defense after 1825.[8]

Nevertheless, this shift gained only momentary expression in officers' correspondence during the 1830s, for they apparently felt too little direct concern over British commercial competition to comment at any length. Indeed, aside from reports and correspondence focused on the Canadian border crises, there were remarkably few comments—public or private, as advice to civilians or in letters to one another—by career officers about foreign affairs or international relations specifically or in general, nor did their frequency increase significantly over the course of the decade. Among the exceptions was an 1833 letter to the *Military and Naval Magazine* warning that British and American commercial success could not continue without conflict: "This competition . . . must end in inequality; then comes the reign of commercial monopoly, which . . . is not to be endured in friendship, or with safety." Like Totten, most American military commentators believed the United States was fortunate to possess a guaranty against direct British aggression through the vulnerability of Canada. Nevertheless, the 1833 author (perhaps, based on his language, strategically minded Quartermaster General Jesup) disclaimed any ambition for territorial conquest, content that "the stake [Canada] thus to be ventured by [British] violation of [inter]national law . . . is a wholesome restraint upon [that country's] commercial cupidity and national jealousy."[9]

Amazingly, aside from reprinted reports and a couple of officers' letters reprinted from civilian newspapers, this article appears to have been the only broad-ranging commentary on the subject of foreign relations and the international state system published by a career army officer during the decade-long run of the army's professional journals. Indeed, like most military comments on foreign affairs, this essay was directed primarily at encouraging generic military preparedness—appropriations, whether for troops or fortifications—rather than analyzing U.S. relations with specific nations or regions. It was not at all difficult for officers to become well-informed about public issues, especially given their ready access to gossip from Washington, and we can assume that they were as knowledgeable as any of their fellow citizens not directly engaged in international commerce. Nevertheless, junior soldiers normally kept silent on paper as well as in public, a tendency that points toward the officer corps' growing sense of political neutrality and subordination, embodied in accountability to the nation-state, as well as the limits of their intellectual and professional curiosity. Such belligerent ideas doubtlessly seemed too outspoken and partisan in nature for professional soldiers—even junior ones, frustrated by sluggish promotion prospects—to feel secure about espousing them publicly. Naval officers (who also wrote in the two professional journals) were more prolific commentators on international relations, probably because their duties brought them into more direct contact with foreign powers, whereas army officers focused on being ready for any contingency by augmenting the size and funding of the national standing army. Doing so certainly implied greater preparedness for war with European powers, but it was just as valuable for the overstretched army's performance of constabulary missions on the Indian frontiers.

Following the decline of the republican internationalism of the 1810s and early 1820s, conservative realism became the order of the day in professional military attitudes toward foreign affairs. A few thoughtful career soldiers, like Edmund Gaines, envisioned the growth of international trade in liberal terms, as a potential force for international peace, but most sought to justify military preparedness and spending by pointing to the uncertainty and tumult of a world of competing nation-states whose commercial interests would probably lead to conflict before they fostered peace. Socialized in ideals of martial glory, professional soldiers believed that competition was an unalterable fact of international life, and the specific circumstances of American relations with particular European nations ultimately meant little in their calculus of military preparation and necessity. Facing congressional pressure for budget cuts amid the economic depression in 1839, engineer Major William H. Chase acknowledged that "there is certainly less disposition for war throughout the civilized world now than twenty years ago," conceding that "the multiplication and extension of commercial relations" between Britain, France, and the United States afforded "strong guarantees for the maintenance of peace." Nevertheless, he, like Gaines, took this tack to conciliate a civilian audience that refused to accept the expense demanded by arguments derived from conservative military assumptions about human nature and the competitive dynamics of the international system.[10]

Employment by the state made experienced professional soldiers acutely aware of the interdependence of politics and the social order and highly conscious of the relationship between domestic and international stability. Experienced senior commanders were not alone in their concern over the unsettled state of European politics and its potential impact on American interests, though more junior soldiers usually expressed their concerns in private. Writing from France while visiting engineering schools in 1840, at a time when tensions over Egypt still ran high between Britain and France, Lieutenant Alexander Swift informed his father (former chief engineer Joseph G. Swift) that the bellicose language of the French press demonstrated "the ticklish condition" of that country's society and politics. Domestic unrest could lead to international aggression, a link that Whiggish officers, or those with any frontier experience, could easily identify between Jacksonian populism and expansionism—the outward projection of domestic social tensions, egalitarian values, and economic uncertainty. The real inequalities white men sought to deny among themselves could be imposed on Indians, and later Mexicans, through dispossession and conquest. Though officers were generally authoritarian, and Whigs generally supported hierarchy, they espoused these values as part of a stable domestic social order, not as excuses for international war, which they thought would undermine domestic stability.[11]

The officer corps was certainly not uniform or united in its attitudes toward international relations. Some soldiers, especially ardent junior officers eager for promotion, found portents of a brighter international future in such instability. In 1842 Lieutenant James Mason, an engineer stationed at Fort Adams in Rhode Island, asserted that the death of the Duke of Orleans would lead to a republic in France. Indeed, Mason looked to a second French revolution to sustain the republican cause: "if the madmen of privilege should again try . . . its suppression . . . [France] can again furnish a committee of public safety composed of the men of questionable morality & colossal intellects." The lieutenant was one of a growing number of young Democrats among the junior officer corps once the Second Party System had matured circa 1840, and he found it "gratifying to see the party of privilege & monopoly in this country in its last gasp." This might have been a reference to the populist Dorr Rebellion for constitutional reform in Rhode Island, with which Mason and other Democrats sympathized, but his superiors, led by former Democrat John Wool and the erstwhile republican internationalist Winfield Scott, had already provided advice and a show of force to help the conservative Charter Party repress the reform movement, under cautious instructions from President Tyler. Despite the effusions of Young America and Manifest Destiny among some Democrats, the army's career officer corps increasingly conflated domestic and international law and order and sought to stabilize U.S. foreign policy through centralization.[12]

The worldview these officers expressed was simultaneously professional and careerist, based ultimately on employment by the nation-state and an acceptance of the consequences thereof. These value systems connected individual, organizational, and occupational self-interest with values of professional responsibility and political accountability. Indeed, these values came together along the Canadian border in a manner more fundamentally professional—meaning accountable or responsive to the demands of the society the army served—than the increasingly bloated plans for the coastal fortification program. (These grandiose plans were ultimately irrelevant, given the budgetary constraints—strong antagonism to raising revenue, or to any form of fiscal deficit—imposed by American liberalism and republicanism.) Nevertheless, the individual officer's normative socialization at West Point and his material desire for career security and promotion in the face of continual congressional inquiries led to a potent sense of personal responsibility and fiscal accountability. This individual imperative ultimately served the larger cause of responsiveness to civil authority, despite the dissatisfaction and anxiety individual commanders felt during crises—a complex, sometimes contradictory, but fundamentally accountable pattern of response that ultimately characterized both the staff and the line of the army. Officers who came to view their responsibilities in terms of national defense—and depended on the national legislature for funding during an economic depression—were more likely to act in ways accountable to the constitutional structure of the American nation-state than to the importunities of local, sectional, or sectoral interests, as Jackson and his subordinates had two decades before. Instead, the rest of *Peacekeepers and Conquerors* will show the officer corps acting as both a leader in and a crucial restraint on U.S. territorial expansion, advancing the interests of American frontiersmen but doing so at the direction of the federal government rather than the behest of private individuals, with whom the corps often came into conflict while attempting to uphold national sovereignty and the authority to initiate war.

THE BEGINNINGS OF THE ANGLO-AMERICAN CRISIS: THE "PATRIOT" REBELLION AND OFFICER REACTIONS TO FILIBUSTERING AGAINST CANADA, 1837–1838

Military relations along the Canadian border mirrored the Anglo-American rapprochement of the late 1810s and the 1820s. The concern American policy makers, including senior western commanders, felt toward British trade with the northwestern Indians during the decade after the War of 1812 is chronicled in *Jackson's Sword*, but senior officers stationed along the Canadian border, closest to British military forces, showed surprisingly few of these anxieties. They may have expressed such concerns, but they felt confident that without overt British action—that is, a renewal of war—the Indians had too little power to halt U.S. expansion. Perhaps they underestimated the influence of British trade farther west, but Alexander Macomb, then commander of the Fifth Military Department headquartered at Detroit, doubted that Britain would oppose the American advance into the Northwest or encourage the indigenes to do so. Like the commanders stationed at Niagara and Detroit after the British backed away from aiding the Ohio Indians in the mid-

Filibusters lounging. From *Frank Leslie's Illustrated Newspaper*, 1856. (Courtesy Library of Congress, LC-USZ62-108152)

1790s—and those during the Canadian border crises between 1837 and 1842—the future commanding general hoped for "a friendly good understanding" with his counterparts and recent adversaries across the border, "where[ever] it can be maintained without injury to the public service and with honor and credit to the army." Hence Macomb showed visiting British officers "every civility and attention in my power," reporting to division commander Jacob Brown that "the greatest harmony has prevailed between the military on both sides." Such concord was less evident among naval commanders, and Macomb complained that the British commodore on Lake Erie seemed determined to break the peace by boarding American vessels.[13]

These breaches were smoothed over, and the brigadier's attention then focused on an extraordinary, albeit short-lived, crisis in local civil-military relations and law enforcement. In April 1817 a committee of Detroit civic leaders complained that marauding soldiers "have been seen at all hours of the night, armed with *guns*, *swords*, and *bludgeons* wandering up and down the settlement, trying to force open the doors of the dwelling houses" and "grossly insulting" the inhabitants. The committee threatened that the citizens would organize in self-defense, but the army apparently dealt with the turmoil, and within six months the civilian customs collector requested a contingent to aid against smuggling. Macomb asked that the request be made in writing and advised the collector that he could not provide troops on a constant basis—reasonable precautions when employing soldiers in civilian law enforcement. Yet military enforcement of federal law became one of the army's principal missions in upholding national sovereignty once Anglo-American rapprochement had eased more dangerous tensions along the border. Fort Niagara, which had been abandoned in 1825 due to the calm in Anglo-American relations and the general shift southward and westward to deal with the Indian frontier and squatter removal, was regarrisoned with an average of two companies between 1828 and 1833. The War Department portrayed this detachment as "a countervailing force" to prevent Canadians from taking advantage of large British troop concentrations to subject Americans to "continued insult and depredation" (robberies), though these insults must have been very minor, given the lack of evidence in military correspondence or other accounts. Nor did Macomb consider these missions trivial irritants: as commanding general in 1831, trying to justify the maintenance of a garrison at Fort Niagara in the face of budget cuts, the native New Yorker emphasized "the effect of deterring persons disposed to engage in illicit commerce from . . . violating the Revenue laws." (Macomb also deployed troops to southwestern Louisiana and Key West for this purpose.)[14]

The Indians might have posed a more difficult case, because some British officers felt a lingering sense of obligation to protect their longtime allies. The Treaty of Ghent recognized and accepted the native custom of moving across the borders established by colonial powers, and the inability to confine the Indians to one side of the border encouraged ongoing worries about British support for the Native Americans, while leaving the door open for a variety of incidents. A closely related border issue was the status of particular locales along the boundary that remained to be surveyed, largely by military engineers. The exchange of forts and other positions in the months immediately after the war's end was fraught with complications and friction, and there were accusations of delay or encroachment on both sides. But these were gradually smoothed over, and rapprochement was achieved, a process in which the increasingly friendly interaction of military officers on the scene was essential to building mutual confidence and minimizing the number and scope of incidents that an increasingly partisan media might exaggerate into a crisis. Friction was ameliorated and tension reduced as much by the frontier diplomacy of military commanders—the most powerful representatives of both national governments along the border—as by senior civilian diplomats or the long-term demands of mutual economic interest.[15]

Nevertheless, after the failure of Mexican offensives against Texas in 1836, the Canadian border became the most dangerous international flash point for the United States. After years of slowly growing unrest, a series of armed rebellions broke out in Upper and Lower Canada (Ontario and Quebec) during the autumn of 1837. The self-proclaimed "Patriots" were quickly dispersed, but many fled to the United States and began to raise money and recruits to return to the fray. Their main force assembled at Buffalo and established a base on Navy Island, on the Canadian side of the Niagara River, that December. Loyal Canadian militia responded by burning the rebel supply vessel *Caroline*, anchored on the American shore, killing an American citizen. From Maine to Michigan, American public opinion erupted in anger and fear. Facing a financial panic and depression, and well aware of the weakness of American coastal defenses, President Martin Van Buren wanted to avoid war and further commercial disruption. He immediately sent a group of experienced professional soldiers to reassure the restive borderers and maintain American sovereignty by securing the frontier against violation from either side, "manifesting to friends and foes," as Major William Worth wrote early in 1838, "the continued disposition of the Government to put forth every energy in maintenance of the laws and the National Faith." For the next four years, professional soldiers were the chief agents of national policy along the northern frontier, battling a series of private attempts to precipitate a war between the United States and Britain by invading Canada. Yet the "Patriot" sympathies of many local civil officials and militiamen—indeed, of many federally appointed civil officials in the border region—deprived federal military commanders of the routine legal authority (the sanction of due process) and manpower they needed to act as a consistent barrier to filibuster forays. Given the delicate balance of American public opinion and the inadequacy of national neutrality law, peacekeeping in the northern borderlands required as much civil-military and federal-local diplomacy, whether persuasive or coercive, as physical force.[16]

By the mid-1830s, traditional American fears that Canada would provide Britain with a base for aggression against the United States were seemingly in decline, as the growth of the American economy, the boom in Anglo-American trade and investment, and the successful conclusion of diplomatic agreements led to self-confidence and a belief in the possibilities of negotiation and coexistence. Some historians have suggested that popular attitudes toward Britain hardened in the South and West during the 1830s because of British support for abolitionism and American banks' indebtedness to their transatlantic counterparts, particularly during the financial panic that began just before the Canadian rebellions; conversely, hostility presumably declined among those who opposed slavery and sought investment, largely in the Northeast. Anglophobia notwithstanding, southerners feared the wartime disruption of the cotton trade and the influx of free states and abolitionist voters that would follow the conquest of Canada; though they projected a fearless façade, they also had to expect British coastal incursions, slave flight, rebellion, and maroonage in case of conflict, as in the Revolution and the War of 1812. Economic relations with Britain and Canada presented similar dilemmas for Anglophobic northerners. Prior to the repeal of the British Corn Laws in 1846, many western farmers valued Canadian markets as a duty-free outlet for their wheat and objected to the potential for competition from Canadian farmers within an expanded United States. Meanwhile, the opening of the Erie Canal reduced some of the attraction of the St. Lawrence River as an outlet for American exports.[17]

Despite occasional boisterous outbursts, American faith in republican institutions and economic growth ultimately worked to encourage peace. Historian Reginald Stuart has observed that "continentalism and self-determination were compatible, not contradictory, components of America's expansionist ideology" concerning Canada: a growing number of Americans expected that Canada would gradually but inevitably move toward independence from Britain and union with the United States as American economic and political influence increased. Confident in the example of their free economy and republican institutions, most Americans were willing to bide their time rather than risk war and economic disruption by subverting British rule directly, and the Van Buren administration refused to use the Patriot crises as grounds to do so. Amid this context, many moderate and conservative Americans shared British views of the Canadian rebels and American filibusters of the late 1830s, seeing them as transgressors of international law and domestic order, Jacksonian democrats gone mad with passion rather than the advance guard of enlightened American republicanism. War with Britain and the Royal Navy was a dangerous gamble when American entrepreneurs believed they could outpace their competition peacefully, and the financial problems created by the Panic of 1837 made war even riskier. For Britain, in addition to the Opium War (1839–1842), the First Afghan War (1839–1842), and the Egyptian crisis with France (1839–1840), these were years of great working-class militancy embodied in the Chartist movement, concurrent crises that diverted some attention from Canadian affairs and Anglo-American relations.[18]

Yet the insurgents presented a significant dilemma for the place of armed force and territorial expansion in the American federal system—a tenuous legal, political, and constitutional balance already stretched to the breaking point by a decade of populist Jacksonian aggression against Indians and Mexico. Many Americans, especially those in the border region, supported the so-called Patriots on ideological grounds, as inheritors of the libertarian revolutionary tradition, or on chauvinist egalitarian grounds of Anglophobia. Popular enthusiasm was intensified by the disruption of the financial panic and the onset of winter (meaning layoffs from outdoor jobs), which left tens if not hundreds of thousands unemployed; in the border states, many of these idle men joined "Hunters' Lodges" that raided into Canada. Federal military officers were then caught in the middle between American filibusters and their civilian supporters (including many local civil officials) and the British authorities and loyal Canadians who wanted to pursue the Patriots into the United States to avenge their raids. The army's sympathies were largely with the British, and professional military commanders believed that the most moral and efficient way to defend American sovereignty was to preempt conflict by preventing filibuster incursions against Canada, rather than trying to stop more powerful British forces from pursuing the Patriots across the border after the fact. The army acted energetically against the insurgents, despite hesitation and passive resistance by many local civil officials, and veteran professional commanders successfully maintained federal authority and contained incidents that otherwise might have led to a disastrous war with Britain. In a contest of coercive frontier diplomacies, the army's national military diplomacy ultimately defeated the regional, nonstate diplomacy (if we can call it that) of the insurgents.[19]

The army's operations along the Canadian border during these tense years provide outstanding examples of several of the principal themes of this book. Their simultaneous efforts at international and domestic peacekeeping demonstrate the complexity and frustration of normally authoritarian national military officers conducting federal as well as international diplomacy on the spot, mediating between local and regional as well as national and international values and interests. They did so with growing professionalism: both subordination, responsibility, and accountability to civilian authority *and* insulation and autonomy from constant civilian intervention. This combination contributed to and reinforced their relative but comparably noteworthy objectivity, both as mediators with national and international vision and as adherents to core ideological values and practices like due process and the rule of law. As the most visible and potent agents of American national power, these professional commanders repeatedly had to confront and constrain aggressive private initiatives along the borders, often in the face of obstruction from local politicians and criticism from their national representatives. As the most powerful and most reliable representatives of federal power in the field, career military officers played a key role, however informally conceived and practiced, as mediators in contests between local and national interests and objectives. Much as on the Indian frontiers, they did so primarily as national rather than local, regional, or sectional agents, displaying a remarkable autonomy and effective insulation from populist civilian beliefs. The concept of national sovereignty, particularly in the form of centralized control over the use of armed force, emerges as the key to understanding the vigor with which career professional soldiers attempted to enforce domestic law and international peace. Their negative reactions to filibustering were ultimately a product of the high value they placed on order and stability, a mind-set developed amid the rules-bound world of the nation's first large bureaucratic hierarchy by men who feared that disorder and challenges to the national state could threaten their employment, social status, and ability to command.

Engineer Colonel Joseph Totten's 1836 report on coastal defense warned that "the military consequences [of American population growth] . . . are so obvious that it [can]not be supposed [that] they are not perfectly understood by our neighbor," which had only 2,000 regular troops in the Canadas when the rebellions broke out. The United States expected to hold Canada hostage in time of war, but American confidence in the balance of power was sorely tested in 1838. The British responded forcefully to the rebellions, American filibusters, and tensions over the boundary between Maine and New Brunswick by massing 20,000 regulars in their North American provinces. Busy with the Seminoles, the United States had less than 200 soldiers along the border in December 1837, stationed at Hancock Barracks in Maine and at Fort Brady on Michigan's Upper Peninsula—the opposite ends of the border, and regions with little Patriot activity. President Van Buren and Secretary of War Poinsett recognized the unreliability of the militia, which would have been an expensive force to employ amid the fiscal crisis that followed the financial panic in the autumn of 1837, and they cautioned Winfield Scott to call only for those he needed, and only from regions "distant from the theater of action" that were uninfected by Patriot zeal. Thus, despite the creation of a new regiment specifically for the northern frontier during the summer of 1838, American commanders never had more than 3,000 regulars on the entire Canadian border during the crises between 1838 and 1842—"hardly enough to fire a shot in honor of our flag," as William Worth put it in February 1839.[20]

Professional soldiers sent to restrain the insurgents recognized that there was no real obstacle preventing the British from sweeping southward in retaliation or pursuit; the abstract confidence of the previous decade quickly evaporated as officers realized that the nation's long-term ability to mobilize overwhelming forces could do little to save the border region from a catastrophic counterstroke. The same lack of troops that hampered their law enforcement operations left professional commanders feeling helpless before the possibility of large-scale retaliation or war, and they hastened to absolve themselves of responsibility for the consequences. "What can a Military Commander do with a mere handful of men, when compelled to act in subordination to civil officers, a majority of whom are notoriously favorable to what is misnamed the Patriot cause?" asked brevet Brigadier General Hugh Brady, commanding the Detroit frontier, in December 1838. "We are envired by Pirates, bold, reckless [and] unscrupulous on the one [American] side, and by an injured people and indignant soldiery on the other [Canadian] with none to appreciate or ameliorate our position," Worth wrote to Winfield Scott in a moment of near panic early in 1839. The stern colonel combined subordination and responsibility to observe that "it is not for us as Soldiers to seek to penetrate the policy of the Government . . . but as a good citizen I cannot resist the belief that we are fast verging toward a contest, for which everything around us denotes total absence of decent preparation, & I can already in my mind's eye, see, for a time, the national honor, stricken to the dust." Worth was especially worried that the consequences would damage the army's credibility and prestige. He implicitly linked personal, national, and professional honor to preservation of the army's organizational jurisdiction over the employment of armed force along the Canadian frontier: "We . . . have no means of preventing the [British] force from overrunning our border fifty miles deep at any point! The thin curtain of Regulars would be pushed aside in an instant . . . if a contest ensues disgrace awaits us; and who amid the torrent of holy indignation will stop to inquire into our means—we may do and die but even that will not rescue our memories."[21]

Junior officers distant from the scene echoed the excited colonel's despair: Zebina Kinsley warned New York congressman Gouverneur Kemble (a strong supporter of the army on the House Military Affairs Committee from 1837 to 1841) that "a war with any European power would show an awful deficiency in the means of defense." Given the unreliability of the militia, which professional officers considered more likely to precipitate war (and then flee or desert) than deter or defeat British aggression, Worth and his compatriots felt that the best they could do was set a good example of upholding national sovereignty and the rule of law. Although his measures might be fruitless in practical terms, they would "have the excellent effect to stimulate the civil authority to the assertion of its honor and dignity, and [to] convince our outraged neighbors, that . . . we [meaning the army's officers, as representatives of the federal government], at least perform our duties in good faith."[22] Worth had real cause for concern, for the British public reacted angrily to American filibustering, and the British government gave a threatening substance to this sentiment by reinforcing its army and navy in North America. Historian Kenneth Bourne observes that elite and official British opinion toward the United States had "seriously deteriorated" since the mid-1820s because of distaste for the growing disorder of American egalitarianism and democracy, and American support for the insurgency seemed to confirm their worst fears about anarchy and chaos spreading from the south. On the eve of the rebellions, Henry Fox, British ambassador to the United States, cautioned the governor of New Brunswick that he saw no intent by the American government to support or promote unrest, but within a couple of months, Fox came to believe that the administration had "both wished and expected [that] the Canadian rebellion would succeed."[23]

The British government reacted to the Patriot movement and the consequent growth of tensions by re-forming its squadron on the Great Lakes, in clear violation of the Rush-Bagot Agreement, and increasing its West Atlantic squadron from twenty-seven ships to forty-one, including several large frigates and steamers. In contrast, the United States remained just as vulnerable on the Atlantic frontier two years after the French war scare as it was on the Canadian border. In November 1837 commanding general Macomb reported to the secretary of war that not a single coastal post, in the fortification system so vaunted by the Corps of Engineers, held even a company's garrison of forty soldiers. In January 1838 Secretary of War Poinsett officially stated to Congress that not a single coastal fortification was in defensible condition: "There is not a fortress on our long line of sea defences capable of resisting an armed brig [a small vessel of ten to twenty guns], not one that may not be taken by a small force." Nor did the army's peacekeeping and neutrality enforcement efforts change that situation; in March 1839 Lieutenant Colonel Ichabod Crane (for whom Washington Irving's character was probably named) warned that he only had enough powder for five rounds per cannon to defend Fort Niagara.[24]

Under these tense circumstances, immediate dangers threatened to supplant confidence in long-term success in the minds of American policy makers, especially among the military men most directly responsible for the nation's security in case of war. The crucial stakes potentially at issue in the Anglo-American contest of the late 1830s and early 1840s were sketched out by Quartermaster General Jesup in a confidential letter to Secretary Poinsett early in 1839. (Jesup had to use his left hand, as the right had been permanently maimed by British fire during the Battle of Lundy's Lane a quarter century before, where he was wounded three times. Readers should keep in mind that Winfield Scott, William Worth, and Hugh Brady were also wounded in the same battle.) The quartermaster's threat assessment sounded much like Andrew Jackson's views of the southern borderlands twenty years earlier, but powerful Britain had replaced weak Spain as the source of foreign contagion and threats to American security: "[The Canadas bear] heavily on our flank and rear . . . the influence which [they] are capable of exercising over the Indians upon our western frontier and the Texan and Mexican states render their geographical position a most powerful check upon us. . . . [Texas and Mexico will] never possess naval power; they must therefore rely on alliances with some great maritime power for the protection of their valuable and growing commerce." The (supposed) American policy of leaving other countries to their own affairs would compel these states to turn to Britain for aid: "her [Canadian] colonies, therefore . . . are a guarantee to her against our commercial, maritime, and political [meaning diplomatic] ascendancy, so long as she holds them." If the United States could seize Canada, however, "our maritime resources would be more than doubled. We should be forever freed from Indian difficulties; and Texas and Mexico . . . would be passive, if not powerless . . . our northern frontier [meaning both the Atlantic and Canadian ones] would be shortened by more than one half, and the resources for its protection augmented in a proportionate degree."[25]

Though exaggerated, Jesup's analysis demonstrates that some American military commanders thought not only in abstract terms of strategic interdependence, like those employed by Edmund Gaines and the engineers on the Fortifications Board, but in specific geostrategic ones closely linked to a consciousness of the role of economics in national power. In this zero-sum view of the world, whatever the United States gained, Britain lost; given their choice circa 1840, the British might have preferred the creation of a durable balance of power on the North American continent through the disintegration of the United States. With attitudes like these, it might seem surprising that the tensions of the early 1840s were not greater, but there were a number of powerful systemic reasons for the peaceful resolution of this ultimately localized crisis: American economic and British diplomatic problems limited the resources each side could devote to military preparations or actual war, commercial and financial ties between the two countries remained strong, and British officials feared that a war would unify the United States and rouse up its latent antagonism to the British presence in North America. To the degree that the confrontation was a real one with explosive potential, however, the successful conciliatory efforts of army officers along the Canadian border were largely responsible for the lack of escalation.[26]

The daily conduct of sensitive law enforcement operations along the Canadian border was charged to highly experienced but, by modern standards, rather junior officers, and they had no civilian diplomats from Washington on the scene to advise them. The army's first direct involvement in the Patriot conflict appears to have been on January 3, 1838, before news of the *Caroline* incident had reached Washington. That day, Secretary Poinsett ordered Inspector General John Wool, a resident of Troy (a suburb of Albany), to assume temporary command of the New York frontier in order to guard federal arsenals and prevent violations of American neutrality. Fresh from his vindication by Winfield Scott regarding the Cherokee, and still on good terms with fellow New Yorker Van Buren, Wool arrived in Buffalo the day before Scott and William Worth (also a New Yorker, stationed at the arsenal at Watervliet, outside Albany). Four days later, Wool was ordered to the Lake Champlain frontier, where he had served as one of Alexander Macomb's principal subordinates against the British invasion in 1814. Scott, an old friend of Van Buren and Poinsett, with whom he had worked during his deployment to South Carolina during the Nullification Crisis in 1832, was at home among New York leaders due to his frequent residence at Elizabethtown (modern-day Elizabeth) in northern New Jersey. Scott rushed from Washington to Buffalo and Detroit in January and February 1838; he returned to tour the Vermont border in January 1839 and briefly visited the Niagara frontier during the final round of substantial Patriot activity that September. Macomb, a New Yorker who had commanded the army forces at Plattsburgh in 1814 and had family upstate, was sent to the frontier during the second surge of filibustering in June 1838; he remained throughout that summer while Scott directed Cherokee removal.[27]

Apart from these brief tours by Scott and Macomb, the delicate practice of northern borderlands diplomacy, and ongoing oversight of geographic flash points in the Patriot insurgency, was left to experienced colonels. The army had only four generals; with Jesup in Florida and Gaines in the West, delegation of authority was unavoidable. Nor did New York challenge national military authority by attempting to place militia generals in command over the regular colonels, as had been the case in 1812 and in Florida in 1836. Thus the Vermont, St. Lawrence, Niagara, and Detroit frontiers were commanded by Wool (whose permanent rank was actually colonel) and regimental commanders Worth (promoted over many senior men to command the Eighth Infantry, raised for duty on the northern border in 1838), Abraham Eustis (commanding the First Artillery, who replaced Wool in Vermont that autumn), and Hugh Brady (longtime commander of the Second Infantry). Brady, like Wool and Worth, brought a wealth of local knowledge to his efforts as a federal diplomat. After spending more than a decade developing contacts while commanding at Detroit, the most mature social center in the Northwest, Brady did not have to depend on self-interested locals or civil officials to understand local public opinion, and he could convey his own sense of the situation directly to national policy makers. With his intimate knowledge of local motives and personalities, Brady would be able to rely on volunteer soldiers and the influence of local social, political, and economic elites more than any other federal commander on the border.[28]

Worth, who had nearly a quarter century of military experience when the rebellions broke out, was the principal field commander on both the Niagara and St. Lawrence frontiers—several hundred miles apart—during the winters of 1837–1838 and 1838–1839, when the Patriot agitation was at its height. Worth had been severely wounded while serving as Scott's aide-de-camp at Lundy's Lane in 1814, and Scott's professional patronage helped him win a series of choice positions; he was the first commandant of cadets at West Point in 1824, where he assisted Scott in testing new infantry drill regulations, and became chief of staff at the Artillery School at Fortress Monroe several years later. In 1832 Worth was promoted to major, over a number of more senior captains, into one of the new ordnance slots, and Scott promptly requested his services as inspector general for the Black Hawk War. The New Yorker's ordnance duty, directing Watervliet Arsenal in Troy, proved undistinguished but brought him into close contact with John Wool, who lived in Troy and was stationed there when not on inspection tours, and with other influential New Yorkers at the nearby state capital. Worth accompanied Scott on the general's first trip to Buffalo in January 1838 and was sent to reinforce Brady in Detroit later that month, before returning to eastern New York to combat the Patriot threat along the St. Lawrence in February. Worth served as Scott's chief of staff during the early stages of the Cherokee removal operation when the Patriot insurgency calmed down that summer, and he was rewarded—skipping the grade of lieutenant colonel entirely—with command of the new Eighth Infantry Regiment, created by Congress in July 1838 to patrol the northern border. Despite several outbursts of excessive pride and zeal, Worth's operational effectiveness along the border led to his appointment as theater commander in what proved to be the final campaign of the Seminole War and as division commander in Scott's army in Mexico.

Hopes for republicanism and the possibility of American territorial expansion characterized these officers' initial reactions to the rebellions. Winfield Scott's first emotion (in December 1837, before being sent to the frontier) was "God grant them success! My heart is with the oppressed of both Canadas." Worth's initial response was somewhat mixed, containing the values of law and order that would sustain his quest to enforce the neutrality laws throughout his tenure on the border. Writing to the general from Detroit shortly after the Battle of Malden (on the Canadian shore opposite the town) in January 1838, the stern major was overcome by emotion: "The flower of the young men of this city have found a *bloody grave*!" he exclaimed sentimentally, including "a noble hearted friend of mine." Like Scott, the New Yorker felt sympathy for the filibusters: "They were firmly of the opinion that they would earn the proud title of liberators of Canada," he reported in tones he would soon find anathema. Yet the authoritarian commander was forced to conclude that the incursion was "a sad affair, unquestionably a violation of law and good order," lamenting that "truly we are little better than a nation of pirates." Worth clearly sensed his own divided loyalties and the dilemmas they posed for his accountability to the neutrality policy, averring that "I can neither write nor speak coolly and hardly rationally." He promised his superior "a rational letter"—that is, one that disregarded his personal sentiments—as soon as he was able. By the time he did so, Worth had overcome his sympathy for the rebels and was prepared to assume the stern mantle of an agent charged with the enforcement of law and national sovereignty.[29]

As we saw with the Seminoles, army officers respected patriotism from almost any source. Unlike American civilians, few professional soldiers believed that the Canadian population was sympathetic to the insurgents, an assumption that encouraged an almost uniform rejection of the Patriots' claims to represent the Canadian people, not unlike officers' rejection of frontiersmen's and filibusters' claims to represent the American people. At a banquet in Houlton, Maine, in September 1838, Lieutenant Colonel Newman Clarke of the newly formed Eighth Infantry, like Worth a veteran of the Niagara campaign a quarter century before, followed a volunteer officer's bellicose reference to the American victory at Chippewa by proposing a toast to "our friends of the Province of New Brunswick . . . loyal to a punctilio; the love of country belongs to them as to all other people." Clarke and his family had already been saluted by a Colonel Ketchum who was visiting from New Brunswick, and their toasts were followed by that of the vice president of the banquet, wishing for continued harmony along the northeastern frontier. Two months later, as the Aroostook crisis over the Maine–New Brunswick boundary heated up, Captain George Nauman advised his brother that "the people of New

Brunswick are loyal and satisfied with their government. . . . They have . . . not the least sympathy with the [rebellious] Canadians."[30]

Captain Robert Anderson, an assistant adjutant general, wrote to Congressman Gouverneur Kemble, a personal friend of Anderson's from his service at West Point and on Winfield Scott's staff: "Instead of allowing the Canadians to work at the Altar of Liberty, forming and fashioning it to suit themselves—we have attempted to force our plan upon them. . . . That many Canadians desire some change—there can be no doubt . . . but they desire reform not revolution—a reform brought about by the quiet, steady action of public sentiment and virtue—not revolution bathed in blood." Anderson referred in particular to the French of Lower Canada: "a quiet, inoffensive people, they have none of that stirring love of liberty which warmed the hearts of our ancestors; it is folly to attempt to thrust liberty upon them." Although they wrote very little about the French Canadians, officers—who were commonly Whiggish and certainly ethnocentric in mind-set—probably shared American civilian doubts that this Catholic peasantry was ready for republicanism. Following the defeat of their uprising at the end of 1837, a set of confidential reports written by senior military leaders in 1839 agreed on French Canadian alienation from British rule but anticipated that further rebellion would occur only in the case of Anglo-American war and a significant American victory. Nor did officers see any disaffection in New Brunswick. William Worth echoed Anderson's astute assessment of the Canadian political climate virtually to the letter, and occasional complaints that the filibusters were "powerfully and numerously instigated from Canada" appear to have been nervous or frustrated reactions to a difficult situation, probably exaggerated in the hope of securing reinforcements.[31]

Worth's antagonism toward the Patriots was almost uniformly shared by his fellow commanders along the border, and their language demonstrates once again the close links between social and political values we observed when examining the role of state and class formation in the creation of the officer's professional identity. Neither soldiers nor civilians made much distinction among the insurgents, and officers on different sections of the frontier used much the same derogatory terms, which resonated with stark contrasts of stability and instability, order and disorder. To begin with, these "brigands" and "banditti" broke the law, both federal statute and international treaty and custom, against intervening in the affairs of another nation with which the United States was at peace. Winfield Scott responded to borderers outraged by the destruction of the *Caroline* that "at no time, could any portion of our people usurp the right of retaliation and revenge; that such would not be in the manner and forms of a civilized people, but according to the practice of savage tribes." Illegitimate usurpation—the use of force outside the guidelines of federal law and professional direction—was also a prominent theme in Worth's dispatches: he warned one subordinate that "the view some of your [civilian] neighbors take of the neutrality law is the very ultraism of nullification." These sentiments were echoed by General Brady on the Detroit frontier, who spoke of "these violators of our Laws" as "marauders" and "desperadoes."[32]

Scott's strictures against the Patriots' "savage" behavior reflected the officer corps' fear of instability and unguided self-interest, and officers of all ages and ranks routinely characterized the rebels in socially and ethically loaded terms as "disorganizers," "agitators," and "miserable" and "unprincipled" "adventurers."[33] Hugh Brady called these "disturbers of peace and good order" the "rabble," and Worth blamed "the floating population that infests the border of every country" for the unrest.[34] Commanders frequently denounced the insurgents as both "reckless and unscrupulous," and their rhetoric sometimes verged on the dehumanizing, implying psychological instability among the Patriots. Worth demonized the filibusters as "these lawless and insane men," while Brady spoke of the "feverish state" of "desperate and uneasy spirits" along the frontier. The biological metaphors of Assistant Surgeon Henry Heiskell show that these sentiments were not confined to combat commanders—an indication of the affinity army medical officers felt for the military dimensions of their professional service. In January 1838 Heiskell wrote to a fellow surgeon from Buffalo that "as soon as the paroxysm subsides, I am in hopes that the reason of the people will be restored once more."[35] But blame for the unrest had to be placed somewhere, and officers' suspicion of popular democracy and self-direction was apparent when they attempted to explain the origins of the raiding. Brady told Scott that the filibusters were "misguided" and "deluded" men who had been deceived by their leaders' "vile and mischievous fabrications," while Worth warned the secretary of war—and reassured the local British commander—that the "miserable youths" were mere "tools, . . . the unfortunate dupes of designing demagogues."[36]

Army commanders also stigmatized the Patriots as greedy cowards, who forsook their obligations to their country and one another in the self-interested pursuit of wealth and personal safety. Quartermaster colonel Henry Whiting claimed that "the eyes of needy [and] unprincipled adventurers began to glisten with rabid hope" when "the Brigand fever" caught them. Robert Anderson labeled the insurgent leaders "cowardly scamps," who preferred "the lights of the lecture rooms, and the sounds of silver falling into the hats passed around for contributions . . . to the flame of the death dealing gun, and the moans of the wounded [and] dying" at the Battle of Windmill Point. Worth, who had secured a tacit understanding with the British commander to allow a rescue attempt there, blamed "cowardice and treachery" for the invaders' "feeble effort" to save their fellows. Vilified by the insurgents and their sympathizers for his seizure of arms earlier in the year, Inspector General Wool condemned the "foul, base, and infamous charges" made by "men who are not guided by principle, honor or honesty." A year into the insurgency, Scott's confidential report to Secretary Poinsett united these themes of attitude and action in a statement that suggests the officer corps' frustration with the very civilians they were charged with protecting: "I have thrown every possible legal obstacle in the way of the mad [and] wicked people called *American Canadian patriots* . . . I have denounced their movements [and] purposes as a stain upon our national honour [and] faith; as dangerous to liberty at home, [and] destructive of all law [and] order. I have laboured to convince them that their projects were absurd [and] impracticable, [and] that every life taken in their unauthorized [and] unlawful enterprizes, would be an atrocious murder—deserving an ignominious execution." Scott went on to contrast the willfulness of the border populace and its civil officials with the long-suffering standing army ordered to police them, "we poor ignorant soldiers [who] only profess to be the creatures [and] servants of the law, by which we live [and] are ready to die."[37].

Class-derived understandings of behavior obviously played an important part in the officer corps' reactions to the Patriot movement. Soldiers' disdain for the filibusters was shared in "respectable" civilian society, the press, and official circles outside the border region; given the clear distinctions they made between proper and improper behavior, Worth and his fellows initially expected that Patriot violations of social norms would end their support among the local populace. After the disorder of February 1838, the New Yorker wrote to Winfield Scott that "the better, and I trust the large portion of the people are greatly shocked at the development of their plans," and he assured the state's governor that "new agitation will . . . be frowned down by a deceived and indignant people." Surgeon Henry Heiskell also demonstrated the intimate connection between these attitudes and the hope that the popular "paroxysm" was coming to an end because of the refugees' disreputable behavior. In January 1838 he wrote to fellow army surgeon Benjamin King that the Canadian refugees were "living on charity and by robbing. . . . The people are heartily tired of their 'Liberator' guests and would be glad to get rid of them." Later that month, Heiskell reported that their "army (if ever such a rabble merit the title) is entirely disbanded—some returning to their homes (if any they have)"; the rest were pilfering from the local civilians, who had welcomed them as heroes. Indeed, Heiskell felt "very certain that the *best cure* for an exuberance of patriotic zeal is to send amongst them a score or two of modern 'patriots.' Dr. Johnson's definition of this abused word (patriot, 'the last resort of a scoundrel') has been verified on this frontier."[38]

These socially weighted value judgments had important practical implications for the conduct of the army's peacekeeping operations along the Canadian border. The economic deprivation that followed the Panic of 1837 first encouraged and then undermined filibustering, when unemployed men multiplied the border population and demanded food from longtime residents, endangering their prosperity. It appears, based on circumstantial evidence, that the socioeconomic status of the average filibuster declined over time (from wave to wave of filibustering activity—during the winter and spring of 1838, the autumn of that year, and the winter and spring of 1839), and this was probably an important factor in turning initially supportive officers like Robert Anderson against the movement. It was natural for military commanders to make a sharp distinction between Patriot rabble-rousers and "respectable" citizens who would uphold law and the social order, and Heiskell's economic calculus was not inaccurate. Yet the asserted affinity between class standing and loyalty to the nation-state—an assumption predicated on professional officers' own experiences and loyalties—ultimately proved faulty, damaging their faith in the utility of civil-military diplomacy and efforts to influence local notables. When Patriot incursions continued long after their initial defeats, army officers were confronted with the unwelcome realization that support for the filibusters was not confined to the lower orders alone. This sharp blow to their hierarchically structured understanding of responsibility and social causation compelled commanders to reassess their strategies for overcoming the insurgency and maintaining the sovereignty of the nation-state they continued to serve.[39]

Indeed, the Jacksonian officer corps' commitment to the internal and external sovereignty of the nation-state was never more evident than in its operations along the Canadian border in 1838 and 1839. Unlike the civilian inhabitants of a frontier region, who were willing to accept the proclamation of a new government as an act of popular sovereignty and voluntary association, federal military officers shared the European and Whig emphasis on social and international order and stability secured by an attachment to the forms and procedures of domestic and international law. Indeed, the conflict between soldiers and filibusters along the northern border illustrates in microcosm the more general contrast between Whig and Jacksonian worldviews articulated by historians like Daniel Howe and Lawrence Kohl. As agents of a highly articu-

Winfield Scott, in full glory, by Giuseppina Vannutelli. (Courtesy Army Art Collection)

lated formal organization serving the national state, professional military officers trusted national institutions and international customs and viewed them as the expression of substantive social and political order and authority, to be questioned only with caution or in extremis. They had no sympathy for "local diplomacy" by nonstate actors, particularly violence against established political authorities and private property by scruffy insurgents.[40]

9

MAINTAINING NATIONAL SOVEREIGNTY AND KEEPING INTERNATIONAL PEACE

Operations to Suppress American Filibusters against Canada, 1838–1841

> The questions of peace and war have much oftener depended on the conduct of military officers on the frontiers, than they have on any negotiations.
> —Edward D. Mansfield, *Life and Services of Winfield Scott*

The army enjoyed firm though quiet support from the Van Buren administration, which, unlike Jackson's, gave it a free hand in the everyday conduct of operations. Congress provided critical assistance in the 1838 Neutrality Act and the law augmenting the army that summer, both requested by Van Buren. (Unlike the partisan politicians Eaton and Cass, Joel Poinsett proved to be the most active reformer and attentive administrator in the War Department since John C. Calhoun.) Nevertheless, Worth and his counterparts were still compelled to mediate the conflict on internal and international fronts with at least five major sets of actors: the "Patriot" filibusters, the local civil authorities, the local public, the British, and the Canadians. Thus, as the New Yorker explained to a subordinate, the army was deployed to reassure all parties and prevent a spiral of retaliation and escalation, "to inspire a sense of security in the People [and] renew and cultivate (in as far as may be consistent with the dignity of the Country) kind and friendly feelings along the border." The complex yet often mutually reinforcing dynamics of this multifaceted struggle were evident in Scott's praise for Worth's rapid march to reinforce Detroit in February 1838: its "excellent effect on our population between Buffalo and Detroit" would "[satisfy] the British authorities that we are in earnest in our

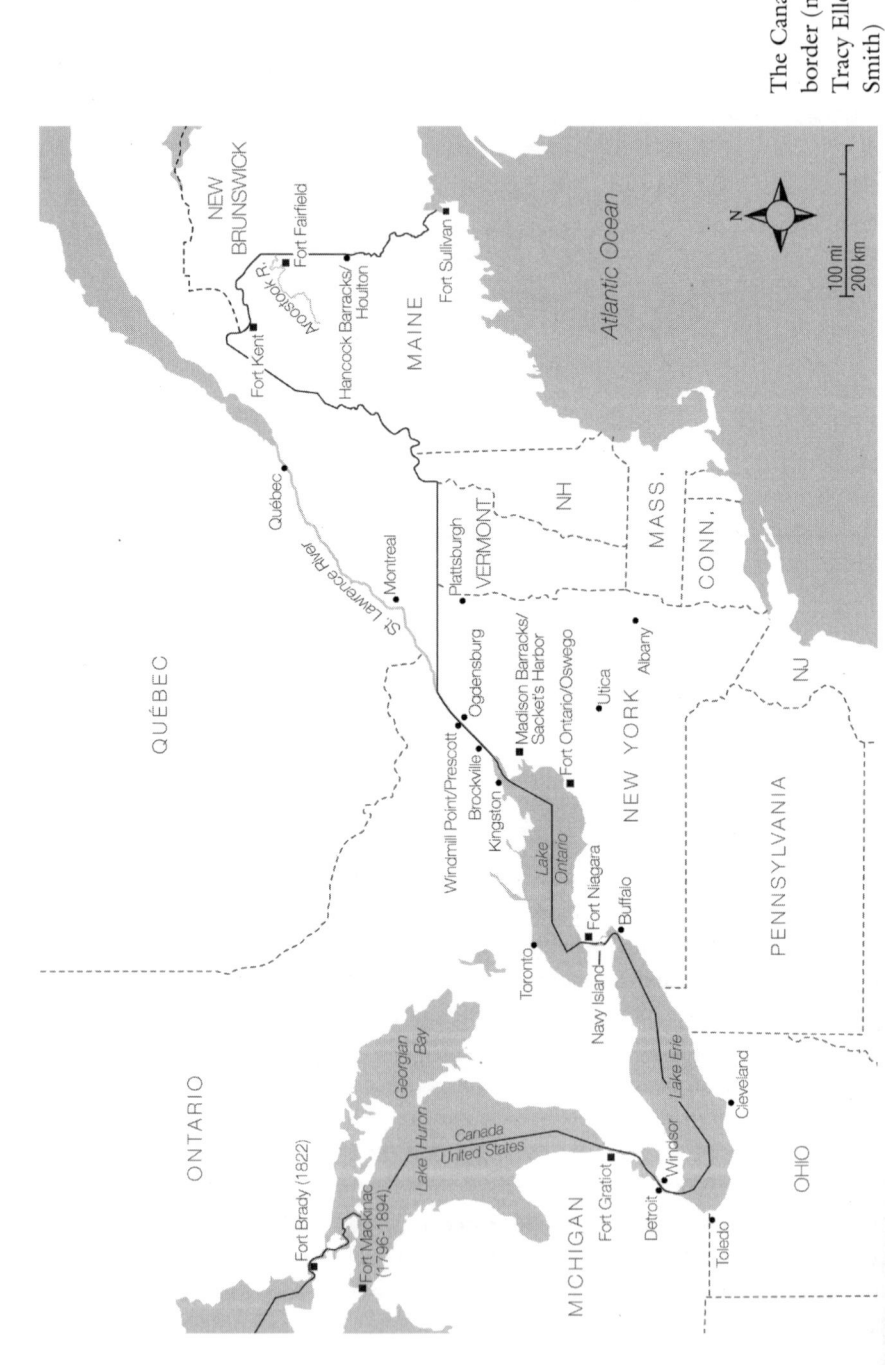

The Canadian border (map by Tracy Ellen Smith)

endeavours to maintain our neutral relations." Even the smallest military presence could have a critical effect on British commanders, as well as American opinion.[1]

Though frequently frustrated by civilian apathy or support for the Patriots, federal military officers constantly solicited the cooperation of leading local citizens and civil officials. They firmly believed that, given "the impossibility on the part of the military authority of enforcing the laws while the mass of the people are so regardless of their obligations . . . the only course which remains, is to endeavour by the exertion of moral influence to bring about a more wholesome state of public opinion, and [to] stimulate the civil authorities to a more vigorous execution of their duties." When this prodding failed, Worth and his counterparts seized arms, arrested leaders, and arranged their meager detachments along the American shore to catch filibusters retreating from the British. In the meantime, Worth assured the British authorities of his determination "to recall such of our own citizens as have strayed from the path of national honour and duty, and to admonish those who have sought the hospitality of our country [the Patriot exiles] of the danger of violating the laws." American professional soldiers recognized that the disorganized raiders stood little chance against the disciplined troops, regular and volunteer, of Britain and the loyalist Canadians. The Patriot "Hunters" were rumored to have enrolled as many as 200,000 men in their ranks, but the principal expeditions usually numbered between 200 and 300 or 500 and 600 men; the largest was probably the initial assemblage at Navy Island, of perhaps a thousand. The forces actually mobilized were clearly incapable of defeating the British by themselves, and the insurgents had to count on stirring up a general rebellion among the Canadians or drawing the United States into war by provoking British retaliation. Even junior officers recognized this dynamic: Lieutenant Morris Miller, a socially well-connected aide to Alexander Macomb who was temporarily serving as one of John Wool's aides along the frontier, wrote to his mother from Sackets Harbor that "the patriots are quiet, as yet, & the British are well prepared to give them a *warm* reception on the other side."[2]

Winfield Scott emphasized these practical considerations as much as the ethical obligations of national faith in his talks with filibuster leader Rensselaer Van Rensselaer, emphasizing "that his men wanted the necessary organization and discipline; that his means of water transportation . . . were totally inadequate, that if . . . he were to effect a landing, he would probably be cut to pieces." As 4,000 British and Canadian troops massed opposite Navy Island (a part of Canada), bombarding the insurgent positions with eleven cannon and mortars, the insurgents withdrew to Buffalo. The general then succeeded in persuading them to disperse and even enlisted some, who apparently lacked other useful employment during the winter, into the U.S. Army, reducing the army's "Patriot problem" by bringing the erstwhile filibusters under the immediate sovereignty of the nation-state and the discipline of its military commanders. Scott was less successful with the twenty cannon the insurgents had amassed, which a militia officer allowed to disappear. Yet the Patriot leaders decided to shift the foci of their offensive east to the St. Lawrence and west to the Detroit frontier, perhaps because, as one later stated, the U.S. government was "making great exertions to thwart our plans."[3]

Professional officers may have expected the British to have little difficulty rebuffing the invaders, but they could not ignore the chance that British forces would pursue the filibusters across the border onto American soil. Indeed, Worth and Brady both feared that this was the Patriots' strategy for ensnaring the United States in war. These concerns were not entirely unfounded. Canadian irregulars, some of whom were certainly organized militiamen, raided across the line on a number of occasions, and in October 1838 the U.S. government felt compelled to warn the British that it could not prevent the invasion known to be planned for the following month. On November 3 Britain's ambassador responded by proposing that the United States give advance sanction to any violation of its territory that might result from pursuit or reprisals, a suggestion Secretary of State John Forsyth rejected out of hand as an abdication of national sovereignty. From Detroit, Brady warned Scott that a formal British declaration that incursions would be considered acts of war would certainly precipitate a conflict because of the filibusters' ability to play on the economic advantages borderers expected from war. "I fear that they will be encouraged by many of our citizens, who have heretofore taken no part with the patriots . . . money is scarce, almost every one is in debt, and they know that war would bring money into this part of the Country, besides giving many of them an opportunity of coming into the service as Generals & Colonels of Militia." These fears were not limited to American commanders: the lieutenant governor of Upper Canada, Colonel George Arthur, expected war even after the Patriots' initial defeats, and a year later, amid the Aroostook crisis over the Maine boundary, he believed it "could scarcely be avoided." (This was also when Worth's fears peaked.) Writing confidentially to Britain's American ambassador in the midst of the Windmill Point incursion of November 1838, Arthur felt certain that "this Canadian contest . . . cannot end without an American war."[4]

Despite different officers, ethnicities, and balances of power, the officer corps' reactions to the crises on the Canadian border provide further evidence of an evolving sense of accountability to national civilian authority, especially when contrasted with Jackson's and Gaines's responses to Washington's inattention to the Florida frontier a generation before. The U.S. Army could have easily precipitated war with Britain; had this been 1820, and Andrew Jackson the commander, it might well have done so. Enforcing national sovereignty and neutrality was a complex mission that posed numerous dilemmas for professional soldiers; these conflicts of objective and allegiance illustrate the nuanced distinctions between the concepts of objective accountability and subjective responsibility and their sometimes contradictory meanings. Federal military officers felt a strong attachment to the national government and loyalty to the dictates of law, but the law proved a malleable abstraction that contained room for a wide variety of interpretations, and the central government gave few instructions as to its objectives. Army officers had great difficulty enforcing the neutrality policy through the formal legal process because they had little recourse against the private assembly of men in arms—Patriots masquerading as hunters—on American soil. The delicate balance of local American public opinion and the inadequacy of federal neutrality law meant that preserving American neutrality was a task for civil-military and international diplomacy as much as military force; Worth warned his subordinates to exercise their "prudence and judgement," recognizing that "as much delicacy and forbearance as firmness will be necessary."[5]

Contemporary readings of the Neutrality Act of 1818 provided only for punishing filibusters, not preventing them, and Poinsett initially instructed Scott that "the Executive possesses no legal authority to employ the military force to restrain persons [from] making incursions" across the international boundary. This interpretation appears to have underestimated the government's authority under both the 1818 Neutrality Act and previous measures from the 1790s, but many radical Jacksonians understood filibustering as the free association of private individuals, a natural reflection of popular sovereignty and the love of freedom unrestrained by the artificial hand of the state or international law. In other words, although the administration did not overtly or even tacitly support the insurgents, it essentially handed off the problem to military commanders while providing them with little guidance beyond the charge to maintain American sovereignty and international peace.[6]

Congress and the executive quickly cooperated to change the neutrality law, and Washington gave its military representatives great latitude in their operations, but career officers remained constrained by their politically cautious but professionally accountable belief that any substantive action, such as arrests or detention, required the legal sanction of due process, meaning approval by civilian officials. Military commanders had no formal or official doctrine to go by under these circumstances, for the government did no more than issue confidential instructions—basically allowing officers to use their discretion; it did not craft "rules of engagement" for peacekeeping or issue official legal opinions on the powers of military officers acting on American soil. National commanders received little assistance from federal legal counsel or diplomatic personnel, and neither the attorney general's office nor the State and Justice Departments sent representatives to the border, which doubtlessly increased the army's caution in dealing with local civilians. (The U.S. district attorneys in the region often proved sympathetic to the insurgents.) Whatever their preferences, the theater commanders were compelled to exercise much the same discretion as their counterparts on the southern and western frontiers. Under orders from Washington to send troops to the village of Big Sodus, Worth instead took the initiative to deploy them to Ogdensburg, which seemed under greater threat of Canadian retaliation, acting "with a knowledge of facts unknown to the [adjutant general], to assume a proper and officerlike responsibility until on accurate advice he could review the subject."[7]

Officers' actions were normally sustained by the War Department, and the army served as the real executive branch along the Canadian border. Despite bursts of hotheaded Jacksonian rhetoric, Congress as a whole recognized the danger of war and did not remain silent in the face of filibuster threats to international peace and national security. The neutrality law of March 10, 1838, permitted the preemptive seizure of property, usually arms and ammunition, when officials had probable cause to suspect that neutrality violations would occur. It explicitly authorized the use of military force to aid civil authorities, but the latter still had to provide writs and warrants for the army to conduct constitutional searches, seizures, and arrests. National military commanders might have acted more "responsibly" and, in the short term, more effectively to prevent a disastrous war with Britain by imposing martial law and using force to round up the filibusters and their sympathizers, but this was politically and ideologically inconceivable, even to professional soldiers socialized in authoritarian hierarchy and discipline. Condemnation of executive usurpation was as much a staple of National Republican and Whig ideology as acclamations of individual liberty were for Democrats, and antagonistic frontiersmen often raised the specter of martial law when frustrated by federal military officers. In this environment, martial law remained a taboo subject for officers' initiative, whatever their personal wishes may have been. Among senior military commanders, only John Wool, fresh from his victorious court-martial following his clash with the Jacksonians over Cherokee removal, advocated going beyond the limits of civil process in his correspondence. When "Radicals" and "ruffians" burned Canadian buildings along the Vermont border in November 1838, Captain Giles Porter, a veteran of twenty years' service, officially advocated "Martial Law" as the only means to preserve American neutrality against "outlaws and pirates," but Porter never received the desired authority to "dispense summary justice" against the "band of incendiaries."[8]

Early in 1839 Worth implied that he would like to detain Canadian refugees in the United States en masse as a precaution against further incursions, but he did so by way of noting the impossibility of such a measure "without further legal enactments," for the colonel believed "they are equally protected by [the laws] with our citizens." Though this might not have been strictly accurate, Worth took the more politically cautious and responsible course. Secretary of War Poinsett requested Winfield Scott's advice about preventative detention that October, but the immediate need had long passed, and it is not clear how Scott responded. On the whole, despite their frustration, Worth and his counterparts demonstrated scrupulous respect for civil rights throughout the Patriot crisis, another illustration of their accountability to civilian authority and the fundamental liberties it prescribed.[9] The officer corps' desire for international harmony and social order had to give way before subordination to the national government and the "free institutions" it represented, and the effective performance of military missions took a backseat to legal, political, and ideological accountability in the practical expression of professional responsibility on the Canadian frontier. Federal military officers may have become emotionally frustrated by their peacekeeping duties, but they did not become substantively alienated from the government and society they served, nor did they lash out counterproductively. And although civilian officials sympathetic to the insurgents sometimes ordered the release of weapons and ammunition, lawsuits against military commanders along the northern border were notably absent, particularly in comparison with the frequent suits against officers enforcing the trade and intercourse acts on the Indian frontiers. (This may have been a legal artifact, because filibusters usually regained their weapons and had few financial damages to recover.)

Unable to round up suspected Patriots preemptively, American commanders often resorted to seizing arms caches and interdicting large-scale filibuster movements along the border. Worth pursued a group of insurgents withdrawing from Navy Island and impounded their weapons; he and General Brady later purchased several local steamers, preventing the Patriots from doing so, and used them to patrol the Detroit, Niagara, and St. Lawrence Rivers to block filibuster movements and intercept those retreating from

British attack—a tactic they often coordinated with British commanders. (Crossing the international border under arms was illegal, though officers had to catch filibusters in the act.) Indeed, an American revenue cutter drove back a Patriot foray along the Niagara River in February 1838, while Brady temporarily detained insurgents retreating from the battle at Fighting Island that month. (These men had lost most of their arms to Worth's pursuit, before Brady informed the British of their advance.)[10]

With many of their supporters drifting back to seasonal employment that spring, the Patriots turned to small-scale raids. A larger foray was frustrated along the Niagara frontier that June, when 200 insurgents fled after a small U.S. force advanced toward them. (At the time, only 90 American soldiers were stationed along the Niagara.) The following month, commanding general Macomb reported "a simultaneous expedition" of British and American regulars "to scour the Thousand Islands [in the St. Lawrence, near its outlet in Lake Ontario] in search of the gang of desperate men [suspected of piracy and arson] said to have collected" there. Brady seized a schooner loaded with arms and ammunition that November, as did a naval officer on Lake Champlain; Worth seized four ships at Ogdensburg, including one laden with arms. Nor did the colonel scruple to restrain the use of private property when he smelled a rat, ordering the steamer *Oneida* (which he later secured for federal use) to depart from Sackets Harbor without picking up civilian passengers and deploying soldiers to enforce his command. Doing so was probably illegal, but Worth must have counted on support from the state and federal executives if the ship's owners chose to go to the expense of filing a lawsuit.[11]

John Wool undertook probably the most tactically sophisticated operation, using patrols by sleds and mounted volunteers against the Patriots when they crossed the Vermont line in February and early March 1838. Clearly well-informed about the insurgents' plans, Wool seized their weapons stockpiles in Vermont after they had overtly violated the law by entering Canada under arms; then he concentrated his forces along the border and halted all movement across it. He gave the insurgents a choice: return peacefully, hand over their arms, and surrender their leaders, or face his soldiers' fire when the British compelled them to retreat. (At that point, the Patriots would have been entering the United States under arms without permission, a clear violation of American sovereignty—in effect, an invasion—that would have given the inspector general a legal rationale, however politically tenuous, for using lethal force.) Six hundred filibusters surrendered to Wool's troops, but they were allowed to disperse because of the difficulty and expense of feeding and prosecuting them, and their leaders apparently escaped through the lines of sympathetic local volunteers. Eight months later, brevet Brigadier General

Abraham Eustis faced down an estimated 1,400 "*revolutionists*" with two companies (no more than 200 soldiers) along the Vermont boundary. Perhaps bearing in mind newspaper criticism of Wool's actions, Eustis demanded only that the insurgents disarm and disperse or face arrest.[12]

Even the most experienced commanders soon felt overwhelmed by the problems of policing a long wooded frontier with just a handful of men. Blockading operations to seal off the border could work only if the Patriots concentrated and the army was given sufficient time to move to the scene. (Fortunately for Anglo-American relations, the filibusters' information security was poor, and several of their major incursions were discovered in advance.) Most of the army was busy in Florida, and because the majority of civil officials and the militia were sympathetic to the insurgents, federal military commanders were deprived of the manpower and legal authority they needed to act as a consistent physical barrier to insurgent expeditions. Winfield Scott had no troops whatsoever during his first tour of the border, and Worth and his counterparts initially had to rely on civilian volunteers and recruits hastily called up from depots to the south. In May 1838, as commanders reflected on the probable course of future operations, Captain George Wright, a sixteen-year veteran, recommended deploying 200 soldiers on each significant front along the Canadian border—Detroit, Niagara, the St. Lawrence, and Vermont: "this number will enforce the laws without violence: a lesser number would be liable to insult." Nevertheless, despite two rounds of filibuster activity, as late as November 1838, Hugh Brady had only "four companies averaging about eighteen men for duty to a company"—70 regular soldiers to guard the entire Detroit frontier.[13]

The small size of the professional officer corps was another constraint on operations against the Patriots. Army commanders on the northern frontier relied on fellow professionals— imbued with similar centralist values and subject to the constraints of military hierarchy and the sanctions of its discipline— for any task that involved leading volunteers or militiamen or negotiating with civil authorities or the British, whereas Poinsett's initial instructions to Scott stressed their employment on administrative duties to reduce costs. With operations in Canada and Florida, the beginnings of the Maine boundary crisis, and ongoing Indian removal and constabulary activities on the western frontier, the officer corps was seriously overburdened in early and mid-1838, and requests for easier duty meant that border commanders faced a constant shortage of regimental officers. Worth, for example, reported that "we are crippled at all points for want of officers," and he frequently took the initiative to requisition those outside his formal command for duty along the boundary.[14]

Like commanders in Florida during these years, Worth had a difficult time keeping some of his subordinates on duty. Several of his letters contain injunctions to officers to remain with their units at all times, while one to the adjutant general conveyed Captain St. Clair Denny's resignation, submitted because Worth had been unable to grant Denny's application for leave, since he was the only officer available at an exposed point. The secretary of war rejected Denny's resignation but granted him one month's leave in which to reconsider; Denny resigned at the end of that month. Border service was unattractive to senior officers as well as junior ones. Lieutenant Colonel Ichabod Crane sought leave on the doubtful grounds that only one field-grade officer was needed along the Niagara; the following year General Eustis, acting commander of the army's Northern Department, assured Robert Anderson of his satisfaction with the quiet state of the frontier, "inasmuch as it insures my prolonged absence from those frozen regions." (Though born in Massachusetts, Eustis owned a plantation in North Carolina and had done much of his service in Virginia and the South.)[15]

The army's most efficient alternative to incarcerating the Patriots was to recruit them into federal military service, where they could be disciplined in the service of national goals. (Both sides probably saw this as a sort of imprisonment, but former insurgents gained pay, food, and housing amid the depths of the depression.) Winfield Scott did so in Buffalo after the filibusters' retreat from Navy Island in January 1838 and in Detroit after their defeat at Fighting Island that February. Canadians usually made up about 1 percent of the army's annual recruiting intake, but this proportion jumped sixfold in 1838 and 1839, and a British officer traveling in the United States on leave estimated that in one group of a hundred recruits, virtually every man had been associated with the rebels. This local reinforcement was insufficient to satisfy the army's manpower needs, however, and during a quiet moment in June 1838, Wool went to Washington to lobby congressmen voting on the annual army bill.[16] Faced with an interminable war in Florida and continuing tensions with Britain, Congress proved that the United States could act as a nation-state, even under the Jacksonians. The Army Act of July 5, 1838, authorized an increase of 4,650 men, including the new Eighth Infantry Regiment, which would serve along the border under Worth's command. In the face of the civil-military and international tensions along the border, reliability, manifested in experience, was the principal criterion for officering the Eighth. This policy demonstrated as much insulation and autonomy from partisan influence—that is, control by the professional army hierarchy over the army's organization—as the officering of the dragoon regiments had evinced partisanship during Jackson's administration. (It is also quite possible that the army's leaders preferred to give some of their veteran subordinates a break, replacing them with lieutenants commissioned directly from civilian life for service in Florida.)

Despite the mass of vacancies already created by the resignations of 1836 and 1837, only six of the new unit's thirty-three officers were appointed directly from civilian life, ranking no higher than second lieutenant. The army minimized promotion politics by transferring experienced infantry officers (almost all West Point graduates), including one captain from each existing regiment, into the Eighth at their existing ranks. These men accounted for twenty-five of the thirty-three officers; only eight received promotions into their new positions. Coming from ordnance duty via Scott's patronage, Worth had already distinguished himself along the northern border. He was the only noninfantry officer in the new regiment (though he had observed ferocious infantry combat at Chippewa and Lundy's Lane and served as the first commandant of cadets at West Point, where he oversaw the testing of new infantry drill regulations) and the only one promoted outside the path of seniority. Eventually, the bulk of three regiments out of the army's fourteen—in theory, approximately 3,000 regulars at the 1838 authorization of 100 per company—was concentrated along the Canadian frontier. Most of the army's new recruits continued to feed the war in Florida, however, and a substantial proportion of the troops along the Canadian border had to be sent to Maine during the Aroostook dispute in 1839. The ratio of soldiers to space was never sufficient to halt Patriot raids through military means alone.[17]

National and personal honor, defined as good faith and integrity in the fulfillment of one's duties and obligations, was one of the core values of the professional officer corps, one that its representatives applied to all the actors in the Patriot drama. "Envired by Pirates . . . with none to appreciate or ameliorate our position," Worth quickly came to see communication with his British counterparts as the most effective means of deterring retaliation against American soil. As early as February 1838, "having in view the peculiar character and extent of our frontier . . . the public and private obligations of every good citizen—the sincerity of the Government . . . and above all a proper regard for the character of our country for honour and good faith," the hard-nosed colonel believed it was his duty to inform "our neighbors" of potential incursions. Hugh Brady did the same when the filibusters occupied Fighting Island, opposite Sandwich on the Detroit frontier. That autumn, Worth reminded Lieutenant Colonel Newman Clarke to advise Captain Sandom of the Royal Navy of "our sincere desire to do all that we might be expected from the most fastidious sense of national and personal honour to guard against every event that might . . . interrupt the friendship of the two countries." The American commander was fully prepared to interpose his troops to oppose any violations of U.S. sovereignty from Canada, but he consistently reported that his communications with the British were "characterized by high courtesy." Consequently, Worth felt certain the British would "act in a corresponding spirit" to restrain retaliation. Indeed, "the rigid discipline . . . & the excellent disposition of the [British and their] commanders" led him to dispute civilian rumors that the British had struck across the border.[18]

Winfield Scott had initiated this unofficial policy of cooperation, and he confirmed it, along with a supporting policy of domestic intelligence gathering, in a confidential circular distributed in April 1839. "Should you, at any time, doubt your means of prevention, under the neutrality laws, you will (as heretofore instructed) not for a moment hesitate to give immediate information . . . to the nearest British commander, in part acquittance of our obligations of good faith towards friendly neighbors." British and Canadian officers sometimes responded in kind to enable the Americans to interpose their troops against retreating filibusters. Nor was communication limited to senior commanders: Lieutenant George Field, an experienced commissary officer from the Third Infantry who was on temporary duty commanding Fort Niagara in May 1838, entertained three British officers at the fort. The army leadership did a remarkable job of identifying officers with local connections for its efforts at public diplomacy; Field, for instance, had been born in Black Rock, on the Niagara River. Equally important, these career officers were willing to shoulder the responsibility for any political embarrassment their cooperation with the British might cause. "Should I have exceeded the bounds of my duty," Worth stated, rather than "permitting any act of mine to be regarded as embarrassing the superior [Scott] militarily or compromising the interest or honour of the country . . . [let it] promptly be disavowed and all the error and the blame rest . . . with me." Indeed, the colonel's aide equated adherence to this policy with upholding "the national faith [and] the honour of the service." Professional accountability and military discipline thus became matters of personal, institutional, and national honor, giving a deeper psychological force to the execution of professional duty.[19]

Military confidence-building measures were aimed at Americans as well as British commanders and Canadians. Communication with local civil authorities and the citizenry was intended to reduce support for the insurgency over the long term. A New Yorker himself, Worth acted to reduce tensions by easing barriers to civilian movement during moments of calm and by limiting the possibility of his officers becoming involved in incidents with angry Canadians during periods of confrontation. After the first winter's crisis had passed, he ordered a Captain Tuthill of the "New York Volunteers" to Niagara Falls to ensure that "there will be no interference [by Patriots or their sympathizers] with the passing and repassing from both sides of persons on business or pleasure." The following day the colonel wrote to a British counterpart at Chippewa—ironically, the site of the battle where Worth had first distinguished himself nearly a quarter century before—asking that restrictions on ferry crossings at Niagara be eased, to encourage "a tranquillizing effect." Worth also worked to prevent Canadian misunderstanding of American military intent. Immediately following the incursion at Windmill Point that autumn, he forbade army personnel to cross the border and instructed his subordinates to "employ civil agents . . . to communicate officially with the opposite side." As winter turned to spring, his aide directed Captain William Montgomery to prohibit junior officers from crossing at points "where [Canadian] irregular forces are stationed" unless they were on duty and in uniform.[20]

Army officers actively facilitated better relations between influential New Yorkers and British officials, particularly in support of legal investigations. In March 1839 Worth provided a citizens' committee investigating arsons on American soil with a letter of introduction to a British lieutenant colonel. British major Richard Webb thanked American major Nathaniel Young for the "kindly feeling expressed" in Young's letter transmitting the names of an American grand jury, which had been conveyed by army surgeon Henry Heiskell. Webb concluded by asking Young to convey "my most cordial thanks" to the jury for its determination to maintain the peace. The two majors apparently socialized in private as well, for an earlier letter inquired about the health of Young's daughter, who had been ill. Young was a successful diplomat in more than one respect: he had been elected "an Honorary Member of the Albany Military Association" in September 1837 and won election to the Delaware state legislature in the fall of 1838, after resigning from the army effective October 31—only the eighth field-grade officer to resign from the combat arms regiments since 1821 (see appendix D).[21]

Worth's communication with the British reached a peak during the Patriot incursion and battle at Windmill Point (November 11–17, 1838), a diplomatic collaboration that demonstrates the American commander's sympathy for U.S. citizens trapped by the British, as well as his devotion to the sovereignty of the nation-state and the rule of international law. The colonel first deployed his forces to prevent British pursuit or Canadian retaliation on U.S. soil, but on November 14 he reported that "I have been applied to by citizens of Ogdensburg to intercede with the commanding officer on the other side to allow these intruders to surrender to me." Worth initially refused: "however disposed to offer personal offices of humanity, I could not reconcile it to a sense of duty to my country to comply," though the coming British attack would probably result "in the annihilation of the invaders."[22]

The stern American changed his mind after a Patriot sortie was repulsed the following day, and for a short time, his feelings of national identity and humanity overcame his strict sense of duty. Worth wrote privately, and thus secretly, to the British commander on the opposite shore: "I hesitate to make any suggestion and officially I am not at liberty to do so; but sh[oul]d you desire to avoid subjecting any valuable lives to sacrifice in an assault . . . I will . . . without authority . . . interpose any offices of humanity you may suggest. . . . [The filibusters] would of course on reaching the jurisdiction of the U. States become prisoners in the hands of the civil authority." Torn between duty and sympathy, the colonel expressed "much doubt whether I should write at all," but his overtures appeared to be rewarded. Worth later reported that his British counterpart, who "had no authority to allow [the insurgents] to withdraw," had "expressed a hope they might escape—we parted perfectly understanding each other. The partisans of these miserable men in Ogdensburgh were urged to take off the remnant that night. Every avenue was left unguarded [by British or American troops]. . . . From my note to Col. Young [the British commander] you will perceive how reluctantly and guardedly I approached the subject; but as an American officer I did not feel at liberty to disregard such an exhibition of the symbol of Hope and Mercy [the white flag of truce and surrender], from Our Countrymen, Guilty though they were."[23]

Worth had commandeered all the private vessels in Ogdensburg, a common practice among American commanders during Patriot incursions. He allowed one boat to try a rescue, but it failed, whether from "cowardice and treachery," as the frustrated colonel, still disdainful toward the insurgents, supposed, or because the British land and sea commanders did not communicate and a British steamer prevented any landing. It seems highly improbable that the British officers would have trusted the American civil authorities to effectively prosecute the filibusters, and Worth's understanding with his counterpart was not repeated. A month later, during the next substantial Patriot offensive, Hugh Brady sent the steamer *Erie* to prevent the insurgents' escape after the Battle of Windsor, on the Canadian shore near Detroit.[24] Worth continued his efforts at mediation after the battle. A week later, the colonel sent the British commander in Kingston a petition for clemency from a group of "gentlemen of the highest intelligence [and] respectability among our citizens." In accordance with military paternalism and understandings of Patriot motives, he believed the petition "truly [set] forth the circumstances of fraud and delusion practised upon the miserable youths who have, thus acted upon, forfeited their lives." The American commander again expressed great uncertainty about the propriety of his role as an intermediary: "This appeal places me in a painful & embarrassing position; on the one hand any effort to stay or divert the free course of justice . . . would justly subject me to the censure of Government, so on the other, I could hardly excuse myself to my countrymen nay to my own heart, were I totally to disregard the humane designs and wishes" of the petitioners. Ultimately, the hard-bitten colonel endorsed the petition for reasons of both policy and humanity:

> Thus circumstanced, I approach you with the frankness that belongs to our profession. . . . I can only add, Sir, the firm conviction that clemency extended to the wretched victims of baseness and duplicity will while illustrating the humane and merciful policy of her Majesty's Government, have the happiest effect in restoring, as we all desire, friendly relations along the entire border [and would] . . . hold up to scorn, contempt, and punishment the great villains in this most unparalleled assault upon a friendly power.[25]

The American commander also sought clemency on behalf of individuals he felt deserving because of their past and present service to the United States. The day before sending this petition, Worth wrote to Captain Williams Sandom of the Royal Navy, commander of the British flotilla on the Great Lakes, in favor of the captured son of one W. Vaughn, a retired American naval officer who had served as a volunteer under Worth during the crisis. The colonel recommended whatever "can be done consistent with the stern principles of justice," remarking that "respect for the misfortunes of this old man and for the zeal . . . in which he performed his Duties, reconcile me to giving him this private note." Worth's actions during the Windmill Point incursion illustrate the moral, ethical, and diplomatic dilemmas faced by an officer charged with peacekeeping. The American commander attempted to satisfy all sides by cooperating with the British while trying to prevent a bloody battle or the stern imposition of British justice—hanging for treason or for the murder of British soldiers—which might spark a backlash in the United States. Worth encapsulated these diplomatic sentiments in a letter to federal customs collector George McWhorter, his go-between with the filibusters, avowing that "when time is blood, action first and reflection after." The colonel hoped his efforts for clemency would be rewarded by renewed allegiance to the sovereignty of the nation-state and the obligations of national and international law, "that every rescued victim would come forth from his prison an apostle of honor, justice, and correct principles, instead of the doctrines of marauders." Indeed, Worth seems to have leaked his letter to McWhorter to the

Kingston Chronicle as evidence of his good faith, which many Canadians had questioned. He was rewarded by public praise and sympathy (as well as his usual share of criticism) on both sides of the St. Lawrence, but he had much less influence on the higher levels of British policy than as a diplomat on the scene; eventually, nine of the prisoners were hung.[26]

The colonel's cooperation with the British did not mean that their relationship was free of conflict. Several potentially dangerous clashes occurred between British commanders frustrated by the Americans' inability to stop the filibusters and American officers determined to defend their nation's sovereignty and the rights of its citizens. The most significant examples were the *Barcelona* and *Weeks* incidents, involving American steamers. Winfield Scott hired the *Barcelona* as soon as it was cut free from the ice in February 1838 to prevent the Patriots from using it, and he told Canadian naval commanders not to fire on the previously suspect vessel as it moved up the Niagara River. Scott then placed cannon opposite Chippewa, aimed at the British vessels, and batteries to reinforce this warning in case of confusion, and there was no trouble.[27] In a more serious confrontation, a British customs collector seized the American civilian vessel *Weeks* at the Canadian river port of Brockville in May 1839. The American steamer *Telegraph* had been fired on and ransacked at this port in June 1838, and to prevent similar transgressions, Worth raced to the Canadian harbor aboard the steamer *Oneida* and demanded that the *Weeks* be released. When ignored, he aimed his guns at the town, which quickly brought the result he sought. The affair produced a great deal of diplomatic recrimination, but General Eustis praised the colonel's "prompt and energetic course."[28]

Worth's fear that his troops would be suborned by British officers or Canadian loyalists was another source of tension, which seems somewhat irrational unless we recognize the strain he was under. In February 1839 the colonel wrote to a British counterpart that an American civilian would provide an affidavit "that efforts are frequently made by persons from Prescott to entice the men from their duty by the promise of high wages." What was worse, the recruiter supposedly appeared in British uniform and was said to be a professional officer. Perhaps in response, Worth told Captain Giles Porter two days later that he had to refuse a British proposal to exchange deserters, despite Porter's agreement to do so, as he was "well satisfied that the power does not rest with us, either to arrest or to deliver up theirs." It is difficult to explain why the authoritarian colonel believed the British would want to suborn discipline among his soldiers, recognized by officers on both sides as a force for order. Perhaps he was merely passing on civilian complaints; his refusal to exchange deserters demonstrates his recognition that military authority had to be tempered with sensitivity to civilian distaste for measures in which the national standing army appeared to act as Great Britain's police force. However, the U.S. Army took care not to anger its British counterparts; in September 1838 a general order directed recruiters to avoid British deserters and ordered commanding officers to prevent their enlisted soldiers from encouraging British defections.[29]

"Professionalism" alone could not provide specific policy answers for complex situations like these. An individual commander had multiple objectives and allegiances he was compelled to balance during moments of great pressure, while operating without any immediate guidance from higher authority. Under these circumstances, professionalism meant a method and approach rather than an inflexible adherence to abstract principles or specific guidelines. It was in this operational autonomy and discretion that the military officer came closest to the civilian "free professional" (doctor, lawyer, or historian) in using his experience and his knowledge of abstract principles to guide his diagnosis of and inferences about a specific problem and its origins, to choose a prescription and carry it into action. Despite the number and intensity of congressional inquiries and the impact of budgetary constraints, army officers operating in the contested borderlands possessed as much autonomy as they did in their daily interactions with one another and their enlisted men in garrison. Having used the state to carve out an exclusive professional jurisdiction, they were granted substantial de facto autonomy in the conduct of their professional practice, not only in daily institutional routines but in the more complex interactions that sustained American national sovereignty and the authority of the nation-state during dangerous crises along its boundaries.

Not surprisingly, while many military professionals today long for the autonomy Worth and his counterparts possessed, these nineteenth-century soldiers felt great anxiety over the lack of guidance from their civilian superiors. Indeed, although this absence of supervision was largely a product of irremediable constraints like technological inadequacy and distance, it is not unreasonable to suggest that Worth and his compatriots were substantially more professional in carrying out their responsibilities to state and society than the politicians to whom they reported. When civilian government was cautious or paralyzed by partisan considerations and conflict, the army effectively took its place along the nation's international boundaries, and it is remarkable how little anger or alienation these officers displayed toward the government and the political system that repeatedly placed them in complex situations fraught with personal and professional uncertainty. This faithful performance of duty stands as a testament to the officer's growing sense of professional obligation and accountability to the nation-state that employed him.

William Jenkins Worth, man of many talents. (Courtesy National Archives)

By the late 1830s, this sense had become the product of institutional employment, socialization, and jurisdiction rather than the personal idiosyncrasies and sectional interests of an Andrew Jackson or his subordinates in the Division of the South a generation before.

Recognizing the limits of their ability to coerce obedience to the nation's neutrality laws, army officers consistently tried to influence local public opinion, especially by praising the "respectable" citizens they expected to support the government's moderation and restraint. Their observations on this score reinforce the picture of an occupational group obsessed with social as well as international order. At a banquet held in his honor in February 1838, John Wool proposed a toast to the citizens of Burlington, "ever faithful to the principles of liberty, law, and order," while Winfield Scott spent most of his initial tour speaking to large crowds about respect for law and order and the role these values played in sustaining republican government. "A number of respectable gentlemen from abroad," obviously from Canada, and probably British officers, attended Wool's banquet, evidence of both international diplomacy and the solidarity of the genteel classes and military commanders of both countries in pursuit of stability and order. In March, Hugh Brady reported that "a meeting of the most respectable citizens of Detroit" had been called to investigate, and implicitly to downplay, Patriot charges of British oppression in Canada. Senior army leaders continued to deploy subordinates with local connections, making their federal frontier diplomacy personal and social as well as military. That July, Vermont native Major Sylvester Churchill, returning with William Worth from duty under Scott in the Cherokee removal, noted in his journal that "Gen. Macomb seems well pleased with my traveling much among, [and becoming] acquainted with the principal inhabitants, as the best means of exerting an influence in preserving order and quiet."[30]

In this federal diplomacy—the army's nationalist inversion of "local diplomacy" to secure local or regional objectives—officers employed their local civilian connections to counter local disaffection from national priorities. Worth's correspondence illustrates that the impetus for these activities came from a nationalist distrust of locally rooted leaders, for he initially feared that the filibusters were "nourished and urged on by persons of high standing in society." Career military commanders normally believed—as authoritarian disciplinarians, they had to believe—that social hierarchy and respect for law went hand in hand, and Worth commented (with some relish) that "many, too late indeed for their reputation and standing in society, are getting heartily ashamed of their part in the affair." The colonel hoped to play on local class distinctions to encourage adherence to law and order: in November 1838 he acknowledged that "many [Patriots] are young men of good family all decent and of the higher order of Yeomanry," but he had turned to blaming disaffection among his soldiers on "the lower classes here." He then advised the self-proclaimed "Gentlemen of Ogdensburg" that "if the good citizens should be pleased to exercise their just influence in society I cannot doubt that very shortly the former relations of good neighborhood will be restored with the opposite border."[31]

Whether the reason was intimidation or sympathy for the Patriots, the reluctance of politically appointed civil officials, including many federal ones, to enforce the law was normally the most serious obstacle the army faced in its efforts to uphold national sovereignty and the rule of law. Indeed, the insurgents and their sympathizers usually faded away when confronted by American military force, and there were no casualties in the peacekeeping and law enforcement operations the army undertook against the filibusters on American soil. Indeed, the tensest confrontation appears to have been in Oswego, on Lake Ontario between the St. Lawrence and Niagara fronts, at the beginning of January 1839, not during one of the Patriot offensives. When a mob refused to allow soldiers to impound several cannon, Captain Thomas Gwynne rushed his company to "the scene of action" but held back when customs collector McWhorter relayed word that the crowd would surrender the guns to civil officials. After this promise fell through, Lieutenant Colonel Newman Clarke dispatched a company from Madison Barracks at Sackets Harbor, with "minute instructions" and twenty-six rounds of ball per soldier, to reinforce Gwynne's company at Oswego. Clarke's "confidence in the discretion" of his subordinates was then rewarded, as the cannon were peacefully turned over to a militia colonel.[32]

The hesitation, vacillation, obstinacy, and obstructionism of local civil officials reflected a conflict between federal and local priorities for which military officers alone could not provide a solution. Professional soldiers accountable to the national government that commissioned them had little sympathy for civilian officials' sense of accountability to their local constituents, which military commanders recognized as an obstacle to peaceful international relations under the circumstances. Winfield Scott warned the War Department that "in general they are either lukewarm [and] inefficient or the open [and] zealous abettors of the violators of law [and] order," and Worth suggested that a suspect customs collector was "but one of many, very many civil officers along the border equally criminal of participation [and] shameful neglect of duty. . . . Many are notoriously active members of the secret societies."[33] Army officers frequently appealed to the War Department for support against refractory civil officials, but the federal government had little effective control over its local appointees short of dismissal, so army officers were forced to bear the burden of what was essentially a federal-local conflict over the direction of national policy. Consequently, Worth and his fellows often had to mediate or choose between competing imperatives of professional responsibility and accountability to political authority, for they took the fundamental principle of civilian supremacy over the military seriously, even when that adherence clearly hampered their immediate ability to sustain the sovereignty of the nation-state they served.

At first, Worth was strongly committed to acting in support of the responsible civilian authorities, feeling "anxious that every energy of the civil arm should first have been put forth and exhausted before our Country should be subjected to this deplorable and humiliating exhibition." The colonel reminded civil officials that he had "constant occasion for the advice [and] cooperation of the United States Civil Officers," and he ordered his subordinates to act in conjunction with the civil authorities "to yield them every aid and support which may be lawfully rendered." Yet he soon warned Scott that if "unsustained and deserted by the civil authorities it will be difficult for the military to render any efficient service by way of prevention, or to convince foreign governments of the sincere desire of our own to do so."[34] As the crisis continued, Worth reacted to the obstructions posed by civil officials by ordering his subordinates to send their correspondence with the civil authorities to headquarters for transmission to the War Department and Congress, "as ample evidence that the Military has not been remiss in the performance of its duties." The colonel always remained diplomatic with those who supported national sovereignty, assuring Governor William Marcy of New York, a Democrat who followed President Van Buren's lead in denouncing the filibusters, that "I am ready to yield prompt obedience to your Excellency's requisition" to guard a state arsenal "& in all other respects to exert in all lawful manner the forces entrusted to my command in aid of such efforts as your Excellency may order." Nevertheless, despite such federal-state diplomacy, Worth's actions were always guided by professional principles of personal and national duty and honor. These values would eventually force him to make a difficult choice between his immediate and ultimate responsibilities and the different loci of accountability they represented, but he grasped this responsibility without hesitation: "In my own judgement my course of Duty is plain, and this duty I shall endeavour to perform regardless of [the] consequences."[35]

A series of events in February 1838 illustrates the mixed cooperation and dual allegiances federal military commanders encountered among local civil authorities. Though legally federal officers, these men had none of the institutional security, political insulation, or professional autonomy of their military counterparts. They were dependent on their local political standing to gain and retain their appointments under the Jacksonian spoils system, and national military officers had to exercise careful, persistent *diplomacy*—a more accurate term than *interagency cooperation*—to secure support for controversial actions that required their legal sanction to meet standards of due process. Indeed, Worth often resorted to persuading subordinate legal officers to act when their superiors would not. Contrary to Secretary Poinsett's initial interpretation of the limits of the 1818 Neutrality Act, the colonel asked A. W.

Rogers, whom he had persuaded to act as U.S. district attorney, for a legal opinion to support his intention to "disarm and disperse [the filibusters] by force if necessary, the civil authority failing to do so." He then reported to Scott that, upon hearing of a Patriot arms cache at Fredonia, "I gave W. Leonard [a deputy U.S. marshal] the necessary militia force" and warned him, "'if you don't seize it, I shall.'" Worth's efforts apparently had some effect, for he praised Leonard's zeal and later gave the civil authorities credit for thwarting the insurgent advance against Hickory Island and Kingston.[36]

Yet military relations with local civil officials remained tense. Worth reproved U.S. district attorney Nathaniel Benton for "publicly and officially" repudiating Leonard's actions in support of federal authority, remarking that "it was with infinite surprise [that] I further learned that you had caused an order to be issued for the re-delivery of arms seized from persons in open violation of the law . . . who no doubt will feel very grateful . . . [that] their arms have been transported to the desired point for unlawful use." The colonel then warned Benton that "I have deemed it my duty to present the whole subject . . . to the consideration of the War Department." He sent the same letter to Leonard's superior, H. N. Garrow, as the circumstances made "it indispensible to the public good that I should be enabled to confer and cooperate with an U. States Marshal or his deputy." Garrow had "publicly repudiated" Leonard's acts and pronounced them unlawful, rendering it "necessary, as a matter of self-defence," for Worth to alert Poinsett to Garrow's obstructiveness. The colonel also appealed to the War Department regarding a U.S. customs collector named Stillman, though he conceded that "ordinarily I should be regarded as travelling beyond my duty in presenting to your notice the conduct of a civil functionary." Worth was certainly not alone in his appeals to the capital: Scott urged the removal of the U.S. marshal for the state of Michigan, and John Wool criticized a deputy customs collector for his Patriot loyalties and threatened Vermont officials that he would inform the president of their misdeeds unless corrected.[37]

These values and attitudes were also expressed by more junior officers. Captain James Duncan reported from Cleveland—which one historian labels "the most active centre" of the Hunters' Lodges—that "two of the three magistrates of the city are most violent patriots, men of but little character, & I doubt if the most solemn obligations of their oaths of office would influence them to give a decisive counter to their avowed prejudices." For career army officers, personal honor and individual integrity were as much about performing one's obligations within an authoritarian institutional hierarchy as about the entropic individualism historians usually associate with these concepts. Professionally, duty and honor were much the same thing—faithful service—and the genteel class values of individual character and honor buttressed the federal military commander's desire to support the authority of the nation-state and the inviolability of its borders, an authority expressed in the officer corps' professional jurisdiction over the direction of organized national force. Class, state, and profession were intimately linked in officers' reactions to borderlands crises.[38]

Federal military commanders encountered the same sort of disaffection and unreliability in the state militia, which they routinely tried to exclude from participation in their operations to uphold national sovereignty. Their calls for deploying regular soldiers in place of the militia displayed the officer corps' affinity for centralization, as Worth came to doubt that the Patriot unrest could be quelled "in the absence of all *reliable* force" to "enforce the just authority of the Government, and [the] supremacy of the Law." As in so many other areas, officers' reactions changed with bitter experience: Worth initially thought the militia "the more appropriate aid to the civil functionaries," given the delicate sensitivities of local public opinion, but he almost immediately began to blame militia officers for allowing the filibusters to steal weapons from arsenals. Indeed, the New Yorker apparently seized artillery from an arsenal to prevent the insurgents from doing so. On the Lake Champlain frontier, some militiamen at Plattsburgh refused to serve under federal authorities, and John Wool hoped to avoid calling up the militia lest they go over to the filibusters. Though he felt compelled to do so late in February 1838, Wool disbanded units that had been called up by their commanders without proper authorization during the Patriot expedition from Vermont at the end of the month. He then asked for a company of regular soldiers to replace the militia he had initially requested, and after a theft of arms in March, he directed his aides to supervise all shipments to and from local arsenals. That autumn, Wool's successor, Abraham Eustis, ordered subordinates to secure several state arsenals, and Captain Giles Porter refused to issue arms to the inhabitants of Alburg, who feared retaliation after filibusters burned Canadian buildings; instead, Porter went to the scene with sixteen soldiers, intending to reassure the citizenry without giving them access to weapons they might hand over to the insurgents.[39]

Indeed, the Patriots seemingly depended on government arsenals for their supply of weapons, and controlling the distribution of arms was a basic dilemma facing the army. On the Detroit frontier, Hugh Brady withdrew a requisition for militiamen "from want of Confidence" in their reliability, after militia officers somehow lost a store of arms to the filibusters, while Winfield

Scott advised Secretary of War Poinsett that, as a rule, the militia "would almost certainly give their arms to the patriots, if not personally unite with them." In February 1838 Worth actually directed a subordinate to refuse district attorney Benton's order to return seized arms to their original possessors (the insurgents), and a year later he refused to allow an auction of condemned arms, which certainly would have been purchased by the filibusters or their sympathizers, without orders from higher up the chain of federal authority.[40]

By 1839, the colonel felt certain that pervasive insurgent sympathies had rendered the militia useless, and he feared that a move to call it to arms that March was driven by Patriot supporters who hoped to precipitate clashes with the British. Worth was able to prevent that call-up, and he persuaded the governor of New York to keep any arms sent for the militia under guard by the army. In Vermont, John Wool initially considered it unwise to seize any weapons his men discovered because of the probable political uproar, but he quickly became frustrated and warned Scott and Poinsett against issuing arms to citizens in northern Vermont, refusing to honor a writ of attachment for the return of captured weapons presented to him by a county sheriff. Wool was roundly criticized by Whig as well as Democratic newspapers in Vermont but refused to respond, having learned in Georgia that he was "sure to come off second best." By the end of 1838, it had become clear to federal military commanders that without centralized control over the use of force, the country would soon be plunged into war with Britain by the very citizen-soldiers American ideology relied on for defense. Yet Worth feared the New York arsenals had been so stripped that there would be insufficient weapons to arm the militia should the British cross the boundary in force.[41]

Worth, Scott, and Wool frequently castigated uncooperative local officials in the idiom of personal and national honor common among career officers. These professional soldiers hoped to develop the same link between nationalism and personal integrity among locally oriented citizen-soldiers. Thus Wool admonished Captain James Platt of the Vermont militia that "your standing and character as an officer" demanded that a stolen box of ammunition be returned: "If it is not you will be suspected of having connived at theft. If I was in your place, I would not for a thousand boxes of ammunition ever have the world suspect me or my company capable of such an act of villainy." When Platt responded with excuses, Wool reiterated his caustic threat: "Sir. The mere cost of the ammunition is nothing compared with the loss of reputation and the suspicion that must ever attach itself to you and your company. I repeat that if you have any regard for your own character and future standing in society you will have the box returned." In Platt's case, local loyalties triumphed, but similar aspersions directed at civil officers brought in several hundred weapons. Nevertheless, the tension aggravated the professionals' already intense distrust of citizen-soldiers. Winfield Scott summed up the army officer's disdain for officials who placed insurgent loyalties ahead of their oaths of office, reporting to Poinsett: "I have scornfully refused, & shall continue so to refuse, to receive or to salute, one of those *traitors to a special trust . . .* because I am the natural guardian of my own personal honour, & do not choose that that shall be defiled by fellowship with such men."[42]

Professional officers conscious of limited appropriations also criticized the militia for its wasteful expense. Like many federal military commanders in Florida, Worth felt sure that local civilians sought militia duty solely for the scarce cash it paid, and he did his best to ensure that the government's money would not be wasted on men he considered unreliable mercenaries. In February 1838 he wrote to the adjutant general that "no time has been lost in reducing the force, & lopping off useless members not provided [for] by law," particularly excess officers (who were paid more). (Here, as in civil-military relations across the board, we can be sure that Worth's frustrating experiences in New York paved the way for his sometimes draconian practices as theater commander in Florida in 1841 and 1842.) A year later Worth noted that a Vermont company was "inclined to disband . . . provided they are [first] mustered for pay," which "would have the effect of flooding the frontier with Militia," unemployed and undisciplined, so he sent a detachment of regular soldiers to take their place and remove the pretext for their mobilization. By the summer of 1838, the principal threat to peace clearly came from American citizens rather than British soldiers, and popular mobilization played no part in Worth's strategy for defending the nation's constitutional sovereignty from the sovereigns enshrined in republican theory. As disillusioned as any of his counterparts in Florida, the colonel knew that a flood of disorderly militiamen would do more harm than good.[43]

In contrast, both Brady and Worth made a clear distinction between the popular militia and the generally more prosperous volunteers, believing that the latter could be trusted with arms. This was much the same distinction these genteel officers made between filibusters and "respectable Citizens— staunch friends of Law and Order," as Worth put it, and they often did so in the same language of social hierarchy and order. Lacking regular troops, Wool relied mostly on civilian volunteers in his operations against the Patriots in Vermont in February 1838, while Brady repeatedly praised a company named after him as "the most respectable young men of Detroit," and Worth applauded a New York battalion for its "zeal, fidelity, and discipline." Indeed, the colonel was a strong believer in the civic and military benefits of training under professional guidance: "[The volunteers] are in a course of instruction

... which will increase their efficiency as soldiers, keep them out of idleness & send them home better citizens," no doubt after being lectured on their duty to observe the neutrality laws.[44]

Worth's characteristic sense of class and profession came together in an official order praising both volunteers and regulars, while highlighting contrasts in the virtues the colonel expected from the two groups:

> The conduct of the Battalion of Volunteers . . . was precisely what was expected from a proud, high minded citizen soldiery, as well acquainted with the law as [with] the manner of enforcing it. The discipline exhibited by these companies reflects the highest credit upon their commanders.
>
> The Battalion of regulars . . . submitted to fatigue and privations with a patience, steadiness, and forbearance, under vexatious circumstances, which would have done credit to veterans [these men were virtually all recent recruits] and does honor to their Officers.

Note how professional officers received "honor"—prestige, status, respect—while enlisted men and volunteer officers got "credit," a market metaphor suitable to businessmen and workers that also implies a delay in payment. Career soldiers "submitted" patiently, with the implication that they behaved well toward the citizenry that was creating such vexing circumstances for them, while volunteers remained "proud" and "high minded" citizens (in contrast to the many immigrant enlisted men—perhaps Canadians—who were not citizens), whose awareness of the law might threaten the discipline commanders cherished. These distinctions notwithstanding, the concrete core of Worth's praise, for volunteers and regular soldiers alike, lay in their good discipline. Yet even here the colonel's words suggest that "the conduct of the Battalion of Volunteers" was *not* "precisely what was expected" of rights-conscious citizen-soldiers by hardened professionals. Among the volunteers, who were unused to subordination, discipline meant a cohesion or sense of common purpose within the unit that encouraged them to do their duty and enforce the laws. For rough-hewn professional soldiers accustomed to subordination, rather than the "high minded" good citizenship demanded when enforcing civil laws, discipline meant restraining their natural irritation and potential aggression against unruly civilians amid "vexatious circumstances": republican citizens did not always do what they were told, as good soldiers expected of good citizens. In practice, Worth shared the class-inflected attitudes of civilians, particularly Whiggish ones, toward enlisted soldiers: volunteer citizen-soldiers, probably of middle-class origins, should be capable of self-discipline, while working-class professionals required the direction of genteel commanders. From this self-congratulatory and self-fulfilling perspective, the discipline of the volunteers "reflected credit" on their leaders much less directly than regular enlisted men did on their commanders.[45]

Surrounded by uncooperative and duplicitous officials, the tension between responsibility to enforce the neutrality policy and accountability to local civil authorities and the principle of civil supremacy frustrated Worth, and by the end of 1838, he adopted an unofficial policy of avoiding association with the local civil authorities whenever possible. The colonel's hard-nosed new approach was directed at the civil authorities as much as identifiable Patriots. Worth actually instructed his subordinates to find evidence of negligence and criminal acts by civil officials, and he was able to secure the arrest of a federal deputy marshal, while refusing orders from civil officers to return or auction captured weapons. Indeed, the colonel intended his soldiers to detain accused civil officials, albeit for immediate transfer to the custody of higher civil authorities. Always verbally diplomatic in public, Worth remained cautious, admonishing subordinates that any military arrest would be "a painful and delicate duty to be performed with great discretion and judgment and under the clearest evidence of criminal design," warning that they must "deliver the person arrested to the civil authority . . . with all possible diligence." Despite his irritation, the experienced colonel knew his confrontational methods could easily prove counterproductive, so he stressed the importance of organizing evidence so that witnesses could not deny it, "for a failure to substantiate the charges . . . would only encourage [the civil officials] to greater exertions in the violation of [their] duty."[46]

Arresting civil officials suggested martial law, and a backlash was sure to ensue, so Worth quickly turned to more indirect methods in order to appear at least superficially obedient to civilian control. In doing so, he actually abandoned the civil populace to its own devices in the hope that a rash of Patriot violence and thievery would cure it of support for the filibusters. When a suspect district attorney complained about a military officer's order that guards prevent an assault on an official messenger, the colonel defended his subordinate's conduct but responded that he would give "specific orders . . . under no circumstances to permit any interference in any brawls or civil difficulties, unless on the written request of a Magistrate." Worth's new approach coincided with the insurgents' turn to arson and banditry while attempting to recover from their battlefield defeats at Windsor and Prescott the previous fall. The colonel decided to classify such incidents as "civil difficulties" beyond his responsibility, asserting that "the Magistracy and people . . . are alone competent to the correction of such evils." By the beginning of 1839, Worth believed that responsibility for the Patriot problem and its resolution rested with the American people: "Should it please our good citizens to withdraw their countenance [and] support there is not a doubt tranquility will be restored." Indeed, his biting letter to customs collector George McWhorter sounded as if it had been written by a British rather than an American officer: "I feel quite assured that your neighborhood is in no danger of being disturbed from Can[ada] and as certain that any further aggressions by your citizens will be duly punished by the offended party. . . . I have neither authority nor inclination to employ the troops in quelling civil brawls." Worth was effectively reclassifying the unrest as a matter for local law enforcement (which depended heavily on the operation of public opinion) rather than federal military intervention, leaving the locality to solve its own problems in the expectation that it would have to accept the government's view of the situation. If civilians wanted to fight among themselves, they would have to police themselves.[47]

By this time, the colonel had begun to worry that disturbances in the social order would infect the army itself, that "the thoroughly corrupt character of a large portion of the frontier inhabitants is fatal to the discipline [and] fidelity of the troops, placed in garrisons in the open towns." His attention to this threat far exceeded his concern about British or Canadian efforts to lure the soldiers from their duty. "You will have to guard against efforts to seduce your men from their duties, and it is desirable that there should be the least practicable association between them and the citizens," he warned subordinates, cautioning Captain Joseph Bonnell that "the constant presence of your officers with the men is indispensable . . . to keep up the discipline and instruction of the company." Worth first tried concentrating his detachments on steamers, which would conserve "men [and] money, keep the troops from contact with the citizens, cause by their movements less excitement, . . . [and] in a manner less obnoxious to . . . the people . . . allow us to concentrate and mature the discipline of the men." Steamers would also obviate civilian complaints about the British naval presence along the St. Lawrence. Nevertheless, Worth still felt obliged to remove his detachments from Ogdensburg to Madison Barracks in Sackets Harbor fifty miles to the south, for he believed that "a systematic plan to debauch and seduce them from their duty, has already been too successfully practiced."[48]

Worth finally came to believe that only fear of chaos would ensure adherence to law and order. This had always been his expectation, demonstrating his recognition that military force alone would fail, given the ideological constraints on American politics and taxation, neutrality legislation, and military budgets. It should be repeated that he did not consider martial law necessary to defeat the insurgency; civilian cooperation would suffice, without exceeding legal due process. As early as February 1838, he advised the adjutant general that "the scandalous excesses . . . will produce a very decisive, and fortunate, reaction in public feeling. . . . [They] have made all true men hug closer to the laws." This optimism proved premature, and a year later Worth instructed Benjamin Pierce that if incidents continued "you will not hesitate to withdraw the troops, and [to] try, as a last expedient, the effects of a due sense of insecurity." Not only had the colonel ceased to cooperate with the civil authorities; he had, by this point, decided to quell the unrest by taking advantage of their fear, by withdrawing the very protection he was normally supposed to provide. In doing so, he turned the weakness of federal neutrality law on its head, showing the local populace that rigid adherence to the letter of the law on his part could be harmful as well as beneficial to their interests. The borderers began "to look with seriousness to these matters, as the brand of the incendiary approaches their own dwellings, and there is reason to hope that in a few days they will compel the refugees to retire," he reported to Scott. "I am firm in the belief that perseverance in keeping the troops back from the line will in a short time bring our people to their senses [and] induce the Magistrates to do their duty." In one of the many ironies of federalism, military accountability to the national government ultimately meant abandoning a portion of the nation's citizens if they persisted in pursuing their local objectives without regard to the decisions made for them by their representatives at the national center.[49]

The colonel was able to undertake this apparently irresponsible course of action because the great majority of the violence was committed by American citizens against one another in robberies by the "Patriots." Worth had come to the conclusion that British or Canadian retaliation was unlikely, and he was careful to assure concerned civilians of this. (Hugh Brady also came to doubt the likelihood of retaliation.) Worth's certainty was based on his excellent relations with his counterparts on the opposite shore and his belief that they could and would restrain Canadian retaliation. The colonel could rely on the centralized authority of the British imperial system (in which the militia was kept under much stricter discipline), and he could turn American decentralization on its head by showing the local gentry a glimpse of the anarchy that awaited a society driven by the fickle winds of Jacksonian populism. Worth's multilateral diplomacy paid off by allowing the United States to defend itself on the cheap. His status as an apolitical agent of the nation-state enabled him to downplay or dismiss local political pressure and demonstrate the federal government's commitment to the principles of national sovereignty and international order. While there were certainly other reasons for British forbearance, the good faith and energetic diplomacy of professional military commanders substantially reduced the friction that could have made accommodation more difficult.[50]

Nor were Worth or any other federal military officers sanctioned for any of their actions along the Canadian border: experience and merit, rather than partisan politics or ideological affinity, drove senior promotions. Despite their contemporary and historical reputations for stronger states' rights sentiments than Jackson, Van Buren and Poinsett backed the professional army throughout the crisis, and they were followed by an equally sympathetic Whig administration in 1841. Scott was promoted commanding general when Macomb died that year, Wool advanced to Scott's former position as brigadier general commanding the army in the north, and Sylvester Churchill took Wool's place as inspector general. Worth rose to theater commander in Florida the same year, bringing the Second Seminole War to an inconclusive but ultimately successful end in 1842. (Abraham Eustis died at age fifty-seven in 1843; Hugh Brady was too old for active service after the insurgency came to an end.) All this occurred under Whig president John Tyler, yet the civil-military tension of 1836 evaporated virtually overnight when Democrat Martin Van Buren replaced Democrat Andrew Jackson in 1837. We can attribute the lack of sanction to Van Buren's fear of war with Britain, to his affable personality (in contrast to Jackson's intensity and authoritarianism), or to the officer corps' accountability to civilian legal norms of due process along the Canadian border, but the army clearly became substantially more autonomous after Jackson's departure from the presidency.

Faced with a dangerous international crisis in which neither white supremacy nor states' rights had any clear role, and which might have justified more aggressive measures against citizens than those in the southern Indian borderlands, army officers, including John Wool, performed more subordinately for Van Buren than for Jackson. Indeed, despite the presence of frontier citizens fully as obnoxious as those in the South, the combination of a more clearly national and international mission, a more temperate president, and an officer corps tempered by a decade of civil-military conflict on the frontiers in southern states made the officer corps more overtly subordinate than ever before. Faced with an international crisis, the officer corps certainly felt more responsible for the outcome and for safeguarding the nation's security; after the resignations of 1836 and 1837, the remaining officers proved more reliable servants of national policy, and the tensions of federalism eased as state and national policy coincided. Thus, despite the many similarities in officer attitudes toward frontier citizens, local civil officials, and citizen-soldiers examined in this chapter and in those on the Seminole conflict, the Canadian border crises offered an experience of civil-military concord at the national level that helped soothe the wounds of the Florida war and Indian removal, providing a memory of harmony that officers could look to for reassurance as the army moved into Texas, toward war with Mexico.

Significant Patriot incursions ended in December 1838, but national military commanders on both sides of the border continued to worry through the spring. Experienced peacekeepers like James Bankhead (who occupied Amelia Island in 1818 and served under Scott in Charleston during the Nullification Crisis) explained the economic dynamics of filibustering: the "indigent idlers . . . who are the only persons to give countenance or support to the patriot cause, will find employment" until winter. Recognizing this pattern, British ambassador Henry Fox raised the insurgent specter again in the autumn of 1839, and Secretary of War Poinsett responded by canceling the redeployment of the Eighth Infantry to Florida, sending Winfield Scott to the border one more time. Rumors of filibuster activity persisted throughout 1840 and enjoyed another revival during the McLeod crisis during the summer of 1841, but the last organized insurgent effort petered out in September 1841. Some reform gradually took hold in Canada, luring many of the disaffected back into the political community, and American interest in northern filibustering dissipated with remarkable speed. There were no attempts to revive the insurgency during the Oregon dispute in 1845 and 1846; indeed, there were no further filibuster incursions from the United States against Canada until the Fenian unrest, which the army helped police and suppress, after the Civil War.[51]

The experienced professional officers of the national standing army succeeded in their peacekeeping mission along the Canadian border. They reassured American citizens that the federal government would defend them from British or Canadian incursions, and they defended the United States from invasion primarily by restraining, or by demonstrating to the British that they were trying hard to restrain, the Americans whose actions might provoke retaliation. Their belief in national good faith was reciprocated by their British counterparts, and the loyal majority of Canadians "relied upon the active interference of the U.S. government to check further outrages by the presence of a regular force." Indeed, the Canadians' trust in American military efforts enabled the United States to avoid mobilizing far larger forces or declaring martial law, as the captain reporting these views advocated. Larger U.S. forces almost certainly would have come from the unreliable militia, whose indiscipline and disaffection easily could have led to international war, while martial

Hugh Brady, federal diplomat on the northwestern frontier. (Courtesy Burton Historical Collection, Detroit Public Library)

law would have sparked indignation and aggravated resistance to national law. Instead, despite bitter frustration, Worth and Wool normally acted well within the bounds of due process. They intimidated but did not fire on the filibusters: the use of deadly force against citizens was as noteworthy for its absence along the northern border as on the western and internal frontiers.[52]

Senior British officials were just as impressed as their local civil and military agents, and the example U.S. officers set in 1838 would reverberate during the "Aroostook War" the following spring. Though known for his acerbic comments about Americans and their politics, the British ambassador to the United States considered federal troops "so usefully employed" in restraining the Patriots that he sought and received a tacit understanding that they would be kept on the border until the Maine boundary crisis was resolved. The senior levels of the British government appreciated U.S. efforts to curb filibustering, and after February 1838, the ministry resisted further calls to reinforce Canada as an unnecessary threat to good relations. British public opinion, though occasionally inflamed by the newspapers, generally followed this path as well, and there was little sustained outcry for action against the United States from any politically significant group. Even the usually bellicose Lord Palmerston was reassured: using language remarkably like that employed by American army officers, the British prime minister opined that "even in the state of Maine the outcry is a factitious [both factional and fictional, apparently] one raised by a few land jobbers & speculators." The diplomatic actions of dedicated career officers on the scene along the international frontier demonstrated that the U.S. government opposed the violence of its lawless constituents, enabling the United States and Britain to avoid a war with potentially immeasurable consequences.[53]

MILITARY PEACEKEEPING AND DIPLOMACY IN THE MCLEOD AND AROOSTOOK CRISES, 1839–1843

The filibuster incursions against Canada effectively died out after 1839, but their repercussions reverberated along the border for several years. The one major instance of Anglo-Canadian retaliation against the insurgents, the destruction of the ship *Caroline* at Navy Island near Buffalo in December 1837, led to a diplomatic crisis three years later, when one of the Canadian militia officers involved, Alexander McLeod, was arrested in a New York tavern for the murder of an American during the raid. In February 1841 the American minister to Britain warned President Van Buren that there would be "*immediate war*" if McLeod were found guilty and executed. In March, Britain assumed responsibility for the raid, but partisan politics led New York's Whig governor, William Seward, to press forward, despite pressure from presidents Van Buren and Tyler, usually states' rights advocates. (In contrast, one of the virtues of career army officers as federal and frontier diplomats was their consistency, since they rarely felt much interest in propitiating the electorate.)

An attempt to bail McLeod from the Lockport jail was met by a mob that set fires, stoned the jail, and fired blank charges from cannon. Winfield Scott undertook another tour of the northern border in March; that August, the War Department directed Scott, just promoted to commanding general, and John Wool, his replacement as brigadier general and commander of the Northern Military Department, to help protect McLeod from mob violence during his trial at Utica, under the direction of local civil authorities.[54]

Governor Seward requested that federal military forces be sent to the arsenal in nearby Rome as a safeguard, but he wanted them to remain in the background to avoid stirring up public anger. Burned by his experiences with Andrew Jackson, Wool assured Scott that "you may rely upon my discretion" not "to compromit [sic] either the United States, or the army" by overreaction. Five days later, he added that the local magistrate had requested a company of federal troops to maintain order amid the rumors and roughnecks in Utica. The brigadier continued to contrast filibustering and vigilantism with the orderly norms of interstate warfare espoused by professional soldiers, declaiming to Governor Seward that he expected "a native border war during the next winter." Wool lamented that "nothing can be more corrupting or debasing to the morals of the people than such a war. If we are to have war let us have it in a way becoming a civilized and just Nation." The federal troops under his command behaved with just such decorum during their stint as national policemen: "the officers are very discreet, and the soldiers orderly and quiet, and do not show themselves or mix with the citizens." According to Wool, Seward asked the brigadier to stay in the vicinity of the trial, but by working with local authorities, he was able to secure a hundred gentlemen volunteers in addition to thirty sheriff's deputies and a group of civilian constables; he then set an example of calm by returning home to Troy. McLeod was quickly found not guilty, and Wool had Captain Robert Anderson (Scott's former aide, now Wool's adjutant) and Lieutenant Horace Brooks join the sheriff of Oneida County to escort the disruptive Canadian out of New York State.[55]

From West Point, cadet James Wall Schureman admonished his sister that "the McLeod affair has shown that a more extended federal jurisprudence is necessary for maintaining good faith toward other nations," a good example of the practical implications of the informal socialization in nationalism at the Military Academy. The Neutrality Act of 1838 had expired, but Wool continued to work to prevent filibustering, recommending that a squad guard the arsenal at Rome and a company remain at Niagara, while Captain Anderson toured the border collecting information about the Patriots. Scott also tried to anticipate trouble that summer, providing detailed instructions to Captain

James Monroe for investigating rumors of a filibuster resurgence in Cleveland, along with directions to work with the U.S. district attorney, marshal, and customs collectors, who might be somewhat more reliable now that they had been appointed by more statist Whigs. Military efforts at domestic intelligence gathering continued into the autumn, when Wool warned Lieutenant Colonel Ichabod Crane, commanding at Buffalo, that the insurgents might prove more active than expected. Like Worth several years before, the brigadier also sought information about the reliability of federal civil officials in the region, asking Crane to send any news about the Buffalo postmaster's sympathy for the insurgents, which Wool promised to forward to the president.[56]

No serious incidents occurred that winter. By February 1842, Wool was advising Scott that the border was quiet and would probably remain so. Perhaps the last reference to active filibusters on the northern frontier came in May 1843 from Hugh Brady, who advised against removing the guard from the Detroit arsenal lest it "tempt those restless spirits to commit depredations, for . . . the same hostile feelings [still] pervade the minds of many on both sides of the river." Perhaps equally important, the brigadier had no barracks to house the troops without reopening Fort Howard at Green Bay. The elderly Brady's focus turned increasingly to maintaining domestic order and institutional autonomy, particularly in local civil-military relations. Like his former counterpart Henry Atkinson, who died in 1842 after thirty-four years in the army, Brady downplayed most potential trouble in the region he oversaw. In June 1843 he sought greater professional autonomy in employing soldiers to remove squatters from public lands where copper had been discovered along Lake Superior, suggesting to commanding general Scott that the War Department give geographic department commanders like himself the discretion to initiate such removal, rather than vesting the authority to request military assistance in a civilian agent.[57]

The brigadier expressed similar skepticism of civilian motives six months later, advising the adjutant general that the citizens requesting a military guard at the Dearborn (Chicago) arsenal did so only to secure customers for their tavern. Failing to gain authority to expel the Lake Superior squatters himself, Brady reverted to caution and subordination; in June 1844 he warned a quartermaster captain, himself a sixteen-year veteran, against interfering with miners in the copper district around newly established Fort Wilkins unless requested to do so by civil officials—and then only if all other means had failed. At the age of seventy-six—his first military service occurring more than fifty years before—the old soldier went on permanent furlough. (In the absence of formal retirement benefits prior to the Civil War, the War Department rewarded elderly officers by allowing them to remain on leave until their deaths.) This left Brady's stand-in, brevet Brigadier General George Mercer Brooke, the genteel commander of the Fifth Infantry Regiment and a thirty-six-year veteran, to articulate a principle of civil-military relations that most commanders stationed on the Canadian border would have echoed. When a businessman asked permission to open a smelting furnace at Fort Wilkins, Brooke first explained the danger to domestic animals (public and private property) and then advised the adjutant general that "it is always better to separate . . . the military from the citizen, as it is nearly certain that from accident or some other cause, collisions and bad feelings will be engendered." Coming on the heels of eight years of frustration in Florida and at least four along the Canadian frontier, Brooke's counsel suggests that the career officer corps had found a balance of professional autonomy and insulation, the latter directed primarily at the enlisted soldiers that genteel commanders presumed unruly, without alienation from civil society. Instead, Brooke expressed a caution born of long experience, an acceptance of accountability for the behavior of the soldiers under his command, and a sense of responsibility for minimizing the potential for civil-military friction.[58]

Just as the Patriot tensions passed their peak, the long-standing dispute over the boundary of northern Maine erupted into the "Aroostook War" between state and Canadian law enforcement officers in January 1839. Perhaps because of the army's success in peacekeeping, the Patriot crisis had done little to spur efforts to increase general American military preparedness. The Eighth Infantry was raised so troops would not have to be diverted from Florida or Cherokee removal, and aside from local initiatives by commanders along the lakes, the United States made no serious preparations to counter British naval concentrations; the economic depression clearly precluded the sort of buildup advocated by Secretary of War Poinsett and the Navy Department. Yet financial difficulties also circumscribed state attempts to practice independent foreign policies. Lord Palmerston doubted "whether it is likely that Maine would undertake an expensive war, when she cannot pay even the cost of a short Demonstration," and the Van Buren administration ultimately assumed Maine's militia expenses from the Aroostook War in return for the state's agreement to cede authority over the future negotiation and defense of its boundaries. Consequently, the British squadron in the western Atlantic was reduced to its former establishment of twenty-eight vessels, none of them ships of the line, by early 1840. Nevertheless, planning for possible conflict entered a new stage of urgency when a Maine posse drove off Canadian loggers, who returned to capture the leader of the posse. The state legislature then authorized Democratic governor John Fairfield to employ force to uphold the state's claims to the region north of the Aroostook River. On February 18 Fairfield dispatched a thousand militiamen to the area, although there were no further physical confrontations or injuries on either side. Eight days later Van Buren told Congress that Maine had the right to halt encroachments on the territory it claimed, and on February 28 Congress appropriated $10 million and authorized Van Buren to muster up to 50,000 volunteers. War appeared imminent.[59]

The army's most significant role in the Maine boundary crisis was that of individual diplomacy—as much federal as international—rather than collective force. President Van Buren dispatched Winfield Scott to Maine with the authority to use force to help Maine expel Canadians from the Aroostook region, but the foundations for peace were already in place. Van Buren, like Jackson, had done little to counter the growing agitation in Maine, where both parties competed for electoral advantage by asserting their chauvinism. Nevertheless, Secretary of State Forsyth and British ambassador Fox agreed on February 27 that Maine would withdraw its forces from the disputed area, and both sides would release their prisoners while negotiations got under way. Van Buren immediately approved, and Palmerston did so as soon as he received word of the agreement, but Scott was the only national agent on the scene with the legitimacy to calm Maine's anger. Once again, as in the Patriot crisis and on the Texas border, the Jacksonians sent officers of the national standing army rather than State Department officials to the scene to conduct federal and international diplomacy and keep the peace. Recognizing the comparative centralization of political authority under the British colonial system, historians Howard Jones and Donald Rakestraw observe that "Scott quickly realized that his primary problem was faction-ridden Maine and not New Brunswick." Though the nationalistic general privately deplored the Fox-Forsyth agreement as an American retreat, he met with Governor Fairfield and state legislators as soon as he arrived in Portland on March 7. Shuttling between Fairfield and New Brunswick governor Sir John Harvey, Scott drafted an armistice to which Fox and Forsyth made few changes. Again, Scott's personal connections played a significant role: Harvey was an old acquaintance from the War of 1812, when he and Scott had both served as adjutants general, arranging truces and prisoner exchanges for their respective armies along the Niagara frontier in 1813. Both Fairfield and Harvey later credited Scott with reestablishing peace.[60]

Despite Scott's crucial diplomatic role, the army as a whole had little to do with the Maine boundary crises, other than planning. Ironically, the establishment of Hancock Barracks and associated roads in 1828 probably encouraged immigration to the region adjoining the Aroostook Valley, swelling popular demands for national action. Nevertheless, no elements of the field army were actually sent to the disputed region until more than two years after the confrontation broke out, after the Patriot insurgency and the McLeod crisis had dissipated. At that time, a pair of companies were deployed to the Aroostook and St. Johns River Valleys, where Fort Fairfield (named after the governor) and Fort Kent were established. Both these positions, never more than blockhouses, were abandoned in 1843. In contrast to the Patriot War, professional commanders left little comment on the Maine boundary dispute or the army's role in it, apparently content to wait on the operations of diplomacy. Indeed, Abraham Eustis, the de facto theater commander at Hancock Barracks, deflected Governor Fairfield's requests for assistance in 1840, forwarding them to the War Department while advising against replacing the Maine posses with regulars. Rather than seeking an enhanced role for the army and saving the government money by demobilizing the militia, fear of civil-military friction and political complications led the brigadier to delay deploying federal troops to uphold American claims for another year. Winfield Scott ultimately ordered him to dispatch companies to Forts Fairfield and Kent to replace the state troops, but Eustis did not do so until Scott reminded him.[61]

As inspector general in 1838, Wool warned that the Houlton garrison of 118 officers and men, the only national military force in Maine during the initial confrontation, was insufficient to do more than deter Canadian militia raids in its immediate vicinity. Yet the minor surge in spending on installations during 1840–1841 receded quickly with the general retrenchment in military expenditures in 1842; a post established at Presque Isle in 1841 was closed two years later, and Houlton itself was abandoned in 1845. Fortunately, the only Anglo-American strife along the Maine border that actually involved army personnel took place in March 1843 near Fort Kent on the St. Johns River, when Captain Lucien B. Webster dispatched several soldiers to aid state law enforcement officers after a Canadian constable arrested an American on territory that had been granted to the United States under the Webster-Ashburton Treaty. The American was recovered without bodily harm to any of the parties involved; Webster sent a conciliatory letter to the Canadian civil authorities and was commended by President Tyler and applauded by a meeting of the local citizenry. The northern frontier remained essentially unfortified, testifying to Congress's long-held belief, shared by most military commanders, that American population growth and consequent economic power made a war with Canada one the United States could win without much preparation.[62]

Junior officers stationed at Maine border posts described much the same comity with their British counterparts as had developed during the Patriot insurgency. Though probably romanticized in retrospect, a First Artillery history published in the late nineteenth century put less emphasis on peacekeeping patrols than on the balls and other "civilities" exchanged with the "corresponding British force" opposite Houlton. Most notable to the author, "the regimental mess . . . was then more nearly a *regimental* mess than it has ever been since, or can ever hope to be again. . . . The regimental band was then at its best." These priorities, which bolstered professional cohesion as well as diplomacy between the military forces sharing the border, were also felt in the disputed regions farther north: commanding Fort Kent, little more than a blockhouse in the northern woods, genteel Captain Webster asked the adjutant general for additional funds to entertain his British counterparts.[63]

Farther south, John Hatheway, a lieutenant of the First who served as Eustis's aide, enjoyed "an elegant dinner" at St. Johns with Colonel Grey, commander of the 71st Highlanders, along with two other American officers during that regiment's commemoration of the Battle of Waterloo in June 1841. Hatheway and three of his comrades then visited Fredericton, capital of New Brunswick, at the invitation of Lady Colbrooke, wife of the governor, for an entire week the following February, dining with a British regiment. Though a self-professed Locofoco (radical Democrat), Hatheway praised the "distinguished attention" they received, and that September he toured New Brunswick for a week with Eustis. The lieutenant continued socializing with his British counterparts during the summer of 1843, and he broke his leg when his carriage flipped over as he returned from such a party. Hatheway wrote nothing substantial about his peacekeeping, policing, or deterrent duties and saw little chance of hostilities. This was not surprising, given the War Department's instructions to Eustis to avoid any intervention "in any matter [where] civil jurisdiction" was asserted by the agents of Maine or New Brunswick, which cautious commanders like Eustis could interpret to mean virtually any matter in the disputed territory. The limits to the army's concern over Canada, and the wartime strategy of mass mobilization this inattention implied, were demonstrated when a number of northern border posts—including Buffalo and Houlton, the principal installations on the Niagara and Maine frontiers—were abandoned in 1845 when the army concentrated against its next opponent in Texas.[64]

MILITARY ATTITUDES TOWARD BRITAIN AND THE LIMITS OF AMERICAN MILITARY EXPANSIONISM

Few professional soldiers sought war with Britain during the Patriot and Aroostook crises. The nationalism and underlying self-interest of career offi-

Abraham Eustis, man of many deployments. (Courtesy Army Transportation Museum, Fort Eustis)

cers dedicated to the service of the state during an era of growing sectional friction did lead some to favor war as a means of unifying American public opinion or spurring efforts toward military preparedness against a foreign threat, but this trope rarely appeared in their letters during the Patriot crisis. The idea appeared more often as sectional tensions increased during the pre–Civil War period, but during the 1840s it remained tightly constrained by the officer corps' predilection for law and order, international as well as domestic. In 1840 the usually responsible Robert Anderson, a fifteen-year veteran, wanted to fight the British to sustain American national unity (presumably against sectional conflict), but his mentor Abraham Eustis cautioned that this was unlikely to occur, much less succeed: "Doubtless *you* would profit by it, & gain more honour & glory, than can be found among the laurels of Florida. But I think we shall *not* be united; & abolitionism, states rights & other hobbies will *not* 'be sunk to old nick.'"[65]

Lieutenant Philip Kearny linked national unity to hatred for Britain during the McLeod crisis, remarking to Anderson that "I am proud to see that that bitterness which the English so unjustly have nurtured towards us for years, has at length kindled as strong a feeling of resentment in the hearts of all our people, & that on this one question of hatred to England all parties will unite to a man." In 1842 Kearny's uncle Stephen, the colonel of the First Dragoons, observed with regret that war between the two countries seemed less likely than before, "because I think war must ensue before our difficulties [with Britain] are settled, and I therefore think the sooner it comes the better!" Though a thirty-year veteran, Colonel Kearny spoke for many junior officers who looked to war as the only certain spur to military preparedness when he declared that "a war would tend to unite the feelings of our people and the public men would then . . . put the country in a state of defense[,] which they will not do in times of peace."[66]

The Anglophobic nationalism of a Philip Kearny, a hot-tempered young officer who had just spent a year in France, had little chance of influencing national policy. Of more serious import, Winfield Scott remarked to Secretary of War Poinsett in 1839 "that [only] a good hot foreign war . . . could save the Union & our free institutions" from the disorder caused by partisanship and cultural radicalism. Scott, who was being considered as a Whig candidate for the presidency after his successes against the nullifiers, the Cherokee, and the Patriots, had made the serious misstep of writing and talking to influential friends in Washington "in express reference to the Canadian excitement." Indeed, the general had asserted "that if a good & sufficient cause of foreign war . . . should be presented, every *American* patriot ought to fall upon his knees & return thanks to Providence for the blessing," because war would "cure" Americans of the "moral distempers" of "peace societies, antimasonry, nullification, Mormon difficulties & abolitionism," the "cankers of a long peace & a calm world." Scott's desire for war quickly evaporated, along with his sympathy for the insurgents, and he responded heatedly, though somewhat disingenuously, to later insinuations by the British ambassador that he was "not disinclined to a war" with England: "I have always earnestly & solemnly protested against being plunged into war by our borderers, wrong end foremost."[67]

Note Scott's distaste for anything smacking of ideological enthusiasm or suspicion of and resistance to the established authority of the nation-state, which he expressed as a fear of division, whether sectional, social, political, or religious. Operating from these mental assumptions, the general and his subordinates quickly came to see the insurgents as undisciplined fanatics maddened by excessive democracy, hardly the appropriate agents for American nationalism or expansion. Robert Anderson, for example, initially sympathized with the filibusters' motives, but as the rebellions disintegrated into banditry, he came to the same conclusion as Worth and Scott, lamenting that "the spirit of patriotism has fallen from its high and honorable designs into the contemptible, cowardly desire to burn & plunder the houses of the defenseless." Professional soldiers were generally realists, and military Anglophobia was not irrational belligerence. Their attitudes were conditioned by both circumstances and worldview, particularly the overall balance of power and the ethical requisites of international order, and by the belief that the United States should be the aggrieved party rather than the aggressor. When Anderson, Scott, and Kearny wrote about war with Britain, they did so as professional military commanders who expected to lead organized national forces against the powerful British threat to American national security and growth, not as advocates or abettors of private plunder.[68]

Belief in the value and necessity of national sovereignty and centralized control over the application of armed power appears to be the key to understanding the emphasis professional soldiers placed on enforcing domestic and international law. Experienced military commanders feared that if these restraints failed, there would be domestic social chaos, at least in the already turbulent border regions, and a war the United States was unprepared for and had no need to fight. The officer corps' quest for social, institutional, and international stability was the most significant restraint on whatever enthusiasm its members initially felt for territorial expansion against Canada or war with Britain. Worth and his fellows were noticeably better disposed toward the rule of national sovereignty and international order on the Canadian frontier than their predecessors had been on the Florida frontier a generation before, and references to the possibility of American expansion against Canada during the Patriot crisis are most notable for their rarity, particularly in comparison to the mood among many civilians.

Territorial expansion became acceptable to the officer corps only when it followed the orderly processes provided for by national and international law, under the direction of professional soldiers serving as executive agents of the American nation-state. Soldiers who would soon hope for war with foreign nation-states over Oregon or Texas withheld their support from a Manifest

Destiny of private individuals acting beyond the restraints of congressional sanction and professional military command. Trying to explain away his initial bellicosity, Scott assured Secretary of War Poinsett that he had always "argued that war could only be legitimately made under a declaration of Congress; that if otherwise brought about, we would probably find our population divided & distracted, which would superadd the disgrace of failure to the taint of breach of treaty & the disorder of its commencement. . . . In short," he excused himself, "in all that I have said & done I have kept strictly in view the constitution, national responsibilities & the high obligations of morality."[69]

Observe Scott's stress on order and good faith, along with his experienced and politically conscious assessment of the likelihood of success or failure. All the senior commanders on the Canadian frontier had fought the British there in 1814, and Brady, Worth, and Scott were all wounded at Lundy's Lane. As an advocate of Anglo-Saxon racial superiority and a man whose penchant for discipline masked an intensely passionate nature, Worth displayed some interest in filibustering against Yucatan or Cuba after the war with Mexico. Yet any sympathy he and his comrades might have felt for the Canadian rebels was curbed by fear of domestic lawlessness and social disorder, mixed with a vague Anglophilia rooted in gentility, along with practical professional considerations about the disadvantageous balance of forces available for immediate action. Worth's ardent ethnocentrism, expressed as recognition of and probably covert admiration for British military capability and derision for that of Mexico, justified expansion to the south as Manifest Destiny but encouraged cooperation with British commanders in Canada. The same ethnocentrism led junior officers to envision the mother country as a potent and worthy adversary, whereas Mexico, which they deemed inferior and unworthy, would likely back down, after they had wasted their time far from their families in torrid Texas.

The juxtaposition of these attitudes and affiliations suggests the difficulty of assigning uniform motives and attitudes to officers of varied backgrounds and careers. Although many professional soldiers spoke belligerently of Britain during the early and mid-1840s, most of them were young company-grade officers, impatient for promotion, who had missed the Seminole War or disdained its limited opportunities for military glory and reputation. Moreover, the military Anglophobia of the 1840s lacked the physical dimension provided a generation before by expeditions to counter British influence over the Indians. Concern about British influence was a minor consideration in some of the dragoon expeditions toward Pembina and across the Plains during the early and mid-1840s, but there was little of the urgency expressed by senior civil and military officials during the decade after 1815. Thus, the Anglophobia expressed by junior army officers during the 1840s had an abstract air—ardent, but without substantive content or practical advice. Most officers in close contact with the British met the putative enemy over dinner, like Hatheway and his fellows on the Maine border. Many if not most of these bellicose junior officers sympathized with the Democratic Party, while the officer corps as a whole tended toward Whiggishness in its values, attitudes, and worldview. The lieutenants of the 1840s grew up amidst the vivid partisan conflict of Jacksonian America and felt much of its urge to choose partisan affiliations, but these divisive affiliations rarely became central to soldiers' identities. Company officers too young to have experienced the frontier civil-military tensions of the 1830s saw Jacksonian support for territorial expansion as an opportunity, while field-grade and general officers harassed and reprimanded by the Jackson administration knew that expansion carried risks and frustration as well as rewards and elation.[70]

The differences between the attitudes of experienced field-grade and general officers and those of their more aggressive junior subordinates, most of whom were lieutenants recently graduated from the Military Academy, suggest that belligerent expansionism, Anglophobia, and eagerness for war declined as career officers gained experience and responsibility and became more thoroughly socialized in the ethos of their profession. In other words, the ideology of expansionism was first and foremost a civilian phenomenon, not a military one, and military interest in expansion rose and fell roughly in tandem with the trajectory of civilian public opinion. However, we must remember that the large proportion of officers who questioned the wisdom of expansion had plenty of civilian company. As in so many other respects, the army was not isolated from American society as a whole in its reluctance to engage in expansion: it displayed a Whiggish worldview entirely compatible with its own professional mind-set and value system as a nonpartisan instrument accountable to the duly constituted national civilian authorities. No single factor can explain officers' diverse reactions to the possibilities of territorial expansion and war. Virtually all the scholars who have touched on this issue maintain that, to use William Skelton's words, "the great majority of the officer corps" eagerly "embraced an aggressively expansionist policy in North America," but this was certainly not the case toward Canada, and as chapters 11 and 12 demonstrate, the picture was much less clear than historians have suggested regarding Texas. Instead, military enthusiasm for expansion varied from crisis to crisis and from officer to officer, depending on the specific circumstances and individuals in question.

These cycles did not follow a linear chronological pattern, and the professional soldiers of the early and mid-1840s seem to have been much more enthusiastic for war with Britain than they were for war with Mexico in 1845 and 1846, or than they had been during actual confrontations with British military power during the Patriot crisis of the late 1830s. Even within the Army of Occupation deployed into Texas in 1845, this expansionist sentiment was substantially less widespread and enthusiastic than most historians have assumed; because war with Mexico seemed so unlikely, the most immediate consideration for many officers was the lengthy separation from their families or the danger to their health along the Texas border.[71] Military expansionism and Anglophobia were situationally dependent. Commanders along the Canadian frontier saw both the disorderliness of filibustering and the power Britain was capable of mobilizing, leading them to reconsider or repress whatever abstract beliefs in American power and the desirability of expansion they might have possessed. An officer's individual status within the army was also critical in determining his stance toward foreign threats and opportunities. Many of the more jingoistic officers were young, often unmarried men just starting their careers, and for them, war was particularly attractive as a rapid means of promotion. This attitude was much less functional for field-grade and general officers, given the small number of high command slots available, their age, and their lower incidence of death in combat, resulting in limited opportunities for promotion. Winfield Scott might have been an exception, given the likelihood that he would lead an army and could parlay victory into the political advancement he so ardently sought, yet Scott proved no more bellicose than his comrades.

All things considered, experienced soldiers had little need for the boisterous belligerence of the sort that led to Anglophobia as a basis for personal, institutional, or national advancement and identity. Their nationalism was founded on their professional allegiances and socialization, rather than chauvinism or racism. No doubt many preferred to envision themselves leading large armies à la Napoleon, but they knew this was unlikely and might endanger their dominance over the direction of national military power. Dutiful service could take many forms for these men; the risks of war were unnecessary for their security, identity, or authority. Their national orientation was focused as much on the maintenance of federal sovereignty within the United States, which Anglophobia threatened as much as sectionalism, as on potential conflicts with Britain. Indeed, the veteran professional commanders actually placed in crisis situations along the Canadian frontier exercised the most restraint in their words and actions, a responsible delicacy derived from the intersection of their institutional mission and values with the practical demands of international diplomacy and civil-military relations in borderlands contested by multiple interests. American expansion hardly looked manifest or feasible to the experienced professional soldiers who watched it unfold along the Canadian boundary in 1838. Their calm and restraint reflected military subordination to the peaceful policies of the national civilian authority and helped sustain peace between Britain and the United States without doing significant injury to the "free institutions" of Americans along the Canadian frontier. Their faithful performance on the nation's northern border fully merits the label professional.

10
THE DILEMMAS OF SOVEREIGNTY AND EXPANSION
Peacekeeping and Law Enforcement along the Texas Border, 1821–1838

The possibility of expansion against Mexico received little if any written consideration by officers during the 1820s and early 1830s. However unstable the governments of Mexico, there was no significant "imperial flux" prior to the American rebellion in 1836; the international boundaries established by the Transcontinental Treaty were fundamentally clear, and incursions across them would constitute cause for war. During the 1820s military comment related to Texas and the Mexican borderlands concentrated on the protection of the Santa Fe trade—admittedly a form of American economic expansion and penetration into the Mexican borderlands—rather than territorial aggrandizement per se: Santa Fe was clearly part of Mexico, and the objective was commercial access and market share.[1] Meanwhile, officers who were ardent expansionists during the 1810s and 1840s cooperated with their Mexican counterparts in pursuit of law and order in the southwestern borderlands. The growth of an informal Comanche empire (much touted by historians of late), akin to that of the Sioux farther north, did not fundamentally shape or reshape U.S. government policy on the southern Plains prior to the war with Mexico, even when the Comanche began season-long raids deep into Mexico south of the Rio Grande and repeated them almost every year after 1833.[2]

The demands of frontier peacekeeping, Indian removal, troop training and discipline, and internal improvements and the fortifications program consumed whatever military attention might otherwise have been devoted to expansion into Texas. In 1824 it was rumored that Andrew Jackson had assumed the leadership of an expedition against the Mexican province, but by this time, the erstwhile general was a civilian, a senator, and a presidential can-

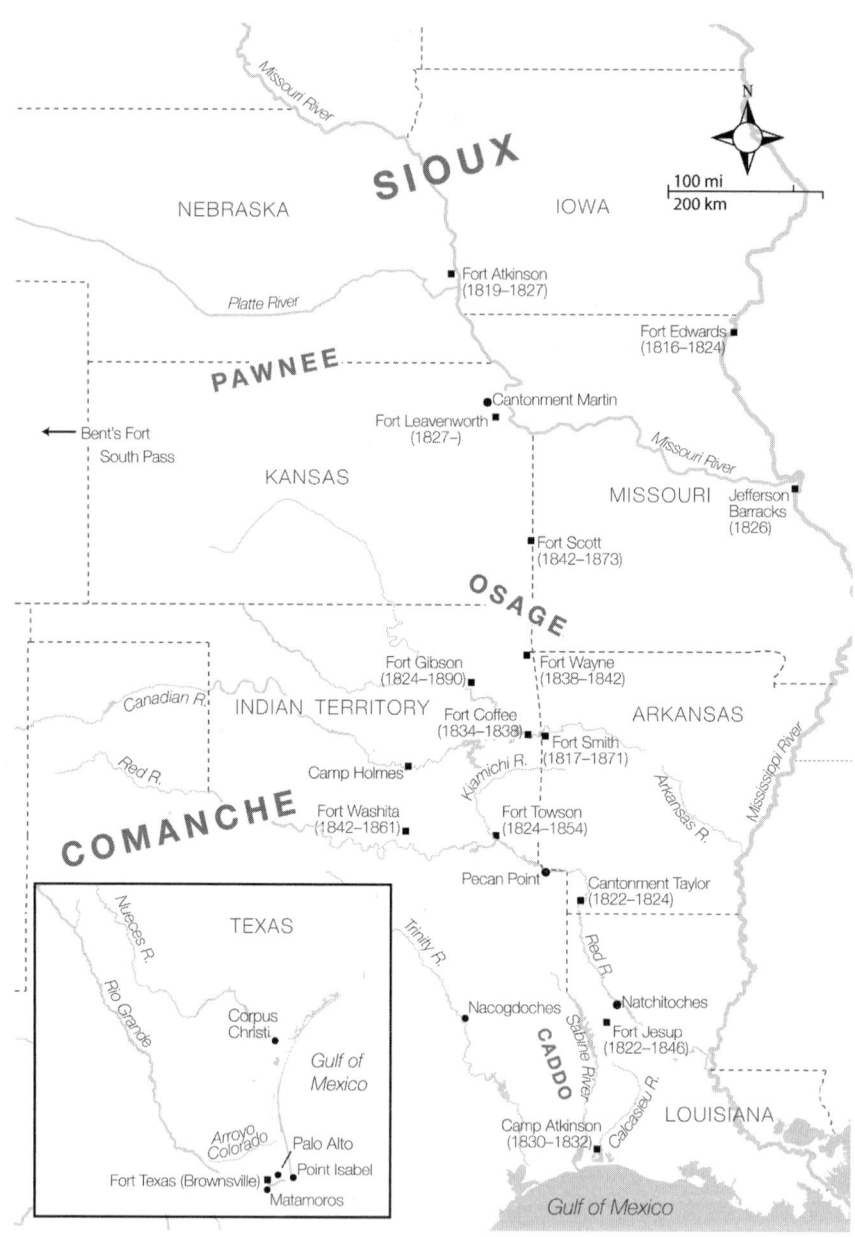

The southwestern frontier (map by Tracy Ellen Smith)

didate, not an army officer. Even Eleazar Ripley, who had resigned from the rank of brigadier general in charge of the southwestern frontier and assumed the presidency of James Long's Texas Republic in 1820, turned to facilitating the peaceful settlement of Texas by Americans after Mexico became a republic.[3] Nevertheless, upholding national sovereignty along the borders of Texas presented the army with multifaceted dilemmas much like those it faced on the Canadian border and the Indian frontiers. The region west of Arkansas was especially prone to disorder, with an increasingly diverse native population competing for resources, no state or territorial civil government, and a weak nation-state across the border in Mexico. Under British, Spanish, or other colonial administrations, this region would have been governed by military commandants and martial law; in the American federal system, responsibility was divided among civilian federal Indian agents, professional soldiers, and the courts.

Much as in the northwestern forests and prairies, the requirements of due process and the threat of intervention by politicians, combined with military resistance to anything smacking of subordination to civilian Indian agents, often made military commanders hesitant peacekeepers and law enforcers along the southwestern border. Under these circumstances, and with little to fear from Mexican retaliation, the army did little to effectively secure U.S. borders and neutrality, whether against smugglers during the 1820s, adventurers and soldiers deserting to join the Texas rebellion in 1836, or Texan incursions into Louisiana in 1838. Not until Philip St. George Cooke's forcible disarmament of Texan raiders on the Santa Fe Trail in 1843 did the army act effectively to uphold national sovereignty against white adventurers in the Southwest. Yet the army did extend national influence onto the southern prairies, and periodically across the southern Plains, through the establishment of several posts in the region that later became Oklahoma and the dispatch of several mounted expeditions during the mid-1830s and mid-1840s. By the 1830s, the United States achieved a dominant position on the prairies not unlike that it had secured in the northern prairies and woodlands of Illinois, southern Wisconsin, and Iowa and along the borders of Missouri. In large part, this was due to the gradual defeat of the seminomadic Osage by the Cherokee and other eastern immigrants, combined with a declining resource base as larger numbers of Indians were compelled to subsist in a shrinking space, compressed by whites from the east and Sioux and Pawnee from the north. Nevertheless, as in the arc from the Missouri border to the Great Lakes, the national army rather than locally rooted or civilian agencies conducted most U.S. diplomatic and peacekeeping efforts in the southwestern borderlands and provided the immediate presence to deter violence, between

Indians or between Indians and whites, when resources failed or routine friction escalated.

Despite a decade of rumors threatening a Cherokee war against whites following their defeat of the Osage, the Cherokee stuck to fighting among themselves, divided into factions created by the debate over removal. Other immigrants—Creek, Shawnee, and Delaware—served the United States against the Florida Seminoles rather than marauding against white frontiersmen or the United States. Despite a decade of whining, white Texans suffered virtually nothing at the hands of Indians from the United States—a pattern that undoubtedly reinforced military skepticism toward frontier Indian panics. Most Texan complaints about Indians were based on rumor rather than fact; the marauding that did occur was often conducted by whites, and apart from the Comanche to the west, Texans rarely had any idea which Indians were responsible for which raids. Osage "depredations" against Missourians (noted in chapter 2) increased in the mid-1830s in response to all these pressures, but perhaps most of all to dispossession by the Cherokee: Osage raids were largely the actions of individuals and small groups, desperate efforts to secure subsistence on the scale of crime (property theft, usually of livestock) rather than war. Nor did American military commanders try to employ Osage robberies as pretexts for action; they neither exaggerated the Osage threat nor sought popularity among frontiersmen by feeding their panic and hate.[4]

On the Plains, facing a series of droughts and the ravages wrought by growing native horse herds during the 1830s and 1840s, the Sioux and Comanche chose easier native and Mexican targets, weakening the objects of future U.S. expansion in the process. Sioux pressure essentially drove the Pawnee to dependence on the United States for survival, and the Pawnee returned the favor by serving as army scouts against the Sioux after the Civil War. The Comanche mounted one offensive against American trade in 1828 and 1829; hurt by army artillery and enticed by American markets, they then returned to peace toward the east and focused their warfare toward the south, launching a series of ever more devastating raids against Texas and other northern Mexican provinces from the early 1830s onward. These campaigns, involving as many warriors as any of the American dragoon expeditions had soldiers, wreaked havoc on the economy of the *norteno* provinces and encouraged many *nortenos*, particularly in New Mexico, to accept or even seek U.S. rule between 1846 and 1848.[5]

These examples suggest that diplomacy and competition for increasingly scarce resources, rather than military power per se, were the keys to U.S. influence in the Southwest prior to large-scale white settlement. Most of the scarcity and competition, which enhanced the influence of U.S. trade and diplomatic subsidies, was due to native population growth, which in turn was due largely to the removal policy implemented by the army east of the Mississippi. Much of the diplomatic influence actually consisted of growing Indian dependence on American trade goods, regardless of the trade and intercourse acts and other government efforts at regulation. Yet diplomacy was not simply a matter of American goods and markets. Nor can we attribute the Comanche's southern thrust to Mexican weakness and American numbers (including citizen-soldiers and Texans, as well as regulars) alone. The Comanche wars with Texas during the 1840s suggest the Indians' potential for violence against whites when the latter's numbers reached a critical mass and threatened scarce resources, a point not yet reached in the Comanche range north of Texas. The antagonism between the Comanche and white Texans also hints at the significance of diplomacy—that is, the willingness to treat the other side as an equal, at least in public negotiations. Unlike British military officials in India and Africa; French ones in Algeria, West Africa, or Sudan; and Russian ones in the Caucasus and central Asia, American military commanders usually managed to coexist peacefully with potential local rivals, like the Comanche on the southern Plains, until the 1860s. This may have been due to the limited number of American settlers; the proximity of Mexico, easily plundered by the nomadic Indians; and the trade between Americans and Indians. In contrast, military self-restraint was rarely present on European imperial frontiers. Indeed, the U.S. Army displayed significant restraint, against Texan wishes, toward the Comanche until after the Civil War—a period of about thirty-five years in which army officers generally preferred a policy of peace toward their most powerful rivals in the region.[6]

Despite their sense of ethnocultural superiority over Indians of all sorts (which probably grew over time as American society became more racialized), professional soldiers were willing to suspend their prejudices during the extended councils that characterized interethnic diplomacy in the North American borderlands. Though this may have been no more than pretense and, in the long run, deception, smoother tongues made for smoother relations. Despite their authoritarianism, military commanders proved remarkably fluent diplomats, often far better at concealing their chauvinism toward Indians than their contempt for whites. In an era when few whites were willing to suspend their disdain for Indians, a small group of traders (for example, the Bent brothers), Indian agents (often former army officers; see appendix C), and professional soldiers provided the oil that greased the wheels of remarkably peaceful relations.

Nor, unlike many of their European counterparts in Africa and Asia, did

Clermont, principal Osage chief. From Catlin, *The North American Indians*

American military commanders take advantage of "flux on the periphery" of Indian polities weakened by the Comanche; they did not use intertribal conflict as a pretext for war and national expansion or for personal or professional aggrandizement prior to significant white settlement. The same proved true, despite settlers' calls for military action, along the borders of Mexican Texas and in the "Indian country" west of Arkansas. As in the Missouri Valley during the 1820s, the army would shield white settlement and show the flag of American power to ward off potential international competitors, but it would not take the initiative to accelerate expropriation in advance of settler demand. Whether military self-restraint subtly accelerated or merely delayed the process of conquest, it meant less violence, and less extreme violence, than under the Republic of Texas—a contrast between regional and national that had been evident since the confrontations between Ohio Indians and Kentuckians, and Creeks and Georgians, during the 1780s. Federal military commanders would pursue similar relations in the state of Texas until the Civil War; their failure, at the hands of impatient Texans socialized in a racism far more extreme than authoritarian military paternalism, was the failure of American federalism.

DISCORD AND COMMOTION EVERYWHERE: PEACEKEEPING AND CIVIL-MILITARY RELATIONS ALONG THE RED AND SABINE FRONTIERS, 1815–1835

American traders, trappers, hunters, and settlers moved quickly up the Red and Arkansas Rivers after the War of 1812, but military officers found it difficult—and perhaps made little effort—to distinguish among squatters, legitimate settlers, and outlaws. In general, the federal government treated these regions as "Indian country" that, for practical purposes, was still under native ownership, so the land remained in the public domain but there were no accurate surveys to demarcate the border with Mexico. As early as 1811, an assortment of unlicensed Indian traders (particularly whiskey sellers) and other intruders and outlaws had collected at Pecan Point, a buffalo crossing claimed by the Caddo Indians on the Red River. In 1816, facing Caddo threats to attack the intruders and Caddo overtures to the Spanish authorities in Texas, U.S. troops were deployed to drive the whites away. This operation had only a temporary effect and was repeated in 1817 and in the autumn of 1818. Indeed, the latter campaign supposedly continued for an entire year, though it probably involved little more than intermittent patrols, given the difficulty of resupplying such an effort.[7]

During 1818 and 1819 Missouri territorial surveyors mapped the land east of the Kiamachi River (which extends north from the Red); though the land was not sold, Arkansas legislators designated it Miller County (named after James Miller, a hero of Lundy's Lane and then the territorial governor) when Arkansas became a separate territory in 1820. The locus of Red River squatter removal operations then shifted west into the future Oklahoma region, beyond territorial jurisdiction. Hoping to conciliate the powerful Osage and the influential Caddo, Secretary of War Calhoun ordered Andrew Jackson to "remove all settlers" and prevent future settlement along the Arkansas River west of the mouth of the Poteau, as well as along the Red River west of its junction with the Kiamachi. Intruders, some of them murderers and marauders, were expelled from west of the Kiamachi in 1819, 1820, and 1821, but the region remained unsurveyed. By 1823, as many as 1,500 squatters had congregated at Pecan Point, which the United States still considered Indian land; orders were issued for the intruders' removal in 1823 and again in 1824, but they had little effect, given the mobility of such transients.[8]

The army began moving up the Arkansas River to the edge of the southern Plains in 1817, when Fort Smith was established at the mouth of the Poteau River on the western border of the Arkansas Territory to police relations between the immigrant Cherokee and the Osage. Once a line of posts had been established across the arc between the Mississippi and Missouri Rivers to the northwest, the southwestern frontier became the focal point for the second major chronological phase of U.S. military expansion after the War of 1812. During the early to mid-1820s, Cantonments Jesup, Towson, and Gibson (named after the quartermaster, paymaster, and commissary generals) were built to extend and uphold U.S. sovereignty by restraining illegal white encroachment while keeping the peace among the Indians. (Cantonments were temporary garrisons; the term was probably employed to reassure frugal congressmen after the expensive surge of military expansion in the Northwest.) Cantonment Jesup replaced Forts Selden and Claiborne to observe Louisiana's Sabine River border with Mexico in 1822, but the army's more immediate regional priority was to facilitate the immigration of southeastern Indians to the newly designated "Indian country" west of the Arkansas Territory, which aggravated the conflict between earlier Cherokee immigrants and the Osage native to the region.[9]

Cantonment Taylor brought the army up the Red River to the Sulphur Fork in 1821, with the goal of protecting a government trading post (or "factory"), keeping peace between the Caddo and Choctaw, and halting white intrusion onto Caddo land. Three years later this post was displaced farther up the Red to the mouth of the Kiamachi and became Cantonment Towson. The rationales for this advance spanned every challenger to U.S. sovereignty:

Indian depredations against whites in Miller County, spurred by failures to restrain white intrusion; slave smuggling; "lawless marauders" who committed "outrageous acts of robbery, violence, and murder"; plus friction between native and immigrant Indians (the Osage and the Kickapoo, who had moved south after ceding their lands in Illinois). Some of the whites in the unsurveyed territory just south of the Red claimed to be Mexican subjects, though these assertions—duplicitous efforts to avoid law of any sort—never went very far, since the majority of the residents sought U.S. protection against Indians. The same year, Cantonment Gibson was established on the Neosho fork of the Arkansas River, northwest of Fort Smith and halfway to the site of modern-day Tulsa, to deter native warfare and prevent hostilities among the Indians from spilling over against white settlements in Arkansas.[10]

The squatters rejected distant national authority, leading to clashes between soldiers and civilians. Shortly after Towson was established, civilians seized several soldiers and beat them while taking them to a magistrate; Major Alexander Cummings dispatched a force that rescued his soldiers. Another affray soon followed, and a gathering of 200 civilians threatened to destroy the post. The major arrested two of their leaders, preventing an attack, but the federal district attorney was unable, or refused, to prosecute due to the difficulty of securing an impartial jury and witnesses. Indeed, Cummings was court-martialed for "resisting the civil authority" after some of the ringleaders secured his indictment in an Arkansas court. The charges were so obviously trumped up that the seventeen-year veteran was able to escape sanction by civil or military court; he was transferred without prejudice to another post and rose to colonel and commander of the Fourth Infantry before his death in 1842.[11]

Brevet Major General Edmund Gaines, Andrew Jackson's former deputy on the Florida border and commander of the army's Western Division or Department during most of the years between 1821 and 1846, provides the best example of an expansionist officer in the southwestern borderlands during this era. But Gaines was also an ardent advocate of law and order. Early in 1823 he informed Secretary of War Calhoun that he believed Mexican reports of banditry in East Texas and advised U.S. action to prevent marauders from using the border as a sanctuary. The general cautioned that "I should not willingly permit any officer of a Foreign Government to charge citizens of the United States" without more proof than the Mexican authorities had presented—a responsible balancing of rights, interests, and law from a man not always known for his nuanced judgments. However, Gaines's penchant for order was clearly evident in his recommendations. "Believing that much good ... will result from proper efforts on the part of our commandants on the Texas frontier to preserve harmony with [the] new Governor," the department commander asked whether he might alert the Mexicans that their officers "pursuing offenders to the Sabine will find [aid] at our military posts; and on application to the civil authority (with proper evidence) may recover the stolen property if found within our limits."[12]

In other words, Gaines was suggesting that the United States provide official military assistance to extradite fugitives to Mexico. Calhoun did not forbid it, so the department commander issued orders to Lieutenant Colonel James Many, a twenty-four-year veteran commanding Fort Jesup near the Sabine, "to *cooperate* with the civil authorities, in the suppression of robberies and murders, and the arrest of offenders, on the frontier confided to your command." That October, Gaines ordered intermittent patrols for "scouring the country, for marauders." The general reiterated these instructions three years later (after returning from command of the Eastern Department) and warned that they "must be implicitly obeyed, without regard to possible [political] consequences." Although "the efficient exercise of military power" might lead to civilian criticism, Gaines told the governor of Louisiana that he believed "every reflecting liberal mind" would support his actions.[13]

On the Red River, Cummings's departure did not end the entropy and civil-military friction rooted in frontier individualism and populist disregard for law. In 1827 the Edwards (or Fredonia) rebellion in Texas brought several of these concerns together, when Americans at Pecan Point again claimed Mexican citizenship, while the Fredonians sought independence from both the United States and Mexico. There were also rumors of a filibuster plot to raid and plunder the Comanche from U.S. territory, and an armed group from New Orleans passed through the Cantonment Towson area en route to Santa Fe, where they claimed to have purchased land. It was almost impossible for U.S. officers to distinguish among the various filibusters and rebels, and the Fredonians sought allies among the Cherokee and other Indians, further confusing matters. Gaines asked commanding general Brown for reinforcements to disperse any Indians gathered on the American frontier while directing Zachary Taylor, the commandant at New Orleans, to "cooperate with the revenue officers and other civil authorities, to prevent violations and evasions of the law; and to suppress any disorders which may grow out of the recent or future disturbances in Texas." Gaines did not specify whether this suppression would involve crossing the international boundary in pursuit of violators, but Brown remedied this lacuna by instructing Many that "the President directs that you carefully refrain from becoming in any way directly or indirectly concerned . . . and that you preserve a strict neutrality within our frontier as far as it is in your power." As usual, "the remoteness of your situation and the absence of definite information" rendered it "impossible to send [more] particular instructions," so the general was compelled to rely on Many's "prudence, intelligence, and knowledge of the country."[14]

Mexican authorities suppressed the Fredonian revolt, and nothing came of the rumored filibusters, but any Indian presence could lead to white complaints. The following year the captain commanding at Cantonment Towson refused a request by an Arkansas militia colonel to remove Shawnee Indians encamped at Pecan Point. Threatened by the colonel, Captain Russell Hyde presented one of the bluntest military condemnations of frontier conduct toward the Indians on record: "If the Commanding Officer . . . is bound to furnish every man with troops . . . who wishes to immortalize himself by plundering an Indian town and killing a few women and children . . . the force in this sector of the country should be substantially increased." The militia colonel, Wharton Rector, had served as a lieutenant in the army for less than a year in 1820 and 1821; due to his political connections, the Jacksonians offered him the plum position of lieutenant colonel of the Second Dragoons in 1836, but Rector chose a less demanding post as paymaster. Farther west, along the Red River, commissary lieutenant William Colquohoun warned his superior that the "Spaniard" posts near Towson needed watching, but the lieutenant's principal concern remained the "desparate and violent" whites who had threatened public officers and property to the point that he suggested abandoning the post. Nevertheless, the chief threat to the army's officers at Towson may well have been their own quarrelsomeness, for Colquohoun was dismissed from the army for striking a superior nine months later. When the fort was abandoned in 1829, local whites burned it down.[15]

Much as in the Northwest, peacekeeping and law enforcement efforts were frequently disrupted by interagency friction and the obstinacy of military commanders who rejected any hint of subordination to Indian agents. Prior to 1822 this discord was often between the Indian agent and the government Indian factor (trader) assigned to the Caddo, but military commanders commonly refused to act without specific orders from the War Department, and enlisted soldiers sent to guard the government factory on Sulphur Fork proved turbulent and insubordinate without commissioned officers to maintain discipline. James Many of the Seventh Infantry, commanding Fort Jesup, proved especially unwilling to assist the Caddo Indian agent, former captain and eight-year veteran George Gray (who figured briefly as Eleazar Ripley's aide in *Jackson's Sword*). Gray, who had ranked well below Many in grade and seniority, wanted a company posted at his agency, and Edmund Gaines instructed Many to establish such a post, but the War Department failed to provide funds to do so.[16]

Gaines then assured Gray that he would order the colonel to periodically send battalion-sized contingents to support diplomatic councils with the Caddo, but Winfield Scott soon replaced Gaines as Western Department commander, per the routine rotation agreed to by the generals. Scott reprimanded Many early in 1828, ordering him to send troops upon request "to support [Gray's] authority, and keep the peace." By the time Gaines returned to command the department, he had become less eager to intervene in civil and Indian affairs, instructing the colonel to respond only if "settlements were actually invaded" by Indians. The following summer Gray asked the War Department to instruct military commanders to provide troops upon his request, without his having to seek specific orders from the secretary of war or the department commander. The department refused, and Many's replacement, Henry Leavenworth, told the agent to go to the civil authorities in Arkansas for assistance against whiskey dealers illegally intruding on Indian land, even though the law clearly intended for the army to provide that aid.[17]

Fort Towson was closed in 1829, partly because of civil-military friction but primarily, given the general retrenchment of Jackson's first administration, due to the cost of resupply after the Red River became almost completely blocked by a mass of wood and other detritus known as the "Red River raft." Yet "disorderly persons" continued to cause turmoil and threaten national sovereignty along both the Red and Sabine borders, and Jackson's Indian removal policy was predicated on concentrating the eastern Indians in the area north of the Red. In 1829 the War Department ordered Many to send a company from Fort Jesup to support revenue officers by patrolling against smugglers along the Calcasieu River along the southern border of Louisiana, and a second company was alerted in case the customs collectors needed additional protection. Commanding general Macomb observed that the officer in command on the Calcasieu could capably serve as customs collector, but he preferred that a civilian hold the position. The troops apparently did not catch many smugglers, and the effort ended two years later due to the cost of supplies, since far southwestern Louisiana was almost as unsettled as the upper Red River.[18]

This savings, plus the anticipated arrival of Indians from the East, led to the reopening of Towson as a full-fledged fort by Stephen W. Kearny's battalion the same year (1831). The rationale for its reopening illustrates the full gamut of national military roles and objectives on the frontiers. The new post was "to afford protection" to the wave of eastern Indians expected to enter the region under the Removal Act of 1830 "against the White people, who may illegally adventure among them"; "to maintain . . . peace among the several Tribes of Indians, and to prevent them from marauding within the limits of the states and Territories" or in Mexico; and "to maintain the sovereignty of the United States . . . by preventing any settlement or intrusion on our Territory," whether by squatters or, less likely, by Mexican Texas. Macomb's operational instructions for the post focused on positive relations with the Indians: "as the object in establishing the post, is in a great measure to benefit the Indians," the post commander was "not in any way to interfere with the Indians"; "no uneasiness should be given to them," and he was to "consult with them" as far as possible. Macomb did not explain how the army was supposed to avoid interfering with the Indians while maintaining peace between different tribes; local commanders would have to work this out for themselves.[19]

Nor did Macomb's language reflect the true thrust of national Indian policy. The government would attempt to resolve the contradictions by exporting them: when the Louisiana Caddo and Texas Cherokee raided each other across the border, the Caddo agent (now Jehiel Brooks, a Kentuckian who had served as a lieutenant between 1818 and 1820) looked to buy the Caddo out—securing substantial illicit benefits for himself—and send them to Texas. James Many cooperated reluctantly and intermittently until his regiment was replaced by the Third Infantry in 1831, and Henry Leavenworth sent soldiers to remove squatters from Caddo land early in 1833. Within two years Many was back, promoted by seniority to colonel of the Third upon Leavenworth's death, to investigate Caddo land claims with a view to liquidation. (There is no biography of Many, but one can assume that he became a plantation owner, like so many other senior officers stationed in the South for extended periods.) Colonel Many judged the Caddo claims valid, but he was confident that pressure from intruders would compel the Indians to sell. Sadly, they did so just before the Texas Revolution, but the Americans were no more eager to see the Caddo in Texas than in Louisiana.[20]

GAINES LOOKS FOR THE SWEET SPOT: THE TEXAS REVOLUTION, 1835–1837

Edmund Gaines's sympathy for Mexican law enforcement efforts did not mean that he had lost the desire for American territorial expansion he had shown on the southeastern borders in the 1810s. As commander of the Western Department, Gaines was the officer most appropriately concerned with scenarios involving Texas, and as Andrew Jackson's protégé from the First Seminole War, it is not surprising that he favored an expansionist foreign policy. Even as he began to question Jackson's removal policy, the Tennessee general wrote to his former patron implying that Texas belonged to the United States as part of the Louisiana Purchase, asserting that the renunciation of American claims under the terms of the Transcontinental Treaty of 1821 had been unconstitutional. The region "must and will be restored to us," Gaines proclaimed: "when the people of Texas . . . demand admission into the union . . . they cannot—[and] will not be refused."[21]

Few other officers appear to have given much thought to the growing unrest in Texas during the early 1830s, even though Mexico increased its garrisons and the United States bound itself by an 1831 treaty to restrain the Indians it was concentrating north of the Red River. In November 1829 Alexander Macomb used the deployment of a company against smugglers as an opportunity to press for a military reconnaissance between the Sabine and Calcasieu Rivers in western Louisiana, requesting a topographical sketch and information regarding Mexican positions and the "facilities of communication" in the region. Nevertheless, President Jackson, who favored annexation, sought to do so by purchase rather than war and ordered American officials to keep a close watch on his friend Sam Houston, who secretly made plans to conquer the region with Indian support in 1832. Houston had risen from the ranks during the War of 1812, where he was severely wounded at Horseshoe Bend, and was retained as a lieutenant after the war but resigned in 1818—ultimately, one of the best examples of the aggressive expansionists who left the national standing army during the decade after the War of 1812.[22]

After a decade and a half of near silence, the officer corps' latent professional interest in the southwestern border was revived by the disorder of the Texas Revolution. The emergence of open hostilities aroused extensive American civilian sentiment in favor of the Anglo-Texans, while Mexican appeals combined with general disorder threatened to unleash Indian raids along the southwestern frontier of the United States. Surprisingly few officers committed their thoughts about the conflict to paper, but those who did provide a variety of perspectives from which to understand how army officers responded to the opportunities and dilemmas of expansion. Two extremes, reflecting the significance of time in service and prefiguring differences in officers' attitudes toward annexation and war a decade later, were presented by senior captain Ethan Allen Hitchcock—former commandant of the Military Academy, a critic of Indian policy and the Seminole War, and an important figure in the U.S. invasion of Mexico a decade later—and Academy cadet Jubal Anderson Early, who would be best known as a Confederate general.

Early, a Virginian then in his third year at West Point, wrote home to his father in a furor over the Mexican attempt to suppress the Texan rebellion.

His views exemplified many attitudes common among American civilians toward the rulers and institutions of Mexico, as well as an ideological consciousness rarely so explicitly and thoroughly articulated among career army officers. The young cadet's letter is worthy of extensive quotation, for contrast with the views of the other officers cited herein and as a reminder of the distance between officers' generally Whiggish, statist values and the more Democratic or Jacksonian ones held by the majority (however slight) of the civilian society from which new junior officers came. The contrast between Early's libertarian individualism, his egalitarianism, populism, chauvinism, and belligerence, and career officers' institutionalism, authoritarianism, and professional neutrality or quiescence toward annexation and expansion exemplifies the distance between professional soldiers and much of society they served.

Like John C. Frémont, Early was the exception who proves the rule. He quit the regular army after only a year, one of the few resignations during the depression that followed the Panic of 1837, and he served during the war with Mexico as a volunteer rather than a regular. Like Frémont, Early's attitudes toward the Texans and his ardent espousal of their cause provide polar counterpoints to those of most other officers during the Jacksonian era, whether in 1836 or a decade later. Unlike most officers who dealt with American frontiersmen, Early (who was nowhere near Texas and had probably never met anyone who had been there) characterized the "Texians" as "respectable adventurers" and took pains to warn his father that they were not "land speculators and fugitives from justice," as opinion in the North often charged. Nor did the young populist believe that the Texans were "attempting to subvert the laws, and overturn their lawful government," as so many Whigs, and Whiggish officers like Hitchcock, proclaimed.[23]

Like resignation, filibustering could actually serve as an outlet for men too bellicose, high-spirited, or opportunistic to accept the army's constraints of discipline and subordination or the slow, rigid promotion process. (This was especially true for enlisted soldiers, who stood to gain much more than officers did.) The small number of officers who resigned to become filibusters represents a sort of outer boundary that shows the rarity of exceptions to the rule of career commitment to national military service. In this sense, filibustering complemented the personal security offered by the army by siphoning off the excessively ambitious, whose actions might pose a threat to its subordination to national policy and support in Congress, aggravating attacks on the officer corps' monopoly over the direction of organized military force. Aside from future Confederate general Albert Sidney Johnston, a second lieutenant and 1826 Military Academy graduate from Kentucky who resigned in 1834, it is unknown how many former officers entered Texan service. Given the mass of resignations during these years, the number could have been substantial, but secondary sources on the army and the Texas Revolution provide little evidence of such an influx.

One study, based on a thorough examination of Texas military rosters, provides four names of West Point graduates who participated in that struggle. Three were New Yorkers: Joseph Cadle, an 1824 graduate and second lieutenant who served almost entirely on the southwestern frontier at Forts Gibson, Towson, and Jesup, was dismissed in 1830 for insubordination and neglect of duty; William Shaler Stillwell, an 1827 graduate who served as a second lieutenant in the Third Infantry at Fort Jesup, resigned in 1833. (Perhaps his name should have been a hint: William Shaler was the State Department's special agent with the Gutiérrez-Magee expedition in 1812 and a fervent expansionist throughout his career.) Hugh McLeod, the third New Yorker, graduated last in the class of 1835 (and was thus the most junior officer in the entire army) and was assigned to the Third Infantry, but he took a leave of absence in March 1836, resigned in July, and commanded the Texan expedition against Santa Fe in 1841. Of the twenty-two officers from the four regiments stationed in the vicinity of the Texas frontier who resigned in 1836, McLeod is the only one who is known to have joined the Texans. McLeod was one of two West Point graduates who actually quit the army to go to Texas—the first officers to go directly from the army to filibustering since Augustus Magee in 1812 (discussed in *Jackson's Sword*). The other was Second Lieutenant John T. Collinsworth, a Tennessean and 1830 graduate in the Fifth Infantry stationed in the Northwest; he resigned in July 1836 and traveled south to become the Texas inspector general but died of natural causes shortly thereafter. These officers, like those who joined filibusters against Texas before 1820, were very junior men, averaging less than six years' service; none had gained promotion to first lieutenant before leaving the army.[24]

Captain Ethan Allen Hitchcock was a veteran with nineteen years' national military service, including duty as commandant at West Point between 1825 and 1832. He was also an articulate intellectual and moral logician, making him unusual among career army officers. However, Hitchcock's attitude toward territorial expansion proved characteristic of American professional soldiers during the 1830s and 1840s. Serving as an aide to General Gaines on the frontier in 1836, the Whiggish Vermonter—grandson of Ethan Allen, who led the Revolution in Vermont and negotiated with the British in pursuit of autonomy from American rule afterward—wrote to his mother:

> The Texas cause looks much better at a distance than it does upon a near approach. . . . The people of Texas made no opposition to Santa Anna or the Mexican government as long as they were not required to comply

with the revenue laws & were permitted to keep slaves (which the Mexican constitution prohibits). [When these conditions changed] the people saw at once an end to their dream of wealth, and accusing the Mexican government of tyranny assailed, abused, and drove off the custom house officers & prepared for defenses. . . . They were immediately joined by a large band of land speculators (who are always prowling around new countries), and this war of independence as it is called is in fact a rebellion.

Not unlike Worth, Wool, and Brady on the northern border, the experienced Vermonter felt that "there are men among [the frontiersmen] bad enough to provoke the Indians to commit depredations even upon themselves," as a pretext for seeking American aid and protection. Thus, Hitchcock went on to discuss the Texans' efforts "to induce General Gaines to take some step which they can represent as an indication" of American support for "their cause, [for] above all they would be glad to involve him directly in it." Indeed, Gaines sent the impressive captain to warn Santa Anna "not to violate our neutrality" or supply the Indians, but Hitchcock's understanding of the crisis was exactly the opposite of Early's: "if [Santa Anna] abstains from enticing the Indians he . . . will deserve success." Although the Vermonter tended to take his moral stances to logical extremes and was as uncharacteristically outspoken as cadet Early, his suspicion of aggressive expansionism was widely shared among officers who left records of their opinions. Thus, when the administration criticized Gaines for being too belligerent toward Texas, the brigadier sent the articulate captain to Washington to explain his actions to President Jackson. This was probably a mistake, since Hitchcock had played the same role four years earlier, acting as an intermediary for Sylvanus Thayer when the Military Academy superintendent faced criticism from Jackson. Hitchcock's intellectualism was not calculated to appeal to Old Hickory.[25]

Among less well-connected officers, Lieutenant Joseph Van Swearingen, deployed from Jefferson Barracks to the Texas border, gradually came to much the same conclusions. The lieutenant's initial concern was across the Atlantic: at the beginning of 1836 he wrote to his sister that he doubted the United States would go to war with France (over American claims for financial reparations for losses during the Napoleonic Wars), "unless we go to Texas and take a hand there." The 1824 Military Academy graduate, the last nineteenth-century officer in a family that sent four men to the War of 1812, doubted that the United States would be able to prevent its citizens from going to Texas, but he accepted rebellion and individual mobility across borders as the price of liberty: without European aid during the Revolution, Americans would not "enjoy the blessings of our Republic." A month later, after the Sixth Infantry was dispatched to Fort Jesup, Van Swearingen downplayed the likelihood of war with either side in the Texas conflict, sounding more dismissive, if not antagonistic, toward the rebels than toward Mexico: the chance of war with the Texans "doesn't concern us in the least, provided they keep to their own side."[26]

On April 1 the lieutenant referred to the Mexican "yoke" in Texas, but otherwise he focused his letter on the limited food grown in western Louisiana, where he claimed the inhabitants thought "only . . . of cotton." Van Swearingen remained uncommitted, despite stories that Mexican troops were killing white women; the rumors worried him, but he believed they were exaggerated. By early June, the lieutenant had entered Texas himself, whether as an official emissary or for pleasure during a short furlough, and exclaimed that he had "never been in so fine a country in my life," vowing that he would resign and settle in Texas if the United States annexed the region. Yet he remained skeptical, reporting numerous fugitives from justice and a "very restless disposition" among the inhabitants. Ambiguity turned to disdain after the Sixth entered Texas. When Van Swearingen resumed correspondence with his sister in September, he claimed the Texans were "unworthy" of the region: "they do nothing but rob one another," and he concluded that "the United States have been much deceived in the cause of Texas." He never got the chance to reap the rewards of expansion; he was killed seizing Florida from the Seminoles at the Battle of Lake Okeechobee, on Christmas Day 1837.[27]

Few senior military leaders left much private comment on the Texas rebellion. Given their temperaments, Scott and Macomb probably opposed or quickly came to oppose it, but they were hardly involved. As a Democrat, John Wool may have felt some support for the rebels, but it probably evaporated during his first exposure to rabid frontier populism in Georgia that autumn. Despite a long history of expansionism, Quartermaster General Jesup, the only other Democrat among the army's principal generals, stated officially that he considered the conflict a civil war (within Mexico) rather than a revolution. Edmund Gaines, longtime commander of the Western Military Department, kept close tabs on the growing unrest in Texas, becoming the key American military player in the drama and the most important American decision maker on the Texas frontier. Gaines played a complex role in this story, for he was an ardent expansionist and eager aggressor; a sometime advocate of leniency, however paternalistic, toward Indians; and a stern enforcer of national and international law against banditry, marauding, and filibustering. As a thirty-five-year veteran of southwestern service and Andrew Jackson's principal subordinate along the Florida border during the years after the War of 1812, Gaines had proved sympathetic to most frontier causes, including expansion. He also had family connections with the revolution: his brother James operated a ferry on the Trinity River and helped write the Texas declaration of independence, while James's son, named Edmund, served in the Texan army. The general's belligerence and impetuosity repeatedly led him to the verge of irresponsibility, yet he refused to cross this line into filibustering or quasi-official aggression like Jackson's—or his own—twenty years before. Unfortunately, Gaines became trapped in much the same toils of Jacksonian politics and duplicity as Wool on the Cherokee frontier, with similar consequences for civil-military relations, and much more damaging ones for Gaines's career.[28]

American military commanders were aware of the tensions growing in 1835. That June, Lieutenant Henry Swartwout, another well-connected New Yorker in the Third Infantry, visited Texas and held discussions with Mexican Indian agent Peter Ellis Bean about Indian raids back and forth across the border. In November, Lieutenant Colonel Josiah Vose and brevet Brigadier General Matthew Arbuckle warned Gaines that armed Americans were gathering along the Sabine, and Arbuckle ordered James Many to stop them from entering Texas. This effort had little effect, but rumors that Mexico had commissioned Indians to attack the frontier spurred the army to action, and Gaines was ordered from Florida to the southwestern border on January 23; however, he did not receive this news until March 28 because of slow communications and his own movements in Florida. After a decade of civilian criticism that the army had been unprepared for the Ho-chunk, Sauk, and Seminole uprisings, Gaines had no intention of enduring the censure aimed at Leavenworth, Atkinson, and Clinch. The following day he wrote to Secretary of War Cass, belligerently proposing to anticipate "any disposition of the Mexicans or their red allies to menace our frontier . . . by crossing our supposed or imaginary national boundary, and meeting the savage marauders [wherever they] are to be found in their approach towards our frontier." Gaines was proposing to establish an American military buffer zone in Mexican territory in East Texas. This proposal encapsulates the different circumstances in which Gaines and the officers stationed on the Canadian frontier found themselves, for it is inconceivable that William Worth or Winfield Scott would have proposed such a measure in the face of British military power and their belief in the legitimacy of the international boundary.[29]

Gaines estimated the number of potential enemies, whether Indian, Mexican, or both, at between 8,000 and 12,000 and suggested that an equal force of mounted troops would be necessary to counter them. Gaines's exaggerated delineation of the potential threat was couched in language so vague as to justify virtually any measure he took. On April 5 he properly ordered the commanders at Forts Towson and Gibson to secure the southern border of the Indian Territory against crossings by the armed forces of either side. Three days later he publicly called on the governors of Arkansas, Mississippi, Louisiana, Tennessee, and Alabama for volunteers, a measure backed by precedent yet illegal without authorization from the president. Gaines requested this authority the same day, but he would not know the response for several weeks; presumably, he remembered that he and Jackson had taken similar action, in anticipation of receiving authorization, on the Florida frontier two decades before. In any case, these public proclamations followed a more responsible tack than his initial letter to the War Department, observing simply that "nothing can be more evident than that an Indian war commencing on either side of the line, will as surely extend to both sides," requiring military preparations for the defense of the frontier.[30]

Gaines received numerous appeals for assistance against Indian depredations from Anglo-Texans residing near Nacogdoches and the Sabine, and on April 13 he was told that the town was probably in Indian hands. He promptly ordered thirteen companies, 400 to 500 men, to the eastern bank of the Sabine, where they took up positions at the site used by James Wilkinson in 1806. He also sent Lieutenant Joseph Bonnell with a patrol to Nacogdoches, which they found peaceful and unoccupied, to sound out the Caddo and Cherokee Indians, who showed no signs of aggression. Gaines nevertheless recommended continuing preparations in order to intimidate the nearby Indians and strike quickly if required. The president responded by giving Gaines the authority to call for militia and to enter Texas as far as Nacogdoches if he felt that doing so was necessary to restrain the Indians. The general was forbidden to cooperate with either of the belligerents, and he was instructed to withdraw from Texas as soon as the safety of the frontier was secured. Gaines anticipated these orders the same day, warning Santa Anna and Sam Houston that he intended to preserve American neutrality and would interpret any military use of Indians living under U.S. sovereignty as an act meriting "summary punishment."[31]

Commanding general Macomb was less concerned about the threat to the frontier, warning the War Department that the rumors of Indian hostility lacked serious foundation and advising that volunteers were unnecessary. Indeed, Macomb had traveled to New Orleans and reported that the governor of Louisiana feared "a scheme of those interested in the Texan speculation" to use the call for militia to send Americans to Texas and perhaps entrap the United States in a war with Mexico. This skepticism did not prevent Macomb from calling for doubling the size of the army, though he justified it by the menace of the Seminoles, slave insurrection, other Indians inspired by the Seminole example, and European threats to the Atlantic coastal frontier. On April 21 the Texan victory at San Jacinto ended the immediate crisis—such as it was—and Gaines withdrew his call for volunteers, none of whom had actually been mustered. Yet he had already advised President Jackson that the United States would have to enter Texas eventually, recommending an immediate offer of statehood. Given the uncertain situation, the administration reciprocated Gaines's concern, and on May 4 Cass notified the general that "the President will sanction the employment of whatever force may be necessary to protect the western frontier of the United States from hostile incursions." The renewal of hostilities between Mexico and Texas in June led Gaines to make a second call for volunteers, but he initially refused Texan appeals to occupy Nacogdoches. Given the constant rumors of Indian war fed to him by the Texans, he changed his mind on July 10 and ordered Lieutenant Colonel William Whistler of the Seventh Infantry to move south from Fort Towson with seven companies (originally drawn from Gibson) to secure the town, though he instructed the colonel to avoid battle unless attacked.[32]

The troops never saw combat, but by early August, continuing rumors led Gaines to worry that "the want of an effective force . . . will endanger the whole of the beautiful and immensely valuable cotton growing region of the Red River" in northwestern Louisiana. Indeed, the general feared that "the prospect of the plunder" would "excite the cupidity" of many white frontiersmen, leading them to join the Indians in general banditry. Gaines therefore alerted General Arbuckle, commander of the Seventh Infantry Regiment at Fort Gibson, to ready additional forces for movement, and he sent an officer into Texas to try to recover deserters who had joined the Texan army (without success). By this time, as many as 1,100 soldiers had been concentrated on or near the Sabine border, along with 155,000 rations, enough to feed them for five months without resupply. Yet officers on the scene proved more skeptical of Texan claims than their commander. At Nacogdoches, Whistler sent Major Bennet Riley, a hard-nosed veteran of the 1823 Arikara expedition (examined in *Jackson's Sword*) and commander of the 1829 Santa Fe Trail escort (discussed later), to scout out the situation and warn the Caddo against violence. Though hardly known for his peace-loving disposition, Riley found no Indian hostilities.[33]

On August 23 President Jackson rejected Gaines's request for volunteers from Tennessee on the grounds that the state's quota was already committed in Florida. Additional call-ups would have disturbed the balance of payments made to the states and their citizens for volunteer services, leading to embarrassing questions (in an election year) about federal patronage and favoritism, given that volunteers or militia had been mobilized in every southern state. (Some similar discord was evident during John Wool's Cherokee operations that autumn.) The president later declared privately that he was trying to prevent Gaines from orchestrating a mass desertion to the Texan side, but there is no evidence that Gaines intended or attempted to do so. Whether Gaines had embarrassed the administration or it had chosen to disavow his actions when they became politically controversial is unclear, but the subsequent friction between Gaines and Jackson was more a clash of strong-willed individuals than of substantive policy differences. With the administration's duplicitous criticism of Duncan Clinch still fresh, Gaines responded to Jackson's restraints in a letter to his subordinate Matthew Arbuckle, asserting the army's "duty to afford the frontier inhabitants . . . [the] protection guaranteed by the constitution of the United States" and claiming that his call for volunteers had been legally sound. At this point, Gaines made his big mistake. In a letter heavily laden with quasi-Jacksonian populism, along with a proto-Whig rhetoric of antipartisanship, Gaines virtually allied himself with Tennessee governor Newton Cannon, longtime leader of the anti-Jackson forces in Tennessee. Gaines proclaimed to the governor:

> Some of the fashionable *party leaders* Editors and others seem very much shocked at my preparatory measures to cross a little muddy branch of the *Sabine Bay* . . . to hold the Savages in check *merely* because some few *white men* have been killed. . . . In reply to such silly effusions of the selfish slaves of party . . . I think it my duty to consider the poorest frontier family . . . entitled to the same . . . protection as the most fashionable of our interior citizens. If I were capable of making an invidious distinction . . . between the rich and the poor—the lordly politician and the humble pioneer . . . I should prove myself unworthy of the trust reposed in me.[34]

Gaines knew that most Texans were American citizens. He may have been displaying a healthy sense of responsibility to the society he served, but his constitutionally elected superiors were not asking him to make class distinctions, interpret the Constitution, or determine national policy toward citizens who had left the United States. Misled by the Texans, easy prey to a self-righteous sense of duty, Gaines greatly exaggerated the magnitude of the crisis, and on September 4 Colonel Whistler reported that, in his opinion, the Texan Indians had no intention of attacking the American frontier. In early October, Gaines left the region to attend the court of inquiry being held to examine his conduct of operations during the first stages of the Second Seminole War the previous winter, and by November, Whistler had had enough of Texan importunities. "No necessity exists for the Seventh Infantry to remain . . . no necessity has ever existed for our occupying Texas," he reported to Arbuckle on November 22. Jackson had come to the same conclusion and ordered the forces at Nacogdoches—still 428 men, the majority of two understrength regiments—to withdraw, bringing the American intervention to an end without combat or casualties. The Seventh Infantry returned to its normal station at Fort Gibson, and most of the Sixth was sent to Florida.[35]

Decades of frontier military command, often as the senior representative of the United States on the scene, had led Gaines to an exaggerated sense of personal responsibility for regional security and defense. Yet the Tennessean did not really act belligerently or irresponsibly in 1836; he did not initiate the move to Nacogdoches independent of civilian authority, nor did he depart from basic government policy to seize pretexts or opportunities to intervene. Indeed, given his past experience with Jackson in Florida, and given the frontier context, one could argue that Gaines exercised laudable caution and responsibility in preparation and execution alike. He called repeatedly for volunteers, but the ideal military situation—concentrating overwhelming force in case of conflict—proved incompatible with the fiscal, political, and diplomatic situation, demonstrating the practical difficulties of ascertaining the balance of professional military responsibility in complex borderlands situations. Much as he and Jackson had done on the Florida frontier a generation before, Gaines provided protection for the flow of American population that both men considered irreversible. Like his mentor twenty years earlier, Gaines was acting without explicit legal and constitutional authorization from the government he was commissioned to serve.

Gaines ultimately proved much less aggressive than Jackson had been in Florida, but Old Hickory's new job left him much more exposed to partisan attack, and he was in a much better position to appreciate the dangers of unauthorized military adventurism, both to the nation's foreign relations and to the election of his successor. The result was a rift between the Tennessee warriors, aggravated by Gaines's opposition to the removal policy and Jackson's suspicion that his subordinate was too friendly with Whigs like Cannon. (In 1840 an embittered Gaines endorsed William Henry Harrison in a letter to the Tennessee governor, which appeared in the *Nashville Whig*.)[36] This rift, combined with the brigadier's repeated calls for costly volunteers based on rumors of Indian hostilities, would lead Democratic as well as Whig presidents to sideline the grizzled veteran over the course of the next decade. In 1837 Secretary of War Poinsett redrew the army's geographic commands in a way that minimized Gaines's responsibilities; President Tyler promoted Gaines's archrival Winfield Scott to commanding general upon Alexander Macomb's death in 1841, and Democrat James K. Polk selected Whigs Scott and Zachary Taylor (once Gaines's subordinate) to lead the invasion of Mexico, while Gaines sat out the war in New York Harbor.

Neither the army nor the administration acted effectively to stop the flow of American volunteers and supplies to Texas, but Gaines did not actively support the Texans, except in the sense that his movement may have released East Texan volunteers or militiamen to move to the primary battlefront; nor did he attack Mexican forces. The prevalence of chattel slavery among the Texans made U.S. annexation, otherwise likely, a sectional flash point, preventing Jackson from launching the army into Texas during an election year.[37] Gaines was certainly excitable, often impetuous, and occasionally petulant when his pride was injured by superiors, but his preparations were responsible ones, given his past experience and his sense of ultimate moral accountability to the citizens of the southwestern frontier. Indeed, his greatest mistake was not in entering Texas, which had been authorized by the president, but in repeatedly calling for large numbers of expensive, politically controversial volunteers, when both his civilian superiors and fellow officers were confident the standing army could handle any difficulties.

Jackson's criticism of his former protégé concealed the reality that Gaines had acted within appropriate bounds, given general American policy objectives and the circumstances on the spot. Like many other actions of the officer corps, Gaines's proactive measures had the potential to cause political and diplomatic embarrassment to the national government to which he was institutionally accountable, but they were not substantially irresponsible in intent or effect. Given the difficulty of communication and the need to grant local commanders substantial operational discretion prior to the advent of the telegraph, it is hardly remarkable that Gaines used his initiative as he did. If anything, it is surprising that officers did not use their discretion to exceed their often (and often purposefully) vague instructions and engage in unauthorized yet politically popular expansionism more frequently. Their growing reluctance to do so displays the sense of politically neutral accountability to national civilian authority that became the hallmark of the officer corps' professionalism.

The success of the Texas Revolution led to continued tensions on the southwestern border throughout the period of this study. Hearing rumors that Mexico had seized American vessels and imprisoned their crews, Gaines reiterated his concerns about protecting American citizens in May 1837: "should it prove to be true," he urged military preparations to "facilitate . . . whatever *effective military remedy* the President of the United States may be pleased to apply." Although he couched his letter in respectfully hesitant language, Gaines clearly assumed that Van Buren would take forceful action. The general bypassed commanding general Macomb and wrote directly to Secretary of War Poinsett, another example of his sense that substantive responsibility was more important than the formal procedures of institutional accountability. (Gaines undoubtedly disdained Macomb, who had been elevated over him to the post of commanding general in 1828, as a bureaucrat who rarely left Washington.)

Gaines's letter was essentially a deployment plan in anticipation of war. As became his habit during this era, the brigadier called for the mobilization of a vast force of mounted volunteers, very few of whom were ever mustered. Nevertheless, in planning to provide for them, Gaines demonstrated the same logistical acuity that marked his views on the coastal fortifications program and the military use of railroads—a broad sense of responsibility for citizen-soldiers that he had learned with Jackson on the frontiers of Florida. Rather than leaving the individualistic volunteers to their own devices, "the United States [would] . . . supply each Battalion with a . . . Regular officer for each branch of the General Staff," which "would contribute to . . . the prompt *instruction, health, comfort,* and *immediate efficiency* of each Battalion." Gaines concluded by proposing locations for recruiting and supply depots and noting the need for an adequate naval force. He then proposed to invade Mexico by land and sea with an army of 50,000 to 100,000 men "until we find them disposed to respect us," though it is not clear whether this immense force was intended for conquest or was a consequence of the officer corps' tendency toward exaggerated projections, aggravated by the general's grandiose personal vision. After his experiences the previous year, Gaines did not attempt to seize the initiative himself, a sign that he was not irredeemably wedded to the pursuit of territorial expansion at the cost of his army career.[38]

Gaines was not alone in his continued attention to the Texan border, however. In April 1837 Macomb instructed brevet Major William Belknap of the Third Infantry to investigate the navigability of the Sabine as a potential supply route for posts that might be established along the river. Although this inquiry may have been merely about reducing costs, the commanding general also sought information on the possibility of obtaining forage for cavalry along the border. The army had never devoted substantial forces to patrolling the Sabine south of the road between Natchitoches and Nacogdoches, most of the river's length, as a border. The Caddo movements the Texans complained about occurred north of that point and north of the army's post at Camp Sabine. A week later Macomb advised Matthew Arbuckle, commanding at

Fort Gibson, that President Van Buren had refused a Texan request, supposedly predicated on fears of the Caddo, for U.S. troops at Nacogdoches. Van Buren realized that the Texans could handle the Caddo, who were few in number and actually quite peaceful; the president had no desire to fuel a sectional debate over the relationship between the United States and Texas. In contrast, Secretary of War Poinsett planned to station five full regiments (out of thirteen in the entire army), including almost all of the four artillery regiments, along the Sabine, with "such Howitzers and field pieces [cannon] as may be deemed necessary and fit for service on the Southwestern frontier . . . especially the mountain Howitzers." (Mountain howitzers were lighter than normal howitzers of their caliber, and most references to artillery pieces in dragoon expeditions and Florida are actually to these guns.) Half the army's mountain howitzers were to be sent to Camp Sabine, and half to Fort Gibson. A total of twenty-two companies were to be deployed south of Camp Sabine, where the road from Opelousas crossed the river. These plans were soon frustrated by the persistence of the war in Florida, but it seems clear that Washington was making plans for new contingencies, foreshadowing a U.S. incursion into Texas, whatever the specific occasion.[39]

Another potential crisis appeared in August 1838 when a rumor of rebellion by Mexicans and Indians near Nacogdoches led Sam Houston to request U.S. troops and cannon from James Many at Fort Jesup. Gaines again sought permission to call up volunteers, vowing that the Texans were "citizens of the same colour, speaking the same language." Colonel Many—one of only a handful of army officers who had served longer than Gaines (forty years versus thirty-nine)—did not prove so receptive. He had investigated Caddo land claims in 1835 and reported them valid; he had investigated rumors of Indian war early in 1837 and found nothing; he had a long history of refusing support to the federal agents assigned to the Caddo; and he was in ill health. Too far down the chain of command to call up the Louisiana militia Houston sought, the colonel properly refused this request for military assistance from a foreign nation, displaying sympathy for the Indians and irritation at Houston's presumption: "I cannot recognize the right of the Republic or the General to give me any order or direction. . . . [Moreover,] the Indians spoken of . . . have been resident in that place much longer than three fourths of the present [white] inhabitants, and . . . they were settled in that Country long before the Independence of Texas was thought of." Nevertheless, Many sent Lieutenant William S. Henry, experienced at working with civilians owing to his duties as the regiment's commissary officer, to confer with Houston, assuring the Texan that he would provide all assistance authorized by the U.S. government, and he advised the Louisiana militia that it would probably be needed to restrain the Indians.[40]

Many's emissary also came to mixed conclusions, blending and balancing racial sympathies and antipathies with the practical concerns of the United States and its army. As a gentleman himself, Lieutenant Henry focused his inquiry among "Gentlemen of high standing" in East Texas. As an officer charged with limiting U.S. liabilities and accustomed to importunate frontiersmen with hyperactive imaginations, Henry confirmed his colonel's predisposition toward inaction by reporting that "the origin of the difficulties was entirely of a domestic nature," a matter of Anglo-Tejano disputes over horse theft. Nevertheless, the lieutenant felt compelled to assert that "there is no doubt in my mind that a very deep and well planned scheme had been laid" against white rule, and that Mexican leaders "had prevailed upon most of the Indian Tribes of Texas to join them." Yet the Indians in question had "permanently located themselves . . . many years ago, long before most of the present [white] inhabitants . . . dreamed of going there." Precise "identification would have been a puzzle" no matter what, so Henry reconciled these disparate conclusions of evidence and attitude by stipulating that "no band of Indians have come (as it was reported [by the Texans]) expressly from our Territory with the avowed intention of joining the Mexicans in War." Indeed, "but a short time will elapse, when Texas will have nothing to fear but herself."[41]

The border zone remained in flux despite Texan victories over local Tejanos, Cherokee, and other Indians. Sam Houston continued to demand that the U.S. Army advance to Nacogdoches, while Texan general Thomas Rusk wanted it to move all the way to the Neches River, but Colonel Many and his lieutenant were echoed by General Arbuckle and Lieutenant Colonel Josiah Vose, who denied the existence of an Indian war in Texas. Many continued to refuse Texan overtures, rejecting their claims of slave unrest even though one of his companies had been deployed since the previous December to deter an uprising in Natchitoches. The Texans, whose rangers had pursued Comanche to the vicinity of Fort Smith, well within U.S. territory, a year before, then took the offensive. Amid a campaign of ethnic cleansing—driving the Texan Cherokee and many Tejanos from the Nacogdoches area in the "Cordova War"—they crossed the border and attacked the Caddo Indians in U.S. territory, occupying Shreveport for several days. Many responded by leading a force of 165 soldiers and two cannon to drive the intruders back into Texas.[42]

This was the closest the army actually came to combat against either Texans or Mexicans along the border between 1820 and 1846, but the Texans withdrew before the colonel arrived. Although soldiers were occasionally sent on patrol to deter Indians who sought to cross the border, the army did not undertake any other significant active operations along the Sabine until the concentration prior to advancing into Texas in 1845. Orders promulgated in December 1838 gave commanders a pretext to build up forces along the Texan border to prevent Indians under U.S. jurisdiction from participating in conflicts in Texas, but there was never a military policy of "hot pursuit" into Texas, as had been the case, for all intents and purposes, toward Spanish Florida a generation before. All the senior field-grade officers on the Texan border shared Many's skepticism: ordered to respond to the Texan ambassador's complaints the following spring, Arbuckle continued to deny that there was any evidence Indians were making war on Texas from the United States. Thus, the army's presence probably did more to deter Texan raiding (whatever the motive) across the border than to reshape the Indian culture of autonomous movement. The local knowledge that Many had developed over nearly twenty years of service along the Louisiana-Texas border probably prevented him, and the United States, from providing further assistance to Texas or being drawn into hostilities with Indians. As on so many other frontiers, the combination of officers' nationalist orientation and their distaste for white frontiersmen moderated national reactions to rumors of Indian violence and ameliorated national Indian policy in general. A generation after the insubordination that led to the First Seminole War, the army's commanders now combined responsible discretion and professional accountability with a growing autonomy from ethnic, sectoral, or sectional political pressure. Their skeptical threat assessments were virtually always correct.[43]

11
CAUTIOUS INTERVENTIONS AND POWER PROJECTION
Southern Plains Diplomacy, Dragoon Expeditions, and the Initial Move into Texas

After decades of avoiding the sustained effort necessary to coerce peace among the Indian tribes, their forced concentration within the shrinking spaces of the plains and prairies west of Arkansas and Missouri gradually led to a shift in U.S. policy. The 1834 intercourse law asserted the most complete U.S. sovereignty over the Indians to date, authorizing the use of military force to prevent or stop violence among the Indians that might otherwise spill over into depredations against whites. Yet this statute had little effect for several years, even for several decades, as the Seminole War drew most of the troops other than the First Dragoons away from the Plains frontier. The decline of the Osage, resulting from the growing Cherokee presence, meant that the focus of army peacekeeping in these regions shifted to the violent factionalism, amounting to a virtual civil war, among the Cherokee after 1838. Brevet Brigadier Generals Matthew Arbuckle and Zachary Taylor, the regional commanders, drew on a generation of experience (for Arbuckle, almost all of it spent along the Arkansas frontier) to resist rumor-mongering and panic rather than forcibly repressing violence among the Cherokee at the cost of diplomatic turmoil, fiscal expense, and injustice to the Indians. The army saw no good reason to try to exploit the Cherokee's civil conflict; instead, the dispute's most overt manifestations were calmed by a council held under Taylor's supervision in 1843, where the treaty and antitreaty (removal and antiremoval) parties agreed to peace.[1]

Like the Osage, the Pawnee, the next major tribe ranging to the north and west, battled virtually every other Indian society in the region, but the Pawnee were centered hundreds of miles west of Fort Leavenworth and the Missouri

Pawnee man. Photograph by A. P. Trott, later in the century. (Courtesy Kansas Historical Society)

frontier and were divided into half a dozen significant subgroups that rarely cooperated militarily. (The Wichita, also known as the Taovayas, Towash, or Pawnee Picts, who ranged between the Arkansas and Red Rivers, were a different group, closer akin to and often allied with the Comanche.) White settlement, and the consequent political demands for expansion at native expense, had not pressed much into the future Kansas region, much less the Platte River Valley where the Pawnee were centered. Under attack by Sioux from the north, the Pawnee tended to range southward to the Arkansas River, clashing constantly with the Osage and other Plains inhabitants, rather than east toward the whites; their wars were normally too distant from the white frontier to concern soldiers, unlike the conflict between the Osage and Cherokee immediately west of the Arkansas settlements. The Pawnee briefly harassed and detained brevet Second Lieutenant George Crosman and an enlisted detail at the Grand Pawnee village as they chased deserters in October 1824, and Henry Atkinson negotiated a peace treaty the following summer. Tensions continued, largely due to white penetration onto the Plains, and Alexander Cummings of the Sixth Infantry, stationed at Cantonment Towson at the southern end of their range, reported whites organizing a filibuster against the Pawnee (in fact, probably the Pawnee Picts, or Wichita) in 1826. Though nothing seems to have come of this rumor, two years later Pawnee warriors attacked the Santa Fe caravans, previously unmolested, and commanding general Macomb began pondering a punitive expedition.

Coming to his office from the Corps of Engineers, with nearly a decade since he had directed such operations, Macomb's principal concern appeared to be avoiding another diplomatic setback like Leavenworth's rebuff by the Arikara five years before. Claiming that the decision to launch an expedition was up to Atkinson, Macomb counseled the brigadier that "you will not . . . undertake any operations against the Indians further than to establish suitable posts for holding them in check, unless you are fully satisfied of your ability to act effectually . . . the campaign should be active and of short duration, making if possible a severe example . . . as too great a moderation will only lead them to despise us." The commanding general went on to worry about the cost of militia and volunteers, versus the chance that Indian scouts might betray an expedition, as the Sioux had done to Leavenworth. Fresh from two years of repressing unrest among the Ho-chunk, Atkinson was left with the comforting thought that "great anxiety will be excited, to know the result of your measures as you proceed."[2] The War Department stepped in to order an investigation into Pawnee intentions, and Lieutenant George Wright was dispatched to the Pawnee villages along the Platte. Following the trend of most officers when confronted with actual native resistance, he concluded that the

Pawnee "will continue to rob and murder . . . until decisive measures are taken by the government." Under pressure from merchants engaged in the Santa Fe trade, President Jackson ordered a military escort for the 1829 caravans, and the Pawnee did not attack them. This inaction, combined with congressional and Jacksonian pressure for retrenchment and Macomb's worries, put paid to any plans for a punitive expedition. A smallpox epidemic in 1831 plus a series of wars with the Comanche, Cheyenne, Arapaho, and Sioux nearly overwhelmed the Pawnee during the following decade.[3]

Thus, although the dragoon expeditions of that decade occasionally encountered Pawnee, they posed little threat to U.S. interests, and the army made little effort to subject them to U.S. control. An 1833 council and treaty sponsored by the United States sought to limit warfare on the eastern Plains by granting shared hunting rights to the Osage, Pawnee, Ioway, Oto, Kickapoo, and Kansa, as well as the immigrant Delaware, Shawnee, Sauk, and Fox, on land formerly claimed by the Pawnee south of the Platte River. In return, the Pawnee were to receive the various elements of the U.S. program to "civilize" Indians, including a hundred guns to defend their villages, if they remained in one place and took up agriculture. Pawnee leaders also engaged in U.S.-sponsored talks with leaders of the Cherokee, Creek, and Choctaw immigrating from the Southeast, and two years later a Pawnee party accompanied Henry Dodge's expedition with the First Dragoon Regiment to negotiate with the Comanche. Nevertheless, the Pawnee had difficulty sharing their land south of the Platte while the Sioux bore down on them from the north, so elements of the tribe, slowly growing weaker, remained at war with most of their neighbors throughout the 1830s and 1840s. (In a rare effort at arms control, an 1825 treaty had bound the Pawnee not to supply guns to other tribes, but this was unlikely in any case, given the threats the Pawnee faced from every direction.)[4]

Despite endemic aggression toward their Indian neighbors, the most powerful of the southern Plains tribes, the Comanche, remained the subject of U.S. diplomacy rather than coercion until the 1850s. Living far from the direct impact of American expansion, confident in their own strength following decades of successful expansion, the Comanche (like the Osage and Cherokee before them) initially saw the United States as a valuable diplomatic partner and a potential font of resources, rather than a competitor for regional hegemony. Insulated from the white settlement frontier by the Pawnee and Osage, and eager to profit from trade with the Americans, the Comanche directed their campaigns against New Mexico, Texas, and beyond the Rio Grande; their warfare against Americans in Texas did not involve the United States until after that polity was annexed in 1845. The Comanche and their cousins the Kiowa, roaming southwest of the Pawnee, had traded with American merchants since the 1790s. They seemed "generally favorable" to the United States until the late 1820s, when the belligerence of some of the Santa Fe traders led elements of these tribes to attack the caravan escorted by four companies of the Sixth Infantry in 1829. On two occasions the infantry, led by hardened veteran Bennet Riley, turned back several large-scale charges, driving the Indians out of musket range and causing significant casualties with grapeshot from their six-pound cannon. Four U.S. soldiers were killed or died of wounds, along with at least eight Comanche or Kiowa. Although the escort entered Mexican territory to rescue the merchants during the first Indian assault, and the Indians retreated on that occasion, the troops did not accompany the caravan to Santa Fe, and it was repeatedly attacked en route and while returning.

Diplomatic restraints notwithstanding, the infantry's inability to pursue the Comanche severely limited its tactical options and potential strategic impact, spurring calls for Congress to authorize cavalry. Yet fiscal retrenchment prevented any appropriations until after the Black Hawk War enhanced congressional support outside the southwestern states and territories. Macomb's instructions to Atkinson show the political constraints: plans to mount the 1829 escort were frustrated because President Jackson believed Congress would have to specifically authorize doing so and would presumably refuse. Macomb's suggestion that two posts be established where the trail crossed the Arkansas and Neosho Rivers also came to naught. Stung by their losses, the Comanche returned to their usual focus on raiding Mexican settlements and trading the goods they stole to American middlemen. Indeed, they did not consistently attack American (as opposed to Texan—a distinction the Comanche drew in blood) merchants or settlements again until the 1850s, when their goodwill toward the Americans had been diluted by the U.S. annexation of Texas.[5]

The Comanche did attack a group of merchants returning from Santa Fe at the end of 1832, and Osage leader Clermont raided the Wichita, frequent allies of the Comanche, the following summer. Worried the Comanche might be drawn into the persistent hostilities between the Osage and the eastern tribes entering the region, the army sent an expedition from Fort Gibson to seek negotiations in 1832. In 1833 five companies (two infantry and three mounted ranger) were dispatched under James Many between the Red and Canadian Rivers, with orders to push the Comanche, Wichita, and Pawnee west or to bring their leaders to Gibson for negotiations if they had already moved up the Red. A force of some 150 or 200 Pawnee seized a ranger; the troops pursued for twelve days but could not catch them. Colonel Many put the best face on the affair by asserting that the Pawnee retreat meant greater security for the emigrant Indians. Later that year, the Mounted Rangers provided the ability to conduct another escort along the Santa Fe Trail, with a company each of rangers and the Sixth Infantry; this time, the Comanche chose not to attack.[6]

In 1834 the War Department pursued a more proactive strategy, dispatching a company of the First Dragoons, who replaced the Mounted Rangers late in 1833, under Captain Clifton Wharton as an escort along the trail. Henry Leavenworth led a much larger expedition—the other nine dragoon companies, plus elements of the Seventh Infantry—directly west to negotiate with the Wichita and Comanche. The escort had its hands full keeping peace by preventing some of the traders from attacking the Comanche they met, but no one was slain. Leavenworth's expedition lost half its strength to desertion, fevers, horse casualties, and finally cholera; the green dragoons had marched to Fort Gibson during the winter, lacked drill manuals and horse equipage with which to train in the spring, and did not depart until June 15. Half the expedition was left in a sick camp three weeks later; Leavenworth died of "bilious fever," perhaps cholera, after being thrown from his horse during a buffalo hunt. Nevertheless, dragoon colonel Henry Dodge led 250 troopers to the Comanche villages on the south fork of the Red River, where he left another hundred soldiers in a second sick camp before turning north to the Wichita villages on the north fork of the Red. Logistically, the operation was a near disaster: by the time the summer was over, nearly a hundred dragoons had died, and the expedition was unable to return along the Missouri through the Sioux country, as Macomb had instructed.

On the positive side, the foray was the deepest and most powerful U.S. military movement to the Southwest to date, and a relative diplomatic success. The Comanche asserted their equality with the Americans through a ceremony in which each warrior shook hands with each dragoon as their two lines passed side by side; yet rarely had 250 Indians gathered on the Plains in a single war party, much less with guns and cannon, as the dragoons did. (The Comanche would begin to do so in a series of devastating raids deep into Mexico over the course of the next decade.) Dodge brought Osage, Cherokee, Creek, Choctaw, Shawnee, and Delaware representatives to his councils with the Wichita and Comanche; told them the United States would provide better trade than the Mexicans; and returned a Wichita girl and a young Kiowa woman, captured by the Osage, to their families. The Wichita girl helped convince her village that the Americans came for diplomacy rather than war. Both young women, along with the Cherokee and Osage, proved valuable interpreters, often translating from English to Caddo and then into one of the

Plains tongues. Perhaps as a result, Lieutenant Thompson Wheelock, journalist for the expedition, labeled Wichita women "infinitely respectable."[7]

A year later (1835) these initiatives led to the Treaty of Camp Holmes, made at the Canadian River near the Cross Timbers that August. Major Richard B. Mason and four companies of the dragoons were reinforced by Matthew Arbuckle (one of the three treaty commissioners) and four companies of the Seventh Infantry to keep the peace among the Indians gathered for the negotiations. The Comanche, Wichita, Osage, and Cherokee agreed that the United States would mediate their disputes and maintain peace between them. U.S. citizens would be free to pass en route to and from Santa Fe, but Indian relations with Mexico presented a momentary sticking point. The Comanche had recently begun to attack northern Mexico on a large scale, and the treaty commissioners, including Arbuckle, gave the Comanche a verbal assurance that the United States would not attack them if they attacked Mexico. (Doing so freed the Comanche from concern for their strategic rear, and was contrary to the spirit of the 1831 treaty between the United States and Mexico.) The relative peace among these Indians (they continued to war with the Pawnee) was primarily due to the near collapse of the Osage after two decades of war and pestilence, but the dragoons had added a new potency to American military diplomacy and power projection on the southern Plains and prairies. Indeed, experienced infantry officers like Captain John Stuart, commanding at Fort Coffee along the Arkansas border, advised that an expedition was necessary in 1835 to fulfill Dodge's promise to meet the Comanche and Kiowa (who did not show up for treaty negotiations) that summer, lest they lose the respect the dragoons, however raw, had inspired the previous year.[8]

Smaller but much better drilled and disciplined, and minus the cholera, the 1835 expedition proved much more successful, losing only one soldier out of three companies during a 112-day march of 1,600 miles to the Rockies and back. The contingent first went up the Missouri, holding councils with the Oto and Omaha before turning west along the Platte and meeting with the principal Pawnee bands and the Arikara, who had been driven south of the Missouri by the Sioux during the previous decade. On the Arkansas River near the Rockies, and at Bent's Fort to the east, the dragoons held talks with the Cheyenne, Arapaho, and Gros Ventres; Dodge chose three Cheyenne to act as "chiefs" in negotiations with the United States, and the Pawnee, Cheyenne, and Arikara agreed to peace. Although this armistice proved short-lived, and the Treaty of Camp Holmes was more important diplomatically, the dragoons had demonstrated their power projection capability, which the Indians may have questioned after the logistical failures of the previous year. Whether because the retrenchment-minded Jacksonians considered this sufficient, or

Dragoons in dress uniform, 1836, by H. Charles McBarron. (Courtesy Army Art Collection)

because the dragoons had to be focused closer to the frontier of white settlement as the infantry was withdrawn for service in the Seminole War, the dragoons did not return to the central or southern Plains on a large scale for nearly a decade.[9]

The dynamics of expansion and civil-military relations in the "Indian country"—essentially modern Oklahoma, west of Arkansas and Missouri—were unusual because white leaders envisioned the region as a gigantic reservation for the tribes being driven from the East (and eventually from Illinois, Iowa, and even Kansas) under the removal policy. Lacking the civilian administration of territories intended to become states, this region was essentially a protectorate policed by the army. Having forced dissimilar Indian groups with incompatible economic systems—agriculture and hunting—into close proximity with one another through the removal policy, one of the principal objectives of military policy in the Southwest was to prevent war between the southeastern agricultural nations being resettled west of Arkansas and the Plains nomads who were already there. Throughout the first postwar generation, the most volatile of the conflicts between native and immigrant tribes was between the Cherokee and the Osage plainsmen. As early as 1819, Major William Bradford warned of war between them and tried to begin negotiations to avert it, knowing that the government wanted to encourage further Cherokee emigration from the Southeast. Indeed, one of the principal reasons for the establishment of Forts Smith and Gibson was to intimidate the Osage—who turned over several perpetrators of crimes against the Cherokee after the posts were built—while the army's regional commander pressed them to centralize their political organization in order to facilitate U.S. control.[10]

Two years later (in 1826), Fort Leavenworth was envisioned in part as a forward operating base in case of war between the Osage natives and Delaware immigrants. Tensions between the plainsmen and their new neighbors continued throughout this period, as the Plains nomads first preyed on the immigrants and were then overwhelmed by the seemingly endless waves of well-organized newcomers. Indeed, Forts Towson (1824) and Washita (1842) were established largely to protect the Choctaw and Chickasaw from the Plains tribes and Anglo-Texan adventurers. The latter post was suggested by civilian Chickasaw agent Gaines P. Kingsbury, a former dragoon lieutenant who had served in Dodge's 1835 expedition, and Matthew Arbuckle; it was seconded by Zachary Taylor, contrary to Winfield Scott's recommendation. Arbuckle had first recommended what would become Fort Washita—on the Red River, about a hundred miles west of Fort Towson—as early as 1833, in response to a query from Macomb pondering Chickasaw expulsion from the Southeast. These deployments demonstrate that military leaders understood and tried to moderate the implications of removal for the western frontier.[11]

The political sophistication and relative acculturation of eastern Indians like the Cherokee did not alter military attitudes or behavior: officers demonstrated much the same attitudes toward the Indians resettled on the southern Plains and prairies as they did toward those elsewhere on the western frontier. During a controversy over whether to relocate Fort Gibson in 1837, Lieutenant Colonel William Whistler of the Seventh Infantry reported that he was "decidedly of the opinion that a large body of troops should be kept in the immediate vicinity . . . or even farther west" to "keep in check" the Creeks, the most embittered of the nations driven from the Southeast. The colonel's report illustrates many of the social and cultural prejudices officers applied to policy, for he clearly saw himself as a national policeman and took the paternalistic and coercive subtexts of his words as a given, justified by the superiority of white civilization. Whistler proclaimed without irony that "the United States has guaranteed . . . a military protection [to the tribes] which they confidently expect, and which should be given to them." A garrison near Gibson would continue to prevent war between the eastern Indians and the Osage, "which will assuredly occur just as soon as the troops are removed." The problem was not limited to the less acculturated Osage, however; Whistler selected a position as central as possible for the replacement post, so that "troops could be thrown" among any of the émigré nations to put down unrest. "The presence of a large body of troops in the centre of the Indian country will have a very salutary effect . . . in keeping down local feuds which might arise among them, and in giving a timely check to any hostile movements toward the whites. . . . The presence of even a small military force has a powerful effect in keeping down disaffection among the Indians."[12]

Intentionally or not, the U.S. government effectively divided, conquered, and made the Indians of the Southeast and Southwest dependent by forcing them together. Whistler declared himself satisfied that the allegiance of the Cherokee and Choctaw could be relied on because of their location between Arkansas and the Plains nations. Thrust suddenly into the limited hunting grounds of the nomads, the eastern agriculturalists could not remain neutral. On the one hand, the colonel believed that "those two tribes alone" would afford the white Arkansans, who wanted the troops at Fort Gibson moved into their state, "more protection than two or three military posts." On the other hand, Whistler felt that there was "scarcely anything that would tend to alienate the feelings of the Indians from our government more than the withdrawal of military protection from them" once they had been thrown among the nomads. The recommendations of the 1840 staff report on western defense were based on a similar assumption, that "the government has . . . contracted the twofold obligation of intervention among, and protection of, the emigrant tribes," a responsibility the army took very seriously as a matter of federal sovereignty and national honor.[13]

The result was constant diplomacy, led by civilian Indian agents but closely backed by military force. The value of Fort Gibson was reaffirmed in 1837 by a treaty crafted there between the Creeks, Osage, Wichita, and Kiowa—the full spectrum of Indians, from eastern emigrants to prairie Osage to Plains nomads—and the United States under the eyes of the Seventh Infantry. That year, Chickasaw agent Kingsbury suggested a regular series of grand councils to bring together representatives from all the nations in the region for confidence building and dispute resolution. Although Secretary of War Poinsett supported the idea at one point, with the proviso that military commanders would oversee the proceedings, the War Department ultimately rejected Kingsbury's proposal because of its cost in rations, gifts, and other subsidies to the attending Indians. Nevertheless, military commanders continued to facilitate smaller diplomatic efforts. These often involved gathering diplomatic and political intelligence on relations within and between ethnic groups, filling in for absent State Department or Customs Service officials and providing an initial federal filter, generally thought objective by the president and the secretary of war, for the vague, often contradictory information arriving from the frontier. In 1841, for example, dragoon lieutenant James H. Carleton was dispatched to look into Texan claims that the Comanche had stolen slaves and sold them to whites living among the Creeks; he then investigated violations of U.S. sovereignty along the Red River boundary, where Texans were crossing the border to sell alcohol to Indians. That year, Benjamin Moore, a mere captain of dragoons, oversaw a council among Choctaw, Chickasaw, Delaware, Shawnee, and Kickapoo, intended to reassure them of U.S. protection against the Texans who had been marauding across the Red River. More important to white citizens and their government, the discussions may have helped restrain Indian retaliation. A year later, Creek leader Rollie McIntosh called a grand council of the tribes in the region, reviving the fear of warfare commonly expressed by whites in the face of any native political activity. Zachary Taylor attended the council but reported, like Henry Atkinson, James Many, and Matthew Arbuckle before him, that the greatest threat to white security was fear itself.[14]

That year (1842), small-scale Osage depredations (essentially the theft of horses and cattle) led to the construction of Fort Scott, halfway between Forts Wayne and Leavenworth along the Missouri line, but no general war ever materialized. Indeed, one correspondent to the *Army and Navy Chronicle* felt so confident of Osage intentions that he warned, "it will be [entirely] the fault of the Government . . . if the present quiet is disturbed." Unstable as it was, the *Pax Americana* encouraged by economic dependence and coercive diplomacy laid the physical groundwork for extending the empire of settlement westward over the Plains. Yet the work of peacekeeping (or peace enforcement) and the ideology of Manifest Destiny were not the same thing, nor were they simply points on the same spectrum. The process of national incorporation, the assertion, extension, and consolidation of American national sovereignty and state formation, led to obligations and dilemmas as well as opportunities and power. Placed in the midst of aggressive white citizens, international powers, and diverse Indian groups competing in an ecology of growing scarcity, responsible professional officers usually saw more uncertainty than control, more dilemmas than opportunities. They advocated coercion against all sources of disorder, white as well as Indian.[15]

The construction of temporary dragoon posts continued in the fourth phase of westward military expansion during the 1840s. Fort Wayne, sixty miles northeast of Fort Gibson on the Arkansas state line, was established in 1838 to restrain conflict between rival Cherokee factions and counter the rumored formation of a Pan-Indian confederation. It lasted until 1842, when Cherokee complaints about its presence—supported by Zachary Taylor of the First Infantry and Lieutenant Colonel Ethan Allen Hitchcock of the Third, whom the War Department had sent to investigate frauds against the Cherokee—caused the garrison's redeployment to the new Fort Scott. Some of the eastern Indians still sought military protection, however: Fort Washita was built the same year, in response to Chickasaw requests for protection from Anglo-Texans and Plains Indians. Similarly, to the north of the Missouri River, the erection of Fort Croghan, near the site of old Fort Atkinson at Council Bluffs, was intended to protect the Potawatomi from the Sioux, while Fort Sanford advanced the army fifty miles up the Des Moines River to protect the growing settlements in Iowa by keeping whites from trespassing on Sauk land.[16]

TENSIONS WITH TEXANS ON THE SANTA FE TRAIL: PHILIP ST. GEORGE COOKE AND THE DRAGOONS IN 1843

Apart from a small, uneventful Santa Fe Trail escort in 1839, the First Dragoons did not resume power projection campaigns on the central or southern Plains until 1843. Indeed, the focus of army attention did not return to the Southwest until 1842, after the Seminole War and the Canadian border crises had wound down and tensions between Texas and Mexico peaked after the Mier and Somervell expeditions against Santa Fe. That March, Ethan Allen Hitchcock reported widespread rumors, circulated by civilian frontiersmen, of a council among "certain Indians of the Cherokee, Shawnee, and Delaware tribes . . . on the subject of [making] war upon Texas" from the north, in conjunction with a Mexican invasion. Zachary Taylor urged the secretary of war to ignore these rumors as unsubstantiated fabrications from self-interested frontiersmen, but he was sent fifteen companies of reinforcements—the Sixth Infantry from Jefferson Barracks and half of the soon-to-be-dismounted Second Dragoons from Leavenworth. This swelled the contingent at Fort Towson from less than 700 men to about 2,000, the army's largest concentration of troops at the time. This move represented the first large-scale commitment of forces to the southwestern border since 1836, and in some respects, it can be considered the origin of Taylor's Armies of Observation and Occupation, soon to be aimed at Texas.[17]

Taylor and Hitchcock were correct: the tribes concentrated in the "Indian Territory" never joined together against Texas; their depredations never exceeded small-scale marauding, mostly horse theft. Yet their occasional raids gave unscrupulous Texans and men claiming to represent that republic excuses for "retaliatory" plunder. Nor was Texas itself innocent: in the process of warring with Mexico, which included the Somervell and Mier expeditions against Santa Fe in 1841 and 1842, the republic issued warrants to its citizens, authorizing them to attack caravans—putatively Mexican, but largely American in composition—on the Santa Fe Trail. In April 1843 sixty dragoons were sent in pursuit of a Missourian with a Texas commission; he escaped, killed a New Mexican merchant in U.S. territory, and was later captured and hung by American civil authorities. Two other Texans, Charles Warfield and Jacob Snively, continued recruiting in Missouri and Arkansas, launching expeditions that clashed with Mexican buffalo hunters and a Mexican army contingent sent to escort the merchant caravan during May and June. This land privateering led to protests by American businessmen and the Mexican government, so the War Department sent four dragoon companies from Fort Leavenworth under Captain Philip St. George Cooke (who had served in Bennet Riley's 1829 escort) to shepherd the principal merchant caravan along the trail that summer, while Captain Nathan Boone led three companies from Fort Gibson across the Plains along the Arkansas and Canadian Rivers.[18]

On June 30 Cooke met and disarmed Snively's force of a hundred Texan privateers in U.S. territory, arousing diplomatic protests from Texas. This incident is worth considering in some detail as an example of officers' increasingly active support for national sovereignty and international order, even when the army was called on to defend Mexican nationals at the expense of white frontiersmen operating under the authority of a polity that many Americans hoped to annex. (Note the military's role in facilitating the penetration of trade in the hinterlands of the emerging global capitalist economy, which scholars usually associate with the navy's commerce protection operations.) Given the importance of Texas to President Tyler—both ideologically and, as was widely recognized at the time, as his only hope for reelection—it might be expected that U.S. policy would seek to minimize friction with the Texans, but this was not the case. Instead, the State Department, the War Department, and the officer corps all sought to protect and promote peaceful trade, refusing to distinguish between U.S. and Mexican citizens in the Santa Fe caravans. Those officers who commented supported Cooke's actions without demur.[19]

Like his commander Bennet Riley fourteen years before, Cooke felt little but scorn for the frontiersmen he encountered on the Plains. Indeed, the captain's experience since the 1829 expedition had only increased his doubts about those who ventured past the frontier without state support, contrary to the trade and intercourse acts reaffirmed by a Jacksonian Congress in 1834. The dragoon's skepticism was an amalgam of pessimism about human nature, distaste for the disorder fostered by restless individualism, and irritation when the army was called on to clean up the mess. During the early stages of the escort, commenting on rumors that Indians had killed several whites on the Plains, Cooke sounded equally doubtful about the desirability and feasibility of protective government action:

> It is not extraordinary that such desperate, heedless, small parties, should meet with such a fate in this lawless wilderness. . . . If the power & almost certain punishments of our best internal government do not prevent daily murders & robberies . . . can they fail to occur here[?] . . . Our government is scarcely bound in duty to protect such rash & vagabond men; unless indeed, it be [the government's] determined policy that any citizen shall traverse at will, the limits of the thousand tribes, who cover the desert territory of her immense empire.

The captain preferred a more cohesive national community and questioned whether the United States should attempt to enforce its writ whenever and wherever citizens sought aid. Cooke had encountered the limits of national hegemony in a world full of nonstate actors: comparing the American and Roman empires, he observed that "the Roman dealt with organized governments [the Parthians and Sassanid Persians] . . . the United States deals with savages, whose imperfectly democratic [meaning inadequately centralized] character of government is not equal to the task of controlling their sparse population on these vast plains." He might have been speaking of the government he served: frustrated and disillusioned by fifteen years of contact with the frontier population, the authoritarian dragoon had come to accept some of the limits to state capacity and personal security imposed by unruly democracy and individualism, whether native or white. Like William Worth on the Canadian border several years before, his final answer was to discipline and coerce those he could, leaving the rest to their individual deserts.[20]

Though "savages" probably meant Indians, Cooke did not view the "vagabond" Texans as fellow whites, Americans, or soldiers. In his 1859 memoir, based on his journals, he engaged in an imaginary dialogue with a "Friend" deriding the Texans' military qualities. This discussion was apparently based on Cooke's dinner with the U.S. consul at Santa Fe, New Mexican merchant Manuel Alvarez, during the escort. Referring to the Texan expedition against Santa Fe, the veteran soldier told the Mexican that the Texans "might easily have captured it . . . if they had only had discipline. It shows the difference between the bravery of bowie-knife broils, and that high courage which supports one amid a long train of difficulties and disasters." The discussion then turned to politics and social values, as the dragoon compared "the *National Intelligencer*, full of sanguine Whiggery—grave [and] dignified," with "the abusive . . . the self-important *Globe*" (the semiofficial Democratic newspaper). Cooke damned a writer for another paper for losing a "Utopian" political pamphlet the captain had written, and claimed he had been fined for, as a cadet at West Point. This juvenile essay prefigured the quasi-aristocratic, antipolitical skepticism of Cooke's later *Romance of Military Life*; the cadet had sought to "cur[e] the dishonesty and rancor of national politics" by electing three men to draw lots to determine who would be president, claiming that the "masses cannot reason, though they may grow corrupt."[21]

Cooke was a scion of Virginia aristocrats who had dedicated his life to military service. Like Worth, he directed his social disdain and professional contempt against all the bowie-knife bravos and disturbers of order he met. The dragoon first met the Texan leader Snively during General Gaines's expedition to Nacogdoches in 1836, observing derisively that "he was a shopkeeper's clerk, and quite insignificant in appearance and demeanor; though, truth to tell, he had just 'come from the army' (which, properly speaking, Texas has never had)." Seven years later, encountering Snively's expedition in territory Cooke thought American, the captain polled his officers, who agreed that he should disarm the intruders; however, the majority of Cooke's subordinates reversed their counsel when the Texan produced his commission. The dragoon's prejudices in favor of state-centered order and propriety then rose to the fore:

> I believed a civilized government would scarcely acknowledge such a document, which without an indication of the forms and customs of regular organization, outrages all the rules of modern warfare. . . . I believed most of [the] ruffian crew before me to be outcast citizens of the United States . . . [there] to assail our peaceful trade; above all, the safety and welfare of my own fellow citizens depended on my decision; I could no longer hesitate.[22]

Cooke then lectured the Texans on the international law of territorial boundaries, showing off his erudition by adverting to a Polish case from 1830, and threatened them with his artillery: "if any leave the grove [to escape disarmament] I shall instantly discharge my howitzers among them, and thus drive you from the woods [where the Texans had taken shelter], and attack you in the plains!" Certainly not what the Texans expected. When Snively argued, the captain formed his dragoons, unlimbered his howitzers, and ordered the soldiers to advance, "sabres drawn." The Texans then surrendered, and Cooke agreed to escort those who wanted to go to the United States. This belligerence notwithstanding, the captain remained conscious of his position as a diplomat. He wanted to arrest Texan leader Charles Warfield and take him to the United States for trial for neutrality violations but decided not to, "fearing to meddle with the municipal law" of Texas; in particular, he thought that doing so might somehow confer legitimacy on Warfield's warrant to grant commissions to American citizens. Cooke then released the other Texans, providing them with substantial food supplies and allowing them to retain some of their weapons for self-defense against Indians. The Texans had in fact hidden their better weapons before the dragoons took them prisoner, and some of them attempted to resume their depredations against the caravans, but they did not try to attack the merchants escorted by U.S. troops. Even after the caravans entered Mexican territory, Cooke's action, combined with his continued presence on the border, dissension among the Texans, and the appearance of a substantial Mexican force escorting the caravan on its return from Santa Fe, effectively put an end to the marauding. Indeed, the presence of the American patrols seemed to encourage further trade, for the captain encountered two smaller caravans later that summer.[23]

Cooke justified his actions not only on abstract grounds of international law and custom but by deriding the Texans as "freebooters," without the discipline that distinguished regular, state-organized, forces: "Everything went to prove that there was no regular military control . . . there was not—save fire arms—the slightest sign of military rank or equipment; but a profusion of bowie knives seemed to mark their character individually & collectively." The dragoon had never held so significant a command, and he felt that he had passed a long-anticipated test:

> [I lay] down to rest with a mind untroubled; satisfied that I have acted only from a stern sense of *duty*—that after having from my childhood devoted myself to the requirement of knowledge in my profession, & of those subjects which to men of enlarged liberal views, are of a kindred nature, I have not failed in the moment of action to correctly perceive & accomplish the duties, the rights and interests of my government in the sphere of trust with which they have honored me.[24]

The hard-nosed captain was not much happier with the merchants he protected, who repeatedly asked him (as they had Bennet Riley in 1829) for escorts beyond U.S. boundaries into Mexican territory, if possible to Santa Fe. Like Riley, Cooke refused to go beyond the point where the caravans appeared to be in immediate danger, maintaining that longer marches would endanger the men and animals in his charge. Though based partly on laudable accountability, and partly on a diplomatic hesitance to enter Mexican territory, this reluctance was also a function of officers' narrowly institutional vision, based on their bureaucratic experience and responsibilities, which made them unnecessarily reliant on their supply of rations when they could have subsisted on buffalo and other game. Probably even more important, the officers' contempt for merchant materialism predisposed them against providing more extended escorts, even when told that the New Mexican governor would not object. (Ironically, Cooke and Riley were refusing to provide public aid to private enterprise, a choice radical Jacksonians presumably would have applauded.)

Yet property, trade, and propriety were central to nineteenth-century visions of civilization and international order, and they had to be protected. Further encounters with the Texans, in which the dragoons disarmed them a second time, only confirmed Cooke's sense that "these men are mere cut-throat outlaws." As Captain B. A. Terrett put it, they were engaged in "a piece of gross impudence" in "their offensive enterprise against our trade." Observing that "their principal men lie like pick pockets on all subjects," Cooke concluded that only "their *show* of authority saved them from a treatment much rougher & richly merited." Though unable to mete out a rougher justice, the captain considered his expedition a success; his troops had "improved in discipline" not only by six weeks in the field but also by the example of proper military behavior. The Texans had argued, but they ultimately gave in to his display of force—a herald of U.S. hegemony on the Plains. Indeed, Cooke assured the adjutant general that the show of force would deter further banditry by whites, while asserting that the Indians in the region—primarily meaning the Comanche, who were even then devastating northern Mexico and Texas—were too few and disorganized to threaten significant caravans. Still skeptical about merchants roaming the wilderness, the captain advised against further escorts, given the limited size of the trade and its tendency, he believed, to benefit Mexicans more than U.S. citizens.[25]

General Gaines strongly supported Cooke's actions, which were criticized in some civilian quarters as a threat to American relations with Texas. For the frontier general, the captain's decisiveness set a valuable example in the army's effort to suppress lawlessness and filibustering along the nation's borders: "It is our bounden duty to put down all predatory movements of this sort of *land privateering*, such as have too long contributed to mark the character of men calling themselves members of American Republics towards each other. We must *destroy, arrest, or disarm* all such lawless combinations, whenever found within or near our *unmarked boundary*." Gaines warned that "no such movements . . . can take place *any where upon the Santa Fe road* without jeopardizing the lives and property of many of our good citizens." The brigadier maintained that Cooke had the discretionary authority to decide whether the bandit party was under American jurisdiction, which included the protection of Mexican citizens engaged in trade along the route. The very fact of army officers' employment by the nation-state invested them with the disinterested authority to make important diplomatic decisions on the spot: "The sacred character of this duty required perfect impartiality on the part of the United States' commander to whom it is confided, and naturally constitutes him, while acting under the authority of the Government, a fit and proper judge . . . to decide how far he can go . . . consistently with the well-known principles of the law of nations." Unlike Cooke, Gaines was eager to extend the protection of American sovereignty the length of the Santa Fe road, warning that the social and economic benefits of liberalism, the free trade and commercialism he expected to foster through railroad construction in the East, ultimately depended on an adherence to the rule of international law that could be enforced only by the military agents of the nation-state:

> I have long acted upon the principle that, for the purposes of protection . . . against predatory bands . . . disposed to violate the known laws of war, or to violate the long-cherished principles of that *free trade* and social intercourse which have done so much for the great cause of

civilization and free government throughout the civilized world, we should not hesitate to consider every foot of land and water near our unmarked boundary . . . as *neutral ground*, and within the reach of our authority.

The cantankerous general could not conclude without a self-justifying reference to past controversies: "I acted upon this principle upon the Sabine frontier in the year 1836, much to the dissatisfaction of certain self-esteemed *abolitionists* . . . but I am never so well satisfied with my own conduct as when I feel myself abused by *political intriguers and land privateers*."[26] Indeed, Gaines sent Cooke out on a second escort seven weeks later, instructing him to:

See these merchants, and assure them of your authority and determination to afford them *protection* until they shall meet a competent escort, or until they shall reach Santa Fe. Assure them of our determination to *protect* them at all hazards—and if in the discharge of this duty you should find *rough or perilous work*, the meritorious services of your officers and your men and your self shall be affectionately remembered by every true hearted soldier and statesman of our country, & more especially of those great and growing states of the valley of the Mississippi, & more especially by your General and friend.[27]

Texan complaints compelled the War Department to convene a military court of inquiry the following year, but the army's stance was made clear by the selection of Cooke's regimental commander, Colonel Stephen W. Kearny, as president of the three-officer court. Kearny had already congratulated Cooke "on your movements this season. They reflect credit upon yourself, upon the Regt, upon the Army, & upon the Country. Your disarming those Texians . . . was an Act which entitled you to the thanks of the authorities in Washington, & which meets with the approval of myself & all officers I have conversed with, whose opinion is worth knowing." A month later Kearny sent Cooke a letter from the adjutant general, conveying Winfield Scott's "approbation of your conduct" and "adding my full & entire concurrence therewith. Your conduct as Commander . . . more particularly your disarming of the Texian freebooters . . . was highly creditable to yourself, & has not only added to your reputation as a Soldier, but to the character of the Regiment & of the Army."[28]

Not surprisingly, the court cleared Cooke of all charges of misconduct, labeling his action "an appropriate exhibition of military force." Captain John Burgwin of Cooke's regiment used the occasion to highlight the link between

Philip St. George Cooke, Kearny's protégé, later in life. (Courtesy U.S. Army Military History Institute)

officers' aspirations for personal prestige and their public service, hoping that Cooke "will get some credit for his service, which I think will be most beneficial in its results." Winfield Scott's annual report reaffirmed this support: "The officers (particularly Captain Cooke) . . . displayed an intelligence, enterprise, and hardihood, which entitle them to very great praise." Two years later Scott recommended Cooke for promotion to the major's slot in the Regiment of Mounted Rifles that had been raised to protect the Oregon Trail: Cooke "has served with uniform honour & efficiency. . . . He is certainly one of the best Cavalry officers in the U. States—intelligent, Scientific, Moral & honourable." Though he did not receive this promotion, Cooke gained an independent command over the battalion of Mormon volunteers that marched to California against Mexico three years later; he was promoted to major, lieutenant colonel, and colonel by 1858, exercising a critical independent command in law enforcement operations in "Bleeding Kansas." During the Civil War, Cooke became the first commander of the Cavalry Corps of the Army of the Potomac. Whatever their personal and professional differences, Edmund Gaines and Winfield Scott certainly agreed on the army's law enforcement obligations in the borderlands, and they recognized professional zeal in their subordinates. Their language demonstrates a similar allegiance to the authority and discipline of the nation-state that promulgated the laws, and on the Santa Fe Trail, like the Canadian border, expansionist administrations accepted the army's judgment that order and stability were preferable to pell-mell expansion and chaos.[29]

ACROSS THE WIDE MISSOURI: POWER PROJECTION REPLACES PEACEKEEPING, IN 1844 AND BEYOND

The last dragoon operations prior to the war with Mexico focused as much on power projection—enforcing peace on U.S. terms—as on peacekeeping. In 1844 Major Clifton Wharton led five companies west from Fort Leavenworth to intimidate the Pawnee, losing only 2 of his 350 soldiers, both to illness. Wharton confidently tried a new route to reach the Pawnee more quickly, crossing the "Big Blue" river, forty yards wide with a swift current and steep banks, in three hours using a rubber raft and wagons fitted with pontoons. He noted the presence of ample wood and water for the passage of a sizable army. Like Jacob Brown two decades before, Wharton claimed the Indians could find no refuge from American cavalry on the prairies. In two councils, he warned the Pawnee against attacking wagon trains headed to Oregon, cautioned them against the use of liquor, and demanded that they move west in accordance with U.S. interpretations of their 1833 treaty. Wharton also met with the Oto; he blamed their robberies of whites on poverty and a lack of control by tribal leaders and advised that the U.S. government appoint a head chief. Like previous dragoon commanders, the major drilled his men and sometimes fired his howitzers (two twelve-pounders) and rockets to impress his hosts, particularly when he visited the Sauk in Iowa. Yet Wharton undermined his own threats and diplomacy—as well as U.S. sovereignty and control over the use of force—with an unrestricted concept of property rights and the commercial market, asserting that white traders could sell arms to anyone they chose, including the Pawnee and their Sioux enemies.[30]

Indeed, some Pawnee apparently planned to rob John C. Frémont's exploring expedition, although others stopped them from doing so. This led to a council where Wharton presented the Indians with gifts, and they spoke in support of friendship between Americans and Pawnee. Nevertheless, while the Pawnee remained at peace with the United States, forays like this were too rare to stop the warfare endemic among the Indians, fed by growing Sioux power and competition for shrinking buffalo herds during a period of extended drought and overgrazing by native horse herds. Pawnee reactions to dragoon shows of force demonstrated the ironies and ambivalence of their growing accommodation to white pressure: when the Pawnee came to receive their annuities, they advanced to meet the dragoons in a two-rank line that Wharton thought they had learned by watching his maneuvers. Early the following year (1845), Nathan Boone's company was dispatched to protect the Creeks from the Pawnee, but no raids materialized. That November, Boone's company deployed to observe the Cherokee and prevent violence between the treaty and antitreaty parties that might spill over into attacks on whites. On the northwestern Plains, two dragoon companies marched through Minnesota to the Red River of the North and Devil's Lake (in the northeastern quadrant of modern North Dakota), aggressively showing the flag to the Sioux (who did not bother to respond, or may have hesitated at the consequences of doing so) and demonstrating an American presence toward the Canadian border.[31]

It is important to remember that junior officers did not always share these strategic motives for expeditionary action. Assistant quartermaster Captain Thomas Swords, for one, was well pleased with the rarity of expeditions to Santa Fe: otherwise, "the Dragoons have a fine prospect before them, of escorting every caravan of traders, that may ask for protection between this and Santa Fe—the only relief will be, the possibility of sometimes getting as far as Santa Fe itself." Even Lieutenant Henry Turner, Kearny's adjutant and one of the most professionally thoughtful junior officers among the dragoons, found the colonel's 1845 expedition to the Rockies "monotonous and laborious." Turner's reactions to the prospect and reality of this movement are representative of both the corps' aggressiveness—the product of officers' desire for fame, glory, and promotion—and its passivity—the consequence of their relative comfort and security as tenured, salaried employees of the nation-state. In February the lieutenant looked forward to the camaraderie of a large expedition toward Oregon, although he ambivalently labeled it "banishment" from family and female society: "I really do long for motion, and would be the happiest man alive could I look forward with certainty to going on camping this summer with a large portion of the Regt." (Turner was particularly eager for an opportunity to return his weight "to reasonable dimensions.") This enthusiasm quickly waned with experience. Turner recognized that "the expedition may be regarded as a profitable one" because of soil samples it had taken, but he was disappointed by the lack of "stirring incidents": "we trudged along our weary way from day to day thinking of nothing but the close of the expedition, which to everyone . . . was highly agreeable." Recognizing the army's contributions to westward expansion, or seeking that recognition from those who controlled appropriations, was not the same thing as enthusing over them.[32]

Kearny's 1845 expedition to the South Pass of the Rockies, the first venture so far across the Plains in a decade, produced a variety of reactions among participants. Kearny believed the Sioux were "much struck with" the "uniform appearance" of the dragoons, who marched 2,200 miles in ninety-nine days without opposition from Pawnee, Cheyenne, or Sioux. The dragoons suffered no deaths while providing emigrant settlers an escort along part of the Oregon Trail east of the mountains. The colonel concluded by reaffirming Henry Atkinson's principles from twenty years before: that occasional mobile expeditions were preferable to static permanent posts on grounds of both economy and effectiveness. Turner privately quipped that Kearny's march was "unprecedented in point of time, rapidity . . . [and] unimportant sacrifices made," but the expedition undoubtedly served as excellent preparation for the march of the Army of the West to New Mexico the following summer. Contact with the emigrants on the Oregon Trail, whom historians usually regard as middle class, reinforced existing attitudes toward white frontiersmen. Philip St. George Cooke came away from the expedition deploring "the wantonness of discontent—a diseased appetite for excitement and change . . . a restless habit of vagrancy" among the white emigrants. Kearny hinted at the same views, while observing that maps made during the expedition showed that Cooke had been in U.S. territory when he halted the Texans in 1843. Kearny recommended the imposition of martial law to prevent white intrusion into Indian country on the Plains (the Oregon Trail excepted), a measure Winfield Scott cautiously endorsed.[33]

The dragoon expeditions of 1845 penetrated to the farthest points north and west yet reached by substantial American combat forces, presaging and in effect training for Kearny's trek to California a year later. The army's western mission, which since the end of the Missouri expedition had been centered on the coerced resettlement of eastern tribes and the protection of resettled Indians from further white aggression, now shifted to the overt pursuit of territorial expansion against Mexico. Presented with significant opportunities for promotion, men like Swords and Turner temporarily changed their tunes: Swords began reading every work related to Mexico that he could get a hold of, noting, "I would like very well to revel in the halls [of Montezuma] for a short time" before returning to sedentary staff life. In May 1846 the newly promoted Captain Turner advised his friend Abraham Johnston that Colonel Kearny "is very anxious to have you with him" in the expedition to New Mexico and California: "tis important that we should acquit ourselves properly. The eyes of the country will be upon us." Johnston was promoted to captain and joined Kearny as an aide-de-camp, but was slain by Mexican lance thrusts while leading a charge at San Pascual in California that December. Like a miniature version of the boisterous nation champing at the bit to expand "the area of freedom," Johnston's horse became exhausted, and his unit lost its cohesion pursuing the Mexicans.[34]

THE ADVANCE INTO TEXAS: MISSIONS AND COMMANDERS, SUBORDINATION AND RELIABILITY

Civilian diplomats worked out incidents like Cooke's in 1843, and the Tyler administration continued to try to annex Texas. By the end of that year, the War Department had concentrated 2,000 regulars in the vicinity of the Texas border. On April 12, 1844, representatives of the United States and Texas signed a treaty of annexation that provided Texas with military protection against Mexico; the western strategic reserve at Jefferson Barracks had been ordered to Fort Jesup, twenty miles east of the Sabine boundary, the previous day. On April 23 the "Corps of Observation" was officially created as an independent command under brevet Brigadier General Zachary Taylor, who was instructed to open confidential communications with Sam Houston without informing his nominal superior Edmund Gaines. Taylor arrived at Fort Jesup on June 17 to find a thousand men in twenty-three companies from the Second Dragoons and the Third and Fourth Infantries—which became the largest force of regular troops concentrated at a single post for an extended period since the War of 1812. Taylor immediately dispatched an officer to contact President Houston while making a reconnaissance of the republic's geography, logistical resources, and attitudes toward annexation. The U.S. Senate rejected the annexation treaty later that month, and the War Department promptly ordered Taylor to cease communications with Houston. Nevertheless, the Tyler administration gave Texas officials an informal, probably unconstitutional, guarantee of assistance in case of Mexican attack. That October, Taylor received orders to prepare for a move into Texas on short notice "in order to restrain any hostile incursions on the part of the border Indians" into Texas, "as required by the provisions of existing treaties." Since the only "border Indians" were those in modern-day Oklahoma, the War Department could have just as easily ordered troops to patrol there. (The Comanche roamed within the boundaries claimed by Texas, and the Apache in New Mexico lived far west of the actual Texan settlements.) Indeed, Taylor wrote to his brother, the assistant commissary general, that he considered the directive "a mere pretext for our troops to cross the Sabine," and he did not attempt to take advantage of the opportunity for aggrandizement.[35]

Following the apparent mandate for expansion in the 1844 elections, President Tyler proclaimed the United States ready for war and sought congressional resolutions (requiring mere majorities rather than a two-thirds vote) for annexation, which he signed three days before Polk's inauguration in March 1845. Later that month the Mexican minister to the United States was withdrawn after presenting a warning that annexation would be considered an act of war. The American minister to Mexico was then expelled, formally breaking diplomatic relations between the two countries. Expecting Texans to consent to annexation, Secretary of War William L. Marcy (the former governor of New York) directed Taylor to prepare to move to the defense of Texas on May 28, and on June 15 George Bancroft, acting secretary of war in Marcy's absence, ordered the brigadier to enter Texas. Taylor received these instructions two weeks later and promptly put his infantry in motion for New Orleans, while the dragoons rode overland to San Antonio. A Texan convention agreed to annexation on July 4, and the first elements of the Army of Observation embarked three weeks later, arriving at Corpus Christi on the last day of July under the command of Ethan Allen Hitchcock. On August 6 Taylor renamed the force the Army of Occupation, a politically infelicitous phrase probably reflecting his practical mind-set and the reality of his mission rather than his Whiggish views.[36]

The specific nature of the army's mission depended on Mexican reactions. On July 7 A. J. Donelson, the U.S. chargé d'affaires to Texas, advised Taylor to advance into disputed territory to the Rio Grande if Mexico declared war. This was a less aggressive course than President Polk had in mind; three weeks later the president wrote to another politician that the army would "occupy the country on the Rio Grande," the boundary Polk claimed for the United States. Yet Secretary of War Marcy's orders, issued July 30, were only to "approach as near the boundary line, the Rio Grande, as prudence will dictate," and certainly not to "employ force to dislodge Mexican troops from any post east of the Del Norte" (the Rio Grande) if the Mexicans had been there at the time Texas was annexed. On August 23 Marcy added that a substantial Mexican crossing of the Rio Grande would be tantamount to a declaration of war; presumably, the brigadier would then repel any incursions against the territory claimed by the United States. Six days later Polk noted the same in his diary, adding that the general would be authorized to pursue defeated Mexican forces across the river and seize Matamoros, "but not to penetrate any great distance into the interior" of Mexico. (Taking Matamoros would compel Mexico to launch any further offensives from deep within its own territory.) On August 30 Marcy issued more complete instructions, allowing the brigadier to use his discretion in choosing a camp, but with the proviso that he leave Mexican outposts between the Rio Grande and the Nueces undisturbed. Yet Taylor was to regard any further Mexican "*attempt*" at crossing the river as an act of war. The last detail may appear insignificant, as it was clearly implied in Polk's position on the location of the boundary, but the only way a Mexican force might fail in such an attempt would be if U.S. forces were actually present along the river to repel it: the implication is that Polk wanted the army to move to the Rio Grande. Nevertheless, as his biographer Charles Sellers observed, the president hoped the general would take the responsibility to do so.[37]

Though no expansionist, Taylor soon suggested measures intended to secure the administration's objectives. Indeed, the brigadier felt certain that a settlement would "be greatly facilitated and hastened by our taking possession at once of one or two points" along the boundary claimed by the United States. Early in October he recommended that the army move south to the Rio Grande, stating that Corpus Christi was much too far from the disputed boundary to "impress the government of Mexico with our readiness to vindicate . . . our title . . . by force of arms, if [it were found] necessary." Taylor advised the adjutant general that "our strength and state of preparation should be displayed in a manner not [to] be mistaken." However, the brigadier stipulated that he did not "feel at liberty, under my [existing] instructions," to advance to the Rio Grande without specific orders unless the Mexicans did so first, examples of both his sense of responsibility for defending U.S. sovereignty and his accountability to diplomatic considerations and civilian decision-making authority. Marcy responded by granting the usual authorization for professional discretion, telling the general to establish winter quarters as close to the Rio Grande "as circumstances will permit," leaving the details to Taylor. The army had only two-thirds of the supply train needed to sustain such a move and was undergoing its first serious bout of disease, so when the general heard that Mexico might agree to negotiations, he decided to wait. Texas formally became the twenty-eighth state in the union on December 29, 1845; American efforts to attain the territories west of Texas by purchase failed two weeks later, and Polk immediately ordered Taylor to the Rio Grande, with instructions to take the offensive if Mexico began hostilities.[38]

Why was Taylor, a Whig, appointed commander of the Army of Observation, and why did he remain commander of the Army of Occupation? As usual, institutional considerations played a significant, perhaps dominant, part, demonstrating the army's insulation from partisan concerns. Henry Atkinson, the most experienced western military diplomat, had died in 1842. With the exception of Edmund Gaines, Taylor was the senior active commander in the Southwest that year, when the Second Dragoons and the Sixth Infantry were concentrated at Fort Towson against rumors of Indian hostilities, and in 1844, when the Army of Occupation was formed. James Many of the Third Infantry and Matthew Arbuckle of the Seventh had both made colonel before Taylor, but Many had gotten along poorly with Texan leaders while stationed on the border during the 1830s, and he was on an extended leave of absence due to ill health. Arbuckle had never distinguished himself in combat or served in the Second Seminole War; he was comfortably situated, conducting ongoing relations with the Indians west of Arkansas while tending his plantation in that state.

Among more distant possibilities, commanding general Scott alternated between Washington and his home in Elizabethtown, New Jersey, and hardly wanted to go to the western wilderness to wait on events; John Wool, brigadier general commanding the army's Eastern Division after his promotion vice Scott in 1841, was similarly ensconced in his headquarters at his home near Albany. (Polk did employ Wool to command the third prong of the American offensive against Mexico in 1846, when he led the Division of the Center from San Antonio through West Texas to Chihuahua before linking up with Taylor at Buena Vista.) William Worth favored expansion to the south, but he was a Whig and Scott's leading protégé; though the most successful up-and-coming officer in the army, Worth had not gained field-grade rank until 1832, sixteen years after Taylor. (Worth would serve as one of Taylor's brigade commanders.) Quartermaster General Jesup was the only senior staff officer with recent experience in frontier diplomacy or combat command, but he had settled back into an administrative routine after his frustrating theater command in Florida and would probably be needed to direct the army's logistical support in case of war.

Institutional considerations notwithstanding, it remains remarkable that Polk felt confident enough in Taylor's sense of duty and subordination to choose a known adherent of the rival Whigs to execute his policies. Yet Polk had little choice within the senior officer corps after its friction with Andrew Jackson over frontier and Indian policy during the 1830s; by 1840, Scott, Gaines, Wool, Taylor, and Worth were all known as Whigs or anti-Jacksonians, which helps account for Wool's ascendance to Scott's brigadiership under the new Whig administration in 1841. All had demonstrated diplomatic restraint along the frontiers. Thomas Jesup was the last open Democrat among the army's senior leaders, but he remained indispensable to the army, and its fiscal accountability to Congress, as quartermaster general. Nevertheless, Gaines had the edge on Taylor in rank, seniority, and actual combat experience. He had been in the army a decade longer than the Kentuckian and had temporarily but successfully commanded the last American army to fight a conventional opponent—during the siege of Fort Erie in 1814, after Jacob Brown and Winfield Scott were wounded at Lundy's Lane. Taylor's War of 1812 experience had been limited to small-scale heroism against western Indians. Indeed, "Rough and Ready's" lack of tactical sophistication is accepted as a truism in virtually every account of the war with Mexico. Thus, one might ask why a Democratic militia general—perhaps no more skillful militarily, but of greater partisan value and reliability, with experienced professional subordinates to conduct operations—was not brought in to command the army sent to intimidate Mexico. Perhaps if Thomas Hart Benton had been sent to do so, he would have been able to replace Scott, as Polk sought to do, unsuccessfully, a year later. But, as a senator, Benton had no intention of leaving Washington before war had begun: the discipline and drill of a garrison in the Texas wilderness were work for a career professional soldier, inured to unpopular decisions and physical hardship by decades of authoritarian command on the frontiers.

Taylor's retention in command suggests several larger dynamics that helped the regular army maintain its monopoly over the operational direction of peacekeeping, coercive diplomacy, and war: inertia; civilian perceptions of, and recognition of military claims to, experience and expertise; and the dilemmas of partisan appointments. Taylor had been hailed as the victor of the Battle of Okeechobee against the Seminoles in 1837, after surviving the backlash from Democratic senators Thomas Hart Benton and Lewis F. Linn against his condemnation of the Missouri volunteers. He had come up with a reasonable (though not particularly successful) campaign plan while commanding U.S. forces in Florida, and he had a reputation as a troop trainer and battlefield leader that few if any militia generals could match. Perhaps most important, especially once the army was on alert for action in Texas, removing him would have raised questions about administration partisanship and provided ammunition for critics of Polk's expansionist policy, whereas his presence in command might be exploited to gain Whig support for Polk's policy of intimidation. When the war began, Taylor's victories at Palo Alto and Resaca de la Palma gave him such fame that he became immune to partisan removal.

Taylor's retention was, above all, a testament to his reliability: though a Whig, he would faithfully execute presidential orders, and because he was a Whig, he would do so cautiously, without getting out in front of the administration's timetable, drawing undesirable attention, and causing political or diplomatic difficulty. Gaines, in contrast, engendered political controversy by rushing to raise a mass of expensive volunteers, something he had been warned against several years before, when frontiersmen had spread false rumors of a Cherokee war along the Arkansas border. (In 1846 Gaines was summarily packed off to a fort in New York Harbor, about as far as he could be sent from the frontier and active service.) Nor did the administration lack other recent examples of military precipitance to cause it concern. In 1842 navy commodore Thomas Catesby Jones (the adjutant general's brother) seized Monterey, California, believing that war had broken out, and in 1843 British general Charles Napier unilaterally escalated tensions with the Baluchi state of Sind into a war of conquest, from which he profited handsomely. Taylor's judgment and reliability, already demonstrated when he discounted rumors and kept the peace on the Cherokee frontier, were mirrored by the reliability of his West Point–trained junior officers, none of whom are known to have resigned due to qualms over the war. Indeed, fewer than forty officers, none ranking higher than captain, resigned in 1845 and 1846, a rate of about 3 percent per annum. History might have been very different had a substantial number of Whiggish officers resigned or otherwise refused to execute Polk's policy, and historians should consider such possibilities rather than assuming reliable civil-military relations as a given.[39]

After a generation of populist Democrats had denounced standing armies and military aristocrats, the ultra-Jacksonian Polk relied on the professional standing army, so closely associated with the Military Academy and Whiggish institutionalism, rather than the militia or state volunteers to lead the execution of his policy. This gap between rhetoric and reality was not new. It had also been the case in the war to remove the Seminole Indians from Florida under the Jackson and Van Buren administrations during the 1830s, and in the command and supervision of every major military operation of that decade. Indeed, at the height of the Jacksonian agitation against the standing army, Secretary of War Lewis Cass, the paladin of popular sovereignty, admitted that the militia "cannot be regarded as our most important means of safety in the event of war," though he still considered it "a valuable auxiliary."[40] As advocates of the regular army had long recognized, the militia and volunteers were eager to gain the hard currency paid for military service but too impatient to get back to their businesses at home to sustain the effort necessary to conquer Seminoles or Mexicans, much less police the borders and frontiers every day. That policing—peacekeeping rather than war—also required more evenhandedness than the vigilante lynch violence often practiced by whites on the frontiers: given their land hunger and Indian distrust, any conciliation or pacification short of conquest was out of the question if white citizen-soldiers from the South were to take the lead. Indeed, federal officials increasingly tried to limit or prevent militia and volunteer call-ups during the decade after 1836, due to those units' indiscipline, expense—commonly estimated at about double the cost of regulars—and unreliability. Though thousands of militiamen and citizen-soldiers volunteered or were mobilized across the South during the Seminole War, their numbers declined greatly after the second year of the conflict, and the fighting and dying needed to implement the Democratic removal policy were largely done by the national standing army that radical Democrats professed to hate.

Though no longer in charge of the regular army forces along the Texas border, Edmund Gaines reacted as precipitously to these events as he had a decade before. Like Jackson a quarter century earlier, Gaines felt capable of interpreting the government's policy himself, assuming responsibility as the senior officer in the region to react to fluid conditions in accordance with the general tone of national policy. (To be fair, Gaines had some reason to do so, since he was the most senior federal executive branch official west of the Mississippi, apart from the superintendent of western Indian affairs in St. Louis.) Taylor's army had been created as a mission-specific task force independent of the newly reestablished Western Division commanded by Gaines. Nevertheless, the old general felt it necessary to go to Taylor's aid and asked the governor of Louisiana for volunteers, hoping to create an army of 50,000 men to march on Mexico City. Gaines had no more legal authority to do this than he had had in 1836, and he was immediately rebuked by the adjutant general. (As in 1836, Gaines also violated the standing order against writing directly to the president or the secretary of war.) Nevertheless, the brigadier promptly repeated his request, aroused to a pitch of urgency by the potential of the "vast geographical limits ... over which [the United States] cannot but extend very soon if we do our duty." Gaines then claimed leadership of the expedition "to the city of Mexico; and thence, if necessary, to California," calling it "*a right*" earned through his preeminence as a frontier commander. (However, unlike Taylor, Scott, Kearny, Worth, and Wool, Gaines had not been entrusted with a major frontier operation in a decade.) Secretary Marcy responded by ordering the general to stop interfering in Taylor's area of responsibility. Gaines then remained silent until May 1, 1846, when his fears for Taylor's army led to a third request to lead an invasion, followed by a series of no fewer than *twelve* requisitions for state volunteers, along with letters purporting to authorize private civilians to raise them.[41]

The exchange that followed demonstrated a broader conflict over the professional responsibilities and autonomy of a departmental commander, as well as Gaines's personal impetuosity and pride. Marcy ordered the general to countermand his requisitions, and Polk ordered him to Washington for a court of inquiry. Militarily, both civilians were worried that Gaines would mobilize a surplus of troops who could not be fed, thus imperiling Taylor's operations. Indeed, Gaines quickly recognized that this might happen, and he actually refused the services of the first division of Louisiana volunteers organized per his request. Yet Gaines's often grandiose vision blinded him to more immediate realities, as well as federal law: he justified his call for volunteers by "the probability of a war with England, or active operations toward the city of Mexico," but ignored the limitations of the army's logistical infrastructure and the political pressures that a large-scale call for volunteers would create. Indeed, the 8,000 volunteers produced by his calls proved almost useless militarily because they had enlisted for only six months, and under the terms of a 1795 law they could be kept in service for only three months. Nor did the law permit military officers to raise troops on their own initiative, or to authorize civilians to do so.[42]

National civil and military leaders had long since tired of Gaines's heedless enthusiasm, and the command of the Army of Occupation was probably entrusted to Taylor precisely because he was a steady, unexcitable general who could and would devote his attention to the specific mission at hand. The command of the Army of Occupation was confided to Taylor in part because he was the senior officer on the spot when President Tyler ordered the first concentration in 1842, in part because of Winfield Scott's endless feud with Gaines, and in part because Taylor, a theater commander in Florida during the Van Buren administration, was clearly the sort of general who would devote his energies to executing the administration's policy, regardless of his own political beliefs. Although Scott was commanding general, that position had evolved largely into one of administration rather than field command—Jacob Brown had not led any of the western expeditions during his tenure, and Alexander Macomb had only briefly appeared in Florida and on the Canadian border—and Scott was already well known as a probable Whig presidential candidate.

Indeed, Tyler probably chose Taylor, and Polk retained him in command, largely because they feared that Gaines's eagerness for expansion might precipitate hostilities unnecessarily or in advance of the administration's timetable, spurring congressional opposition. Historian Piero Gleijeses recently demonstrated how little public debate actually occurred over the army's presence or mission in Texas; most newspapers and congressional debaters were focused on the possibility of war with Britain over Oregon and expected Mexico to back down without a fight (as did most officers). Polk had no desire to disturb this quiet; the unflappable Taylor would neither make nor provoke a fuss, so the administration could try to secure the Rio Grande boundary under the radar and let Mexico stew over the difficult decision for war or peace. Gaines, in contrast, considered his actions justified by the urgency of the moment and demanded the professional autonomy his experience had taught him was necessary for frontier command: "The War Department seems to be of the opinion that there is no discretionary power lodged in me to act without positive instructions." His response invoked a worst-case scenario without precedent since 1815, and a situation he himself had downplayed a decade before. "I therefore ask, for information, if a servile insurrection should occur; if an irruption should be made by large tribes of Indians . . . would it be my duty to refuse all aid until I should have received orders from Washington?" These complaints were straw men, and everyone knew it.[43]

Yet Gaines had long ceased to rely on the standing army as the primary instrument of national security. He seems to have become mentally dissociated from the army since his court of inquiry and the change in the geographic command structure aimed at him in 1837. With few operational or administrative responsibilities while Atkinson, Arbuckle, Kearny, and Taylor dealt with the western frontiers, Gaines spent much of the intervening decade lobbying for his long-range strategic plans for national and coastal defense. His calls for volunteers, whose officering and expense would certainly arouse plentiful comment and partisan debate, created precisely the sort of attention the Polk administration wanted to avoid. As in the years between 1815 and 1818 along the Florida border, Gaines's sense of professional responsibility for national security overwhelmed his sense of professional subordination and accountability to civilian authority. Ironically, this occurred as much because of Gaines's lack of trust in the professional standing army, led by his enemy Scott, to guarantee national security as because of his expansionism. Any other army general would have seen a volunteer mobilization as a last resort, because of volunteers' expense and poor discipline, and because senior commanders wanted to ensure that the officer corps maintained a monopoly over the direction of American military force. Gaines was the exception that proves the rule.

Dragoons meet Comanches, 1834. From Catlin, *The North American Indians*

No hostilities had actually occurred when Gaines called for volunteers. The general pridefully and "carelessly submit[ted]" to "the reprimands with which you have honored me," proclaiming that he did not "wish to have the place of any general or other officer . . . I . . . was born at a time, and reared among men who had not learned the art of marching to distinction by trampling under foot the claims of their dearest friends or brother soldiers." (Gaines and Taylor were old friends.) The court of inquiry found that Gaines had exceeded his authority but recommended leniency because of his long service and patriotism, so Polk put an end to the problem by ordering Gaines to command the Eastern Division in New York, noting in his diary that this would "put it out of his power to further embarrass the Government." Gaines later shot back by publishing a private letter from Taylor explaining that commander's decision to make an armistice following the Battle of Monterrey, after Polk had reprimanded Taylor for doing so. The old general continued to seek permission to command an expedition to Mexico City but was ignored. He resumed formal command of the Western Department in December 1848, after Taylor's election to the presidency, and died of cholera the following June after fifty years of distinguished if controversial service, having provided ample evidence of the paradoxes of professional subordination to civilian control. The first volunteer units did not arrive on the Rio Grande until several days after the initial battles at Palo Alto and Resaca de la Palma.[44]

Zachary Taylor, calm and commanding. (Courtesy Library of Congress, LC-USZ62-71730)

12
MANIFEST DESTINY MEETS MILITARY PROFESSIONALISM
The Army Faces Britain and Mexico, 1844–1846

Consciousness of British power led professional soldiers to cite Britain and Oregon far more often than they did Mexico and Texas throughout the half decade before the outbreak of the Mexican War. The reason for this attention was simple: the consensus among most career officers was that Mexico would cave in without a fight, while Oregon seemed a much chancier game in the face of British determination and the power of the Royal Navy. Few professional soldiers left evidence that they shared the faith of civilian expansionists (or the fears of some Canadian officials) that American economic power could influence or coerce a Britain weakened by the social ills of industrialization. British power made that nation more likely to resist American expansion, a probability that must have seemed all the greater to men predisposed by experience (the War of 1812) and ethnicity to see fellow Anglo-Saxons as their most potent antagonists. Hence, writing only a month before the Battle of Palo Alto, Lieutenant William Barry told Captain James Duncan of the Army of Occupation, "I have no idea that you will burn a cartridge [in Texas]—you may possibly see the enemy, but I fancy no more." Yet Barry warned his friend that "54 40 won't go down" in Britain, asking whether Duncan thought "we are any nearer Oregon now, or [are] likely to be, than a year ago."[1]

Belligerence and Anglophobia were much more common among younger, less experienced junior officers and Military Academy cadets, who were impatient for promotion and frustrated by public criticism of the army during the early 1840s, than among more established senior commanders like those on the Canadian border during the Patriot and Maine crises. Nevertheless, several soldiers expressed remarkably hostile sentiments that illustrate the survival of Anglophobia in the career officer corps, particularly when professional interests were at stake. Two years before Barry's letter, Lieutenant Henry Hunt wrote to Duncan that "we are getting into a fever here about the Oregon question. I hope it may lead to a war that will drive the d[amne]d inveterate mercenaries from our continent. I . . . hope that once engaged it may be continued . . . until England loses not only Oregon but the Canadas." As statements like these suggest, officers were politically divided over the desirability of annexing Oregon, particularly to the 54° 40 latitude line, much as they were divided over war with Mexico or had been divided over the French claims issue a decade before, but they expressed these opinions, like their party affiliations, in private. Barry was a Whig; soldiers like Duncan, who was inclined toward the Democratic Party, were much less skeptical of the prospects and desirability of expansion against either Great Britain or Mexico. (Duncan was also commander of a horse artillery battery and could look forward to testing himself and earning laurels in battle, while Barry was a commissary officer.) Yet Whiggishness and belligerence were sometimes united, usually in the pursuit of promotion. Professionally minded Lieutenant Henry Turner, Stephen W. Kearny's adjutant, considered Polk's election "a disappointment to all [the] *intelligent* people of the country" but proved eager once war began. The conflict fulfilled Turner's expectations: he was promoted to captain during the expansion of 1846 and earned a brevet promotion to major for battlefield gallantry in California.[2]

Yet even Anglophobic junior officers displayed comparatively little of the ardent republican internationalism of their early national predecessors and contemporary civilian expansionists. More significant was the prospect of "early" promotion and the desire for the societal approval, embodied in martial glory, denied them in the long Seminole conflict. Awareness of British power also shaped soldiers' views in ways distinct from those of more sanguine civilians. The Anglophobia common among many company-grade officers had militarily rational roots produced by half a decade of tension with the most powerful nation in the world. Yet however belligerent their language, boisterous proclamations of European weakness (like those made by civilian expansionists) remained much less common among military observers than fears of British aggressiveness and power. This cautious professional perspective helps account for the lack of strong ideological republicanism or deep emotional Anglophobia in the officer corps as a whole, for most soldiers appear to have seen the world as a competitive system in which aristocratic, monarchical Britain was only one potential opponent, though by far the strongest and most dangerous.

Regardless of the crisis in question, there were positive as well as negative reasons for these bellicose assessments of Anglo-American relations. Professional soldiers considered Britain both a more dangerous and a more "worthy" opponent than Mexico; most expected Mexico to back down, whereas Britain was the world's greatest power and had a long track record of aggression and victory, in North America and elsewhere. Many junior and some field-grade officers resented or were jealous of British power and hoped to confound it in combat, while others thought that war with Britain was inevitable because of commercial rivalry. The very ethnic and cultural familiarity of Britain made many soldiers more eager to win the societal sanction of glory by defeating fellow Anglo-Saxons; some longed to avenge the defeats of the War of 1812 or to regain the public esteem and internal cohesiveness they believed that conflict's victories had brought to the army. Individual, professional, and national interest and honor could all furnish closely entwined reasons for career soldiers to favor war, but the republicanism, whether anxious or optimistic, commonly espoused by civilian expansionists was virtually invisible in their ruminations.

The Anglophilia common among experienced soldiers survived the Oregon dispute, as it had those of the late 1830s. In the spring of 1845 Captain W. W. S. Bliss, a twelve-year veteran whose uncle had been wounded at Lundy's Lane, related his pleasure that "the Oregon question does not excite as much angry remark as at first." (Bliss would soon become adjutant general and de facto chief of staff for Zachary Taylor.) One of his professional mentors agreed: a year later Sylvanus Thayer proclaimed himself "happy to find the Oregon question settled" when he returned from touring Europe. Veterans of the War of 1812, so often wounded by British steel, felt a respect for their former adversaries and a kinship born of mutual service in the name of international law and order during the Patriot War.[3] The best examples of this fellow feeling appeared during the early 1840s in a series of anniversaries organized by civilians along the northern border to heal recent wounds by commemorating events from the War of 1812. In the summer of 1843 a ceremony at Plattsburgh dedicated a group of monuments over the graves of British and American officers who had been killed at the battle there in September 1814. Former colonel John McNeil, distinguished commander of the Eleventh Infantry Regiment at Chippewa and Lundy's Lane (battles in which he won brevet promotions to lieutenant colonel and colonel and received a wound that lamed him for life), introduced General Wool. As a young major, the proud brigadier had commanded American soldiers during the Battle of Plattsburgh and won a brevet to lieutenant colonel; he dedicated a monument to a British colonel who had "gallantly" fallen at the head of his men while invading the United States, perhaps within Wool's sight.

These officers spanned the political spectrum. The Whig William Worth—severely wounded at Lundy's Lane along with McNeil, Jacob Brown, Henry Leavenworth, Thomas Jesup (three times), Hugh Brady, and Winfield Scott (whom Worth had served as aide-de-camp that blood-stained evening)—had initiated this process of reconciliation by ordering the British colonel's remains transferred from an unmarked grave several years before. (The curious reader should note that these *seven* future army leaders were *all* wounded at Lundy's Lane.) McNeil, a Jacksonian and federal surveyor of the Port of Boston since his resignation from the command of the First Infantry in 1830, proclaimed it "a pleasing spectacle to see the living brave doing honor to the memory of the illustrious dead." Wool, a Democrat at odds with the Jacksonians since his command in the Cherokee country, responded that "the duty assigned me . . . is no less gratifying . . . than it is honorable," declaring that the monument would "furnish themes of praise to the end of time." These veterans had little need, either psychologically or as a basis for national or professional identity, for the national chauvinism of the sort that led to belligerent Anglophobia, or that encouraged Anglo-Saxon racialism before the outbreak of war with Mexico. (Paradoxically, however, the most Whiggish of the three, Worth, was a racialist advocate of Manifest Destiny toward Latin America.) Their nationalism was founded on their professional allegiances and socialization in service to the nation as embodied in the national state, rather than aggressive racial romanticism or international antagonism.[4]

These friendly, if not quite pacific, tendencies notwithstanding, British strength and the contingencies of the international situation made rumors of war with Britain a much more common topic in soldiers' letters during the early and mid-1840s than those concerning Mexico. As late as the beginning of 1846, company-grade officers entering their thirties rested their hopes for expansion of the army, and the consequent promotions, primarily on the Oregon dispute. (Unfortunately for them, the regiment of mounted riflemen organized to secure the new territory was officered primarily by western Democrats commissioned directly from civilian life.) Yet on the whole, soldiers' expectations regarding Britain, and the possibility of war in general, remained more defensive than offensive. As late as January 1846, Winfield Scott was urging defensive preparations to guard the coastline against British attack, lamenting that Mobile and the Potomac were completely ungarrisoned, while the fortifications at Baltimore, Philadelphia, Charleston, and New Orleans averaged less than a hundred soldiers apiece. At West Point, the cadets of the Dialectic Society debated the rather abstract topic of whether the United States should intervene to protect American republics against European interference, not the advisability of imminent territorial expansion and war. (Nor did that debate leave much of a mark: the cadet who reported it left no comment on the countries or events in question, or on the arguments and conclusions.)[5]

British methods and actions were closely scrutinized by commanders who anticipated hostilities with Mexico. The attention they gave to British experience and example illustrates the continuing links between offensive and defensive motives among American military officers, government policy, and public opinion. American expansionists objected to British efforts to prevent the annexation of Texas and California, even as they envied or admired Britain's skill and success at empire building, though they certainly would have rejected any assertions of moral equivalence. Indeed, American professional soldiers sometimes seemed jealous of Britain's imperial prowess, leading to some morally dubious conclusions at odds with the proclaimed values of their nation: Lieutenant Robert Allen asserted that "we can afford to take all of Oregon and California, and still not be as well versed as John Bull in the game of theft." Similarly, engineer lieutenant P. G. T. Beauregard believed that "if our government would only adopt the British policy 'to conquer by spreading the brand of discord amongst our enemies' . . . in a very short time [they] would be very anxious to have Mexico itself annexed to our 'Glorious Republic.'"[6]

Once the war began, most commanders expected it to end quickly unless Mexico received foreign support. Several junior officers mentioned the possibility of foreign intervention; like civilian policy makers, they expected any aid for Mexico to come from Britain. In the fall of 1844, Lieutenant William Tecumseh Sherman reported rumors that England was supplying Mexico with arms to retake Texas, and the following summer he opined, "I have no doubt that there is some underhanded work between the British government and that of Mexico to secure the independence of Texas, provided she will abolish slavery." Most important, England's international power and influence led topographical engineer George Meade and his fellow captain Ephraim Kirby Smith (of the Fifth Infantry) to recognize that the solutions to the Oregon and Texas disputes were interdependent. The United States would probably not be able to fight Britain and Mexico at the same time, and when the Oregon dispute was settled, Britain effectively gave the United States a green light to pressure Mexico. Unlike some civilian expansionists, few professional soldiers were unrealistic enough about the balance of power to expect to force Britain's hand by a demonstration of military strength against Mexico.[7]

APATHY AND SUBORDINATION: ATTITUDES TOWARD THE OCCUPATION OF TEXAS AND WAR WITH MEXICO

The army's most obvious mission, the one that gave its officers their strongest sense of professional identity, was the prospect of wartime command, but it is remarkable how little eagerness for, or even interest in, war and territorial expansion is expressed in the letters and diaries of the company-grade officers stationed along the Mexican border in 1845 and 1846. Indeed, such quietude stands in sharp contrast to the belief almost universally expressed by historians that (in William Skelton's words) "the officer corps greeted the outbreak of fighting in 1846 with an enthusiasm bordering on mania." The ten-month interlude between annexation and the onset of hostilities gave military commanders plenty of time to reflect on the probable consequences of war, but they wrote surprisingly little about their expectations of battle and its aftermath; nor did they give much attention to more technical professional subjects like the strength, organization, and capabilities of the Mexican army. Once they arrived in Texas, most regulars mentioned the Army of Occupation's intensified regimen of training and drills only briefly and soon came to find them boring—"the dull routine of a life of military instruction," to quote one lieutenant. Most of their letters and diary entries are descriptions of camp life and the flora, fauna, and climate of Texas, not unlike those left by civilian Americans. Much as in Florida during the Seminole War, their most prominent concerns—sources of dissatisfaction rather than belligerence—seem to have been personal health and separation from wives and families back east. Nevertheless, even after taking family and health considerations into account, the general quietude of military commanders concerning the highly charged questions of annexation and war, so full of import for their futures, is nothing short of amazing, unless we connect their reactions to the imperatives of employment by the nation-state and the desire to maintain orderly international relations conducive to direction by its officers.[8]

This inattention was certainly not new. The army's professional periodicals mirrored this apparent lack of interest in the broad issues of war and peace: aside from reprinted reports to Congress by general officers and staff bureau chiefs, I found only a single article by an officer published in the army's professional journals that contains any sort of broad philosophical analysis of American foreign policy. Like an article by engineer major William Chase—the only other public statement of this sort by an officer below general grade that I could find—this soldier professed a policy of peace and nonintervention while warning of the necessity of preparation for war, standard yet abstract themes in the official reports and correspondence of senior officers throughout this era. The corollary to this lack of assertiveness was a lack of explicit attention to military planning for specific contingencies. Official reports said little about the possibility of war with Mexico, much less its ramifications for the army, and the army performed nothing even remotely akin to a detailed "threat assessment" regarding Mexico until early in 1846, when commanding general Winfield Scott submitted several strategic plans to the War Department. Until then, the movements of the Armies of Observation and Occupation were essentially those of frontier diplomacy writ large.[9]

By 1844 the *Army and Navy Chronicle*, which had survived the depression of the late 1830s, had shut down for lack of circulation, leaving the officer corps without a forum for public debate on professional issues. This fact cannot be dismissed as an anomaly, because it illustrates the officer corps' failure to sustain a professional journal even as the nation moved toward a conventional war and the army moved toward expansion, precisely the time one would expect military commanders to take an increased interest in their profession and its prospects. Nor did Henry Halleck's 1846 *Elements of the Art and Science of War*, which contained extensive discussions about international relations and has been celebrated by historians as the first general treatise on warfare by an American, fill this gap. A prescriptive work intended to alert the public to the need for preparedness and thereby improve the army's status and appropriations, it dealt in abstractions, with a concrete focus on fixed fortifications rather than actual diplomatic crises or military contingencies facing the nation. In the very broadest sense, the consensus of historians that "the great majority of officers . . . supported the expansionist surge" is probably correct at the level of the unspoken assumptions conditioned by officers' nationalism and ethnocentrism. In other words, few national soldiers actually objected to the growth of American wealth and power—and probably the size of the army and opportunities for promotion—represented by the acquisition of additional territory. To do so would have required a countercultural critical sensibility rare among any privileged elite. Yet military commanders supported expansion quietly, without ideological fervor and with proper professional respect for civilian control over the military, rather than pressuring the administration, through writing or action, to move more quickly or aggressively. In contrast to the corps' overt support for the conquest of Spanish Florida before 1820, the regulars of the 1840s made no effort to initiate action independent of the civil government.

Nor did Taylor or other Whigs in the officer corps, who opposed the annexation of Texas and war with Mexico, seek to undermine the administration's expansionist policies, despite Polk's partisan paranoia. In comparison with other educated Americans working in the public sphere, few military commanders put the slogans of Manifest Destiny and Young America in their writings, be they official, anonymous but public, or private missives to friends and family. Insofar as this silence reflected an objective, politically neutral dedication to national service and constitutional government, it was a laudable example of professional accountability, although the officer corps can certainly be judged less than fully responsible in its apparent inattention to the professional expertise that would enable it to do its job once policy had been decided.[10] We find a similarly mixed picture of ambitious enthusiasm and responsible disinterestedness when examining the specific responses of soldiers stationed in Texas in 1845 and 1846. Initially, many officers looked forward to deploying to Texas in the hope of distinguishing themselves in combat. Most expected a rapid American victory in any conflict that might occur, but their overwhelming consensus, much like Polk's expectation and American public opinion more generally, was that Mexico would back down and nothing would happen. In fact, despite their desire for glory and promotion, these career soldiers were far from united on the desirability of annexation and war. Many thought territorial expansion a national good, and a majority probably hoped for an increase in the army's size, which would mean more command slots and promotions; but a substantial minority expressed opposition to annexation and expansion, whether from principle or personal inconvenience.

Though few officers resigned during the occupation of Texas, resignation patterns were not fundamentally different from those during the Seminole War in the preceding decade: resignations were tendered almost entirely for reasons of personal health and welfare. Indeed, most of the resignations in 1845 and 1846 (about 30 out of more than 540 regimental officers—a rate of less than 6 percent over the two years combined) were due to the former rather than the latter; unlike in 1836, few officers resigned in 1845 or 1846 because they had been ordered to Texas from cushy urban posts. (The creation of separate staff branches in 1838, and the consequent decline in detached service by regimental officers, certainly contributed to this change.) Perhaps self-interest should have logically predisposed soldiers to hope for war, but their response to the possibility of war was far from monolithic: as a group, they were certainly national and ethnic chauvinists, but they did not express expansionist sentiments very ardently, articulately, or often. The principal determinants of their reactions to deployment in Texas were personal considerations of health, family, and career (roughly in that order of precedence), not partisan or ideological beliefs. Uncertainty rather than enthusiasm dominated their emotions, for distant, humid, minimally populated South Texas was an unattractive post unless there was a war to be fought. Nevertheless, despite an economy recovered from the depression that had put an end to the resignation crisis of 1835–1837, few officers resigned to pursue civilian economic opportunities, and it appears that none did so because of moral qualms, a strong indication of their dedication to national service and military careers.

There are a number of explanations for this surprising lassitude in the face of what William Worth described as the first opportunity in thirty years to seriously practice his profession. Practically speaking, the slow, uncertain timing of the army's advance through Texas was the most concrete factor that inhibited military enthusiasm for annexation and war. The army was not actually directed to advance to the Rio Grande until mid-January 1846. The order arrived February 4, but delays caused by heavy rains and inadequate naval and logistical support kept the army in Corpus Christi until March 6, and it did not arrive opposite Matamoros—only a hundred miles to the south—until March 28.[11] Even then, nearly six weeks of tension passed before the Battle of Palo Alto. Few regulars actually expected war until that final month; they assumed that at some point Mexico would cave in to American demands, so they waited, impatient but impotent, for news of diplomatic or military movement. The company-grade officers of the Army of Occupation were stuck waiting, month after month, in the sand, as illness began to spread through camp, with neither the glory and promotion of combat nor the comforts of familiar posts and family. Professional camaraderie had its limits, and social isolation went unrelieved by the presence of wives or kin, so perhaps it was only natural that most officers' primary concern became the effect deployment would have on their family lives.

Career soldiers also limited their discussion of war and its potentialities because of their institutional position as employees of the national government, an important professional consideration that was not dependent on the specific circumstances of their service in Texas. The growth of accountability to civilian authority was both the most successful and the most important dimension of the army's professional development during the Jacksonian era. By the mid-1830s, chastened by frontier frustrations and the overbearing Jackson administration, most veterans had come to believe that they should avoid active involvement in partisan politics, and the officer corps' disinterested reaction to the vigorous public debates surrounding the annexation of Texas illustrates the pervasiveness of this mind-set a decade later. Junior officers—a growing number of whom commented on elections and expressed partisan preferences as the Second Party System developed—often mentioned the possibility of annexation in a casual way, as simply another rumor in the world of public affairs. Some of this indifference was probably rooted in the education professional soldiers received at the Military Academy, which stressed engineering and mathematics almost to the exclusion of government and the liberal arts, but officers had enough political connections, and left enough private commentary on politics and public policy questions, to lead historians to expect a more in-depth analysis of issues that affected them so directly, like war and peace.

Many regulars possessed Whig loyalties and affinities, and some of them privately opposed the Polk administration's policy of expansion and annexation, but few espoused such views in writing, much less in public. This dynamic began at the top: in September 1845 topographical engineer captain George Meade reported a widespread rumor that "General Taylor . . . is a staunch Whig, and opposed *in toto* to the Texas annexation, and therefore does not enter heart and soul into his present duties. . . . He is said to be very tired of this country, and the duty assigned to him, and is supposed will return [to the East] on the arrival of General Worth." Yet Meade was careful to warn his wife that "all this . . . is mere rumor and is *entre nous*." Lieutenant Colonel Ethan Allen Hitchcock, a confidant of Taylor's who opposed annexation on moral grounds, initially suspected that the general wanted a fight in order to make himself famous. Hitchcock had suggested the same of William Worth in Florida (where Worth's success won him a brevet to brigadier general) and demonstrated similar contradictions in his own actions. The Vermonter commanded a regiment in the Army of Occupation before securing sick leave a month before the first battles, and he returned to the theater of operations at the end of 1846 with enough vigor to win two brevet promotions for battlefield gallantry while serving as Winfield Scott's inspector general during the advance on Mexico City. Indeed, virtually the only public objection to the war's morality by an army officer came from an engineer who never served in Mexico; in the August 1846 edition of the *American Whig Review*, Lieutenant Edward Hunt, a year out of West Point, labeled the conflict "a war of sheer aggression." Yet he avowed subordination to civilian control, defending the army from critics of the conflict by portraying the standing force as a neutral instrument of national policy.[12]

Decades later, portraying himself as "bitterly opposed" to the war—a position that is not much in evidence in his letters from Texas, though he was clearly not an avid expansionist—Ulysses Grant opined that "generally the officers of the army were indifferent" to the question of annexation. Unlike the civilian editors and politicians studied by historian Thomas Hietala, army officers junior and senior wrote virtually nothing about the costs or benefits of annexation and war for the United States as a whole. Few spoke of the war as a means of national unification or as a moral good in itself, as several had done regarding a possible war with Britain at the beginning of the decade; nor did they discuss the impact of imperialism and colonialism on American society and its institutions. Though perhaps morally irresponsible, this quiescence also manifested the reality—reflective of their growing sense of professional accountability and subordination to the nation-state that employed them, to which they had sworn an oath—that they would not refuse to serve in the execution of an expansionist policy many personally doubted.[13]

The corps' self-image as a disinterested, nonpartisan group dedicated to national goals led to a similar silence—again in significant contrast to the outspokenness of men of affairs in the civilian world—on the potential for sectional gain or conflict inherent in annexation. There were exceptions to this quietude, often couched in tones of irony or distaste, usually among Whiggish soldiers who feared the divisive impact of sectional quarrels over expansion. Thus, Captain William C. DeHart, a socially well-connected officer who had served for eight years as Winfield Scott's aide-de-camp, observed that southern Democrats in Congress were much less enthusiastic over Oregon than Texas, remarking derisively that "politicians are like eels, slimy enough to slip by any thing, or through any place." This was not simply antipolitical military authoritarianism; it was a realistic appreciation of the sectional politics of expansion, the reality that the army was subject and subordinate to representatives elected by constituencies with widely differing views, which produced frustrating uncertainty for the nation's military commanders throughout the era explored in this book.[14]

Lieutenant William Tecumseh Sherman of the Third Artillery, whose foster father (and future father-in-law) was a prominent Ohio politician, showed an awareness, however inaccurate, of the domestic political implications of war that was unusual in the correspondence of company officers. In September 1844 the young lieutenant wrote to his future wife that "we are never to have a war that costs money. Our government talks and bullies a good deal, but when they talk of money they are frightened [and w]ithout it war cannot be carried on." Despite his personal Whiggishness, Sherman dismissed abolitionist fears that annexation was a project to extend slavery and opined that Texas would become a free state, though his personal enthusiasm for "so fortunate a war" seems to have had little to do with extending "the Area of Freedom." (It is not clear whether the Whig Sherman was using Andrew Jackson's slogan ironically.) Indeed, the sometimes naïve lieutenant "much doubted" that Texas "will be received into our confederacy if she is impudent [enough] to advance her frontier to the Rio Grande," presumably because he expected the Whigs to vote it down. Aside from Sherman, few professional soldiers commented on slavery as an issue in the annexation crisis or shared the hopes proclaimed by civilian expansionists that Texas would serve as a racial safety valve and an alternative to emancipation. Lieutenant Napoleon Tecumseh Dana (Seventh Infantry Regiment) and Captain Philip Barbour (Third Infantry) noted that several officers' slaves had fled across the Rio Grande to freedom, and Barbour felt that officers would have to resort to white servants as a result, but they viewed these losses as personal rather than political events. Lieutenant William S. Henry (Third Infantry Regiment), who had long supported Texan aspirations, referred briefly to the extension of the "'area of freedom'" and "'Liberty and Union, now and forever, one and inseparable,'" when the American flag was raised on the banks of the Rio Grande, but he did not comment on the meaning of these potent Jacksonian tropes.[15]

Much of this inarticulateness can be attributed to the officer corps' nascent professional ethic, which stressed national service in the politically and ideologically neutral form of "duty" rather than "mission." Recent historians have reenvisioned the impetus for Manifest Destiny in fears for the survival of the Jeffersonian social order amidst the growing urbanization and industrialization of the Market Revolution. Yet few American professional soldiers expressed social or economic republicanism; their republicanism meant disinterested service, self-sacrifice, and antipartisanship—Whiggish tropes more than Jacksonian ones, which suited their sense of nationalism and complemented their desire for career security, regardless of electoral change. In other words, most career military officers aspired to a surprisingly objective professional accountability to the nation-state rather than a subjective responsibility rooted in emotional or ideological loyalty to the ideals of agrarian republicanism, "free institutions" and Jacksonian democracy, or the romanticized ethnocultural community of the Anglo-Saxon race.[16]

As William Skelton has noted, their concept of political engagement can perhaps best be encapsulated in the phrase "army politics," implying not complete political passivity, isolation, or alienation, nor simple self-interestedness, but public nonpartisanship combined with a focus on the institutional bureaucratic politics of promotions, postings, and the allocation of resources and power among different branches of the service. Their demands on civilian society were usually limited to autonomy in the direction of military operations, increases in compensation, limitations on entry into the officer corps by maintaining the requirement for specialized education and professional socialization at West Point, hope for faster promotions through expansion of the army, and longing for public recognition and acclaim. Officers left analyses of the war's costs and benefits to civilian society to the growing political and editorial professions, which thrived on divisions in the national community that the officer corps hoped to minimize. As Skelton cogently observes, career soldiers were "in the political world but not of that world."[17]

CLASS, NOT RACE OR RELIGION: PREWAR ATTITUDES TOWARD MEXICO AND MEXICANS

Service along the Texas border during the 1820s and 1830s seems to have engendered few strong sentiments among the officers who led the army into the new state. Most regular officers understood that the American annexation of Texas was the principal cause of Mexican anger and the war, and many (perhaps the majority) recognized that the United States was ultimately the aggressor, but the conclusions they drew from this judgment depended primarily on self-interest, both personal and national. For West Point cadet James Wall Schureman, annexation was an opportunity that the nation should have taken advantage of sooner: "We were in hopes for some time that Texas would be annexed to the Union, in which case a [war] with Mexico would have followed. . . . Our swords are getting rusty in their scabbards, and we want something to do to brighten them," he wrote to his sister in 1844. The defeat of that year's annexation bill meant that "the Oregon question is for the present our only chance." A different form of self-interest led cadet William Dutton to hope that Texas would choose independence instead of annexation: "I presume that their climate will be the death of many [soldiers] . . . if they should be stationed there."[18]

Like most officers, the more experienced George Meade expected that the United States would wait for Mexico to initiate hostilities, but he felt that "we [meaning the United States] would like nothing better than some excuse to pounce upon them." Lieutenant Robert Allen accepted American responsibility for the confrontation without real qualms or anxiety because, like most officers, he expected Mexico to back down when confronted by manifestly superior American power: "Mexico may bluster and we may bully but there will be no fight. We have stolen Texas—no doubt of that." The desire for war and doubts that it would occur were both echoed in cadet Samuel Raymond's letter to his sister Mary, which succinctly sums up the average professional soldier's attitude toward the career opportunities presented by crisis: "Since the treaty for the annexation . . . is signed we may have a little brush but no great things need be expected . . . in case there should be[,] I should like to be . . . one who would go."[19]

Young officers wanted a quick taste of martial elation before they returned to dull peacetime routine and the frustrations of frontier constabulary duty. Frustrated soldiers blamed Mexican intransigence for the interminable negotiations that kept them "at a dead standstill, doing nothing, which we could be doing as well anywhere else." Philip Barbour wrote impatiently, "There will not be a hostile gun fired, but we shall have to drag through a hot and tedious summer here without our families, infinitely worse than all the horrors of war. It is nonsense for our government to temporize any longer with . . . Mexico." This personal anxiety spurred officers' eagerness to seek battle as soon as Congress authorized it. Napoleon Dana's words reflected the thoughts of many soldiers irritated by the inactivity: "Our government cannot in honor hold out the olive branch to Mexico when she is making so many brags and trying to borrow money to fight us. . . . If Mexico, in her ignorance, is not overawed . . . we must wait until Congress . . . can declare war . . . if [Mexico's] answer is not satisfactory, she will soon be driven to terms. . . . Then and not until then can we be happy. All depends on treacherous Mexico."[20]

It was much less troubling for officers to blame the Mexican government than the American one that employed the army. Experienced commanders had little need of Anglophobia or Anglo-Saxon racialism either as a rationale for doing their duty against Britons or Mexicans or as a basis for national identity, because their nationalism was founded on existing professional socialization and allegiances. Much as on the Canadian frontier, officers' conscious attitudes toward their likely adversaries prior to the outbreak of war with Mexico were conditioned primarily by class sensibilities rather than race, religion, or ethnicity. Growing exposure to the Mexican peasantry and their mestizo culture aroused increasingly racist attitudes among veterans once the war began, but they showed relatively little antagonism, racialist or otherwise, or even curiosity toward Mexico and its inhabitants beforehand. Nor did they demonstrate very much interest in Mexico's military capabilities, foreign policy and international affairs, the issues involved in war, or their own professional preparation. Aside from William Worth, I have found only one statement explicitly supporting the view that the officer corps "had come to accept the idea of a distinct Anglo-Saxon race," as described by historian Reginald Horsman. This statement was in a letter from Lieutenant Richard Stoddard Ewell, a Virginian who applied such distinctions to every ethnic and religious group he encountered: writing to his sister several years before the war, Ewell briefly compared the "ignorant French & Spanish" with "the more enlightened Anglo-Saxon race." Nor did the issue of whether the United States could or should absorb large nonwhite populations appear in officers' papers before the war. In sum, while the career professional soldiers of the officer corps shared much of the ethnic chauvinism of other mid-nineteenth-century Americans, they can hardly be considered articulate racialists eager to advance the cause of Anglo-Saxon civilization and progress through Manifest Destiny.[21]

This moderation was entirely in keeping with the officer corps' lack of ideological fervor and introspection in other realms. Unlike many civilian Americans in the era of the Second Great Awakening, few officers expressed strong religious sentiments or antagonisms. While some expressed disdain for Catholicism, others admired the beauty and hierarchy of its liturgy, and few commented at any length on Catholicism as a dimension of Mexican society and culture before the war began. William Skelton and Edward M. Coffman have both observed that Protestants got along well with the genteel Catholics in the officer corps (about 10 to 15 percent of its total), and Coffman has suggested that "the army took a tolerant attitude toward Catholics" in the ranks. Thus, nativism in the officer corps seems to have been primarily a matter of class and ethnicity, especially as these characteristics were associated with the army's growing percentage of foreign-born enlisted men—an enduring source of complaint from many commanders—rather than religion per se. While some authors have assailed the army and its officers as fundamentally nativist, the premier historian of the army's enlisted soldiers, Dale Steinhauer, does not discuss nativism or anti-Catholicism at any length.[22]

The Mexicans that officers came in contact with before the war were usually of a higher social class and a more European ethnic background than the Mexican population as a whole, and officers applied their social concepts of gentility and respectability to Tejanos and Anglos alike. They often found the latter wanting. Soldiers like Lieutenant John Porter Hatch considered the Mexicans of Corpus Christi "much the most respectable portion of the inhabitants," in sharp contrast to the Anglo-Texans, who were mostly smugglers or camp followers of one form or another—"rascals," in Napoleon Dana's words, "the best of [whom] looked as if they could steal sheep." Dana was referring specifically to the former secretary of war. A year before, Lieutenant Benjamin Alvord had labeled Sam Houston—a lieutenant himself a quarter century before—"a rowdy" whose reelection as Texan president was "enough to damn the Republic in the eyes of the decent portion" of the American people. Other regulars commented favorably on Mexican officers and their treatment of American prisoners of war, and American officers' views of Mexican women were usually free of egregious racism, however sexually motivated or sexist. Class blinders and a lack of direct contact prevented commanders from commenting at any length about the Mexican peasantry before the war, although they sometimes praised opposing troops for their precision in drill—a perspective not unlike their view of American enlisted men, whom they praised principally for discipline and loyalty rather than the more independent qualities they expected from officers and gentlemen.[23]

From the officer corps' perspective, the most important fact about the Mexicans was that they were not Indians (or they were not viewed as such before the war). The war would be primarily conventional, and professional soldiers impatient for glory could hope that their victories would be respected and acknowledged by the American people, unlike those in the recent Seminole War. In this sense, it was professionally counterproductive for officers to emphasize the mestizo quality of the Mexican population. Thus, although encountering the disorder of an impoverished and politically corrupt Mexico spurred greater racialization in officers' attitudes, they initially identified Mexican officers—their professional counterparts and opponents, dressed in Napoleonic uniforms much like their own—as gentlemen of European blood, however tainted by the cruelty most Anglo-Americans associated with Spanish descent. Army officers could be counted on to stress the character of Mexican officers rather than enlisted men, because the officers led and commanded the troops. Whatever the officers' true feelings toward Mexicans, particularly toward the mestizo majority, they had little incentive to portray their adversaries as degraded barbarians, because they knew from the Seminole War that no glory could be won defeating enemies the public considered savages.

Regardless of the diplomatic situation, professional soldiers took it for granted that Mexico was no match for the United States, and this confidence led most of them to assume that war was unlikely. As early as August 1843, Winfield Scott warned the adjutant general that "we are but in the beginning of Texas rumours & fancies. . . . In less than a month we shall have fresh rumours from that quarter requiring the remainder of our army . . . but I am absolutely certain that either Genl. T[aylor] or W[orth], at the head of 2,000 men would be an overmatch for any Mexican army that can pass the Rio Bravo in the next 6 or 12 months. . . . I am equally confident that there will be no land battle in that period . . . unless England should aid Mexico." This confidence discouraged detailed war planning; once victory in northern Mexico failed to bring peace, the American course of action was pretty plain, and the route to Mexico City was pretty obvious. Prior to the war Scott was worried about the health of American troops stationed in Texas or along its borders and implied that the force deployed there might be reduced by half, given the absence of military danger and the possibility of conflict with Britain over Oregon. In 1845 most officers expected the advance to the Rio Grande to go uncontested, and at first most regulars believed this intimidation would compel Mexico to submit to American dictates. "I do not think they can be so insane as to provoke a war by an act of hostilities," George Meade remarked. "There are many ridiculous reports . . . of our being cut to pieces by the Mexicans," Napoleon Dana wrote. "We will have no fight. This is almost a certainty. . . . We are too strong for her and are growing stronger and stronger every day. She cannot fight us. . . . She cannot raise the means."[24]

Few officers said much about the sources of their self-confidence, but one of Dana's letters to his wife contains an assessment of Mexican capabilities that is rare in both detail and acuity. In addition to the disparity in population, this infantry lieutenant listed American advantages in artillery, troop discipline and cohesion, and logistics and noted that Mexican reinforcements would have to cross the desert from Monterrey and would suffer devastating attrition, as indeed occurred in January and February 1847 during Santa Anna's advance on Buena Vista. Given these disparities, the lieutenant thought Mexico would surrender its claims to Texas for nothing more than the promise of protection from Indian attacks across the new border. Lieutenant Ulysses Grant, of the Fourth Infantry, went a good deal further in his optimism, contending that "the poorer and less ambitious and . . . most numerous class of Mexicans are much better pleased with our form of government than their own; in fact they would be willing to see us push our claims past the Rio Grande if we would promise not to molest them in their homes and possessions." Although Grant's assessment of Mexican nationalism proved inaccurate, there was significant *norteno* interest in annexation or status as an American protectorate. In his memoirs, Grant identified the distinction between the Mexican army and his own in terms that illustrate the values of specialization and accountability that American officers absorbed as they became more professionally expert and committed: "The Mexican army of that day was hardly an organization"; its defeat was due to the irresponsibility and "lack of experience among the[ir] officers . . . [who] simply quit" when the tide of battle turned against them.[25]

The disorder of failed states could pose as many problems (and perhaps much the same ones) as the indiscipline of nonstate actors. Political instability in Mexico accounted for much of the officer corps' assurance, but it also fostered uncertainty and discontent with the sluggish progress of negotiations. Like Grant, who mentioned the rebellion in Yucatan, William Tecumseh Sherman believed that Mexico "is unable to carry on war, her government is hardly secure, their provinces are rebelling." Other officers emphasized that instability in Mexico would lengthen their stay in Texas without producing a battle in which they might win glory or promotion. George Meade was upset that the "infernal revolution" led by General Mariano Paredes in December

1845 might derail negotiations and keep the army concentrated in Texas, far from its home stations. Lieutenant Dana felt the same way, and as he became more aggravated by the delay, he actually came to hope that Mexico could "quiet her internal disturbances and form a permanent government" before Congress met again so that affairs would "approach a crisis much more rapidly." But other aspiring soldiers were pleased with the Paredes coup because it seemed to augur peace. Cadet William Dutton attributed Mexico's refusal to yield to the personal ambition of Santa Anna, and in February 1846 he reported to his fiancée that "now that Santa Anna is shut up at Perote no one thinks of any difficulty."[26]

This recognition of Mexican political discord did not prevent American professional soldiers from feeling some anxiety over the exposed position of their small army. With each new advance, some officer would worry that "we certainly ought not with so small a force [to] be left here to face the whole Mexican nation," as Ephraim Kirby Smith put it on March 29. Upon their arrival at Corpus Christi the preceding fall, both Grant and Dana had wondered whether "we will . . . get a whipping" from the larger Mexican forces feared to be nearby, and a similar concern was shared by some of their counterparts outside Texas. Like Smith, George McClellan thought that "the Government has placed Genl Taylor in a very dangerous situation." McClellan, finishing his last year at West Point and often cited as an exemplar of the officer corps' war fever, doubted the steadiness of the army's foreign-born enlisted men and expected heavy casualties among the officers as a result. The future commander of the Army of the Potomac observed ambiguously that "if so many officers are killed the whole of our class will be ordered down there at once to supply the vacancies"; his less-illustrious classmate William Dutton remained completely pessimistic about the prospects for glory "in such a cause and in such a place." Dutton's romanticism was dedicated to his fiancée rather than Manifest Destiny; he graduated but was compelled to resign that November, apparently because of a life-threatening illness.[27]

The prospect of war also threatened to disrupt the orderly relations between officers and enlisted men built up in times of peace, and the attitudes of some officers toward the enlisted men under their command reflected this uncertainty. McClellan's pessimistic appraisal of the army's enlisted men was a compound of ethnic and class prejudice toward "these wretched Dutch and Irish immigrants" and concern over their lack of combat experience (which McClellan's genteel self-discipline would presumably overcome). His dour estimate was shared by Dutton, but officers actually serving in the Army of Occupation were more confident of their men's élan and contempt for the enemy. Indeed, Ephraim Kirby Smith noted the soldiers' "disappointment"

Camp of the Army of Occupation at Corpus Christi. Lithograph by Captain Daniel P. Whiting, in his *Army Portfolio* (1847)

when the Mexicans retreated from the Arroyo Colorado on March 20, while Dana boasted that "our men are anxious for the fray" and "in just the humor for the business." Desertion was a much more urgent concern than demoralization, but officers felt they had the problem under control. Nevertheless, enlisted men (like officers) talked with their Mexican counterparts and with women washing clothes across the narrow Rio Grande, and several soldiers were shot in the act of swimming to the other side. Dana reassured his wife that "the good men are highly incensed by it. The whole army are said to behave admirably. . . . Good men are always placed on the picket guard and show the deserters no mercy." The ardent lieutenant concluded that "the severity has put a stop to desertion."[28]

These fears of defeat and desertion were short-lived, however. Arriving opposite Matamoros in March, Captain Philip Norbourne Barbour, son of John Quincy Adams's secretary of war, noted that from "a military point of view General Taylor has committed a blunder . . . in coming here with so small a force." Nevertheless, Barbour remarked that "it is truly surprising to see with what indifference, not to say contempt, our Officers and men look upon the Mexican batteries frowning upon us. No one seems to think a disaster . . .

possible, and most of the Army are disappointed that General Taylor does not create a pretext for taking [Matamoros]." The previous November, Ephraim Kirby Smith had described the Comanche as "a much more formidable enemy than the Mexicans," while Lieutenant John Porter Hatch of the Third Infantry laughed at being outnumbered three to one in April. "We would not ask to fight a smaller number than this and I have not the slightest doubt that we would then thrash them so that they would never again dare look an American in the face," he boasted to his sister. Only a year out of the Military Academy, Hatch transferred to the Regiment of Mounted Rifles that July and was brevetted twice for gallantry on the road to Mexico City. He stuck with the army through the 1850s and the Civil War, earning brevets to brigadier general and permanent lineal rank as a colonel during a career that spanned more than four decades and included divisional command.[29]

OPPORTUNITIES AND DISTRACTIONS: THE PROFESSION GOES TO WAR

Few of the junior officers mentioned here had seen combat service, despite the close of the Second Seminole War only four years before. Combat command meant the chance to show one's courage and win public acclaim; given the era's romantic notions of warfare, it is not surprising that they looked forward to glory and promotion—commonly united in the form of honorary promotions for battlefield gallantry—rather than the deaths that would make such benefits possible. Camaraderie and the opportunity to command troops were also major inducements for professional soldiers to welcome the concentration of force brought on by the prospect of war; because many field-grade officers were past middle age, their incapacity for active service meant that younger men could command units larger than they would have been responsible for in peacetime. Indeed, less than a third of the prewar field-grade officers served with their regiments in Mexico, and in the artillery, only one of twelve did so, leading Congress to authorize a second major in each regiment so that younger men could gain promotion and hold rank befitting their responsibilities as battalion or de facto regimental commanders. Yet the system was not entirely dysfunctional: age aside, a number of regimental field-grade officers were detailed to senior staff positions in Washington, and a disproportionate number of these men remained in the United States to handle administrative and logistical duties. The captains who led battalions in Mexico were experienced professionals who quickly proved their ability to command in combat; their experienced lieutenants had no difficulty leading companies. And, although their rank and pay did not match their responsibilities, the army's system of promotion by seniority, without mandatory retirement, gave them a security unmatched in Jacksonian America. (In other words, they too could eventually look forward to going on permanent medical leave, in lieu of receiving a pension.)

Given routine illness, leaves of absence, temporary duty, and staff and other details, first lieutenants had often commanded companies in peacetime, and even more so during the Seminole War; captains had often commanded "battalions" of two, three, or four small companies when two of the three field-grade officers in their regiments were stuck commanding geographic departments or doing administrative or staff jobs. War with Mexico offered many senior lieutenants the chance to command full-strength (100-man) companies, and senior captains had the rare professional opportunity to command battalions of 400 to 600 men, or even full regiments of approximately a thousand. The Army of Occupation that finally advanced from Corpus Christi to the Rio Grande was approximately 3,500 strong, the largest single concentration of regular troops in one place for an extended period since the Revolutionary War. The influx of recruits forwarded from stateside depots led soldiers like Ephraim Kirby Smith to declare that "I shall have a pretty good command for a captain, and if there is anything to be done, I think I shall have a chance." Smith had been dismissed from the army for brutality toward enlisted men in 1829 but was recommissioned in 1831; he took command of an elite battalion of light infantry at Churubusco and Molino del Rey, where he was slain at the head of an assault.[30]

Examining life in the Army of Occupation gives us a final glimpse of cohesion and dissension in the army officer corps, suggesting that professionalization was still a work in progress in the spring of 1846. The opportunity for command and service with old friends initially encouraged the growth of camaraderie and regimental esprit de corps among the soldiers of the Army of Occupation. This cohesion was evident in a letter from John Porter Hatch to his sister Eliza: "I consider myself very fortunate in being sent here for it is very probable that I may not see so many regulars together in many years. Many old officers have never before seen so many troops at one time. . . . My regiment is one of the best in the service . . . and there is a great deal of regimental pride in it. There is a very good feeling among the officers [and] most of us mess together." Such esprit and cohesion were competitive as well as comradely: Napoleon Dana felt that his own regiment was "decidedly" superior to Hatch's. Regimental pride had direct consequences for officers' glory and promotion during the war, for proud units fight better. The effect could be a perverse one, however. In 1845 William Tecumseh Sherman was stationed in South Carolina with the Third Artillery Regiment. He thought of exchanging posts with an infantry officer in Louisiana before the move to Corpus Christi, but Sherman's loyalty to his unit and preference for the artillery as a combat arm disposed him against doing so. He ended up going to California by sea instead and gained nothing more from the war than a generic brevet for "meritorious service" while helping to administer the new territory on the Pacific. Dana was severely wounded at Cerro Gordo in 1847, for which he was brevetted to captain. Like Sherman and many of the other future notables mentioned here, Dana resigned in 1855 and reentered the army as a general during the Civil War.[31]

This crisis-induced cohesion was not universally felt, and it waned as months passed without combat during the autumn of 1845. While a fair number of officers actively sought duty in Texas, significant numbers tried to avoid it. Promotion-minded officers on the scene did not altogether mind this disruption of the army's command structure. In September 1845 Hatch asserted that "promotions from resignations are quite rapid," presumably in comparison to peacetime, when it usually took ten to fifteen years to rise to captain. The young lieutenant maintained that "it is a good thing to get rid of them if they can't stay away from their wives. . . . There are plenty of good men glad to fill their place." As noted above, Hatch's estimate of resignations was more perception than reality, but it helped ease his frustration with the interminable waiting. Still, the unmarried lieutenant hinted that he would not mind a transfer to Florida, because "I find myself already wishing we were not quite so much out of the world," so distant from the civil society of genteel women he had enjoyed before Texas. Even more characteristically, both Ulysses Grant and George Meade wrote constantly about securing leaves of absence to visit their loved ones, and both commented extensively on the efforts of other officers to do so.[32]

The concerns most commonly expressed by regular officers awaiting the war were highly parochial, centered around its probable impact on the officer corps, the army (which they usually identified with the officer corps), and, above all, their personal happiness and advancement. "A camp where there is no active service is a dull and stupid place," reported Meade. "It seems we are not even to have the consolation of a little glory, but are to remain here rusting in idleness, or rather in drilling and parading." (Meade later received a brevet promotion for gallantry at Monterrey.) At first officers volunteered eagerly for reconnaissance patrols or went on extended hunting trips, but these diversions ceased to provide much relief from boredom as the weather worsened and sickness began to spread. The stalemate between the United States and Mexico appeared interminable to soldiers caught in this aggravating situation. Between the intermittent negotiations and political turmoil in Mexico itself, their consensus was that they would probably end up sitting on the border for several years, exposed to conditions much less healthy or hospitable than they were used to, even in frontier garrisons (where many of their wives lived), without the compensations of public acclaim that actual combat would bring. This dismal prospect was the most compelling factor behind their constant attention to the weather, climate, and disease.[33]

Under the circumstances, the most urgent concern for most officers seems to have been separation from their loved ones, a natural source of uneasiness that was exacerbated by the long wait spent in uncertainty. George Meade and Napoleon Dana both considered it out of the question for wives to join the army's encampment, given the poor living conditions and lack of privacy there. (Indeed, under the circumstances, Dana found the presence of women in camp "very annoying," probably because of the jealousy and frustration he felt at being separated from his own family.) Most officers seem to have discouraged their wives from joining them, and based on their letters, it appears that only a handful (between two and four) actually did so. Indeed, the need for masculine cohesion amidst feminine scarcity apparently prevented some officers from taking comfort in campfire talk of home. "I suppose you know that, in a camp like this, where we are supposed to be awaiting active service, allusions to wives and children are considered in bad taste, and one who is always talking about his wife is an object of ridicule," Meade wrote to his own. Other soldiers were unable to restrain their obsession with domestic comforts: unmarried Lieutenant John J. Peck, of the Second Artillery, quipped that "we have so many married officers . . . who are crazy to get back to their families [that] their continued grumbling renders the rest of us nervous." Indeed, Zachary Taylor confirmed in a letter to his daughter that "one of the principal diseases now among the officers . . . is homesickness." The aging general (then sixty-one) typified the officer corps in this regard, as well as in his lack of enthusiasm for expansion: "All the pomp & parade of [the Army of Occupation is] lost on me; I now sigh for peace & quiet with my family around me."[34]

Even the most professional soldiers found it difficult to sustain their initial elation as the months dragged by, and restlessness bred demoralization, dissension, and talk of resignation. In January 1846 James Wall Schureman relayed the news that "the excitement of the contemplated campaign, the ardor for distinction, and all the soldier's incentives have one by one vanished and left them sad and gloomy. . . . The state of the Army of Occupation is the prostration of a patient after the fever has subsided; our Regiment has cause to be thankful that it is not there." George Meade's attitudes probably typified the feeling among officers after several months of encampment. Meade was consumed with longing for his wife, Margaretta, but he hoped to draw some prestige out of his sacrifice, writing to her that "I hope for a war and a speedy battle, and I think that one good fight will settle the business; and really, after coming so far and staying so long, it would hardly be the thing to come back without some laurels." Lieutenant Peck had always expected a fight and had enjoyed the excitement of the advance to the Rio Grande, but he grew restless when it did not produce the battle he wanted: "unless we have some fighting soon I shall get wholly dissatisfied and wish to return. If we could [just] have one good battle and then return!" Sherman shared these sentiments, but even at the end of January he doubted that the opportunity would arise. Unwilling to wait much longer, he seems to have decided that there was no other worthy mission for him to perform: "The proposed invasion of Mexico . . . holds out but a slim prospect to the military aspirant," and "as the prospect of a peaceful year is strong . . . it therefore becomes me to make all possible preparation to leave the service." (Sherman ultimately resigned in 1853, after his service in California provided the connections to enter banking.) Similarly, when it appeared that war with Britain had been avoided in January, a number of officers in the First Dragoon Regiment (soon to lead the conquest of New Mexico) prepared for or spoke of resignation, although none actually did so. Their attention soon turned to a new, more easily defeated adversary.[35]

The close quarters and tedium of camp life diminished the corps' enthusiasm while officers awaited the outcome of diplomacy. The combination of renewed acquaintances and boredom also encouraged the reemergence of ills that had characterized the peacetime army throughout this era, providing further evidence of the officer corps' distraction from the task before it. Colonel Josiah H. Vose, commander of the Fourth Infantry and a thirty-three-year veteran we last met in Florida, died of a stroke or heart attack after drilling his men for the first time in several years in July 1845; his successor, William Whistler, a forty-four-year veteran, was soon arrested and sent home for appearing drunk on parade.[36] Old enemies resurrected their feuds amid the boredom. The most notorious of these was between the two brigade commanders, Daniel Twiggs and William Worth, who quarreled over guard postings. Indeed, the papers of Ethan Allen Hitchcock, acting colonel of the Third Infantry at the time, contain an exchange of letters suggesting that Worth issued a challenge to Twiggs, which was quickly resolved without bloodshed. Their otherwise rather trivial dispute ultimately centered on the authority of Worth's brevet rank as a brigadier general versus the seniority of Twiggs's permanent rank as a colonel. Officers split into two factions over this issue, already a long-standing subject of controversy in the army, prompting the ever-litigious Hitchcock to send the president of the Senate a memorial against brevet rank (and thus against his current enemies, Worth and Scott) containing the signatures of 158 officers, nearly half the complement of the Army of Occupation. Winfield Scott supported his protégé Worth's claims for the authority of brevet rank, which Scott had upheld for decades against Edmund Gaines, but President Polk decided in favor of the Democratically inclined Twiggs, spurring the irate Worth to submit his resignation and leave for Washington to argue his case.[37]

Worth was one of the army's most skilled and distinguished commanders. His unblemished record included brevets for gallantry at both Chippewa and Lundy's Lane in 1814, when he was only twenty; serving as commandant at West Point and chief of staff at the Artillery School; suppressing the Patriot filibusters in upstate New York in 1838; and bringing the Seminole War to a successful conclusion in 1842. Worth was filled with ambition for glory, and he was an ardent expansionist who wrote articulately about his desire for war and his belief that Mexicans were culturally and ethically inferior. He must have doubted that anything momentous would happen while he was absent, yet most of his subordinates believed he had exceeded the bounds of professional propriety: Philip Barbour remarked that "his resigning at this time is considered by nearly the whole army a false step from which he can never recover and, should we have an engagement, [it] will dim forever the luster he has thrown around his name." Worth returned to the army as soon as he heard of the Mexican advance across the Rio Grande, but he arrived too late to command his troops at Palo Alto and Resaca de la Palma. Even then, the officer corps resumed quarreling as soon as the shooting stopped. The best example was the controversy between Captain James Duncan, supported by Worth, and Winfield Scott (who had once been Worth's patron, as Worth had been Hitchcock's) during the occupation of Mexico City. Ironically, Duncan and Worth—two of the army's most proficient soldiers—were supporting a politically appointed, militarily incompetent volunteer, General Gideon Pillow. When Scott had his three subordinates arrested, Worth sought a court-martial against the commanding general. Scott was then relieved of command by a jealous president eager to discredit the potential Whig candidate. Not surprisingly, during the 1850s, the officer corps was consumed by disputes over brevets awarded or not awarded for service in the war.[38]

Taylor was sent to the border without any substantial guidance beyond his initial instructions to take up a defensive position (which became Fort Texas, around which Brownsville would be built) opposite Matamoros. The previously close cooperation between Taylor and American chargé d'affaires Andrew Jackson Donelson apparently ceased once the army moved south. This left Taylor, whom his most recent biographer characterizes as "one of the least [diplomatically] sensitive senior officers in the army," alone to handle the tensions exacerbated by the American advance into territory claimed by Mexico. While this decision may indicate that Polk hoped to precipitate a war through Taylor's agency, the general's performance suggests that his apparent stolidity reflected a sense of dutiful accountability to civilian political direction, calling his alleged diplomatic incapacity into question. Taylor was certainly not the diplomat Scott was, but his reluctance to credit rumors of Indian war on the southwestern frontier earlier in the decade showed that he could be counted on to act coolly, unlike the impulsive Gaines. Nor was he politically active like Scott, who was widely spoken of as a Whig presidential candidate and schemed for that position as early as 1839.[39]

As with President Monroe's loose handling of Andrew Jackson in 1818, lax instructions provided a clear prescription for war, but Taylor showed noteworthy patience under the circumstances. Upon his arrival opposite Matamoros on March 28, Taylor sent William Worth with a dispatch for Mexican commander Francisco Mejia. Mejia's representative, General Romolo de la Vega, informed Worth that Mexico considered the American army's march across the Nueces to the Rio Grande an act of war but had not formally declared war. Indeed, Vega refused Worth's request to see the U.S. consul in Matamoros. Harassed by guerrillas and bandits since the army's arrival in late March, the hard-nosed Taylor ordered the Rio Grande blockaded on April 14 after receiving General Pedro de Ampudia's ultimatum to withdraw behind the Nueces and his declaration that the American advance had created a state of war. The brigadier also deployed several small infantry patrols "to scour the country" along the northern bank of the Rio Grande "and capture or destroy any [Mexican] parties that they might meet." Taylor intended to complicate the resupply of Matamoros and thus force the Mexicans' hand, compelling them to withdraw (probably to Monterrey) or to cross the Rio Grande to expel the Army of Occupation. Such a move would give the United States a pretext for resolving the boundary dispute through war, but the brigadier also suggested an "armistice pending the final settlement of the question between the governments." Thus, though Taylor may have precipitated the Mexican advance with his blockade, he did not exceed Polk's instructions by doing so.[40]

On April 23 Mexican president Paredes formally declared a "defensive war" against the United States, based on the American occupation of the disputed territory. The following day General Ampudia notified Taylor that hostilities had begun—actually the fourth time a Mexican commander had done so—

and 1,600 Mexican troops crossed the Rio Grande to cut the American line of communication to the depot at Point Isabel on the coast. On April 25 a U.S. patrol was ambushed by Mexican regulars, leading Taylor to notify the War Department that war had begun and to call for eight regiments of volunteers from Texas and Louisiana, per the War Department authorization he (rather than Gaines) had been given. On April 30 the main Mexican army began to cross the Rio Grande, and the following day Taylor took the majority of his army to reopen his supply line to Point Isabel. On May 3 Mexican artillery began to bombard Fort Texas, mortally wounding Major Jacob Brown (no relation to the former commanding general), for whom Brownsville would be named. Four days later Taylor began the return march from Point Isabel, riding in a wagon driven by a slave. The first major battle of the war was fought at Palo Alto the following day, four days before the formal American declaration of war, which was a response to the news of the April 25 ambush.[41]

The army's tone changed as fighting became imminent. "I could not in honor leave now," Meade vowed, "no one could leave . . . with reputation" intact. Grant echoed Meade, but he also reassured his fiancée Julia (who saw the army as a poor career choice) that his interest in the military was temporary and would be abandoned if there were no laurels to be won: "I could not think of such a thing now . . . but I do not think that I will stand another year of idleness in camp." Grant was brevetted twice for gallantry during the battles around Mexico City but resigned in 1854. It is important to note, however, that William Skelton's comprehensive statistics show only a small and temporary spike in resignations during the early to mid-1850s: scholars must not exaggerate the resignations occurring during this period due to the prominence of future Civil War generals among them. Whatever the frustrations, resignations were rare in the Army of Occupation, and the corps remained properly quiescent until events provided its commanders with the opportunity to unleash their energies against Mexico. The final reactions of the officers awaiting combat were anxiety, confidence, a sense of duty, and a desire for vengeance. Many had already experienced combat on a small scale in the Seminole War. For others, the first semblance of battle had come on March 20, during Worth's crossing of the Arroyo Colorado thirty miles north of Matamoros. A sizable Mexican force was deployed on the opposite bank, and Worth prepared to cross under fire, but the Mexicans withdrew before he did so. Despite some "anxious faces," Ephraim Kirby Smith watched "in breathless silence" and "saw no one who was not cheerful and apparently eager for the game to begin." Smith called the crossing "perhaps one of the most exciting hours of my life," while the usually ardent Lieutenant John Peck referred to "long faces" and felt "all the painful and breathless expectancy of battle" as he watched "the two hundred doomed men" of the vanguard cross the arroyo.[42]

A month later, when Captain Seth Thornton escaped from a Mexican ambush but did not return to camp, Philip Barbour wrote that "I very much fear that he has . . . taken his own life. . . . He has often told me that he would blow his own brains out before he would surrender." Several days later the captain remarked that "we are all anxious to avenge the death of our gallant companions," reflecting on the mysterious workings of Providence and reaffirming his faithfulness to his wife. Barbour's words show neither elation nor alienation from the task at hand: "I go to meet the enemy with my feelings all schooled to do my duty regardless of personal consequences." Barbour was killed in action at Monterrey that September after earning a brevet promotion at Palo Alto. Despite the indifference that seemed to pervade the Army of Occupation, this mind-set of dutiful service ultimately characterized career officers' attitudes toward war with Mexico. Very few of these men put their ideas of what combat might be like on paper, but they generally accepted it as the soldier's lot and expected their comrades to perform courageously, regardless of their beliefs about national policy.[43]

This dutiful subordination was also present in the reactions of the army's commander. Taylor's response to the Mexican crossing of the Rio Grande was in full accord with his instructions and the intent of President Polk's policy to annex Texas to the boundary claimed by the United States and compel Mexico to go to war to take it back. Though his choice not to wait for volunteer reinforcements or call for them earlier was potentially rash, Taylor's confident decision to overrule the consensus of his senior subordinates and pursue the Mexicans after the stalemate at Palo Alto paid off with victory at Resaca de la Palma and national acclaim for the professional army and its officers. Although the small peacetime scale of West Point meant that the new national regiments Congress raised for the war (the Ninth through Sixteenth Infantries, the Voltigeurs, and the Third Dragoons) were officered mostly by men commissioned directly from civilian life, the regulars received unprecedented credit for their skill and bravery, and the war was fought primarily under their direction. All four of the major offensive thrusts against Mexico were commanded by veteran stalwarts of the national standing army who have appeared throughout this book. Stephen W. Kearny led the Army of the West through New Mexico to California, and John Wool led the Division of the Center from San Antonio through Chihuahua to reinforce Taylor at Buena Vista. In the principal armies, Taylor and Scott gave their ranking regulars, Twiggs, Worth (another Whig), and Wool (a disaffected Democrat), priority over the volunteer major generals who owed their commissions to partisan prominence; the regulars entrusted one another with the largest divisional commands and the principal responsibility for leading assaults throughout their campaigns.[44]

Apart from attempting to replace Scott with Thomas Hart Benton, Polk's appointments were really efforts to provide temporary patronage and postwar political advantage to state-level Democrats by excluding prewar regulars from promotion to new slots; he was not trying (or at least realized that he lacked sufficient support) to replace the professionals altogether or to refashion the permanent regular army along partisan lines. West Pointers continued to fill vacancies in the old regiments, and unlike 1815 or 1821, there was no postwar reduction in force among the officers of the antebellum corps. Only a handful of the officers commissioned into the temporary regiments were given the opportunity to transfer into permanent regiments, which were all retained after the war, and only a handful of prewar regular army veterans risked the security of their careers by transferring into temporary regiments or left the army during the postwar drawdown (and none did so involuntarily). Thus, regulars kept their commissions when the temporary regiments were disbanded after the war, and the commissioning sources of the professional officer corps changed very little. By 1860, West Point graduates made up three-quarters of the officer corps, up from three-fifths in 1830 and probably an all-time peak. (As I emphasize in *Jackson's Sword*, this meant that the U.S. Army officer corps had a more consistent education and socialization than any of its European counterparts, the naval officer corps, or any of the American civilian professions.) Ironically, the war's greatest impact on the regular army was an enhanced reputation that effectively preempted Democratic critiques like Polk's after the war. The politicization of wartime appointments notwithstanding, victory cemented West Point's status as the primary peacetime commissioning source during the nineteenth century, and it predisposed both Democratic and Republican politicians to seek men with regular experience for most senior commands at the outset of the Civil War.

The interplay between officers' personal and professional frustration and their development of an objective, politically neutral accountability was both dialectical and symbiotic. The growth of the generally antiexpansionist Whig Party and its criticism of the army during the Second Seminole War, combined with constant Democratic condemnation of the army and its officers during the 1830s and 1840s, may have made the officer corps more hesitant to draw congressional fire by taking overt positions on the question of expansion. Yet the irritation professional soldiers stored up while waiting for war to begin seems to have reinforced the desire to prove themselves that was spurred by congressional disparagement. These attacks had little real effect on the officer corps—although some allowances were reduced in 1842, after Congress had substantially increased the officer corps' compensation in 1838—but they certainly added to soldiers' disenchantment with Congress and popular politics, even among those who favored the Democratic Party (from which most critics came). Nevertheless, the officer corps remained properly subordinate until events gave its members the opportunity to prove themselves by unleashing their energies against Mexico. Morale suffered during the wait, but by the time the war began, there was no questioning the officer corps' eagerness to fight. Until then, career officers' hope for promotion lay more in resignations among those dismayed by poor conditions and separation from family than in deaths in a war they did not expect to fight.

The officer corps' overwhelming reaction to service in the Army of Occupation was sheer boredom, and few regulars found any relief in close attention to their professional duties or analyses of the political and diplomatic context they were performed in. (The camaraderie of old friends helped, but the army sat at Corpus Christi for more than six months.) When the war came, the officer corps fought skillfully, courageously, and successfully, but conflict seemed so unlikely that few soldiers could sustain much enthusiasm until hostilities actually began. Until then, the predominant attitude was George Meade's hope "that the whole affair will be settled before spring, [to] enable me and many other victims to rejoin our disconsolate wives." Military leadership was a career for these men, and they served their nation faithfully and effectively when the time came, as they had sworn to do.[45]

THE MEANING OF PROFESSIONAL MISSION: OBJECTIVITY MEANS ACCOUNTABILITY

Army officers had not always exhibited the restraint toward border crises detailed in the preceding chapters. Indeed, the penchant for (quasi-)independent action displayed by Andrew Jackson in Florida was characteristic of many senior and middle-ranking officers before 1820. These soldiers were men of affairs from well-connected families with multiple links to regional and national elites; they would make their marks as leaders in gentry society wherever they were stationed and regardless of the restrictions supposedly placed on their conduct by the army's subordination to civilian political control. They owed their high appointments and rapid promotions (mostly but not exclusively during the War of 1812 and the expansions that preceded it) to the primacy of social connections and political influence in a society structured by webs of personal patronage. Their interests naturally extended beyond military affairs to the political arena, and their income came as much from private resources, usually as landholders, as from their salaries as public servants. The elite of the Jeffersonian army, and even more so of the wartime Madisonian one, was part of the national elite. Officers were gentlemen trained in the art of command as much by experience in the household or the southern plantation as by that on the parade ground or battlefield; independence, and with it the potential for irresponsibility, came as naturally to their actions as to their rhetoric.

The officer corps was reshaped qualitatively as well as quantitatively during the decade after the War of 1812. Army officers' increasingly unenthusiastic responses to the very real opportunities for personal and institutional aggrandizement presented by expansion demonstrate the close links among class and nation-state formation, jurisdictional monopoly, institutional maturity, and the growing sense of professional accountability in the development of the commissioned officer corps between 1815 and 1846. The men who dominated the army's commissioned ranks after the reduction in force of 1821, when West Point began to provide the majority of the army's new lieutenants, could not pursue their dreams of heroism and conquest as independently as their predecessors during the First Seminole War. They lacked the social, political, and regional prominence and the ferociously "independent" ambition of self-made frontier magnates like Andrew Jackson or James Wilkinson (the commanding general from 1796 to 1808, and a notorious intriguer), who used these qualities to bypass the legal and constitutional channels of national civilian authority in quest of personal, sectional, and national aggrandizement.

Like the boundary between civil and military careers, the boundary between soldier and filibuster became much firmer and more costly to cross. Though nominated for education at the Military Academy through political connections, the company-grade officers of the 1830s and 1840s were not gentry leaders or party politicians themselves. Socialized through education and experience as professional military commanders and nonpartisan nationalists, they increasingly made the army a long-term career rather than a temporary avocation. By the 1830s, given the availability of increasingly secure careers in the army's bureaucratic hierarchy, unrestrained individualism no longer seemed so viable or attractive a mode of action and personal advancement to men from middling social origins who aspired to genteel status and prestige amid the more fluid, less deferential society of Jacksonian America. Although most scholars have depicted the resignations of the mid-1830s as evidence of deficient professionalization, the departure of officers who sought commercial opportunities actually reinforced this dynamic and facilitated professional development.

Personal and class anxiety and the corollary quest for security were powerful motivating forces among the professional soldiers of the Jacksonian era. As American society became more fluid and democratic, many officers felt a growing uncertainty, and ultimately a threat to their economic prospects and their (related) ability to command social respect. However, rather than resigning their commissions to pursue uncertain opportunities in the rapidly growing yet highly competitive (and thus insecure) civilian marketplace, army officers responded with a strong distaste for disorder and a pursuit of structured advancement through a bureaucratic hierarchy—in short, through careerism in its institutional form—to combat this sense of constraint. For the army officer corps, the answer to personal uncertainty and the means of social ascent lay in a fledgling bureaucracy, sponsored and given legitimacy by the sovereign sanction of the nation-state, that could fuse officers' material needs for security at a socially "respectable" level with their pretensions to disinterested social service, authority, and legitimacy.

The West Point motto "Duty, Honor, Country" came to mean that soldiers won personal and professional honor, glory, and reputation by dutifully serving the policies formulated by elected civilian officials, whether as peacekeepers and law enforcers or as directors of conquest, without regard for immediate self-interest (the desire to gain glory and promotion by fomenting expansion and war) or personal moral or ideological qualms about these policies. More generally, the army's self-conception (and its dependent position) as an instrument of the state and its functional organization as a translocal bureaucratic hierarchy led career officers to accept, articulate, and elaborate many of the leading characteristics of late-nineteenth-century corporate thought and organization well before the Civil War, foreshadowing the postbellum reintegration of individual ambition and the locus of community obligation into the functionally and institutionally, rather than geographically, based forms of social organization that characterize modern America. In effect, the growth of army bureaucracy and the officer corps' allegiance to the nation-state that gave it employment led to the creation of the first national managerial class, an elite whose claim to authority was ultimately based on state sponsorship and power rather than individual or collective wealth, partisan affiliation, social connections, or local prestige. The officer corps saw itself as part of the national gentry, but this association was increasingly phrased as a matter of center and periphery, nation and locality, in which officers who shared the genteel values of the social, cultural, and political elite derived their status and authority from state sponsorship based on functional jurisdiction, rather than local or regional networks or family wealth and prestige.

The professional rhetoric of neutral duty, service, and responsibility proved materially and psychologically attractive for such men. According to historian Thomas Hietala, during the 1840s "many Democratic expansionists viewed the acquisition of land and markets as essential to their program for sustaining the unique character [of] American social and political life" by reproducing the locally oriented, regionally and sectionally differentiated republican society of yeoman farmers, the "parallelism" and "segmentation" adumbrated by historian Robert Wiebe. While neither insensible to these desiderata nor incapable of profiting from their pursuit, professional soldiers no longer lived within the Jeffersonian world the civilian expansionists were attempting to preserve and restore. Their service within increasingly formalized bureaucratic institutions led them to a broadly Whiggish perspective (though rarely to active Whig partisanship) that valued order, restraint, and stability in all aspects of personal, national, and international life. As the putatively neutral servants of the nation-state, army officers essentially sat out what Hietala calls the central cultural debate of the decade. Hietala suggests that midcentury American expansionism grew as much from a domestic sense of malaise following the panic and depression of the late 1830s and early 1840s as from the boundlessness of the mid to late 1840s cited by previous historians. From this perspective, both "ambitious and anxious policy makers welcomed war and expansion as alternatives to basic structural changes in American economics and politics" brought on by the emergence and prospect of urbanization, industrialization, and the commercial Market Revolution.[46] This potentially disruptive response was unnecessary for professional soldiers because they derived their material and psychological security from essentially permanent service in an organization that suffered little from the downturns inherent in the capitalist economy (a phenomenon that was becoming increasingly apparent by 1840).

Conversely, we should not underestimate the degree to which this occupational security was linked to the territorial expansion so many officers questioned. The Whigs opposed expansion but favored an effective military establishment because of their conservative temperament, while the Democrats' policies gave the army active employment and a practical raison d'être despite the nation's generally peaceful relations with Europe and the Democrats' populist antagonism toward standing armies and professional monopolies. All things considered, the officer corps acted subordinately and accountably in following civilian America in the pursuit of expansion, yet it did so with a responsible professional caution and self-restraint. This mindset, professional as well as careerist, was an important reason behind the otherwise surprising rarity of warlike or expansionist sentiments in the officer corps. Though usually given a negative connotation, the word *careerist* acquires a much more positive meaning when viewed from this perspective. The personal and occupational security provided by a national bureaucracy encouraged subordination and accountability as well as laxity and insulation, and in an era of simple military technology, with few systemic military threats, political accountability (or at least partisan neutrality) was a more important professional quality than technical or tactical expertise or capability per se. This professional accountability was especially evident in the lack of extended substantive comment on controversial political questions from soldiers stationed in Texas (and in Florida a decade before), in significant contrast to their constant individual preoccupation with separation from their wives and the prospect of disease. Professional military commanders could hardly be unaware of the partisan debates that would shape the policies they executed, but they usually kept their thoughts to themselves (or in private correspondence), and found it in poor taste if their comrades did not.

Ultimately, men with careers as secure as those of U.S. Army officers did not need an aggressive ideology like Manifest Destiny to advance themselves—they had a definite stake in orderly national expansion but did not need to take the risks of urging or precipitating aggression. Here, the adjective *orderly* was as important as the fact of expansion itself. Though certainly patriots and nationalists, and chauvinistic in a generic sense, army officers would not have benefited from—and indeed, might have found their status threatened by—a war led by private enterprisers like filibusters, or a disastrous defeat (like that William Worth feared along the Canadian border) for which the regular army would be blamed. In officers' minds, national success required national direction, and local settlers and filibusters could not be allowed to dictate American foreign policy through actions unrestrained by allegiance to the national structure created by the Constitution. Finally, we should remember that the sectional issues and allegiances brought to the forefront of American life by expansionism eventually destroyed the First Republic the army served. Though army officers were no more visionary than civilians, they deserve some credit for their restraint in advocating the expansion that ultimately splintered their profession and nation.

Changing occupational circumstances exerted a profound influence on the trajectories and nuances of officers' responses to the foreign policy problems they confronted. The army was the first public-sector employer on a national scale in the United States, and its leaders espoused centralist, indeed statist, values that served, but were also shaped by, their duties and interests. In general, like civilian bureaucrats facing change, career military men often think war risky because of the likelihood that it will disrupt the organizational stability built up in times of peace. This consideration commonly grows in strength as an army becomes more institutionally mature, and the anxiety it produces is perhaps strongest when such an army is reaching the point of organizational and occupational monopoly but its officers still feel some uncertainty over the outcome of their efforts to secure this jurisdiction.

Thus, paradoxical though it may seem, self-interest made the professional soldiers of the Jacksonian era less likely to seek expansion and war or to willfully violate foreign borders than their Jeffersonian predecessors. Commanders before and after 1820 spoke in the cautious idioms of legalism and conservative realism as they sought to defend American sovereignty along the frontiers. Yet officers committed to army careers and increasingly sensitive to the fragility of social order and their place within it came to fear that native filibusters posed a more immediate danger to American national honor and security than the supposed "insults" of European powers. The officer corps' practical function as the principal defender and enforcer of national and federal sovereignty along the nation's borders fostered a strong personal and institutional interest in enhancing the federal government's power and legitimacy, and the officer corps' ongoing search for personal and organizational security bred a yearning for order and stability that regulars routinely expressed in the conservative idiom of national sovereignty and the rule of law. When their vocation was challenged by citizen-soldiers and filibusters, professional soldiers responded by stressing the necessity for centralized national control over the organized use of military force.

These biases were clearly present in their disdain for Canadian and Texan rebels and for squatters and settlers in Indian lands, all of whom elevated doctrines of natural right (or Manifest Destiny) and popular democracy (within the ethnocentric strictures of their concepts of citizenship) over the rule of domestic and international law, while attempting to usurp the regulars' jurisdiction as the only legitimate managers of organized violence. Filibusters were a danger to international peace, a threat to law and order within the United States, and a socially disruptive demonstration of the limits of the government's sovereignty over its own people. In contrast, foreign aggression could be deterred or combated by military preparation, which provided employment, prestige, and promotion for officers and posed less danger of conflict with frontier citizens and their representatives in Congress. The army's

The death of Major Samuel Ringgold at Palo Alto, 1846. Lithograph by James Baillie. (Courtesy Library of Congress, LC-USZ62-67)

accountability to civilian political control—to the Constitution and the democratic values and rule of law it ultimately represented—and its lack of zeal for expansion flowed directly, though apparently paradoxically, from its employment by the nation-state. The officer corps' role as the principal defender of national sovereignty meshed comfortably with officers' individual and organizational search for security, legitimacy, and authority, not in a monolithic ideological enthusiasm for Manifest Destiny and empire.

The officer corps, which directed and led the American conquest of Spanish Florida during the 1810s (albeit in general agreement, and often in cooperation, with those civilians, mostly southerners and filibusters, who took a strong interest in the subject), proved content to follow the gradual trajectory of American public opinion in coming to imagine and accept the conquest of the Mexican Southwest. If Taylor had any personal motive for aggressiveness, it was to win laurels for the regular army before the volunteers arrived, an institutional rather than an ideologically expansionist motive that was not in any way the reason for the army's presence opposite Matamoros. In the highly partisan context of Jacksonian America, a Democratic president elected on a platform of aggressive expansionism chose to entrust the command of the force he intended to occupy Texas (if not to precipitate war with

Mexico) to Taylor, a known Whig, and then left it under his command even when Taylor's opposition to expansion became well known. Jackson's impact on the nation's foreign policy was independent and strategic, Gaines's was disruptive but controllable, and Taylor's was subordinate and essentially tactical (a matter of policy implementation). There, in a nutshell, lies the difference in foreign policy activism, bellicosity, and accountability to national civilian political authority between the officer corps of 1818 and that of 1846.

CONCLUSION
Army, State, and Profession in Nineteenth-Century American History

During the nineteenth century, the balance of initiative and influence in the borderlands of the United States shifted from European, Indian, nonstate, and American civilian actors toward U.S., white, state, and military ones. Conquest and occupation, the defeat or deterrence of international, Indian, and nonstate actors, extended formal U.S. sovereignty, facilitating and accelerating the growing political and economic hegemony of racially defined U.S. citizens acting through the nation's representative state institutions (Congress and executive branch agencies). Rather than decentralization and entropy, territorial expansion under national auspices, increasingly by or under the direction of national executive agents, meant the extension and elaboration of nation-state sovereignty: a trajectory of greater administration, surveillance, discipline, rationalization, and centralization, both formally and informally. Thus, the action of national military forces, increasingly permanent and professional, meant greater political and, ultimately, social, economic, and cultural stability and cohesion, as well as constraint over those who resisted white democracy and market capitalism. Physical nationalization—political, diplomatic, and military—also meant social, economic, and cultural stabilization, which meant the reproduction and consolidation of eastern models in the nation's southern and western peripheries and a growing nationalization and rationalization in all these spheres.

This process was remarkably peaceful, compared to European colonialism, Andrew Jackson's wars against the Creeks and Seminoles, or the wars against the Indians of the trans-Mississippi West after 1850. Yet, as legal and political historian William Novak observes, "the storied history of liberty in the United States, with its vaunted rhetoric of unprecedented rights of property, contract, [and] mobility . . . was built directly upon a strong and consistent willingness to employ the full, coercive, and regulatory powers of law and government." The actions of the army officer corps, like the municipal regulations Novak explores, demonstrate "the power of a deeply rooted American tradition of police and regulatory governance [that proved] vital to social and economic development." As political scientist Ira Katznelson opines, the American "state was flexible, effective, and efficient"—responsive to societal goals and accountable to political representatives. The professional officer corps of the national standing army was a prime example of this responsibility, capability, and accountability.[1]

Contrary to its frequent caricature as a mere "night watchman," the early republican state was a creative force, through the extension and elaboration of existing patterns as well as the destruction of obstacles. Nevertheless, localism, localities, and federalism did impose limits and constraints on the nation-state and its autonomy and cohesion, even in the conduct of military operations and foreign relations. Local, territorial, and state officials, political leaders, businessmen, and leaders and representatives of nonwhite ethnic groups all pursued "local diplomacy," with local or locally rooted objectives that were often contrary to, or in contradiction of, national objectives embodied through the federal government. The United States was a true nation-state, not just a national state (which is primarily a matter of scale). White man's democracy and federalism, two of the principal structures national agents advanced through their actions in the West, presented multiple, often sectionally, sectorally, or socially stratified axes for citizen representation and action, sometimes independent of the nation-state and its officers. Advancing white supremacist democracy while restraining its excesses, or at least those that threatened national sovereignty and cohesion, repeatedly fostered tensions in the American system of representative government between relatively subjective social-political responsibility to a set of values and "the people" (white frontiersmen) as a whole and a more objective accountability to the specific institutions and procedures of national governance under the Constitution and the rule of law. Elected representatives pressed for both responsibility (perhaps better understood as responsiveness to popular pressure and public opinion) and accountability; professional soldiers had to find a balance that remained faithful to society's values while enabling the sustained application of those values over the long term, which often required imposing patience and restraint to prevent entropy and disintegration.

The national standing army made a significant, perhaps decisive impact on the nation's borders and frontiers. Despite repeated filibusters and illegal incursions onto Indian land, no lasting competitor states emerged in the interstices of the North American borderlands: apart from Texas, which sought annexation by the American federal union, no sustained alternatives to the United States survived among white settlers. Despite the Constitution and the Northwest Ordinance, this was hardly a foregone conclusion in 1787 or during the 1790s, when Georgians, Tennesseans, and Kentuckians repeatedly intrigued with Spain, Britain, and France to join with or seize territory from Spain, separate from the United States, and create new polities—hopefully republican ones, but probably militarily and economically dependent on European powers as patrons. The defeat of the "Burr conspiracy," so easily caricatured, obscures the very real fragility of the early republic in the borderlands, where the agents of European empires competed for influence while republican claims to personal autonomy encouraged American citizens to seek the best bargain they could.

Western land was "free" among whites, in the Turnerian and exceptionalist sense of encouraging individualism and democracy, only if it was seized and secured against Indians and international threats. "Free land" depended on establishing conditions of "free security": freedom from significant threat of European intervention, and thus the freedom to expropriate Indians and Latinos. Indeed, national military forces could almost put themselves out of business if success (military or otherwise) enabled the reduction of national government, in order to minimize taxation and federal constraint over western expansion. But the years before 1821, and the Jacksonian-era filibusters of the mid to late 1830s, taught political leaders, local as well as national, that peace and stability depended on repressing internal as well as external sources of conflict. Caveats and cavils notwithstanding, states' rights advocates like Martin Van Buren took this lesson just as closely to heart, when they assumed the reins of national authority, as the more nationally oriented Whigs. In the process, the career army officer corps secured structural (institutional) authority and normative (professional) legitimacy as the usual directors of organized armed force, whether over volunteers—the military forces organized by the states—or against filibusters—private citizens aggressively pressing the logic of libertarian individualism and white supremacy. With the exception of the Texas Revolution, the American nation-state gained an effective monopoly over the direction of military force, as well as the conduct of foreign relations, after 1820.

Military and diplomatic conquest permitted economic and ultimately cultural hegemony. If sustained by sovereign authority and national power, international borders—whether demarcated by forts or enforced by military patrols against filibusters, bandits, and unlicensed Indian trade—became a shield against foreign intervention in disputes within the territory claimed by the United States, permitting more extensive penetration and settlement of once-distant hinterlands by white farmers. Because European powers like Britain, Spain, and France privileged borders patrolled by national, professional military forces as a core attribute and legitimator of sovereignty, the establishment of firm borders was essential to European recognition of U.S. independence in the practice of international relations. As long as the United States was unable to control its borders, European powers would feel that the new nation lacked the sovereign qualities of a formally equal state and might feel justified to intervene within its boundaries, much as the United States did in Spanish Florida. The ability to secure the borders, proved by federal military forces in the Northwest Territory in 1794 and, with more difficulty, in the Southwest Territory and its successors between 1793 and 1807, was also crucial to the political and economic expansion and social stability of the new republic. European recognition of American legitimacy within the international system meant that the racialized democracy that ruled the new republic could proceed essentially unhindered against the indigenous populations within the territory it claimed, expanding opportunities for members of that democracy at the expense of those outside its racialized confines.

The federal government's successful assertion of national sovereignty, so often led by the army, made the Louisiana Purchase a reality, rather than a field for continuing international competition. Similar efforts put Pinckney's Treaty with Spain (1795) into effect, enabling the creation of the cotton kingdom in the Old Southwest, and secured the American plantation empire by driving Spain, and the nonstate actors who rebelled against Spanish rule, from Florida and the Gulf littoral. Indeed, of the four major fields of early- and mid-nineteenth-century federal policy initiative—banking, revenues (the tariff), transportation ("internal improvements"), and territorial expansion—only the last was a clear and sustained success, not disputed or rolled back by antistatist Jacksonians and Democrats during the 1830s and 1840s.

External pressure (both international and domestic) increased professional cohesion and commitment within the officer corps. Professional soldiers sometimes considered themselves—and in many ways they were—truer republicans than many civilians, particularly those in the borderlands, where career military officers brought a sense of disinterested service to a unitary national public interest, amidst a population often driven by individualism (or family and kin motives) and the quest for commercial gain. Aside from their distrust of centralized power, particularly that lodged in national government and standing military forces, most frontiersmen were populist democrats, nineteenth-century liberals, and expectant capitalists rather than classical republicans; they were heralds of the Gilded Age, while national military officers simultaneously looked back to republicanism and heralded the Progressive Era. The professional officer corps was a force for and an instrument of ordered liberty, doing as much as any other national agency to establish and maintain the "public conditions of private freedom."[2]

As such, the army officer corps was a significant force for national cohesion and union in the public sphere that emerged in the early national borderlands. The national state, composed of military executive branch officials as well as elected civilian representatives, acted as a link between the Eastern Seaboard center and the frontier peripheries, providing a national information and communications network for local elites and aspirants to elite status, who sought intelligence about national trends, resources, and constraints, as well as for the state itself. While we should not strain for analogies, this process was not fundamentally dissimilar, at least in its ultimate impact, from the social, political, and economic surveillance that encouraged and sometimes enabled coordination, administration, and (gradually) rationalization in early modern Europe and nineteenth-century European colonies. As sociologist Emile Durkheim explained later in the nineteenth century, the state in this sense was an expression, a rationalization, of social-economic interdependence and complexity, in and through the Market Revolution, the Second Party System, and the growth of economic and professional specialization and social and institutional density. Indeed, the development and activities of the army officer corps as a national administrative cadre anticipated some of the patterns later identified with Progressivism.[3]

The professional officer corps was not isolated from early- and mid-nineteenth-century American society, nor was it alienated from that society's core political ideologies of republicanism and democracy, as they ultimately merged in the belief in popular (majoritarian) sovereignty. Privately and as individuals, officers often expressed core civilian social values of liberalism, individualism, and majoritarian democracy. Yet as national military officers, they publicly preferred older, more communal values of republicanism, popular sovereignty expressed and moderated through the procedures of representative government under the checks and balances of the Constitution; these values were more conducive to the hierarchical authority and disinterested service they considered necessary to sustain order, whether social or institutional. Indeed, there is little evidence that they sought a more unitary civilian control centered in the presidency, like that advocated by pathbreaking political scientist Samuel Huntington in his classic work *The Soldier and the State* as most conducive to military professionalism. These officers remembered

Andrew Jackson's incursions on their operational autonomy and feared the destabilizing consequences of a plebiscitary majoritarianism.[4]

The career officer corps was simultaneously part of the broad American middle class and part of the American elite: they were members of the "respectable" middle class (not the petite bourgeoisie or lower middle class) economically; genteel in their career security and the relative financial security it provided; and elite in their cosmopolitan, metropolitan social connections and cultural gentility, with parallel political connections and influence, however indirect. Professional soldiers stationed in the capital became part of Washington society; elsewhere, perhaps particularly in the less socially mature West, local elites and members of the middle class aspiring to gentility looked to federal military officers as representatives of the East Coast metropole and the national state, whether they wanted favors, news, or the emotional satisfaction (and perhaps prestige) of connecting to something larger than their locality. Yet the officer corps was not a simple class fragment, whether of an elite or a more general middle class; it was a distinct social formation—a remarkably autonomous state-sponsored profession, socially and culturally modeled on the quasi-aristocratic ideal of the European gentleman, with an unusually strong interest in hierarchical, ultimately statist forms of order and authority.[5]

During the 1820s, 1830s, and 1840s, officers' genteel authoritarianism and their conservative, hierarchical sense of patriotism, consisting of disinterested service and paternalistic responsibility—essentially, noblesse oblige—were increasingly tempered by a professional sense of socially objective accountability, not primarily to their civilian class counterparts (southern planters or northern businessmen), as was so often the case among European officers, but to the institutions, forms, and processes of constitutional democracy. Indeed, their "objective" accountability to the nation-state, embodying a sense of responsibility to society as a whole rather than to a particular elite, may have been encouraged, even made possible, by the divided constitutional structures Huntington deplored. This occurred because professional soldiers were compelled to account to multiple centers of political power that represented multiple social and ideological constituencies, much as James Madison envisioned in *Federalist Number Ten*. As political scientist Peter Feaver recently observed, such a division of civilian authority between legislative and executive branches "may be a necessary part of *democratic*, as opposed to merely *civilian*, control of the military."[6]

Unfortunately, some leading military historians of the West, who do the specialist work on which assessments of the army's significance must rest, have contributed to misconceptions about the army's missions and impact and, by extension, to misconceptions about the role and significance of the nineteenth-century American state. Philosophically, this may be a laudable attempt to avoid national chauvinism and triumphalism, but most often it seems to be due to their conclusion that the army was not very creative, imaginative, or effective at Indian fighting, and thus not very good at the conquest that most presume was its mission. The problem here is primarily in distinguishing scale and scope—that is, between intermediate efficiency and ultimate effectiveness. In military terms, this is the difference between tactics—the mixture of fire and movement employed in the face of an enemy—and strategy—the gradual pursuit of attrition and logistical exhaustion, versus the pursuit of immediate victory in battle. No one would argue that the army was well adapted, or that it even sought to adapt itself, to warfare on Native American terms. Facing small parties of skilled outdoorsmen, the conventionally oriented army found it difficult to deter Indian raids or to find, catch, and prevent the Indians' escape when it was on the offensive. Individually, its usually inexperienced soldiers were no match for native warriors. Collectively, the army's reconnaissance, intelligence, and terrain utilization (so effective in the war with Mexico) were often sorely lacking against the Indians; its artillery was often unable to keep up and reach them; and after the Civil War, its individual weapons were often outmatched when Indians purchased repeating rifles (usually from U.S. citizens) and the army did not. The historic strength of American military supply systems often became a liability, as expected logistical requirements burdened offensive columns and slowed their advance. The army usually lacked the Indians' agility and had trouble coordinating its power to gain and retain the initiative.[7]

Yet the army did not lose wars to the Indians. It did not merely win "a few wars" or secure "occasional successes."[8] It eventually won virtually every war the United States and its citizens had with the Indians. There were a few exceptions: the "Arikara War" of 1823, the "Third Seminole War" of the 1850s, and the war with the Sioux and Cheyenne that ended in 1868. But only the last was truly a defeat for the United States or for the expressed will of a substantial number of citizens. The historian is hard-pressed to identify other wars—not skirmishes, battles, or campaigns, but *wars*—that ended with Native American polities less subject to U.S. power than before conflict began. This was not because the United States mobilized overwhelming forces of citizen-soldiers when the army had difficulty: military historian Bruce Vandervort has observed, and I have suggested in reference to the Black Hawk and Second Seminole Wars, that the power of citizen-soldiers was "by and large an illusion."[9]

The United States was successful because the national standing army was persistent. Unlike the state and local militia or volunteer citizen-soldiers, the national standing army was paid for the long term, it had no crops or businesses to care for, and it was reinforced by new recruits when soldiers were slain, enabling it to persist and exploit the Indians' lack of resources and logistical depth, which aggravated their political divisions. The army was reluctant to change its tactical and operational methods (which often worked if battle was joined), but some leaders (like George Crook, who conducted several of the army's most significant campaigns) did so in the field, and in most cases the army gradually penetrated "Indian country" to destroy native resources and settlements and exploit the Indians' dependence on a limited resource base. Whether or not it defeated the Indians in battle, the army was never permanently defeated in battle itself, and its losses were much more easily replaced, so it could eventually defeat the Indians through combat attrition and material and psychological exhaustion. The army bounced back from catastrophic battlefield defeats under Josiah Harmar and Arthur St. Clair to victory under Anthony Wayne; it bounced back from Dade's defeat to drive most of the Seminoles from Florida; and it bounced back from Custer's last stand to confine the Sioux to the ghettoes of Pine Ridge and Wounded Knee.

Native tactical skill in skirmishes and battle did not prevent the army from winning campaigns and wars. In modern wars, characterized by resource depth on at least one side (in this case, the United States), battles and tactics—the dramatic focus of much of the written history of the Indian wars—are often less decisive than operations, campaigns, and strategy (the level of politics and mobilization). (The operational level of warfare links—or should link—the tactical and strategic, usually through movement before and after battle.) Historically, the U.S. Army has proved mediocre at the tactical level but has excelled at the strategic one of synchronizing resources for persistent, gradually decisive power projection. Nor were the Indians able to turn their tactical advantages into an insurgency, which is ultimately societal and political: they were hard to catch, but the wars were intercultural, essentially international, without the counterinsurgent problem of losing popular support when violence and casualties outweigh expected benefits. (One might say that this was because the "occupation" was of American territory, but Whigs, northerners, and easterners hardly felt the same commitment as Democrats and frontiersmen.) Indeed, the army proved surprisingly and significantly capable of exploiting divisions within and between tribes, while the Cherokee were the only tribe that appealed with any effect to American public opinion. Indian advantages remained fundamentally tactical and military rather than strategic, political, social, or economic. Thus, even leading military historians of the West who criticize the army's tactical and operational methods observe that economic factors—in military terms, operational and strategic logistics—are often most decisive, in asymmetrical conflicts between simple and complex societies as well as those between symmetrical conventional opponents.

The success of insurgencies and revolutionary warfare ultimately depends on persistence: either a depth of political will or a lack thereof on the part of counterinsurgent and counterrevolutionary states, so that these states are unwilling to deploy their potential power—the depth of their economic and military logistical resources—against the militarily weaker insurgents. Tactics are not the critical distinction: the military forces of large states can employ "guerrilla warfare" and "guerrilla tactics," as the United States sometimes did toward the Indians. As leading western military historian Robert Utley observes, the army was often more tactically successful when it did so, but institutional, psychological, and cultural considerations (rooted in the factors Utley himself emphasizes) and the variety of potential future missions often make it difficult, and undesirable over the long term, for complex conventional institutions to adopt unconventional methods on an extensive or exclusive scale. Nor did the Indians pose a threat to U.S. national survival, so the imperative for tactical and institutional adjustment was much less urgent than it might be for a state defending itself against domestic insurgency. Despite all the white fears and the exaggerations of army officers seeking augmentation, the loosely organized Indians were ultimately a raiding or marauding force, capable of discouraging white intrusion and settlement but not of taking the strategic offensive into densely settled regions, where white numbers would prove overwhelming, even when organized as militia.

Nor did the national standing army take a backseat to the citizen-soldier volunteers or militia (or even the railroad) in the active conquest of the West. One can point out that white civilians destroyed most of the very loosely organized natives of southern and central California with little national military assistance, and that citizen-soldier volunteers and militias proved sufficient to repress (and massacre) the Native Americans of California, Colorado, and the Pacific Northwest during the Civil War. Yet few settlers, and particularly few farmers, possessed the skills, stamina, or individual ferocity of the Indian warrior. Indeed, citizen-soldiers commonly ran away when they encountered Indians who fought back, whether in Ohio in 1790 and 1791 or during the opening skirmishes of the Black Hawk (1832) and Snake (1864) wars, to name a few instances. The belief that farmers, untrained citizen-soldiers, and vigilantes could defeat warrior societies in battle, or even protect their isolated farmsteads from raiders, is a prime form of American military exceptionalism, and the emphasis on nonstate actors, military or economic, is a species of the exceptionalist myth of American statelessness.

The Seminole Wars and the Plains campaigns of the mid and late 1850s, like all those after the Civil War—the Modoc War and the pursuit of the Paiute, Bannock, and Nez Perce, the conquest of the northern and southern Plains Indians and the Mimbréno and Chiricahua Apache—were fought almost entirely by national military forces. Indeed, native auxiliaries—Indians who joined U.S. forces to fight traditional enemies—contributed far more to victory in these conflicts than did citizen-soldiers, providing scouting and tracking that few whites or the army could supply. The railroad and the buffalo hunter deprived the Plains Indians of subsistence, but not the Apache, Modoc, Paiute, Bannock, or Nez Perce. (Nor, though subjugated by citizen-soldier forces during the Civil War, did the Navajo, Mescalero Apache, or natives of the Pacific Northwest depend on bison.) And while the army's ability to concentrate and coordinate power projection for major campaigns was greatly enhanced by the railroads, the army also had to disperse its regiments into small, inefficient detachments to guard the construction crews and stations. Nor did the railroads lead into Apache country: strategic concentration—when possible, given the small size of the army and its extensive responsibilities across the West—still had to be followed with operational and tactical execution.[10]

Despite its tactical and operational limitations of mobility and reconnaissance, as well as its officers' ambivalence toward white frontiersmen and the process of conquest, the national standing army *did* deter or quell native resistance to white expansion in the Upper Mississippi Valley and beyond. State and territorial volunteers and militia usually proved incompetent in this task, unless they were able to operate with genocidal freedom against fragments of native societies. The national standing army provided protection at a cost, in both lives and taxes, that was acceptable to most citizens, East and West. Civilian War Department officials as well as military commanders agreed that regular troops were less expensive per soldier than the volunteers or militia, and once Jacksonian expansionism led Congress to pay for regular mounted troops, citizen-soldiers lost their principal military advantage over the regular army. Indeed, though citizen-soldiers still served as the equivalent of colonial or early national "rangers" in mountainous regions, they only became a significant military force on the central and northern Plains at Sand Creek. (Texas, with its strong tradition of state military forces rooted in the Republic, remained something of an exception with its rangers and associated vigilantes, but these did not win the Red River War.) And citizen-soldiers never proved willing to serve over sustained periods: though they sometimes—if organized, and if advance intelligence of an Indian attack was available—sprang to action for local defense, they rarely went far from their families and businesses. They sometimes launched raiding expeditions but rarely carried out sustained seasonal campaigns if the Indians avoided contact.[11]

One cannot logically argue that some group—in this case, settlers—was militarily "irresistible" when it did not act militarily. Utley refers to settlers as *politically* irresistible, and though this was true in the end, scholars need to look more closely at cases in which the government resisted western citizens' demands, as in the Upper Missouri Valley during the 1820s (examined in *Jackson's Sword*). However, one must ask what the settlers actually sought from their government. Did they seek arms, ammunition, and pay to seek out and destroy the Indians on their own? No, particularly if doing so would take more than a couple of weeks. Instead they sought federal military protection, from the standing army. How quickly they got it, and the form it took—a fort to defend a community or an offensive expedition against an Indian tribe—depended on contingent circumstances, including the policies of senior army leaders and the extent of the army's duties and operations already under way. The dispersion of the army into battalion posts, compelled by settlers demanding local protection—and thus acknowledging their inability or unwillingness to protect themselves—slowed the army's ability to react quickly to significant trouble.[12]

The army was certainly not an independent causal factor, nor was it independent of subordination to civilian political authority, constituted through the racially delimited processes of white democracy. The army's actions were hardly sufficient to foster the white settlement of the West, but they were necessary: there is little in the historical record to suggest that white citizens would have made the continual sacrifice of livelihood and personal independence, if not life, to defeat or coerce the Indians onto reservations themselves. Nor, with the exception of California, were trans-Mississippi settler populations dense or widespread enough to quell substantial Native American resistance, either through citizen-soldier mobilizations or daily aggression by individual bullies and vigilante groups (as occurred with the Indians of the Old Northwest during the 1830s) until quite late in the period of white expansion. What might have happened to the early settlers in each region had there been no outside military force to call on for assistance? Despite a decade of pressure, the inhabitants of Deadwood did not drive the Sioux from the Black Hills: political pressure from the white intruders, and the unusually eager belligerence of military commanders, particularly those on the scene like George Armstrong Custer, led the War Department to order the army into the Black Hills. Nor had similar pressure from a far larger white population, against Indians already defeated in war, driven the Creeks from Alabama or the Cherokee from Georgia during the 1830s; nor did such pressure, or the acts of citizen-soldiers, prevent the repeated return of Ho-chunk, Potawatomi, Sauk, and Fox to land they had ceded during the 1820s and 1830s. When Black Hawk's return east of the Mississippi led to a settler panic in 1832, militia first attacked peaceful Indians and then fled when attacked themselves, preventing a diplomatic solution. Four years later, thousands of Alabama militiamen floundered about in a panic until experienced regular generals, Winfield Scott and Thomas Jesup, arrived to take control of operations and capture the Creeks rising up against white oppression. The combination of white greed and land hunger provided the motive and created the pretext for territorial expansion; it did not provide sufficient violence or power to succeed without national assistance.

The Sioux had expanded across the Plains over the course of a century, and they defeated the U.S. Army in 1866: we face a vast causal dissonance between ethnohistorians, who emphasize Native American strength and agency like that of the Sioux prior to 1877, and the western historians who accentuate the military potential of white settlers. Both interpretations cannot be correct for the same place and time. The psychological pressure against Native Americans came from persistence not just by settlers but by the army that answered their calls for protection. Protected effectively at the strategic level (though often inefficiently at the tactical level), settlers had the opportunity to gradually erode the Indians' resource base, creating the economic and psychological pressure that, again in conjunction with military pressure, enabled U.S. cultural and diplomatic pressure. One perspective argues that gradual erosion was the critical factor, diminishing the Indians' ability to resist, but the Indians did not go quietly, submitting to preordained or inevitable defeat: as Utley observes, these warrior societies "accepted reservations only after heavy-handed violence." Sometimes, particularly in California during the 1850s, that violence came from settlers, commonly in the form of vigilantism and atrocity, but victory through settler violence was not the norm in the West, particularly after 1865. Cowboys almost never fought Indians: the army took care of that, allowing the cowboys to fight one another or clash with sheep men and sodbusters, in what Richard Maxwell Brown, a historian of American violence, labels "western wars [or civil wars] of incorporation."[13]

Some chain that links cause and effect is necessary to explain the historical sequence of events. If Indians could raid, as they were accustomed to do, then perhaps reservations were not the "only alternative to extinction": surely the Comanche, Apache, Navajo, and other Indians who raided so successfully in Mexico and Texas could have continued to subsist by raiding small communities of American settlers, as the Yaqui continued to do in Mexico until repressed by national military power after 1900. Westering settlers were *not* militarily irresistible, and their resource impact did not undermine native ecosystems overnight. When the Indians resisted the settler tide, national military forces provided the margin of white victory. At no point in the process of conquest was military pressure—primarily from the national standing army—absent. Thirty-five years ago, Utley observed that the frontier army "figured prominently" in the conquest of the West. Following western military historian Robert Athearn, he quoted William Tecumseh Sherman's reasonable assessment that "the Army has been a large factor, but . . . not the only one." This interpretative moderation proved very short-lived. Frontiersmen, "rather than the soldiers," Utley promptly went on, "deprived the Indians of the land and the sustenance that left him no alternative but to submit. . . . Thus the frontier army was not, as many of its leaders [and mid-twentieth-century myth] saw it, the heroic vanguard of civilization, crushing the savages." Yet in citing Sherman, and no doubt trying to escape the perceived limits of military history, Utley put his emphasis on the railroad, rather than accepting the general's assessment that the iron horse "*became*" (in the future transitive) the greater force in white expansion.[14]

Not until then could frontiersmen flourish in sufficient numbers to deprive the Indians of their sustenance—nor did they do so in Apacheria or to the Modocs and Paiutes in the years shortly after the Civil War. When the Indians submitted, it was not simply because they lacked food but because military pressure, usually from the regular army, prevented them from gathering food or seizing sufficient quantities from settlers. Settlers did not prevent the Indians from doing so: settlers complained about Indian raids and demanded that politicians dispatch the army to compel the Indians to return to the reservations. Perhaps the settlers could have done so, but with the significant exception of the period 1849–1865, and occasional vigilante action against very small Indian parties or individuals, neither settlers nor citizen-soldiers chased and caught Indian raiders or refugees themselves. Indeed, the growing authority of the professional standing army, and the consequent autonomy of the nation-state from settler pressure, is perhaps best demonstrated by the almost complete success with which post–Civil War commanders resisted the employment of citizen-soldiers against the Indians.

Utley concludes that "the army's particular contribution was to precipitate a final collapse that had been ordained by other forces." "Precipitate" may be a reasonable term, but "ordained" is a very strong word that denotes a dangerously imbalanced assessment of causation. In most cases, the army actually preceded the "other forces," including the railroads and the majority of settlers, into the trans-Mississippi West. Army, state, and society agreed that American expansion was desirable, but they had different visions of pace and process, and the army and the state had resources—power—the settlers lacked, both individually and in the aggregate. Native resources came under great pressure as settlement grew, but neither individual farmers, isolated and vulnerable (and all the more likely to cry out for army protection), nor gaggles of settler militia defeated the Sioux. Scalp hunters did not defeat the Apache. Nor did the railroad do so: Sherman's reference to the railroads as "instrumentalities rather than the substantial causes" of economic development, which has long been echoed by economic historians assessing the railroads' contribution to American growth, can be extended to their role in military operations, where they enhanced the army's ability to concentrate and sustain a campaign but had little tactical effect.[15]

Rather than dismissing the contingencies of politics and policy and contributing to the myths of Manifest Destiny, statelessness, and American exceptionalism—particularly that in which the organized agency of the people (the government) persistently proves hapless, superfluous, or counterproductive—scholars might more closely investigate the economic and political timing and geography of settlement and policy. A quarter century ago, leading western historian Clyde Milner distinguished the "frontier of national [U.S.] expansion" as the conclusion to five stages of the European frontier in North America and argued that "the federal government of the United States played perhaps the most significant role in the closing of the Trans-Mississippi frontier, because of its program of political domination developed to close the cis-Mississippi frontier." More recently, military historian Bruce Vandervort observed that the critical factor in the defeat of the Native Americans (and Africans resisting European colonialism) was the development of "more highly centralised governments" that could combine demographic, technological, and resource advantages. We need to reincorporate the national state, and its agents of coercion, into our understanding of the western wars of incorporation that included the conquest of Native America. Recognizing the extent of the army's agency, while explaining its limits and constraints, is one step toward recovering a sense of the nineteenth-century state, one that would help scholars better comprehend the sources, nuances, and consequences of frontier and conquest.[16]

In the early American borderlands, the professional army officer corps provided all three of the key factors sociologist Anthony Giddens considers necessary for the concentration of coercive resources and power in the nation-state: surveillance, specialized administration, and organized armed force. The surveillance and discipline underpinned by the national standing army did not create cultural or ideological hegemony over whites or Indians, nor did it produce a complete nation-state monopoly of force and constant physical domination, but it did permit the mediation and moderation of conflicts, particularly interethnic and international ones. The American state proved capable of administering its boundaries and hardening them to borders when necessary. As political theorist Franz Neumann observed and political scientist Stephen Skowronek recognized, "no greater disservice has ever been rendered political science than the statement that the liberal state was a 'weak state.' It was precisely as strong as it needed to be in the circumstances."[17]

The United States, particularly the executive agencies of the national state, did not pursue expansion and aggression without heed to cost; it commonly deferred expansionist initiatives until white settlement and demands for protection reached a politically critical mass. U.S. relations with the Sioux, the Crow, the Ojibwa, or any other tribe cannot be understood independent of the contingent circumstances and objectives of each encounter. The United States did not lack power to deploy to the West prior to the Civil War; it lacked interest sufficient to deploy the power necessary to secure hegemony. More precisely, most of the substantial agencies of organized power, whether public or private, were busy in the East: they had higher priorities. We can reasonably identify the absence of U.S. hegemony in one region or another, or over one tribe or another, as a contingent objective reality for that region or tribe, but we should not default or extrapolate to assert some general limitation to U.S. power, any more than we should presume the pervasiveness and inevitability of "irresistible" settlers. The critical question was *when* national power, normally latent, would be mobilized and directed against a particular tribe or region. This was essentially a political question among U.S. citizens and their representatives, the outcome determined by the dynamics of racialized democracy and federalism. Sadly, contingency lay as much in the timing and extent of white intrusion as in native agency.

Early national army officers lacked a consistent expansionist, much less imperial, vision, not to mention an articulation of it meriting the label ideology. Like British imperial soldiers, they did little long-term systemic planning and expressed surprisingly few enduring principles for men with such education and responsibility. Their attitudes and operations in the borderlands were more reactive than initiatory. Nevertheless, in terms of public land policy, the combination of white man's democracy and the national territorial expansion led by the officer corps meant that centralized power could be employed in the pursuit of future decentralization—Jefferson's "empire of liberty" and Jackson's "area of freedom." At the same time, political decentralization via control over land policy at the state level often meant growing economic consolidation and stratification at the hands of state and local oligarchies, particularly coteries within the planter class of the South. Military friction with white frontiersmen was intermittent, not constant, and was subject to biases of class and gentility: the crises in this book were challenges to national sovereignty, and federal military officers usually tried to be sensitive to local public opinion and to work with local elites who could influence their success and their careers. The greatest civil-military friction probably occurred at the approximate midpoint between the initial civilian dependence on military power for security and the full, essentially postfrontier maturation of civil society in a region.

As early American historians Peter Onuf and James Lewis have observed, the original purposes of the American constitutional system included exporting conflict and coercion to national borders. As such, the army officer corps acted as a leading force in white and U.S. national imperialism, but it also served, surprisingly often, as a force for interethnic and intercultural peace in the face of white man's democracy, territorial expansion, expropriation, and conquest. Apart from economic or resource constraints and Native American opposition itself, probably no other force acted as so frequent and substantial a restraint on white intrusions against Indian land. The same was true to an even greater degree in the army's operations to restrain filibusters against Spanish, British, and Mexican territory. In the process, the national standing army was the principal force on the ground along the northern border that kept the United States out of a potentially devastating war with Britain during the crises between 1838 and 1842. Indeed, the career professional officer corps proved truer republicans than many civilians, whose increasing individualism and materialism, in conjunction with racialized democracy, meant aggressive territorial expansion that threatened to foster social, political, and economic entropy (and eventually civil war), to undermine if not negate national sovereignty and invite international war, sometimes with more powerful states like Britain, which could severely damage the United States and retard its future development.[18]

The role played by the standing army on the nation's frontiers shows that classical republicans were right about the relationship between liberty and power. Political power mattered: stratification was not just economic or class but racialized, mediated by the ability to claim national citizenship. The standing army restrained the ability of frontier citizens to take advantage of democracy, liberalism, and the libertarian elements of republicanism to invade foreign or Indian lands for their own gain, whatever the cost to their fellow citizens elsewhere in the nation. The irony is that aggressive frontier citizens turned out to be far less "virtuous"—less disinterested, more materialistic—representatives of the republican tradition and the American nation as a whole than the authoritarian military officers who sought to restrain them: civilians criticizing the army expressed the individualistic values of liberalism much more than the public vision of classical republicanism.

Yet the national standing army also served as one of the physical underpinnings of Madison's pluralistic, liberal vision of an extended republic of diverse interests balancing one another. The army extended the republic through war, conquest, and occupation; the army preserved the republic's cohesion by maintaining national sovereignty through its many and varied constabulary operations in the new borderlands; and the army sustained national survival and future extension by maintaining national sovereignty and international law against American citizens as well as international threats or rivals. In and of itself, in its intentions, the army's role was socially, politically, and ideologically "objective," or neutral: the question was to what use American citizens put the army, and which citizens were able to secure the power to do so, through the representative mechanisms of American constitutional democracy. The United States was in some significant ways more of a nation-state—a nation as well as a state—than many of its European and Latin American contemporaries, which were *national* states (states organized and administered on a national scale) but not yet nations to the degree that racist democracy fostered (among the whites who defined themselves as citizens) in the United States. Even leaving aside multinational European empires like Austria, and despotisms like that in tsarist Russia, one could still compare the United States with the France depicted by historian Eugen Weber—a "nation" of remarkable parochialism among the vast majority of its largely peasant population. Though many individual officers shared the subjectivity and chauvinism of civilian citizens—a subjectivity that set limits to the state autonomy and influence desirable in a political democracy—the source of that subjectivity, of territorial expansion, conquest, and empire, was the racialized culture of nineteenth-century America. Professional soldiers were complicit in that culture but did not make it; if anything, the officer corps acted to restrain its iniquities.[19]

Democratic civilian control shaped American military missions and organization at every turn. Congressional control of the purse strings compelled fiscal accountability, and the power of congressional inquiry—which the executive branch rarely challenged during this period—spurred professional soldiers toward accountability in the execution of national policy. This often meant serving the interests of white supremacy, slavery, and the dispossession of Native Americans, and career officers often felt discomfort, or at least distaste, when performing such tasks. Yet their experience of civilian self-assertion through frontier civil-military tension and congressional inquiry habituated them to dutiful subordination to civil authority. The question, as the most sophisticated scholars of American civil-military relations have recognized, is to which civil authority military men would give their support. The American constitutional system gave them many possibilities: national, state, or local; executive or legislative. (The judiciary was not yet a well-developed branch of government, and when Andrew Jackson chose not to enforce John Marshall's decision in favor of the Cherokee, no army officer was going to seize the initiative to do so.) The partisan political system, which sometimes posed very real ideological choices, provided at least two more sets of options, and sectional divisions gave them several more. Opportunities for state, local, and sectoral military service were always present in the militia or as volunteers, vigilantes, and filibusters, so service in the U.S. Army and Navy implied a national orientation and allegiance, a greater sense of accountability to national authority than was the norm among nineteenth-century Americans. This did not necessarily preclude serving the interests of a state, region, locality, or section, especially if an officer came from and served in a frontier region, but between 1821 and 1846, professional military allegiance increasingly centered on the federal government. Avowals of sectional loyalty, whether southern or western (or to the frontier), virtually disappeared. With limited structural tension between the executive and the legislature, the principal question remaining was whether federal military officers would engage in the growing partisanship that characterized the development of party systems—the Federalists and Republicans and the Whigs and Democrats—in the early republic.

There is little evidence of extensive partisanship among career army officers; based on the limited evidence available, their partisan affinities seem to have been divided about evenly between the Whigs and the Democrats, much like the loyalties of civilian Americans. As a body, the career officer corps was essentially nonpartisan, and the most extensive evidence suggests antipartisanship or even antagonism toward politics per se in the officer corps, in which the term "demagogue" was commonly applied to politicians. This antipolitical stance originated largely in reaction to civilian condemnation of military hierarchy and the consequent disparagement of military professionalism and professional military education.[20] Faced with attacks on their numbers and pay, officers responded by asserting the necessity of military professionalism for national defense and security. National Republican and Whig support notwithstanding, this approach proved insufficient, given the limited international threats to American security after 1815 and 1821: expertise in conventional war fighting was not enough to protect the officer corps from reproach and reduction, as occurred in those years. Professional soldiers had to turn to other missions and other skill sets to secure their livelihoods and status, and the most obvious alternative was expansion against Native Americans, one of the principal objectives of the Jeffersonian Republican and Jacksonian Democratic parties. Yet politicians from those parties would continue to claim, all evidence to the contrary, that citizen-soldiers could do the work of expansion.

During the 1820s, professional soldiers were compelled to fall back on nonmilitary tasks, like civil engineering work for transportation projects, to supplement their roles preparing for conventional conflict and leading assaults on Native America. Though military participation in surveys for private projects later became a source of Jacksonian censure, by 1838 the Democrats found that too few citizen-soldiers were willing to undertake the arduous, extended service necessary for the expansion they demanded. Thus, although Democratic administrations appointed the junior officers in the regiments they created during the 1830s, 1840s, and 1850s, commissioning many partisan supporters directly from civil life, the regular army survived the Jacksonian assault with higher pay and a larger staff, and without losing its nearly monopolistic control over the operational and tactical direction of national military power. In practice, Democratic congressmen voted for the army almost equally with Whigs. Indeed, rather than demonstrating a reliance on citizen-soldiers, partisan Democratic opportunities to commission junior officers depended on expanding the national standing army (in 1833 and 1836) or taking advantage of unusual situations like the resignations between 1835 and 1837. Nor did these appointments transform the officer corps or the army: disproportionately large numbers of Democratic appointees resigned within several years of receiving their commissions, while none of the national regiments created for the war with Mexico was retained in 1848. After 1837, Military Academy graduates clearly proved more committed and persistent than officers commissioned directly from civilian life, and even a hundred partisan commissions in the four regiments created in 1855 did not prevent the proportion of West Pointers from reaching an all-time high in 1860, at more than 75 percent of the officer corps.[21]

In the meantime, the continual friction between soldiers and civilians on the frontiers led officers to an overtly nonpartisan, often antipartisan, accountability to the national civil authority (the executive branch and Congress), a representative arbiter that actually insulated them from direct citizen pressure, at least as much as anywhere else in democratizing America. Though unable to reduce the army's size, Jacksonian attacks on the regulars' attempts to monopolize the direction of organized armed force, particularly during the Seminole War, led most officers to avoid public controversy and stress their subordination to civilian authority. Most professional military commanders felt a Whiggish affinity for social hierarchy, order, and stability, derived in large part from their aggravating experiences with disorderly egalitarian democrats on the frontier, but they tended to confine the public expression of their views, drawn from professional concerns for the effective performance of their duties to the nation, to situations where that performance was at issue. Thus, although many officers felt qualms over the morality of warring with Mexico, they expressed these qualms privately to one another, rather than publicly opposing administration policy. The consequence was a distinctly professional, or institutional, politics geared toward preserving and enhancing the numbers, status, and professional jurisdiction of the career officer corps.

Officers' interest in partisan politics probably increased as the Second Party System matured during the years of the Second Seminole War, but strong partisan allegiances remained exceptional—and, to many officers, exceptionable—and subordinate to their allegiance to the national civil authority, whatever its partisan composition. The officer corps managed a delicate balancing act that fostered a self-reinforcing cycle of legitimacy, insulation, and autonomy. Before 1821, the officers Jackson commanded may have been too closely identified with the advancement of southern territorial expansion; after 1830, the increasingly professional soldiers he led as commander in chief refused to act as his partisans but continued to serve the expansion willed through the representative process. Nor, despite Jacksonian criticism and the frontier frustration that culminated in Florida, did they seek Whig patronage, which would have undermined their insulation, autonomy, and legitimacy regardless of Whig success. Accountability meant objectivity, and objectivity meant partisan neutrality. Objective subordination and accountability were evident in virtually every dimension of their work: in their service in Florida and Mexico; in their law enforcement efforts against filibusters and their peacekeeping efforts on the frontier and in Kansas during the 1850s; in more overt assertions of national sovereignty, like their performance in the Nullification Crisis and the expedition to compel Mormon adherence to national law between 1857 and 1859; and in comparison to their civilian counterparts during the secession crisis.[22]

A process of professionalization and change, however gradual and uneven, characterized American military history and institutions between 1783 and 1861. By 1820, a de facto consensus on policy and appropriations had developed, favoring a small peacetime standing force to undertake constabulary operations and to serve as a cadre for teaching larger wartime forces organized through the states. This consensus was encouraged by the very positive relations between middle- and upper-class civilians and career military officers, both in Washington and on the nation's peripheries, where the army was recognized as a connection to the national center and an embodiment of national feeling and affinity. More egalitarian or locally oriented citizens, particularly along the frontiers, often resented the imposition of restraint by the nation-state; this meant that local civil-military relations and the constabulary work of professional soldiers in the borderlands were fraught with the complications presented by federalism, socioeconomic pluralism and stratification, and different approaches to territorial expansion. The consequent tensions spurred the officers of the regular army toward greater allegiance to the nation-state that sponsored their profession. These trends and phenomena reflected the American social and political context in which military officers acted, especially the constitutional structure of checks and balances and the hostility of liberal and republican ideology to centralized power (and thus to taxation and military establishments), but also the international and national security contexts of aggressive expansion against Indians and Mexico, amid relative security from conventional European threats.

American military history during this period illustrates, and even spotlights, the complex subtleties of nineteenth-century American society and culture: the relationships among states, nation (or nationalism), and the nation-state, between federalism and sectionalism (East-West or center-periphery as much as North-South), between localism and nationalism. Nineteenth-century American military history demonstrates the realities of growing interdependence, institutional development, and stratified access to social, political, and economic opportunity and power. The military history of nineteenth-century America illustrates both the racialized hierarchies and exclusions of that polity and, perhaps more revealingly, the gradually growing organization, nationalization, and rationalization of American life. The development of enduring national military institutions and the growing concentration of the direction of organized armed force in national, increasingly professional, and incipiently bureaucratic hands, rather than those of Indians, filibusters, local militias, or vigilantes, were early harbingers of the appearance and pervasive penetration of translocal functional organizations throughout American society later in the century. Indeed, this early- to mid-nineteenth-century process of military institutionalization and rationalization anticipated the era of vertical and horizontal integration (in business) and the Progressive reforms of Secretary of War Elihu Root circa 1900.

Not all the consequences were positive. For better or worse, army officers were in the forefront of the design and construction of the early national transportation infrastructure and the forced expulsion of the Native Americans across the Mississippi, crucial stages in the nation's economic growth and the so-called Market Revolution that spurred the advance of the plantation economy and slavery into Indian lands. This capitalist development—the fulfillment of Jefferson's vision, however flawed, of an "empire of liberty"—was expected to permit the elision of social tensions through territorial expansion and the replication of a simple agrarian society across the continent. Professional soldiers advanced the American empire across the South and the Plains into Texas, the Southwest, and California; their efforts would consolidate the inland empire of the Plains, the Southwest, and the Great Basin after the Civil War. Their administrative abilities enabled the United States to project its power into central Mexico without facing the costly guerrilla warfare that extensive foraging for supplies might have stirred among the Mexican people had the army been unable to rely on West Point–educated logisticians and officers socialized in self-discipline and accountability. Much the same can be said of the Civil War, brought on in large part by tensions over the disposition of the western "empire for liberty" that officers had done so much to win. In the struggle to preserve the "last, best hope of mankind," extensive corruption and inefficiency, largely due to the vastly multiplied scale of operations and the influx of administrators without professional socialization, did not prevent the eventual formation of one of the nineteenth century's most effective systems of supply to support the projection of one of its most powerful military forces. That army, its top commanders almost exclusively West Point graduates, destroyed the Confederacy, which had questioned majoritarian democracy and threatened the national union that loyal officers considered, to quote William Tecumseh Sherman, the starting point for the welfare of "all future generations."[23]

The officers of the national standing army were leading actors in the evolution, for good and ill, of the American nation during the nineteenth century. They did so with a distinctive interpretation of protean American values, tightening the bonds of the national union and furthering the process many historians refer to as the political, social, economic, and cultural "incorporation of America." This was neither ironic nor an anomaly. Professional soldiers served the nation's democratically elected representatives, for better or worse, both in conquering the Native Americans and in crushing slavery, by successfully projecting and consolidating national power, which ultimately proved destructive for the parallel paths of social development (essentially those of North and South) that underpinned the Jacksonian republic. Transformed by its own processes of socialization and the nationalist republicanism that followed the War of 1812, the national standing army became a bastion of nationalism and national power against the classical "small republics" of Jackson's South. Yet its officers fought in the cause of liberty as well as democracy and order, pursuing a moderate Enlightenment republicanism that envisioned the American union as the torchbearer of an empire of ordered liberty more comprehensive and cohesive than Jefferson had ever imagined.[24]

Professional socialization in nationalism and scientific-technical disciplines, combined with the hierarchical institutional discipline intended to assure subordination and accountability to the constitutional, democratic civilian authority of the central government, encouraged the officers of the national standing army to see themselves as the objective representatives of that government, pursuing national order and harmony at its direction even when that direction took paths we might deem undemocratic, intolerant, or unjust. In this they reflected, but also influenced, the shifting balances among liberty, democracy, and order in American life: the balances among democratic majoritarianism, republican community, and liberal individualism, between the pursuit of a liberty whose content is always contested and the illiberal means often thought necessary to secure its blessings. Spurred by the intrinsic security concerns of the nation-state, by nation-state sponsorship of military institutions, and by continuing territorial expansion and the internal tensions it fostered and reflected, the nationalization of American military institutions during the decades between the Constitution and the Civil War prefigured the greater institutionalization, rationalization, and nationalization of American life during the Gilded Age and the Progressive Era. Chronologically, this trajectory was substantially more advanced in the military realm than in others, yet the forcible reunification of the United States during the Civil War set a national and institutional tone for future social, political, and economic development, a tone obscured by the apparent dominance of laissez-faire principles during the Gilded Age, but hardly absent even then.[25]

In sum, some elements of national executive power proved highly significant in nineteenth-century America. American governance was not just a matter of "courts and parties," patronage, or legislative largesse to corporations and individuals. Unlike most of the civilian executive branch, which undoubtedly suffered in efficiency and accountability under the partisan spoils system, the career officer corps of the national standing army gained remarkable insulation and autonomy, whether measured against that context or in terms of operations and outcomes. This insulation and autonomy developed despite continual contestation, primarily local and primarily on the nation's frontiers, by citizens, citizen-soldiers, filibusters, local civil officials, and some congressmen. Indeed, this friction spurred national military commanders to greater accountability and subordination to constitutional national civilian authorities and thus to greater responsibility to representative democracy at the national level. The public character of American democracy, combined with officers' socialization in nationalism and disinterested service, reinforced their relative objectivity—and integrity—as public servants. Whatever they thought of the boisterous, turbulent democracy of Jacksonian America, subordination to the Constitution and the rule of law required soldiers to work with citizens and their representatives, regardless of party. They accepted federalism and the separation of powers as inescapable realities, and found some solace and shelter in the latter. In doing so, they carried forward the values and virtues of classical republicanism while advancing liberalism, democracy, and capitalism through the effects of the territorial expansion they directed.

The career officer corps of the national standing army was not physically or mentally isolated or mentally or politically alienated (which is what most scholars imply when they refer to isolation). It was certainly not equally supportive of every segment of the citizenry: socialized in values of nationalism and gentility, disinterestedness and obligation, most officers disdained unruly, rabidly materialistic frontiersmen and the self-interested politics they identified—like many other Americans—with the new parties. This is not to depict officers as paragons of virtue: they had strong personal, institutional, and professional interests and sought to profit from investments in the growing commercial economy. Their relationship to individualism and the market, to liberalism and democracy, was complex, often ambiguous, sometimes ambivalent. But none were permanently isolated from the trends in their parent society and its culture, and very few were truly alienated. The army officer corps was part of the American middle class, part of American federalism, the separation of powers, and constitutional representative government, but it was entrusted with an insulation and autonomy unusual during the growth of liberal democracy in the early republic. Unlike many agencies of civilian government, the officer corps was not "captured" by a class, economic interest group, party, or section. Professional military commanders accepted and promoted the rule of law and representative government, hoping to maintain and enhance national cohesion and power through their execution of policies determined by civilians.

They succeeded. The army's actions enhanced national cohesion and restrained political and social fragmentation. Professional soldiers kept the United States out of war, against the efforts of filibusters and despite the violence of frontiersmen, unless the elected national civilian authorities wanted war. When war came, their administrative expertise, particularly as logisticians, and tactical capability enabled the United States to successfully project national power over distances far greater than it had in 1776 or 1815. Their experienced leadership and disciplined ability, not the enthusiasm of volunteer citizen-soldiers, defeated Mexico; both sides entrusted them with command during the Civil War, and their logistical expertise, largely retained by the Union, gave the United States a crucial advantage in execution (and not just raw resources) over the Confederacy.

The outcome was more ordered liberty and vast territorial expansion, with only one truly significant case of fragmentation, which the career officer corps helped resolve in the Civil War. Indeed, professional soldiers proved essential to Madisonian liberal expansion and Jackson's expanded "area of freedom," within the constitutional union treasured by Jackson and the founders of the republic. Citizen-soldiers lacked the experience, the resources, and the persistence to defeat the Indians, Mexico, or the Confederacy. They were too sectional (or partisan) and too expensive for anything short of a major war. Organization was necessary for victory, and expertise was necessary for effective organization. Centralization was necessary to preserve decentralization without entropy.

At the national level, civilian politicians recognized the value of forces for national organization and cohesion, for disciplined agents of the national will expressed through the constitutional representative process. Congress and the executive granted the national standing army and its career officer corps permanence and autonomy: political insulation, operational discretion, and a de facto monopoly of command in order to achieve the objectives civilian officials assigned. These relations were fraught with tension, but the standing army and its officers served the nation, even when they restrained some elements of the people. They could hardly avoid doing so, in order to serve the people as a whole.

Alexander Ramsay Thompson monument, West Point Cemetery. Photograph by the author

APPENDICES

APPENDIX A

The Spectrum of Coercive Diplomacy and Deterrence

Here I suggest a schematic range of actions and intended consequences to clarify some of the confusion surrounding phrases such as "constabulary operations," "operations other than war," "military operations other than war," "stability operations," "stability and support operations," "gunboat diplomacy," and "coercive diplomacy" (a concept invented in analyses of Cold War diplomatic crises). As a historian, I am much more interested in the specific action or form of deployment and the message it was intended to convey than in precise definitions of specific concepts, so I do not distinguish sharply between deterrence and coercive diplomacy or between peacekeeping and peace enforcement, except that in each pairing, the latter is more active and perhaps more aggressive. I also accept the general distinction that deterrence and peacekeeping are intended to prevent actions, whereas coercion (sometimes referred to as "compellance") and peace enforcement are intended to change existing behavior.

Above all, the following list is intended to show a spectrum from passivity to violence, from indirection to direction, from implication to action, from generally small scale to larger scale, and from lesser to greater demands on the targeted populace, using specific historical deployment types as examples. I do not attempt to make moral distinctions, because virtually all army officers justified these actions as law enforcement and expressed their moral qualms privately.

1. Simply being garrisoned in an area—passive presence. This constitutes a passive form of point or "wide area" security, in today's terms, but it implies the potential for more active power projection: "We are here."
2. Showing the flag more actively, through small-scale (squad- to company-

sized) presence patrols or the presence (usually in the guise of guards, on a small scale) at negotiations.
3. Focused movements, usually to specific places of political significance—usually Indian or squatter villages. This represents a move from peacekeeping to the potential for peace enforcement.

   A. More specifically, and thus implicitly more aggressively, showing the flag—an implied threat: "We know where you are, and we can reach you."
   B. A more explicit show of threat intended to intimidate, but still passive coercion, such as warnings to leave an area or otherwise change behavior.

4. Active coercion, via larger and more extended or more frequently sustained expeditions, often couched in terms of peacekeeping or peace enforcement, but potentially culminating in conquest, either overt or de facto. These actions can be "punitive" or "law enforcement" in nature (in both cases, retaliating for individual incidents or for several incidents or a pattern thereof).

   A. Remove Indians or squatters from a village or from an area.
   B. Detain them.
   C. Burn their crops and/or dwellings.
   D. Do so with the authority (usually implied in orders to "use your discretion") to employ lethal force if resisted.

APPENDIX B

Officers Who Became Civilian Territorial or Senior Federal Executive Branch Officials, 1814–1846

Name	Dates and Highest Rank as Regular Officer	Civilian Positions and Dates
William Clark	1792–1796, 1804–1807; lieutenant (Senate rejected Jefferson's nomination as lieutenant colonel)	Missouri territorial governor, 1813–1820; federal superintendent of Indian affairs, St. Louis, 1822–1838 (died)
John Miller	1812–1818; colonel (Ohio, distinguished at Fort Meigs, 1813)	Public land registrar, Missouri, 1818–1825; state governor, 1828–1832; House of Representatives, 1837–1843
Thomas A. Smith	1803–1818; colonel (commanded Ninth Military Department in St. Louis)	Public land office receiver of money, Missouri, 1818–
Richard Keith Call	1814–1822; captain (Jackson protégé)	Florida territorial council, 1822; territorial militia general, 1823; territorial delegate, 1823–1825; U.S. receiver of public lands in west Florida, 1825; territorial governor, 1835–1839 and 1841–1845

(*continued*)

Name	Dates and Highest Rank as Regular Officer	Civilian Positions and Dates
Robert Butler	1812–1821; adjutant general, Southern Division (Jackson), declined reduction to lieutenant colonel	U.S. surveyor general of public lands, Florida, 1824–1849
James Gadsden	1812–1821; inspector general, Southern Division (Jackson), Senate rejected nomination as adjutant general	Florida territorial council, 1824; treaty commissioner to Seminoles, 1823 and 1832; chief negotiator for land purchase from Mexico, 1853
Joseph Lee Smith	1812–1821; colonel (Conn.), disbanded after dispute with Alexander Macomb	Superior court of east Florida, 1822–
John McNeil	1812–1830; colonel (N.H.), hero at Lundy's Lane	U.S. surveyor, Port of Boston, 1830–1850 (died) (only field-grade officer who resigned to enter federal civil service, 1821–1846)
John McIntosh	1808–1820; major (Ga.)	U.S. Customs collector, Darien, Ga., 1824–
Charles Mason	West Point, 1829–1831; lieutenant (first in class)	Chief justice, superior court of Iowa territory, 1838–1847
James Miller	1808–1819; colonel (Mass.), hero at Lundy's Lane	Arkansas territorial governor, 1819–1825; U.S. Customs collector, Salem, Mass., 1825–1851 (died)
George Izard	1794–1803, 1812–1815; major general	Arkansas territorial governor, 1825–1828 (died)
Robert Crittenden	1814–1815; lieutenant	Arkansas territorial secretary and acting governor, 1819–1829 (brother of Senator John J. Crittenden)

William Bradford	1812–1824; major (only field-grade officer who resigned, 1822–1830)	Ran twice for Arkansas territorial delegate to Congress while still in uniform; Arkansas territorial militia general, 1824–
Henry Conway	1812–1820; lieutenant (related to Sevier political family)	Defeated Bradford for Arkansas territorial delegate, 1823–1827 (mortally wounded by Crittenden in 1827 duel)
William O. Allen	1812–1818; captain	Arkansas territorial militia general, 1820–
John Nicks	1808–1821; lieutenant colonel, Seventh Infantry Regiment (stationed in Ark.)	Arkansas territorial militia general, 1827–
Joseph Selden	1812–1820; brevet lieutenant colonel	Federal judge in Arkansas (killed in 1824 duel)

Data drawn from army biographical sources and state political histories. Note that the terminal dates for many civil offices are not given in the army sources. I included states of origin when these were relevant to federal civil appointments.

These cases show the movement from federal military service to civilian federal executive branch employment between 1815 and 1821. Their average military service was 9.3 years; only seven of these eighteen men exceeded 9 years in the army. Only two left the army after 1822, and one of them (Bradford) was the only field-grade officer to resign from the entire line of the army (the infantry and artillery) between 1822 and 1830. Six of these men were first appointed to civil office by James Monroe, two by John Quincy Adams, and one (McNeil) by Andrew Jackson. McNeil was the only field-grade officer to resign his army commission to enter the federal civil service between 1821 and 1846, after he supported a newspaper backing Jackson in 1828. Bradford and McNeil were two of only six field-grade officers in the line who resigned between 1822 and 1837.

These men's practical significance was as territorial governors (commanders of territorial militias) and as generals of militia, and in the acquisition and sale of public lands from Indians and to whites, above all in Florida, where Jackson's influence was critical.

APPENDIX C
Army Officers Who Served as Indian Agents, 1814–1846

Agency	Name	Dates as Regular Officer	Dates as Agent
Apalachicola (Florida)	(Captain) John Phagan	1813–1815	1826–1833
Caddo	(Lieutenant) Jehiel Brooks	1818–1820	1830–1834
Cherokee (West)	(Colonel) David Brearley	1808–1811, 1812–1820	1820–1823
	(Captain) George Vashon (ex-Delaware and Shawnee)	1812–1819	1830–1834
	(Lieutenant) Pierce M. Butler	1819–1820	1841–1845
Chickasaw (East)	(Colonel) Robert Carter Nicholas	1808–1819	1820–1823
Chickasaw (West)	(Lieutenant) Gaines P. Kingsbury (West Point graduate)	1832–1836	1837–1839
Choctaw (West)	(Captain) F. W. Armstrong	1812–1817 (U.S. marshal, Alabama, 1823–1827)	1831–1835
Creek (West)	Brearley (ex-Cherokee West)	1820–1821	1826–1829
	(Lieutenant) Wharton Rector	1836–1842, paymaster (exchanged with Harney for LTC 2nd Dragoons)	1835–1836

(*continued*)

Agency	Name	Dates as Regular Officer	Dates as Agent
Delaware and Shawnee	Vashon	—	1829–1830
Green Bay	(Colonel) John Bowyer	1792–1815	1816–1821
Osage	(Lieutenant) John F. Hamtramck (West Point graduate)	1819–1822	1826–1830
Prairie du Chien (Fort Winnebago subagency)	Three serving officers	—	1834–1837
Sault Ste. Marie	(Captain) Waddy V. Cobbs	1813–1848	1834–1837 (acting)
Seminole	(Lieutenant Colonel) Gad Humphreys	1808–1821	1822–1830
	Phagan (also Apalachicola)	—	1830–1833
Upper Missouri (Sioux subagency)	(Lieutenant) George Kennerly	1813–1819; 1823, sutler (Fort Atkinson); 1828–1842 (Jefferson Barracks); 1846–1848, assistant quartermaster	1824–1828
Totals and averages	13 total, not including acting agents: 3 colonels, 1 lieutenant colonel, 3 captains, 6 lieutenants	Average, 6.5 years (5.5 minus Bowyer); average date of separation, 1820	Average, 4 years

Data drawn from comparison of army biographical sources with Edward E. Hill, *The Office of Indian Affairs, 1824–1880: Historical Sketches* (New York: Clearwater Publishing, 1974).

Thirteen was a significant number of agents, but it was only a small minority of the total number and a very small minority of the officers who were disbanded in 1815 or 1821 or who resigned. However, former officers figured prominently as agents for tribes being removed to the West and for those in Florida. Only two of the thirteen left the army after 1821; they were also the only West Pointers among the thirteen. None of these men became career officials in the Indian service: only three of the thirteen served more than the four-year average. Only three received their appointments after 1831, and only three served after 1836, suggesting that former officers were no longer a significant constituency for federal patronage after Jackson's first administration.

APPENDIX D
Combat Arms Field-Grade Officer Resignations, 1822–1846

Name	Year Resigned	Reason, if Known	Length of Service (Years)	New Occupation
Major William Bradford	1824	To engage in territorial politics	12	Territorial militia general, Arkansas
Colonel John McNeil	1830	To take civil service position	18	U.S. surveyor, Port of Boston
Colonel William Lawrence	1831		30	
Major George Bender	1833	Probably because of loss of quartermaster staff assignment	21	Chief clerk, Ordnance Department (a responsible position in Washington, where he had been stationed)
Colonel Duncan L. Clinch	1836	Criticism from War Department over conduct of operations in Florida	28	Planter, Georgia congressman, candidate for governor
Lieutenant Colonel John Bliss	1837		25	
Major Nathaniel Young	1838	To run for office	25	Delaware state legislator
Lieutenant Colonel Sullivan Burbank	1839		27	
Colonel Enos Cutler	1839		31	

This table is based on the Army Registers. I looked at all of them except for those from 1842 and 1844, but the 1843 and 1845 registers do not show any field-grade officer departures except for men known to have died. I did not include Henry Dodge, who served as colonel of the First Dragoon Regiment from 1833 to 1836 (when he was appointed territorial governor of Wisconsin), because his commission and departure were both exceptionally political.

Their average time in service was twenty-five years (discounting Bradford, the first and most junior officer to resign; after him, there were no resignations for six years). Except for Lawrence, these men all received their commissions in the 1808 buildup or the War of 1812. The army had a minimum of thirty-three field-grade officers (a colonel, lieutenant colonel, and major for each regiment), and it added regiments in 1833, 1836, and 1838; thus, the eight who resigned during the decade 1830–1839 represent a resignation rate of less than 3 percent per annum. The nine who resigned during the quarter century between the 1821 reduction in force and the beginning of war with Mexico in 1846 represent a rate of about 1 percent per annum.

APPENDIX E
Schematic Illustrations of the Dynamics of U.S. Territorial Expansion

The relationships between historians' interpretations of civilian expansionism and limited government ideology, state capacity, and military effectiveness are illustrated in this diagram.

	If we emphasize civilian preferences for aggressive territorial expansion	If we emphasize civilian preferences for limited government (or simply low taxes)
If we view the American state as powerful	A: the modern popular culture vision of a powerful army eagerly overwhelming the Indians—not held by modern historians	B: civilians wanted a small army, but it proved sufficient to achieve their objectives—my view
If we view the American state as weak	C: extralegal citizen violence (filibusters and vigilantes) defeats the Indians—not likely against strong resistance	D: the political scientists' "state of courts and parties," in which an indirect actor distributes patronage and subsidies—in this case, primarily easy access to public lands—an incentive for C

The criteria shaping case D would also fit the standard modern "western history" interpretation in college textbooks, with population growth and the consequent ecological damage (reduced access to food) defeating the Indians. Examples of the outcomes of these relationships are shown in the next diagram.

457

	Aggressive civilian public opinion	Passive civilian public opinion
Aggressive federal government	A: the "Indian wars"—the conquest of the Northwest Territory during the 1790s, the Seminole Wars, and the Black Hawk War, each won by the national standing army with some citizen-soldier and allied Indian assistance	B: the Missouri expeditions (discussed in *Jackson's Sword*)—only the fur companies were really interested in expansion, but there was poor cooperation with military commanders; lack of public interest ultimately ended federal efforts, leading to a case C situation and compromise with the Indians for the fur companies
Relatively passive government	C: the Southwest Territory during the 1780s and 1790s—expansion primarily through civilian violence, but with less success than in case A	D: no expansion

The great majority of the case studies in this book (and most examples of U.S. territorial expansion) are examples of case A. Apart from the Texas Revolution, examples of case C usually proved less complete and enduring: the critical question was whether the demands of public opinion were sufficient to produce a shift to case A, with the intervention by national military forces needed to complete and consolidate expansion. The larger question for students of American territorial expansion is how often the dog did not bark: cases B and D. Since the federal government rarely initiated sustained expansionist efforts without some impetus from public opinion, case B proved quite rare; the purchase of Alaska, deemed "Seward's Folly" by many newspapers at the time, was perhaps the great exception. These dynamics were significantly distinct from those of European imperialism during the nineteenth century, which was usually initiated by central governments (sometimes to distract or mobilize public opinion) or by military or civil officials on the scene, often in collaboration with some interested party (businessmen, small groups of European colonists, or indigenous groups seeking aid against rivals), but with very little general public interest or support.

APPENDIX F

Major Campaigns or Deployments against Indians, apart from Seminole Wars

Year	Objective and Opponent	Force	Commander
1815	Survey Florida boundary, vs. Creeks	Two regiments (800 soldiers)	Gaines
1819	Advance up Mississippi, vs. Winnebagos	Most of one regiment (300–400 soldiers)	Leavenworth
1823	"Arikara War" (punitive expedition)	Elements of one regiment (230 soldiers), 500–750 Sioux allies	Leavenworth
1826	Arrest Winnebagos	Elements of a regiment	Leavenworth
1827	"Winnebago War" (intimidate and arrest Winnebagos)	580 regulars, plus a mix of 650 additional regulars, militia, and allied Indians	Atkinson (second such command, counting 1825 Missouri expedition)
1829	Escort Santa Fe caravans, vs. Pawnee and Comanche	Four companies (approx. 200 soldiers)	Riley (second such experience, counting Arikara expedition)
1831	Intimidate Black Hawk's band	Ten companies (approx. 400 soldiers), 1,500 militia	Gaines (second such command)
1832	Black Hawk War	560 regulars, Mounted Rangers (federal volunteers), 750 Indian allies, 3,000+ militia; plus 22 regular companies and 200 recruits who arrived too late for action	Atkinson Scott arrived too late for action

(*continued*)

459

Year	Objective and Opponent	Force	Commander
1836	Second Creek War	1,100 regulars (some from Florida), as many as 9,000 militia	Scott (with Jesup as principal subordinate)
1838	Concentrate Cherokee for removal	2.5 regiments (approx. 1,000 soldiers), plus large militia forces	Scott (third such command, including 1836 Seminole War)
1840	Remove Winnebagos	1,100 soldiers (elements of four regiments)	Worth (second such experience, including 1838 Cherokee concentration)

Thus, there were eleven such campaigns, or an average of one every 2.5 years between 1815 and 1840, and they averaged 640 soldiers (essentially two regiments) per deployment. This does not include several deployments in anticipation of possible campaigns, which did not result in active operations in the field. Substantial operations were undertaken against the Creeks in 1815, 1817–1818 (as the Red Sticks, the real target of the "First Seminole War"), and 1836–1842 (as fugitives in Florida after their 1836 uprising). The Winnebago were the only Native Americans besides the Seminoles to be threatened by substantial expeditions over extended periods, in 1819, 1826–1827, and 1840. It should be noted that the dragoon expeditions onto the Plains during the 1830s and 1840s were not undertaken against specific geographic objectives (like opening rivers to white access) or with the expectation of combat, as in the deployments listed above. The dragoon expeditions that were sent several times a year to remove or intimidate different groups of Indians (Ioway, Osage, Oto, Potawatomi, Sauk, Sioux, and Winnebago) on the Missouri frontier, in Iowa, and in the future Indian Territory consisted of only a company or two (50 to 200 soldiers), indicating that they did not expect resistance.

APPENDIX G

Major Expeditions or Deployments to Project American Power against Non-Indian Opponents

Year	Mission, Objective, Opponent	Force*	Commander
1816	Destroy "Negro Fort," a sanctuary for fugitives from slavery on Apalachicola River in Spanish Florida	One regiment, Creek allies, navy gunboats	Clinch (at Jackson's direction)
1817	Occupy Amelia Island in Spanish Florida, vs. filibusters	250 soldiers, navy brig	Bankhead
1818–1820	Prepare attack against Spanish St. Augustine	Two regiments plus artillery	Jackson, Gaines
1818	Advance into Neutral Ground to prepare for contingencies on Texas frontier	360 soldiers	Ripley
1836	Prepare for contingencies on Texas frontier (occupy Nacogdoches)	Up to 20 companies (1,100 soldiers)	Gaines
1839–1843	Prepare to defend Maine boundary against Canadians or British (Aroostook War)	Several companies, mostly militia during the immediate crisis	Scott
1842–1846	Prepare for contingencies in Texas (advance to Rio Grande)	Began with approx. 2,000 soldiers (three regiments)	Taylor

*Calculating force averages would not be meaningful due to the wide variation in missions and expected opposition.

APPENDIX H

Major Campaigns or Deployments Upholding National Sovereignty against U.S. Citizens

Year	Opponent	Force and Action Taken	Commander
1819	The Long filibusters against Texas	Several companies; other units arrested some filibusters	William Beard
1825–1826	Georgia, over Creek lands	One regiment*	Gaines
1830–1833	Georgians, during gold rush in Cherokee lands, and Alabamians trespassing on Creek lands	Up to 14 companies (550 troops); conducted arrests and detentions, shot one citizen	Several majors (Wager, McIntosh)
1832–1833	Nullification	Approx. one regiment total	Scott, Bankhead
1838	Texans raiding the Caddo in western Louisiana	165 soldiers (arrived after the Texans withdrew)	James Many
1838–1839	Filibusters against Canada; British or Canadian retaliation	Elements of several regiments (maximum of 3,000 soldiers); disarmed and detained filibusters	Scott, Wool, Worth, Brady, Macomb, Eustis
1842	The "Dorr War"—constitutional conflict in Rhode Island (not upholding U.S. sovereignty per se)	Four companies (as many as 400 soldiers)	Bankhead

(*continued*)

463

Year	Opponent	Force and Action Taken	Commander
1843	Texans raiding the Santa Fe Trail	Four companies (150 soldiers); disarmed Texans	Philip St. George Cooke

Note: This table does not include company-scale squatter removal operations, which were more frequent than similarly sized expeditions against Indians until about 1834, or company-sized operations to aid civilian authorities in domestic law enforcement. Only four cases resulted in physical action, with only one use of lethal force.

*Most of these troops probably remained in west and northwest Georgia between 1827 and 1829 to intimidate either Georgians or Creeks.

NOTES

Note that I have cited documents in the sources where I initially found them, but many official letters are duplicated, whether in the *American State Papers*, published National Historical Publications and Records Commission editions, or multiple National Archives record groups. Researchers should note that many documents cited in the registers of letters received by the War Department (M222) are not preserved in the microfilm of the letters themselves (M22).

ABBREVIATIONS

AFS	*Armed Forces and Society*
AGOLR	Letters Received by the Office of the Adjutant General, M566 and M567, RG 94 (only the author is cited, unless the adjutant general was not the addressee)
AGOLS	Letters Sent by the Office of the Adjutant General (Main Series), 1800–1890, M565, RG 94 (only the addressee is cited, unless the adjutant general was not the author)
AHR	*American Historical Review*
AJ	Andrew Jackson
AM	Alexander Macomb (commanding general, 1828–1841)
ANC	*Army and Navy Chronicle* (13 vols., Washington, D.C., 1835–1842)
ANC&SR	*Army and Navy Chronicle and Scientific Repository* (3 vols., Washington, D.C., 1842–1844)
ASPIA	*American State Papers . . . Class II, Indian Affairs*, 2 vols. (Washington, D.C.: Gales and Seaton, 1832–1861) (available online)
ASPMA	*American State Papers: Documents, Legislative and Executive, of the Congress of the United States, Class V, Military Affairs.* 7 vols. [covering the years 1794–1836] (Washington, D.C.: Gales and Seaton, 1832–1861) (available online)
BHC	Burton Historical Collection, Detroit Public Library

CAJ	John Spencer Bassett, ed., *Correspondence of Andrew Jackson*, vol. 2, *May 1, 1814 to December 31, 1819* (Washington, D.C.: Carnegie Institution of Washington, 1927)
COK	*Chronicles of Oklahoma*
DH	*Diplomatic History*
EPG	Edmund P. Gaines
FHQ	*Florida Historical Quarterly*
GAHQ	*Georgia Historical Quarterly*
HA	Henry Atkinson
HB	Hugh Brady
HQALR	Letters Received by the Headquarters of the Army [the commanding general's office], 1827–1903, M1635, RG 108 (only the author is cited, unless the commanding general was not the addressee)
HQALS	Letters Sent by the Headquarters of the Army (Main Series), 1828–1903, M857, RG 108 (only the addressee is cited, unless the commanding general was not the author; this was my most important source for operations between 1828 and 1834)
HSP	Historical Society of Pennsylvania, Philadelphia
JAH	*Journal of American History*
JCC	John C. Calhoun (secretary of war, 1817–1825)
JER	*Journal of the Early Republic*
JMH	*Journal of Military History*
JSH	*Journal of Southern History*
LC	Library of Congress
MNM	*Military and Naval Magazine of the United States* (6 vols., Washington, D.C., 1833–1836)
MPP	James D. Richardson, comp., *Compilation of the Messages and Papers of the Presidents*, vols. 1–3 (New York: Bureau of National Literature, 1897)
MVHR	*Mississippi Valley Historical Review*
NA	National Archives (Archives I), Washington, D.C.
NASPMA	Benjamin Franklin Cooling, ed., *The New American State Papers, 1789–1860: Military Affairs*, 19 vols. (Wilmington, Del.: Scholarly Resources, 1979)
NYPL	New York Public Library, New York City
NYSL	New York State Library, Albany
OHS	Ohio Historical Society, Columbus
PAJ	Harold D. Moser et al., eds., *The Papers of Andrew Jackson*, 7 vols. to date (Knoxville: University of Tennessee Press, 1980–).
PJCC	Robert L. Meriwether and W. Edwin Hemphill, eds., *The Papers of John C. Calhoun*, vols. 2–9 (Columbia: University of South Carolina Press, 1963–1976)
PLDU	William R. Perkins Library, Duke University

RG	Record Group
RJ	Roger Jones (adjutant general, 1825–1852)
SHC	Southern Historical Collection, University of North Carolina, Chapel Hill
SWHQ	*Southwestern Historical Quarterly*
SWK	Stephen W. Kearny
SWLR: Reg	Letters Received by the Secretary of War, Registered Series, 1801–1870, M221, RG 107 (only the author is cited, unless the secretary of war was not the addressee)
SWLR: Unreg	Letters Received by Secretary of War, Unregistered Series, 1789–1861, M222, RG 107 (only the author is cited, unless the secretary of war was not the addressee)
SWLS	Letters Sent by the Secretary of War Relating to Military Affairs, 1800–1889, M6, RG 107 (only the addressee is cited, unless the secretary of war was not the author)
SWLS: C	Confidential and Unofficial Letters Sent by the Secretary of War, 1814–1847, M7, RG 107 (only the addressee is cited, unless the secretary of war was not the author)
SWLS: PUS	Letters Sent to the President by the Secretary of War, 1800–1863, M127, RG 107
THS	Tennessee Historical Society, Nashville
TP	Clarence E. Carter and John P. Bloom, eds., *The Territorial Papers of the United States*, 28 vols. (Washington, D.C.: U.S. State Department and National Archives, 1934–1975) (available online)
USAMHI	United States Army Military History Institute, Carlisle, Pennsylvania
USMA	United States Military Academy Library, Special Collections, West Point, N.Y.
WBS	Notes summarizing documents, received from William B. Skelton
WDLS	Western Department, Letters Sent (this is actually Letters Sent by Brevet Major General Edmund Pendleton Gaines and Staff, 1819–1826, Entry 5806, RG 393, but many older sources refer to it as Western Department, Letters Sent, or as Letters Sent, Western Department)
WHQ	*Western Historical Quarterly*
WLC	William L. Clements Library, University of Michigan, Ann Arbor
WMQ	*William and Mary Quarterly*, 3rd series
WS	Winfield Scott (commanding general, 1841–1861)
ZT	Zachary Taylor

PREFACE AND ACKNOWLEDGMENTS

1. The term *nonstate actors* can mean any people not acting under the authority of the nation-state, though it usually refers to their actions in the international arena, as in frontiers and borderlands. The modern term *nongovernmental organizations* (NGOs) has a similar meaning but usually refers to groups acting peacefully (e.g., those working in disaster relief, poverty assistance, and economic development), whereas present-day usage tends to refer to armed persons not under nation-state authority as nonstate actors. Indians were almost by definition nonstate actors, but I use the term primarily to mean whites, whether U.S. citizens (usually frontiersmen) or European or Latin American adventurers, who were usually armed, aggressive, and not acting under the authority of internationally recognized nation-states. Indeed, most of their significant actions were contrary to national or international law (or at least its evolving customs and principles)—much like criminals, pirates, and terrorists today. The movement of American farmers, usually armed, across international boundaries without passports was considered invasion under international custom; Native Americans saw intrusion on their lands the same way, and federal law actually sided with the Indians, however inadequately it was enforced.

2. *Removal* originated as a term during the 1820s, if not before, and the Jacksonians used it to obscure the coercive nature of their policies, meaning that a person or group would "remove"—a contemporary synonym for *move*—from point A to point B. Many historians use *removal* as if the army were pushing the Indians west at bayonet point; others appear to use it without any sense of irony, as though the Indians simply chose to "remove" from one place to another like the whites moving west. The army did forcibly drive the Seminoles and Creeks west, and at one point or another it used force against most of the northwestern tribes addressed in chapter 2, but not the Choctaw or Chickasaw; it forcibly concentrated the Cherokee, but their movement west was then conducted by Cherokee leaders under John Ross. If the reader rejects my characterization of Indian removal as ethnic cleansing, see more specific examples in Jean Pfaelzer, *Driven Out: The Hidden War against Chinese-Americans* (Berkeley: University of California Press, 2008), and Elliott Jaspin, *Buried in Bitter Waters: The History of Racial Cleansing in the United States* (New York: Basic Books, 2008). The latter examines the "expulsion" (ethnic cleansing) of African Americans from towns in the South and Lower Midwest during the late nineteenth century, a process enlarged in mob actions (usually labeled "race riots") against urban African American neighborhoods and the destruction of African American towns (e.g., Rosewood, Florida) during the early twentieth century. Historians of Texas will recognize parallel examples in nineteenth-century violence against Mexicans.

CHAPTER ONE: NATIONAL MILITARY EXPANSION
ON THE WESTERN FRONTIER

1. A. S. Kanya-Forstner, *The Conquest of the Western Sudan: A Study in French Military Imperialism* (Cambridge: Cambridge University Press, 1969), 8–9. See also Hew Strachan, *The Politics of the British Army* (Oxford: Clarendon Press, 1997), 76–80; J. A. deMoor and H. L. Wesseling, eds., *Imperialism and War: Essays on Colonial Wars in Asia and Africa* (Leiden, Netherlands: Brill, 1989), 79; E. Willis Brooks, "Nicholas I as Reformer: Russian Attempts to Conquer the Caucasus, 1825–1855," in *Nation and Ideology: Essays in Honor of Wayne S. Vucinich*, ed. Ivo Banac et al. (New York: Columbia University Press, 1981), 245; David Mackenzie, "Russian Expansion in Central Asia: St. Petersburg versus the Turkestan Generals," *Canadian Slavic Studies* 3 (1969): 303–306; C. M. Andrew and A. S. Kanya-Forstner, "Centre and Periphery in the Making of the Second French Empire, 1815–1920," *Journal of Imperial and Commonwealth History* 16, 3 (1988): 9–34; Kenneth J. Perkins, *Qaids, Captains, and Colons: French Military Administration in the Colonial Mahgrib, 1844–1934* (New York: Africana Publishing, 1981); C. A. Bayly, *Imperial Meridian: The British Empire and the World, 1780–1830* (London: Longman, 1989); David M. Anderson and David Killingray, eds., *Policing the Empire: Government, Authority, and Control, 1830–1940* (Manchester: Manchester University Press, 1991).

2. For attitudes toward the justifications for and operations of law during the Jacksonian period, see Lawrence Frederick Kohl, *The Politics of Individualism: Parties and the American Character in the Jacksonian Era* (New York: Oxford University Press, 1989), chap. 4, and Daniel Walker Howe, *What Hath God Wrought? The Transformation of America, 1815–1848* (New York: Oxford University Press, 2007), chap. 11.

3. See Thomas C. Leonard, "Red, White, and Army Blue: Empathy and Anger in the American West," *American Quarterly* 26 (May 1974): 176–190, for the post–Civil War era.

4. Francis Paul Prucha, *American Indian Policy in the Formative Years: The Indian Trade and Intercourse Acts, 1790–1834* (Cambridge, Mass.: Harvard University Press, 1962), 134; ZT to Superintendent of Western Indian Affairs William Clark, July 2, 1835, quoted in K. Jack Bauer, *Zachary Taylor: Soldier, Planter, Statesman of the Old Southwest* (Baton Rouge: Louisiana State University Press, 1985), 67; SWK to HA, May 26, 1837, quoted in Martha Royce Blaine, *The Ioway Indians* (Norman: University of Oklahoma Press, 1979), 168; SWK, Capt. T. F. Smith, and Capt. Nathan Boone (the commission to select the route of the western military road) to Cass, December 11, 1836, communicated to the House of Representatives March 24, 1838, *NASPMA*, 2:12–13.

5. Douglas M. Peers, *Between Mars and Mammon: Colonial Armies and the Garrison State in India, 1819–1835* (London: I. B. Tauris, 1995), 4, 7, 45; John Connor, *The Australian Frontier Wars, 1788–1838* (Sydney: University of New South Wales Press, 2002); James Belich, *The New Zealand Wars and the Victorian Interpretation of Racial Conflict* (Auckland, New Zealand: Auckland University Press, 1986); Alan

Ward, "Law and Law Enforcement on the New Zealand Frontier, 1840–1893," *New Zealand Journal of History* 5 (October 1971): 128–149. See note 1 for French and Russian imperial military government and civil-military relations.

6. Robert M. Utley, "Culture Clash on the Western North American Indian Frontier: Military Implications," in *The Military and Conflict between Cultures: Soldiers at the Interface*, ed. James C. Bradford (College Station: Texas A&M University Press, 1997), 103.

7. The principal trade and intercourse acts were dated July 22, 1790 (1 *Stat.* 137–138), May 19, 1796 (1 *Stat.* 469–474), March 30, 1802 (2 *Stat.* 139–146), and June 30, 1834 (4 *Stat.* 729–735). Despite the problems inherent in the term, I generally refer to Indian polities as "tribes" because "nations" might be more confusing in its implications about internal cohesion or sovereignty. We should note, however, that eighteenth- and early-nineteenth-century whites commonly referred to Indian polities and ethnic groups as "nations" (much more so than "races"), regardless of whether they intended to accord the Indians the sovereignty and respect they gave to European nation-states. Given both the complexity of Sioux social and political organization and the uncertainty in the sources, I generally refer to Sioux rather than Lakota or Dakota (which are dialects) or the seven major political subdivisions, such as the Teton or Yankton. This also reflects U.S. government perception and practice, in that military officers and civilian officials were often unable or unwilling to distinguish among large native cultural groups. Since my work explores the perspectives and actions of U.S. Army officers, I have tried to balance modern sensitivity to the intricacies of ethnicity, particularly among nonstate or tribal societies, and the unfortunate reality that my subjects rarely recognized such distinctions. The tension between the desire to split groups (to recognize distinctions) and the need to lump them together (to synthesize and aggregate) remains a dilemma for American military officers today in places with tribal societies and weak states with a limited sense of nationalism, like Afghanistan.

8. See especially David LaVere, *Contrary Neighbors: Southern Plains and Removed Indians in Indian Territory* (Norman: University of Oklahoma Press, 2000).

9. See especially P. Richard Metcalf, "Who Should Rule at Home? Native American Politics and Indian-White Relations," *JAH* 61 (December 1974): 651–665.

10. Mary W. M. Hargreaves, *The Presidency of John Quincy Adams* (Lawrence: University Press of Kansas, 1985), 201.

11. Robert Wooster, *The American Military Frontiers: The United States Army in the West, 1783–1900* (Albuquerque: University of New Mexico Press, 2009), xv. For attitudes toward enlisted soldiers, see Dale R. Steinhauer, "'Sogers': Enlisted Men in the U.S. Army, 1815–1860" (Ph.D. diss., University of North Carolina, 1992), especially chaps. 1–3 (the best work on enlisted men during this era), and Dale T. Knobel, *Paddy and the Republic: Ethnicity and Nationality in Antebellum America* (Middletown, Conn.: Wesleyan University Press, 1986).

12. Gary Clayton Anderson, *The Conquest of Texas: Ethnic Cleansing in the Promised Land, 1820–1875* (Norman: University of Oklahoma Press, 2005). John Gre-

nier, *The First Way of War: American War Making on the Frontier, 1607–1814* (Cambridge: Cambridge University Press, 2005), maintains that white military success against the Indians depended on the operation of volunteer "rangers" as scouts and raiders, but his argument is much less persuasive for the period after 1787. White Kentuckians, for example, were able to secure control of their future state without national military assistance. But the Kentuckians were unable to halt Indian raids across the Ohio River until Anthony Wayne led his Legion of the United States to occupy and destroy the Miami villages, and they earned a rather mixed record in the War of 1812. Meanwhile, the Chickasaws, rather than white Georgians, were the most effective force against the Creeks during the 1790s. Perhaps Kentucky volunteers could have driven the Indians from Ohio through raids or the gradual spread of white populations northward in conjunction with such raids, but there is no evidence that they were doing so. Perhaps George Washington's decision to employ national regulars (Wayne's Legion) foreclosed that possibility, but Washington wanted to maintain as much control as possible over the northwestern expansion of white settlement. Nor did the Kentuckians effectively use their abilities as scouts and rangers to protect the Harmar and St. Clair expeditions, which were destroyed by Ohioan ambushes in 1790 and 1791; see Paul David Nelson, "General Charles Scott, the Kentucky Mounted Volunteers, and the Northwest Indian Wars, 1784–1794," *JER* 6 (Fall 1986): 219–251, for their military limitations.

13. Bruce C. Vandervort, *The Indian Wars of Mexico, Canada, and the United States, 1812–1900* (London: Routledge, 2006), 21; Connor, *The Australian Frontier Wars*. Vandervort notes that the outcome in New Zealand was much more like that in the United States because the British army rather than citizens retained primary responsibility for the conquest of the Maori and other indigenous peoples. John Grenier's most important point in *The First Way of War* is that American warfare against the Indians was comparatively unrestrained, or total, focusing on raids and "food fights" to destroy Indian resources. While this is true, national and professional control usually restrained the extremes of atrocity common among citizen-soldiers, at least prior to the Civil War. On the one hand, Mark Grimsley, "'Rebels' and 'Redskins': U.S. Military Conduct toward White Southerners and Native Americans in Comparative Perspective," in *Civilians in the Path of War*, ed. Mark Grimsley and Clifford J. Rogers (Lincoln: University of Nebraska Press, 2002), argues that the army acted much more harshly against Indians than civilians in the Confederacy during the Civil War. On the other hand, Grimsley is writing only about the post–Civil War period, and he acknowledges that "it is fortunate that the U.S. government chose to make the regular army its principal instrument . . . rather than to continue the large-scale use of western volunteer troops" (155), as it had between 1861 and 1865. Of the six massacres Grimsley cites, three were by regular troops (two during surprise attacks on villages at the Washita and Marias, and the third at Wounded Knee), two were by citizen-soldiers (Sand Creek and Bear River in 1863), and one was by a white mob (the Camp Grant massacre in Arizona in 1871).

Durwood Ball, *Army Regulars on the Western Frontier, 1848–1861* (Norman: University of Oklahoma Press, 2001), emphasizes brutality in the army's campaigns against Indians during the 1850s, but two of the three known atrocities by regular army troops before the Civil War were initiated by William S. Harney, a man of violent passions if not something of a sadist (he fled after being indicted for the murder of a slave in St. Louis in 1834, though he was acquitted in a partisan court the following year). The first of these atrocities was Harney's summary execution of several "Spanish Indians" in southern Florida in 1840, followed by a massacre akin to those at the Marias and Washita against the Brulé Sioux at Ash Hollow in 1855. See George R. Adams, *General William S. Harney, Prince of Dragoons* (Lincoln: University of Nebraska Press, 2001), 47–51, chaps. 5, 8; and Tony R. Mullis, *Peacekeeping on the Plains: Army Operations in Bleeding Kansas* (Columbia: University of Missouri Press, 2004), chap. 3. Brigadier General George Wright also ordered summary executions in the Pacific Northwest during the 1850s; see Carl P. Schlicke, *General George Wright, 1803–1865: Guardian of the Pacific Northwest* (Norman: University of Oklahoma Press, 1988), chap. 10. Some engagements during the 1850s resembled massacres in the unevenness of the forces involved, and the "battle" of Bad Axe that ended the Black Hawk War has sometimes been referred to as a massacre, though this was due to the participation of citizen-soldiers and allied Indians and the combat situation (a pursuit); see Wooster, *The American Military Frontiers*, 128, regarding two extremely lopsided engagements in California. Given the rarity of warfare against the Indians between 1815 and the 1850s, the army's treatment of prisoners during the Seminole Wars needs further investigation as the principal test case available.

14. Based on official records, the commission of homicide (i.e., killing by individuals outside of combat and unrelated to their military duties) by regular troops against Indians also seems to have been rare. See Big Warrior to AJ, April 16, 1816, *PAJ*, 4:20–21, for one example—a sergeant who killed a Creek woman. After being released by a civilian judge, the sergeant was reduced in rank and confined in the guardhouse at Fort Montgomery for four months, but he remained in the army until his discharge three years later. I have not found any examples from the post-1820 period; no doubt there were murders of Indians by regular soldiers, but this suggests their rarity and their origin in individual quarrels and depredation.

15. "Agents of Empire" is the title of chapter 16 of Francis Paul Prucha, *The Sword of the Republic: The United States Army on the Frontier, 1783–1846* (New York: Macmillan, 1969), 319.

16. See, however, Dan Flores, "Bison Ecology and Bison Diplomacy: The Southern Plains from 1800 to 1850," *JAH* 78 (September 1991): 465–485; Andrew C. Isenberg, *The Destruction of the Bison: An Environmental History, 1750–1920* (Cambridge: Cambridge University Press, 2000); and Pekka Hämäläinen, "The Rise and Fall of Plains Indian Horse Cultures," *JAH* 90 (December 2003): 833–862. These works provide superb ecological analyses, exploring Native American agency in ecosystem change before the advent of significant agrarian settlement or buffalo hunting by whites. Concise recent analyses of the role of army, Indians, and civilians in the destruction of the buffalo are David D. Smits, "The Frontier Army and the Destruction of

the Buffalo, 1865–1883," *WHQ* 25 (Autumn 1994): 312–338, which overstates the army's role and employs the logic of conspiracy theory; William A. Dobak, "The Army and the Buffalo, a Demur: A Response to David D. Smits's 'The Frontier Army and the Destruction of the Buffalo,'" and David D. Smits, "More on the Army and the Buffalo: The Author's Reply," *WHQ* 26 (Summer 1995): 197–208; and William A. Dobak, "Killing the Canadian Buffalo, 1821–1881," *WHQ* 27 (Spring 1996): 33–52. Thoughtful discussions that go beyond simply asserting agency to demonstrate the significance of native power on the northern Plains during the early and mid-nineteenth century include Richard White, "The Winning of the West: The Expansion of the Western Sioux in the Eighteenth and Nineteenth Centuries," *JAH* 65 (September 1978): 319–343; Gary C. Anderson, *Kinsmen of Another Kind: Dakota-White Relations in the Upper Mississippi Valley, 1650–1862* (Lincoln: University of Nebraska Press, 1984); and Anthony R. McGinnis, *Counting Coup and Cutting Horses: Intertribal Warfare on the Northern Plains, 1738–1889* (Lincoln: University of Nebraska Press, 1990).

17. Utley, "Culture Clash on the Western North American Indian Frontier," 104; Sherman to Thomas Ewing Jr., February 3, 1861, in Brooks D. Simpson and Jean V. Berlin, eds., *Sherman's Civil War: Selected Correspondence of William T. Sherman, 1860–1865* (Chapel Hill: University of North Carolina Press, 1999), 54. Recent western history textbooks take a more balanced approach; see, for example, Richard White, *"It's Your Misfortune and None of My Own": A New History of the American West* (Norman: University of Oklahoma Press, 1991); Robert V. Hine and John Mack Faragher, *The American West: A New Interpretive History* (New Haven, Conn.: Yale University Press, 2000); and Richard W. Etulain, *Beyond the Missouri: The Story of the American West* (Albuquerque : University of New Mexico Press, 2006).

18. Robert M. Utley, *Frontiersmen in Blue: The United States Army and the Indian, 1848–1865* (New York: Macmillan, 1967), 2; Robert M. Utley, *The Indian Frontier of the American West, 1846–1890* (Albuquerque: University of New Mexico Press, 1984), 3.

19. William B. Skelton, *An American Profession of Arms: The Army Officer Corps, 1784–1861* (Lawrence: University Press of Kansas, 1992), 70; Bayly, *Imperial Meridian*, 6, 114; Anthony Giddens, *The Nation-State and Violence: Volume Two of a Contemporary Critique of Historical Materialism* (Berkeley: University of California Press, 1985), 192.

20. Ibid.

21. See Daniel J. Herman, "Romance on the Middle Ground," *JER* 19 (Summer 1999): 279–291, for a critique of romanticized views of cultural interaction. This critique does not seem to have had much impact among historians, who are eager to find contingency and agency and limits to white or state power, regardless of actual historical outcomes. The introduction to *Jackson's Sword* explains my understanding of "borderlands" as zones of imperial contact rather than zones of cultural interaction, as the majority of scholars emphasize. Peter Sahlins, *Boundaries: The Making of France and Spain in the Pyrenees* (Berkeley: University of California Press, 1989), provides a

pathbreaking perspective that can be used to support either side, depending—of course—on timing.

22. Like the British and French, the Americans often chose or promoted Indian leaders with whom to negotiate, and many Native American societies accepted this mechanism as a means to facilitate negotiations; see John W. Hall, *Uncommon Defense: Indian Allies in the Black Hawk War* (Cambridge, Mass.: Harvard University Press, 2009), 53–54. Conversely, the practice usually aggravated factionalism within native polities. See "The Army of the United States," *North American Review* 28 (October 1826): 274, for a contemporary recognition of these differences in the relations between European and American military officers and their governments and the greater isolation of the European officers. Thus the most proximate comparisons would actually be to the British settler colonies in Canada, Australia, and New Zealand. The last of these was barely under way during the period of my study, while British rule was sufficiently distant and authoritarian to provoke rebellions in Canada in 1837, compelling the U.S. Army to police the border against extralegal incursions (filibusters) by American citizens, as detailed in chapters 8 and 9. Canada became increasingly self-governing after 1846 but did not become a Dominion until 1867. Britain devolved responsibility for frontier defense onto the Australian colonies after 1838; see Connor, *The Australian Frontier Wars*.

23. Given the formality of official documentation and the limits of officers' personal correspondence, which rarely discussed peacekeeping or policing in depth, the scholar may well find fiction, like the police novels of Joseph Wambaugh, or even film and television valuable resources for imagining the complexities of peacekeeping situations. I have sometimes found sociological studies of police forces (twentieth and nineteenth century) just as valuable for reflecting on the dilemmas and dynamics of peacekeeping—especially the issue of discretion, a principal question in the study of policing—as the often bare-bones accounts of U.S. diplomacy with Native Americans, not to mention classic diplomatic history or international relations or peacekeeping theory. See, for example, James Q. Wilson, *The Varieties of Police Behavior* (Cambridge, Mass.: Harvard University Press, 1968); Jonathan Rubinstein, *City Police* (New York: Farrar, Straus and Giroux, 1973); Robert Reiner, *The Politics of the Police*, 4th ed. (New York: Oxford University Press, 2010); William Ker Muir Jr., *Police: Streetcorner Politicians* (Chicago: University of Chicago Press, 1977); and George E. Berkeley, *The Democratic Policeman* (Boston: Beacon, 1969). Valuable though perhaps conceptually dated historical studies include Wilbur R. Miller, *Cops and Bobbies: Police Authority in New York and London, 1830–1870* (Chicago: University of Chicago Press, 1973); Roger Lane, *Policing the City: Boston, 1822–1885* (Cambridge, Mass.: Harvard University Press, 1967); and James F. Richardson, *The New York Police, Colonial Times to 1901* (New York: Oxford University Press, 1971). A novel by Jessamyn West, *The Massacre at Fall Creek* (New York: Harcourt Brace, 1975), provides a thought-provoking fictional account of frontier tensions, largely from the perspectives of white settlers and Indians.

24. Thomas R. Hietala, *Manifest Design: Anxious Aggrandizement in Late Jacksonian America* (Ithaca, N.Y.: Cornell University Press, 1985), 7–8.

25. James W. Silver depicts a relatively benign Gaines in "A Counter-proposal to the Indian Removal Policy of Andrew Jackson," *Journal of Mississippi History* 4 (October 1942): 207–215, but what Silver considered benevolent in 1942 is no longer seen in such an innocuous light.

26. Byron Farwell, *Eminent Victorian Soldiers: Seekers of Glory* (New York: W. W. Norton, 1985), 50, 91, 178, 190, 286, 329. See also V. G. Kiernan, *Colonial Empires and Armies, 1815–1960* (Phoenix Mill, U.K.: Sutton Publishing, 1998), 133, who also notes that land was granted to Russian commanders for victories in Persia and central Asia in the 1820s, as well as territory taken from Turkey in 1878.

27. Lt. Phillip Roots Thompson to Lt. Abraham Robinson Johnston, March 21 and April 23, 1840, and Lt. William Eustis to Johnston, May 3, 1842, Abraham Robinson Johnston Papers, USMA. Wooster, *The American Military Frontiers*, 66, observes that officers practicing land speculation could feed civilian anger over perceived inequality, particularly when officers had inside information or when the land came from the "military reservations" established for official purposes around army posts. See Edward M. Coffman, *The Old Army: A Portrait of the American Army in Peacetime, 1784–1898* (New York: Oxford University Press, 1986), chap. 2, for the most comprehensive discussion of officer vices, and Tony R. Mullis, *Peacekeeping on the Plains: Army Operations in Bleeding Kansas* (Columbia: University of Missouri Press, 2004), chap. 5, for conflicts of interest involving land speculation in Kansas during the 1850s. The army did engage in its share of fraud and embezzlement, whether in construction and supply contracting or the distribution of soldiers' pay, but I would suggest that a combination of the professional military ethos, genteel self-image, and sanctions greater than those to which civilians were subject meant less dishonesty than was the norm in the liberalizing economy of Jacksonian America. The behavior of civilian supply contractors for the army before 1820 and that of civilian contractors engaged in Indian removal (to say nothing of civilian dealings with Indians in general) present the most immediate contrasts; one could surely add the practice of electoral politics during the Second and Third Party Systems.

28. Louis Pelzer, *Marches of the Dragoons in the Mississippi Valley* (Iowa City: State Historical Society of Iowa, 1917), provides a thorough narrative and bibliography of primary sources; see also Prucha, *Sword of the Republic*, chap. 18. The Second Dragoon Regiment, created in 1836, served in Florida until 1842 and was dismounted to save money in 1843 and 1844.

29. David B. Ralston, *Importing the European Army: The Introduction of European Military Techniques and Institutions into the Extra-European World, 1600–1914* (Chicago: University of Chicago Press, 1990); Duane Champagne, *Social Order and Political Change: Constitutional Governments among the Cherokee, the Choctaw, the Chickasaw, and the Creek* (Stanford, Calif.: Stanford University Press, 1992); William G. McLoughlin, *Cherokee Renascence in the New Republic* (Princeton, N.J.: Princeton University Press, 1986); William G. McLoughlin, *After the Trail of Tears: The Cherokees' Struggle for Sovereignty, 1839–1880* (Chapel Hill: University of North Carolina Press, 1993); Matthew W. Kimmel, "The Cherokee, Choctaw, and Creek Lighthorse

Police: Bridging Tribal and Anglo Laws" (M.A. thesis, University of Arkansas, 1996). Note that the British and French had also chosen Indian "alliance chiefs," and many Native American societies accepted this as a way to facilitate negotiations; see Hall, *Uncommon Defense*, 53–54.

30. Clyde A. Milner II also recognizes that "the government often anticipated white demands for more land"; see "Indulgent Friends and Important Allies: Political Process on the Cis-Mississippi Frontier and Its Aftermath," in *The Frontier in History: North America and Southern Africa Compared*, ed. Howard Lamar and Leonard Thompson (New Haven, Conn.: Yale University Press, 1981), 146. Francis Paul Prucha, "The Settler and the Army in Frontier Minnesota," *Minnesota History* 29 (September 1948): 231–246, provides an unusually explicit look at the sequence of military and civilian advance on the western frontier, generally concluding that forts followed civilian demand. Michael J. Brodhead, "Notes on the Military Presence in Nevada, 1843–1988," *Nevada History* 32 (1989): 261–277, and Merrille G. Burlingame, "The Influence of the Military in the Building of Montana," *Pacific Northwest Quarterly* 29 (April 1938): 135–150, arrive at similar conclusions, but note that the army often conducted topographical and road surveys in advance of settlement. Paul A. Hutton, "'Fort Desolation': The Military Establishment, the Railroad, and Settlement on the Northern Plains," *North Dakota History* 56 (Spring 1989): 21–30, emphasizes the autonomy of the army's objectives—its desire to extend railroads in advance of settlement in order to enhance strategic and operational mobility, and as an opportunity to concentrate troops to improve training. Gary S. Freedom, "The Role of the Military and the Spread of Settlement in the Northern Great Plains, 1866–1891," *Midwest Review* 9 (Spring 1987): 1–11, concludes that in the Dakotas and Montana, six forts were established before settlement (though in two of them, no settlement occurred nearby), while nine forts followed settlement. Ernest F. Dibble, "Giveaway Forts: Territorial Forts and the Settlement of Florida," *FHQ* 78 (Fall 1999): 207–233, observes that the army preceded and enabled (often through surveys) civilian settlement throughout most of Florida.

Looking broadly at all military efforts and contributions in western Kansas, Leo E. Oliva concludes that both sides have overgeneralized from limited samples, noting that "the primary contribution of the army to settlement was military—protection of routes of travel, campaigns against Indians, and the like" (73). See Oliva, "Frontier Forts and the Settlement of Western Kansas," in *Kansas and the West: Bicentennial Essays in Honor of Nyle H. Miller*, ed. Forrest R. Blackburn et al. (Topeka: Kansas State Historical Society, 1976), 59–73. In contrast, John B. Garver Jr., an army officer but also a student of historical geographer D. W. Meinig, concludes after 800 pages that "the Army was one of the most influential frontier institutions in the full process and pattern of Anglo-American conquest and colonization of the Kansas area." See Garver, "The Role of the United States Army in the Colonization of the Trans-Missouri West: Kansas, 1804–1861" (Ph.D. diss., Syracuse University, 1981). See also Earl A. Shoemaker, *The Permanent Indian Frontier: The Reason for the Construction and Aban-*

donment of *Fort Scott, Kansas, during the Dragoon Era* (n.p.: National Park Service, 1986). There appear to be no analogous studies for the Pacific slope or the Southwest.

31. See Andrew R. L. Cayton, "'Separate Interests' and the Nation-State: The Washington Administration and the Origins of Regionalism in the Trans-Appalachian West," *JAH* 79 (June 1992): 39–67. Cayton is really talking more about southern than western sectionalism—his "west" means frontier Georgia and, especially, Tennessee—and the Carolinians moving into Tennessee, who lacked support from the national standing army in their wars with the Creeks and Cherokee. For western sectionalism after 1820, see William Appleman Williams, *The Roots of the Modern American Empire: A Study of the Growth and Shaping of Social Consciousness in a Marketplace Society* (New York: Vintage Books, 1969).

32. See Henry P. Beers, "The Army and the Oregon Trail to 1846," *Pacific Northwest Quarterly* 28 (October 1937): 339–362; Kenneth Bourne, *Britain and the Balance of Power in North America, 1815–1908* (Berkeley: University of California Press, 1967), chap. 5; Wilbur D. Jones and J. Chal Vinson, "British Preparedness and the Oregon Settlement," *Pacific Historical Review* 22 (November 1953): 353–364; and, more generally, Frederick Merk, *Albert Gallatin and the Oregon Problem: A Study in Anglo-American Diplomacy* (Cambridge, Mass.: Harvard University Press, 1950); Frederick Merk, *The Oregon Question: Essays in Anglo-American Diplomacy and Politics* (Cambridge, Mass.: Harvard University Press, 1967); and David M. Pletcher, *The Diplomacy of Annexation: Texas, Oregon, and the Mexican War* (Columbia: University of Missouri Press, 1973).

33. This issue, once manifested largely as "the safety valve question," is less often addressed than was once the case: see especially Stanley Elkins and Eric McKitrick, "A Meaning for Turner's Frontier," *Political Science Quarterly* 69 (September and December 1954): 321–353, 565–602; William F. Deverell, "To Loosen the Safety Valve: Eastern Workers and Western Lands," *WHQ* 19 (August 1988): 269–285; and Carville Earle and Changyong Cao, "Frontier Closure and the Involution of American Society, 1840–1890," *JER* 13 (Summer 1993): 163–179.

34. Frank N. Schubert, *Vanguard of Expansion: Army Engineers in the Trans-Mississippi West, 1819–1879* (Washington, D.C.: Government Printing Office, 1980), x.

35. Richard G. Wood, *Stephen H. Long, 1784–1864: Army Engineer, Explorer, Inventor* (Glendale, Calif.: Arthur H. Clark, 1966), 40–55; Long to Thomas A. Smith, May 12, 1818, in *The Northern Expeditions of Stephen H. Long: The Journals of 1817 and 1823 and Related Documents*, ed. Lucile M. Kane, June D. Holmquist, and Carolyn Gilman (n.p.: Minnesota Historical Society Press, 1978), 333–351; see also Stephen H. Long, *Voyage in a Six-Oared Skiff to the Falls of the St. Anthony in 1817* (St. Paul: Minnesota Historical Society, 1889).

36. Roger L. Nichols and Patrick L. Halley, *Stephen Long and American Frontier Exploration* (London: Associated University Presses, 1980), 181–212; Long to JCC, enclosure, April 20, 1819, *PJCC*, 4:32; Wood, *Stephen H. Long*, 82. See also Kane, Holmquist, and Gilman, *The Northern Expeditions of Stephen H. Long*.

37. Schubert, *Vanguard of Expansion*, 5–9. Lieutenants Aeneas Mackay and David B. Douglass accompanied Cass and Schoolcraft as escort commander and topographical engineer; Lieutenant John Pierce later took Mackay's place; see Willard Carl Klunder, *Lewis Cass and the Politics of Moderation* (Kent, Ohio: Kent State University Press, 1996), 34–37. For the explorers' influence on public opinion about the Plains, see Roger L. Nichols, "The Army and Early Perceptions of the Plains," *Nebraska History* 56 (Spring 1975): 121–135, and Martyn L. Bowden, "The Great American Desert and the American Frontier, 1800–1822: Popular Images of the Plains," in *Anonymous Americans: Explorations in Nineteenth-Century Social History*, ed. Tamara Hareven (Englewood Cliffs, N.J.: Prentice-Hall, 1971); for change and continuity in military views of the Plains after the Civil War, see Hutton, "'Fort Desolation.'"

38. Bonneville, July 29, 1831, HQALS. William H. Goetzmann, *Army Exploration in the American West, 1803–1863* (New Haven, Conn.: Yale University Press, 1959), 147–158, contains a good brief account, as do Edgeley W. Todd, "Benjamin Bonneville," in *Mountain Men and the Fur Trade of the Far West*, ed. LeRoy R. Hafen (Glendale, Calif.: Arthur H. Clark, 1968–1972), 5:45–63, and Hiram M. Chittenden, *The American Fur Trade of the Far West* (New York: F. P. Harper, 1902), 1:421–433.

39. Bonneville to AM, July 29, 1833, and to Secretary of War Lewis Cass, September 30, 1835, in *The Adventures of Captain Bonneville, U.S.A., in the Rocky Mountains and the Far West, Digested from His Journal by Washington Irving*, ed. Edgeley W. Todd (Norman: University of Oklahoma Press, 1961), 381, 394–395.

40. At least one officer had hoped to join Bonneville; see Rep. James Findlay, March 28, 1832, HQALS, regarding the application of Lt. Samuel Torrence of the Fourth Infantry. Bonneville had already departed by the time Torrence's application was received.

41. July 5, 1838, 5 *Stat.* 256–260. See Samuel J. Watson, "Professionalism, Social Attitudes, and Civil-Military Accountability in the U.S. Army Officer Corps, 1815–1846" (Ph.D. diss., Rice University, 1996), chap. 8, which relies on documents from John Abert and Isaac Roberdeau, the topographical engineer commanders, for a more extended discussion of the Corps of Topographical Engineers as a branch, and its relationship with the rest of the army. Goetzmann, *Army Exploration*, remains the standard treatment of scientific and cartographic surveying expeditions. See also William H. Goetzmann, "The Corps of Topographical Engineers in the Exploration and Development of the Trans-Mississippi West" (Ph.D. diss., Yale University, 1957), and *Exploration and Empire: The Explorer and the Scientist in the Winning of the West* (New York: Knopf, 1966); Edgar S. Wallace, *The Great Reconnaissance: Soldiers, Artists, and Scientists on the Frontier* (Boston: Little, Brown, 1955), covering only the period 1848–1861; James P. Ronda, *Beyond Lewis and Clark: The Army Explores the West* (Tacoma: Washington State Historical Society, 2003); Milford F. Allen, "United States Government Exploring Expeditions and Natural History, 1800–1840" (Ph.D. diss., University of Texas, 1958); Philip D. Thomas, "The United States Army as the Early Patron of Naturalists in the Trans-Mississippi West, 1803–1820," *COK* 56 (Summer 1978): 171–193; John B. Garver Jr., "Practical Military Geographers and Mappers of the Trans-Missouri West, 1820–1860," in *Mapping the North American Plains:*

Essays in the History of Cartography, ed. Frederick C. Luebke, Francis W. Kaye, and Gary Moulton (Norman: University of Oklahoma Press, 1987), 111–126; Adrian G. Traas, *From the Golden Gate to Mexico City: The U.S. Army Topographical Engineers in the Mexican War, 1846–1848* (Washington, D.C.: Government Printing Office, 1993); and, more generally, Edmund W. Gilbert, *The Explorations of Western America, 1800–1850: A Historical Geography* (New York: Cooper Square, 1966).

42. Vincent Ponko, "The Military Explorers of the American West, 1838–1860," in *North American Exploration*, vol. 3, *A Continent Comprehended*, ed. John Allen Logan (Lincoln: University of Nebraska Press, 1997), 332–334, 342–345; Vernon Volpe, "The Origins of the Frémont Expeditions: John J. Abert and the Scientific Exploration of the Trans-Mississippi West," *The Historian* 62 (Winter 2000): 244–263. However, Ponko reverts to interpreting the Corps of Topographical Engineers as an agency created by "those interested in overland expansion" (342). This was one motive among several, including the army's requirements in Florida, for Congress's decision to expand the topographical engineer branch and separate it from the Corps of Engineers in 1838.

43. James W. Abert, *Expedition to the Southwest: An 1845 Reconnaissance of Colorado, New Mexico, Texas, and Oklahoma* (Lincoln: University of Nebraska Press, 1999), vi, 36, 70, 35, viii (also printed as "Journal of Lieutenant J. W. Abert, from Bent's Fort to St. Louis, in 1845," 29th Cong., 1st sess., Sen. Doc. 438).

44. Tom Chaffin, *Pathfinder: John Charles Frémont and the Course of American Empire* (New York: Hill and Wang, 2002), 379–381; Traas, *From the Golden Gate to Mexico City*, chap. 2. Goetzmann, *Army Exploration*, 68, asserts that "almost to a man . . . the officers of the Corps [of Topographical Engineers] were in accord with the policy of Manifest Destiny," but I have found no evidence in the papers of career regulars that they supported Frémont's employment as a special agent to stir rebellion in California. Frémont's journals and reports are collected in Donald Jackson and Mary Lee Spence, eds., *The Expeditions of John Charles Frémont*, 3 vols. (Urbana: University of Illinois Press, 1970–1984); see also John C. Frémont, *Memoirs of My Life* (Chicago: Belford, Clarke, 1887); Andrew Rolle, *John Charles Frémont: Character as Destiny* (Norman: University of Oklahoma Press, 1991); Ponko, "The Military Explorers of the American West," 342–364; Ross Calvin, ed., *Lieutenant Emory Reports: A Reprint of Lieutenant W. H. Emory's Notes of Military Reconnaissance* (Albuquerque: University of New Mexico Press, 1951); and Abert, *Expedition to the Southwest*. Allan Nevins, *Frémont, Pathmarker of the West* (1928; reprint, Lincoln: University of Nebraska Press, 1992) remains valuable.

CHAPTER TWO: SUBORDINATION AND DISCRETION

1. See William B. Skelton, *An American Profession of Arms: The Army Officer Corps, 1784–1861* (Lawrence: University Press of Kansas, 1992), chap. 16, and William B. Skelton, "Army Officers' Attitudes towards Indians, 1830–1860," *Pacific Northwest*

Quarterly 67 (July 1976): 113–124, concerning army officers' attitudes toward Amerindians and Indian warfare. Far more has been written on this subject for the post–Civil War era; see especially Thomas C. Leonard, "Red, White, and Army Blue: Empathy and Anger in the American West," *American Quarterly* 26 (May 1974): 176–190, and Sherry L. Smith, *The View from Officers' Row: Army Perceptions of Western Indians* (Tucson: University of Arizona Press, 1990), whose attention to the nuances and variety of military views of the Indians has no parallel for the antebellum era. The fundamental continuities of Euro-American attitudes can be traced in Colin G. Calloway, *Crown and Calumet: British-Indian Relations, 1783–1815* (Norman: University of Oklahoma Press, 1987): British civil and military officials may have been less overtly ethnocentric (xii), but they thought "Indians had to be treated like children and to be governed by a mixture of firmness and indulgence, kindness and deceit" (59–60). American military commanders doubted the long-term value of indulgence and believed that, practically and morally, firmness was preferable to the use of deceit, but they acted much like the British in attempting to balance firmness with kindness. On the whole, American officers seem to have been more willing to ascribe the characteristics of Indian culture to race than to environment, but like the British, "most regarded [the] destruction [of Indian cultures] as both necessary" to the advance "and inevitable" in the progress of white society (128; see also 86, 111).

For further context, see Roy Harvey Pearce, *Savagism and Civilization: A Study of the Indian and the American Mind*, 2nd ed. (Berkeley: University of California Press, 1988); Robert F. Berkhofer, *The White Man's Indian: Images of the American Indian from Columbus to the Present* (New York: Alfred A. Knopf, 1978); Brian W. Dippie, *The Vanishing American: White Attitudes and U.S. Indian Policy* (Middletown, Conn.: Wesleyan University Press, 1982), chaps. 2, 3; Ronald N. Satz, *American Indian Policy in the Jacksonian Era* (Lincoln: University of Nebraska Press, 1974); Ronald T. Takaki, *Iron Cages: Race and Culture in Nineteenth-Century America* (New York: Alfred A. Knopf, 1979); Richard Drinnon, *Facing West: The Metaphysics of Indian-Hating and Empire-Building* (Minneapolis: University of Minnesota Press, 1980); Reginald Horsman, *Race and Manifest Destiny: The Origins of American Racial Anglo-Saxonism* (Cambridge, Mass.: Harvard University Press, 1981), chap. 10; and Michael Paul Rogin, *Fathers and Children: Andrew Jackson and the Subjugation of the American Indian* (New York: Alfred A. Knopf, 1975). Rogin provides the most explicit emphasis on white paternalism and its use as a justification for the expropriation of the Amerindians.

2. Thomas Jefferson to Benjamin Hawkins, August 13, 1786, in *Papers of Thomas Jefferson*, ed. Julian P. Boyd, 38 vols. (Princeton, N.J.: Princeton University Press, 1950–), 10:240.

3. Roger L. Nichols, "The Army and Early Perceptions of the Plains," *Nebraska History* 56 (Spring 1975): 121–135; Dan Flores, "Loving the Plains, Hating the Plains, Restoring the Plains," in *The Future of the Southern Plains*, ed. Sherry L. Smith (Norman: University of Oklahoma Press, 2003), 221; Paul A. Hutton, "'Fort Desolation': The Military Establishment, the Railroad, and Settlement on the Northern Plains,"

North Dakota History 56 (Spring 1989): 21–30. For civilian contrast, see Klaus J. Hansen, "The Millennium, the West, and Race in the Antebellum American Mind," *WHQ* 3 (October 1972): 373–390, and Rush Welter, "The Frontier West as Image of American Society: Conservative Attitudes before the Civil War," *MVHR* 46 (March 1960): 593–614.

   4. See Bernard W. Sheehan, *Seeds of Extinction: Jeffersonian Philanthropy and the American Indian* (New York: Norton, 1974), chap. 1, 123–124, 147 (quotation), 174, 217.

   5. Leonard, "Red, White, and Army Blue"; Sheehan, *Seeds of Extinction*, 149–152, 198, 201, 207, 212, 240. Leonard (184) notes that he was unable to find an officer who had resigned because of moral qualms.

   6. AM to brevet Brigadier General John Miller, June 30, 1816, Macomb Family Papers, BHC. See also AM to Capt. John Fowle, May 22, 1818, and to Lt. Col. Henry Leavenworth, August 11, 1819, ibid.

   7. AJ to JCC, September 2, 1820, *PAJ*, 2:388; Smith, January 5, 1820, file S-167, SWLR: Reg. See C. A. Bayly, *Imperial Meridian: The British Empire and the World, 1780–1830* (London: Longman, 1989), and Douglas M. Peers, *Between Mars and Mammon: Colonial Armies and the Garrison State in India, 1819–1835* (London: I. B. Tauris, 1995), especially 1–4, 53, for official beliefs that British rule rested ultimately, even primarily, on military force in the pre-Victorian, late Victorian, and even the supposedly less militaristic early and mid-Victorian years. See Benjamin Claude Brower, *A Desert Named Peace: The Violence of France's Empire in the Algerian Sahara, 1844–1902* (New York: Columbia University Press, 2009), for similar views among French officers in North Africa.

   8. V. G. Kiernan, *Colonial Empires and Armies, 1815–1960* (Phoenix Mill, U.K.: Sutton Publishing, 1998), chap. 4, 153–160. See the works cited in note 1 to chapter 1 for similar behavior among French, Russian, and Dutch officers. For British examples, see Ian Hernon, *Britain's Forgotten Wars: Colonial Campaigns of the 19th Century* (London: Sutton Publishing, 2003); H. T. Lambrick, *Sir Charles Napier and Sind* (Oxford: Clarendon Press, 1952); Robert A. Huttenback, *British Relations with the Sind, 1799–1843: An Anatomy of Imperialism* (Berkeley: University of California Press, 1962); Byron Farwell, *Eminent Victorian Soldiers: Seekers of Glory* (New York: W. W. Norton, 1985); and Graham Dawson, *Soldier Heroes: British Adventure, Empire, and the Imagining of Masculinities* (London: Routledge, 1994).

   9. Smith to Major Reynolds M. Kirby, June 10, 1818, Lewis Cass Papers, WLC. John W. Hall, *Uncommon Defense: Indian Allies in the Black Hawk War* (Cambridge, Mass.: Harvard University Press, 2009), 61, contains a similar example from Fort Howard in 1832. See Dale R. Steinhauer, "'Sogers': Enlisted Men in the U.S. Army, 1815–1860" (Ph.D. diss., University of North Carolina, 1992), chap. 6, and Mark A. Vargas, "The Military Justice System and the Use of Illegal Punishments as Causes of Desertion in the U.S. Army, 1821–1835," *JMH* 55 (January 1991): 1–19, regarding the extraordinary forms and frequency of violence in army discipline and by officers against enlisted men more generally.

10. AM to Brown, May 25 and August 17, 1816, Brown Letterbooks, LC.

11. HA to AM, October 25, 1829, HQALR.

12. EPG to JCC, December 4, 1817, *ASPIA*, 2:161; EPG to Secretary of War Joel R. Poinsett, August 17, 1838, enclosure in EPG to Rep. Newton Cannon, August 24, 1838, Gaines Papers, Tennessee State Library.

13. Boundaries delineated in sec. 1 of the laws of May 19, 1796 (1 *Stat.* 469), March 30, 1802 (2 *Stat.* 139–141), and June 30, 1834 (4 *Stat.* 729); other restrictions in the laws of July 22, 1790 (1 *Stat.* 137–138), May 19, 1796 (1 *Stat.* 469–474, quotations from secs. 16 and 17), March 30, 1802 (2 *Stat.* 139–146), and June 30, 1834 (4 *Stat.* 729–735).

14. Riddle to Lt. Col. William Trimble, June 15, 1817, William Allen Trimble Papers, OHS; Francis Paul Prucha, *American Indian Policy in the Formative Years: The Indian Trade and Intercourse Acts, 1790–1834* (Cambridge, Mass.: Harvard University Press, 1962), 82–83, 134 (quotation); Edward M. Coffman, *The Old Army: A Portrait of the American Army in Peacetime, 1784–1898* (New York: Oxford University Press, 1986), 72. See also Edwin C. Bearss and Arrell M. Gibson, *Fort Smith: Little Gibraltar on the Arkansas* (Norman: University of Oklahoma Press, 1969), chap. 7.

15. Prucha, *American Indian Policy*, 134; Secretary of War Cass to AJ, November 30, 1829, *ASPMA*, 6:153; House Claims Committee report, April 9, 1832, *ASPMA*, 5:7–10; ZT to Thomas Sidney Jesup, July 15, 1834, Jesup Papers, LC.

16. HA to JCC, November 26, 1819, *ASPIA*, 2:204, and *PJCC*, 4:433; Baker to EPG, September 15, 1824, Daniel Baker Papers, BHC; SWK to RJ, September 15, and WS comment, November 10, 1845, in 29th Cong., 1st sess., Sen. Doc. 1, 213. In 1857 Philip St. George Cooke recommended returning to a government factory system for trade with the Indians, along with "a complete non-intercourse" policy "maintain[ed] by terror of summary punishments"; Cooke, *Scenes and Adventures in the Army, or, the Romance of Military Life* (Philadelphia: Lindsay and Blakiston, 1857), 128. See Francis Paul Prucha, "The Army and the Fur Trade," in *Indian Policy in the United States: Historical Essays* (Lincoln: University of Nebraska Press, 1981), for a survey of the relationship.

17. Herman J. Viola, *Thomas L. McKenney: Architect of America's Early Indian Policy, 1816–1830* (Chicago: Sage Books, 1974), 223–224. In *Indian Affairs and the Administration State in the Nineteenth Century* (Cambridge: Cambridge University Press, 2010), political scientist Stephen J. Rockwell asserts the effectiveness and thus the significance of civilian Indian agents as instruments of territorial expansion, going so far as to avow that through them, "big government won the West" (1). In doing so, Rockwell effectively critiques the weak-state thesis but consistently dismisses or ignores military power, beginning with the non sequitur that nineteenth-century America was not dominated by the military (25). That this was true hardly means that civilian administration could overcome violent resistance without some force, or at least the threat of force, or the denial of resources. While it may be possible to maintain that the army "rarely operated as the first line of expansion" (3–4), Rockwell touts the post office and customs agents as alternative causal forces. Customs agents did not

serve on the western land frontier, and I doubt that even Richard John, who brought the post office to light as a critical agency of American state building, would maintain that the post office preceded the army into regions contested by Native Americans. Presumably, Rockwell means that federal Indian agents or treaty commissioners led the negotiations in which Indians ceded their lands, but of the twenty-two treaty signers he lists (105), less than a quarter prove to be Indian agents. The rest were territorial governors, secretaries of war, and three generals of the national standing army.

Focused on a sustained, often counterintuitive defense of the civilian administration of Indian policy on every front, while trying to overcome the vast majority of existing scholarship, Rockwell never presents any evidence of research into the army's activities, apart from its conduct of removal in the 1830s. Although I note in chapter 5 that the army did not physically escort the Cherokee along the Trail of Tears, it certainly intimidated them into concentrating in camps to be removed, often burning their homes and chaining them to one another to do so. The fact that the Indians calculated the odds and chose not to resist does not mean that they were simply responding to the carrot of civilian blandishments. In Florida, Rockwell substitutes road building (153) for violence as the army's most important role in the Seminole War, implying that white settlement would have driven the Seminoles from Florida without war or the national standing army. This is swinging the pendulum much too far. The ultimate failure of Rockwell's civilian administration, beyond its corruption (which he denies) and financial cost, came precisely in the need for wars against the Seminoles and Creeks to enforce the supposedly voluntary removal against their violent opposition.

18. Satz, *American Indian Policy in the Jacksonian Era*, 166, 186–187, 158–159, 193.

19. Ibid., 189, 193; AM to brevet Brigadier General John McNeil, September 23, 1816, to Brown, September 7, 1818, and to JCC, February 8, 1819, Macomb Family Papers, BHC; Snelling to HA, May 31, 1827, quoted in Marcus L. Hansen, *Old Fort Snelling, 1819–1858* (Minneapolis: Ross and Haines, 1958), 132. Hall, *Uncommon Defense*, provides plentiful evidence of agents' attachment to individual tribes, sometimes at the expense of coordinated U.S. diplomacy.

20. HA to RJ, November 21, 1834, 6th Military Department, Letters Sent, 1834–1846, Entry 45, RG 393, NA; EPG to Jacob Brown, 1827, *ASPMA*, 4:132–133; EPG to AM, July 6, 1837, in James W. Silver, "A Counter-proposal to the Indian Removal Policy of Andrew Jackson," *Journal of Mississippi History* 4 (October 1942): 214–215. Silver's footnote says 1833, but the context makes it clear that the date was 1837, as he says in the text.

21. Southern Division adjutant general Robert Butler to agents Return J. Meigs, John McKee, Benjamin Hawkins, and William Cocke, May 26, 1816, Division of the South, Letters Sent, 1816–1821, Entry 72, RG 98, NA; HA to Edwin James, July 28, 1838, 6th Military Department, Letters Sent; K. Jack Bauer, *Zachary Taylor: Soldier, Planter, Statesman of the Old Southwest* (Baton Rouge: Louisiana State University Press, 1985), 67–68; EPG to AM, July 6, 1837, in Silver, "A Counter-proposal," 214–215; Satz, *American Indian Policy in the Jacksonian Era*, 190.

22. Prucha, *American Indian Policy*, chap. 6, especially 117–118, 121–125, 128–133; Whistler and Capt. John Stout to AM, September 30, 1837, *ASPMA*, 7:978–980; Ewell to his brother Benjamin, February 2, 1841, Ewell Papers, LC. See also Lt. Col. William A. Trimble, November 27, 1818, file T-45, SWLR: Reg. Zachary Taylor shared this view of the Cherokee; see ZT to RJ, December 23, 1842, and March 28, 1843, cited in Brainerd Dyer, *Zachary Taylor* (Baton Rouge: Louisiana State University Press, 1946), 138–140. Whistler's father also rose to colonel, but he began his military career as a British private and was captured at Saratoga in 1777. Given their peacekeeping mission, it is remarkable how rarely the papers of frontier military officers explicitly discuss the flow of arms to the Indians. They appear to have taken native armament for granted, as part of a hunting culture and economy, and with equivalent, largely inaccurate weapons (smoothbore muskets), they expected their soldiers' drill, discipline, and cohesion to defeat resistance through volleys and advances with the bayonet. Military commanders did pay some attention to the Seminoles' sources and supplies of powder and lead in Florida, particularly during the Second Seminole War, but they were also willing to give hostile Seminoles powder during the later years of the war in the hope of persuading their surrender and emigration. But the army seized Indian weapons only when concentrating Indians for removal (and often returned them once removal had been completed) and upon capturing them in combat; it did not conduct preemptive weapons seizures along the western frontier, where no treaties forbade Indian armament.

23. Prucha, *American Indian Policy*, 132; Francis Paul Prucha, *The Great Father: The United States Government and the Indians* (Lincoln: University of Nebraska Press, 1984), 168.

24. EPG to Brown, July 20, 1826, file G-131, SWLR: Reg. See the quotations from General Nelson A. Miles in Leonard, "Red, White, and the Army Blue," 180, nn. 11, 12, for a senior commander's perspective from the late nineteenth century much like Gaines's.

25. Hall, *Uncommon Defense*, 59; B. Frank Emery, "Fort Saginaw," *Michigan History Magazine* 30 (July–September 1946): 476–503; Joseph M. Sweninger, "'A Lingering War Must Be Avoided': The Defense of the Northern Frontier, 1812–1871" (Ph.D. diss., Ohio State University, 1998), 65 (table 3.2), 121 (table 4.1).

26. EPG to Brown, July 20, 1826, file G-131, SWLR: Reg. Half a decade later, Gaines repeated his doctrine to Colonel Willoughby Morgan; see Calvin Reese, "The United States Army and the Indian: Low Plains Area, 1815–1854" (Ph.D. diss., University of Southern California, 1963), 182. See also Henry Leavenworth, February 19, 1834, HQALS, and Secretary of War Joel R. Poinsett to Congress, December 30, 1837, *NASPMA*, 1:259.

27. Gary Clayton Anderson, *Kinsmen of Another Kind: Dakota-White Relations in the Upper Mississippi Valley, 1650–1862* (Lincoln: University of Nebraska Press, 1984), 88–99, 120–128, 134–136; Gary Clayton Anderson, "The Removal of the Mdewakanton Dakota in 1837: A Test Case for Jacksonian Paternalism," *South Dakota History* 10 (Fall 1980): 314, 320, 323–325; Patrick J. Jung, *The Black Hawk War of*

1832 (Norman: University of Oklahoma Press, 2007), 46–47. The consensus of recent historians is that the Sioux responded more to the opportunities of the Plains than the pressure of the Ojibwa; see Gary Clayton Anderson, "Early Dakota Migration and Intertribal War: A Revision," *WHQ* 11 (January 1980): 17–36. Nevertheless, the two societies remained intermittently at war throughout this era.

28. Charles J. Kappler, comp., *Indian Affairs: Laws and Treaties* (Washington, D.C.: Government Printing Office, 1904), 2:250–255, 268–273; Bruce E. Mahan, *Old Fort Crawford and the Frontier* (Iowa City: State Historical Society of Iowa, 1926), chap. 7; HA to EPG, June 15, 1827, quoted in Roger L. Nichols, *General Henry Atkinson: A Western Military Career* (Norman: University of Oklahoma Press, 1965), 121. See also Evan Jones, *Citadel in the Wilderness: The Story of Fort Snelling and the Northwest Frontier* (New York: Coward-McCann, 1966). Allowing the Indians to sort out their differences was not always an acceptable route for officers, particularly if the violence thereby facilitated came too close to genteel white sensibilities: in 1831 Captain James H. Gaile resigned when facing a court of inquiry for allowing Indians to conduct a scalp dance *within* his post (Hansen, *Old Fort Snelling*, 131). Hansen spells the officer's name as "Gale," but the biographical dictionaries show only one Gale or Gaile as a captain in that year, and the symmetry is too great to be a coincidence.

Like many historians exploring the trajectory of specific native societies, Michael J. Witgen emphasizes the agency and power of his subjects, the Ojibwa, particularly the number of Ojibwa warriors compared to the army's small presence in Michigan and Wisconsin. Nevertheless, despite the scope of his research, Witgen's "An Infinity of Nations: How Indians, Empires, and Western Migration Shaped National Identity in North America" (Ph.D. diss., University of Washington, 2004) is focused overwhelmingly on the seventeenth century and on Minnesota in the nineteenth century. However, Witgen also acknowledges that the Ojibwa gave the United States land for a post (Fort Brady) at Sault Ste. Marie in 1820 and surrendered warriors who killed four fur traders in 1825. The initial Ojibwa land cession, in Wisconsin in 1829, may have been a matter of misunderstanding or white deception about what the Ojibwa had agreed to, but their final Wisconsin cession, in 1837, cannot be seen in such a light, since it was soon followed by Ojibwa emigration from the territory. The army had little direct responsibility for the decline of the Ojibwa, but growing resource competition and scarcity, as well as attrition at the hands of the Sioux, had the same fundamental impact: de facto conquest and domination. As usual, interpretation depends very much on perspective, but it is difficult to agree that the Ojibwa were gaining strength during the 1820s and 1830s.

29. Hall, *Uncommon Defense*, 72–75; James E. Wright, *The Galena Lead District: Policy and Practice, 1824–1847* (Madison: State Historical Society of Wisconsin, 1966).

30. Mark Wyman, *The Wisconsin Frontier* (Bloomington: Indiana University Press, 1998), 137, 143; Lucy Eldersveld Murphy, *A Gathering of Rivers: Indians, Métis, and Mining in the Western Great Lakes, 1737–1832* (Lincoln: University of Nebraska Press, 2000), 101, 103, 109–112, 124–125, 128; Nichols, *General Henry Atkinson*, 120–121; Hall, *Uncommon Defense*, 79.

31. Brown to Secretary of War James Barbour, annual report communicated to Congress by the president, December 4, 1826, *ASPMA*, 3:618; Hall, *Uncommon Defense*, 79; Nichols, *General Henry Atkinson*, 122; Jung, *The Black Hawk War*, 41–42. See also Mahan, *Old Fort Crawford*, chap. 8; Patrick J. Jung, "Forge, Destroy, and Preserve the Bonds of Empire: Euro-Americans, Native Americans, and Métis on the Wisconsin Frontier, 1634–1856" (Ph.D. diss., Marquette University, 1997), chaps. 4–6; and Martin Zanger, "Red Bird," in *American Indian Leaders: Studies in Diversity*, ed. R. David Edmunds (Lincoln: University of Nebraska Press, 1980).

32. Nichols, *General Henry Atkinson*, 125–132; Jung, *The Black Hawk War*, 44–45; Hall, *Uncommon Defense*, 78–83; HA to EPG, September 28, 1827, in Sen. Doc. 1, 20th Cong., 1st sess., 156–163 (quotation at 162–163). See also EPG to Secretary of War Barbour, August 16, 1827, Western Department, Letters Sent, Entry 5806 (Letters Sent by Brevet Major General Edmund Pendleton Gaines and Staff, 1819–26), RG 393, NA.

33. HA, proclamation of September 22, 1827, in Nichols, *General Henry Atkinson*, 159; AM to Secretary of War Peter B. Porter, November 1828, quoted in Francis Paul Prucha, *The Sword of the Republic: The United States Army on the Frontier, 1783–1846* (New York: Macmillan, 1969), 167; Brown to Barbour, "Confidential," August 13, 1827, Brown Papers, WLC; Lt. John R. Vinton (Brown's aide-de-camp) to HA, October 16, 1827, AGOLR; Assistant Adjutant General Robert Butler to HA, August 14, 1827, Western Department, Letters Sent (by Brevet Major General Edmund Pendleton Gaines and Staff, 1819–26); SWK to McNeil, November 14, 1827, Kearny Papers, Missouri Historical Society, quoted in Nichols, *General Henry Atkinson*, 135. See also Lewis Cass, August 19, 1828, HQALS; Andrew Jackson Turner, "The History of Fort Winnebago," in *Collections of the State Historical Society of Wisconsin*, ed. Reuben Gold Thwaites, vol. 14 (Madison: Democrat Printing, 1898); Louise P. Kellogg, "Old Fort Howard," *Wisconsin Magazine of History* 18 (December 1934): 125–140.

34. Nichols, *General Henry Atkinson*, 138–139, 147; Wyman, *The Wisconsin Frontier*, 144–146; Murphy, *A Gathering of Rivers*, 130; Agent Joseph Street to Major John Fowle, and response, February 7, 1828, AGOLR; Hall, *Uncommon Defense*, 88–89; Mahan, *Old Fort Crawford*, 143–150. McNeil's services, which went back to the War of 1812, were rewarded with a post as federal surveyor for the port of Boston when he resigned in 1830.

35. Wyman, *The Wisconsin Frontier*, 148; Jung, *The Black Hawk War*, 48–50; Judith A. Boughter, *Betraying the Omaha Nation, 1790–1916* (Norman: University of Oklahoma Press, 1998), 25, 34–35; Mahan, *Old Fort Crawford*, 152–155; Nichols, *General Henry Atkinson*, 145.

36. Hall, *Uncommon Defense*, 98–99, 105, 117–118; Kappler, *Indian Affairs*, 2:305–310; Bauer, *Zachary Taylor*, 65. See Catherine Price, "Lakotas and Euroamericans: Contrasted Concepts of 'Chieftainship' and Decision-making Authority," *Ethnohistory* 41 (Summer 1994): 447–463, for a discussion of the difficulty U.S. officials had negotiating with the Sioux, whose leadership, already decentralized, rotated

according to situation. Much the same was true for the Ojibwa, Winnebago, and Potawatomi; see Thomas G. Conway, "Potawatomi Politics," *Journal of the Illinois State Historical Society* 65 (Winter 1972): 395–418, and, more generally, P. Richard Metcalf, "Who Should Rule at Home? Native American Politics and Indian-White Relations," *JAH* 61 (December 1974): 651–665. Primary sources and historians usually portray the Sauk and the Ioway as enemies but sometimes associate them in violence against whites; that association may have been due to white confusion, given the geographic proximity of the two tribes.

37. Murphy, *A Gathering of Rivers*, 161; HA, July 26, 1830, HQALS; Mahan, *Old Fort Crawford*, 198–200; Jung, *The Black Hawk War*, 58; HB to WS, June 21, 1831, 7th Military Department, Letters Sent, Entry 56, RG 393, NA.

38. Lt. George A. McCall to his father, June 19 and July 1 and 5, 1831, in George A. McCall, *Letters from the Frontiers, Written during a Period of Thirty Years Service in the Army of the United States* (1868; reprint, Gainesville: University Presses of Florida, 1974), 228–241; Jung, *The Black Hawk War*, 62–63; Black Hawk, *Autobiography*, ed. J. Gerald Kennedy (New York: Penguin, 2008), 28–29. See EPG to AM, March 25, 1831, AGOLR, for the contrast with Gaines's approach to the Cherokee.

39. Jung, *The Black Hawk War*, 73–86, 139, 162, 172.

40. Ibid., 65–67, 70, 49, 174–177, 164; Wyman, *The Wisconsin Frontier*, 148–153; Kappler, *Indian Affairs*, 2:345–351; AJ, July 24, 1832, and EPG, June 22, 1832, HQALS; Willard Carl Klunder, *Lewis Cass and the Politics of Moderation* (Kent, Ohio: Kent State University Press, 1996), 69. Scholarly accounts include Jung, *The Black Hawk War*; Hall, *Uncommon Defense*; Roger L. Nichols, *Black Hawk and the Warrior's Path* (Arlington Heights, Ill.: Harlan Davidson, 1992); Nichols, *General Henry Atkinson*, chaps. 8, 10; Prucha, *Sword of the Republic*, 163–167, chap. 11; and William T. Hagan, *The Sauk and Fox Indians* (Norman: University of Oklahoma Press, 1958). Ellen M. Whitney, ed., *The Black Hawk War, 1831–1832*, 2 vols. (Springfield: Illinois State Historical Library, 1970–1978), provides a thorough collection of documents.

41. ZT, quoted in Frank E. Stevens, *The Black Hawk War, Including a Review of Black Hawk's Life* (Chicago: Frank E. Stevens, 1903), 197–198; HB to WS, June 26, 1832, 7th Military Department, Letters Sent.

42. Cooke, *Scenes and Adventures*, 156–159, 162, 164; Holmes to paymaster Major J. H. Hook, April 16 and September 28, 1832, in James S. Hutchins, ed., "'Dear Hook': Letters from Bennet Riley, Alphonso Wetmore, and Reuben Holmes, 1822–1833," *Bulletin of the Missouri Historical Society* 36 (1980): 218–219. See Hall, *Uncommon Defense*, for the most thorough and thoughtful exploration of Indian service as U.S. auxiliaries, for any period.

43. ZT to Jesup, December 4, 1832, Taylor Papers, ser. 2, reel 1, LC. Despite his criticism of the militia and his apparent confidence in the regulars, Taylor closed by hinting that the army's tactical capability had not developed as much as the post–War of 1812 reformers had hoped: "I do not consider the line of the army, as efficient now, as it was at the beginning of that war." However, this is the only statement I have seen attributing substantial tactical efficiency to the army on the eve of the War of 1812.

Reading Taylor's correspondence to Jesup and during the Seminole War should give the lie to the myth that he was a simple farmer guided by his staff officers—a misconception that dominates his image, among scholars as well as the general public, even today. Some of this image is a legacy of Taylor's self-portrayal as Old Rough and Ready, the democratic Whig, in election campaign literature. Some of it, particularly among military historians, is due to contrasts these historians have drawn with Winfield Scott. Neither source is rooted in Taylor's correspondence as a military commander or as president: he appears to have been just as thoughtful as any of his fellow field-grade officers of the line. Bauer, *Zachary Taylor*, provides a more accurate portrait, particularly of Taylor as president, but his military career remains in need of critical reassessment. One small beginning is Wesley A. Moerbe, "The Truth about Zachary Taylor in Mexico" (undergraduate senior thesis, USMA, 2004).

44. Cooke, *Scenes and Adventures*, 167, 171, 175–178.

45. Ibid., 195, 156, 172; McCall to George Cadwalader, January 18, 1833, Cadwalader Family Papers, HSP.

46. William E. Unrau, *The Kansa Indians: A History of the Wind People, 1673–1873* (Norman: University of Oklahoma Press, 1971), 157–158; Mary Ellen Rowe, *Bulwark of the Republic: The American Militia in the Antebellum West* (Westport, Conn.: Praeger, 2003), 94–96; Dorothy J. Caldwell, "The Big Neck Affair: Tragedy and Farce on the Missouri Frontier," *Missouri Historical Review* 64 (July 1970): 391–412; Greg Olson, *The Ioway in Missouri* (Columbia: University of Missouri Press, 2008), 100.

47. HA to AM, July 31 and August 2, 1829, cited in Martha Royce Blaine, *The Ioway Indians* (Norman: University of Oklahoma Press, 1979), 155; HA, August 11, 1829, HQALS; *ASPMA*, 4:156.

48. Blaine, *The Ioway Indians*, 161–162; Olson, *The Ioway in Missouri*, 107, 118.

49. Blaine, *The Ioway Indians*, 167–168 (SWK to HA, May 19 and 26, 1837, quoted on 168), 204. For biographies of Kearny, see Dwight L. Clarke, *Stephen Watts Kearny, Soldier of the West* (Norman: University of Oklahoma Press, 1961), and Durwood Ball, "Stephen W. Kearny," in *Soldiers West: Military Biographies from the Western Frontier*, ed. Durwood Ball and Paul R. Hutton, rev. ed. (Norman: University of Oklahoma Press, 2009). For the expansionism, often loosely controlled by central or civilian authority, of European military commanders, see the works cited in note 8.

50. See the correspondence in 6th Military Department, Letters Sent. For example: HA to RJ, May 5 and 29, June 6 (first quotation), 28, and 30, and July 9, 1836, and June 16, 1837; to Capt. Matthew Duncan (First Dragoons), May 9, 1836; to EPG, May 23, 1836, May 3, 1838, and November 11, 1839; to Superintendent of Western Indian Affairs William Clark, May 26, 1836; to brevet Major William Hoffman, June 20, 1836; to brevet Brigadier General George M. Brooke, June 21, 1836; to SWK, June 21 and July 29, 1836, and May 20, 1839; to Missouri governor Daniel Dunklin, July 9, 1836; to Capt. John Breckinridge Grayson, acting assistant adjutant general, Western Division, June 17, 1839 (second quotation).

51. HA to SWK, June 21 (first quotation) and July 7, 1836; to RJ, July 9 1836 (second and third quotations); and to Dunklin, July 9, 1836, 6th Military Depart-

ment, Letters Sent; Willis B. Hughes, "The Heatherly Incident of 1836," *Bulletin of the Missouri Historical Society* 13 (January 1957): 161–180; Rowe, *Bulwark of the Republic*, 106–108; R. David Edmunds, *The Potawatomis: Keepers of the Fire* (Norman: University of Oklahoma Press, 1978), 251–252. The wave of rumors among whites has led to a similar confusion among scholars; reading different secondary accounts can give the impression that there were half a dozen incidents with half a dozen tribes that summer or fall, in each of which two whites were killed, but they all refer to the same incident.

52. HA to RJ, August 3, 1836; to AM, November 21 and December 20, 1837; and to Missouri governor Lilburn W. Boggs, November 28 and December 14, 1837, 6th Military Department, Letters Sent (see also HA to Boggs, August 2, and to SWK and EPG, November 28, 1837); Willard H. Rollings, *The Osage: An Ethnohistorical Study of Hegemony on the Prairie-Plains* (Columbia: University of Missouri Press, 1992), 280; Henry P. Beers, *The Western Military Frontier, 1815–1846* (1935; reprint, Philadelphia: Porcupine Press, 1975), 124; "Application of Missouri for the Payment of Four Companies of Mounted Volunteers Employed on the Northwestern Frontier of the State in 1836," February 14, 1837, *ASPMA*, 7:967–969; HA, April 22, 1838, AGOLR; Louis Pelzer, *Marches of the Dragoons in the Mississippi Valley* (Iowa City: State Historical Society of Iowa, 1917), 82, 86; R. Douglas Hurt, *Nathan Boone and the American Frontier* (Columbia: University of Missouri Press, 1998), 194; "Dragoon Expedition," *ANC* 9 (October 31, 1839): 286; Olson, *The Ioway in Missouri*, 119.

53. HA to Dodge, July 26, 1836; and to AM and to SWK, December 20, 1837, 6th Military Department, Letters Sent. Of course, state governors retained authority over the militias of their states; indeed, Dunklin refused to call up the militia in response to Atkinson's request that October (HA to EPG, October 8, 1836, ibid.). In Florida, this trend accelerated after Jesup replaced Governor Richard K. Call as theater commander, although Call continued to mobilize the militia during local emergencies, and Jesup eventually extended some of the authority he had been granted by the Jackson and Van Buren administrations to the governor. Jesup's correspondence in the Generals' Papers, Entry 159, RG 94, NA, provides extensive evidence of War Department and army efforts to restrain militia and volunteer mobilizations during the Second Seminole War.

54. Prucha, *The Great Father*, 248; Howard I. McKee, "The Platte Purchase," *Missouri Historical Review* 32 (January 1938): 129–147; Lt. Col. Enos Cutler, May 13, 1834, HQALS; Edmunds, *The Potawatomis*, 251–254, 267–271; Olson, *The Ioway in Missouri*, 118; Kappler, *Indian Affairs*, 2:468–470; HA to RJ, June 30, 1836; to EPG and to AM, July 7, 1837; to Potawatomi subagent Edwin James, July 28, 1837; to Sauk and Ioway subagent A. S. Hughes, July 31, 1837; and to Boggs, August 2, 1837, 6th Military Department, Letters Sent.

55. "Dragoon Expedition," *ANC* 9 (October 31, 1839): 285–286; Prucha, *The Great Father*, 252–253; Pelzer, *Marches of the Dragoons*, 87. See also R. David Edmunds, "Potawatomis in the Platte Country: An Indian Removal Incomplete," *Mis-

souri Historical Review 68 (July 1974): 375–392; James A. Clifton, *A Place of Refuge for All Time: Migration of the American Potawatomi into Upper Canada, 1830–1850* (Ottawa: National Museums of Canada, 1975); and John P. Bowes, *Exiles and Pioneers: Eastern Indians in the Trans-Mississippi West* (Cambridge: Cambridge University Press, 2007), chap. 2. See HB to Major John L. Gardner, January 27, 1840, 7th Military Department, Letters Sent, for a further example of supplying rations on grounds both diplomatic and humanitarian.

56. Lt. John Beach to Major John Green, January 17, 1837, and ZT to SWK, February 14, 1837, 6th Military Department, Letters Sent; HB to RJ, May 9 and 20 and July 12, 1836, 7th Military Department, Letters Sent.

57. HA, January 5 and May 14, 1833, HQALS.

58. HA, January 5 (three separate letters), April 30, and May 9, 1833, and Dodge, March 14, 1833, HQALS; Beers, *The Western Military Frontier*, 90–92; Mahan, *Old Fort Crawford*, 205–206, 217–220; Kappler, *Indian Affairs*, 2:498–500; WS to A. C. Dodge, February 7, 1841, Oshkosh Papers, State Historical Society of Wisconsin; Worth to WS, May 10, 1840, file W-181, reel 150, AGOLR. See Grant Foreman, *The Last Trek of the Indians* (Chicago: University of Chicago Press, 1946), for the only general treatment of the removal of the northwestern tribes. The Nullification Crisis, the conflict over squatter removal in Alabama, and the French claims crisis do not appear to have been factors in the inertia that allowed the Sauk, Fox, and Winnebago to remain, since the regiments involved in those crises were artillery units already stationed on the coast or in the Southeast.

59. SWK, report of 1835 expedition, quoted in "Fort Des Moines, No. 1, Iowa," *Annals of Iowa* 3 (April–June 1898): 357; Pelzer, *Marches of the Dragoons*, 49–58; Hurt, *Nathan Boone*, 175–182; see also William E. Whittaker, ed., *Frontier Forts of Iowa: Indians, Traders, and Soldiers, 1682–1862* (Iowa City: Iowa University Press, 2009).

60. Beers, *The Western Military Frontier*, 122, 139–140, 143–144; Bruce E. Mahan, "Old Fort Atkinson," *Palimpset* 22 (November 1921): 341; Pelzer, *Marches of the Dragoons*, 90–91; Kappler, *Indian Affairs*, 2:546–549; "Fort Des Moines, No. 2," *Annals of Iowa* 4 (October 1899): 175–176.

61. Mahan, *Old Fort Crawford*, 221–225; Sumner, November 9, 1843, AGOLR; Pelzer, *Marches of the Dragoons*, 96.

62. Sweninger, "'A Lingering War Must Be Avoided,'" 249 (table 7.1).

63. Scott and Allen quoted in Prucha, *Sword of the Republic*, 384–385 (emphasis added); Allen to SWK, January 4, 1845, 29th Cong., 1st sess., House Doc. 168, 5.

64. Sumner to acting assistant adjutant general, August 23, 1845, 29th Cong., 1st sess., Sen. Doc. 1, 217–220; Nancy L. Woolworth, "Captain Edwin V. Sumner's Expedition to Devil's Lake in the Summer of 1845," *North Dakota History* 28 (April 1961): 79–98. There is no known relation between the author and the Watson in question. The métis are examined in John Mack Faragher, "Americans, Mexicans, Métis: A Community Approach to the Comparative Study of North American Frontiers," in *Under an Open Sky: Rethinking America's Western Past*, ed. William Cronon, George Miles, and Jay Gitlin (New York: W. W Norton, 1992), 90–109.

65. Wyman, *The Wisconsin Frontier*, 160–61; Anderson, *Kinsmen of Another Kind*, 157, 173; Anderson, "The Removal of the Mdewakanton Dakota," 310–333.

66. Anderson, "The Removal of the Mdewakanton Dakota," 329; HA to Plympton, September 4, 1838, 6th Military Department, Letters Sent; Hansen, *Old Fort Snelling*, 125, 194–195.

CHAPTER THREE: FEDERAL AUTHORITY UNDER ATTACK

1. Brian W. Dippie, *The Vanishing American: White Attitudes and U.S. Indian Policy* (Middletown, Conn.: Wesleyan University Press, 1982), chap. 5, especially 60. Arthur H. DeRosier Jr., *The Removal of the Choctaw Indians* (Knoxville: University of Tennessee Press, 1970), chaps. 3, 6, presents the most extensive and positive treatment of the "policy of moderation." Reginald Horsman, *The Origins of Indian Removal, 1815–1824* (Lansing: Michigan State University Press, 1970), was one of the first scholars to observe the continuity between Jeffersonian and Jacksonian policy; see also Richard Drinnon, *Facing West: The Metaphysics of Indian-hating and Empire Building* (Minneapolis: University of Minnesota Press, 1980). Focusing on legal developments, particularly the courts, Stuart Banner, *How the Indians Lost Their Land: Law and Power on the Frontier* (Cambridge, Mass.: Harvard University Press, 2005), provides the most recent support for Horsman's continuity thesis.

Apart from several articles on the 1830 Removal Act, the national politics of Indian removal has not received the explicit attention evident in monographs on state politics (the most numerous studies of Jacksonian politics available). See Ronald N. Satz, *American Indian Policy in the Jacksonian Era* (Lincoln: University of Nebraska Press, 1974), 39–56; David J. Russo, *The Major Political Issues of the Jacksonian Period and the Development of Party Loyalty in Congress, 1830–1840*, vol. 62, pt. 5 (Philadelphia: Transactions of the American Philosophical Society, 1972), 13–14; and Leonard A. Carlson and Mark A. Roberts, "Indian Lands, 'Squatterism,' and Slavery: Economic Interests and the Passage of the Indian Removal Act of 1830," *Explorations in Economic History* 43 (2006): 486–504. Fred S. Rolater, "The American Indian and the Origin of the Second American Party System," *Wisconsin Magazine of History* 76 (Spring 1993): 180–201, provides the clearest analysis; John Ashworth, *Slavery, Capitalism, and Politics in the Antebellum Republic: Conflict and Compromise, 1820–1850* (Cambridge: Cambridge University Press, 1995), 369–381, provides the most broad ranging. Mary Hershberger, "Mobilizing Women, Anticipating Abolition: The Struggle against Indian Removal in the 1830s," *JAH* 86 (June 1999): 15–40, ultimately focuses on how mobilizing to oppose removal led women into abolitionism, rather than on the politics of removal per se. Removal is virtually invisible in the standard and otherwise comprehensive accounts of political party formation during the Jacksonian era: Richard P. McCormick, *The Second American Party System: Party Formation in the Jacksonian Era* (Chapel Hill: University of North Carolina Press, 1966), and

Michael F. Holt, *The Rise and Fall of the American Whig Party: Jacksonian Politics and the Onset of the Civil War* (New York: Oxford University Press, 1999).

2. The Indian treaties of the era covered by this book are printed in vol. 7 of *Statutes at Large* and Charles J. Kappler, comp., *Indian Affairs: Laws and Treaties* (Washington, D.C.: Government Printing Office, 1903–1929), vol. 2. See Lawrence Frederick Kohl, *The Politics of Individualism: Parties and the American Character in the Jacksonian Era* (New York: Oxford University Press, 1989), chap. 4, and Daniel Walker Howe, *What Hath God Wrought? The Transformation of America, 1815–1848* (New York: Oxford University Press, 2007), chap. 11, for the most extensive explorations of Jacksonian attitudes toward law.

3. For context, see especially Ronald T. Takaki, *Iron Cages: Race and Culture in Nineteenth-Century America* (New York: Alfred A. Knopf, 1979); Alexander Saxton, *The Rise and Fall of the White Republic: Class Politics and Mass Culture in Nineteenth-Century America* (London: Verso, 1990); Reginald Horsman, *Race and Manifest Destiny: The Origins of American Racial Anglo-Saxonism* (Cambridge, Mass.: Harvard University Press, 1981); and the special issue of *JER* 19 (Winter 1999) on race in the early republic.

4. For public land policy, see Paul W. Gates, *History of Public Land Law Development* (Washington, D.C.: Government Printing Office, 1968); Malcolm J. Rohrbaugh, *The Land Office Business: The Settlement and Administration of American Public Lands, 1789–1837* (New York: Oxford University Press, 1968); Daniel Feller, *The Public Lands in Jacksonian Politics* (Madison: University of Wisconsin Press, 1984); Melvin T. Kanazawa, "Possession Is Nine Points of the Law: The Political Economy of Early Public Land Disposal," *Explorations in Economic History* 33 (April 1996): 227–249; and more broadly, Laura Jensen, *Patriots, Settlers, and the Origins of American Social Policy* (Cambridge: Cambridge University Press, 2003).

5. Francis Paul Prucha, *American Indian Policy in the Formative Years: The Indian Trade and Intercourse Acts, 1790–1834* (Cambridge, Mass.: Harvard University Press, 1962), 186.

6. See the works of sociologist Everett C. Hughes, especially *Men and Their Work* (Glencoe, Ill.: Free Press, 1958), for the concept of "dirty work," especially that dealing with death and morally debatable actions, like killing, delegated to professionals by society.

7. See Ronald P. Formisano, "State Development in the Early Republic: Structure and Substance, 1780–1840," and David Waldstreicher, "The Nationalization and Racialization of American Politics: Before, beneath, and between Parties, 1790–1840," in *Contesting Democracy: Substance and Structure in American Political History, 1775–2000*, ed. Byron E. Shafer and Anthony J. Badger (Lawrence: University Press of Kansas, 2001), for interpretations of the Republican victory as one of the expansionist periphery (the South and the West) over the centralizing Federalists. Leonard J. Sadosky, *Revolutionary Negotiations: Indians, Empires, and Diplomats in the Founding of America* (Charlottesville: University Press of Virginia, 2009), argues that Federalist borderlands policy had a direct impact on mobilizing the South and the West

against the Federalists. This argument has long been made about the Jacksonians, first as a movement of the West and since the 1960s as one of the South; Formisano and Waldstreicher connect the reaction against the Federalists with that against the National Republicans. See Andrew R. L. Cayton, "'Separate Interests' and the Nation-State: The Washington Administration and the Origins of Regionalism in the Trans-Appalachian West," *JAH* 79 (June 1992): 39–67, for a similar argument emphasizing southern resentment against President Washington's deployment of the army against Indians in Ohio rather than in Tennessee or Georgia.

8. AJ to JCC, June 15, 1820, *CAJ*, 3:25–26.

9. AJ to JCC, July 9 and 26 and November 30, 1820, *CAJ*, 3:29–31, 33–34; Call to AJ, July 8, 1820, *PAJ*, 4:372–373, and July 12 and 16 and August 17, 1820, Jackson Papers, LC. See also George Birch, "Private Journal," Birch Family Papers, HSP.

10. AJ to William Rabun, May 7, 1818, *PAJ*, 4:202.

11. Ibid.; Vandeventer to AJ, and Jackson's endorsement (n. 3), June 2, 1818, *PAJ*, 4:216–217. The murderers ultimately escaped punishment.

12. AJ to HA, February 27, 1820, file J-200, and Bell, April 22, 1822, SWLR: Reg.

13. Birch journal, November 3, 1820, Birch Family Papers; Eustis, July 23, 1822, file E-18, SWLR: Reg.

14. Arbuckle, January 12, 1823, file A-113, and Eustis to Duval, September 15, 1822, file E-44, SWLR: Reg. Horsman, *The Origins of Indian Removal*, was perhaps the first scholarly work to suggest the continuities I emphasize here.

15. William G. McLoughlin, *Cherokee Renascence in the New Republic* (Princeton, N.J.: Princeton University Press, 1986), 309–314; Prucha, *American Indian Policy*, 186. On the one hand, Alfred A. Cave, "Abuse of Power: Andrew Jackson and the Indian Removal Act of 1830," *The Historian* 65 (Winter 2003): 1330–1353, emphasizes that the law required fair negotiation and did not permit the coercion that characterized the actual removal process. On the other hand, while some congressmen may have voted for the act in the hope that it would moderate frontier practice, it is difficult to believe that anyone at all familiar with the events detailed in this chapter could have failed to anticipate coercion. Indictments of removal must ultimately be moral rather than legal; Jackson, like most frontiersmen, had long since displayed his contempt for the rule of law when it protected Indians.

16. Monroe, March 30, 1824, and January 27, 1825, *MPP*, 2:804, 850; Michael D. Green, *The Politics of Indian Removal: Creek Government and Society in Crisis* (Lincoln: University of Nebraska Press, 1982), 54, 67, 97–99, chap. 4. Georgia politics is examined in Ulrich B. Phillips, *Georgia and State Rights* (1901; reprint, Yellow Springs, Ga.: Antioch Press, 1968), chap. 4; Porter L. Fortune Jr., "George M. Troup: Leading State Rights Advocate" (Ph.D. diss., University of North Carolina, 1949); Jack N. Averitt, "The Democratic Party in Georgia, 1824–1837" (Ph.D. diss., University of North Carolina, 1956); and David A. Nichols, "Land, Republicanism, and Indians: Power and Policy in Early National Georgia, 1790–1825," *GAHQ* 85 (Summer 2001): 199–226. See Tim Alan Garrison, *The Legal Ideology of Removal: The Southern Judiciary and the Sovereignty of Native American Nations* (Athens: University of Georgia

Press, 2002); Deborah A. Rosen, *American Indians and State Law: Sovereignty, Race, and Citizenship, 1790–1880* (Lincoln: University of Nebraska Press, 2007); Lisa Ford, *Settler Sovereignty: Jurisdiction and Indigenous People in America and Australia, 1788–1836* (Cambridge, Mass.: Harvard University Press, 2010); and Mary Young, "The Exercise of Sovereignty in Cherokee Georgia," *JER* 10 (Spring 1990): 43–63, regarding the extension of state jurisdiction over Native Americans; more generally, see Michael D. Green, "Federal-State Conflict in the Administration of Indian Policy: Georgia, Alabama, and the Creeks, 1824–1834" (Ph.D. diss., University of Iowa, 1973). Forrest McDonald, *States' Rights and the Union: Imperium in Imperio, 1776–1876* (Lawrence: University Press of Kansas, 2000), ably assesses the shifting balance of power between federal and state claims to sovereignty during this era.

17. Kappler, *Indian Affairs*, 2:214–217; see also Benjamin W. Griffith Jr., *McIntosh and Weatherford: Creek Indian Leaders* (Tuscaloosa: University of Alabama Press, 1988), chaps. 13–16. The most recent account of McIntosh's execution is Andrew K. Frank, "The Rise and Fall of William McIntosh: Authority and Identity on the Early American Frontier," *GAHQ* 86 (Spring 2002): 18–48. Students of European empires might recall Lord Lugard's rueful (or perhaps wistful) observation about British diplomacy in Africa: "Treaties were produced by the cartload in all approved forms of legal verbiage—impossible of translation. . . . It mattered not that tribal chiefs had no power to dispose of communal rights." Frederick Lugard, *The Dual Mandate in British Tropical Africa*, 5th ed. (London: Frank Cass, 1965), 15.

18. Lynn Hudson Parsons, "'A Perpetual Harrow upon My Feelings': John Quincy Adams and the American Indian," *New England Quarterly* 46 (September 1973): 339–379; Brown to WS, July 5, 1825, Jacob Brown Papers, WLC.

19. JCC to Crowell, January 18, 1825, *ASPIA*, 2:578; Green, *Politics of Indian Removal*, 101–104.

20. Adams, May 19, 1825, in *Memoirs of John Quincy Adams, Comprising Portions of His Diary from 1795 to 1848*, 12 vols., ed. Charles F. Adams (Philadelphia: J. B. Lippincott, 1874–1877), 8:8; EPG to Cadwalader, June 1, 1825, Thomas Cadwalader Papers, box 75, series 3, Cadwalader Family Collection, HSP.

21. EPG to Troup, May 31, Troup to EPG, June 14, and Andrews to Secretary of War Barbour, June 2 and 7, 1825, in House Report 98, 19th Cong., 2nd sess. (serial 161): 169–170, 592, 173, 178–179.

22. Andrews to Barbour, June 12, to the Georgia commissioners, June 27 and July 1, and to the *National Journal*, September 9, 1825, ibid., 182, 672–677, 639–649. Andrews's report to the War Department is in ibid., 305–347. Andrews did not note his military commission or rank in his letter to the *National Journal*, which exposed the dirty laundry of each individual Georgia commissioner at length. This omission was probably an attempt to prevent attacks on the army or on the administration for employing it, much as modern military officers and civil government officials state that their views do not represent those of the government.

23. Butler to Frances Parke Lewis, July 1, 1825, Edward G. W. Butler Papers, PLDU; Butler to the Georgia commissioners, July 1 and 3, 1825, serial 161: 678, 681;

Butler to Lewis, July 11, 1825, Butler Papers, PLDU. Butler's journal from May 30 to September 18, mostly addressing the negotiations between Gaines and the Creeks, is in serial 161: 575–588. Butler stuck with Gaines for six more years, resigning as a lieutenant in 1831 after eleven years' service, more than seven of them as Gaines's aide. Butler's connections led to his recommissioning as colonel of the Third Dragoon Regiment in 1847; he resigned when it was demobilized following the war with Mexico.

24. EPG to Barbour, September 26, serial 161: 560–561, and June 15 and August 9, 1825, files G-70 and G-105, SWLR: Reg. The treaty states that "the period of removal shall not extend beyond" September 1, 1826, but that was generally understood as the date by which the Creeks had to begin leaving, during which time Georgia and its citizens had to forgo intrusion.

25. AJ to Edward G. W. Butler, July 25 and December 8, 1825, *PAJ*, 5:94, 125; EPG to Troup, July 28, 1825, *ASPIA*, 2:801; Iverson Brooks, in House Executive Document 59, 19th Cong., 2nd sess., 373. See James W. Silver, "General Gaines Meets Governor Troup: A State-Federal Clash in 1825," *GAHQ* 27 (September 1943): 248–270, and Green, *Politics of Indian Removal*, 105–116, for narratives; much of the correspondence between Gaines and Troup was published in *Niles' Weekly Register* that summer and fall.

26. Edward J. Harden, *The Life of George M. Troup* (Savannah, Ga.: E. J. Purse, 1859), 393–394; *Niles' Weekly Register* 29 (September 10, 1825): 17–18; WS to William S. Hamilton, September 30, 1825, Scott Papers, LC. See also EPG to Troup, August 16 and 29, 1825, published in the *Georgia Journal*, in serial 161: 550–554.

27. AJ to Edward G. W. Butler, November 10, 1825, *PAJ*, 5:121; EPG to Thomas Cadwalader, October 9, 1825, Cadwalader Papers, box 75, series 3, Cadwalader Family Collection, HSP.

28. Butler to AJ, July 14, 1826, *PAJ*, 5:184.

29. Mary W. M. Hargreaves, *The Presidency of John Quincy Adams* (Lawrence: University Press of Kansas, 1985), 200; Dippie, *The Vanishing American*, 63; DeRosier, *The Removal of the Choctaw Indians*, chap. 6 (quotation); Adams to Secretary of State Monroe, September 5, 1814, in *Writings of John Quincy Adams*, ed. Worthington Ford (New York: Macmillan, 1913–1917), 5:116.

30. Hargreaves, *The Presidency of John Quincy Adams*, 200; Grant Foreman, *Indian Removal: The Emigration of the Five Civilized Tribes of Indians* (Norman: University of Oklahoma Press, 1932), 157.

31. Hargreaves, *The Presidency of John Quincy Adams*, 116–131; serial 161: 706–708; Kappler, *Indian Affairs*, 2:264–268. See "Journal of a Meeting between General Gaines and the Creek Nation, 30 Oct.–1 Nov. 1825," in serial 161: 708–712, and Richard J. Hryniewicki, "The Creek Treaty of Washington, 1826," *GAHQ* 48 (December 1964): 425–441. Hryniewicki concludes that "the federal government . . . ultimately won the struggle" (439), but this is true only in the most extreme and superficial sense, in that Georgia did not resist militarily: after all the shouting, the United States did Georgia's will. The role of state representatives at treaty negotiations, which could legally be conducted only under federal auspices, had been a prob-

lem during the 1790s, largely with the Georgians (who wanted to bully the Creeks). The Georgians had negotiated their own treaties with the Indians (i.e., obtained land cessions from them) during the 1780s, prior to the first trade and intercourse act. The 1796 and 1802 acts attempted to resolve this clash by authorizing state agents to negotiate the compensation "for their claims to lands within such state, which shall be extinguished by the treaty." Though this could be interpreted in several ways, federal agents would negotiate the land cessions and had the authority to forbid their state counterparts from participating, as Gaines appears to have done in 1826. See David Andrew Nichols, *Red Gentlemen & White Savages: Indians, Federalists, and the Search for Order on the American Frontier* (Charlottesville: University Press of Virginia, 2008), chap. 7; Sadosky, *Revolutionary Negotiations*, chaps. 5, 6; 1 *Stat.* 472 and 2 *Stat.* 143.

32. Crawford to Smith, November 21, 1826, in Chase C. Mooney, *William H. Crawford, 1772–1834* (Lexington: University Press of Kentucky, 1974), 336; Troup, January 29, 1827, SWLS.

33. John R. Vinton, January 30, 1827, SWLS; Brown to WS, February 1, 1827, Brown Letterbook, LC.

34. Green, *Politics of Indian Removal*, 133–138; Vinton journal, February 13 and 19, 1827, John R. Vinton Papers, PLDU.

35. Adams, December 2, 1828, *MPP*, 3:982; WS to Brown and Brown to WS, February 5 and 8, 1827, Brown Letterbook, LC; Brown to his son Jacob Brown Jr., April 13, and to Secretary of War James Barbour, August 13, 1827, Brown Papers, WLC. Brown and Scott had both supported John C. Calhoun during the early stages of the 1824 campaign and turned to John Quincy Adams when Calhoun dropped out. Vinton's diary, like Brown's papers, demonstrates the northern sectionalism that support for Adams represented among some officers during the 1820s.

CHAPTER FOUR: THE ARMY AND THE JACKSONIANS TANGLE ON THE SOUTHERN FRONTIER

1. Mary W. M. Hargreaves, *The Presidency of John Quincy Adams* (Lawrence: University Press of Kansas, 1985), 207.

2. Crowell to Secretary of War John Eaton, June 25, 1829, HQALR; May 28, 1830, 4 *Stat.* 411–12; Alfred A. Cave, "Abuse of Power: Andrew Jackson and the Indian Removal Act of 1830," *The Historian* 65 (Winter 2003): 1333, 1336, 1351.

3. David Williams, *The Georgia Gold Rush: Twenty-niners, Cherokees, and Gold Fever* (Columbia: University of South Carolina Press, 1993), 32; Brady to Eaton, June 12 and 28, and to AM, July 18, 1830, HQALR. See EPG to AM, March 25, 1831, AGOLR, for similar disdain toward the prospectors.

4. Eaton to AM, February 24 and March 16, and Commanding Officer U.S. Troops, Cherokee Nation, June 26, 1830, HQALS.

5. Gilmer to AJ, June 17, 1830, in James W. Covington, ed., "Letters from the Georgia Gold Regions," *Collections of the Georgia Historical Society* 39 (1955):

404–407; William G. McLoughlin, *Cherokee Renascence in the New Republic* (Princeton, N.J.: Princeton University Press, 1986), 431–432; Brady, July 13, 1830, SWLS.

6. Tommy R. Young II, "The United States Army in the South, 1789–1835" (Ph.D. diss., Louisiana State University, 1973), 298–315; John Crowell, July 6, 1829, Georgia governor John Forsyth, July 7, 1829, brevet Brigadier General George Mercer Brooke, February 20, 1830, HQALS; Williams, *The Georgia Gold Rush*, 32–33; Wager, September 15 and 30, 1830, HQALR. Theda Perdue and Michael D. Green, *The Cherokee Nation and the Trail of Tears* (New York: Viking, 2007), 74, state that the United States did nothing to prevent intrusion in the Cherokee gold country. The 1830 removal operations were a one-time effort, but they involved a substantial commitment of forces at a time when the administration was demanding extreme restraint on spending. There was undoubtedly a mélange of state and federal political factors involved in the decision to deploy the army; the desire to mollify the Cherokee so they might sign a removal treaty was probably uppermost. Neither the decision to deploy nor that to end the operation was up to the army.

7. Roley McIntosh and other Creeks to AJ, March 7, 1829, *PAJ*, 7:83–85.

8. Eaton, March 17, 1830, House Doc. 89, 21st Cong., 1st sess. (serial 197): 42; Wager, November 10, 1830, SWLS.

9. Regimental commanders chose their adjutants and could nominate commissary and quartermaster officers within their regiments; they could support or undermine individual requests for leave or for recruiting and other detached duties in socially attractive eastern cities; they could harass subordinates by assigning them to court-martial duties that might require travel and absence from family. Geographic division and department commanders, staff bureau chiefs, and the commanding general could do much the same, and all these men received frequent requests for preferential assignments from officers' civilian friends and patrons, often including prominent politicians, often channeled through the War Department. (The language of these requests was entirely social, based on genteel friendship and consideration of family needs, rather than partisan. If anything, this demonstrates, like nominations to West Point, the persistence of social elites and their connections across party lines.) No doubt more extensive investigation would uncover instances of War Department sanctions against individual officers, but military commanders appear to have retained substantial autonomy to approve or deny individual assignment preferences, and general officers seemingly deferred to regimental commanders in most cases. (In other words, regimental commanders, like the staff bureau chiefs, exercised substantial autonomy within the army, a third layer of insulation reinforcing the insulation of the army within the executive branch and the executive branch within the nation and the nation-state as a whole.) The types of detached duty, such as transportation surveys, and leaves granted during the Second Seminole War (respectively examined in *Jackson's Sword* and chapter 7 herein) indicate that the War Department acted primarily to reward rather than punish, and it proved very hesitant to rescind preferential assignments.

10. Covington, "Letters from the Georgia Gold Regions," 409; Wager, February 8, 1831, and September 26, 1830, HQALR.

11. Wager, August 10 and November 2, 1832, HQALS.

12. Charles J. Kappler, comp., *Indian Affairs: Laws and Treaties* (Washington, D.C.: Government Printing Office, 1904), 2:341–343; Wager to AM, September 9, 1832, file W-137, AGOLR.

13. Frank L. Owsley Jr., "Francis Scott Key's Mission to Alabama in 1833," *Alabama Review* 23 (July 1970): 184, 187; Mary Elizabeth Young, *Redskins, Ruffleshirts, and Rednecks: Indian Allotments in Alabama and Mississippi, 1830–1860* (Norman: University of Oklahoma Press, 1961), 76–77; Armistead, May 21 and July 18, 1832, North Carolina governor Montfort Stokes, July 18, 1832, commanding officer, Fort Armstrong, October 27, 1832, Governor Swain (of North Carolina), March 14, 1833, and commanding officer, Fort Dearborn, February 16, 1833, HQALS; Bruce E. Mahan, *Old Fort Crawford and the Frontier* (Iowa City: State Historical Society of Iowa, 1926), 200.

14. Michael D. Green, *The Politics of Indian Removal: Creek Government and Society in Crisis* (Lincoln: University of Nebraska Press, 1982), 175–176; Young, *Redskins, Ruffleshirts, and Rednecks*, 77; U.S. Deputy Marshal Jeremy Austill, November 26, Wager, November 27, and WS, December 4, 1832, HQALS; RJ to McIntosh, August 26, 1833, James S. McIntosh Papers, PLDU.

15. Green, *The Politics of Indian Removal*, 180; *Charleston Courier*, October 19 and December 15, 1833; Albert J. Pickett, *History of Alabama* (Birmingham, Ala.: Webb Book Company, 1900), 686–687.

16. McIntosh to Solicitor William Pickett, Eighth Federal Circuit Court, and to R. L. Crawford and Anstill, October 15, 1833, McIntosh Papers.

17. McIntosh to AM, October 21, 1833, McIntosh Papers. See also McIntosh to R. L. Crawford, October 23, 1833, ibid., and serials 247, 256, and 292, U.S. Congress, Serial Set.

18. Manning to Secretary of War Lewis Cass, October 20, 1833, file M-214, AGOLR.

19. WS to Cass, November 20, 1833, quoted in Young, *Redskins, Ruffleshirts, and Rednecks*, 80; Cass to McIntosh, October 29, 1833, McIntosh Papers, and November 23, 1833, Fourth Infantry Regiment Letters Sent and Received, 1823–1835, Entry 1136, RG 391, NA; Owsley, "Francis Scott Key's Mission to Alabama," 188. Cass's letter to McIntosh on November 23 affirmed that Jackson considered the United States responsible for soldiers' legal expenses.

20. Owsley, "Francis Scott Key's Mission to Alabama," 191.

21. McIntosh to Cass, November 8, 1833, McIntosh Papers; Richard R. John, *Spreading the News: The American Postal System from Franklin to Morse* (Cambridge, Mass.: Harvard University Press, 1995).

22. Twiggs, November 20, 1833, Eustis, November 22, 1833, and Twiggs, January 4, 1834 (quotation), HQALS. Macomb was the author of *A Treatise on Martial Law and Courts-Martial* (Charleston, S.C.: J. Hoff, 1809), which emphasized the subordination of military to civil law (see especially 27–29).

23. Abert to Cass, June 9, 1833, quoted in Young, *Redskins, Ruffleshirts, and Red-*

necks, 81. See the Records of the Topographical Engineers, Central Office, Entry 318 in Records of the Chief of Engineers, RG 77, NA, for a box with reports and correspondence relating to Abert's direction of the removal of the Shawnee and Ottawa from Ohio to Missouri during the autumn of 1832. Abert was put in charge after John F. Lane, a politically well connected but very junior (brevet) second lieutenant assigned as disbursing agent, quarreled with the civilian superintendent. Abert's employment in the removal process suggests both the government's lack of civilian personnel with administrative and logistical experience and the possible career benefits of serving in civil as well as military capacities. The topographical engineers, subordinated to the fortification-oriented Corps of Engineers since their birth, gained autonomy as a separate bureau in 1832 and became a separate "corps" (or branch) six years later, when Abert became their colonel by seniority. Presumably, the topographical engineers' quest for autonomy benefited from his service in removal.

24. EPG to Belton, August 23, 1832, WDLS.

25. Wager to Rep. Edward Lucas, December 19, 1833, Edward and William Lucas Papers, PLDU; McIntosh, May 9, 1836, file M-138, AGOLR.

26. WS to Cass, November 20, 1833, in Young, *Redskins, Ruffleshirts, and Rednecks*, 80; Leonard A. Carlson and Mark A. Roberts, "Indian Lands, 'Squatterism,' and Slavery: Economic Interests and the Passage of the Indian Removal Act of 1830," *Explorations in Economic History* 43 (July 2006): 486–504.

27. Stuart Banner, *How the Indians Lost Their Land: Law and Power on the Frontier* (Cambridge, Mass.: Harvard University Press, 2005), chaps. 4–6; Perdue and Green, *The Cherokee Nation and the Trail of Tears*, 51. See Jill Norgren, *The Cherokee Cases: The Confrontation of Law and Politics* (New York: McGraw-Hill, 1996), for the ambiguous decisions of the Supreme Court.

28. See especially Fred S. Rolater, "The American Indian and the Origin of the Second American Party System," *Wisconsin Magazine of History* 76 (Spring 1993): 180–201, and Ronald N. Satz, *American Indian Policy in the Jacksonian Era* (Lincoln: University of Nebraska Press, 1974), 39–56.

29. Cave, "Abuse of Power," 1331.

30. Ibid., 1344, 1332; Donald B. Cole, *The Presidency of Andrew Jackson* (Lawrence: University Press of Kansas, 1993), 115. See also Rolater, "The American Indian and the Origin of the Second American Party System," 200–201. Stephen J. Rockwell, *Indian Affairs and the Administration State in the Nineteenth Century* (Cambridge: Cambridge University Press, 2010), downplays the trade-off between speed and ultimate cost in removal. Rockwell is at pains, however counterintuitive and contrary to existing historiography, to interpret Jacksonian patronage and rotation in office in the most positive light, ignoring white opposition to removal and rejecting the extensive accusations of corruption (accepted by virtually every historian) as unfounded, personally or politically motivated calumnies. Employing passive language and a single case study for evidence, he maintains that "bureaucratic delays [and] frauds . . . all furthered the ends" of removal. In other words, patronage worked because agents knew they could benefit from removal but had little time in which to do so, so they pushed it hard.

In effect, Rockwell seems to consider patronage an asset to policy because government actors, or their private-sector allies, knew they could personally profit from their actions. He calls this commitment; I call it conflict of interest. But removal was one area where the Jacksonians would advance "monopoly" and the privilege extended by government. See ibid., especially 200, 205, 168, 171–172, 211 (quotation).

Rockwell undoubtedly demonstrates the power of the U.S. government, but not its autonomy or its bureaucratic efficacy in any sense recognized by any other scholar. That removal occurred does not vitiate its corruption and expense: policy effectiveness in outcome (the achievement of policy objectives) is not the same thing as ethical or efficient policy execution. Rockwell's administrative state lacks continuity, consistency, system, specialized expertise (except as mediators, implicitly if not overtly corrupt, between special interests), and autonomy from local, sectional, sectoral, or partisan interests. To portray Indian removal as effective policy utterly ignores opportunity costs in government, politics, and social and economic impact. Republican virtue, ethics and transparency in government, equal access to public resources (Jacksonian antimonopoly), and the rule of law were all subordinated to removal, one of the most damning case studies in the sorry record of Jacksonian public administration.

The Indian agents lacked the nationalist socialization army officers received at the Military Academy; they had less time in their short tenures to become socialized or acclimated or to gain local knowledge (of the Indians as well as the white frontiersmen they served) through experience in the field; they were not subject to the additional sanctions of military law and the Articles of War; and they were appointed through partisan patronage, as rewards for services rendered and expected. In fact, Rockwell demonstrates the capture of the civilian Indian policy apparatus by southern and western frontier interests—politically embodied in Jackson's Democratic Party—and their fraudulent, selfish manipulation of government resources, contrary to the very statutes that authorized them to pursue removal. This is evidence of *de*-professionalization in the civil service and *for* the state of courts and parties thesis—simply for more powerful parties. In effect, Rockwell's argument supports Daniel Carpenter's denial of bureaucratic autonomy in the Jacksonian civil service; see Daniel P. Carpenter, *The Forging of Bureaucratic Autonomy: Reputations, Networks, and Policy Innovation in Executive Agencies, 1862–1928* (Princeton, N.J.: Princeton University Press, 2001). Nor would I argue otherwise—for the civil service. But the majority of removal was conducted and overseen by military officers, *not* civilian agents.

31. Rolater, "The American Indian and the Origin of the Second American Party System," 197; John Ashworth, *Slavery, Capitalism, and Politics in the Antebellum Republic: Conflict and Compromise, 1820–1850* (Cambridge: Cambridge University Press, 1995), 369–381; Daniel Walker Howe, *What Hath God Wrought? The Transformation of America, 1815–1848* (New York: Oxford University Press, 2007), 386. See William B. Skelton, "Officers and Politicians: The Origins of Army Politics in the United States before the Civil War," *AFS* 6 (Fall 1979): 22–48, and *An American Profession of Arms: The Army Officer Corps, 1784–1861* (Lawrence: University Press of Kansas, 1992), chap. 15 (statistics on 295), for the only published assessments of offi-

cer politics. See Samuel Watson, "What Do We Mean by Partisan? Army Officers and Politics during the Evolution of the Second Party System" (unpublished paper presented to the Southwestern Historical Association, April 1, 1999), for a narrative and analysis of officers' changing political views between about 1820 and 1845.

32. William B. Skelton, "The Commanding Generals and the Question of Civil Control in the Antebellum U.S. Army," *American Nineteenth-Century History* 7 (June 2006): 153–172.

33. EPG to Secretary of War Barbour, August 25, 1827, and to Col. Willoughby Morgan, January 23, 1832, cited in Calvin Reese, "The United States Army and the Indian: Low Plains Area, 1815–1854" (Ph.D. diss., University of Southern California, 1963), 177, 182.

34. EPG to Jacob Brown, 1827, *ASPMA*, 4:129–133.

35. See, for example, Grant Foreman, *Indian Removal: The Emigration of the Five Civilized Tribes of Indians* (Norman: University of Oklahoma Press, 1932), 8. Despite the age of Foreman's work, it remains more detailed than most histories, and Foreman's assessments and conclusions have not been fundamentally altered.

36. December 1, 1830, SWLS: PUS. Choctaw removal has sometimes been referred to, perhaps casually, as a "test case," which might imply that Jackson would have ceased removal had it "failed"; that was highly unlikely.

37. I use the term *expropriation* as essentially synonymous with removal. Regardless of the means, dispossession was the intent and effect of Indian land cessions. The combination of these treaties, which were often fraudulent and almost always coerced, with the pressure of economic dependency and coercion, "private" bullying and rowdyism, the threat and imposition of state sovereignty, and the threat and use of state and national troops makes expropriation an appropriate term for the process as a whole. I also use the term *emigration*, which suggests voluntary action, largely to avoid the overuse of *removal* and *expropriation*; however, I have attempted to limit my use of *emigration* to specific movements away from a place of origin, the physical process of moving west from the lands expropriated by the United States.

38. 1 *Stat.* 592.

39. Francis Paul Prucha, *The Great Father: The U.S. Government and the American Indians* (Lincoln: University of Nebraska Press, 1984), 1:218; Arthur H. DeRosier Jr., *The Removal of the Choctaw Indians* (Knoxville: University of Tennessee Press, 1970), 138, 142–143; Satz, *American Indian Policy in the Jacksonian Era*, 72–73.

40. Cave, "Abuse of Power," 1344; Satz, *American Indian Policy in the Jacksonian Era*, 73; EPG to AJ, March 20, 1830, AGOLR, cited in James W. Silver, "A Counter-proposal to the Indian Removal Policy of Andrew Jackson," *Journal of Mississippi History* 4 (October 1942): 214.

41. Satz, *American Indian Policy in the Jacksonian Era*, 74–76.

42. Foreman, *Indian Removal*, 73, 69, 94.

43. DeRosier, *The Removal of the Choctaw Indians*, 147–148, 183–184; Satz, *American Indian Policy in the Jacksonian Era*, 78–81; Foreman, *Indian Removal*, 69–70, 98.

44. Satz, *American Indian Policy in the Jacksonian Era*, 78; Foreman, *Indian Removal*, 94.

45. DeRosier, *The Removal of the Choctaw Indians*, 147, 156; Gibson to Lt. Edward Deas, September 20, 1835, quoted in Gaston Litton, ed., "The Journal of a Party of Emigrating Creek Indians, 1835–1836," *JSH* 7 (May 1941): 227; Grant Foreman, ed., *A Traveler in Indian Territory: The Journal of Ethan Allen Hitchcock*, with a foreword by Michael D. Green (Norman: University of Oklahoma Press, 1996); W. A. Croffut, ed., *Fifty Years in Camp and Field: The Diary of Major-General Ethan Allen Hitchcock, U.S.A.* (New York: G. P. Putnam's Sons, 1909), 136–144, 156–158. Although Hitchcock was assigned this investigation by a Whig administration, his conclusions reverberated across party lines; he was careful to issue it just after his promotion to lieutenant colonel.

46. Cole, *The Presidency of Andrew Jackson*, 112; Arrell M. Gibson, *The Chickasaws* (Norman: University of Oklahoma Press, 1971); brevet Brigadier General Duncan L. Clinch to RJ (re Seminole removal), April 1, 1835, Letterbook, 1835–1836, Clinch Letterbooks, LC; Charles Winslow Elliott, *Winfield Scott: The Soldier and the Man* (New York: Macmillan, 1937), 327; Amanda L. Paige, Fuller L. Bumpers, and Daniel F. Littlefield Jr., *Chickasaw Removal* (Ada, Okla.: Chickasaw Press, 2010).

47. Green, *The Politics of Indian Removal*, 184–185. John T. Ellisor provides an extremely thorough narrative of the military conflict in "The Second Creek War: The Unexplored Conflict" (Ph.D. diss., University of Tennessee, 1996). Green provides the best account of the preremoval crisis, but Ellisor, *The Second Creek War: Interethnic Conflict and Collusion on a Collapsing Frontier* (Lincoln: University of Nebraska Press, 2010), presents the most comprehensive analysis.

48. Foreman, *Indian Removal*, 119–121.

49. Ibid., 167, 169.

50. Ibid., 167–170, 181–182. See Litton, "The Journal of a Party of Emigrating Creek Indians," in which Lieutenant Edward Deas describes a much less harrowing experience by a group that left before the second "Creek War" broke out. They had good weather for all but the last week of the two-month journey and were not plagued by significant shortages, sickness, or white marauders en route.

CHAPTER FIVE: THE ARMY AND THE CHEROKEE REMOVAL

1. See Jean Pfaelzer, *Driven Out: The Hidden War against Chinese-Americans* (Berkeley: University of California Press, 2008), and Elliott Jaspin, *Buried in Bitter Waters: The History of Racial Cleansing in the United States* (New York: Basic Books, 2008), on the ethnic cleansing of towns in the American South, West, and Lower Midwest during the late nineteenth century; see also James W. Loewen, *Sundown Towns: A Hidden Dimension of American Racism* (New York: Touchstone, 2006). Many late-nineteenth- and early-twentieth-century "race riots" are recognizable to European historians as pogroms, like those in east-central Europe and Russia against the Jews.

2. See Theda Perdue and Michael D. Green, *The Cherokee Nation and the Trail of Tears* (New York: Viking, 2007), chaps. 4 and 5, for a concise narrative of the Georgia threat and the Cherokee response between 1830 and 1836. See Sarah H. Hill, "'To Overawe the Indians and Give Confidence to the Whites': Preparations for the Removal of the Cherokee Nation from Georgia," *GAHQ* 95 (Winter 2011): 479–480, on the militia's lack of uniforms. The treaty and amendment are in Charles J. Kappler, comp., *Indian Affairs: Laws and Treaties* (Washington, D.C.: Government Printing Office, 1903–1929), 2:439–449. See Theda Perdue, "The Conflict Within: Cherokees and Removal," in *Cherokee Removal, Before and After*, ed. William L. Anderson (Athens: University of Georgia Press, 1991), 55–74, regarding factionalism among the Cherokee, which pitted the small acculturated elite (including Ross) and the majority of full-blooded, subsistence-economy Cherokee against a minority of aspiring "new men," who hoped to secure wealth through accommodation.

3. Cass to Wool, June 20, 1836, *ASPMA*, 7:549. See Gary E. Moulton, *John Ross: Cherokee Chief* (Athens: University of Georgia Press, 1978); Gary E. Moulton, ed., *The Papers of Chief John Ross*, vol. 1, *1807–1839* (Norman: University of Oklahoma Press, 1985); and, more briefly, Walter H. Conser Jr., "John Ross and the Cherokee Resistance Campaign, 1833–1838," *JSH* 44 (May 1978): 191–212.

4. Lawrence Hauptman's statement that Wool was "long experienced" in such situations is in error; see "General John E. Wool in Cherokee Country, 1836–1837: A Reinterpretation," *GAHQ* 85 (Spring 2001): 24. See William B. Skelton, "The Commanding General and the Problem of Command in the United States Army, 1821–1841," *Military Affairs* 34 (December 1970): 117–122, regarding the evolution of that office during this era.

5. Harwood P. Hinton, "The Military Career of John Ellis Wool, 1812–1863" (Ph.D. diss., University of Wisconsin, 1960), 87–93, 96; Wool to Butler, November 6, 1836, *ASPMA*, 7:559.

6. Wool to Dunlap, August 4 and 12, 1836 (not 1837, despite the document), *ASPMA*, 7:550–551.

7. Hinton, "The Military Career of John Ellis Wool," 100–101; Carl J. Vipperman, "The Bungled Treaty of New Echota: The Failure of Cherokee Removal, 1836–1838," *GAHQ* 73 (Fall 1989): 543.

8. Hauptman, "General John E. Wool"; Wool to Cass, July 5, 1836, AGOLR.

9. Wool to Harris, August 27, 1836, *ASPMA*, 7:552.

10. AJ to Wool, September 7, 1836, Harris to Wool, July 30, 1836, and Wool to Butler, November 6, 1836, *ASPMA*, 7:554, 560. See Vipperman, "The Bungled Treaty of New Echota," for the contradictions of administration policy. Wool arrested Jones on his own, rather dubious, authority. C. A. Harris is in sore need of a biography.

11. Wool to AJ, August 30, to Harris, September 1 (quoted in Wool to Butler, November 6), and to Harris, August 27, 1836, *ASPMA*, 7:553, 561, 552. Wool also warned against temporizing and self-deception in letters to Harris, August 15, 1836, Cass, September 18, 1836, and Poinsett, March 31, 1837, *ASPMA*, 7:551, 557, 564. See also Hinton, "The Military Career of John Ellis Wool," 94–98; Hauptman, "Gen-

eral John E. Wool," 13–15. See *NASPMA*, 8:297–302, for the administration's reluctance to authorize militia call-ups in Alabama during February and March 1836, as Creek unrest grew.

12. Wool to Cass, September 10, 1836, AGOLR.
13. AJ to Wool, September 7, 1836, *ASPMA*, 7:554.
14. 1 *Stat.* 472; Cass to Wool, September 3, 1836, and Cherokee address, September 30, 1836, *ASPMA*, 7:555–556, 566–567.
15. Harris to Wool, October 12 and 17, 1836, Wool to Harris, November 2, and to Butler, November 6, 1836, *ASPMA*, 7:557, 564, 568, 562; Lumpkin and John Kennedy to J. Mason, September 9, 1837, in Wilson Lumpkin, *The Removal of the Cherokee Indians from Georgia* (New York: Dodd, Mead, 1907), 134.
16. Wool to Butler, November 23, and response, December 24, 1836, *ASPMA*, 7:563; Hinton, "The Military Career of John Ellis Wool," 104–106, 109–110, 114–115; Wool to Warren, November 21, 1836, Wool Papers, LC, and to Tallmadge, November 20 and 25, 1836, Nathaniel Tallmadge Papers, LC. The secondary sources all refer to the *Nashville Republican*; Wool's letter of complaint refers to the *Athens Republican*.
17. Hinton, "The Military Career of John Ellis Wool," 117–119 (Wool to Lt. Chileab S. Howe, December 8, 1836, and to Tallmadge, January 6, 1837, quoted on 118–119).
18. Butler to Wool, January 9, 1837, quoted in Hinton, "The Military Career of John Ellis Wool," 118–119; Lumpkin and John Kennedy to Harris, January 30, 1837, in Lumpkin, *The Removal of the Cherokee Indians*, 95.
19. Hinton, "The Military Career of John Ellis Wool," 119–126 (Wool to Tallmadge, January 6, 1837, quoted on 119).
20. Ibid., 122–124 (Wool quoted on 122).
21. Wool, April 20, 1837 (misfiled in reel 19 for 1816–1817), SWLR: Unreg. Wool to Poinsett, August 6, 1837, *ASPMA*, 7:565, states that the general had not renewed his request for recall since November 1836, but the tone and language of his April 20 letter clearly suggest that he wanted relief. Wool's personal letters from the early 1830s in the Francis Baylies Papers (Old Colony Historical Society, Taunton, Mass.), particularly those to his then-friend Lewis Cass, show an egalitarian democrat and, indeed, a partisan Democrat.
22. Wool to Poinsett, August 6, 1837, *ASPMA*, 7:565. Daniel Walker Howe, *What Hath God Wrought? The Transformation of America, 1815–1848* (New York: Oxford University Press, 2007), 484, observes that Van Buren's "instincts . . . were deeply conservative."
23. *ASPMA*, 7:546; testimony in court of inquiry, *ASPMA*, 7:534–540, summarized on 543.
24. AJ, February 14 and 18, 1837, *MPP*, 4:1509–1511. The inquiry into the Florida campaigns by Scott and Gaines, which lasted months, is in *ASPMA*, 7:125–465; that into the Creek campaign, which the court used to vindicate Scott and condemn Jesup, is in *ASPMA*, 7:794–894.

25. "Defence of Brigadier General Wool," *ASPMA*, 7:567–571.
26. Ibid.
27. Wool to Butler, November 6, 1836, *ASPMA*, 7:560. Indeed, even the pleas of Alabama governor Clement Clay for authority to mobilize militia against the threat of Creek depredations were downplayed by the administration during February and March 1836; see *NASPMA* 8:297–302.
28. John Wool to Sarah Wool, January 9, 1837, box 1, folder 1, Wool Papers, NYSL.
29. Ronald N. Satz, *American Indian Policy in the Jacksonian Era* (Lincoln: University of Nebraska Press, 1974), 158–159. See Hinton, "The Military Career of John Ellis Wool," and Durwood Ball, *Army Regulars on the Western Frontier, 1848–1861* (Norman: University of Oklahoma Press, 2001), for Wool's service in the 1850s.
30. "Opinion of the Court," September 14, 1837, *ASPMA*, 7:540–541. See Ball, *Army Regulars*, for Wool's peacekeeping and law enforcement duties against filibusters in California in the 1850s.
31. William Lindsay to Anna Lindsay, April 29, 1837, William Lindsay Papers, State Historical Society of Wisconsin; Reynolds to his sister Rebecca, April 13, 1837, Thaddeus Banks Papers, SHC; Vipperman, "The Bungled Treaty of New Echota," 553. Lindsay spelled his name with an *a*, not an *e* (as Vipperman spells it).
32. Lindsay to Secretary of War Poinsett, July 7, 1837, quoted in Vipperman, "The Bungled Treaty of New Echota," 554–555, and to Anna Lindsay, September 28, 1837, Lindsay Papers. Hill, "'To Overawe the Indians and Give Confidence to the Whites,'" 474–475, presents a Georgian perspective in which George Gilmer, the governor during the 1830 gold rush who returned to the office in 1837, attempted to restrain the Georgia "home guards," as he had done during the previous crisis.
33. Lindsay to Anna Lindsay, March 5 and 14, April 2, May 29, June ?, and July 15, 1838, Lindsay Papers.
34. Lumpkin, *The Removal of the Cherokee Indians*, 226–228; Vipperman, "The Bungled Treaty of New Echota," 556.
35. Charles Winslow Elliott, *Winfield Scott: The Soldier and the Man* (New York: Macmillan, 1937), 346, 349. Sources that cite three or five regiments are referring to all the regiments with companies involved in the removal: following common practice in the Southeast—where companies from different regiments were stationed and operated together depending on contingencies—companies were ultimately dispatched from six different regiments. The cumulative force was approximately two and a half regiments, primarily from the First and Second Artillery and the Fourth Infantry.
36. Capt. William G. Williams, "Memoir Relative to the Cherokee Nation within the Limits of N. Carolina and Its Immediate Vicinity," sent to volunteer Colonel T. T. Hubert, February 8, 1838, quoted in Duane H. King and E. R. Evans, "Tsali: The Man behind the Legend," *Journal of Cherokee Studies* 4 (Fall 1979): 207–208.
37. WS, orders, May 17, 1838, and address to the Cherokee, undated, in Winfield Scott, *Memoirs of Lieut.-Gen. Winfield Scott, L.L.D., Written by Himself*, 2 vols. (New York: Sheldon, 1864), 1:320–325.

38. Ibid. Apart from short sections in the Scott biographies, there are surprisingly few accounts of army operations to concentrate and remove the Cherokee in 1838; see also Richard F. Ivy, *The Distinguished Light of Abraham Eustis: A Biography of an 1800 Artillery General* (Yorktown, Va.: Citizen Publications, 1993), 169–173.

39. Kirby to Webster, June 11, 1838, and Foster to Larnard, July 2, 1838, Lucien B. Webster Papers, USAMHI.

40. Webster to his wife Frances, June 9, 1838, Webster Papers; Elliott, *Winfield Scott*, 327.

41. Churchill diary, July 3, 1838, Sylvester Churchill Papers, LC; WS to War Department, November 6, 1838, quoted in King and Evans, "Tsali: The Man behind the Legend," 216–218.

42. WS to War Department, November 6, and to Foster, November 7, 1838, quoted in King and Evans, "Tsali: The Man behind the Legend," 216–218.

43. WS to War Department, November 6, 1838, quoted in ibid., 216–217.

44. WS to Foster, November 7, 1838, quoted in ibid., 217–218; Charles Lanham, *Letters from the Alleghany Mountains* (New York: George Putnam, 1849), 112–113; John R. Finger, "The Saga of Tsali: Legend versus Reality," *North Carolina Historical Review* 56 (January 1979): 11; James Mooney, *Myths of the Cherokee, Nineteenth Annual Report of the Bureau of American Ethnology, Part I* (Washington, D.C.: Government Printing Office, 1900), 157 (last quotation). The estimated number of fugitives from removal changed several times, generally downward.

45. Foster, unnumbered order, November 21, and Foster to WS, December 3, 1838, William S. Foster Papers, McClung Historical Collection, East Tennessee Historical Society. Finger, "The Saga of Tsali," suggests that the Cherokee were not compelled to execute the killers and may have done so based on the traditional law of blood for blood, but he also recognizes that the Cherokee probably realized that executing the men would improve their standing in American eyes. Blood vengeance was no longer Cherokee law, and the Cherokee, like other Native American tribes, were bound by treaty to turn over those who violated white law to white officials, so the decision to execute the killers themselves was out of the ordinary. See John Phillip Reid, *A Law of Blood: The Primitive Law of the Cherokee Nation* (New York: New York University Press, 1970), for the traditional law of the eighteenth century, and Duane Champagne, *Social Order and Political Change: Constitutional Governments among the Cherokee, the Choctaw, the Chickasaw, and the Creek* (Stanford, Calif.: Stanford University Press, 1992), for formalization and change in Cherokee law during the early nineteenth century.

46. Foster to WS, November 24, 1838, enclosure C to file S-568, December 28, 1838, AGOLR.

47. Foster, November 24, 1838, enclosure E to file S-568, December 28, 1838, AGOLR.

48. WS, December 28, 1838, file S-568, AGOLR. See also John R. Finger, *The Eastern Band of Cherokees, 1819–1900* (Knoxville: University of Tennessee Press, 1984), 26; Paul Kutsche, "The Tsali Legend: Culture Heroes and Historiography," *Ethnohistory*

10 (Autumn 1963): 329–357; King and Evans, "Tsali: The Man behind the Legend," 194–239, which concentrates the key documents, including those cited herein, from the Foster Papers and several record groups in the National Archives; and William Martin Jurgelski, "New Light on the Tsali Affair," in *Light on the Path: The Anthropology and History of the Southeastern Indians*, ed. Thomas J. Pluckhahn and Robbie Ethridge (Tuscaloosa: University of Alabama Press, 2006), 133–164. The civilian Cherokee removal commissioners permitted Euchella's band to remain in the East; they, along with the Oconaluftee, eventually became the Eastern Band of the Cherokee Nation. Foster's proclamation referred to thirty people in the band, whereas his letters tended to use the number sixty. Lanham, *Letters from the Alleghany Mountains*, 112, suggests that a hundred fugitives were able to take advantage of the exemption, and I would suggest that accommodation during this incident contributed to the Oconaluftees' ability to remain in North Carolina: despite their citizenship under the 1819 treaty, every bit helped when Indians were seeking rights in the white man's democracy.

49. Churchill diary, July 3, 6, 8, 1838, Churchill Papers, LC; Scott, *Memoirs*, 328.

50. Scott, *Memoirs*, 329; Elliott, *Winfield Scott*, 354, 352; Erasmus D. Keyes, *Fifty Years Observation of Men and Events, Civil and Military* (New York: Scribner's, 1884), 133; Webster to Frances, June 9, 1838, Webster Papers.

51. Letter dated November 26, 1838, in George A. McCall, *Letters from the Frontiers, Written during a Period of Thirty Years Service in the Army of the United States* (1868; reprinted with an introduction by John K. Mahon, Gainesville: University Presses of Florida, 1974), 359–360.

52. Vinton to Thomas Sidney Jesup, March 6, 1838, 1836–1838 Letterbook, John R. Vinton Papers, PLDU; Vinton, journal, May 27 and June 2, 1838, Vinton Papers.

53. WS to Vinton, June 29, and Vinton to WS, July 3, 1838, Vinton Papers.

54. Vinton to WS, July 3, 1938, Vinton Papers.

55. WS to Vinton, July 5, 1838, Vinton Papers. Keyes, *Fifty Years Observation*, 134, states that Scott's initial letter seemed "wantonly unjust and insulting," and that Keyes persuaded Scott to soften its tone.

56. See Russell Thornton, "Cherokee Population Losses during the Trail of Tears: A New Perspective and a New Estimate," *Ethnohistory* 31 (Fall 1984): 289–300, for the historiography and an estimate based on population growth that did not occur as a result of the losses during the Trail of Tears. See Perdue and Green, *The Cherokee Nation and the Trail of Tears*, 130–131, for Scott's letters to the Cherokee leaders, which show an unusual sympathy for white merchants bidding on contracts to supply the Cherokee and an unusual lack of sympathy for the "strong [Cherokee] men, women, girls and boys not only capable of marching twelve or fifteen miles a day, but to whom the exercise would be beneficial." Whether Scott felt responsible for fiscal accountability, or whether he envisioned the Cherokee as subordinates under his command, these letters represent an exception to the norm of army empathy toward the Cherokee and other southeastern Indians.

57. Sherman to Hugh B. Ewing, March 10, 1844, William Tecumseh Sherman Papers, OHS (WBS).

CHAPTER SIX: "THIS THANKLESS... UNHOLY WAR"

1. Sheer Justice [pseud.], "Battle of the Okee-Chobee—The Army," *ANC* 6 (March 8, 1838): 154. The weekly, privately published (though officially subsidized) *Army and Navy Chronicle* was the army's only professional journal and its primary means of public communication. Contributors normally wrote anonymously; in rare instances, officers used their real names (usually in letters from senior officers reprinted from other newspapers or official documents). Many of the letters published in the *Army and Navy Chronicle* were sent first to fellow officers and civilian friends (often ex-officers) or were reprinted from local newspapers in the South or from semiofficial national papers like the *National Intelligencer* and the *Washington Globe*; I indicate this only if the circumstance or newspaper is of particular note.

2. Edward M. Coffman, *The Old Army: A Portrait of the American Army in Peacetime, 1784–1898* (New York: Oxford University Press, 1986), 52; William B. Skelton, *An American Profession of Arms: The Army Officer Corps, 1784–1861* (Lawrence: University Press of Kansas, 1992), 216–217; James M. Denham, "'Some Prefer the Seminoles': Violence and Disorder among Soldiers and Settlers in the Second Seminole War, 1835–1842," *FHQ* 70 (July 1991): 38–54.

3. Sam Jones [pseud.], "Florida," *ANC* 9 (August 29, 1839): 131; A Subaltern of the 7th [pseud.], "The Seventh Infantry," *ANC* 9 (August 22, 1839): 116; An Officer of the Line [pseud.], "Florida War," *ANC* 9 (August 29, 1839): 132. There was little close study of Napoleon at West Point prior to the 1850s; even then, there was less real study and analysis than most authors assume, since most of them are hoping to explain generalship during the Civil War.

4. I refer to the senior commander in Florida as the "theater commander," although this was an ad hoc, temporary position created by assignment from the president, rather than a permanent institutional position in the army's regular hierarchy of command prior to the reestablishment of "military departments" (with Florida as the Ninth) in 1837. This chapter does not discuss controversies over command, strategy, or tactics in any detail; they are covered well in John K. Mahon, *History of the Second Seminole War, 1835–1842* (Gainesville: University Press of Florida, 1967), and are summarized in Joe Knetsch, "Strategy, Operations, and Tactics in the Second Seminole War, 1835–1842," in *America's Hundred Years' War: U.S. Expansion to the Gulf Coast and the Fate of the Seminole, 1763–1858, Essays in Honor of J. Leitch Wright, Jr.*, ed. William S. Belko (Gainesville: University Press of Florida, 2010). The only thorough account of the war before Mahon's was by ex-Lieutenant John T. Sprague, *The Origin, Progress, and Conclusion of the Florida War*, introduction by John K. Mahon (1848; reprint, Gainesville: University Press of Florida, 1964). The most recent account is John Missall and Mary Lou Missall, *The Seminole Wars: America's Longest Indian Conflict* (Gainesville: University Press of Florida, 2002), a synthesis that provides more attention to politics and less to archival sources and operations. Virginia B. Peters, *The Florida Wars* (Hamden, Conn.: Archon Books, 1979), and Joe T. Knetsch, *Florida's*

Seminole Wars, 1817–1858 (Charleston, S.C.: Arcadia, 2003), examine all three Seminole wars, necessarily with less attention to each individual conflict.

See James W. Covington, *The Seminoles of Florida* (Gainesville: University Press of Florida, 1993); Edwin C. McReynolds, *The Seminoles* (Norman: University of Oklahoma Press, 1957); and J. Leitch Wright Jr., *Creeks and Seminoles: Destruction and Regeneration of the Muscogulge People* (Lincoln: University of Nebraska Press, 1986), for narratives of Seminole and Mikasuki history. The voice of northern dissent against the removal of the Seminoles is best represented by Joshua Giddings, *The Exiles of Florida* (1858; reprint, Baltimore: Black Classics Press, 1997), originally published in the aftermath of the Third Seminole War; see also Linda K. Kerber, "The Abolitionist Perception of the Indian," *JAH* 62 (September 1975): 276–283; George Klos, "Blacks and the Seminole Removal Debate, 1821–1835," *FHQ* 68 (July 1989): 55–78; and Mary Hershberger, "Mobilizing Women, Anticipating Abolition: The Struggle against Indian Removal in the 1830s," *JAH* 86 (June 1999): 15–40. Seminole perspectives have received increasing attention during the last decade; see especially Brent R. Weisman, *Unconquered People: Florida's Seminole and Miccosukee Indians* (Gainesville: University Press of Florida, 1999); Patricia Wiles Wickman, *The Tree that Bends: Discourse, Power, and the Survival of the Maskókì People* (Tuscaloosa: University of Alabama Press, 1999); Patricia Wiles Wickman, *Osceola's Legacy*, rev. ed. (Tuscaloosa: University of Alabama Press, 2006); Susan A. Miller, *Coacoochee's Bones: A Seminole Saga* (Lawrence: University Press of Kansas, 2003); and Samuel Watson, "Resisting Removal: Seminole Strategy, 1812–1842," in Belko, *America's Hundred Years' War*.

A number of journal articles concerning the Second Seminole War have been published in the fifteen years since I began writing this book. See the extensive and varied works of Florida state archivist Joe T. Knetsch, which would take an entire page to list, especially his collection *Fear and Anxiety on the Florida Frontier: Articles on the Second Seminole War, 1835–1842* (Dade City, Fla.: Seminole Wars Foundation, 2008), and, most recently, Matthew T. Pearcy, "'The Ruthless Hand of War': Andrew A. Humphreys in the Second Seminole War," *FHQ* 85 (Fall 2006): 123–153. Recent published primary sources include Frank Laumer, ed., *Amidst a Storm of Bullets: The Diary of Lt. Henry Prince in Florida, 1836–1842*, foreword by John K. Mahon (Tampa: University of Tampa Press, 1998), and John Missall and Mary Lou Missall, eds., *This Miserable Pride of a Soldier: The Letters and Journals of Col. William S. Foster in the Second Seminole War* (Tampa: University of Tampa Press for the Seminole Wars Historic Foundation, 2005). In addition to the collections cited here, I benefited from research in the letterbooks and papers of the theater commanders (particularly Jesup and Worth) in RG 94 and 393 at the National Archives, the William L. Perkins Library at Duke University (particularly the John R. Vinton Papers), the Georgia Historical Society, the Virginia Historical Society, the William G. Belknap Papers at the Firestone Library at Princeton University, the Florida State Archives in Tallahassee, and above all, the P. K. Yonge Library at the University of Florida. This chapter cannot pretend to be more than a survey of the dynamics and dilemmas of civil-military relations during the Second Seminole War; I intend to employ most of this research in a future book.

5. The officers engaged in civil engineering were young lieutenants, a few captains, and the Bureau of Topographical Engineers (for whom the surveys served as professional training and provided data in case of foreign invasion). On the whole, those who resigned rather than perform combat service during the Second Seminole War—a significant component in the argument by historians Robert Angevine and Robert Wettemann that the army lacked a fully martial identity before 1838—were a young, junior, and often politically well-connected subset of the army. Their socialization at West Point had not outweighed the opportunities available to them due to family political connections, with Jacksonians as well as Whigs, which had further undermined their military socialization by enabling them to avoid company and field duty. Yet they resigned in 1836 and 1837, whereas the law limiting duty assignments on civilian surveying projects was not passed until 1838: the resignation crisis ended due to the economic panic and depression that began in 1837, or perhaps because all those so inclined had already resigned in 1836 and 1837. Had this legislation truly been necessary to redirect the army's professional focus, one would expect to see a wave of resignations after its passage by officers who lacked such focus, but that did not happen. The officers who might have resigned in 1838 had already done so, and others ultimately went to Florida, however grudgingly. Thus, the 1838 law—actually an omnibus measure intended to strengthen the army with more soldiers, better pay, and specialized staff officers in the midst of the Seminole War, Cherokee removal, and the Canadian border crisis with Britain—in which the repeal of General Survey Act provisions was a single paragraph, probably attached as an amendment, confirmed a shift in officer assignments that the Seminole War had already spurred. Indeed, Jackson and his secretaries of war had repeatedly issued but failed to enforce orders for officers on leave or detached duty (such as transportation surveys) to return to regimental duty, but they often permitted exemptions for those with political connections. That behavior hardly meshes with Wettemann's claim that the Jacksonians compelled the army to do its military duties. Robert Angevine, *The Railroad and the State: War, Politics and Technology in Nineteenth-Century America* (Stanford, Calif.: Stanford University Press, 2004), chap. 5; Robert Wettemann, "A Part or Apart: The Alleged Isolation of Antebellum U.S. Army Officers," *American Nineteenth-Century History* 7 (June 2006): 193–217; July 5, 1838, 5 *Stat.* 256–260.

6. Statistics in Mahon, *History of the Second Seminole War*, 325; Clinch to RJ, October 8, 1835, Clinch Letterbook, 1835–1836, LC; WS to Capt. F. M. Robertson of the Augusta (Ga.) Volunteers, May 26, 1836, published in *ANC* 2 (June 16, 1836): 380.

7. McCall to his father, February 9 and May 1, 1836, in George A. McCall, *Letters from the Frontiers, Written during a Period of Thirty Years Service in the Army of the United States* (1868; reprint, Gainesville: University Press of Florida, 1974), 295, 301; "Florida War," *ANC* 8 (March 10, 1839): 155; Worth to WS, February 14, 1842, quoted in Sprague, *The Origin, Progress, and Conclusion of the Florida War*, 441–445; McCall to "my dear E," February 27, and to his father, March 28, 1842,

in *Letters from the Frontiers*, 396, 398. Note that only eighteen regular officers were actually killed in action or mortally wounded during the war, and seven of these died in its opening engagement, the "Dade Massacre" of December 28, 1835 (Skelton, *An American Profession of Arms*, 214, 409n86). Mahon, *History of the Second Seminole War*, 321, gives the number as seventy-four, but this is an aggregate figure that includes ten surgeons (one killed in action in Dade's battle) and all others who died in Florida from any cause and those who died outside the territory from disease or illness contracted there. One marine lieutenant died (killed in action), as did three naval officers (of disease), one of them a surgeon. At least two officers of the regular army committed suicide while in Florida, but they were said to be suffering from heat- or fever-induced delirium at the time (Mahon, *History of the Second Seminole War*, 174, 182). Another "drowned himself during temporary insanity caused by wounds received in Florida" while in Charleston harbor (Sprague, *The Origin, Progress, and Conclusion of the Florida War*, 532). The preeminent work on the Dade ambush is Frank Laumer, *Dade's Last Command*, foreword by John K. Mahon (Gainesville: University Press of Florida, 1995).

8. WS, official letter published in *ANC 2* (June 2, 1836): 346 (originally in the semiofficial *Washington Globe*); Mahon, *History of the Second Seminole War*, 207, 293, 238, 235.

9. Assistant Surgeon Thomas Henderson to Assistant Surgeon Benjamin King, February 6 and 13, 1838, Benjamin King Papers, LC; McCall to his father, February 9, 1836, in *Letters from the Frontiers*, 295; Jesup to Secretary of War Poinsett, February 11, 1838, in Sprague, *The Origin, Progress, and Conclusion of the Florida War*, 199–201; "On the Florida War," *ANC 9* (November 7, 1839): 291 (reprinted from the *National Intelligencer*). Jesup's command was often referred to as the "Army of the South," but this too was informal. For troop strength estimates, see Assistant Surgeon John B. Wells to King, February 10, 1840, King Papers (20,000); Capt. Robert Anderson to Col. Abraham Eustis, June 11, 1840, Robert Anderson Papers, USMA (30,000); Sam Jones [pseud.], "Florida War," *ANC 9* (October 31, 1839): 285 (50,000–60,000); untitled anonymous correspondence to *ANC* 11 (August 27, 1840): 137 (100,000). There were no more than about 5,000 Indians, including Red Stick Creeks, Mikasukis, blacks of various status and ethnicity, and a variety of smaller Muskogean and Hitchiti-speaking groups, throughout Florida, meaning no more than 1,500 to 2,000 warriors.

10. Captains J[ohn B.] Clark and M[ichael]. M. Clark to Benjamin King, May 18, 1841, and February 17, 1842, King Papers; "On the Florida War," *ANC 9* (November 7, 1839): 291; letter (author's name illegible, perhaps anonymous) to King, February 10, 1838, King Papers. Many European imperial and colonial wars produced similar demoralization and malaise among military officers if they did not quickly achieve decisive victories. See Benjamin Claude Brower, *A Desert Named Peace: The Violence of France's Empire in the Algerian Sahara, 1844–1902* (New York: Columbia University Press, 2009), 46–50; E. Willis Brooks, "Nicholas I as Reformer: Russian Attempts to Conquer the Caucasus, 1825–1855," in *Nation and Ideology: Essays in*

Honor of Wayne S. Vucinich, ed. Ivo Banac et al. (New York: Columbia University Press, 1981), 235, 248; and J. A. deMoor and H. L. Wesseling, eds., *Imperialism and War: Essays on Colonial Wars in Asia and Africa* (Leiden, Netherlands: Brill, 1989), 61–62, for French, Russian, and Dutch examples.

11. Mahon, *History of the Second Seminole War*, 300; McCall to "my dear M," January 16, 1842, in *Letters from the Frontiers*, 393–394; Jesup to Poinsett, December 15, 1837, HQALR.

12. Dr. (Assistant Surgeon) L[ewis]. A. Birdsall to Benjamin King, July 17, 1841, King Papers (first quotation); Hunter diary (no dates given), quoted in Reynold M. Wik, "Captain Nathaniel Wyche Hunter and the Florida Indian Campaigns, 1837–1841," *FHQ* 39 (July 1960): 71 (hereafter cited as Hunter diary, with page number); Junius [pseud.], "A Visitor to Sam Jones's Camp" (parts 3 and 4), *ANC* 10, 21 and 22 (May 21 and 28, 1840): 331–332 (third quotation), 347; Capt. George H. Pegram to Lt. Robert Anderson, February 3, 1841, Robert Anderson Papers, LC. Birdsall had just left Florida and was in a fever; he apologized for sending "such a crazy letter." Lt. William Chapman used language much like Hunter's in a letter to his future wife, Helen Blair, May 17, 1838, in "A West Point Graduate in the Second Seminole War: William Warren Chapman and the View from Fort Foster," *FHQ* 68 (April 1990): 473. For a rare and outstanding official history, see Mary C. Gillett, *The Army Medical Department, 1818–1865* (Washington, D.C.: Government Printing Office, 1987), especially chaps. 2, 3, regarding the army's health and efforts to improve it during the 1820s and the Seminole War.

13. Lt. Charles E. Woodruff (who was unmarried) to James Banks (a purser in the U.S. Navy), June 25, 1839, Charles Woodruff Papers, USAMHI; "On the Florida War," *ANC* 9 (November 7, 1839): 290; George Pegram to Robert Anderson, January 18, 1841, Anderson Papers, LC; Morris Miller to Sarah Miller, April 29, 1835, Morris S. Miller Papers, USMA; Hunter diary, 69 (n. 30). See also Lt. William Chapman to Helen Blair, May 17, 1838, in "A West Point Graduate in the Second Seminole War," 473, and Assistant Surgeon John B. Wells to Assistant Surgeon Benjamin King, February 10, 1840, King Papers.

14. Skelton, *An American Profession of Arms*, 136 (figure 7.1); Lt. Joseph R. Smith to his wife Juliet, March 6, 1838, in John K. Mahon, ed., "Letters from the Second Seminole War," *FHQ* 36 (April 1958): 338–342. See also Pegram to Anderson, January 18 and February 3, 1841, Anderson Papers, LC.

15. See Skelton, *An American Profession of Arms*, 144, regarding appointments directly from civil life (i.e., without passing through West Point first). Seven sergeants were appointed lieutenants in 1838, the only enlisted men to receive commissions between 1821 and 1847 (ibid., 147–148).

16. Ibid., 138–139. The officering of the Battalion of Mounted Rangers in 1832, which became the First Dragoon Regiment the following year, presents the only clear exception, since there were plenty of brevet second lieutenants on supernumerary status awaiting permanent commissions. The Mounted Rangers were originally an ad hoc, though federal, volunteer force mobilized for the Black Hawk War; the army's

difficulties in catching Black Hawk provided the impetus needed by advocates of professional mounted troops. The battalion's volunteer officers, commissioned in significant part through local political connections during an election year, were given the opportunity to transfer into the new dragoon regiment and accounted for most of its company officers, along with Colonel Henry Dodge, a leader of illegal intruders on Sauk and Fox land only a year or two before. Such were the possibilities of Jacksonian democracy—or opportunism—but most of the former volunteer officers soon resigned, and their replacements were almost entirely West Pointers or veteran field-grade officers well-disposed toward them, including Stephen W. Kearny as colonel.

17. Hunter diary, 69 ("ignominy"); "Florida War," *ANC* 7 (August 16, 1838): 105; Quasi Major [pseud.], "The Seminole War" [a public letter addressed to the secretary of war], *ANC* 7 (October 18, 1838): 249; A Subaltern of the 7th [pseud.], "The Seventh Infantry," *ANC* 9 (August 22, 1839): 116; Lt. Thomas Boylston Adams to Major Rufus Lathrop Baker, April 12, 1836, Rufus Lathrop Baker Papers, USMA ("drudgery"); Lewis Birdsall to Benjamin King, July 17, 1841, King Papers; Agricola [pseud.], "The Army," *ANC* 5 (October 26, 1837): 267; A Subaltern [pseud.], "Florida War—No. 3," *ANC* 8 (February 21, 1839): 124. The first three citations from the *ANC* all use the term "inglorious." See also Capt. George McCall to "my dear M," January 16, 1842, in *Letters from the Frontiers*, 393: "how ignoble and pitiful a service . . . against a handful of savages." See Skelton, *An American Profession of Arms*, 255–256, 318–325, 346–347, regarding the officer corps' general lack of interest in (if not disdain for) Indian fighting.

18. WS, Order No. 48, May 17, 1836, in *ANC* 2 (June 16, 1836): 379.

19. Brevet Brigadier General Duncan L. Clinch to brevet Major Richard A. Zantzinger, January 18 and March 31, 1835, Order Book, Fort King, 1834–1835, Clinch Letterbooks, LC; Denham, "'Some Prefer the Seminoles'"; Lt. R[obert] A[uchmuty] Wainwright to Lt. William Warren Chapman, March 17, 1837, William Warren Chapman Papers, USMA. See also James M. Denham, *"A Rogue's Paradise": Crime and Punishment in Antebellum Florida, 1821–1861* (Tuscaloosa: University of Alabama Press, 1997). For white society in Florida, see Edward E. Baptist, *Creating an Old South: Middle Florida's Plantation Frontier before the Civil War* (Chapel Hill: University of North Carolina Press, 2002); Paul E. Hoffman, *Florida's Frontiers* (Bloomington: Indiana University Press, 2002); and Arthur W. Thompson, *Jacksonian Democracy on the Florida Frontier* (Gainesville: University of Florida Press, 1961).

20. Mahon, *History of the Second Seminole War*, 298, 203 (Jesup's paranoia about white renegades); Capt. J[ohn B.] Clark to Benjamin King, May 18, 1841, King Papers; letter, *ANC* 11 (August 27, 1840): 137.

21. Denham, "'Some Prefer the Seminoles,'" 45–47 (quotation, possibly apocryphal, from Worth published in the Tallahassee *Florida Sentinel*, October 31, 1843). For examples of officers' tacit support for acts of revenge by soldiers under their command, see ibid., 43, 48. A similar sequence of events seems to have taken place on Black Creek near Fort Heilman and Gorey's Ferry late in 1839; see "Florida War: Affairs at Black Creek," *ANC* 9 (October 24, 1839): 266.

22. Mahon, *History of the Second Seminole War*, 259, 316–317; Skelton, *An American Profession of Arms*, 319; Davenport to ZT, September 2, 1839, file T-316, AGOLR; Vose to RJ, April 13, 1838, House Exec. Doc. 434, 25th Cong., 2nd sess., 3. During periods of truce, the War Department issued frequent, albeit largely ineffectual, orders that the army protect the Seminoles from white aggression; for example, see Poinsett to Jesup, May 25, 1837, *TP*, 25:392. See Lt. Col. Ethan Allen Hitchcock to Secretary of War John C. Spencer, March 20, 1842, Ethan Allen Hitchcock Papers, LC, and ZT to RJ, December 23, 1842, and March 28, 1843, cited in Brainerd Dyer, *Zachary Taylor* (Baton Rouge: Louisiana State University Press, 1946), 138–140, regarding the rumors of a Cherokee uprising.

23. Matthew T. Pearcy, ed., "Andrew A. Humphreys' Seminole War Field Journal," *FHQ* 85 (Fall 2006): 214. See also John F. Marszalek, *Sherman: A Soldier's Passion for Order* (New York: Free Press, 1993), 35, 47.

24. Clinch Letterbooks, 1834–1835, LC (quotations from letters of January 22 and October 9, 1835, to the adjutant general and the War Department); Rembert W. Patrick, *Aristocrat in Uniform: General Duncan L. Clinch* (Gainesville: University Press of Florida, 1963), 73–74, 97. The Order Book for Fort King, 1834–1835, included in Clinch's Letterbooks, contains a hodgepodge of letters copied in 1836 that demonstrate the trajectory of Clinch's views.

25. Mahon, *History of the Second Seminole War*, 109–111, 184–185, 227–229; Clinch Letterbooks, 1836, LC; George C. Bittle, "The Florida Militia's Role in the Battle of Withlacoochee," *FHQ* 44 (April 1966): 303–311; "Clinch's Reply to Governor Cass," *Niles' Weekly Register* (July 15, 1837): 315–317.

26. "Clinch's Reply to Governor Cass," *Niles' Weekly Register* (July 15, 1837): 315–317.

27. AM to Call, August 23, 1837, entry 476-z, Southern Historical Collection, University of North Carolina; Phelps to his father John, July 10, 1837, in "Letters of Lieutenant John W. Phelps, U.S.A., 1837–1838," *FHQ* 6 (October 1927): 75; K. Jack Bauer, *Zachary Taylor: Soldier, Planter, and Statesman of the Old Southwest* (Baton Rouge: Louisiana State University Press, 1985), 83; *ASPMA*, 7:987–988. See also McCall to his father, February 1, 1836, in *Letters from the Frontiers*, 294. Regular officers made few distinctions between volunteers and militia, and since this book is about officers' perceptions, I have followed their practice. The militia was usually employed in local defense rather than active operations, but it would be difficult to distinguish between the two groups in terms of tactical effectiveness and relations with the standing army.

28. Clinch to RJ, January 11, 1836, Clinch Letterbook, 1835–1836, LC; Sheer Justice [pseud.], "Battle of the Okee-Chobee—The Army," *ANC* 6 (March 8, 1838): 154; P. [pseud.], "The Army," *ANC* 6 (February 15, 1838): 108–109; letter (author's name illegible, probably anonymous) to Benjamin King, February 10, 1838, King Papers (presumably he meant "Missourians"); Henderson to King, February 13, 1838, King Papers; Canard [pseud.], "Florida War," *ANC* 11 (July 23, 1840): 62. See also "Gen. Taylor, and the Missouri Volunteers," *ANC* 8 (April 11, 1839): 236, and Mentor [pseud.], untitled letter, *ANC* 9 (October 17, 1839): 246, whose extensive cri-

tique includes the unjust accusation that the volunteers fled "at the commencement of the battle" of Okeechobee. For the Missourians' view, see John K. Mahon, "Missouri Volunteers at the Battle of Okeechobee: Christmas Day 1837," and Phillip Thomas Tucker, "A Forgotten Sacrifice: Richard Gentry, Missouri Volunteers, and the Battle of Okeechobee," *FHQ* 70 (October 1991): 166–176, 150–165.

29. Sheer Justice, "Battle of the Okee-Chobee," 155; Canard [pseud.], "Florida War," *ANC* 11 (July 30, 1840): 67.

30. WS, "Order No. 1," in *ANC* 2 (March 17, 1836): 168.

31. Clinch to RJ, January 18, 1835, and record of council of officers to determine course of action toward the volunteers at the blockhouse, April 29, 1836, Order Book, Fort King, 1834–1835, in Clinch Letterbooks, LC; Mahon, *History of the Second Seminole War*, 113, 159–160, 171, 179, 264.

32. "Many Officers of the Army," *ANC* 3 (November 3, 1836): 285 (reprinted from the *National Intelligencer*, n.d.); Mahon, *History of the Second Seminole War*, 264. The letter's intent is unclear—it takes the form of a request for guidance and is phrased in terms of great propriety, but its implications were plain for all to see. See also Patrick, *Aristocrat in Uniform*, chaps. 7, 8; Secretary Butler's instructions to Jesup in *ASPMA*, 6:992–1002; Tom Knotts, "History of the Blockhouse on the Withlacoochee," *FHQ* 49 (January 1971): 245–255; and Herbert J. Doherty, *Richard Keith Call, Southern Unionist* (Gainesville: University Press of Florida, 1961), chap. 7.

33. Henderson to Benjamin King, February 6 and 13, 1838, King Papers; Mentor [pseud.], untitled letter, *ANC* 9 (October 17, 1839): 246.

34. "Florida War," *ANC* 11 (October 1, 1840): 220; WS to Capt. F. M. Robertson of the Augusta (Ga.) Volunteers, May 26, 1836, published in *ANC* 2 (June 16, 1836): 380; Quasi-Major [pseud.], "The Seminole War," *ANC* 7 (October 18, 1838): 249–250; Mahon, *History of the Second Seminole War*, 325. See also Justice [pseud.], "Gen. Scott and the Volunteers," *ANC* 2 (June 16, 1836): 378; Sheer Justice [pseud.], "Battle of the Okee-Chobee—The Army," *ANC* 6 (March 8, 1838): 154–155; "Florida War," *ANC* 9 (December 19, 1839): 394–395; and "Florida War—Captain Thistle's Plan," *ANC* 8 (March 28, 1839): 201–202, which derides an ex-volunteer's idea for raising civilian woodsmen to supplant the army. It is intriguing that the only volunteer many regulars truly respected was Brigadier General Joseph M. Hernandez, a Floridian of Spanish descent who was praised for his military effectiveness and genteel personal bearing. See, for example, John Phelps to his father, July 10, 1837, in "Letters of Lieutenant John W. Phelps," 81.

35. Agricola [pseud.], "The Army," *ANC* 5 (October 26, 1837): 268; A Subaltern [pseud.], "Florida War, No. 4," *ANC* 8 (April 4, 1838): 220.

36. Chapman to Blair, November 19, 1837, and February 28, 1838, in "A West Point Graduate in the Second Seminole War," 458–459, 470–471; Wright, *Creeks and Seminoles*, 253; anonymous letter published in *ANC* 6 (April 5, 1838): 216–217. See also Thomas Henderson to Benjamin King, February 6, 1838, King Papers. Thomas C. Leonard, "Red, White, and the Army Blue: Empathy and Anger in the American West," *American Quarterly* 26 (May 1974): 176–190, provides evidence of a height-

ened attraction to primitivism and the image of the noble savage among officers in the post–Civil War era. This may well have been due to the qualities nineteenth-century whites commonly associated with nomads like the Plains Indians, as well as the "empathy and anger" Leonard sees in officers' reactions to the modernization of Anglo-American society. See also Sherry L. Smith, *The View from Officers' Row: Army Perceptions of Western Indians* (Tucson: University of Arizona Press, 1990), which emphasizes the diversity of late-nineteenth-century opinion.

37. John W. Phelps to his father, July 10, 1837, in "Letters of Lieutenant John W. Phelps," 67–68, 73; McCall to his father, February 9, 1836, in *Letters from the Frontiers*, 301; Hitchcock cited in *Fifty Years in Camp and Field: The Diary of Major General Ethan Allen Hitchcock, U.S.A.*, ed. W. A. Croffut (New York: G. P. Putnam's Sons, 1909), 77–82, 120 (June 22, 1840); Allen [probably Capt. George W. Allen] to Heintzelman, August 9, 1840, Samuel P. Heintzelman Papers, LC; Hunter diary, 74. The American treaties with the Seminoles in 1823 (establishing a reservation area in Florida), 1832, and 1833 are in Charles J. Kappler, comp., *Indian Affairs: Laws and Treaties* (Washington, D.C.: Government Printing Office, 1903–1929), 2:203–207, 344–345, 394–395.

38. Lt. John King Fenno Mansfield to Edward Deering Mansfield, September 18, 1836, J. K. F. Mansfield Papers, USMA. Mentor [pseud.], untitled letter, *ANC* 9 (October 17, 1839): 244–246, also provides good examples of this language. See the quotations from Colonel Richard Irving Dodge in Leonard, "Red, White, and Army Blue," 181, for sentiments similar to Hunter's from the post–Civil War era.

39. "An Officer of the 4th Artillery," *ANC* 6 (January 25, 1838): 55 (originally published in the *Charleston Courier*); Joseph T. Glatthaar, *Forged in Battle: The Civil War Alliance of Black Soldiers and White Officers* (New York: Free Press, 1990), 7–8; James G. Hollandsworth Jr., *The Louisiana Native Guards: The Black Military Experience during the Civil War* (Baton Rouge: Louisiana State University Press, 1995), 12–14. William Skelton identifies the officer of the Fourth Artillery as "almost certainly Lieutenant John W. Phelps" (*An American Profession of Arms*, 324), but according to Phelps, rumor identified Major John L. Gardner as the author. When Gardner denied authorship, an alarmed Phelps exclaimed, "Now it is fixed upon me!" Phelps diary, February 12 and March 4, 1838, John W. Phelps Papers, NYPL. Phelps's motive for refusing the brevet promotion to captain is unknown. It is not clear whether there was a direct connection between Phelps's resignation and Brown's sentencing on November 2, 1859, but officers' resignations were usually dated on the last day of the month, indicating their submission several months in advance, so the timing is doubly suggestive. Intriguingly, during the Civil War, one white enlisted soldier wrote of Phelps that he "is very much liked here by the men and hated professionally by the officers. He . . . seems to think as much of a private as an officer" (Hollandsworth, *The Louisiana Native Guards*, 13n3).

40. Wall to Robert Anderson, August 19, 1836, Anderson Papers, LC.

41. "An Officer of the 4th Artillery," 56; letter ["not intended to be published," according to the editor], *ANC* 6 (April 5, 1838): 216–217; Hunter diary, 73–74.

42. Thomas Lawson to Benjamin King, August 18, 1837, King Papers; Mahon, *History of the Second Seminole War*, 204; Jesup to War Department, June 7, 1837, *ASPMA*, 7:872; Marszalek, *Sherman*, 37. See also "Gen. Macomb's Arrangement," *ANC* 9 (July 11, 1839): 25. See A Lieutenant of the 2d Artillery [pseud.], "Seminole War—Treaty of Payne's Landing," *ANC* 6 (May 1, 1838): 344–346, for an answer to "Officer of the 4th Artillery" that invoked duty and the "inevitability" of "progress" and "destiny" in favor of prosecuting the war.

43. Mentor [pseud.], untitled letter, *ANC* 9 (October 17, 1839): 246.

44. "Seminole War," *ANC* 5 (August 3, 1837): 72–74; Jesup to RJ, March 18, 1837, *TP*, 25:381. The record of communications between Jesup (and his successors as theater commander) and the government in Washington is scantier than one would expect; there are no official records of interagency deliberations in the early and mid-nineteenth century executive branch—no cabinet diary and, of course, no National Security Council. Nor did Jackson and Van Buren leave diaries like those of John Quincy Adams and James K. Polk (though Polk's diary is hardly the font of information one would hope for, at least regarding diplomacy and national security). The bibliographical notes in James C. Curtis, *The Fox at Bay: Martin Van Buren and the Presidency, 1837–1841* (Lexington: University Press of Kentucky, 1970), and Major L. Wilson, *The Presidency of Martin Van Buren* (Lawrence: University Press of Kansas, 1984), explore the limits of the sources; the Library of Congress's *Calendar of the Papers of Martin Van Buren* (Washington, D.C.: Government Printing Office, 1910) has only four citations to Seminoles or the war.

45. Mahon, *History of the Second Seminole War*, 199–202, 207, 235, 257; Jesup cited in Richard F. Ivy, *The Distinguished Light of Abraham Eustis: A Biography of an 1800 Artillery General* (Yorktown, Va.: Citizen Publications, 1993), 164; Jesup to Poinsett, February 11, 1838, quoted in Sprague, *The Origin, Progress, and Conclusion of the Florida War*, 200.

46. Van Buren, third annual message to Congress, December 2, 1839, *MPP*, 4:1754; Frank F. White Jr., "Macomb's Mission to the Seminoles: John T. Sprague's Journal Kept during April and May, 1839," *FHQ* 35 (October 1956): 130–193 (a thorough contemporary account by Macomb's aide-de-camp); Major Ethan Allen Hitchcock to his brother Samuel, August 22, 1842, Hitchcock Papers; Hitchcock, *Fifty Years in Camp and Field*, 122–129. Hitchcock's letter recounts his efforts to persuade the War Department to adopt a pacific policy, against Armistead's wishes. Hitchcock sent his letter to the secretary of war after receiving Worth's approval, though it is not clear whether he did so while Armistead was still in command. Given Hitchcock's vanity and lack of respect for senior officers and the chain of command, he may well have done so. Hitchcock, who attempted to draw public attention to the frauds he uncovered while serving as special agent to the commissioner of Indian affairs during the late 1830s and early 1840s, had pronounced removal "despicable," vowing that "I can hardly help wishing the right to prevail, which [means], in this case . . . praying for the Indians" (Hitchcock to the Rev. William G. Eliot Jr., March 1, 1841, Hitchcock Papers). This distaste may help account for Hitchcock's tardiness in join-

ing his regiment when it moved to Florida in 1840, although personal convenience was probably equally important. During the 1850s he criticized white settlers warring on Indians in Oregon in terms much like those officers used in Florida. See Ethan Allen Hitchcock, *A Traveler in Indian Territory*, ed. Grant Foreman (1930; reprint, Norman: University of Oklahoma Press, 1996), and Skelton, *An American Profession of Arms*, 315–316, 324–325.

47. Lt. Alfred Sully to Thomas Sully, May 22, 1842, Alfred Sully Papers, Beinecke Library, Yale University; Capt. William L. McClintock to Robert Anderson, May 1, 1841, Anderson Papers, LC; McCall to his father, March 28, 1842, in *Letters from the Frontiers*, 398; Poinsett to Rep. Gouveneur Kemble, August 17, 1841, Poinsett Papers, Gilpin Collection, HSP.

CHAPTER SEVEN: "THE DUTY OF A SOLDIER TO OBEY"

1. Henderson to Benjamin King, February 6, 1838, Benjamin King Papers, LC; Jacob Rhett Motte, *Journey into the Wilderness: An Army Surgeon's Account of Life in Camp and Field during the Creek and Seminole Wars, 1836–1838*, ed. James F. Sunderman (Gainesville: University Press of Florida, 1963), 144; letter to *ANC* 11 (August 27, 1840): 137–138; "On the Florida War," *ANC* 9 (November 7, 1839): 290 (reprinted from the *National Intelligencer*). See also Lt. Robert Christie Buchanan, journal entry, December 19, 1837, in Frank F. White Jr., ed., "A Journal of Lt. Robert C. Buchanan during the Seminole War," *FHQ* 29 (October 1950): 142. Officers commonly used the term "citizens" (often abbreviated "cits"), but almost never "civilians." They frequently did so sarcastically, but use of the term indicates a responsible understanding that civilians were citizens, to whom the army and its commanders were ultimately accountable.

2. Hunter diary (no dates given), quoted in Reynold M. Wik, "Captain Nathaniel Wyche Hunter and the Florida Indian Campaigns, 1837–1841," *FHQ* 39 (July 1960): 68, 73–74, n. 47 (hereafter cited as Hunter diary, with page number); John K. Mahon, *History of the Second Seminole War, 1835–1842* (Gainesville: University Press of Florida, 1967), 315.

3. Clinch to Eaton, February 9, 1836, Order Book, Fort King, 1834–1835, Clinch Letterbooks, LC.

4. "Gen. Taylor, and the Missouri Volunteers," *ANC* 8 (April 11, 1839): 236; Sheer Justice [pseud.], "Battle of the Okee-Chobee—The Army," *ANC* 6 (March 8, 1838): 154; Canard [pseud.], "Florida War," *ANC* 11 (July 23, 1840): 62; J. K. F. Mansfield to Edward D. Mansfield, September 18, 1836, J. K. F. Mansfield Papers, USMA. See Chester L. Kieffer, *Maligned General: The Biography of Thomas Sidney Jesup* (San Rafael, Calif.: Presidio Press, 1979), for further information on this controversy.

5. "Gen. Macomb's Arrangement," *ANC* 9 (July 11, 1839): 25; "Florida War," *ANC* 7 (August 16, 1838): 105; A Subaltern [pseud.], "Florida War, No. 4," *ANC* 8 (April 4, 1839): 220. Note the similarity between the second of these and Motte,

Journey into the Wilderness (compiled after the war from notes assembled while in the field), 144.

6. Thomas Jesup to RJ, August 13, 1837, quoted in Kieffer, *Maligned General*, 180; William Wall to Robert Anderson, August 19, 1836, Robert Anderson Papers, LC; Joseph R. Smith to his wife Juliet, March 24, 1838, in "Letters from the Second Seminole War," ed. John K. Mahon. *FHQ* 36 (April 1958): 341.

7. Wainwright to William Chapman, March 17, 1837, William Chapman Papers, USMA; Sylvester Churchill, February 23, 1837, and May 7, 1839, Journals 1 and 3, Sylvester Churchill Papers, LC; Abraham Eustis to Frederic Eustis, April 6, 1838, Abraham Eustis Papers, USAMHI. See Richard F. Ivy, *The Distinguished Light of Abraham Eustis: A Biography of an 1800 Artillery General* (Yorktown, Va.: Citizen Publications, 1993), 146–149, for Eustis's relations with the volunteers under his command. Criticism of Jesup can be found in "Gen. Jesup and the Military Academy," *ANC* 6 (February 8, 1838): 93, and in three letters in *ANC* 6 (March 1, 1838). Jesup was not a West Pointer, and many graduates felt that he was aiding and abetting (however unconsciously) Jacksonian assaults on the institution they considered the core of the army. *ANC* 9 (August 22, 1839) alone contained three letters, from soldiers of the Second and Seventh Infantries and the Third Artillery, either defending their units and officers or appealing for regimental relief.

8. Pegram and McClintock to Robert Anderson, January 18 and May 1, 1841, Anderson Papers, LC.

9. Quotation from citizens' petition to Secretary of War Poinsett, March 18, 1837, House Doc. 225, 25th Cong., 3rd sess. See Tommy R. Young II, "The United States Army in the South, 1789–1835" (Ph.D. diss., Louisiana State University, 1973), for by far the most thorough account of the army's role in supporting slavery, and Tommy R. Young II, "The United States Army and the Institution of Slavery in Louisiana, 1803–1835," *Louisiana Studies* 13 (Fall 1974): 201–222. Macomb wrote to a wide range of officers between 1829 and 1831 about troop deployments to forestall slave rebellions, although in a couple of cases, he refused civilian requests for troop deployments due to the excessive dispersal and disciplinary difficulties they produced. Gaines also had an active correspondence with civilian leaders on this subject.

10. Jesup to RJ, March 6, 1837, quoted in Daniel F. Littlefield, *Africans and Seminoles: From Removal to Emancipation* (Westport, Conn.: Greenwood Press, 1977), 19; Jesup to Poinsett, March 26, 1837, *ASPMA*, 7:827; Jesup, letter published in *ANC* 8 (February 7, 1839): 65–66; "On the Florida War," *ANC* 9 (November 7, 1839): 291; Jesup to Poinsett, May 8, 1837, Thomas Sidney Jesup, General's Papers, Entry 159, RG 94, NA. See also Daniel F. Littlefield, *Africans and Creeks: From the Colonial Period to the Civil War* (Westport, Conn.: Greenwood Press, 1979).

11. Order No. 79, April 5, 1837, and Jesup to Poinsett, June 16, 1837, Jesup, General's Papers, Entry 159, RG 94, NA.

12. Mahon, *History of the Second Seminole War*, 206; Jesup to Poinsett, September 23, 1837, Jesup, General's Papers, Entry 159, RG 94, NA; third quotation from Kieffer, *Maligned General*, 182 (source uncited); Littlefield, *Africans and Seminoles*, 26.

13. Kieffer, *Maligned General*, 28; Jesup to Wilkins, May 30, 1844, Thomas Sidney Jesup Papers, LC. In general, see Mahon, *History of the Second Seminole War*, 200–206.

14. Churchill journals, passim, Churchill Papers, LC; ZT to RJ, June 2, 1838, quoted in Littlefield, *Africans and Seminoles*, 49 (see also 40–53); Mahon, *History of the Second Seminole War*, 251–252; Kenneth W. Porter, "Negroes and the Second Seminole War, 1835–1842," *JSH* 30 (November 1964): 446.

15. Worth, August 19, 1841, quoted in Porter, "Negroes and the Second Seminole War," 446; Littlefield, *Africans and Seminoles*, 71, 82, 85. Many officers were slaveholders themselves, and some colonels and generals owned large plantations worked by numerous slaves. The officer corps was generally racist and abetted a number of attempts to recover ex-slaves, but I find it more remarkable that senior commanders sometimes refused to do so. I attribute this reluctance primarily to their sense of honor and good faith rather than beliefs about the morality of slavery—they had made agreements with the Seminoles and would not break them simply to help some greedy planters make money. See also Jane F. Lancaster, *Removal Aftershock: The Seminoles' Struggles to Survive in the West, 1836–1866* (Knoxville: University of Tennessee Press, 1994).

16. Miller to his mother Maria and his sister Sarah, ? and April 29, 1835, Morris Smith Miller Papers, USMA; *ANC* 6 (May 10, 1838): 297; John T. Sprague, *The Origin, Progress, and Conclusion of the Florida War*, introduction by John K. Mahon (1848; reprint, Gainesville: University Press of Florida, 1964). Sprague resigned his lieutenancy in the Marine Corps in 1837 and immediately entered the army, where he rose to colonel (with two brevets for service in Florida, where he was an aide to William Worth) before retiring in 1870.

17. Sam Jones [pseud.], "United States Military Academy," *ANC* 8 (January 24 and February 21, 1838): 50–51, 122–124; Junius [pseud.], "A Visit to Sam Jones's Camp, Part II," *ANC* 10 (May 7, 1840): 301, and "Part VII," *ANC* 11 (July 23, 1840): 59. See also Mahon, *History of the Second Seminole War*, 236–237. See Sylvester Churchill, March 8, 1837, Journal 1, Churchill Papers, LC, and "Mentor," *ANC* 9 (October 17, 1839): 245, for other examples of sentimental attitudes toward Seminole families and children. Mahon (*History of the Second Seminole War*, 303–304) notes a bit of doggerel that humorously detailed the army's efforts to catch Sam Jones, whom "Junius" used to parody army policies of all sorts in his seven-part series in the *Army and Navy Chronicle*. Another example of officers' humor employed in gentle dissent was Anti-Puff [pseud.], "Puffing," *ANC* 7 (November 29, 1838): 348, which chided Winfield Scott for his pretentions to the presidency.

18. Canard [pseud.], "Florida War," *ANC* 11 (July 30, 1840): 67; Alan Taylor, *Liberty Men and Great Proprietors: The Revolutionary Settlement on the Maine Frontier, 1760–1820* (Chapel Hill: University of North Carolina Press, 1990), 189–194, 205; Alan Taylor, "'A Kind of Warr': The Contest for Land on the Northeastern Frontier, 1750–1820," *WMQ* 46 (January 1989): 3–26; Eric F. Lott, *Love and Theft: Blackface Minstrelsy and the American Working Class* (New York: Oxford University Press,

1995); Alexander Saxton, *The Rise and Fall of the White Republic: Class Politics and Mass Culture in Nineteenth-Century America* (London: Verso, 1990); Alexander Saxton, "Blackface Minstrelsy and Jacksonian Ideology," *American Quarterly* 27 (March 1975): 3–28. For comparison with European ambivalence, see Mikail Mamedov, "'Going Native' in the Caucasus: Problems of Russian Identity, 1801–64," *Russian Review* 67 (April 2008): 275–295; more generally, Susan Layton, *Russian Literature and Empire: Conquest of the Caucasus from Pushkin to Tolstoy* (Cambridge: Cambridge University Press, 1994); and, of course, Tolstoy's "The Prisoner of the Caucasus," updated in the film *Prisoner of the Mountains* (dir. Sergei Bodrov, 1996).

19. Taylor, *Liberty Men and Great Proprietors*, 189 (quotation modified to fit officers' situation).

20. Ibid., 190, 205. Army regulations forbade writing to newspapers, and the Articles of War forbade contemptuous statements against the president and Congress, so pseudonyms were essential.

21. Mahon, *History of the Second Seminole War*, 135, 160, 204, 209; Jesup to Harney, June 8, 1837, file J-117, AGOLR.

22. Hatheway to his sister Elizabeth, March 4, 1838, in *Frontier Soldier: The Letters of Maj. John S. Hatheway, 1833–1853*, ed. Ted Van Arsdol (Vancouver, Wash.: Vancouver National Historic Reserve Trust, 1999), 38; Mahon, *History of the Second Seminole War*, 204, 209, 225. The employment of bloodhounds is discussed in Kieffer, *Maligned General*, 172; K. Jack Bauer, *Zachary Taylor: Soldier, Planter, and Statesman of the Old Southwest* (Baton Rouge: Louisiana State University Press, 1985), 87; Mahon, *History of the Second Seminole War*, 204, 239, 265–267, 307; James W. Covington, "Cuban Bloodhounds and the Seminoles," *FHQ* 33 (October 1954): 111–119; and John Campbell, "The Seminoles, the 'Bloodhound War,' and Abolition, 1796–1865," *JSH* 77 (May 2006): 259–302, which I had the pleasure to referee.

23. Mahon, *History of the Second Seminole War*, 278, 283–284; Phelps diary, February 3, 1838, John W. Phelps Papers, NYPL. See Col. Abraham Eustis and Capt. William L. McClintock to Robert Anderson, February 8, 1841, and December 31, 1840, Anderson Papers, LC, for examples of approval. Harney's hanging of the Cuban fisherman was also a point along the spectrum of authoritarian brutality; army officers frequently punished enlisted soldiers by means verging on torture, and the officers of the Second Dragoons gained a widespread reputation for mistreating enlisted men. Only two factors stand out to distinguish the Second Dragoons from other regiments in Florida: lack of Military Academy socialization among its officers, and rapid turnover, demonstrating a lack of commitment to the military profession. Harney was one of the last officers commissioned without Military Academy socialization between 1818 and 1832; Nathaniel Wyche Hunter, whose dissenting views have already been mentioned, was one of only four Academy graduates in the regiment when it was raised, and he was the only one of the four remaining in the regiment a decade later. Despite the economic depression, the Second Dragoons suffered a high rate of officer attrition during its early years; by 1841, only nine of its twenty-six original company officers remained. In the worst case of violence, Captain Marshall Howe beat Private James

Jones to death during a march but was acquitted of manslaughter by a civilian court; the commanding general insisted on a court-martial, but Howe's peers convicted him only of cruelty, and he was suspended for a year. The seniority system then allowed him to rise steadily to the rank of colonel and regimental commander before retiring twenty-five years later. In 1844 a lieutenant of the First Dragoons, Abraham Johnston, initiated court-martial proceedings against Harney for "arbitrary and unmilitary conduct" and "conduct prejudicial to good order and military discipline" in a series of violent acts against enlisted soldiers. The court-martial sentenced Harney to be publically reprimanded and suspended from his rank and command for four months; Winfield Scott condemned Harney as a "conspicuous violator of law and morals" but released him to his regiment, which was on its way to Texas.

See William B. Skelton, *An American Profession of Arms: The Army Officer Corps, 1784–1861* (Lawrence: University Press of Kansas, 1992), 271–273, 278–281; Dale R. Steinhauer, "'Sogers': Enlisted Men in the U.S. Army, 1815–1860" (Ph.D. diss., University of North Carolina, 1992), chap. 6, especially 261–264; George R. Adams, "General William Selby Harney: Frontier Soldier, 1800–1889" (Ph.D. diss., University of Arizona, 1983), 74–78, 97, 102–103, 130–132; Felix P. McGaughy Jr., "The Squaw Kissing War: Bartholomew M. Lynch's Journal of the Second Seminole War, 1836–1839" (M.A. thesis, Florida State University, 1965), 98, 101, 179; EPG to Johnston, September 13, 1844, Abraham Robinson Johnston Papers, USMA; and General Order No. 39, August 13, 1845, General Orders and Circulars, AGO, 1809–1860, M-1094, reel 5, RG 94, NA.

24. Mahon, *History of the Second Seminole War*, 299, 302, 307; Worth to Ethan Allen Hitchcock, March 10, 1841, Hitchcock Papers, LC; Adams, "General William Selby Harney," 74–78, 130–132. Most pecuniary incentives were directed toward citizen-soldiers and Indian allies like the Lower Creeks; regular soldiers were not offered a bounty ($100 apiece) for Seminole warriors until Worth's final offensive in 1842. Skelton, *An American Profession of Arms*, 318–322, points to an increasing hardening of attitudes beginning with the later stages of the Seminole War and accelerating, along with exterminationist sentiment among civilian frontiersmen, during the 1850s. Although the distinction may be slight, I would hesitate to endorse Reginald Horsman's conclusion in *Race and Manifest Destiny: The Origins of American Racial Anglo-Saxonism* (Cambridge, Mass.: Harvard University Press, 1981), 205, that the conflict became racialized: army officers continued to use the rhetoric of savagery and civilization rather than one more closely linked to inherent racial differentiation. In comparison, Thomas-Robert Bugeaud, commander of the French forces occupying Algeria during the same years, declared that he would "renounce . . . legal niceties," causing his biographer to conclude that "official sanction of unrestricted violence" led the army "to act with untrammeled ferocity." Anthony Thrall Sullivan, *Thomas-Robert Bugeaud, France, and Algeria, 1784–1849: Politics, Power, and the Good Society* (Hamden, Conn.: Archon Books, 1983), 101, 124–125. See also Benjamin Claude Brower, *A Desert Named Peace: The Violence of France's Empire in the Algerian Sahara, 1844–1902* (New York: Columbia University Press, 2009).

25. This is a prominent theme in Thomas C. Leonard, "Red, White, and Army Blue: Empathy and Anger in the American West," *American Quarterly* 26 (May 1974): 176–190, regarding the army after the Civil War.

26. Hunter diary, 74.

27. Omicron [pseud.], "General Jesup, the Secretary of War, and the Military Academy," *ANC* 6 (March 1, 1838): 138.

28. Jesup to Secretary of War William Wilkins, May 22, 1844, quoted in Kieffer, *Maligned General*, 233.

29. Lt. Joseph R. Smith diary entry, November 11, 1837, in "Letters from the Second Seminole War," 332; Chapman to Helen Blair, February 27, 1838, in Edward C. Coker and Daniel L. Schafer, "A West Point Graduate in the Second Seminole War: William Warren Chapman and the View from Fort Foster," *FHQ* 68 (April 1990): 468; P. [pseud.], "Battle of the Kissimmee—The Army: Honor to Whom Honor Is Due," *ANC* 6 (March 1, 1838): 141; Wik, "Captain Nathaniel Wyche Hunter," 74.

30. John F. Marszalek, *Sherman: A Soldier's Passion for Order* (New York: Free Press, 1993), 31; Anderson, draft of application to join company, November 26, 1841, Anderson Papers, LC; Anderson to Alden, February 12, 1842, HQALR. The post of assistant adjutant general conveyed a brevet rank—in Anderson's case as a captain.

31. Lt. Bradford Alden to Anderson, February 9, 1842, Anderson Papers, LC.

32. Sam Jones [pseud.], "Florida War," *ANC* 9 (October 31, 1839): 285. See also Skelton, *An American Profession of Arms*, 325.

33. The army's journals were fertile sources of professional discourse, but few historians have given them the attention they deserve. The *Military and Naval Magazine of the United States* was published monthly from March 1833 until December 1835 (the month the Second Seminole War began). It was supplanted by the *Army and Navy Chronicle*, a weekly newspaper of sixteen densely packed pages that ran from the beginning of 1835 through 1844; it was renamed the *Army and Navy Chronicle and Scientific Repository*, without a significant change in focus, in 1842. By the second volume (July–December 1835), the *Chronicle* was slightly more than half naval in content; by 1836, army-oriented material took up more than two-thirds of the space, with more than half the total devoted to the Seminole War alone.

34. See Skelton, *An American Profession of Arms*, 195, on the incidence of courts-martial. While I believe that Skelton's numbers understate the amount of personal tension among officers by focusing on courts-martial rather than the much more common courts of inquiry or other manifestations of controversy, it is clear that there was no upward spike in disciplinary proceedings during the war, and I have not found any primary or secondary evidence of courts directed against officers on the basis of statements made about the war.

35. "Major Dade's Battleground," *ANC* 3 (September 8, 1836): 156; "Celebration of Independence at Fort Towson," *ANC* 7 (August 16, 1838): 109; Alvord, address delivered December 29, 1838, and partially reprinted in *ANC* 8 (April 18, 1839): 249. Alvord's full text was published in New York (by Wiley and Putnam, 1839) and is available at the Library of Congress. One of the earliest examples of an

epitaph was that by the officers of the First Dragoons at Fort Des Moines for "The Late Lieutenant J. F. Izard," *ANC* 2 (May 19, 1836): 316–317, slain during Edmund P. Gaines's attempted crossing of the Withlacoochee on February 28. (Izard's fellows at Fort Leavenworth published a memorial to him several weeks later.) Other examples include that of officers at Jefferson Barracks in St. Louis ("Battle of the Okee-Chobee," *ANC* 6 [March 15, 1838]: 172).

36. An Officer of the Line [pseud.], "Florida War," *ANC* 9 (August 29, 1839): 132.

37. See Skelton, *An American Profession of Arms*, 182–183, 194, 213 (tables 11.1–11.4), for median career lengths, promotion rates (time in grade), and means of attrition.

38. Anonymous letter published in *ANC* 6 (April 5, 1838): 216–217. This officer probably meant that he had served thirty-one years without attaining the rank of major, not that he had been a captain for that long, which was almost certainly not so. The average officer was promoted about once per decade—about as often as academic professionals today—so statistically, the captain was only slightly behind the norm. Knowing that would have been of little comfort, however.

39. Pressed by partisan vitriol, nonpartisanship often became antipartisanship, but alienation from democratic politics was restrained by professional socialization in nationalism and duty and the need to protect the army, which was dependent on civilian government for its funding. Most officers combined an informed skepticism toward partisan politics with a professional identity of disinterested nationalist virtue, a "disengaged belief" in the ultimate legitimacy of representative government and an "engaged disbelief" as soldiers defending the army and its service to the nation, while trying to avoid entanglement in divisive partisan rhetoric and electioneering. Indeed, the army's officers may have been more characteristic of the American middle classes than we tend to think, partaking of what several historians have labeled a "vernacular liberalism," dutifully engaged and genteelly skeptical of division and corruption, rather than raptly absorbed and constantly inserting partisanship into daily life. See Glenn C. Altschuler and Stuart M. Blumin, *Rude Republic: Americans and Their Politics in the Nineteenth Century* (Princeton, N.J.: Princeton University Press, 2000); Glenn C. Altschuler and Stuart M. Blumin, "'Where Is the Real America?' Politics and Popular Consciousness in the Antebellum Era," *American Quarterly* 49 (June 1997): 225–267; Glenn C. Altschuler and Stuart M. Blumin, "Limits of Political Engagement in Antebellum America: A New Look at the Golden Age of Participatory Democracy," *JAH* 84 (December 1997): 855–885; and Samuel Watson, "What Do We Mean by Partisan? Army Officers and Politics during the Evolution of the Second Party System" (unpublished paper presented to the Southwestern Historical Association, April 1, 1999).

40. See Thomas L. Haskell, *Objectivity Is Not Neutrality: Explanatory Schemes in History* (Baltimore: Johns Hopkins University Press, 1998), for the complex relationship between these two very loaded concepts.

41. The concept of "army politics" was first advanced by William B. Skelton, "Officers and Politicians: The Origins of Army Politics in the United States before the Civil

War," *AFS* 6 (Fall 1979): 22–48; see also Skelton, *An American Profession of Arms*, chap. 15.

42. March 1, 1843, 5 *Stat.* 606. Most scholars writing about civil-military relations during the early 1840s tend to emphasize the congressional pressure for reductions in numbers, appropriations, and compensation embodied in legislation such as "Black's bill." Officers themselves certainly wrote more about that bill (introduced repeatedly during the Twenty-seventh Congress) than the new provision for nominations to West Point, but the system of congressional nominations proved far more significant. ("Black's bill" was never passed.)

43. "Notes and Reminiscences of an Officer of the Army, No. IX," *ANC* 11 (September 24, 1840): 202.

CHAPTER EIGHT: CHANGING MILITARY ATTITUDES TOWARD FOREIGN RELATIONS

1. See especially Reginald C. Stuart, "Special Interests and National Authority in Foreign Policy: American-British Provincial Links during the Embargo and the War of 1812," *DH* 8 (Fall 1984): 311–328; William Earl Weeks, "New Directions in the Study of Early American Foreign Relations," *DH* 17 (Winter 1993): 73–95; Jay Gitlin, "Private Diplomacy to Private Property: States, Tribes, and Nations in the Early National Period," *DH* 22 (Winter 1998): 85–99; Peter J. Kastor, "'Motives of Peculiar Urgency': Local Diplomacy in Louisiana, 1803–1821," *WMQ* 58 (October 2001): 819–848; Peter J. Kastor, *The Nation's Crucible: The Louisiana Purchase and the Creation of America* (New Haven, Conn.: Yale University Press, 2004); and Nathan J. Citino, "The Global Frontier: Comparative History and the Frontier-Borderlands Approach in American Foreign Relations," *DH* 25 (Fall 2001): 677–693. Joshua M. Smith, *Borderland Smuggling: Patriots, Loyalists, and Illicit Trade in the Northeast, 1783–1820* (Gainesville: University Press of Florida, 2006), provides a case study of the Maine maritime frontier, focused on the years before 1815.

2. See Stephen Peter Rosen, "Alexander Hamilton and the Domestic Uses of International Law," *DH* 5 (Summer 1981): 183–198, and Daniel G. Lang, *Foreign Policy in the Early Republic: The Law of Nations and the Balance of Power* (Baton Rouge: Louisiana State University Press, 1985), regarding the identification of domestic and international law and order in the mind and actions of an earlier conservative.

3. Thomas R. Hietala, *Manifest Design: Anxious Aggrandizement in Late Jacksonian America* (Ithaca, N.Y.: Cornell University Press, 1985), 195–196.

4. WS, August 20, 1820, file S-37, SWLR: Reg.

5. See Jesup to Secretary of War Eaton, October 20, 1830, *ASPMA*, 4:634; Wool to AM, October 23, 1830, *ASPMA*, 4:462, reprinted in *ANC* 13 (February 12, 1842): 49; Samuel J. Watson, "Knowledge, Interest, and the Limits of Military Professionalism: The Discourse on American Coastal Defense, 1815–1860," *War in History* 5 (Fall 1998): 280–307; and Jamie W. Moore, *The Fortifications Board 1816–1828*

and the Definition of National Security (Charleston, S.C.: The Citadel, 1981). Mark A. Smith, *Engineering Security: The Corps of Engineers and Third System Defense Policy, 1815–1861* (Tuscaloosa: University of Alabama Press, 2009), argues that the Corps of Engineers pursued a more militarily rational strategy than I discerned in my article, but he does not present evidence that the American coastal fortifications were any better prepared in terms of guns actually mounted and gunners present for duty.

6. See Brown, October 6, 1820, file B-59, and EPG, July 27, 1820, file G-144, SWLR: Reg.; ZT to Quartermaster General Jesup, June 18, 1821, Zachary Taylor Papers, LC. Lester D. Langley, *Struggle for the American Mediterranean: United States–European Rivalry in the Gulf-Caribbean, 1776–1904* (Athens: University of Georgia Press, 1976), 57, states that there was little American reaction to the French and Spanish incursions. I have found none among army officers regarding the Tampico invasion; several of the commentaries written by Gaines, Wool, and engineer major William Chase in 1839 and 1840 refer to the bombardment of Veracruz, primarily to discuss the French use of guns firing explosive shells ("Paixhans guns").

7. ZT to Jesup, January 20, 1824, series 2, reel 1, Taylor Papers, LC; John M. Belohlavek, *"Let the Eagle Soar!" The Foreign Policy of Andrew Jackson* (Lincoln: University of Nebraska Press, 1985), 20. See ibid., chap. 1, and Douglas M. Astolfi, *Foundations of Destiny: A Foreign Policy of the Jacksonians, 1824–1837* (New York: Garland, 1989), chap. 1, for the decline of expansive republican internationalism among Jacksonians in the 1820s, especially concerning Latin America and the Pan-American Congress. The cooling of relations between the United States and Latin America is noted in nearly all works on American diplomacy of the period; see especially John J. Johnson, *A Hemisphere Apart: The Foundations of United States Policy toward Latin America* (Baltimore: Johns Hopkins University Press, 1990). Dexter Perkins, *The Monroe Doctrine, 1826–1867* (Baltimore: Johns Hopkins University Press, 1933), refers to the 1830s as "the period of quiescence" in American assertions of the doctrine.

8. Watson, "Knowledge, Interest, and the Limits of Military Professionalism." As the army's premier visionary, Gaines wrote numerous memorials to Congress and the public on coastal defense, internal improvements, and the role of the militia, all full of connections to the international situation. In contrast, apart from official papers and campaign materials from 1852, surprisingly few of Winfield Scott's thoughts on international relations have survived. This may be due to his partisan political ambitions or simply to the absence of a large concentration of personal papers like those available for Jesup and Wool, but it may also be because Scott focused his professional attention specifically on military developments such as tactical, administration, and logistical regulations. Intellectually, Gaines thought in breadth, Scott in depth, and Wool and Jesup somewhere in between.

9. "On Popular Prejudices against Military Establishments," *MNM* 1 (July 1833): 302–303. For similar fears among civilian policy makers and newspaper editors, see Hietala, *Manifest Design*, chap. 3; Kinley J. Brauer, "The United States and British Imperial Expansion, 1815–1860," *DH* 12 (Winter 1988): 19–37; American Minister to Mexico Waddy Thompson to Secretary of State Daniel Webster, April 29, 1842, in

Richard W. Van Alstyne, "Empire in Mid-Passage, 1845–1867," in *From Colony to Empire: Essays in the History of American Foreign Relations*, ed. William Appleman Williams (New York: J. Wiley, 1972), 100; Andrew Jackson to Sam Houston, March 15, 1844, in *The Writings of Sam Houston, 1813–1863*, 8 vols., ed. Amelia W. Williams and Eugene C. Barker (Austin: University of Texas Press, 1938–1943), 4:265–267; and Secretary of State John C. Calhoun (December 1844), cited in Kinley J. Brauer, "1821–1860: Economics and the Diplomacy of American Expansionism," in *Economics and World Power: An Assessment of American Diplomacy since 1789*, ed. William H. Becker and Samuel F. Wells (New York: Columbia University Press, 1984), 98. See Judith B. Williams, *British Commercial Policy and Trade Expansion, 1750–1850* (Oxford: Clarendon Press, 1972), for the British side, and Peggy K. Liss, *Atlantic Empires: The Network of Trade and Revolution, 1713–1826* (Baltimore: Johns Hopkins University Press, 1983), more generally. The centrality of commerce in American foreign policy calculations of this era has become a common scholarly theme; see Astolfi, *Foundations of Destiny*, chap. 3; Belohlavek, *"Let the Eagle Soar!"*; and Brauer, "1821–1860: Economics and the Diplomacy of American Expansionism," 55–118.

10. William H. Chase, "Harbor of Pensacola," *Pensacola Gazette*, March 21, 1839, in *ANC* 8 (April 18, 1839): 244. See also Chase, March 10, 1845, article from unidentified newspaper in Henry Halleck's "Military Note Book," Henry Halleck Papers, LC.

11. Alexander Swift to Joseph Swift, November 12, 1840, Alexander Swift Papers, USMA.

12. Mason to Lt. George L. Welcker, August 9, 1842, Lenoir Family Papers, SHC. However, see Richard C. Rohrs, "American Critics and the French Revolution of 1848," *JER* 14 (Fall 1994): 359–377, for an examination of conservative attitudes toward European democratic revolutions that contains numerous parallels to the foreign policy attitudes of Whiggish officers during the 1830s and 1840s. Wool, Scott, and Zachary Taylor provide characteristic—and the most important—examples of the shift in officer attitudes toward foreign relations and international order. Edmund Gaines became an outlier, as chapters 10 and 12 will show; Thomas Sidney Jesup remained a republican internationalist, but the Second Seminole War was his only borderlands command.

13. AM to Jacob Brown, July 13, and to Miller, June 30, 1816, Alexander Macomb Letterbook, 1807–1819, BHC; AM to Morris S. Miller, July 29, 1815, Macomb Family Papers, BHC; AM to Brown, June 21 and July 27, 1816, Brown Letterbooks, LC; AM to Crawford, July 25, 1816, Macomb Letterbook, BHC.

14. James May, Stephen Henry, and Robert Abbott to AM, April 1817, and AM to William Woodbridge, November 12, 1817, William Woodbridge Papers, BHC; Secretary of War Peter B. Porter to President John Quincy Adams, November 24, 1828, Sen. Doc. 1, 20th Cong., 2nd sess., serial set 181, and December 26, 1828, SWLS: PUS; Assistant Surgeon Zena Pitcher to Capt. Alexander R. Thompson, April 20, 1830, Alexander R. Thompson Papers, WLC; Secretary of War John Eaton, January 7, 1831, Secretary of the Treasury S. D. Ingham, April 2, 1830, Secretary of War Peter B. Porter, December 17, 1828, and Major George M. Brooke, January 10, 1829,

HQALS. In contrast, an examination of the Brown Letterbooks (LC) for 1821–1828 and of Macomb's letters sent as commanding general between 1828 and 1834 (HQALS) shows little concern for the Canadian border as a law enforcement problem.

15. William R. Manning, ed., *Diplomatic Correspondence of the United States: Canadian Relations*, vol. 1, *1784–1820* (Washington, D.C.: Carnegie Endowment, 1940), 228–229, 234–235, 717–723, 788–789, 794–795.

16. Worth to Secretary of War Joel R. Poinsett, February 12, 1838, Worth's Official Letterbook, LC. All subsequent citations to Worth's letters are from this source, unless otherwise noted. His letterbooks are extant only for February 1838 to April 1839, but they provide the most detailed information available on officers' reactions to the Patriot conflicts.

17. D. W. Meinig, *The Shaping of America, A Geographical Perspective on 500 Years of History*, vol. 2, *Continental America, 1800–1867* (New Haven, Conn.: Yale University Press, 1993), 533–546. See Sam W. Haynes, *Unfinished Revolution: The Early American Republic in a British World* (Charlottesville: University Press of Virginia, 2011), for the most comprehensive exploration of American attitudes toward Britain between 1815 and 1846.

18. Brauer, "1821–1860: Economics and the Diplomacy of American Expansionism," 68–71, 95; Reginald C. Stuart, *United States Expansionism and British North America, 1775–1871* (Chapel Hill: University of North Carolina Press, 1988), 84, 144. See Albert Corey, *The Crisis of 1830–1842 in Canadian-American Relations* (New Haven, Conn.: Yale University Press, 1941), chap. 6, and Stuart, *United States Expansionism*, 143–144, for examples of conservative civilian opinion. See Donald F. Warner, *The Idea of Continental Union: Agitation for the Annexation of Canada to the United States, 1849–1893* (Lexington: University of Kentucky Press, 1960), regarding expansionist views later in the century.

19. Like most scholars and contemporary observers, I use the term "Patriots" interchangeably to refer to the initial rebels, their American supporters in the winter of 1837–1838, the Canadian Refugee Relief Association, the "Sons of Liberty," the "Hunters' Lodges," and any other organizations devoted to filibustering against Canada during this period. General and military histories of the Patriot rebellions include Oscar A. Kinchen, *The Rise and Fall of the Patriot Hunters* (New York: Bookman Associates, 1956); Michael Mann, *A Particular Duty: The Canadian Rebellions, 1837–1839* (Salisbury, England: Russell, 1986); and Mary Beacock Fryer, *Volunteers, Redcoats, Rebels, and Raiders: A Military History of the Rebellions in Upper Canada* (Toronto: Dundurn Press, 1987). See Hamish A. Leach, "A Politico-Military Study of the Detroit River Boundary Defense during the December 1837–March 1838 Emergency" (Ph.D. diss., University of Ottawa, 1963), for a more focused study, and Colin Read, *The Rising in Western Upper Canada, 1837–8: The Duncombe Revolt and After* (Toronto: University of Toronto Press, 1992), for a more scholarly one.

Few works explore the American local or regional civilian response to the insurgency in any depth; see especially Marc L. Harris, "The Meaning of Patriot: The Canadian Rebellion and American Republicanism, 1837-1839," *Michigan Historical Review* 23 (Spring 1997): 33-69; Stuart D. Scott, "The Patriot Game: New Yorkers and the Canadian Rebellion of 1837-1838," *New York History* 78 (July 1987): 281-295; and John J. Duffy and H. Nicholas Muller, *An Anxious Democracy: Aspects of the 1830s* (Westport, Conn.: Praeger, 1982). Like other works on American filibustering, Robert E. May, *Manifest Destiny's Underworld: Filibustering in Antebellum America* (Chapel Hill: University of North Carolina Press, 2002), focuses on the period between the war with Mexico and the Civil War, although May observes that "federal intervention proved decisive" to undermining the insurgency (11).

Apart from the works cited below, most of the literature on Anglo-American relations during this era predates the 1950s. For accounts of the diplomacy of the crisis (and leading up to the Webster-Ashburton Treaty in 1842), see Corey, *The Crisis of 1830-1842*; Howard Jones, *To the Webster-Ashburton Treaty: A Study in Anglo-American Relations, 1783-1843* (Chapel Hill: University of North Carolina Press, 1977); Kenneth R. Stevens, *Border Diplomacy: The Caroline and McLeod Affairs in Anglo-American-Canadian Relations, 1837-1842* (Tuscaloosa: University of Alabama Press, 1989); and Howard Jones and Donald A. Rakestraw, *Prologue to Manifest Destiny: Anglo-American Relations in the 1840s* (Wilmington, Del.: Scholarly Resources, 1997).

20. Totten to Gratiot, March 29, 1836, *ASPMA*, 6:391; Kenneth Bourne, *Britain and the Balance of Power in North America, 1815-1908* (Berkeley: University of California Press, 1967), 79, 118; Joseph M. Sweninger, "'A Lingering War Must Be Avoided': The Defense of the Northern Frontier, 1812-1871" (Ph.D. diss., Ohio State University, 1998), 156-157; Poinsett to WS, January 5, 1838, *MPP*, 4:1620; Worth to WS, February 9, 1839.

21. HB to RJ, December 6, 1838, in Francis Paul Prucha, ed., "Reports of General Brady on the Patriot War," *Canadian Historical Review* 31 (March 1950): 56-68 (all subsequent letters from HB are from this source, unless otherwise noted); Worth to WS, February 9, 1839.

22. Worth to WS, February 9, 1839; Kinsley to Kemble, February 2, 1838, Gouverneur Kemble Papers, USMA; Worth to Lt. Col. Benjamin K. Pierce, February 14, 1839. Kinsley was seeking reappointment to the army at this time.

23. Bourne, *Britain and the Balance of Power in North America*, 69; Fox to Sir John Harvey, November 30, 1837, and Lt. Gen. John Colborne, January 19, 1838, quoted in ibid., 81.

24. Ibid., 79, 89; AM to Poinsett, annual report communicated to Congress by the president December 4, 1837, House Executive Doc. 3, 25th Cong., 2nd sess.; Poinsett, "Report on the Protection of the Frontiers," January 9, 1838, Sen. Doc. 88, 25th Cong., 2nd sess.; Crane to RJ, March 18, 1839, enclosure to Col. James Bankhead to Crane, March 20, 1839, file B-147, reel 150, AGOLR. This reel contains the consolidated correspondence related to the Patriot war. All references to Jones as addressee are to the adjutant general.

25. Jesup to Poinsett, March 21, 1839, Letters Received by the Secretary of War: Confidential, RG 107, NA. There is a similar draft in the folder titled "Reading Notes"

in box 10, Thomas Sidney Jesup Papers, LC. Jesup had also authored a plan for the seizure of Halifax in 1812 (Jesup to Rep. Charles J. Ingersoll, May 20, 1845, Jesup Papers, LC).

26. An ex–Canadian official pointed out this zero-sum equation in absolute terms, much like those used by senior American policy makers who were afraid of British domination in Texas: the United States "would exclude British manufactures . . . take the cotton of the Southern States [for domestic production] . . . seduce to their shores English artisans, and soon . . . supplant many English fabrics in other Countries. . . . In fifty years, perhaps half that time, the United States would thus cause the downfall of Great Britain." See James Fitzgibbon, memorandum to the War Office, June 18, 1838, quoted in Bourne, *Britain and the Balance of Power in North America*, 56–57, 70. See also Lt. H. D. Fanshawe's reports to the Admiralty in late 1841 and Col. George Arthur (lieutenant governor of Upper Canada), "Memorandum upon the Defence of Canada" (circa September 1841), cited in ibid., 95, 113.

27. Harwood P. Hinton, "The Military Career of John Ellis Wool, 1812–1863" (Ph.D. diss., University of Wisconsin, 1960), 139–140. Both Corey, *The Crisis of 1830–1842*, and Stevens, *Border Diplomacy*, assert that American officials were totally unprepared for the onset of border strife or war. Corey states that "it is an open question . . . whether [Van Buren] or any of his advisers were acutely aware of the possible implications of the border troubles, or of the vast discontent there, or of the deep-lying sympathy of the border people for the Canadian rebel cause" in late 1837 (36, 46–47). However, the first of several strategic reconnaissances to evaluate American defenses and the vulnerabilities of Canada was actually put in motion at the initiative of Secretary of War Poinsett before the crisis began, when Macomb ordered Scott and Wool to inspect the northern borders in October 1837 (AM to WS, October 18, 1837, HQALS). See also the Private and Confidential Letters Sent by Major General Alexander Macomb, 1837–1841, Entry 6, RG 108, NA. Macomb's family was engaged in land speculation in northern New York, and he commanded the Fifth Military Department, headquartered at Detroit, between 1815 and 1821; see Allan S. Everest, *The Military Career of Alexander Macomb* (Plattsburgh, N.Y.: Clinton County Historical Association, 1989), 1, which is the only modern biography.

28. Brady's Letterbooks (Entry 56, RG 393, NA) provide abundant material on the Patriot conflict. Brady had served as a regiment commander for twenty-five years in 1837, but his first military service dated to a lieutenancy in Anthony Wayne's Legion in 1792. Wool began his military career as a captain in 1812, was brevetted for gallantry during the war, and emerged as an inspector general in 1816, a post he held until his promotion to brigadier in the line in 1841. His formal rank as inspector general was colonel; he had received a brevet promotion to brigadier general for ten years' service in 1826.

29. WS to Worth, December 12, 1837, cited in Charles Winslow Elliott, *Winfield Scott: The Soldier and the Man* (New York: Macmillan, 1937), 336n14; Worth to WS, January 11, 1838, Winfield Scott Papers, LC.

30. Clarke's toast quoted in "Tribute of Respect," *Bangor Republican*, reprinted

in *ANC 7* (October 4, 1838): 214; Capt. George Nauman to William H. Nauman, December 27, 1838, Nauman Family Papers, HSP.

31. Anderson to Kemble, January 12, 1839, Robert Anderson Papers, LC; Bourne, *Britain and the Balance of Power in North America*, 97; Worth to Secretary of War Poinsett, February 12, 1838. Stuart, *United States Expansionism*, and Gordon Stewart, *The American Response to Canada since 1776* (East Lansing: Michigan State University Press, 1992), 42–44, suggest the confusion of American attitudes toward and responses to the Patriot rebellions, which were commonly based on the American experiences of political revolution and independence rather than an understanding or acceptance of distinct Canadian perspectives. See Allan Greer, *The Patriots and the People: The Rebellion of 1837 in Rural Lower Canada* (Toronto: University of Toronto Press, 1993), and Joseph Schull, *Rebellion: The Rising in French Canada, 1837* (Toronto: Macmillan, 1971), for discussions of the French Canadian rebels. I have not found any other comments about the French Canadians or the possibility of expansion into Canada in officers' correspondence of this period. Stuart, *United States Expansionism*, 140–141, observes that "the French seemed unlikely recruits for republicanism" to anti-Catholic Anglo-Americans. (See my discussion of officers' reactions to Mexicans in chapter 12 for an analysis of their views on Catholicism, which depended largely on class rather than specifically religious factors.) See also Sydney F. Wise and Robert C. Brown, *Canada Views the United States: Nineteenth Century Political Attitudes* (Seattle: University of Washington Press, 1962).

32. Major (paymaster and volunteer aide-de-camp) Benjamin F[ranklin] Larned to Robert Anderson, April 23, 1839, Anderson Papers, LC; Col. James Bankhead, November 28 and December 8, file B-702, reel 150, AGOLR; WS to Poinsett, January 12, 1839, in C. P. Stacey, ed., "A Private Report of General Winfield Scott on the Border Situation in 1839," *Canadian Historical Review* 21 (December 1940): 412; Worth to Capt. William R. Montgomery, December 19, 1838 (and also to Abraham Eustis, November 10, 1838); HB to Jones, December 6, to WS, February 26, and to Jones, June 29, 1838.

33. HB to Jones, February 26, 1838, and Anderson to Kemble, January 12, 1839, Anderson Papers ("disorganizers"); Worth to WS, February 13, 1838, and March 21, 1839 ("agitators"); Worth to Poinsett, March 3, 1838, in Stacey, "Private Report of Scott," 408, ("miserable"); Lt. Col. (deputy quartermaster general) Henry Whiting to Robert Anderson, March 14, 1840, Anderson Papers ("unprincipled"); Worth to Jones, February 23, 1838 ("adventurers").

34. HB to Jones, June 8, 1838, and to WS, January 14, 1838; Worth to Lt. Col. Newman Clarke, November 1, 1838. See also Worth to Wool, February 14, 1838; HB to WS, December 8, 1838; and Bankhead to WS, March 26, 1839, file B-152, reel 150, AGOLR, regarding "disturbance of the peace."

35. Worth to WS, February 9, 1839, and to Poinsett, February 12, 1838; HB to Jones, June 27 and 8, 1838; Heiskell to Assistant Surgeon Benjamin King, January 18, 1838, Benjamin King Papers, LC. Robert Anderson also wrote of "the *patriot* fever" (Anderson to Kemble, January 12, 1839, Anderson Papers).

36. HB to WS, February 2 and 15, January 14 (see also Larned to Robert Anderson, April 23, 1839, Anderson Papers), and March 14, 1838; Worth to Poinsett, November 15, 1838 (accusing U.S. customs collector Stillwell as "one of the great offenders"), and to the British Officer Commanding at Kingston, November 23, 1838 (transmitting a petition from "gentlemen of the highest intelligence and respectability among our citizens" for clemency for some of the filibusters taken prisoner at the Battle of Windmill Point).

37. Whiting to Robert Anderson, March 14, 1840, and Anderson to Kemble, January 12, 1839, Anderson Papers; Worth to Abraham Eustis, November 20, 1838; Wool to Lt. Horace B. Sawyer, U.S. Navy, September 27, 1838, box 4, folder 10, John E. Wool Papers, NYSL; WS to Poinsett, January 12, 1839, in Stacey, "Private Report of Scott," 411. Brady also denounced the filibusters' "wicked threats" (HB to Jones, February 22, 1839). See also Corey, *The Crisis of 1830–1842*, chap. 6, and Stuart, *United States Expansionism*, 143. The Wool Papers contain an abundance of material on the Patriot war.

38. Worth to WS, February 20, 1838, and to Gov. William Marcy, March 5, 1838; Heiskell to Assistant Surgeon King, January 18, 26, and 31, 1838, King Papers, LC.

39. Corey, *The Crisis of 1830–1842*, 70, suggests that economic conditions during the Panic of 1837 and its aftermath were "the key to the discontent" among American borderers, and he notes that of the 140 named filibusters taken prisoner by the British near Windmill Point in November 1838, "practically every man was a laborer, dependent for the most part upon seasonal employment" (78). Sixty-five actually described themselves as "laborers," and only one as a "gentleman." Interestingly, Patriot leaders offered them $8 a month, virtually the same wages as a private in the U.S. Army at the time. Robert May has made some intriguing connections between these wage rates and other forms of compensation in his "Young American Males and Filibustering in the Age of Manifest Destiny: The United States Army as a Cultural Mirror," *JAH* 78 (December 1991): 874, 880. He argues that filibustering held the same emotional attractions as service in the army but offered greater material opportunities, which often drew deserters and discharged soldiers. See also Tom Chaffin, "'Sons of Washington': Narciso López, Filibustering, and U.S. Nationalism, 1848–1851," *JER* 15 (Spring 1995): 82. Duffy and Muller stress the social and psychological dimensions of the Patriot movement in *An Anxious Democracy*, observing that Vermont professionals almost uniformly opposed the movement because of fear of disorder, whereas many entrepreneurs supported it, even against their own financial interests (50). David A. Gerber, *The Making of American Pluralism: Buffalo, New York, 1825–1860* (Urbana: University of Illinois Press, 1989), does not discuss the border crises.

40. Lawrence Frederick Kohl, *The Politics of Individualism: Parties and the American Character in the Jacksonian Era* (New York: Oxford University Press, 1989); Daniel Walker Howe, *The Political Culture of the American Whigs* (Chicago: University of Chicago Press, 1979).

CHAPTER NINE: MAINTAINING NATIONAL SOVEREIGNTY AND KEEPING INTERNATIONAL PEACE

1. Worth to Capt. Giles Porter, February 17, 1839, Worth's Official Letterbook, LC (all subsequent citations to Worth's letters are from this source, unless otherwise noted); WS to Worth, February 12, 1838, Winfield Scott Papers, LC. See *MPP*, 4:1607, for Van Buren's request for a larger army with a larger staff; ibid., 1616, for Van Buren's request that Congress pass a stronger neutrality law; and ibid., 1698–1699, for his neutrality proclamations of January and December 1838.

2. Worth to WS, December 12, 1838, and to Capt. Williams Sandom of the Royal Navy, November 1, 1838; Albert Corey, *The Crisis of 1830–1842 in Canadian-American Relations* (New Haven, Conn.: Yale University Press, 1941), 98; Morris Miller to Mrs. Maria Miller, October 30, 1838, Morris Smith Miller Papers, USMA. Corey (75–76) suggests that estimates of 40,000 to 50,000 are more accurate than 200,000. I doubt the lower numbers as well, following the military historian's accustomed skepticism about reported troop strengths, given the difficulties of supplying such numbers.

3. WS to Poinsett, February 3, 1838, cited in Charles Winslow Elliott, *Winfield Scott: The Soldier and the Man* (New York: Macmillan, 1937), 339; Donald E. Graves, *Guns across the River: The Battle of the Windmill, 1838* (Toronto: Robin Brass, 2001), 35, 41–43; Ernest A. Cruikshank, "The Invasion of Navy Island in 1837–8," *Papers and Records of the Ontario Historical Society* 23 (1937): 7–84.

4. Corey, *The Crisis of 1830–1842*, 107; HB to WS, December 25, 1839, in Francis Paul Prucha, ed., "Reports of General Brady on the Patriot War," *Canadian Historical Review* 31 (March 1950): 56–68 (all subsequent letters from HB are from this source, unless otherwise noted); Arthur to Lt. Gen. John Colborne (commander and governor in chief of Canada), April 5, 1838, to J. F. Love, February 14, 1839, and to Ambassador Henry S. Fox, confidential, November 15, 1838, quoted in Kenneth Bourne, *Britain and the Balance of Power in North America, 1815–1908* (Berkeley: University of California Press, 1967), 80. See Kenneth R. Stevens, *Border Diplomacy: The Caroline and McLeod Affairs in Anglo-American-Canadian Relations, 1837–1842* (Tuscaloosa: University of Alabama Press, 1989), 58, 138–140, and WS to Poinsett, January 12, 1839, cited in C. P. Stacey, ed., "A Private Report of General Winfield Scott on the Border Situation in 1839," *Canadian Historical Review* 21 (December 1940): 412–414, for examples of retaliatory actions by the Canadians and British. See Worth to WS, February 13, 1838, to A. W. Rogers (recently acting U.S. district attorney), February 14, 1838 (marked "confidential"), and to Lt. Col. Benjamin K. Pierce, March 20, 1839, for his fears that the filibuster raids were intended to precipitate a conflict and would succeed. (See also Major Benjamin F. Larned, paymaster and volunteer aide-de-camp, to Robert Anderson, April 23, 1839, Robert Anderson Papers, LC.) Worth's 1838 letters to J. D. Vaux (a civilian, position unknown), March 3, to WS, December 12, to Eustis (undated, between December 12 and 19), and to John Hine, December 27, note his deployments to prevent retaliation or pursuit by British forces. A letter to the adjutant general (January 8, 1839) notes his dispositions to meet

the threat of Canadian irregulars, and one sent to Lt. Horace B. Sawyer, U.S. Navy, by Worth's acting assistant adjutant general (hereafter abbreviated AAAG), February 19, 1839 (also in Worth's Official Letterbook, LC, as are subsequent letters from Worth's AAAG), implies that any retaliation would come from them rather than regular "*Troops.*"

5. Worth to Poinsett, February 12, 1838, to Capt. William Montgomery, November 4, 1838, and to Lt. Homans, U.S. Navy, February 26, 1838.

6. See Corey, *The Crisis of 1830–1842*, 49n17, for Poinsett's instructions to Scott, which were relayed to the British.

7. Worth to Eustis, December 1838.

8. Wool, no addressee, January 16, 1838, box 4, folder 10, John Wool Papers, NYSL; Porter to Eustis, November or December 30, 1838, file P-270, enclosure to Eustis, January 1, 1839, file E-2, reel 150, AGOLR. See Matthew Warshauer, *Andrew Jackson and the Politics of Martial Law: Nationalism, Civil Liberties and Partisanship* (Knoxville: University of Tennessee Press, 2006), chap. 2, on denunciations of Andrew Jackson's 1814 declaration of martial law during the 1824 and 1828 elections, and chaps. 6–7 on the evolution of martial law and other wartime emergency measures, primarily after 1840. Military governors at Vincennes, Detroit, and Natchez during the 1790s enforced civilian law, not military law or the Articles of War, although the situation at Detroit was confused by the question of its fort, essentially a military reservation of the sort that often produced localized conflict between commanders and local inhabitants across the frontier. General James Wilkinson used military force to detain civilians (including a judge) without civil process or authority at New Orleans in 1806, to deny writs of habeas corpus, and to deport several civilians to Washington, but he did not attempt to try them himself, and his actions were rejected by an 1807 Supreme Court decision (Warshauer, *Andrew Jackson and the Politics of Martial Law*, 21). Reginald C. Stuart, *Civil-Military Relations during the War of 1812* (Santa Barbara, Calif.: Praeger Security International, 2009), asserts that "half-way martial law" was common between 1806 and 1815, usually taking the form of civilian officials (such as Jefferson during the embargo) employing military power to enforce civilian law. Although undesirable in principle, this aid to the civil power is not martial law in the usual sense of military courts or tribunals that apply their own rules of evidence and procedure, or in the sense of Jackson seizing power by unilaterally declaring martial law in New Orleans.

9. Worth to Capt. Giles Porter, February 17, 1839; WS, October 26, 1839, SWLS: C. Poinsett intended to have Van Buren seek a law authorizing preventative detention and deportation to the interior of the United States.

10. Corey, *The Crisis of 1830–1842*, 81; Mary Beacock Fryer, *Volunteers, Redcoats, Rebels, and Raiders: A Military History of the Rebellions in Upper Canada* (Toronto: Dundurn Press, 1987), 73, 91, 115; Graves, *Guns across the River*, 42–43, 69, 105.

11. Fryer, *Volunteers, Redcoats, Rebels, and Raiders*, 87; AM to Marcy, July 9, 1838, Macomb Family Papers, BHC; Capt. Justin Dimick to Capt. John H. Winder, November 7, 1838, enclosure to Eustis, file E-136, reel 150, AGOLR. See also HB to WS, February 26, 1838, to Poinsett, November 23, 1838, and to Jones, December 6, 1838.

The "simultaneous expedition" was probably not joint in the sense of patrols with soldiers of both nations; rather, each army searched the islands within its territory. Nevertheless, this was the first case of direct cooperation in international peacekeeping by U.S. forces since the joint patrols with Spanish detachments in the Louisiana Neutral Ground in 1810 and 1812. See also William L. Haskin, *The History of the First Regiment of Artillery: From Its Organization in 1821, to January 1st, 1876* (Portland, Me.: B. Thurston, 1879), 287–288, for an officer's report that British and American troops patrolled side by side along the border road north of Plattsburgh during the winter of 1838–1839, when their officers held sleigh races open to public viewing.

12. Harwood P. Hinton, "The Military Career of John Ellis Wool, 1812–1863" (Ph.D. diss., University of Wisconsin, 1960), 153–155; Eustis, November 8, 1838, file E-136, reel 150, AGOLR.

13. HB to WS, January 14, 1838, to Jones, February 10, June 27 and 29, and November 22, 1838, and to Poinsett, November 22 and 23, 1838; Wright, May 16, 1838, file W-227, reel 150, AGOLR.

14. Poinsett to WS, January 5, 1838, *MPP*, 4:1620; Worth to WS, February 15, 1838, to Jones, February 9, 1838, to HB, February 9, 1838, and to Lt. Homans, U.S. Navy, February 26, 1838; Worth's AAAG, Lt. James H. Prentiss, to Lt. Horace Sawyer, USN, February 19, 1839.

15. Worth to Capt. William Montgomery, November 4, 1838, to Capt. Joseph Bonnell, December 30, 1838, to Jones, March 21, 1839, and to Denny, April 9, 1839; Crane to Jones, March 18, 1839, enclosure to Col. James Bankhead to Crane, March 20, 1839, file B-147, reel 150, AGOLR; Eustis to Anderson, January 21, 1840, Anderson Papers.

16. Robert W. Coakley, *The Role of Federal Military Forces in Domestic Disorders, 1789–1878* (Washington, D.C.: Center of Military History, 1988), 117; Stanley S. Graham, "Life of the Enlisted Soldier on the Western Frontier, 1815–1845" (Ph.D. diss., North Texas University, 1972), 36–37; Frederick Marryat, *A Diary in America*, 2 vols. (London: Longman, 1839), 2:43; Henry Heiskell to Benjamin King, January 26, 1838, Benjamin King Papers, LC; Francis Paul Prucha, *The Sword of the Republic: The United States Army on the Frontier, 1783–1846* (New York: Macmillan, 1969), 318. See "Young American Males and Filibustering in the Age of Manifest Destiny: The United States Army as a Cultural Mirror," *JAH* 78 (December 1991): 857–886, for the opposite side of the coin, in which filibusters drew on army soldiers discharged after the Mexican War or in California during the 1850s.

17. Thomas Wilhelm, *History of the Eighth U.S. Infantry, from Its Organization, in 1838*, 2nd ed. (n.p.: Eighth Infantry Regiment, 1873), 10–17. Artillery officers often complained that infantry promotions were faster because there were fewer lieutenants to slow promotion by seniority than in artillery regiments. Thus, artillery officers were probably unhappy with the organization of the Eighth.

18. Worth to WS, February 9, 1839, and February 25, 1838, to Abraham Eustis, November 14 and 16, 1838, and to WS, April 10, 1839; Graves, *Guns across the River*, 43; Worth to Clarke, November 1, 1838.

19. WS, circular, April 15, 1839, Anderson Papers; Capt. William R. Montgomery to Eustis, November 9, 1838, enclosure to Eustis, November 9, 1838, file E-139, reel 150, AGOLR; Field to Capt. George Wright, May 16, 1838, enclosure to Wright, May 16, 1838, file W-227, reel 150, AGOLR; Worth to WS, February 25, 1838; Lt. James Prentiss to Lt. Col. Benjamin Pierce, January 23, 1839, transmitting Worth's instructions to communicate with the British. See also Worth to Wool, February 14, 1838, to WS, March 5, 1838, and to John Hine, December 27, 1838. For other examples of Worth's cooperation with the British military authorities, see his letters to WS, February 25 and March 5, 1838, to a British colonel Cameron, March 5, 1838, to Capt. Charles Thomas, March 9, 1838, and to Lt. Col. Newman Clarke, November 1, 1838. See Col. James Bankhead, November 28, 1838, file B-702, reel 150, AGOLR, for a discussion of intelligence gathering through paid and unpaid agents.

20. Lt. H. [probably either Francis or George] Taylor, Adjutant, to a Capt. Tuthill of the New York Volunteers, March 4, 1838, Worth Letterbook, LC; Worth to [British] Col. Cameron, March 5, 1838, and to Capt. Joseph Bonnell, December 30, 1838; Worth's AAAG to Montgomery, February 21, 1839.

21. Worth to a British Lt. Col. Taylor, March 19, 1839; British Major Richard P. Webb to Young, June 14 and May 1, 1838, and J. B. Van Schaick to Young, September 18, 1837, Nathaniel Young Papers, LC.

22. Worth to Eustis, November 14 and 16, 1838. See also Allan Macdonald, adjutant general of the New York militia, to Young, November 24, 1838, Young Papers, and Fryer, *Volunteers, Redcoats, Rebels, and Raiders*, 87–90.

23. Worth to [British] Col. Young, November 15, 1838, and to Eustis, November 20, 1838.

24. Worth to Eustis, November 20, 1838; Fryer, *Volunteers, Redcoats, Rebels, and Raiders*, 117.

25. Worth to British Officer Commanding at Kingston, November 23, 1838.

26. Worth to Sandom, November 22, 1838, and to McWhorter, November 23, 1838; Stevens, *Border Diplomacy*, 40. Worth's letter to McWhorter was published in *ANC* 8 (January 3, 1839): 6, along with the editorial from the *Kingston Chronicle* in his favor.

27. All secondary sources go back to Winfield Scott, *Memoirs of Lieut.-Gen. Winfield Scott, L.L.D., Written by Himself*, 2 vols. (New York: Sheldon, 1864), 1:313–316, regarding this incident. Scott warned the commanders of the British ships (placed to prevent Patriot movements) against firing on the *Barcelona*, but he did not inform them that he had chartered the ship himself. He did inform the local Canadian militia commander, a Colonel Hughes, that there were no rebels or contraband on the *Barcelona*, but his memoirs do not say that he told Hughes he had chartered the *Barcelona*. It may well be that Scott omitted this information from his memoirs because he thought it was a given, but he explicitly noted his communication about the absence of rebels or contraband. My interpretation is that Scott probably told Hughes he had chartered the vessel and expected Hughes to tell the ship commanders; this sense of a chain of command prevented him from communicating fully to all the Canadians

involved. I would attribute this to punctilio or error rather than anything "strange" (as Elliott, *Winfield Scott*, 341, puts it).

28. Stevens, *Border Diplomacy*, 21, 59.

29. Worth to Young, February 2, 1839, and to Porter, February 4, 1839. General Order No. 38 of September 18, 1838, is referred to in Worth's letters, though like many orders, it is not listed in the microfilm edition of General Orders and Circulars (M1094, RG 94, NA). Hugh Brady observed significant desertion occurring from each side of the river over the ice during the winter of 1839–1840. In one case, an American non-commissioned officer pursued a deserter into Canada; the local British commander did not object, but the lack of an international agreement for returning deserters prevented further action (HB to Major John L. Gardner, January 27, 1840, 7th Military Department, Letters Sent, Entry 56, RG 393, NA). Nor would the governor of Michigan extradite an American deserter from Canada, as one of Brady's subordinates seems to have arranged informally with a British officer (January 28, 1840, ibid.).

30. Wool's toast reported in "Respect to Gen. Wool," reprinted from the *Burlington Free Press* in *ANC* 6 (March 1, 1838): 131; HB to WS, March 14, 1838; Churchill diary entry, July 26, 1838, Journal 2, Sylvester Churchill Papers, LC.

31. Worth to WS, February 26, 1838, to Poinsett, March 3, 1838 (in Stacey, "Private Report of Scott," 408), to Eustis, November 10, 1838, to WS, March 10, 1839, and to "A. Bacon and other Gentlemen of Ogdensburg," November 17, 1838.

32. Gwynne to Worth, January 1, 1839, and Clarke to Worth, January 4, 1839, file C-29, reel 150, AGOLR.

33. WS to Poinsett, January 12, 1839, and Worth to Poinsett (private), December 25, 1838, in Stacey, "Private Report of Scott," 411, 409.

34. Worth to WS, February 19, 1838, to Nathaniel Benton, February 17, 1838, to Capt. William Montgomery, November 4, 1838, and to WS, February 17, 1838. See Capt. George Wright to Lt. George Field, May 13, 1838, enclosure in Wright, May 16, 1838, file W-227, reel 150, AGOLR, for an example of these offers of assistance to the civil authorities during Worth's absence.

35. Worth to Capt. Giles Porter, February 17, 1839, to Marcy, November 3, 1838, and to A. W. Rogers, February 14, 1838.

36. Corey, *The Crisis of 1830–1842*, 49n17; Worth to Rogers, "Confidential," February 14, 1838 (see also Worth to WS, February 19), and to WS, February 17 and 26, 1838.

37. Worth to Benton, February 17, 1838, to Garrow, February 17, 1838, and to Poinsett, November 15 and December 25, 1838; WS to Poinsett, December 16, 1838, in Stacey, "Private Report of Scott," 409; Hinton, "The Military Career of John Ellis Wool," 160. Other examples of Worth's criticism of civil officials can be found in his letters to WS, February 17, 1838, concerning the postmaster at Erie; to the Adjutant General of New York, January 7, 1839, concerning a state militia colonel; to U.S. Customs Collector George McWhorter, January 7, 1839, concerning that officer's collusion with the Patriots in permitting them to retake a cannon that Worth had seized; and to Capt. Porter, January 24, 1839, as well as letters from Worth's AAAG con-

cerning deputy U.S. customs collector Whittmore. Brady was more general in his comments; see his letters to WS, March 14, 1838, and to Jones, November 22 and December 6, 1838.

38. Graves, *Guns across the River*, 57; Duncan (unaddressed), January 2, 1839, Official Letterbook, James Duncan Papers, USMA.

39. Worth to WS, February 17 and 13, 1838, and to the Adjutant General of New York, January 7, 1839; Hinton, "The Military Career of John Ellis Wool," 147, 145, 156, 159; Eustis to Poinsett, November 17, 1838, file E-173, and Porter to Eustis, November or December 30, 1838, enclosure in Eustis, January 3, 1839, file E-2, reel 150, AGOLR.

40. HB to WS, February 15, 1838, and WS to Poinsett, December 15, 1838, in Stacey, "Private Report of Scott," 409–410; Worth to Jones, February 8, 1838, and to WS, February 17, 1838.

41. Worth to Jones, January 24, 1839; AAAG to Capt. George Wright, February 1, 1839; Worth to WS, March 21, 1839, and to Governor William Seward, March 28, 1839; Hinton, "The Military Career of John Ellis Wool," 143, 146–147, 156–157; Wool to Lt. Horace B. Sawyer, September 10 and 27, 1838, and to Col. William L. Stone (a New Jersey militia officer), September 13, 1838, box 4, folder 10, Wool Papers; Worth to WS, February 9, 1839. See also Graves, *Guns across the River*, 33, 46–47, regarding thefts of weapons from arsenals.

42. Wool to Platt, March 12 and 13, 1838, in Hinton, "The Military Career of John Ellis Wool," 158–160; WS to Poinsett, January 12, 1839, in Stacey, "Private Report of Scott," 411.

43. Worth to Jones, February 8, 1838, and to WS, April 10 and 17, 1839. Wool was also concerned with the militia's expense; see Hinton, "The Military Career of John Ellis Wool," 145. Worth displayed a similar impatience in Florida, where he ordered that civilians "who have made themselves obnoxious to the military" (for reasons unstated) be removed from the military reservation at Fort Brooke. See James M. Denham, "'Some Prefer the Seminoles': Violence and Disorder among Soldiers and Settlers in the Second Seminole War, 1835–1842," *FHQ* 70 (July 1991): 43, 45–47 (quotation from Worth, apparently published in the *Florida Sentinel* on October 31, 1843). Apart from Alexander Macomb, Worth is the only major senior army officer of this era to lack an analytical biography, even in dissertation form. Edward S. Wallace, *General William Jenkins Worth: Monterey's Forgotten Hero* (Dallas: Southern Methodist University Press, 1953), lacks both context and analysis. One reason for this, and for the absence of a monograph on Macomb, is the lack of personal papers, but the use of official correspondence from the National Archives, combined with letters to and from other officers in their personal papers, would enable scholars to write these studies.

44. Worth to Brig. Gen. King (adjutant general of New York), January 30, 1839 (asking that the volunteers be permitted to retain their arms as the municipal guard of Ogdensburg); Hinton, "The Military Career of John Ellis Wool," 150–155; HB to WS, January 6 and February 15, 1838, and to Poinsett, November 23, 1838; Worth to Gov. William Marcy, March 5, 1838, and to WS, February 15, 1838.

45. Worth, Order No. 12, March 3, 1838, Nathaniel Young Papers, LC.

46. Worth to Capt. William Montgomery, November 4, 1838, and to Nathaniel Benton, November 14, 1838 (concerning a Deputy Marshal Malcolm).

47. Worth to Bishop Perkins, February 21, 1839, to Lt. Col. Benjamin Pierce, April 10 and March 20, 1939, and to George McWhorter, January 7, 1839.

48. Worth to Poinsett, March 8, 1839, to Capt. Montgomery, November 4, 1838, to Bonnell, December 30, 1838, to WS, February 14, 1839, and to Messrs. Bacon, Hill, and Sherman (the trustees of Ogdensburg), March 9, 1839. His letter to Scott of March 10, 1839, repeated his concern for the discipline of the troops; see especially Worth to Capt. George Wright, February 14, 1839, in Wilhelm, *History of the Eighth U.S. Infantry*, 20. Letters to Lt. Col. Pierce (March 20 and 21, 1839) order the troop withdrawals, though the latter gave Pierce discretion in deciding whether to do so.

49. Worth to Jones, February 23, 1838 (see also Worth to WS, February 20, and to Gov. Marcy, March 5, 1838), to Pierce, March 21, 1839, and to WS, March 21 and April 10, 1839. Worth also expressed this belief in a letter to Governor Jenison of Vermont (April 17, 1839). The army's relations with local civilians had improved by 1841, albeit under a less rigid commander: at a banquet held in his honor, James Bankhead of the Second Artillery praised "the kind and friendly feelings that had subsisted between the citizens of Buffalo and the officers of the regiment under his command." See "Dinner to Col. J. Bankhead, U.S.A.," correspondence and article reprinted from the *Buffalo Journal* in *ANC* 12 (September 2, 1841): 273.

50. Worth to John Hine, December 27, 1838, and to Messrs. Bacon, Hill, and Sherman (the trustees of Ogdensburg), March 9, 1839; HB to Jones, June 8, 1838.

51. Bankhead to WS, March 26, 1839, file B-152, reel 150, AGOLR; WS, October 26, 1839, SWLS: C; Fryer, *Volunteers, Redcoats, Rebels, and Raiders*, 128.

52. Capt. Giles Porter to Eustis, November or December 30, 1838, file P-270, enclosure to Eustis, January 3, 1839, file E-2, reel 150, AGOLR.

53. Corey, *The Crisis of 1830–1842*, 115; Bourne, *Britain and the Balance of Power in North America*, 82, 85, 88–89 (Palmerston to Lord Landsdowne, April 25, 1840, on 85).

54. Andrew Stephenson to Van Buren, February 9, 1841, Martin Van Buren Papers, LC; Corey, *The Crisis of 1830–1842*, 130–133; Howard Jones and Donald A. Rakestraw, *Prologue to Manifest Destiny: Anglo-American Relations in the 1840s* (Wilmington, Del.: Scholarly Resources, 1997), 48–50, 55.

55. WS, August 23, 1841, SWLS: C; Wool to WS, September 24 and 29, 1841 ("Confidential"), and to Seward, October 1, 1841, box 54, Wool Papers. See also Capt. Robert Anderson, instructions to Lt. Horace Brooks, September 30, 1841, Anderson Papers, LC.

56. James Schureman to Mary Schureman, December 15, 1841, James Wall Schureman Papers, LC; Wool to WS, October 5, 11, 16, and 18, 1841, and to Crane, November 16, 1841, box 54, Wool Papers; WS to Monroe, July 8, 1841, Winfield Scott Papers, WLC; see also HB to WS, July 16 and 22, 1841, 7th Military Department, Letters Sent, Entry 56, RG 393, NA. Wool repeated his instruc-

tions for Crane to Brady on December 10; Jones and Rakestraw, *Prologue to Manifest Destiny*, 62.

57. Wool to WS, February 8, 1842, box 54, Wool Papers; HB to RJ, May 9, 1843, and to WS, June 7, 1843, 7th Military Department, Letters Sent, Entry 56, RG 393, NA. An entire generation of general officers and regimental commanders died during the following decade. Like Atkinson, brevet Brigadier General John R. Fenwick (commander of the Fourth Artillery and a significant player in the development of army tactical systems) died in 1842, after thirty-one years in the army and a previous twelve in the marines; Abraham Eustis died a year later, after thirty-five years' service. Stephen W. Kearny died of yellow fever in 1848, after thirty-six years' service; Edmund Gaines (after fifty years' service) and William Worth (thirty-six years) died the following year. Zachary Taylor (forty years' service) died of food poisoning in 1850, after ascending to the presidency. Brady died in 1851 at age eighty-three, after forty-four years of military service. He first entered the army in 1792 at age twenty-four, was disbanded in the reduction of 1796, recommissioned in 1799, disbanded in 1800, and gained his final commission in 1812, as colonel of the Twenty-second Infantry Regiment. Brady fought at Fallen Timbers, Chippewa, and Lundy's Lane, where he was severely wounded, and he served more than thirty years on the northern and northwestern frontier, largely at Detroit. Brooke entered the army in 1808, was brevetted twice for his gallantry at the siege of Fort Erie in 1814, where he was severely wounded, and served in Florida, on the northwest frontier, and against Mexico. Brooke died in San Antonio five weeks before Brady died in Detroit. Brevet Brigadier Matthew Arbuckle, commander of the Seventh Infantry, died the same year, after fifty-two years' service, and Colonel James Many (commander of the Third Infantry, though on extended sick leave) died in 1852, after nearly fifty-four years in the army. Adjutant General Roger Jones also died in 1852, three days after reaching forty years of army service. (He also served three years as a marine officer between 1809 and 1812.) Brevet Brigadier John DeBarth Walbach, commander of the Fourth Artillery after Fenwick's death, served in German armies from 1782 until 1796, entered the U.S. Army in 1799 or 1801 (the records are unclear), and died in service in 1857. Thomas Sidney Jesup died in 1860 after forty-two years' service, at which point only Wool, Scott, William Whistler (colonel of the Fourth Infantry Regiment), and William Gates (colonel of the Second Artillery) remained from the War of 1812 generation that had forged the professional army. Whistler retired in 1861 after sixty years' service, the longest in the army's history; the others retired in 1863. Gates was senior with fifty-seven years' service, and Scott served a mere fifty-five years.

Though these men (who averaged nearly forty-seven years of national military service) were too infirm for field duty, their actual duties usually involved diplomacy (federal, interagency, and international) and administration, areas in which their experience and connections increased their effectiveness over time—there was no need for them to chase Indians across the Plains or through the Florida swamps. This is pointed out not to deny the need for a system of retirement but to observe that there were few deployments large enough to demand officers of their rank during the 1850s—the younger dragoon and cavalry colonels could command those. Indeed, William S. Harney had been in the army thirty-seven years when he commanded an expedition against the Sioux in 1855, and Wool supervised the capture of Norfolk in 1862, his fiftieth year as an officer. Nor was Jesup incapable as quartermaster general, nor Scott as the strategist who devised the Anaconda Plan to strangle the Confederacy.

58. HB to RJ, December 21, 1843, HB to Capt. Robert E. Clary, June 17, 1844, and Brooke to RJ, August 29, 1844, 7th Military Department, Letters Sent, Entry 56, RG 393, NA.

59. Palmerston to Landsdowne, April 25, 1840, quoted in Bourne, *Britain and the Balance of Power in North America*, 85; Jones and Rakestraw, *Prologue to Manifest Destiny*, 14–15; J. Chris Arndt, "Maine in the Northeastern Boundary Controversy: States' Rights in Antebellum New England," *New England Quarterly* 62 (June 1989): 216–217. See Bourne, 88–89, 115, regarding British naval preparations on the lakes.

60. Jones and Rakestraw, *Prologue to Manifest Destiny*, 17; Arndt, "Maine in the Northeastern Boundary Controversy," 217; Michael D. Wagner, "'A Few Days Late in Coming': Major General Winfield Scott's Role in the Aroostook War," *Maine History* 34 (1995): 174–175. The February memorandum, along with the agreement Scott crafted, is in Edward D. Mansfield, *Life and Services of Winfield Scott* (New York: A. S. Barnes, 1852), 328–330, 338–340. The role of Scott's political connections is not clear. In his memoirs, which most students have taken at face value, the general attempted to project an image of nonpartisanship by claiming that neither Fairfield nor the Maine Whigs knew he was a Whig, which seems far-fetched if not absurd. One must remember that the egotistical general always portrayed himself in the best light, which often meant depicting others as less sophisticated naifs acting on Scott's lead. It is possible that partisan allegiances were not quite clear enough early in 1839 for us to be sure which party held the legislative majority; in any case, Whigs could more easily accept Scott's lead because he was a Whig, while Democrats could view him as a national representative of a Democratic administration, even though he was a Whig. All we can say for certain is that the Whigs trusted or came to trust Scott, and that Fairfield and the Democratic majority in the state legislature—and perhaps, in the back of his mind, Van Buren—were happy to have a Whig take the lead and provide cover for the state's retreat or in case the negotiations went sour. See Scott Kaufman and John A. Soares Jr., "'Sagacious beyond Praise'? Winfield Scott and Anglo-American-Canadian Border Diplomacy, 1837–1860," *DH* 30 (January 2006): 70.

61. Joseph M. Sweninger, "'A Lingering War Must Be Avoided': The Defense of the Northern Frontier, 1812–1871" (Ph.D. diss., Ohio State University, 1998), 137–138, 239; Eustis, May 7 and October 15, 1840, AGOLR.

62. Assistant Adjutant General Edmund Schriver to AM, December 26, 1838, *NASPMA*, 2:48; AM to Cass, "Statement of Fortifications in Maine," December 26, 1832, *ASPMA*, 5:127; Van R. Baker, ed., *The Websters: The Letters of an American Army Family in Peace & War, 1836–1853* (Kent, Ohio: Kent State University Press, 2000), 48; Capt. L[ucien] B. Webster to Lt. Col. B[enjamin] K. Pierce, March 13, 1843, reprinted in *ANC&SR* 1 (April 6, 1843): 407–409; Corey, *The Crisis of 1830–1842*, 151–153.

63. Haskin, *The History of the First Regiment of Artillery*, 73; Webster, November 5, 1841, AGOLR.

64. Hatheway to his sister Bet (Elizabeth), July 12, 1841, February 15 and October 16, 1842, and January 8 and July 3, 1843, in *Frontier Soldier: The Letters of Maj. John S. Hatheway, 1833–1853*, ed. Ted Van Arsdol (Vancouver, Wash.: Vancouver National Historic Reserve Trust, 1999), 50–51, 53–54, 56, 59; Eustis, September 4, 1841, SWLS.

65. Eustis to Anderson, March 14, 1840, Anderson Papers.

66. Philip Kearny to Anderson, January 10, 1841, Anderson Papers; SWK to his nephew Ravaud, February 24, 1842, in "A Group of Kearny Letters," *New Mexico Historical Review* 5 (January 1930): 26.

67. WS to Poinsett, January 12, 1839, and Poinsett to WS (Fox's remarks), December 15, 1838, in Stacey, "Private Report of Scott," 411. See William B. Skelton, *An American Profession of Arms: The Army Officer Corps, 1784–1861* (Lawrence: University Press of Kansas, 1992), 301–304, concerning officers' hostility to the Mormons and their autonomous government in Utah. Philip Kearny served as Macomb's aide-de-camp in November 1840 and as Scott's between December 1841 and April 1844. It is unclear when Scott made the remarks he referred to in his letter to Poinsett; the general spoke of doing so "last winter," which may have meant as far back as December 1837. Several senior officers noted Scott's rise to political prominence with interest. Lieutenant Colonel Henry Whiting observed that there was a "Scott meeting" in Detroit (Whiting to Anderson, March 14, 1840, Anderson Papers), and Eustis asked Anderson (then acting as Scott's aide) to "present me to him cordially, with the assurance that I am quite as much his friend now as I ever can be when he is President; as please God, he shall be one of these days" (Eustis to Anderson, January 21, 1840, Anderson Papers).

68. Anderson to Kemble, January 12, 1839, Anderson Papers. See Richard P. McCormick, "The Jacksonian Strategy," *JER* 10 (Spring 1990): 1–17, for a proposed synthesis of Jacksonian-era politics that stresses the parties' avoidance of sectional controversy as a means of preserving the Union. See Sam W. Haynes, *Unfinished Revolution: The Early American Republic in a British World* (Charlottesville: University Press of Virginia, 2011), for the most thorough examination of American Anglophobia between 1815 and 1846.

69. WS to Poinsett, January 12, 1839, in Stacey, "Private Report of Scott," 411.

70. See William B. Skelton, "Officers and Politicians: The Origins of Army Politics in the United States before the Civil War," *AFS* 6 (Fall 1979): 22–48; Skelton, *An American Profession of Arms*, chap. 15; and Samuel Watson, "What Do We Mean by Partisan? Army Officers and Politics during the Evolution of the Second Party System" (unpublished paper presented to the Southwestern Historical Association, April 1, 1999).

71. Skelton, *An American Profession of Arms*, 329, 330.

CHAPTER TEN: THE DILEMMAS OF SOVEREIGNTY AND EXPANSION

1. See John S. Galbraith, "The 'Turbulent Frontier' as a Factor in British Expansion," *Comparative Studies in Society and History* 2 (January 1960): 150–168; R. E. Robinson and J. A. Gallagher, *Africa and the Victorians: The Official Mind of Imperialism* (London: Macmillan, 1961); Bruce Vandervort, *Wars of Imperial Conquest in Africa, 1830–1914* (Bloomington: Indiana University Press, 1998); and Bruce Vandervort, *Indian Wars of Mexico, Canada, and the United States, 1812–1900* (London: Routledge, 2006), for the concepts of "imperial flux" or "flux on the peripheries" (of empire)—meaning turbulence in borderlands, particularly among nonstate, often tribal actors—drawing in imperial powers seeking order and stability (on their own imperial terms, of course). In nineteenth-century European colonial empires (e.g., the British, French, and Russian), aggressive military commanders "on the spot" often took advantage of such crises as opportunities for imperial expansion and personal aggrandizement. See A. S. Kanya-Forstner, *The Conquest of the Western Sudan: A Study in French Military Imperialism* (Cambridge: Cambridge University Press, 1969); Anthony Thrall Sullivan, *Thomas-Robert Bugeaud, France, and Algeria, 1784–1849: Politics, Power, and the Good Society* (Hamden, Conn.: Archon Books, 1983); C. M. Andrew and A. S. Kanya-Forstner, "Centre and Periphery in the Making of the Second French Empire, 1815–1920," *Journal of Imperial and Commonwealth History* 16, 3 (1988): 9–34; Benjamin Claude Brower, *A Desert Named Peace: The Violence of France's Empire in the Algerian Sahara, 1844–1902* (New York: Columbia University Press, 2009); J. A. deMoor and H. L. Wesseling, eds., *Imperialism and War: Essays on Colonial Wars in Asia and Africa* (Leiden, Netherlands: Brill, 1989); V. G. Kiernan, *Colonial Empires and Armies, 1815–1960* (Phoenix Mill, U.K.: Sutton Publishing, 1998); David Mackenzie, "Russian Expansion in Central Asia: St. Petersburg versus the Turkestan Generals," *Canadian Slavic Studies* 3 (1969): 286–311; Hew Strachan, *The Politics of the British Army* (Oxford: Clarendon Press, 1997); Ian Hernon, *Britain's Forgotten Wars: Colonial Campaigns of the 19th Century* (London: Sutton Publishing, 2003); H. T. Lambrick, *Sir Charles Napier and Sind* (Oxford: Clarendon Press, 1952); Robert A. Huttenback, *British Relations with the Sind, 1799–1843: An Anatomy of Imperialism* (Berkeley: University of California Press, 1962); Byron Farwell, *Eminent Victorian Soldiers: Seekers of Glory* (New York: W. W. Norton, 1985); and Graham Dawson, *Soldier Heroes: British Adventure, Empire, and the Imagining of Masculinities* (London: Routledge, 1994). For a contemporary critique, see Richard Cobden, *How Wars Are Got up in India: The Origin of the Burma War* (London: William and Frederick G. Cash, 1853).

2. Historians of the Comanche emphasize imperial flux, or "flux on the peripheries" of nation-states and empires, during the 1830s and 1840s, but I have seen little evidence, either in their works or in official U.S. government sources, that the rise of the Comanche altered or decisively influenced U.S. policy. The political push to protect the Santa Fe Trail began as that route was established during the mid-1820s;

the Regiment of Mounted Rangers and its successor, the First Dragoon Regiment, were formed as much to carry out operations in the arc between the Mississippi and Missouri Rivers, and in the Osage-Pawnee area west of Missouri and the Arkansas Territory, as for operations along the Santa Fe Trail. See the works by Smith, Weber, Delay, and Hämäläinen cited in note 5 below. Remarkably innovative, thought provoking, and wide ranging, these works demonstrate far more concern and policy action by Mexico than by the United States. This chapter shows both the extent and the limits of U.S. government response to the Comanche in the most potent dimension of U.S. power projection: operations by the national standing army. See Douglas C. Comer, *Ritual Ground: Bent's Old Fort, World Formation, and the Annexation of the American Southwest* (Berkeley: University of California Press, 1996), for a still wider perspective.

3. Douglas M. Astolfi, *Foundations of Destiny: A Foreign Policy of the Jacksonians, 1824–1837* (New York: Garland, 1989), 62; Ripley, Au[gust] 1823, no addressee, at www.tamu.edu/ccbn/dewitt/adp/archives/documents/ripley_emigrate.html.

4. David LaVere, *Contrary Neighbors: Southern Plains and Removed Indians in Indian Territory* (Norman: University of Oklahoma Press, 2000); Willard H. Rollings, *The Osage: An Ethnohistorical Study of Hegemony on the Prairie-Plains* (Columbia: University of Missouri Press, 1992); Louis F. Burns, *A History of the Osage People* (Tuscaloosa: University of Alabama Press, 2004); Edwin C. Bearss and Arrell M. Gibson, *Fort Smith: Little Gibraltar on the Arkansas* (Norman: University of Oklahoma Press, 1969). See Gary C. Anderson, *The Conquest of Texas: Ethnic Cleansing in the Promised Land, 1820–1875* (Norman: University of Oklahoma Press, 2005), for a detailed and insightful discussion of Texan Indian relations.

5. Dan Flores, "Bison Ecology and Bison Diplomacy: The Southern Plains from 1800 to 1850," *JAH* 78 (September 1991): 465–485; Andrew C. Isenberg, *The Destruction of the Bison: An Environmental History, 1750–1920* (Cambridge: Cambridge University Press, 2000); Pekka Hämäläinen, "The First Phase of Destruction: Killing the Southern Plains Buffalo, 1790–1840," *Great Plains Quarterly* 21 (Spring 2001): 101–114; Pekka Hämäläinen, "The Rise and Fall of Plains Indian Horse Cultures," *JAH* 90 (December 2003): 833–862; Ralph A. Smith, "The Comanche Bridge between Oklahoma and Mexico, 1843–1844," *COK* 39 (Spring 1961): 52–69; Ralph A. Smith, "Indians in American-Mexican Relations before the War of 1846," *Hispanic American Historical Review* 43 (February 1963): 34–64; David J. Weber, "American Westward Expansion and the Breakdown of Relations between *Pobladores* and '*Indios Bárbaros*' on Mexico's Far Northern Frontier, 1821–1846," *New Mexico Historical Review* 56 (July 1981): 221–238; Brian Delay, "Independent Indians and the U.S.-Mexican War," *AHR* 112 (February 2007): 36, 54, 57, 60–61; Brian Delay, "The Wider World of the Handsome Man: Southern Plains Indians Invade Mexico, 1830–1846," *JER* 27 (Spring 2007): 83–113; Brian Delay, *War of a Thousand Deserts: Indian Raids and the U.S.-Mexican War* (New Haven, Conn.: Yale University Press, 2008), especially chaps. 3, 5, 9, 10 and pp. 68, 170, 214–216; Pedro Santoni, *Mexicans at Arms: Puro Federalists and the Politics of War, 1845–1848* (Fort Worth: Texas

Christian University Press, 1996), 215–218. See also Pekka Hämäläinen, *The Comanche Empire* (New Haven, Conn.: Yale University Press, 2008), and Pekka Hämäläinen, "The Politics of Grass: European Expansion, Ecological Change, and Indigenous Power in the Southwest Borderlands," *WMQ* 67 (April 2010): 173–208. Though truly wide ranging and often brilliant in his analysis, Hämäläinen sometimes overreaches in his portrayal of Comanche power, particularly in relation to the United States.

6. Anderson, *The Conquest of Texas*. The Sioux and the Comanche also benefited from their mobility, which limited their exposure to the diseases brought by whites that devastated more sedentary, agriculturally based Indian societies. See Clyde W. Dollar, "The High Plains Smallpox Epidemic of 1837–38," *WHQ* 8 (January 1977): 15–38. For the expansionism, often loosely controlled by central or civilian authority, of European military commanders during the 1830s and 1840s and beyond, see the works cited in note 1 above, especially Kiernan, *Colonial Empires and Armies*, 68, 107, 109, and in note 1 to chapter 1.

7. Grant Foreman, *Indians and Pioneers: The Story of the American Southwest before 1830* (New Haven, Conn.: Yale University Press, 1930), 159–175; Harry F. Middleton Jr., "Frontier Outpost: A History of Fort Jesup, Louisiana, 1822–1846" (M.A. thesis, Louisiana State University, 1973), 11–17.

8. JCC to AJ, December 15, 1818, *ASPIA*, 2:704; Capt. Richard Easter (aide-de-camp) to commanding officer, 9th Military Department (Brigadier General Daniel Bissell, at St. Louis), January 5, 1819, Division of the South, Letters Sent, 1816–1821, Entry 72, RG 98, NA; Middleton, "Frontier Outpost," 25, 128; Major William Bradford, statement, March 25, 1824, *ASPIA*, 2:557; Lt. Richard Wash to Colonel Matthew Arbuckle, October 31, 1823, *TP*, 19:564–565.

9. Robert A. Wooster, "Military Strategy in the American West, 1815–1860" (M.A. thesis, Lamar University, 1979), 59–60; Francis Paul Prucha, *American Indian Policy in the Formative Years: The Indian Trade and Intercourse Acts, 1790–1834* (Cambridge, Mass.: Harvard University Press, 1962), 169; Brad Agnew, *Fort Gibson: Terminal on the Trail of Tears* (Norman: University of Oklahoma Press, 1980).

10. Foreman, *Indians and Pioneers*, 176–194, 203–204; Lt. Henry Smith to Adjutant General Charles J. Nourse, January 16, 1824, WDLS; Henry P. Beers, *The Western Military Frontier, 1815–1846* (1935; reprint, Philadelphia: Porcupine Press, 1975), 69; Arrell M. Gibson, *The Kickapoos: Lords of the Middle Border* (Norman: University of Oklahoma Press, 1963), 100.

11. Cummings to HA, April 8, 1825, and to Adjutant General Charles J. Nourse, April 28, 1825, *TP*, 20:30–34, 46–47; Foreman, *Indians and Pioneers*, 207–208.

12. EPG, March 11, 1823, file G-136, SWLR: Reg.

13. EPG to Many, March 2, 1823, and to the governor of Louisiana, March 24, 1826, WDLS. Captain George Birch conducted one such patrol in December 1824; see Birch journal, Birch Family Papers, HSP. Middleton, "Frontier Outpost," 110, suggests that there were daily patrols from Cantonment Jesup. If so, they could not have gone more than ten miles from the post, and there is no evidence of smaller patrol

bases deployed from Jesup, as was done during the later stages of the Second Seminole War. Middleton observes that these patrols achieved little success.

14. Calvin Reese, "The United States Army and the Indian: Low Plains Area, 1815–1854" (Ph.D. diss., University of Southern California, 1963), 149–153, 317–318; Foreman, *Indians and Pioneers*, 250–253; Middleton, "Frontier Outpost," 130; EPG to Brown, February 24, 1827, WDLS; EPG to ZT, March 1, 1827, quoted in K. Jack Bauer, *Zachary Taylor: Soldier, Planter, and Statesman of the Old Southwest* (Baton Rouge: Louisiana State University Press, 1985), 46; Brown to the commandant of Cantonments Towson, Jesup, and Gibson (Many), February 22, 1827, Brown Letterbooks, LC.

15. Hyde to RJ, November 17, 1828, *TP*, 20:784–785; Colquohoun to Major James Hook, February 24, 1829, HQALS. Hyde and Colquohoun were also accused of refusing to render aid to New York law enforcement officers, contrary to orders from their regimental commander Matthew Arbuckle, for the arrest of "Colonel" William King (a militiaman, not the former commander of the Fourth Infantry Regiment, who had died in 1826) in relation to the abduction and murder of William Morgan, an apostate Freemason (Arbuckle to commanding officer, Cantonment Towson, February 3, 1828, and attached statements, SWLR: Unreg).

16. Middleton, "Frontier Outpost," 9–12, 21–22, 27–29; Ripley, October 20, 1818, SWLS; EPG to Many, July 1827, WDLS. Middleton uses the spelling *Grey*; F. Todd Smith (see note 20) uses *Gray*, as do the army biographical dictionaries.

17. Middleton, "Frontier Outpost," 127–135; EPG to Many, November 14, 1830, WDLS; WS to Many, January 1828, cited in Middleton, "Frontier Outpost," 131.

18. EPG to the governor of Louisiana, March 24, 1826, WDLS; War Department Annual Report, December 8, 1829, *ASPMA*, 4:154; Secretary of War Eaton to Many, November 20, 1829, and AM to Secretary of the Treasury S. D. Ingham, April 2, 1830, HQALS.

19. AM to Eaton, November 12, 1831, and to SWK, January 14, 1831, HQALS.

20. Middleton, "Frontier Outpost," 135, 142–144; Many to Secretary of War Cass, January 6, 1835, in House Report 1035, 27th Cong., 2nd sess., 95–96; F. Todd Smith, *The Caddo Indians: Tribes at the Convergence of Empires, 1542–1854* (College Station: Texas A&M University Press, 1995), 117–122; F. Todd Smith, *From Dominance to Disappearance: The Indians of Texas and the Near Southwest, 1786–1859* (Lincoln: University of Nebraska Press, 2005), 147–153; Charles J. Kappler, comp., *Indian Affairs: Laws and Treaties*, 4 vols. (Washington, D.C.: Government Printing Office, 1903–1929), 2:432–434. Under the treaty, the Caddo were to leave the United States forever, presumably to enter Texas—a provision that violated the agreement the United States made with Mexico in 1831.

21. EPG to AJ, March 20, 1830, AGOLR.

22. Many, November 20, 1839, HQALS; Reese, "The United States Army and the Indian," 319–324.

23. Jubal Anderson Early to his father, November 8, 1835, Jubal Anderson Early Papers, LC. See Bruce Collins, "The Ideology of the Ante-bellum Northern Demo-

crats," *American Studies* 11 (April 1977): 103–112; John Ashworth, *"Agrarians" and "Aristocrats": Party Political Ideology in the United States, 1837–1846* (Atlantic Highlands, N.J.: Humanities Press, 1983); Lawrence Frederick Kohl, *The Politics of Individualism: Parties and the American Character in the Jacksonian Era* (New York: Oxford University Press, 1989); and Jean H. Baker, *Affairs of Party: The Political Culture of Northern Democrats in the Mid-Nineteenth Century* (Ithaca, N.Y.: Cornell University Press, 1983), for the Democratic worldview. See Thomas R. Hietala, *Manifest Design: Anxious Aggrandizement in Late Jacksonian America* (Ithaca, N.Y.: Cornell University Press, 1985), and John Higham, *From Boundlessness to Consolidation: The Transformation of American Culture, 1848–1860* (Ann Arbor, Mich.: William L. Clements Library, 1969), for explications of the themes observed in Early's letter; see also William H. Goetzmann's survey of American foreign policy, *When the Eagle Screamed: The Romantic Horizon in American Diplomacy, 1800–1860* (New York: John Wiley and Sons, 1966).

24. Paul N. Spellman, *Forgotten Texas Leader: Hugh McLeod and the Texan Santa Fe Expedition* (College Station: Texas A&M University Press, 1999); Bill Walraven and Marjorie K. Walraven, "The 'Sabine Chute': The U.S. Army and the Texas Revolution," *SWHQ* 107 (April 2004): 573–601. The Walravens suggest that Olwyn Trask was an officer who entered Texan service, but Trask is not present in the Army Register or other biographical sources. They also refer to Lieutenant George Wright, but the only regular officer of this name remained in service until after the Civil War. I refer to Americans entering Texas to support the rebellion against Mexican rule as filibusters, because that was their status under U.S. neutrality law and universal international custom: they were nonstate actors entering another country, with which their sovereign was at peace, without permission from the internationally recognized government of the polity they entered.

For another approach to determining the incidence of filibustering among regular officers, I sampled the antebellum officer corps, which totaled about 600 men in the early 1830s. I examined the Cullum biographical registers of Military Academy graduates for every fifth class of West Pointers—who made up 70 percent of the officer corps by 1836—beginning in 1820. The entries for the classes of 1820, 1825, and 1830 provide no evidence of filibustering. Phillip Roots Thompson, class of 1835, went to Nicaragua with William Walker after he was cashiered for misconduct (drunkenness and violence toward enlisted soldiers) in 1855. Of the 165 graduates in these four classes, only one, McLeod, went to Texas; counting Thompson, two filibustered at some point in their careers. Far more became engineers, lawyers, jurists, politicians, editors, educators, doctors, or businessmen. Far more served in the army for twenty, thirty, or forty years; served as volunteers under national command in the war with Mexico; were killed or mortally wounded in action in the army; or served against filibusters. About the same proportion that filibustered (1 percent) actually committed suicide. I then examined the Cullum registers for each Military Academy class between 1830 and 1839. Besides McLeod, George B. Crittenden (class of 1832), of the Kentucky political family, went to Texas after resigning in 1833; however, it is not clear whether he participated in the Texas Revolution, although he was captured in the 1841 expedition against Santa Fe. After being released, supposedly at Andrew Jackson's personal request, Crittenden reentered the army as a captain in the Regiment of Mounted Rifles in 1846, serving until he resigned to join the Confederacy in 1861; he resigned after repeated accusations of drunkenness and two battlefield defeats. His brother William L. Crittenden, an 1845 graduate, resigned in 1849 and filibustered to Cuba with Narciso Lopez, where he was captured and executed by Spanish authorities in 1851. Another former officer who went to Texas, after the United States recognized it as an independent nation, was Roswell W. Lee of Massachusetts, an 1833 graduate of West Point. Lee was cashiered for signing false statements in 1838, moved to Texas the following year, served in the Texas army and militia until 1861, and remained in the state until his death in 1873. Lee is notable as an example of those who used Texas as a refuge, seeking to start anew after dereliction or failure; he is also notable because he remained a nationalist, or a northern man, and did not serve in the Confederate rebellion against the constitutional government of the United States. See Mark E. Nackman, "Anglo-American Migrants to the West: Men of Broken Fortunes? The Case of Texas, 1821–1846," *WHQ* 5 (October 1974): 441–455, for this interpretation of motives for moving to Texas. Henderson Yoakum, who graduated from West Point in 1832 and resigned in 1833, served in the Tennessee militia along the Sabine in 1836, as a Tennessee volunteer in the Cherokee country in 1838, and as a Texan volunteer at Monterrey during the war with Mexico. He later became one of the first Anglo historians of Texas, but he did not move there until 1845 (see the *Handbook of Texas Online*).

There is no biographical source as detailed as the Cullum registers for officers who did not graduate from West Point, but they constituted a shrinking minority of the officer corps. Whichever methodology one uses, even allowing for the classes I did not sample and the officers commissioned directly from civilian life (mostly before 1821 and after 1835), the pattern is quite clear. See Robert E. May, "Young American Males and Filibustering in the Age of Manifest Destiny: The United States Army as a Cultural Mirror," *JAH* 78 (December 1991): 857–886, for a similar view of filibustering as a safety valve, both for soldiers and for American men, constrained by economic boom and bust and family domesticity, more generally; May emphasizes desertion by enlisted soldiers and de-emphasizes officer interest in filibustering in his book *Manifest Destiny's Underworld: Filibustering in Antebellum America* (Chapel Hill: University of North Carolina Press, 2002). See also see Amy S. Greenberg, *Manifest Manhood and the Antebellum American Empire* (Cambridge: Cambridge University Press, 2005), which does not discuss the army or its personnel apart from the war with Mexico.

25. Ethan Allen Hitchcock to his mother Mrs. Lucy Hitchcock, April 9, 1836, Ethan Allen Hitchcock Papers, Vermont Historical Society Collections, reprinted in "Ethan Allen Hitchcock and the Texas Rebellion: A Letter Home," ed. Marshall M. True, *Vermont History* 45 (Spring 1977): 104–105; W. A. Croffut, ed., *Fifty Years in Camp and Field: The Diary of Major-General Ethan Allen Hitchcock, U.S.A.* (New York: G. P. Putnam's Sons, 1909), chaps. 10, 16, 17. For further context, see William

G. Shade, "'The Most Delicate and Exiting Topics': Martin Van Buren, Slavery, and the Election of 1836," *JER* 18 (Fall 1998): 459–484; Michael A. Morrison, "Martin Van Buren, the Democracy, and the Partisan Politics of Texas Annexation," *JSH* 61 (November 1995): 695–724; Michael A. Morrison, "The Westward Curse of Empire: Texas Annexation and the American Whig Party," *JER* 10 (Summer 1990): 221–249; and John H. Schroeder, "Annexation or Independence: The Texas Issue in American Politics, 1836–1845," *SWHQ* 84 (October 1985): 137–164. Morrison stresses the value Whigs placed on international law and national faith.

26. Joseph Van Swearingen to Elizabeth Van Swearingen, January 6 and February 14, 1836, box 87, folder 14, Florida Manuscripts, P. K. Yonge Library, University of Florida.

27. Ibid., April 1 and 13, June 2 and 14, and September 29, 1836. Another Van Swearingen, a captain in the levies raised for Arthur St. Clair's expedition against the Ohio Indians, was killed in 1791. Four men named Swearingen from Ohio and Indiana served as captains and lieutenants in the War of 1812. Henry Van Swearingen was wounded in the capture of Fort George, Upper Canada, in 1813. James S. Swearingen entered U.S. service in 1803 and was mentioned in relation to the Burr conspiracy, but he gained a paymaster position in 1808 and rose to colonel as one of the quartermaster generals in 1814. *Philadelphia Aurora*, January 8, 1807; deposition of Surgeon David Davis, January 1, 1807, enclosure in James Wilkinson, January 8, 1807, SWLR: Unreg.

28. Jesup to Cass, February 15, 1836, *ASPMA*, 7:152–153; EPG to RJ, November 12, 1835, *ASPMA*, 6:146; Anderson, *The Conquest of Texas*, 111.

29. Swartwout to Many, June 12, 1835, Fort Jesup Letters Received, and Arbuckle and Vose to EPG, November 24, 1835, 2nd Military Department Letters Sent, 1834–1843, both in M1302, RG 393, NA; EPG to Cass, March 29, 1836, AGOLR. Anderson, *The Conquest of Texas*, 99, refers to Swartwout as Swartmont, but this is contrary to all army biographical sources. It is worth noting that Henry Leavenworth, commander of the Third Infantry Regiment between 1826 and 1834, was a New Yorker. New York was the most populous state and contributed a proportional number of officers to the national standing army.

30. EPG to Cass and to the governors of Louisiana, Mississippi, Alabama, and Tennessee, April 8, 1836, *ASPMA*, 6:419–420. Ibid., 416–427, contains the most relevant correspondence.

31. James W. Silver, *Edmund Pendleton Gaines: Frontier General* (Baton Rouge: Louisiana State University Press, 1949), 196–199; Bonnell to EPG, April 20, 1836, AGOLR; EPG to Cass, April 20, 1836, House Executive Doc. 351, 25th Cong., 2nd sess., 771–773; Cass to EPG, April 25, 1836, AGOLS, and May 12, 1836, House Executive Doc. 256, 24th Cong., 1st sess., 54–55; EPG to Santa Anna, April 25, 1836, John W. Gaines Papers, THS.

32. AM to Cass, April 25, 1836, *ASPMA*, 6:424; EPG to AJ, May 10, 1836, AGOLS; Cass to EPG, May 4, 1836, *ASPMA*, 6:420–421; EPG to Tennessee governor Newton Cannon, June 28, 1836, Gaines Papers, THS; EPG, orders, July 10,

1836, in M. L. Crimmins, ed., "Texas Items in the *Army and Navy Chronicle*, 1836," *SWHQ* 49 (January 1946): 393–394.

33. EPG to Arbuckle, August 10, 1836, Gaines Papers, THS; *ANC* 3 (September 8, 1836): 157; Riley to EPG, August 24, 1836, AGOLR; Beers, *The Western Military Frontier*, 156. It is important to account for the contrast between the rapid move to the Texas border and the months of delay in deploying significant regular forces on the Canadian frontier in the first half of 1838. Regiments were already present at Forts Gibson and Leavenworth, serving as the strategic reserve Jacob Brown had intended when the latter post was established, whereas the troops stationed at either end of the Canadian border could not be shifted to Detroit and the Niagara. The Second Infantry was deployed in Florida and at frontier outposts northwest of Detroit, and the artillery companies that had not been sent from Maine to Florida had to remain to protect the northeastern border from the British, or at least from civilian fears of British attack. Climate also played a major role: The winter of 1837–1838 was a campaign season in Florida, as Thomas Jesup launched what he hoped would be his final offensive. In contrast, the heat of the spring and summer of 1836 produced lulls in U.S. operations in Florida, and it proved easier to move large numbers of troops in the southwestern heat than the northern snow.

34. Silver, *Edmund Pendleton Gaines*, 204–210; EPG to Arbuckle, August 10 (first quotation), and to Cannon, August 28 (second quotation), 1836, Gaines Papers, THS.

35. Silver, *Edmund Pendleton Gaines*, 211–213; Whistler to Arbuckle, November 22, 1836, 2nd Military Department Letters Sent, 1834–1843, M1302, RG 393, NA; Jackson's order of November 12, 1836, was noted in *ASPMA*, 6:807. See Reese, "The United States Army and the Indian," 328–334, and Francis Paul Prucha, *The Sword of the Republic: The United States Army on the Frontier, 1783–1846* (New York: Macmillan, 1969), 307–311, for summaries of these operations.

36. EPG to Cannon, published in the *Nashville Whig*, September 11, 1840, in Silver, *Edmund Pendleton Gaines*, 160.

37. According to Walraven and Walraven, "The 'Sabine Chute,'" 575, desertions from units stationed on the border "rose markedly" in 1836. The authors suggest that deserters moving to Texas were not detained, but this would have been impossible once they crossed the border, whereas deserters remaining in the United States could be pursued and returned to service. They list forty-eight deserters from the Third Infantry and twenty-two from the Sixth Infantry whose names were also found on Texan military rosters; this was also true of forty-two men discharged from the Third Infantry and thirty-seven from that regiment who were neither discharged nor charged with desertion (in other words, those thirty-seven were off the rolls entirely—the most likely candidates for a corps of American military "volunteers"). Most damningly, they note that ninety-three soldiers of the Sixth Infantry deserted during the six months the regiment was stationed on the Sabine, from April to September 1836—a desertion rate of approximately 25 percent. This was tremendously high even for that era, when annual desertion rates were 10 to 20 percent. The authors also observe that nine

of the deserters were returned to the United States by Texan authorities, five to pay for muskets they had taken.

All this being said, the fact remains that there is no hard evidence that officers allowed enlisted men to go to Texas, as has sometimes been suggested. Desertion was difficult to prevent, especially near international borders; fighting for land and liberty (personal as well as Texan) in Texas was certainly more attractive than desertion within the United States, which was already common and often ended in unemployment. It may be intriguing to imagine officers sending soldiers as "volunteers" to Texas, but that is not how the army worked or how its officers thought. Officers wanted command and discipline, and they would hardly reinforce these goals by sending groups of soldiers, whom they rarely trusted as a class to begin with, to join a rebellion against a nation with which the United States was at peace, without officers to maintain discipline and order. If they did so, they could hardly expect the soldiers to return, which would create a fast track to the disintegration of the army on the frontier. All the hard evidence of officers' attitudes and behavior, on the Canadian, Florida, and Texas frontiers from 1783 through 1846, runs counter to this thesis.

38. EPG to Secretary Poinsett, May 22, 1837, HQALR. It is not clear whether Gaines sent this letter to Macomb for transmission to Poinsett first, but it was addressed to the secretary.

39. Belknap, April 7, Arbuckle, April 14, and Jesup, April 18, 1837, HQALS.

40. EPG to Poinsett, August 8 and 19, 1838, Gaines Papers, THS; Middleton, "Frontier Outpost," 137, 163–170; EPG to Poinsett, August 20, 1838, Many to RJ, August 16, 1838, and to Houston, August 17, 1838, Headquarters Army of the Southwestern Frontier Letters Sent, M1302, RG 393, NA. Amazingly, Many denied knowledge of the 1831 treaty requiring the United States and Mexico to prevent Indians on their territory from initiating hostilities in the neighboring nation; one almost suspects dishonesty, presumably because Many's back was up at Houston's demanding tone. Many did not serve on the Canadian border during the War of 1812, which probably accounts for his obscurity. Originally commissioned in the artillery, he was transferred to the infantry in 1821 to make room for more capable artillerists, while recognizing that he possessed some seniority and merit. He went on de facto disability leave soon after 1838 and remained colonel of the Third Infantry until his death in 1852.

41. Henry to Many, August 25, 1838, Headquarters Army of the Southwestern Frontier Letters Sent, M1302, RG 393, NA. Anderson, *The Conquest of Texas*, 166, suggests that this officer was William S. Harney, but Harney was the lieutenant colonel of the Second Dragoons and was stationed in Florida.

42. Arbuckle to RJ, September 25, 1838, in Anderson, *The Conquest of Texas*, 166; Vose to headquarters, Fort Gibson, November 1, 1838, 2nd Military Department Letters Received, M1302, RG 393, NA; Beers, *The Western Military Frontier*, 157–159; Smith, *The Caddo Indians*, 138–144; Mary W. Clarke, *Chief Bowles and the Texas Cherokees* (Norman: University of Oklahoma Press, 1971); Paul D. Lack, "The Cór-

dova Revolt," in *Tejano Journey, 1770–1850*, ed. Gerald E. Poyo (Austin: University of Texas Press, 1997), 89–110.

43. Reese, "The United States Army and the Indian," 335–337; Arbuckle to Texas ambassador Anson Jones, April 13, 1839, 2nd Military Department Letters Sent, 1834–1843, M1302, RG 393, NA.

CHAPTER ELEVEN: CAUTIOUS INTERVENTIONS
AND POWER PROJECTION

1. Ronald N. Satz, *American Indian Policy in the Jacksonian Era* (Lincoln: University of Nebraska Press, 1974), 229. See Thurman Wilkins, *Cherokee Tragedy: The Ridge Family and the Decimation of a People*, 2nd rev. ed. (Norman: University of Oklahoma Press, 1986); William G. McLoughlin, *After the Trail of Tears: The Cherokees' Struggle for Sovereignty, 1839–1880* (Chapel Hill: University of North Carolina Press, 1993), chap. 2; Stanley W. Hoig, *The Cherokees and Their Chiefs in the Wake of Empire* (Fayetteville: University of Arkansas Press, 1998), chap. 15; Brad Agnew, *Fort Gibson: Terminal on the Trail of Tears* (Norman: University of Oklahoma Press, 1980), chap. 13; Grant Foreman, *Advancing the Frontier, 1830–1860* (Norman: University of Oklahoma Press, 1933), chaps. 14, 15; and Grant Foreman, ed., *A Traveler in Indian Territory: The Journal of Ethan Allen Hitchcock, Late Major-General in the United States Army* (1930; reprint, Norman: University of Oklahoma Press, 1996).

2. Dale L. Morgan, *The West of William H. Ashley* (Denver: Old West Publishing, 1964), 258n26; Charles J. Kappler, comp., *Indian Affairs: Laws and Treaties*, 4 vols. (Washington, D.C.: Government Printing Office, 1903–1929), 2:258–260; Cummings to EPG, June 22, 1826, TP, 20:266–267; HA, December 9, 1828, HQALS. In 1825 civilian commissioners negotiated treaties with the Kansa (who had harassed the Missouri expedition in 1818–1819) and the Osage to open a road, authorized by Congress earlier that year, that became the Santa Fe Trail. The Indians agreed to permit travelers to pass unmolested for meager compensation: a one-time payment of $500 for the Kansa and $800 for the Osage (Kappler, *Indian Affairs*, 2:246–250).

3. Richard E. Jensen, "The Wright-Beauchamp Investigation and the Pawnee Threat of 1829," *Nebraska History* 79 (Fall 1998): 133–143; Wright to Capt. John Bliss, April 11, 1829, AGOLR.

4. Kappler, *Indian Affairs*, 2:416–418; George E. Hyde, *The Pawnee Indians* (Denver: University of Denver Press, 1951), chaps. 6, 7.

5. Stanley Noyes, *Los Comanches: The Horse People, 1751–1845* (Albuquerque: University of New Mexico Press, 1993), 115 ("generally favorable"), 207–213; HA, March 26, 1829, HQALS. The 1829 expedition is described in Philip St. George Cooke, *Scenes and Adventures in the Army, or, the Romance of Military Life* (Philadelphia: Lindsay and Blakiston, 1857), chaps. 6–12; Otis E. Young, *The West of Philip St. George Cooke, 1809–1895* (Glendale, Calif.: Arthur H. Clark, 1955), 31–52; and Otis E. Young, *The First Military Escort on the Santa Fe Trail, 1829, from the Journal and*

Reports of Major Bennet Riley and Lieutenant Philip St. George Cooke (Glendale, Calif.: Arthur H. Clark, 1952).

6. Pekka Hämäläinen, *The Comanche Empire* (New Haven, Conn.: Yale University Press, 2008), 145; Elizabeth Ann Harper, "The Taovayas Indians in Frontier Trade and Diplomacy, 1779–1835," *Panhandle-Plains Historical Review* 26 (1953): 61–65; Thomas W. Kavanaugh, *The Comanches: A History, 1706–1875* (Lincoln: University of Nebraska Press, 1996), 220; Colonel Henry Dodge, March 14, 1833, HQALS; Carolyn T. Foreman, "Colonel James B. Many, Commandant at Fort Gibson, Fort Towson, and Fort Smith," *COK* 19 (June 1941): 124–126.

7. Henry Leavenworth, February 19, 1834, HQALS; Lt. Thompson B. Wheelock, "Journal of Colonel Dodge's Expedition," *ASPMA*, 5:373–382; S. C. Stambaugh, "Expedition of the Dragoons to the West," August 26, 1834, reprinted in *Niles' Weekly Register* 47 (October 4, 1834): 1202. See also Young, *The West of Philip St. George Cooke*, 72–83; Noyes, *Los Comanches*, 138–141, 237–247; and Agnew, *Fort Gibson*, chap. 9.

8. Kappler, *Indian Affairs*, 2:435–439; Harper, "The Taovayas Indians in Frontier Trade and Diplomacy," 66–68; Stan Hoig, *White Man's Paper Trail: Grand Councils and Treaty-Making on the Central Plains* (Boulder: University of Colorado Press, 2006), 51–54; Grant Foreman, ed., "The Journal of the Proceedings at Our First Treaty with the Wild Indians, 1835," *COK* 14 (December 1936): 412; Stuart to Lt. Seawell, March 28, 1835, Letters Received from Fort Coffee, 1834–1838, M1302, RG 393, NA; Agnew, *Fort Gibson*, chap. 10.

9. "From the Dragoons," *Niles' Weekly Register* 49 (October 17, 1835): 1256; Lt. Gaines P. Kingsbury, 1835 expedition journal, *ASPMA*, 6:130–146; Louis Pelzer, ed., "Captain Ford's Journal of an Expedition to the Rocky Mountains," *MVHR* 12 (March 1926): 556–568.

10. Bradford, February 4 and March 28, 1819, files B-7 and B-286, and March 4, 1820, file B-178, SWLR: Reg. The Cherokee-Osage wars, and the army's efforts to keep the peace between them, are the largest conflict of the period not discussed at length here. See Grant Foreman, *Indians and Pioneers: The Story of the American Southwest before 1830* (New Haven, Conn.: Yale University Press, 1930), for the most extensive account of the Cherokee-Osage conflict.

11. David LaVere, *Contrary Neighbors: Southern Plains and Removed Indians in Indian Territory* (Norman: University of Oklahoma Press, 2000), 85; ZT to RJ, June 21, 1841, AGOLR; K. Jack Bauer, *Zachary Taylor: Soldier, Planter, Statesman of the Old Southwest* (Baton Rouge: Louisiana State University Press, 1985), 100–101; Jones to ZT, March 9, 1843, and ZT to Jones, March 29, 1843, cited in Brainerd Dyer, *Zachary Taylor* (Baton Rouge: Louisiana State University Press, 1946), 137; Arbuckle to AM, June 6, 1833, *ASPMA*, 7:984.

12. Whistler and Capt. John Stout to AM, September 30, 1837, *ASPMA*, 7:978–979. See also Col. Matthew Arbuckle to AM, June 6, 1833, *ASPMA*, 7:984; SWK, Smith, and Boone to Cass, December 11, 1836, *NASPMA*, 2:11–13; and Totten, Thayer, Talcott, and Cross to Secretary of War Poinsett, March 14, 1840, *NASPMA*, 2:136.

13. Whistler and Stout to AM, September 30, 1837, *ASPMA*, 7:978–980; Totten, Thayer, Talcott, and Cross to Poinsett, March 14, 1840, *NASPMA*, 2:136.

14. Kappler, *Indian Affairs*, 2:489–491; Satz, *American Indian Policy*, 221; LaVere, *Contrary Neighbors*, 79, 85–87; Aurora Hunt, *Major James Henry Carleton, 1814–1873: Western Frontier Dragoon* (Glendale, Calif.: Arthur H. Clark, 1958), 47–48; LaVere, *Contrary Neighbors*, 92, 96–97.

15. "Defence of the Frontier," *ANC&SR* 3 (April 25, 1844): 527; Major Ethan Allen Hitchcock to Secretary of War John C. Spencer, January 9, 1842, cited in Dyer, *Zachary Taylor*, 137–138; Calvin Reese, "The United States Army and the Indian: Low Plains Area, 1815–1854" (Ph.D. diss., University of Southern California, 1963), 148, 155–156.

16. Arrell M. Gibson, *The Kickapoos: Lords of the Middle Border* (Norman: University of Oklahoma Press, 1963), 160–165; Foreman, *Advancing the Frontier*, chaps. 4, 5; Henry P. Beers, *The Western Military Frontier, 1815–1846* (1935; reprint, Philadelphia: Porcupine Press, 1975), 139–140, 143–144. See Hitchcock to Secretary of War John C. Spencer, January 9, 1842, cited in Dyer, *Zachary Taylor*, 137–138, regarding Forts Wayne and Scott.

17. Hitchcock to Secretary of War John C. Spencer, March 20, 1842, Ethan Allen Hitchcock Papers, LC; Spencer to ZT, March 26, 1842, SWLS; ZT to RJ, December 23, 1842, and March 28, 1843, cited in Dyer, *Zachary Taylor*, 138–140; Foreman, *Advancing the Frontier*, chaps. 14, 15. See Joseph M. Nance, *After San Jacinto: The Texas-Mexican Frontier, 1836–1841* (Austin: University of Texas Press, 1963), and *Attack and Counterattack: The Texas-Mexican Frontier, 1842* (Austin: University of Texas Press, 1964), for narratives of the ongoing border strife and military preparations and expeditions.

18. Harry C. Myers, "Banditti on the Santa Fe Trail: The Texan Raids of 1843," *Kansas History* 19 (Winter 1986): 286–289; Young, *The West of Philip St. George Cooke*, 109–110.

19. W. Julian Fessler, ed., "Captain Nathan Boone's Journal," *COK* 7 (March 1929): 58–105; R. Douglas Hurt, *Nathan Boone and the American Frontier* (Columbia: University of Missouri Press, 1998), 197. See also Henry P. Beers, "Military Protection of the Santa Fe Trail to 1843," *New Mexico Historical Review* 12 (April 1937): 113–133, and Otis E. Young, "Dragoons on the Santa Fe Trail in the Autumn of 1843," *COK* 32 (Spring 1954): 42–51.

20. Cooke, June 15, 1843, in William E. Connelly, ed., "A Journal of the Santa Fe Trail," *MVHR* 12 (June 1925): 85–86.

21. Cooke, *Scenes and Adventures in the Army*, 248, 252–253.

22. Cooke, June 22, 1843, in Connelly, "A Journal of the Santa Fe Trail," 92, and June 30, 1843, ibid. (September 1925): 228–230.

23. Ibid., 230–235.

24. Ibid., 232–234.

25. Young, *The West of Philip St. George Cooke*, 41–52; Cooke, July 8, 13, and 21, September 15, and November 21, 1843, in Connelly, "A Journal of the Santa Fe

Trail," 232–234, 242, 246, 248, 251, 254–255. One might argue that Cooke expected Texas to join the United States, and this is why he thought banditry would end, but his opinions about the limits of domestic order and policing, cited above, suggest otherwise, especially given his view of the Texans' character. For the Texan perspective, see Snively's report in Sen. Doc. 1, 28th Cong., 2nd sess., 96–112, and the citations in Leo E. Oliva, *Soldiers on the Santa Fe Trail* (Norman: University of Oklahoma Press, 1967), 44–45.

26. EPG to ZT, July 27, 1843, *St. Louis Evening Gazette*, reprinted in *ANC&SR* 2 (August 17, 1843): 206–207. See William R. Manning, ed., *Diplomatic Correspondence of the United States: Inter-American Affairs, 1831–1860*, vol. 12, *Texas and Venezuela* (Washington, D.C.: Carnegie Endowment, 1939), 42, 58, 65–68, 298, 312–316, 332–338, for the relevant diplomatic exchanges.

27. EPG to Cooke, August 21, 1843, Cooke Family Papers, Virginia Historical Society.

28. SWK to Cooke, October 24 and November 29, 1843, ibid.

29. SWK, "Opinion of the Court," undated, but sent to Cooke October 25, 1844, ibid.; Burgwin to Abraham Johnston, July 27, 1843, Abraham Robinson Johnston Papers, USMA; Scott's report quoted in RJ to Cooke, April 26, 1844, and WS, unaddressed, March 1846, Cooke Family Papers. See also Jeffrey V. Pearson, "Philip St. George Cooke," in *Soldiers West: Military Biographies from the Western Frontier*, rev. ed., ed. Durwood Ball and Paul R. Hutton (Norman: University of Oklahoma Press, 2009). See Norma Lois Peterson, *The Presidencies of William Henry Harrison and John Tyler* (Lawrence: University Press of Kansas, 1989), chaps. 12, 13, regarding American policy toward Texas during the early 1840s; see Durwood Ball, *Army Regulars on the Western Frontier, 1848–1861* (Norman: University of Oklahoma Press, 2001), chap. 9, concerning Cooke's service in Kansas.

30. Wharton journal, published as "The Expedition of Major Clifton Wharton in 1844," *Collections of the Kansas State Historical Society* 16 (1925): 273, 275, 280, 283.

31. Ibid., 284–287, 291, 294–296, 303; [Lt.] James Henry Carleton, *The Prairie Logbooks: Dragoon Campaigns to the Pawnee Villages in 1844, and to the Rocky Mountains in 1845*, ed. Louis Pelzer (1943; reprint, Lincoln: University of Nebraska Press, 1983); Hurt, *Nathan Boone and the American Frontier*, 205–209.

32. Swords, August 7, 1843, and Turner, October 30 and February 11, 1845, to Lt. Abraham Robinson Johnston, Johnston Papers. See also Turner to Johnston, February 2, 1845, ibid.

33. Turner to Johnston, October 30, 1845, Johnston Papers; Cooke, *Scenes and Adventures in the Army*, 330–331; SWK to RJ, September 15, 1845, in Sen. Doc. 1, 29th Cong., 1st sess., 213; see also Hamilton Gardner, "Captain Philip St. George Cooke and the March of the 1st Dragoons to the Rocky Mountains in 1845," *Colorado Magazine* 30 (October 1953): 246–269. The dragoon expeditions of the mid-1840s are described in detail in Carleton, *The Prairie Logbooks*; see also Hunt, *Major James Henry Carleton*, and Adam Kane, "James Henry Carleton," in Ball and Hutton, *Soldiers West*.

34. Swords, August 18, 1845, and Turner, May 1846, to Johnston, Johnston Papers.

35. ZT to Houston and ZT to Capt. Lloyd Beall, both June 17, 1844, enclosed in Taylor, June 18 and July 15, 1844, AGOLR; Major Lorenzo Thomas (assistant adjutant general) to ZT, September 17, 1844, cited in Dyer, *Zachary Taylor*, 148, 150; ZT to Assistant Commissary General Joseph P. Taylor, January 29, 1845, Zachary Taylor Papers, LC.

36. Bancroft to ZT, June 15, 1845, Sen. Doc. 1, 29th Cong., 1st sess., 69–70; Richard W. Van Alstyne, "Empire in Mid-Passage, 1845–1867," in *From Colony to Empire: Essays in the History of American Foreign Relations*, ed. William Appleman Williams (New York: J. Wiley, 1972), 103, 109. See also Bauer, *Zachary Taylor*, 111–116; Michael A. Morrison, "The Westward Curse of Empire: Texas Annexation and the American Whig Party," *JER* 10 (Summer 1990): 221–249; and, more generally, David M. Pletcher, *The Diplomacy of Annexation: Texas, Oregon, and the Mexican War* (Columbia: University of Missouri Press, 1973), and William H. Goetzmann, *When the Eagle Screamed: The Romantic Horizon in American Diplomacy, 1800–1860* (New York: John Wiley and Sons, 1966).

37. Donelson to ZT, July 7, 1845, in Manning, *Diplomatic Correspondence of the United States*, 12:454–455; Polk to Robert Armstrong (U.S. consul, Liverpool), July 28, 1845, James K. Polk Papers, LC; Marcy to ZT, July 30 and August 23 and 30, 1845, House Executive Doc. 60, 30th Cong., 1st sess., 82–85; Polk diary entry, August 29, 1845, in *The Diary of James K. Polk, during His Presidency, 1845 to 1849*, ed. Milo M. Quaife (Chicago: A. C. McClurg, 1910), 1:8–9; Charles Sellers, *James K. Polk, Continentalist, 1843–1846* (Princeton, N.J.: Princeton University Press, 1966), 330. Piero Gleijeses, "A Brush with Mexico," *DH* 29 (April 2005): 247, observes that Polk's diary and personal papers are "equally opaque" about his intentions toward Mexico and that historians have placed too much reliance on Polk's diary, which is, after all, no more than a summary or précis.

38. Marcy to ZT, July 8, 1845, SWLS; ZT to Jones, October 4, 1845, House Executive Doc. 196, 29th Cong., 1st sess., 93–95; Marcy to ZT, October 16, 1845, ibid., 76–77; Assistant Quartermaster General Trueman Cross to Assistant Quartermaster General Henry Stanton, Sept. 10, 1845, cited in Bauer, *Zachary Taylor*, 121; ZT to Jones, November 7, 1845, and Marcy to ZT, January 13, 1846, House Executive Doc. 196, 29th Cong., 1st sess., 97, 77–78.

39. Samuel J. Watson, "Professionalism, Social Attitudes, and Civil-Military Accountability in the U.S. Army Officer Corps, 1815–1846" (Ph.D. diss., Rice University, 1996), 1288–1305, chap. 15; EPG to Senator Lewis F. Linn and Representative A. G. Harrison, August 14, 1837, *NASPMA*, 1:288; ZT to RJ, December 23, 1842, and March 28, 1843, cited in Dyer, *Zachary Taylor*, 138–140; Gene A. Smith, *Thomas Catesby Jones: Commodore of Manifest Destiny* (Annapolis, Md.: Naval Institute Press, 2000), chap. 6; H. T. Lambrick, *Sir Charles Napier and Sind* (Oxford: Clarendon Press, 1952); Byron Farwell, *Eminent Victorian Soldiers: Seekers of Glory* (New York: W. W. Norton, 1985), chap. 2; Robert A. Huttenback, *British Relations*

with the Sind, 1799–1843: An Anatomy of Imperialism (Berkeley: University of California Press, 1962).

40. Cass, annual report, November 21, 1831, *ASPMA*, 4:712.

41. EPG to Marcy, August 15, 1845, Sen. Doc. 378, 29th Cong., 2nd sess., 22–23; RJ to EPG, August 27, 1845, AGOLS; EPG to Jones, September 2, 1845, Sen. Doc. 378, 29th Cong., 2nd sess., 27–31; Marcy to EPG, September 13, 1845, AGOLS; EPG to Marcy, May 1, 1846, Sen. Doc. 378, 29th Cong., 2nd sess., 56–57. See Jones to EPG, May 29, 1844, AGOLS, for Scott's order on communications through the chain of command. General Order No. 40 of July 11, 1842, had eliminated the Eastern and Western Divisions, while increasing the seven departments reestablished in 1837 to nine. This had essentially reduced Gaines's command to that of a colonel without a regiment; though clearly a move by Scott against his enemy, it promised easier communications without the irascible Gaines acting as an intermediary. Gaines was popular in the Southwest, and the divisions were probably reestablished to give him a command suitable to his rank so that he could not complain of being passed over by Taylor (his junior) for command of the Corps of Observation.

42. Marcy to EPG, May 18 and June 2, 1846, Sen. Doc. 378, 29th Cong., 2nd sess., 51, 61; EPG to Marcy, May 21, 1846, AGOLR.

43. Gleijeses, "A Brush with Mexico"; EPG to Marcy, June 7, 1846, AGOLR.

44. EPG to Marcy, June 7, 1846, AGOLR; Quaife, *The Diary of James K. Polk*, 2:97–98; James W. Silver, *Edmund Pendleton Gaines: Frontier General* (Baton Rouge: Louisiana State University Press, 1949), 267–269.

CHAPTER TWELVE: MANIFEST DESTINY MEETS
MILITARY PROFESSIONALISM

1. Reginald C. Stuart, *United States Expansionism and British North America, 1775–1871* (Chapel Hill: University of North Carolina Press, 1988), 92–93; Barry to Duncan, April 3, 1846, James Duncan Papers, USMA. See Frederick Merk and Lois Bannister Merk, *The Monroe Doctrine and American Expansionism, 1843–1849* (New York: Alfred A. Knopf, 1966), chap. 4; Frederick Merk and Lois Bannister Merk, *Albert Gallatin and the Oregon Problem: A Study in Anglo-American Diplomacy* (Cambridge, Mass.: Harvard University Press, 1950); and Frederick Merk and Lois Bannister Merk, *The Oregon Question: Essays in Anglo-American Diplomacy and Politics* (Cambridge, Mass.: Harvard University Press, 1967), concerning Oregon. Douglas M. Astolfi, *Foundations of Destiny: A Foreign Policy of the Jacksonians, 1824–1837* (New York: Garland, 1989), chap. 7, narrates the antecedents of the Oregon conflict during the 1820s and 1830s. Melvin Clay Jacobs, *Winning Oregon: A Study of an Expansionist Movement* (Caldwell, Idaho: Caxton Printers, 1938), chaps. 4, 5, discusses the congressional debates, mostly of the 1840s. Merk and Merk, *The Monroe Doctrine and American Expansionism*, chap. 5, covers British activities concerning California; see Wilbur D. Jones, *The American Problem in British Diplomacy, 1841–1861* (Athens:

University of Georgia Press, 1974), and Kenneth Bourne, *Britain and the Balance of Power in North America, 1815–1908* (Berkeley: University of California Press, 1967), concerning British policy toward Texas and Oregon between 1842 and 1846.

See editor John Jones in the *Daily Madisonian* (President Tyler's house organ), March 14, 1842, and Rep. Chesselden Ellis in the *Congressional Globe*, January 25, 1845, 28th Cong., 2nd sess., cited in Thomas R. Hietala, *Manifest Design: Anxious Aggrandizement in Late Jacksonian America* (Ithaca, N.Y.: Cornell University Press, 1985), 64, 67, 98, for examples of civilian expansionists who expected to coerce Britain by threatening to withhold American exports and an example of the expansionist belief that Britain had been weakened by the social turmoil of industrialization. The Polk administration apparently shared some of this confidence; see ibid., 75. For a more general context on American expansionism during the 1840s, see Charles Sellers, *James K. Polk, Continentalist, 1843–1846* (Princeton, N.J.: Princeton University Press, 1966); Norman A. Graebner, *Empire on the Pacific: A Study in American Continental Expansion* (New York: Ronald Press, 1955), which emphasizes California; William H. Goetzmann, *When the Eagle Screamed: The Romantic Horizon in American Diplomacy, 1800–1860* (New York: John Wiley and Sons, 1966); Frederick Merk and Lois Bannister Merk, *Fruits of Propaganda in the Tyler Administration* (Cambridge, Mass.: Harvard University Press, 1971); Edward P. Crapol, *John Tyler: The Accidental President* (Chapel Hill: University of North Carolina Press, 2006); and David M. Pletcher, *The Diplomacy of Annexation: Texas, Oregon, and the Mexican War* (Columbia: University of Missouri Press, 1973).

2. Hunt to Duncan, March 17, 1844, Duncan Papers, USMA; Turner to Lt. Abraham Johnston, October 30, 1844 (quotation) and May 1846, Abraham Robinson Johnston Papers, USMA. See Sam W. Haynes, *Unfinished Revolution: The Early American Republic in a British World* (Charlottesville: University Press of Virginia, 2011), for the most comprehensive examination of American Anglophobia between 1815 and 1846.

3. William B. Skelton, *An American Profession of Arms: The Army Officer Corps, 1784–1861* (Lawrence: University Press of Kansas, 1992), 328–329, 339; Bliss to Lt. Col. Ethan Allen Hitchcock, May 18, 1845, Ethan Allen Hitchcock Papers, LC; Thayer to J. R. Chadbourne, June 28, 1846, Sylvanus Thayer Papers, USMA.

4. "The Battle of Plattsburgh," *Plattsburgh Republican*, reprinted in *ANC&SR* 2 (October 5, 1843): 433–442 (quotations from 434 and 436–437). See also Lt. Col. Newman S. Clarke's toast quoted in "Tribute of Respect," *Bangor Republican*, reprinted in *ANC* 7 (October 4, 1838): 214.

5. Secretary of War William L. Marcy, January 2, 1846, HQALS; William T. Dutton to his cousin and fiancée Lucy Matthews, January 27, 1846, William Dutton Papers, USMA.

6. Allen to Thomas Berryman (a civilian friend), August 3, 1845, Robert Allen Papers, USMA; Beauregard to Webster [probably Capt. Lucien B. Webster], September 15, 1845, and to Col. Joseph Totten, May 14, 1846, P. G. T. Beauregard Papers, LC.

7. Sherman to Ellen Ewing (his future wife), September 17, 1844, and June 9, 1845, in *Home Letters of General Sherman*, ed. M. A. DeWolfe Howe (New York:

Charles Scribner's Sons, 1909), 26, 29; Meade to his wife Margaretta, January 10 and February 24, 1846, in *The Life and Letters of George Gordon Meade, Major-General United States Army*, ed. George Gordon Meade (New York: Scribner's, 1913), 1:44, 49; Capt. Ephraim Kirby Smith (brother of Edmund Kirby Smith) to his wife, April 19, 1846, in *To Mexico with Scott: Letters of Captain E. Kirby Smith to His Wife*, ed. Emma Jerome Blackwood (Cambridge, Mass.: Harvard University Press, 1917), 37. (The name of Smith's wife is not given therein.)

See Merk and Merk, *The Monroe Doctrine and American Expansionism*, chaps. 2, 3, regarding European efforts to keep the United States and Texas apart, and chap. 7, concerning the possibility of European intervention during the war, which the authors show was minimal. See also Lester D. Langley, *The Struggle for the American Mediterranean: United States–European Rivalry in the Gulf-Caribbean, 1776–1904* (Athens: University of Georgia Press, 1976), chap. 3, concerning the Anglo-American diplomatic rivalry over Texas. Richard W. Van Alstyne, "Empire in Mid-Passage, 1845–1867," in *From Colony to Empire: Essays in the History of American Foreign Relations*, ed. William Appleman Williams (New York: J. Wiley, 1972), 101, notes that Mexican confidence increased as tensions over Oregon grew and suggests that a Mexican invasion threat in the fall of 1844 was intended to force Texas into the arms of Britain to prevent its annexation by the United States (103). See Hietala, *Manifest Design*, 205–207, for expansionist hopes that Britain would be intimidated by the American performance in Mexico. Ronald Hyam, *Britain's Imperial Century, 1815–1914: A Study of Empire and Expansion* (New York: Palgrave Macmillan, 2002), 14, suggests that Britain's greatest foreign policy concerns during the nineteenth century were the growing power of the United States and Russia; he observes (following Bourne, *Britain and the Balance of Power in North America*) that British policy makers feared the U.S. threat to Canada and, in effect, chose to avoid conflict (ibid., 64, 69, 231–235). In this interpretation, the Oregon compromise represented "a colossal if not final blow to any British attempt to establish a balance of power in North America" (ibid., 64–65).

Scholars studying British naval power tend to be less pessimistic about British prospects, given the weakness of American coastal defenses despite the fortifications system. See C. J. Bartlett, *Great Britain and Seapower, 1815–1853* (Oxford: Clarendon Press, 1963); Howard Fuller, *Clad in Iron: The American Civil War and the Challenge of British Naval Power* (Westport, Conn.: Praeger Security International, 2008); and Samuel J. Watson, "Knowledge, Interest, and the Limits of Military Professionalism: The Discourse on American Coastal Defense, 1815–1860," *War in History* 5 (Fall 1998): 280–307. Mark A. Smith, *Engineering Security: The Corps of Engineers and Third System Defense Policy, 1815–1861* (Tuscaloosa: University of Alabama Press, 2009), argues that American coastal fortifications were technologically capable of effective resistance, but my article notes the lack of artillery and trained artillerymen in most American fortifications, which would have required months to remedy.

8. Skelton, *An American Profession of Arms*, 294; Lt. Napoleon Jackson Tecumseh Dana to his wife Sue, November 1, 1845, in *Monterrey Is Ours! The Mexican War*

Letters of Lieutenant Dana, 1845–1847, ed. Robert H. Ferrell (Lexington: University Press of Kentucky, 1990), 29. The only exception to this historiographical consensus seems to be Ronald Spiller, "From Hero to Leader: The Development of Nineteenth Century American Military Leadership" (Ph.D. diss., Texas A&M University, 1993), 44, 129. See Thomas Bangs Thorpe, *Our Army on the Rio Grande* (Philadelphia: Carey and Hart, 1846), for an extended contemporary account; Edward J. Nichols, *Zach Taylor's Little Army* (Garden City, N.Y.: Doubleday, 1963), for a popular narrative; and Samuel J. Watson, "Manifest Destiny and Military Professionalism: A New Perspective on Junior U.S. Army Officers' Attitudes toward War with Mexico, 1844–1846," *SWHQ* 99 (April 1996): 466–498, for an analysis, although my emphasis on officers' quest for personal comfort, and their apparent lack of interest in their opponents or the international situation, now seems a bit overdrawn because, as a graduate student, I tended to seek contrasts (perhaps more than connections) between my work and that of William Skelton.

9. Skelton, *An American Profession of Arms*, 131. The article in question is "Of Popular Prejudices against Military Establishments," *MNM* 1 (July 1833): 292–303. See also Major William Chase, March 10, 1845, article from an unidentified newspaper, in Henry Halleck, "Military Note Book," Henry Halleck Papers, LC. The outstanding exception to this lack of discussion was [brevet Second Lt. Daniel H. Hill], "The Army in Texas," *Southern Quarterly Review* 9 (April 1846): 434–457, later supplemented by [Hill], "The Army in Texas—No. 2," *Southern Quarterly Review* 14 (July 1848): 183–197, but these articles were devoted almost exclusively to attacking the staff bureaus and the government for providing inadequate logistical support to the Army of Occupation. Hill's primary theme was that parsimony had precluded preparedness, but neither American aims nor the enemy were discussed.

10. Skelton, *An American Profession of Arms*, 330. See John C. Pinheiro, *Manifest Ambition: James K. Polk and Civil-Military Relations during the Mexican War* (Westport, Conn.: Praeger Security International, 2007), and Richard Bruce Winders, *Mr. Polk's Army: The American Military Experience in the Mexican War* (College Station: Texas A&M University Press, 1997), for Polk's perspective. Pinheiro maintains that the principal threats to American victory were atrocities (largely by volunteer citizen-soldiers) that might have stirred up a popular insurgency, or an overly harsh military government doing so; the danger of disobedient officers disrupting policy; and Polk's partisanship, which culminated in undermining Winfield Scott after Polk was unable to secure Senate approval to appoint Thomas Hart Benton over the army's commanding general. Admitting the effectiveness of American military government in Mexico (including substantial restraint and some punishment of soldier depredations and atrocities) and, tacitly, that few officers were actually disobedient (or could be faulted for using their discretion, as Scott so effectively did in pursuing a peace treaty), Pinheiro ultimately concludes that the majority of civil-military friction during the war with Mexico was due to Polk's ideological fervor, partisanship, and personal intensity. These qualities combined to produce paranoia and micromanagement, threatening to disrupt or destroy the negotiations that eventually produced peace.

The proof lies in the facts of execution, not in the assumptions and blinders of Polk's ideology: if "Young Hickory" was truly fearful of military tyranny, military partisanship, or Whig gains from the war, why did he not send some of the many Democratic politicians with administrative or executive experience to serve as civilian governors for the occupied territories? (Of course, that may have been unfeasible because their actual administrative experience was rather limited, particularly in comparison to that of veteran army officers.) Pinheiro shows that the American military government was both principled and effective; while ideologues anticipated tyranny, the reality on the ground was dutiful execution and as much restraint as could be expected. (The exception was John C. Frémont, a Democratic partisan commissioned directly from civilian life due to his father-in-law's influence.) Though Pinheiro faults Zachary Taylor for making an armistice at Monterrey, the general was following administration policy: secure northern Mexico, then negotiate. Trying to pursue the Mexicans and advance overland from Monterrey to Mexico City would have caused the U.S. Army heavy casualties (as it had caused the Mexican army when Santa Anna advanced from central Mexico to Buena Vista), and doing so was unnecessary, given American amphibious capabilities.

Despite, or perhaps in tune with, his historical reputation as a strong executive and a capable strategist, Polk consistently condemned Taylor and Scott whether they used their initiative or held back to avoid criticism, making already tough situations more difficult for his generals, repeatedly and unnecessarily. Perhaps Polk somehow understood the abstractions of military strategy better than Winfield Scott, but Taylor and Scott, supported by veteran staff officers, certainly had as much diplomatic and logistical experience as the president, and the complexity and contingency of events required a degree of autonomy in policy implementation that even the most brilliant president could not manage from thousands of miles away. Fortunately, Polk ultimately accepted his generals' efforts, which achieved his objectives at remarkably little cost.

11. Worth to Surgeon General Thomas Lawson, November 1, 1845, Thomas Lawson Papers, LC. Note that Lawson had come to oppose the expropriation of the Seminoles, so it is possible that he opposed expansion and was engaged in an argument with Worth. See John S. D. Eisenhower, *So Far from God: The U.S. War with Mexico, 1846–1848* (New York: Random House, 1989), 50–51, on the lack of naval support, which Taylor felt was necessary to escort his unarmed supply and reconnaissance vessels. Taylor had 285 supply wagons in September and 307 six months later, for a force of 3,550 men. The siege train and staff traveled by sea to Port Isabel. See Assistant Quartermaster General Cross to Assistant Quartermaster General Stanton, September 10, 1845, cited in K. Jack Bauer, *Zachary Taylor: Soldier, Planter, and Statesman of the Old Southwest* (Baton Rouge: Louisiana State University Press, 1985), 121, and ZT to RJ, March 8, 1846, House Executive Doc. 60, 30th Cong., 1st sess., 118–119.

12. Meade to Margaretta Meade, September 18, 1845, in *Life and Letters of George Gordon Meade*, 26; Hitchcock, diary entries for September 8 and 20 and November 2, 1845, in *Fifty Years in Camp and Field: The Diary of Major-General Ethan Allen Hitchcock, U.S.A.*, ed. W. A. Croffut (New York: G. P. Putnam's Sons, 1909),

200–203; Edward B. Hunt, "Army Attack and National Defense," *American Whig Review* 4 (August 1846): 147. Holman Hamilton, *Zachary Taylor: Soldier of the Republic* (Indianapolis: Bobbs-Merrill, 1941), 167, reports that Taylor's thoughts of retirement were common gossip in the Army of Occupation. Skelton, *An American Profession of Arms*, 330, 332, gives several examples of officers who opposed the war on moral grounds, including Meade, Hitchcock, and Ephraim Kirby Smith, though he rightly points out that these were exceptions and that each of these officers hoped to see combat once war was certain. See William Tecumseh Sherman to Ellen Ewing, September 17, 1844, and June 9, 1845, in *Home Letters of General Sherman*, 27, for an explicit statement of Whig partisan preference combined with dedication to public neutrality.

13. Ulysses S. Grant, *Memoirs and Selected Letters: Personal Memoirs of U.S. Grant, Selected Letters, 1839–1865* (New York: Library of America, 1990), 4.

14. DeHart to Capt. Charles F. Smith, January 6, 1846, Charles Ferguson Smith Papers, USMA. See Hietala, *Manifest Design*, 205, for examples of congressional Democrats who spoke of war as a moral good (at least in the context of opportunities for territorial expansion) that would reenergize a society grown soft; see also John H. Schroeder, "Annexation or Independence: The Texas Issue in American Politics, 1836–1845," *SWHQ* 84 (October 1985): 137–164. Skelton, *An American Profession of Arms*, offers only one citation (340) of an officer from the Mexican War era who directly advocated war as a means of national unification: Lt. John J. Peck, October 31, 1845, cited in Richard F. Pourade, ed., *The Sign of the Eagle: A View of Mexico—1830 to 1855* (San Diego: Union-Tribune Publishing, 1970), 7–9. I have found several others, but all are from 1838 to 1842 and regarding Britain. See Charles Royster, "Founding a Nation in Blood: Military Conflict and American Nationality," in *Arms and Independence: The Military Character of the American Revolution*, ed. Ronald Hoffman and Peter J. Albert (Charlottesville: University Press of Virginia, 1984), 25–49, and Steven Watts, *The Republic Reborn: War and the Making of Liberal America, 1790–1820* (Baltimore: Johns Hopkins University Press, 1987), for examinations of war as a means of social and civic regeneration or revitalization. Drawing together the work of Watts and Hietala, it is easy to see how "republican regeneration" and national unity would aid in the Jacksonians' project to restore a pure Jeffersonian republic. See Marvin Meyers, *The Jacksonian Persuasion: Politics and Belief* (New York: Vintage, 1957), chap. 2, on the "restoration theme" in Jacksonian thought and rhetoric.

15. Sherman to Ellen Ewing, September 17, 1844, and June 9, 1845, in *Home Letters of General Sherman*, 26, 29; Sherman to his brother John, August 29, 1845, in *The Sherman Letters: Correspondence between General and Senator Sherman from 1837 to 1891*, ed. Rachel Sherman Thorndike (New York: Charles Scribner's Sons, 1894), 28; Dana to Sue Dana, April 11 and 17, 1846, in *Monterrey Is Ours*, 42, 45; Barbour journal entry, April 4, 1846, in *Journals of the Late Brevet Major Philip Norbourne Barbour and His Wife Martha Isabella Hopkins Barbour Written during the War with Mexico—1846*, ed. Rhoda van Bibber Tanner Doubleday (New York: G. P. Putnam's Sons,

1936), 42; Henry diary entry, March 28, 1846, in *Campaign Sketches of the War with Mexico* (New York: Harper and Bros., 1847), reprinted in Grady McWhiney and Sue McWhiney, eds., *To Mexico with Taylor and Scott, 1845–1847* (Waltham, Mass.: Blaisdell Publishing, 1969), 14.

See Frederick Merk and Lois Bannister Merk, *Slavery and the Annexation of Texas* (New York: Alfred A. Knopf, 1972), and Hietala, *Manifest Design*, chaps. 2, 6, regarding civilian expansionists' expectations for sectional and national gain and their belief that annexation might hold the nation together by acting as an alternative to abolition. See John Schroeder, *Mr. Polk's War: American Opposition and Dissent, 1846–1848* (Madison: University of Wisconsin Press, 1973), and Ernest M. Lander, *Reluctant Imperialists: Calhoun, the South Carolinians, and the Mexican War* (Baton Rouge: Louisiana State University Press, 1979), for a view of the sectional and, indeed, intrasectional dimensions of opposition to the war in the United States. See Paul A. Varg, *New England and Foreign Relations, 1789–1850* (Hanover, N.H.: University Press of New England, 1983), chaps. 10, 11, for a discussion of the primary center of dissent against Manifest Destiny. Robert E. May, *The Southern Dream of a Caribbean Empire, 1854–1861*, 2nd ed. (Gainesville: University Press of Florida, 2002), provides a thorough examination of attempts at pro-slavery expansionism during the 1850s.

16. See Hietala, *Manifest Design*, especially chap. 4; Major L. Wilson, *Space, Time, and Freedom: The Quest for Nationality and the Irrepressible Conflict, 1815–1861* (Westport, Conn.: Greenwood Press, 1974), chap. 5; and, more generally, Drew R. McCoy, *The Elusive Republic: Political Economy in Jeffersonian America* (Chapel Hill: University of North Carolina Press, 1980). Wilson's conceptualization of the differences between Democrats and Whigs has been elaborated in Lawrence Frederick Kohl, *The Politics of Individualism: Parties and the American Character in the Jacksonian Era* (New York: Oxford University Press, 1989), and Daniel Walker Howe, *What Hath God Wrought? The Transformation of America, 1815–1848* (New York: Oxford University Press, 2007). The only explicit reference to republicanism I found among junior officers associated with the Army of Occupation was William S. Henry's diary entry for April 23, 1846, in *To Mexico with Taylor and Scott*, 25, regarding Taylor's response to the Mexican ultimatum of April 22: "a capital paper; truly republican." See Marc W. Kruman, "The Second American Party System and the Transformation of Revolutionary Republicanism," *JER* 12 (Winter 1992): 509–537; Major L. Wilson, "Republicanism and the Idea of Party in the Jacksonian Period," *JER* 8 (Winter 1988): 419–432; and Major L. Wilson, "The 'Country' versus the 'Court': A Republican Consensus and Party Debate in the Bank War," *JER* 15 (Winter 1995): 619–647, on changes and continuities in republican values and rhetoric during the Jacksonian era.

17. Skelton, *An American Profession of Arms*, chap. 15 (quotation on 283). See Daniel Walker Howe, *The Political Culture of the American Whigs* (Chicago: University of Chicago Press, 1979), chaps. 3, 6; Howe, *What Hath God Wrought?* 584; and Thomas Brown, *Politics and Statesmanship: Essays on the American Whig Party* (New York: Columbia University Press, 1985), chaps. 1, 2, 5, for the persistence of antipartisanship—or at least a distaste and skepticism for aggressive partisanship—among

Whigs. See Glenn C. Altschuler and Stuart M. Blumin, *Rude Republic: Americans and Their Politics in the Nineteenth Century* (Princeton, N.J.: Princeton University Press, 2000); "'Where Is the Real America?' Politics and Popular Consciousness in the Antebellum Era," *American Quarterly* 49 (June 1997): 225–267; and "Limits of Political Engagement in Antebellum America: A New Look at the Golden Age of Participatory Democracy," *JAH* 84 (December 1997): 855–885, for the "disengaged belief"—or, more cynically, the "engaged disbelief"—many ordinary Americans held in the Second Party System.

18. Schureman to Mary Schureman, April 10, 1844, Schureman Papers, LC (the word for which I have substituted "war" was illegible); Dutton to Lucy Matthews, March 6, 1845, Dutton Papers, USMA.

19. Meade to Margaretta Meade, September 4 and October 10, 1845, in *Life and Letters of George Gordon Meade*, 23, 30; Allen to Thomas Berryman (a civilian friend), August 3, 1845, Robert Allen Papers, USMA; Samuel H. Raymond to Mary Raymond, May 5, 1844, Samuel Raymond Papers, USMA.

20. Dana to Sue Dana, October 26, 1845, in *Monterrey Is Ours*, 28–29; Barbour journal entry, April 15, 1846, in *Journals of the Late Brevet Major Philip Norbourne Barbour*, 37; Dana to Sue Dana, October 24, 1845, in *Monterrey Is Ours*, 28. See also Peck, April 20, 1846, in *Sign of the Eagle*, 20.

21. Worth to Thomas Lawson, November 1, 1845, Lawson Papers, LC; Skelton, *An American Profession of Arms*, 330–331; Reginald Horsman, *Race and Manifest Destiny: The Origins of American Racial Anglo-Saxonism* (Cambridge, Mass.: Harvard University Press, 1981); Ewell to his sister Rebecca Ewell, July 30, 1844, Benjamin Ewell Papers, LC. Worth provides Skelton's only citation to racial Anglo-Saxonism before the outbreak of war and the advance into Mexico. This is not to say that there are no others amid Skelton's decades of research notes, but the trope is far rarer than a scholar familiar with civilian attitudes, or one expecting belligerence, and thus racial and ethnic chauvinism, from military officers, might expect. In contrast, about half the citations Skelton presents for officers' opposition to the war (332) are from after the war had begun, when one would expect patriotism and a desire to avenge slain comrades to silence dissent. In other words, veterans wanted to win, and they wanted to avenge dead comrades, but they did not forget how or why the war began—nor did they move from private dissent to public insubordination or disruption of the war effort. Remembering the American origins of the war, rather than aggressively promoting white supremacy, probably helped them maintain restraint among their enlisted soldiers, limiting depredations and atrocities that might have spurred stronger Mexican resistance.

James M. McCaffrey, *Army of Manifest Destiny: The American Soldier in the Mexican War, 1846–1848* (New York: New York University Press, 1992), chap. 5, describes the predominantly negative reactions to Mexicans and their culture found among American regular and volunteer troops during the invasion. Nevertheless, his citations are overwhelmingly from volunteers: only one of his examples of American military racism is from a regular army officer during 1846. See Hietala, *Manifest Design*, chap.

5, regarding the restraining influence of American racial attitudes on expansion into the Mexican heartland. For context, see especially Arnoldo De León, *They Called Them Greasers: Anglo Attitudes toward Mexicans in Texas, 1821–1900* (Austin: University of Texas Press, 1983), and Ronald T. Takaki, *Iron Cages: Race and Culture in Nineteenth-Century America* (New York: Alfred A. Knopf, 1979).

22. Edward M. Coffman, *The Old Army: A Portrait of the American Army in Peacetime, 1784–1898* (New York: Oxford University Press, 1986), 79–80; Skelton, *An American Profession of Arms*, 162 (table 9.6); Dale R. Steinhauer, "'Sogers': Enlisted Men in the U.S. Army, 1815–1860" (Ph.D. diss., University of North Carolina, 1992), chap. 2. Steinhauer's tables 8.9–8.12, 9.1, 9.5, and 9.6 (348–353, 367, 380–381) demonstrate that foreign-born soldiers were promoted to noncommissioned officer ranks, recognized with certificates of merit during the war with Mexico, and killed in action at rates proportionate to their numbers in the army.

The brief against the army is argued most strongly in Peter F. Stevens, *The Rogue's March: John Riley and the St. Patrick's Battalion, 1846–48* (Dulles, Va.: Brassey's, 1999), which asserts that "Protestant U.S. Army officers" were "among the most strident" nativists (23) and that nonnativists were a minority among junior officers (64). Yet Stevens also has abolitionists and nativists supporting Polk, a slaveholder whose party welcomed immigrants, and he does not cite Skelton, Coffman, or Steinhauer. Nor does Stevens provide actual examples of strident nativism, either from officers' personal papers or from official documents. Certainly, no officer is known to have written publicly in favor of nativism. He cites several examples of officers (including Philip Barbour, John Hatch, and Ulysses Grant, albeit in October 1846) referring to "popery" and "mummery" (80), but such language was, frankly, not uncommon or particularly "strident" in 1846; elsewhere, Stevens acknowledges Grant's lack of nativism and his admiration for Irish soldiers (55, 64, 67). See also Robert Ryal Miller, *Shamrock and Sword: The Saint Patrick's Battalion in the U.S.-Mexican War* (Norman: University of Oklahoma Press, 1989), which states accurately (given the vagueness of the words in question) that nativism was "widespread" in the army (161) but does not extrapolate further. My caution regarding the pervasiveness of nativism in the army does not extend to the brutality officers frequently inflicted on enlisted soldiers, which is attested to by all scholars; however, I interpret that brutality as a manifestation of authoritarianism, not primarily or even very disproportionately nativist, anti-Irish, or anti-Catholic. For context beyond the many works on political nativism, see Dale T. Knobel, *Paddy and the Republic: Ethnicity and Nationality in Antebellum America* (Middletown, Conn.: Wesleyan University Press, 1986).

23. Hatch to his sister Eliza Hatch, October 28, 1845, John Porter Hatch Papers, LC; Dana to Sue Dana, September 22, 1845, in *Monterrey Is Ours*, 13–14; Alvord to M. C. M. Hammond, October 8, 1844, James Henry Hammond Papers, LC. See also Henry diary entry, April 3, 1846, in *To Mexico with Taylor and Scott*, 19. See Coffman, *The Old Army*, 78–81, and Skelton, *An American Profession of Arms*, 162–163, for brief summaries of officers' religious preferences. See also Ted C. Hinckley, "American Anti-Catholicism during the Mexican War," *Pacific Historical Quarterly* 31 (May

1962): 121–138, who argues that the war was not motivated or greatly shaped by religion. About 40 to 50 percent of regular army enlisted men were foreign born, the largest proportions coming from Ireland and Germany. Both groups were largely Catholic.

24. WS to Jones, August 25, 1843, HQALS; Meade to Margaretta Meade, December 17, 1845, and February 24 and March 2, 1846, in *Life and Letters of George Gordon Meade*, 39, 48, 50; Dana to Sue Dana, September 16, 1845, in *Monterrey Is Ours*, 12.

25. Dana to Sue Dana, September 16 and 22, 1845, in *Monterrey Is Ours*, 12, 14; Grant to his fiancée and future wife Julia Dent, October 10, 1845, and March 3, 1846, in *The Papers of Ulysses S. Grant*, ed. John Y. Simon (Carbondale: Southern Illinois University Press, 1967), 1:56–57, 75; Grant, *Memoirs and Selected Letters*, 114–115. See Meade to Margaretta Meade, April 15, 1846, in *Life and Letters of George Gordon Meade*, 58–59, and Peck, February 6, 1846, in *Sign of the Eagle*, 11–12, for additional examples of confidence. Merk and Merk, *The Monroe Doctrine and American Expansionism*, 149, observe that editorial opinion in the United States was divided over whether the advance to the Rio Grande would preserve peace or precipitate war. See William A. DePalo Jr., *The Mexican National Army, 1822–1852* (College Station: Texas A&M University Press, 1997), regarding the problems of that force. See Pedro Santoni, *Mexicans at Arms: Puro Federalists and the Politics of War, 1845–1848* (Fort Worth: Texas Christian University Press, 1996), 216–218, regarding discussions about annexation or a U.S. protectorate between northern Mexicans and U.S. officers, including Ethan Allen Hitchcock and Winfield Scott.

26. Sherman to Ellen Ewing, June 9, 1845, in *Home Letters of General Sherman*, 29; Meade to Margaretta Meade, January 10 and 20, 1846, in *Life and Letters of George Gordon Meade*, 44–45; Dana to Sue Dana, October 24 and 26, 1845, in *Monterrey Is Ours*, 28; Dutton to Lucy Matthews, February 26, 1845, Dutton Papers, USMA. See also Peck, November 1, 1845, in *Sign of the Eagle*, 9; Capt. William C. DeHart to Capt. Charles F. Smith, January 6, 1846, Charles Ferguson Smith Papers, USMA; and Lt. James B. Dyer [listed as Alexander B. Dyer in all army biographical sources] journal entry, February 17, 1845, James B. Dyer Papers, LC.

27. Smith to his wife, March 29, 1846, and August 28, 1845, in *To Mexico with Scott*, 35, 14; Dana to Sue Dana, August 29, 1845, in *Monterrey Is Ours*, 3; Grant to Julia Dent, October 1845, in *The Papers of Ulysses S. Grant*, 1:59; McClellan to his sister Frederica, May 3 and 13, 1846, McClellan Papers, LC; Dutton to Lucy Matthews, May 18, 1846, Dutton Papers, USMA. See also Peck, February 10, 1846, in *Sign of the Eagle*, 12.

28. McClellan to Frederica McClellan, May 3, 1846, McClellan Papers, LC; Dutton to Lucy Matthews, May 18, 1846, Dutton Papers, USMA; Smith to his wife, March 17, 1846, in *To Mexico with Scott*, 30–31; Dana to Sue Dana, April 21, 22, and 11, 1846, in *Monterrey Is Ours*, 46, 48, 41.

29. Barbour journal entry, March 30, 1846, in *Journals of the Late Brevet Major Philip Norbourne Barbour*, 23; Smith to his wife, November 2, 1845, in *To Mexico with Scott*, 21; John Hatch to Eliza Hatch, April 3, 1846, Hatch Papers, LC. See also

Henry diary entry, March 28, 1846, in *To Mexico with Taylor and Scott*, 13, and Peck, April 16, 1846, in *Sign of the Eagle*, 19.

30. Smith to his wife, August 28, 1845, in *To Mexico with Scott*, 14. See Skelton, *An American Profession of Arms*, 277–278, regarding Smith's dismissal. The peacetime companies, consisting of approximately 40 soldiers, were increased to 100 by the war legislation of May 13, 1846.

31. Hatch to Eliza Hatch, October 14 and 28, 1845, Hatch Papers, LC; Dana to Sue Dana, September 23, 1845, in *Monterrey Is Ours*, 15; Sherman to Ellen Ewing, June 9, 1845, in *Home Letters of General Sherman*, 29–30. See also Peck, February 10, 1846, in *Sign of the Eagle*, 12.

32. Hatch to Eliza Hatch, September 10, 1845, Hatch Papers, LC.

33. Meade to Margaretta Meade, November 3 and October 21, 1845, in *Life and Letters of George Gordon Meade*, 35, 33.

34. Meade to Margaretta Meade, December 18, 1845, in *Life and Letters of George Gordon Meade*, 40; Dana to Sue Dana, September 26 and 30 (quotation) and October 15 and 19, 1845, in *Monterrey Is Ours*, 16, 25, 27; Peck, October 31, 1845, in *Sign of the Eagle*, 10–11; ZT to his daughter Mary Elizabeth Taylor, December 15, 1845, quoted in Hamilton, *Zachary Taylor*, 168.

35. Schureman to Susan Schureman, January 26, 1846, Schureman Papers, USMA; Meade to Margaretta Meade, February 18, 1846, in *Life and Letters of George Gordon Meade*, 48; Peck, April 16, 1846, in *Sign of the Eagle*, 19; Sherman to Ellen Ewing, January 31, 1846, in *Home Letters of General Sherman*, 31; Capt. Thomas Swords to Lt. Abraham Johnston, January 26, 1846, Johnston Papers, USMA.

36. Similarly, William Hoffman of the Seventh Infantry, a thirty-two-year veteran, died of illness in Corpus Christi four months after his promotion to lieutenant colonel. His son William won two brevets for gallantry in combat outside Mexico City and served until 1870, directing the army's prisoner of war effort during the Civil War. Another son, Saterlee, was killed in action at Churubusco less than six months after receiving his commission. A third son, Alexander, preceded his father in death, succumbing to illness in St. Augustine in 1844 after spending six years in the army. Vose and Whistler also sent sons into the officer corps.

37. Bauer, *Zachary Taylor*, 148; Edward S. Wallace, *General William Jenkins Worth: Monterey's Forgotten Hero* (Dallas: Southern Methodist University Press, 1953), 71. See Worth to Twiggs, December 25; Twiggs to Worth, December 26 and 27; Lt. H[enry]. H. Sibley to Twiggs, December 28; Capt. C[harles]. A. May to Major W[illiam]. G[oldsmith]. Belknap, December 28; and Belknap to Twiggs, two letters dated December 28, 1845, all in Hitchcock Papers, LC. Belknap and May spoke as "the authorized friend[s]" of Worth and Twiggs, respectively; this term was commonly used to designate go-betweens and seconds in duels and the negotiations leading up to them. The two colonels did not "meet," but Belknap (vice Worth) did call on Twiggs to withdraw his note of the twenty-seventh, "with the view of making such explanations as may be satisfactory." This was done, and Belknap's second note excused Worth's conduct as overhasty.

38. Journal entry, April 9, 1846, in *Journals of the Late Brevet Major Philip Norbourne Barbour*, 31–32. See also Capt. William C. DeHart to Capt. Charles F. Smith, May 27, 1846, Charles Ferguson Smith Papers, USMA, and Eisenhower, *So Far from God*, 38–39, 62. See Skelton, *An American Profession of Arms*, 330–331, regarding Worth; see Peck, October 31, 1845, in *Sign of the Eagle*, 5, for an example of an officer who felt that Worth "wishes something to do" and "would prefer a little trouble" (presumably with the Mexicans, not Twiggs).

39. Bauer, *Zachary Taylor*, 129.

40. Minutes of Worth-Vega meeting, March 28, 1846, Ampudia to ZT, April 12, 1846, and ZT to Ampudia, April 12, 1846, House Executive Doc. 60, 30th Cong., 1st sess., 134–140; ZT to RJ, April 15 and 26, 1846, House Executive Doc. 196, 29th Cong., 1st sess., 118, and House Executive Doc. 60, 30th Cong., 1st sess., 141.

41. Samuel Flagg Bemis, *A Diplomatic History of the United States*, 3rd ed. (New York: Holt, Rinehart and Winston, 1965), 241; ZT to RJ and to Ampudia, April 23 and 22, 1846, House Executive Doc. 197, 29th Cong., 1st sess., 2–4. See Bauer, *Zachary Taylor*, 148–158, for a concise summary of the events leading up to Palo Alto and Resaca de la Palma.

42. Meade to Margaretta Meade, February 24, 1846, in *Life and Letters of George Gordon Meade*, 49; Grant to Julia Dent, March 3, 1846, in *The Papers of Ulysses S. Grant*, 1:75; Skelton, *An American Profession of Arms*, 216 (table 11.1); Smith to his wife, March 17, 1846, in *To Mexico with Scott*, 30–31; Peck, March 27, 1846, in *Sign of the Eagle*, 15.

43. Journal entries, April 22, 27, and May 1, 1846, in *Journals of the Late Brevet Major Philip Norbourne Barbour*, 42, 47, 50–51. These officers believed the Mexicans could have made the crossing a costly one, although the Americans would have forced the position. See also Henry diary entry, March 28, 1846, in *To Mexico with Taylor and Scott*, 12–13. See Dana to Sue Dana, September 15, 1845, in *Monterrey Is Ours*, 12, and Meade to Margaretta Meade, April 22, 1846, in *Life and Letters of George Gordon Meade*, 68, for other examples of an officer swearing vengeance.

44. Winders, *Mr. Polk's Army*, presents the most aggressive argument that Polk transformed the army through partisan appointments during the war, but the commissions he refers to are all temporary wartime ones: the Mounted Rifles was the only regiment raised between 1846 and 1848 that survived the war, and the rationale for that regiment was to escort emigrants on the Oregon Trail, as it did in 1849. Winders's attention to wartime appointment politics leads him to assert that "political influence often played an important part in [regular] officers' advancement" before the war (56)—a highly inaccurate portrait of regular army life and antebellum civil-military relations. Officers grumbled constantly, so the perception of influence was certainly present, but regular army promotion was almost entirely by an extraordinarily rigid system of seniority. Winders's only example of a political promotion in the antebellum army is John C. Frémont, such a rare and glaring exception to the rule that it generated considerable outrage among officers, but even Frémont was promoted in the new Mounted Rifles, not one of the old regiments. Indeed, Frémont had *not* been pro-

moted between his commissioning in 1838 and 1846; he received a brevet for leading his first two expeditions, which was neither unreasonable nor subversive of seniority. And, of course, career regulars pushed Frémont out of the army less than two years after his promotion; he never actually commanded in the Mounted Rifles.

As William Skelton has pointed out after an exhaustive reading of the manuscript sources, most of the politicking in the regular army was for choice duty assignments, not the rare opportunity for promotion into new and possibly temporary units. Timothy D. Johnson, *A Gallant Little Army: The Mexico City Campaign* (Lawrence: University Press of Kansas, 2007), appendix 2, shows that a plurality of the army that won the surrender of Mexico City was composed of prewar regulars: thirteen of fourteen prewar regular army regiments were represented, though most by only five or six of their ten companies, versus eight of the eleven national regiments (including the Mounted Rifles) formed for the war and only three state volunteer regiments (albeit very large ones).

45. Meade to Margaretta Meade, November 12, 1845, in *Life and Letters of George Gordon Meade*, 36. See Dutton to Lucy Matthews, May 18, 1846, Dutton Papers, USMA, for an extensive example of this dutiful attitude, so similar to the corps' neutrality on political questions.

46. Hietala, *Manifest Design*, 7–8, 270; Robert H. Wiebe, *The Segmented Society: An Introduction to the Meaning of America* (New York: Oxford University Press, 1975); Robert H. Wiebe, *The Opening of American Society: From the Adoption of the Constitution to the Eve of Disunion* (New York: Alfred A. Knopf, 1984), chaps. 16, 17.

CONCLUSION

1. William J. Novak, *The People's Welfare: Law and Regulation in Nineteenth-Century America* (Chapel Hill: University of North Carolina Press, 1996), 17, 235; Ira Katznelson, "Flexible Capacity: The Military and Early American State-Building," in *Shaped by War and Trade: International Influences in American Political Development*, ed. Ira Katznelson and Martin Shefter (Princeton, N.J.: Princeton University Press, 2002), 89.

2. Peter Karsten, "Armed Progressives: The Military Reorganizes for the American Century," in *Building the Organizational Society: Essays on Associational Activities in Modern America*, ed. Jerry Israel, with an introduction by Samuel P. Hays (New York: Free Press, 1972); Magali Sarfatti Larson, *The Rise of Professionalism: A Sociological Inquiry* (Berkeley: University of California Press, 1977); James L. Abrahamson, *America Arms for a New Century: The Making of a Great Military Power* (New York: Free Press, 1981); Novak, *The People's Welfare*, 17. Marc W. Kruman, "The Second American Party System and the Transformation of Revolutionary Republicanism," *JER* 12 (Winter 1992): 509–537; Major L. Wilson, "Republicanism and the Idea of Party in the Jacksonian Period," *JER* 8 (Winter 1988): 419–432; and Major L. Wilson, "The 'Country' versus the 'Court': A Republican Consensus and Party Debate in the Bank

War," *JER* 15 (Winter 1995): 619–647, explore changes and continuities—the continued emphasis on virtue and community consensus, now to be bolstered and expressed through parties to buttress republicanism—in republican values and rhetoric during the 1830s.

3. Michael Mann, *The Sources of Social Power: The Rise of Classes and Nation-States, 1760–1914* (Cambridge: Cambridge University Press, 1993); Philip Corrigan and Derek Sayer, *The Great Arch: English State Formation as Cultural Revolution* (Oxford: Basil Blackwell, 1985); Christopher Dandeker, *Surveillance, Power, and Modernity: Bureaucracy and Discipline from 1700 to the Present Day* (New York: St. Martin's Press, 1990); Alf Ludtke, *Police and State in Prussia, 1815–1850* (Cambridge: Cambridge University Press, 1989); Bernard S. Silberman, *Cages of Reason: The Rise of the Rational State in France, Japan, the United States, and Great Britain* (Chicago: University of Chicago Press, 1993); C. A. Bayly, *Empire and Information: Intelligence-Gathering and Social Communication in India, 1780–1870* (Cambridge: Cambridge University Press, 1990); Larson, *The Rise of Professionalism;* Abrahamson, *America Arms for a New Century.*

4. The most historically nuanced approach might take a tip from former officer Donald Connelly, who observes that the key question in American civil-military relations is not military subordination to civilian authority but to which civilian authority (e.g., the executive or Congress) the military has been more responsive; see Donald Connelly, *John M. Schofield and the Politics of Generalship* (Chapel Hill: University of North Carolina Press, 2006), xii, for a summary assessment of the relationship between officers and American politics (nineteenth century and today) that accords well with my own. Samuel Huntington considered this "dual control" a weakness that hindered professional development; I hope I have shown otherwise.

5. These interactions, with the middle classes and elites of every jurisdiction in which officers found themselves, occurred primarily at social events—dinners, parties, dances, picnics, sleigh rides, and genteel card games. Yet an officer's conveyance or interpretation of news or even "gossip" from "the court" at Washington—as it was often labeled even during the early Jacksonian period—from "the East," or, if in Washington, from "the West" was understood through political filters, or at least within political contexts. In the absence of real-time communications technology, such news was part of the educated man's (and woman's) personal intelligence network; this made military officers valuable contacts, regardless of ideological conviction. (Some historian should write a monograph on the role of rumor in Jacksonian political culture, to complement existing works on formal and informal partisan networks and structures.) These social connections, as well as partisan ones, could lead to federal civil appointments or appointments to the Military Academy and thus federal military positions.

For plentiful examples of junior officers' interaction with civilian elites, both in the borderlands and in Washington, see Erasmus D. Keyes, *Fifty Years Observation of Men and Events, Civil and Military* (New York: Scribner's, 1884); Joseph E. Chance, ed., *My Life in the Old Army: The Reminiscences of Abner Doubleday* (Fort Worth: Texas Christian University Press, 1998); and Robert Garth Scott, ed., *Forgotten Valor: The*

Memoirs, Journals, & Civil War Letters of Orlando B. Willcox (Kent, Ohio: Kent State University Press, 1999). See Cheryl Conover, ed., "A Kentuckian in 'King Andrew's' Court: The Letters of John Waller Barry, Washington, D.C., 1831–1835," *Register of the Kentucky Historical Society* 81 (Spring 1983): 168–198, and Wilson, "The 'Country' versus the 'Court,'" for examples of references to the "court" at Washington; Lieutenant Barry was the son of Jackson's first postmaster general.

6. Peter D. Feaver, *Armed Servants: Agency, Oversight, and Civil-Military Relations* (Cambridge, Mass.: Harvard University Press, 2003), 301.

7. Robert M. Utley, *The Indian Frontier of the American West, 1846–1890* (Albuquerque: University of New Mexico Press, 1984), 41, 166, criticizes the army's lack of creativity and imagination in developing tactics to defeat the Indians. Utley implicitly recognizes that operational persistence was the decisive factor, observing that "when they worked, [the army's] offensives worked with a vengeance" (167), but he seems unwilling to let go of his causally secondary tactical assessment: "in the end it was not combat success but convergence, unremittingly prosecuted," that won the Red River War and ended Comanche, Cheyenne, Kiowa, and Arapaho resistance on the southern Plains (178). Perhaps Utley sought to raise the analysis of the Indian wars above the tactical level so beloved by buffs—a worthy objective; my point is that it was the national standing army, not settlers or citizen-soldiers, that conducted these campaigns and converged on the Red River. Indeed, Utley recognizes this when he observes that the western volunteer forces of the Civil War melted away at its end, even before they might have been demobilized (77–79).

8. Robert M. Utley, "Culture Clash on the Western North American Indian Frontier," in *The Military and Conflict between Cultures: Soldiers at the Interface*, ed. James C. Bradford (College Station: Texas A&M University Press, 1997), 104. I do not disagree with the majority of the generalizations and hypotheses about military effectiveness Utley presents: that simple societies (the Indians) fare best when they stick to their own military methods rather than trying to adopt those of their complex opponents (the United States), and that U.S. victory "depended less on purely military factors than upon economic, political, diplomatic, and psychological factors" (105). The key word here is "purely." Utley's other hypothesis, that complex societies are most successful when they adopt the military methods of their simpler opponents, has substantial historical validity *at the tactical level* and may seem reasonable in light of the recent resurgence in asymmetrical warfare, "guerrilla warfare," and revolutionary warfare in the twentieth and twenty-first centuries, but it strikes me as far too sweeping, even for a generalization. Nor does it address the strategic level of politics and mobilization, where the fate of insurgencies is most often decided. It might be apt to contrast two of Mao Tse-tung's best-known statements: that the guerrilla is a fish that can survive only in the sea of the people, and that political power grows from the barrel of a gun. Rarely can the support of the people be fully divorced from the power of the gun, or vice versa.

9. Bruce Vandervort, *The Indian Wars of Mexico, Canada, and the United States, 1812–1900* (London: Routledge, 2006), 8. The citizen-soldier mobilizations of the

1850s (in California and the Pacific Northwest) and 1860s were the result of white belligerence and the inability of the democratic nation-state to restrain it, both generally deplored by regular officers. An investigation into the reasons why the nation-state lost so much of its control over the organized employment of armed force in the West between 1848 and 1865 would contribute significantly to our understanding of change and continuity in nineteenth-century America; for parallels east of the Mississippi, see David Grimsted, *American Mobbing, 1828–1861: Toward Civil War* (New York: Oxford University Press, 1998).

10. See Robert Angevine, *The Railroad and the State: War, Politics and Technology in Nineteenth-Century America* (Stanford, Calif.: Stanford University Press, 2004), chaps. 7–9, for an outstanding discussion of the symbiotic relationship between the railroads and the army later in the century that emphasizes the railroads' limitations as well as advantages.

11. Gary C. Anderson, *The Conquest of Texas: Ethnic Cleansing in the Promised Land, 1820–1875* (Norman: University of Oklahoma Press, 2005). John Grenier, *The First Way of War: American War Making on the Frontier, 1607–1814* (Cambridge: Cambridge University Press, 2005), maintains that white military success against the Indians depended on the operation of volunteer "rangers" as scouts and raiders, but his argument is much less persuasive for the period after 1787. The white Kentuckians, for example, were able to secure control of their future state without national military assistance, but they were unable to halt Indian raids across the Ohio River and earned a rather mixed record in the War of 1812. Meanwhile, the Chickasaws, rather than the white Georgians, were the most effective force against the Creeks during the 1790s. Perhaps Kentucky volunteers might have driven the Indians from Ohio through raids or through the gradual growth of the white population along the northern banks of the Ohio River and its spread northward in conjunction with such raids, but there is no evidence that they were doing so, nor did they volunteer to use their abilities as scouts and rangers to protect the Harmar and St. Clair expeditions, which were destroyed by Ohioan ambushes in 1790 and 1791. Perhaps George Washington's decision to employ national regulars (Anthony Wayne's Legion of the United States) foreclosed that possibility, but Washington wanted to maintain as much national control as possible over the northwestern expansion of white settlement. See Andrew R. L. Cayton, "'Separate Interests' and the Nation-State: The Washington Administration and the Origins of Regionalism in the Trans-Appalachian West," *JAH* 79 (June 1992): 39–67, for a contrast with the Southwest Territory.

12. Utley, "Culture Clash on the Western North American Indian Frontier," 104. Robert M. Utley, *Frontiersmen in Blue: The United States Army and the Indian, 1848–1865* (New York: Macmillan, 1967), ultimately appears to recognize that Sherman's desire for white frontier communities to protect themselves was just that—a wish rather than a reality (see especially 348–349).

13. Robert M. Utley, *Frontier Regulars: The United States Army and the Indian, 1866–1900* (New York: Macmillan, 1973), 421; Utley, "Culture Clash on the Western North American Indian Frontier, 104; Utley, *The Indian Frontier of the American*

West, 63. See especially Richard Maxwell Brown, "Western Violence: Structure, Values, Myth," *WHQ* 24 (February 1993): 4–20, and Richard Maxwell Brown, *No Duty to Retreat: Violence and Values in American History and Society* (New York: Oxford University Press, 1991), for the concept of "western civil wars of incorporation."

14. Utley, *The Indian Frontier of the American West*, 170; Utley, *Frontier Regulars*, 420–421; Vandervort, *The Indian Wars of Mexico, Canada, and the United States*; Evelyn Hu-DeHart, *Yaqui Resistance and Survival: The Struggle for Land and Autonomy, 1821–1910* (Madison: University of Wisconsin Press, 1984). In *Frontiersmen in Blue*, Utley observes that "the U.S. Army played a key, often decisive, role," but only "in the quest" to balance expansion and humanity (5). He provides a more balanced conclusion in that work (349) than in *Frontier Regulars*.

15. Utley, *Frontier Regulars*, 421; Robert G. Athearn, *William Tecumseh Sherman and the Settlement of the West* (Norman: University of Oklahoma Press, 1956), 327–344; Robert Fishlow, *Railroads and American Economic Growth: Essays in Econometric History* (Baltimore: Johns Hopkins University Press, 1964). Athearn concludes that "farmers . . . plows . . . and barbed wire, followed the army as a clean-up corps that accomplished the final obliteration" of the Indians (322). He observes that Sherman had long contended "that the impact of settlement and density of population would offer the *ultimate* [my emphasis] solution to the Indian problem. His part in western development had been more concerned with controlling the Indians during the time that settlement was edging forward" (328). This is a more nuanced and more accurate portrait than Utley's, but even Athearn stresses Sherman's expectation that settlers would ultimately defend themselves, which I consider the general's genuflection to national myth. (See ibid., 335, 328, 343, for contemporary hints to the contrary, based on the presumed character of the settlers.) Even if Sherman truly believed this, he may well have been wrong, except in the case of very small Indian bands or individuals. When eventually reduced to individual scale, Indian "marauding" would be handled by civilian sheriffs and police forces, but this was a long way off in 1865 or 1877, whereas students of the Jacksonian period can present an outstanding example of settler incapacity in the Second Seminole War. Athearn's final conclusions were the sort Utley reacted against: "vainly the military commander sought justice, equity, and a more ordered progression of events" (346–347). One does not have to idolize the army as a heroic vanguard of civilization, crushing savages, to recognize that national military commanders sought greater order and, in practice, greater equity in the face of herrenvolk democracy and rampant individualism.

16. Clyde Milner, "Indulgent Friends and Important Allies: Political Process on the Cis-Mississippi Frontier and Its Aftermath," in *The Frontier in History: North America and Southern Africa Compared*, ed. Howard Lamar and Leonard Thompson (New Haven, Conn.: Yale University Press, 1981), 138, 146; Vandervort, *The Indian Wars of Mexico, Canada, and the United States*, 16; Bruce Vandervort, *Wars of Imperial Conquest in Africa, 1830–1914* (Bloomington: Indiana University Press, 1998).

17. Anthony Giddens, *The Nation-State and Violence: Volume Two of a Contemporary Critique of Historical Materialism* (Berkeley: University of California Press, 1985),

14–16; Franz Neumann, *Democratic and Authoritarian States* (1957), epigraph in Stephen Skowronek, *Building a New American State: The Expansion of National Administrative Capacities, 1877–1920* (Cambridge: Cambridge University Press, 1982), 19.

18. Peter S. Onuf and Nicholas Onuf, *Federal Union, Modern World: The Law of Nations in an Age of Revolutions, 1776–1814* (Madison, Wis.: Madison House, 1993); James E. Lewis Jr., *The American Union and the Problem of Neighborhood: The United States and the Collapse of the Spanish Empire, 1783–1829* (Chapel Hill: University of North Carolina Press, 1998).

19. Eugen Weber, *Peasants into Frenchmen: The Modernization of Rural France, 1870–1914* (Stanford, Calif.: Stanford University Press, 1976). For further comparison, see Peter Sahlins, *Boundaries: The Making of France and Spain in the Pyrenees* (Berkeley: University of California Press, 1989); Gilbert M. Joseph and Daniel Nugent, eds., *Everyday Forms of State Formation: Revolution and the Negotiation of Rule in Modern Mexico* (Durham, N.C.: Duke University Press, 1994); and Florencia E. Mallon, *Peasant and Nation: The Making of Postcolonial Mexico and Peru* (Berkeley: University of California Press, 1995). We should further note the rapidity with which the former Confederate states were readmitted to the Union and southerners' eagerness to establish themselves as American patriots in international affairs, even as their self-justifying "Lost Cause" became widely accepted among Americans in the North.

20. See Glenn C. Altschuler and Stuart M. Blumin, *Rude Republic: Americans and Their Politics in the Nineteenth Century* (Princeton, N.J.: Princeton University Press, 2000); Glenn C. Altschuler and Stuart M. Blumin, "'Where Is the Real America?' Politics and Popular Consciousness in the Antebellum Era," *American Quarterly* 49 (June 1997): 225–267; and Glenn C. Altschuler and Stuart M. Blumin, "Limits of Political Engagement in Antebellum America: A New Look at the Golden Age of Participatory Democracy," *JAH* 84 (December 1997): 855–885, for concepts of "disengaged belief" and "engaged disbelief" among civilians in the Second Party System. See also Samuel J. Watson, "What Do We Mean by Partisan? Army Officers and Politics during the Evolution of the Second Party System" (unpublished paper presented to the Southwestern Historical Association, April 1, 1999). Thus, the more general Whiggishness of the officer corps was fundamentally a matter of affinity: Jacksonian egalitarianism, populism, suspicion of institutions, and antagonism toward monopolies created or sustained by government certainly contrasted with Whig avowals of stability, hierarchy, and the rule of law. As historian Daniel Walker Howe observes, "much more than Democrats, Whigs worried about lawlessness, violence, and demagogy. Duties seemed to them as important as rights." Whigs "emphasized that the people had imposed legal limitations on their own sovereignty." Daniel Walker Howe, *What Hath God Wrought? The Transformation of America, 1815–1848* (New York: Oxford University Press, 2007), 583, 599. Officers lived these Whiggish values and feared the entropic effects of Jacksonian decentralization, but civilian friendships, socialization at home as youths, or exuberant nationalism made many—apparently a slight majority, proportionate to that in the civilian electorate—Democrats in partisan affinity. Most important, their

nationalist duties, their nationalist military socialization (at West Point or in carrying out their duties), and their desire to protect the army from partisan attack made them almost universally nonpartisan in their service. See Lawrence Frederick Kohl, *The Politics of Individualism: Parties and the American Character in the Jacksonian Era* (New York: Oxford University Press, 1989), chap. 4, and William B. Skelton, *An American Profession of Arms: The Army Officer Corps, 1784–1861* (Lawrence: University Press of Kansas, 1992), chap. 15 (statistic on 295).

21. Skelton, *An American Profession of Arms*, 295, 138–139.

22. Samuel J. Watson, "Manifest Destiny and Military Professionalism: A New Perspective on Junior U.S. Army Officers' Attitudes toward War With Mexico, 1844–1846," *SWHQ* 99 (April 1996): 466–498 (though my emphasis on officers' quest for personal comfort and their apparent lack of interest in their opponents or the international situation now seems overdrawn); Tony R. Mullis, *Peacekeeping on the Plains: Army Operations in Bleeding Kansas* (Columbia: University of Missouri Press, 2004); Marvin Ewy, "The United States Army in the Kansas Border Troubles, 1855–1856," *Kansas Historical Quarterly* 32 (Winter 1966): 385–400; Samuel J. Watson, "Continuity in Civil-Military Relations and Expertise: The U.S. Army during the Decade before the Civil War," *JMH* 75 (January 2011): 221–250, which contains a survey of the historiography and statistics on officer resignations in 1861. By far the best treatment of the army during the 1850s is Durwood Ball, *Army Regulars on the Western Frontier, 1848–1861* (Norman: University of Oklahoma Press, 2001); Ball shows the persistence of the complex dynamics of the 1820s, 1830s, and 1840s, particularly with regard to rendering responsible service during constabulary missions, but he puts far more emphasis on partisanship, politicization, and sectionalism than Skelton and I do. Like Richard Bruce Winders, *Mr. Polk's Army: The American Military Experience in the Mexican War* (College Station: Texas A&M University Press, 1997), or John C. Pinheiro, *Manifest Ambition: James K. Polk and Civil-Military Relations during the Mexican War* (Westport, Conn.: Praeger Security International, 2007), writing about the army during the war with Mexico, Ball greatly exaggerates the politicization of commissioning and promotion, which remained dominated by Military Academy graduation and the seniority rule during peacetime. Only a handful of "Mr. Polk's officers," commissioned directly from civilian life into new regiments created for the duration of the war in 1846 and 1847, remained in the postwar army two years later, and the proportion of West Pointers in the officer corps *increased* from 60 to 75 percent between 1830 and 1860, despite about four regiments' worth of officers commissioned directly from civilian life into the seven permanent regiments raised in 1833, 1836, 1846, and 1855.

Ball's emphasis on southern officers with Democratic and sectional loyalties (William S. Harney, George Pickett) is outweighed by his own evidence: despite the shifting demands of Democratic presidents for action or inaction, Ball's narrative shows that the army performed with objective accountability in Kansas, where Edwin Vose Sumner and Philip St. George Cooke, authoritarian commanders imbued with a strong sense of national duty, tried to keep the peace. Chastened by Pierce administration censure, John Wool ultimately drew back from efforts to restrain filibustering or vigilante atrocities against Indians in California, which demonstrates the difficulty of enforcing the laws when the national command authority combines with public opinion against doing so. The significance of George Pickett's belligerence against the British on Vancouver Island has to be tempered by the Virginian's rank—lieutenant—while the brutally belligerent William Harney, Pickett's commander and supporter, was certainly a more exceptional figure in the army than Winfield Scott. Much like Martin Van Buren during the Maine boundary crisis in 1839 and Andrew Jackson during the Nullification Crisis in 1832, Democratic president James Buchanan dispatched Whig general Winfield Scott to make peace.

Ball's focus on western operations and national political context limits his attention to the distinctiveness of the army's professional culture. While army officers, like other Americans, were certainly more sectionally conscious in the 1850s than before, Ball's emphasis on the motives and policies of Presidents Pierce and Buchanan leads him to exaggerate politicization and sectional loyalties within the army and to underestimate the continuing, though certainly diminished, strength of its antipartisanship and nationalism. Rather than suggesting that "constabulary duty in the West politically destabilized the regular army" (138) or that the defection of officers to the Confederacy "indicated structural flaws and ideological weaknesses in the institutional army" (208), I would argue, as Ball usually does, that officers were divided by the same forces as other Americans. There were, however, proportionately fewer defections from the army in 1861 than from other national institutions, including Congress, federal civil officials from the South, and southern-born students in northern schools. In other words, the army reflected the nation; it was not isolated from national trends, but its professional institutions and culture provided a degree of insulation and autonomy. The sectional politics of the 1850s certainly "shadowed all frontier commanders" (208), but presidential motives cannot be conflated with those of the army officer corps, and the change was much more presidential—compare Taylor and Fillmore with Pierce and Buchanan—than military.

Ball also exaggerates the military glory—which most officers associated with war against Europeans—to be gained in fighting Indians and Mormons. It therefore remains unclear how, why, and how much army attitudes had actually changed since the 1830s and early 1840s, when officers expressed great distaste for their duties in Indian removal and the Second Seminole War and generally sought to perform them as humanely as possible. Sharing the same history as other white Americans, the professional soldiers of the 1850s were probably more romantic, expansionist, bellicose, and racist than those before the war with Mexico, but the racism that "motivated" (138) these operations was more national than specifically military, and their execution by regulars was generally less harsh than that by citizen volunteers or vigilantes. Yet Ball ultimately arrives at a balanced judgment and rightly places ultimate responsibility with the representative institutions the army was constitutionally obligated to serve, concluding that "a professional army, however well supported and trained, could not make up for the failures and imprudence of poorly conceived diplomatic, political, and social policy" (208). The army attempted to serve the nation that created it as responsibly as it could, but in the 1850s, subordination and accountability to national political institutions (the dictates of president and Congress) often made impartiality or objectivity in the execution of duty impossible. The army reflected the nation.

23. Charles Sellers, *The Market Revolution: Jacksonian America, 1815–1846* (New York: Oxford University Press, 1991); Michael Paul Rogin, *Fathers and Children: Andrew Jackson and the Subjugation of the American Indian* (New York: Alfred A. Knopf, 1975); Sherman quoted in Henry Steele Commager, ed., *The Blue and the Grey: The Story of the Civil War as Told by Participants*, 2 vols. (Indianapolis: Bobbs-Merrill, 1950), 2:929.

24. See Robert H. Wiebe, *The Segmented Society: An Introduction to the Meaning of America* (New York: Oxford University Press, 1975), and Robert H. Wiebe, *The Opening of American Society: From the Adoption of the Constitution to the Eve of Disunion* (New York: Alfred A. Knopf, 1984), for the origin of the concept of "parallelism," or distinctive social development in parallel—nonintersecting—spaces on the American continent; Major L. Wilson, *Space, Time and Freedom: The Quest for Nationality and the Irrepressible Conflict, 1815–1861* (Westport, Conn.: Greenwood Press, 1974); and Alan Trachtenberg, *The Incorporation of America: Culture and Society in the Gilded Age* (New York: Hill and Wang, 1982). For evidence of graduates' success outside the army, see the army biographical dictionaries; United States Military Academy, *The Centennial of the United States Military Academy at West Point, New York*, 2 vols. (Washington, D.C.: Government Printing Office, 1904); R. Ernest Dupuy, *Men of West Point: The First 150 Years of the United States Military Academy* (New York: William Sloane Associates, 1951); and Dale E. Hruby, "The Civilian Careers of West Point Graduates, Classes of 1802–1833" (M.A. thesis, Columbia University, 1965). There is also a list solely of educators graduated under Sylvanus Thayer in the Thayer Papers, USMA, which includes 51 of the 488 graduates from the classes of 1818–1833. Thirty-three of them were presidents, principals, or superintendents, suggesting that West Point graduates were given administrative positions because of their executive and managerial experience. These men served all over the country and taught all subjects, but mostly mathematics and the natural sciences, up to the level of Yale and Brown.

25. See Mark R. Wilson, *The Business of Civil War: Military Mobilization and the State, 1861–1865* (Baltimore: Johns Hopkins University Press, 2006), chap. 6, for the most extensive assessment apart from my own.

SELECTED BIBLIOGRAPHY

NATIONAL ARCHIVES, WASHINGTON, D.C.

"Entry" means a collection's number in the record group (RG) inventories published by the Archives. "M" followed by a number is the microfilm number for the collection in question.

Records of the Office of the Chief of Engineers, RG 77
    John J. Abert, papers referring to Shawnee removal, Records of the Topographical Bureau, 1818–1867, Central Office, Entry 318
    Letters and Papers Received by the Chief of Engineers, 1789–1831, Entry 20
    Letters and Reports of Col. Joseph G. Totten, 1803–1864, Entry 146
Records of the Office of the Adjutant General, RG 94
    Confidential Inspection Reports, 1812–1826, Entry 20
    General Orders and Circulars of the War Department and General Headquarters of the Army, 1809–1860, M1094
    Letters Received by the Office of the Adjutant General, 1805–1821, M566
    Letters Received by the Office of the Adjutant General, 1821–1860, M567
    Letters Sent by the Office of the Adjutant General (Main Series), 1800–1890, M565
    Thomas Sidney Jesup Papers, Generals' Papers, Entry 159 (these are the letters to and from the theater commander in Florida during the early years of the Second Seminole War)
Records of United States Army Commands, 1784–1821, RG 98
    5th Military Department, Letters Sent, 1815–1821, Entry 67
Records of the Office of the Secretary of War, RG 107
    Confidential and Unofficial Letters Received, 1832–1846, Entry 21
    Confidential and Unofficial Letters Sent by the Secretary of War, 1814–1847, M7
    Letters Received by the Secretary of War, Registered Series, 1801–1870, M221
    Letters Received by Secretary of War, Unregistered Series, 1789–1861, M222
    Letters Sent by the Secretary of War Relating to Military Affairs, 1800–1889, M6
    Letters Sent to the President by the Secretary of War, 1800–1863, M127

Register of Confidential and Unofficial Letters Received, 1832–1846, Entry 20
Registers of Letters Received by the Office of the Secretary of War, Main Series, 1800–1870, M22
Records of the Headquarters of the Army (the commanding general's office), RG 108
Letters Received by the Headquarters of the Army, 1827–1903, M1635
Letters Sent by the Headquarters of the Army (Main Series), 1828–1903, M857
Letters Sent by Major General Alexander Macomb, 1828–1830, Entry 4
Private and Confidential Letters Sent by Major General Alexander Macomb, 1837–1841, Entry 6
Proceedings of the Military Board, 1832–1835, Entry 54
Register of Officers Reporting at the Adjutant General's Office, 1837–1841, Entry 58
Semi-Official Letter Book of Major General Alexander Macomb, 1828–1832, Entry 5
Unregistered Letters Received, 1821–1902, Entry 23
Records of the Office of the Inspector General, RG 159
Inspection Reports, 1814–1842, M624
Records of U.S. Regular Army Mobile Units, 1821–1942, RG 391
Fourth Infantry Regiment Letters Sent and Received, 1823–1835, Entry 1136
Second Infantry Regiment Letters Sent, 1825–1832, Entry 1065
Sixth Infantry Regiment Letters Sent, 1821–1841, Entry 1203
Sixth Infantry Regiment Letters Sent, 1824–1833, Entry 1204
Sixth Infantry Regiment Letters Sent and Received, 1817–1824, Entry 1202
Records of the U.S. Army Continental Commands, 1821–1920, RG 393
Headquarters Records of Fort Gibson, Indian Territory, 1830–1857, M1466
Letterbooks of Walker K. Armistead and William J. Worth, in 9th Military Department (Provisional), Letters Sent, 1838–1845, Entry 72 (these are the letters by the theater commanders in Florida during the latter years of the Second Seminole War)
Letters Sent by Brevet Major General Edmund Pendleton Gaines and Staff, 1819–1826, Entry 5806
Records of Headquarters, Army of the Southwestern Frontier, and Headquarters, Second and Seventh Military Departments, 1835–1853, M1302
6th Military Department (Henry Atkinson), Letters Sent, 1834–1846, Entry 45
7th Military Department (Hugh Brady), Letters Sent, 1828–1846, Entry 56

MANUSCRIPT COLLECTIONS

Robert Alves, Greenwich, Connecticut (private collection)
Thomas Sidney Jesup
Beinecke Rare Book and Manuscript Library, Yale University
Alfred Sully

Burton Historical Collection, Detroit Public Library
- Daniel Baker
- Hugh Brady
- Lewis Cass
- Macomb Family Papers
- Alexander Macomb Letterbook, 1807–1819
- John Mason
- Winfield Scott
- Zachary Taylor
- Henry Whiting
- William Woodbridge

William L. Clements Library, University of Michigan, Ann Arbor
- Jacob Brown
- Lewis Cass
- H. A. S. Dearborn
- Amos B. Eaton
- Maskell C. Ewing (Ewing Family Papers)
- Thomas Sidney Jesup
- Theodore Laidley (Laidley Family Papers)
- John Love
- Winfield Scott
- Alexander R. Thompson

Firestone Library, Princeton University
- William Goldsmith Belknap

Florida State Archives, Tallahassee
- Richard Keith Call Papers
- Governors' Correspondence and Letterbooks (vols. 1–3: 1836, 1840–1841, 1845)
- Records of the Territorial Legislative Council (RG 910, Series 876 and 877)

Georgia Historical Society, Savannah
- William Whann Mackall (Mackall Family Papers)
- Richard B. Screven

Library of Congress, Washington, D.C. (Manuscript Division; many in the Miscellaneous Manuscripts Collection)
- Robert Anderson
- Jacob Brown
- Sylvester Churchill
- Duncan Lamont Clinch
- George Croghan
- George W. Cullum
- James B. Dyer
- Jubal Anderson Early
- Richard Stoddard Ewell
- Edmund Pendleton Gaines

        Ulysses S. Grant
        Henry Wager Halleck
        John Porter Hatch
        Samuel P. Heintzelmann
        Ethan Allen Hitchcock
        Henry J. Hunt
        Andrew Jackson
        Thomas Sidney Jesup
        Roger Jones
        Benjamin King
        Thomas Lawson
        Alexander Macomb
        George Brinton McClellan
        Montgomery C. Meigs
        Alfred Mordecai
        John Pickell
        James K. Polk
        Eleazar Wheelock Ripley
        James Wall Schureman
        Winfield Scott
        Nathaniel Tallmadge
        Zachary Taylor
        Martin Van Buren
        John Ellis Wool
        William Jenkins Worth
        Nathaniel Young
Maryland Historical Society, Baltimore
        Robert Christie Buchanan
Massachusetts Historical Society, Boston (microfilm courtesy of John Morris)
        Jacob Brown
McClung Historical Collection, East Tennessee Historical Society, Knoxville
        William S. Foster
Newberry Library, Chicago
        Stephen Watts Kearny
New Jersey Historical Society, Newark
        Winfield Scott
New York Public Library, New York City
        James Monroe
        John W. Phelps
New York State Library, Albany
        Charles Kitchel Gardner
        John Ellis Wool

Old Colony Historical Society, Taunton, Massachusetts
    Francis Baylies Papers (letters to and from John E. Wool)
Historical Society of Pennsylvania, Philadelphia
    Military Papers of Captain Thomas J. Baird (Edward Carey Gardiner Collection)
    Birch Family
    Cadwalader Family
    Edmund Pendleton Gaines
    George A. McCall
    George Gordon Meade
    Nauman Family
    Daniel Parker
    Poinsett Papers (Gilpin Collection)
William R. Perkins Library, Duke University
    Edward G. W. Butler
    Andrew Jackson
    Thomas Sidney Jesup
    Edward and William Lucas
    James S. McIntosh
    William W. Pew Journal
    John Rogers Vinton
Southern Historical Collection, University of North Carolina, Chapel Hill
    William S. Basinger
    William Davenport
    Alexander Macomb
    Edmund Kirby Smith
Earl Gregg Swem Library, College of William and Mary
    Patrick Henry Galt letters (Galt Family Papers II)
Tennessee Historical Society, Nashville
    Edmund Pendleton Gaines (John W. Gaines Papers)
United States Army Military History Institute, Carlisle, Pennsylvania
    William T. H. Brooks
    Abraham Eustis
    Maskell C. Ewing
    Charles J. Nourse
    Edwin Vose Sumner (Carlisle Papers)
    Lucius B. Webster
    Charles E. Woodruff
United States Military Academy Library, Special Collections, West Point, New York
    Edmund Brooke Alexander
    Robert Allen
    Charles Benjamin Alvord
    Robert Anderson

Jacob W. Bailey
Rufus Lathrop Baker
Philip Norbourne Barbour
Alexander H. Bowman
Braxton Bragg
William Chapman
Thomas Jefferson Cram
Napoleon Tecumseh Dana
Dialectic Society Journal, 1840–1844
James Duncan
William Dutton
Charles Winslow Elliott Collection (Winfield Scott Papers)
Maskell C. Ewing
William Frazer
Ulysses S. Grant
Henry Wager Halleck
Robert Hazlitt
George W. Hazzard
Abner Riviere Hetzel
Ethan Allen Hitchcock
Washington Hood
Joseph F. Irons
Abraham Robinson Johnston
Gouverneur Kemble
Minor Knowlton
Alexander Macomb
Dennis Hart Mahan
John K. F. Mansfield
Morris Smith Miller
John Michael O'Connor
Charles Petigru
John Pope
Samuel H. Raymond
Jeremiah Mason Scarrit
James Wall Schureman
Winfield Scott
Charles Ferguson Smith
Frederick Augustus Smith
Isaac Ingalls Stevens
Alexander J. Swift
Joseph Gardner Swift
Sylvanus Thayer

Joseph G. Totten
  William Jenkins Worth
Virginia Historical Society, Richmond
  George Rush Clarke and William Beverley Clarke (Beverley Family Papers)
  Philip St. George Cooke
  William W. Hoxton (Randolph Family Papers)
  Winfield Scott
  Christopher Q. Tompkins Diary and Letterbook
State Historical Society of Wisconsin, Madison
  William Lindsay
  Winfield Scott
P. K. Yonge Library of Florida History, University of Florida, Gainesville (mostly in the Florida Manuscripts)
  Duncan Lamont Clinch
  William Davenport
  William S. Foster
  Thomas Sidney Jesup Orderbook
  Reynolds M. Kirby Diary
  Joseph R. Smith
  Joseph Van Swearingen

BOOKS, ARTICLES, AND DISSERTATIONS

Abbott, Andrew. *The System of Professions: An Essay on the Division of Expert Labor.* Chicago: University of Chicago Press, 1988.

Abernethy, David B. *The Dynamics of Global Dominance: European Overseas Empires, 1492–1980.* New Haven, Conn.: Yale University Press, 2000.

Abert, James W. *Expedition to the Southwest: An 1845 Reconnaissance of Colorado, New Mexico, Texas, and Oklahoma.* Introductions by John Miller Morris and H. Bailey Carroll. Lincoln: University of Nebraska Press, 1999.

Abrahamson, James L. *America Arms for a New Century: The Making of a Great Military Power.* New York: Free Press, 1981.

Abrahamsson, Bengt. *Military Professionalization and Political Power.* Beverly Hills, Calif.: Sage, 1972.

Abrams, Philip. "Notes on the Difficulty of Studying the State." *Journal of Historical Sociology* 1 (March 1988): 58–89.

Adams, George R. *General William S. Harney, Prince of Dragoons.* Lincoln: University of Nebraska Press, 2001.

Adelman, Jeremy, and Stephen Aron. "From Borderlands to Borders: Empires, Nation-States, and the Peoples in between in North American History." *American Historical Review* 104 (June 1999): 814–841.

Adler, William D., and Andrew J. Polsky. "The State in a Blue Uniform." *Polity* 40 (Summer 2008): 348–354.

Agnew, Brad. *Fort Gibson: Terminal on the Trail of Tears.* Norman: University of Oklahoma Press, 1980.

Albers, Patricia, and Jeanne Kay. "Sharing the Land: A Study in American Indian Territoriality." In *A Cultural Geography of North American Indians*, ed. Thomas E. Ross and Tyrel G. Moore. Boulder, Colo.: Westview Press, 1987.

Altschuler, Glenn C., and Stuart M. Blumin. *Rude Republic: Americans and Their Politics in the Nineteenth Century.* Princeton, N.J.: Princeton University Press, 2000.

Alvord, Benjamin. *Address before the Dialectic Society of the Corps of Cadets, in Commemoration of the Gallant Conduct of the Nine Graduates of the Military Academy, and Other Officers of the United States Army, Who Fell in the Battles Which Took Place in Florida.* New York: Wiley and Putnam, 1839.

American State Papers: Documents, Legislative and Executive, of the Congress of the United States, Class V, Military Affairs. 7 vols. Washington, D.C.: Gales and Seaton, 1832–1861.

Anderson, David M., and David Killingray, eds. *Policing the Empire: Government, Authority, and Control, 1830–1940.* Manchester: Manchester University Press, 1991.

Anderson, Gary C. *The Conquest of Texas: Ethnic Cleansing in the Promised Land, 1820–1875.* Norman: University of Oklahoma Press, 2005.

———. *Kinsmen of Another Kind: Dakota-White Relations in the Upper Mississippi Valley, 1650–1862.* Lincoln: University of Nebraska Press, 1984.

Anderson, Gary Clayton. "The Removal of the Mdewakanton Dakota in 1837: A Test Case for Jacksonian Paternalism." *South Dakota History* 10 (Fall 1980): 310–333.

Anderson, William L., ed. *Cherokee Removal, Before and After.* Athens: University of Georgia Press, 1991.

Andrew, C. M., and A. S. Kanya-Forstner. "Centre and Periphery in the Making of the Second French Empire, 1815–1920." *Journal of Imperial and Commonwealth History* 16, 3 (1988): 9–34.

"The Army of the United States." *North American Review* 28 (October 1826): 245–274.

Arndt, Jochen S. "Treacherous Savages & Merciless Barbarians: Knowledge, Discourse, and Violence during the Cape Frontier Wars, 1834–1853." *Journal of Military History* 74 (July 2010): 709–735.

Aron, Stephen. "Lessons in Conquest: Towards a Greater Western History." *Pacific Historical Quarterly* 63 (May 1994): 125–147.

Astolfi, Douglas M. *Foundations of Destiny: A Foreign Policy of the Jacksonians, 1824–1837.* New York: Garland, 1989.

Athearn, Robert G. *William Tecumseh Sherman and the Settlement of the West.* Norman: University of Oklahoma Press, 1956.

Atkinson, James R. *Splendid Land, Splendid People: The Chickasaw Indians to Removal.* Tuscaloosa: University of Alabama Press, 2004.

Babington, Anthony. *Military Intervention in Britain: From the Gordon Riots to the Gibraltar Incident.* London: Routledge, 1990.

Bailey, John W. *Pacifying the Plains: General Alfred Terry and the Decline of the Sioux, 1866–1890.* Westport, Conn.: Greenwood Press, 1979.

Baldwin, Peter. "Beyond Weak and Strong: Rethinking the State in Comparative Policy History." *Journal of Policy History* 17 (January 2005): 12–33.

Ball, Durwood. *Army Regulars on the Western Frontier, 1848–1861.* Norman: University of Oklahoma Press, 2001.

Ball, Durwood, and Paul R. Hutton, eds. *Soldiers West: Military Biographies from the Western Frontier.* Rev. ed. Norman: University of Oklahoma Press, 2009.

Balough, Brian. *A Government Out of Sight: The Mystery of National Authority in Nineteenth-Century America.* Cambridge: Cambridge University Press, 2009.

Banner, Stuart. *How the Indians Lost Their Land: Law and Power on the Frontier.* Cambridge, Mass.: Harvard University Press, 2005.

Barbuto, Richard V. *Niagara 1814: America Invades Canada.* Lawrence: University Press of Kansas, 2000.

Barfield, Thomas J. *The Perilous Frontier: Nomadic Empires and China.* Oxford: Basil Blackwell, 1989.

Barr, Daniel P., ed. *The Boundaries between Us: Natives and Newcomers along the Frontiers of the Old Northwest Territory, 1750–1850.* Kent, Ohio: Kent State University Press, 2006.

Bassett, John Spencer, ed. *Correspondence of Andrew Jackson.* Vol. 2, *May 1, 1814 to December 31, 1819.* Washington, D.C.: Carnegie Institution of Washington, 1927.

Baud, Michiel, and Willem Van Schendel. "Toward a Comparative History of Borderlands." *Journal of World History* 8 (Fall 1997): 211–242.

Bauer, K. Jack. "The Battles on the Rio Grande: Palo Alto and Resaca de la Palma, 8–9 May 1846." In *America's First Battles, 1776–1965,* ed. Charles E. Heller and William A. Stofft. Lawrence: University Press of Kansas, 1986.

——— . *Zachary Taylor: Soldier, Planter, and Statesman of the Old Southwest.* Baton Rouge: Louisiana State University Press, 1985.

Baumann, Robert F. *Russian-Soviet Unconventional Wars in the Caucasus, Central Asia, and Afghanistan.* Fort Leavenworth, Kans.: U.S. Army Combat Studies Institute, 1993.

Bayly, C. A. *Empire and Information: Intelligence-Gathering and Social Communication in India, 1780–1870.* Cambridge: Cambridge University Press, 1990.

——— . *Imperial Meridian: The British Empire and the World, 1780–1830.* London: Longman, 1989.

Bearss, Edwin C., and Arrell M. Gibson. *Fort Smith: Little Gibraltar on the Arkansas.* Norman: University of Oklahoma Press, 1969.

Becker, William H., and Samuel F. Wells, eds. *Economics and World Power: An Assessment of American Diplomacy since 1789.* New York: Columbia University Press, 1984.

Beckett, Ian. *The Victorians at War.* London: Hambleton and London, 2003.

Beers, Henry P. "The Army and the Oregon Trail to 1846." *Pacific Northwest Quarterly* 28 (October 1937): 339–362.

———. *The Western Military Frontier, 1815–1846.* 1935. Reprint, Philadelphia: Porcupine Press, 1975.

Belich, James. *The New Zealand Wars and the Victorian Interpretation of Racial Conflict.* Auckland, New Zealand: Auckland University Press, 1986.

———. *Replenishing the Earth: The Settler Revolution and the Rise of the Anglo-World, 1783–1939.* Oxford: Clarendon Press, 2009.

Belko, William S., ed. *America's Hundred Years' War: U.S. Expansion to the Gulf Coast and the Fate of the Seminole, 1763–1858.* Gainesville: University Press of Florida, 2010.

Belohlavek, John M. *"Let the Eagle Soar!" The Foreign Policy of Andrew Jackson.* Lincoln: University of Nebraska Press, 1985.

Berkeley, George E. *The Democratic Policeman.* Boston: Beacon, 1969.

Berkhofer, Robert F. *The White Man's Indian: Images of the American Indian from Columbus to the Present.* New York: Alfred A. Knopf, 1978.

Binnema, Ted, and William A. Dobak. "'Like the Greedy Wolf': The Blackfeet, the St. Louis Fur Trade, and War Fever, 1807–1831." *Journal of the Early Republic* 29 (Fall 2009): 411–440.

Black, Jeremy. *America as a Military Power: From the American Revolution to the Civil War.* Westport, Conn.: Praeger, 2002.

———. *War in the Nineteenth Century, 1800–1914.* Cambridge: Polity Press, 2009.

———. *Western Warfare, 1775–1882.* Bloomington: Indiana University Press, 2001.

Blackwood, Emma Jerome, ed. *To Mexico with Scott: Letters of Captain E. Kirby Smith to His Wife.* Cambridge, Mass.: Harvard University Press, 1917.

Blaine, Martha Royce. *The Ioway Indians.* Norman: University of Oklahoma Press, 1979.

Bolton, S. Charles. *Arkansas, 1800–1860: Remote and Restless.* Fayetteville: University of Arkansas Press, 1998.

Bond, Brian, ed. *Victorian Military Campaigns.* New York: Praeger, 1967.

Bourne, Kenneth. *Britain and the Balance of Power in North America, 1815–1908.* Berkeley: University of California Press, 1967.

Bowes, John P. *Exiles and Pioneers: Eastern Indians in the Trans-Mississippi West.* Cambridge: Cambridge University Press, 2007.

Bradford, James C., ed. *Command under Sail: Makers of the American Naval Tradition, 1775–1850.* Annapolis, Md.: Naval Institute Press, 1985.

———. *The Military and Conflict between Cultures: Soldiers at the Interface.* College Station: Texas A&M University Press, 1997.

Bradshaw, Brendan, and John Morrill, eds. *The British Problem, c. 1534–1707: State Formation in the Atlantic Archipelago.* New York: St. Martin's Press, 1996.

Bragg, Braxton. "Notes on Our Army." *Southern Literary Messenger* 10 (February 1844): 86–87, 155–157, 246–251, 283–287, 372–377, 750–753; 11 (February 1845): 39–47, 104–105.

Brantlinger, Patrick. *Rule of Darkness: British Literature and Imperialism, 1830–1914.* Ithaca, N.Y.: Cornell University Press, 1988.

Brauer, Kinley J. "The Great American Desert Revisited: Recent Literature and Prospects for the Study of American Foreign Relations, 1815–1860." *Diplomatic History* 13 (Summer 1989): 395–417.

———. "The United States and British Imperial Expansion, 1815–1860." *Diplomatic History* 12 (Winter 1988): 19–37.

Bright, Charles C. "The State in the United States in the Nineteenth Century." In *Statemaking and Social Movements: Essays in History and Theory,* ed. Charles C. Bright and Susan Harding. Ann Arbor: University of Michigan Press, 1984.

Brower, Benjamin Claude. *A Desert Named Peace: The Violence of France's Empire in the Algerian Sahara, 1844–1902.* New York: Columbia University Press, 2009.

Brower, Daniel R., and Edward J. Lazzerini, eds. *Russia's Orient: Imperial Borderlands and Peoples, 1700–1917.* Bloomington: Indiana University Press, 1997.

Brown, Alan S. "The Role of the Army in Western Settlement: Josiah Harmar's Command, 1785–1790." *Pennsylvania Magazine of History and Biography* 93 (April 1969): 161–178.

Brown, Charles H. *Agents of Manifest Destiny: The Lives and Times of the Filibusters.* Chapel Hill: University of North Carolina Press, 1980.

Brown, Richard D. *Knowledge Is Power: The Diffusion of Information in Early America, 1700–1865.* New York: Oxford University Press, 1989.

Brown, Richard Maxwell. "Western Violence: Structure, Values, Myth." *Western Historical Quarterly* 24 (February 1993): 4–20.

Brown, Thomas. *Politics and Statesmanship: Essays on the American Whig Party.* New York: Columbia University Press, 1985.

Burbank, Jane, Mark von Hagen, and Anatolyi Remnev, eds. *Russian Empire: Space, People, and Power, 1700–1930.* Bloomington: Indiana University Press, 2007.

Burroughs, Peter. "Imperial Defence and the Victorian Army." *Journal of Imperial and Commonwealth History* 15, 1 (1986): 55–72.

Burt, A. L. *The United States, Great Britain, and British North America, from the Revolution to the Establishment of Peace after the War of 1812.* New Haven, Conn.: Yale University Press, 1940.

Bushman, Richard L. *The Refinement of America, 1750–1850: Persons, Houses, Cities.* New York: Alfred A. Knopf, 1993.

Byler, Charles. *Civil-Military Relations on the Frontier and Beyond, 1865–1917.* Westport, Conn.: Praeger Security International, 2006.

Cain, P. J., and A. G. Hopkins. *British Imperialism: Innovation and Expansion, 1688–2000.* London: Longman, 2001.

Caldwell, Dorothy J. "The Big Neck Affair: Tragedy and Farce on the Missouri Frontier." *Missouri Historical Review* 64 (July 1970): 391–412.

Calhoun, Daniel H. *Professional Lives in America: Structure and Aspiration, 1750–1850.* Cambridge, Mass.: Harvard University Press, 1965.

Calhoun, Frederick S. *The Lawmen: United States Marshals and Their Deputies, 1789–1989*. Washington, D.C.: Smithsonian Institution, 1989.

Calloway, Colin G. *Crown and Calumet: British-Indian Relations, 1783–1815*. Norman: University of Oklahoma Press, 1987.

———. "The End of an Era: British-Indian Relations in the Great Lakes Region after the War of 1812." *Michigan Historical Review* 12 (Fall 1986): 4–20.

Callwell, C. E. *Small Wars, Their Principles and Practice*. 3rd ed. 1906. Reprinted with an introduction by Douglas Porch. Lincoln: University of Nebraska Press, 1996.

Cannadine, David. *Ornamentalism: How the British Saw Their Empire*. New York: Oxford University Press, 2001.

Carlson, Leonard A., and Mark A. Roberts. "Indian Lands, 'Squatterism,' and Slavery: Economic Interests and the Passage of the Indian Removal Act of 1830." *Explorations in Economic History* 43 (July 2006): 486–504.

Carp, E. Wayne. *To Starve the Army at Leisure: Continental Army Administration and American Political Culture, 1775–1783*. Chapel Hill: University of North Carolina Press, 1984.

Carpenter, Daniel P. *The Forging of Bureaucratic Autonomy: Reputations, Networks, and Policy Innovation in Executive Agencies, 1862–1928*. Princeton, N.J.: Princeton University Press, 2001.

Carroll, Francis M. *A Good and Wise Measure: The Search for the Canadian-American Boundary, 1783–1842*. Toronto: University of Toronto Press, 2001.

Carter, Clarence E., and John P. Bloom, eds. *The Territorial Papers of the United States*. 28 vols. Washington, D.C.: U.S. State Department and National Archives, 1934–1975.

Cave, Alfred A. "Abuse of Power: Andrew Jackson and the Indian Removal Act of 1830." *Historian* 65 (Winter 2003): 1330–1353.

Cayton, Andrew R. L. "'Separate Interests' and the Nation-State: The Washington Administration and the Origins of Regionalism in the Trans-Appalachian West." *Journal of American History* 79 (June 1992): 39–67.

Cayton, Andrew R. L., and Fredrika J. Teute, eds. *Contact Points: American Frontiers from the Mohawk Valley to the Mississippi, 1750–1830*. Chapel Hill: University of North Carolina Press, 1998.

Cell, John W. *British Colonial Administration in the Mid-Nineteenth Century: The Policy-making Process*. New Haven, Conn.: Yale University Press, 1970.

Chaffin, Tom. *Pathfinder: John Charles Frémont and the Course of American Empire*. New York: Hill and Wang, 2002.

Champagne, Duane. *Social Order and Political Change: Constitutional Governments among the Cherokee, the Choctaw, the Chickasaw, and the Creek*. Stanford, Calif.: Stanford University Press, 1992.

Childress, David T. "The Army in Transition: The United States Army, 1815–1846." Ph.D. diss., Mississippi State University, 1974.

Citino, Nathan J. "The Global Frontier: Comparative History and the Frontier-

Borderlands Approach in American Foreign Relations." *Diplomatic History* 25 (Fall 2001): 677–693.

Clark, Kevin. "Hard Corps: Native American Resistance, Leadership, and Tactics in Florida, 1835–1838." M.A. thesis, University of North Carolina, 2000.

Clarke, Dwight L. *Stephen Watts Kearny, Soldier of the West.* Norman: University of Oklahoma Press, 1961.

Clayton, Anthony. *France, Soldiers, and Africa.* London: Brassey's, 1988.

Coakley, Robert W. *The Role of Federal Military Forces in Domestic Disorders, 1789–1878.* Washington, D.C.: Center of Military History, 1988.

Cobden, Richard. *How Wars Are Got up in India: The Origin of the Burma War.* London: William and Frederick G. Cash, 1853.

Coffman, Edward M. *The Old Army: A Portrait of the American Army in Peacetime, 1784–1898.* New York: Oxford University Press, 1986.

Cohen, Eliot A. "The Unequal Dialogue: The Theory and Reality of Civil-Military Relations and the Use of Force." In *Soldiers and Civilians: The Civil-Military Gap and American National Security*, ed. Peter D. Feaver and Richard H. Kohn. Cambridge, Mass.: MIT Press, 2001.

Coker, Edward C., and Daniel L. Schafer. "A West Point Graduate in the Second Seminole War: William Warren Chapman and the View from Fort Foster." *Florida Historical Quarterly* 68 (April 1990): 447–475.

Cole, Donald B. *The Presidency of Andrew Jackson.* Lawrence: University Press of Kansas, 1993.

Collins, Bruce. "The Ideology of the Ante-bellum Northern Democrats." *American Studies* 11 (April 1977): 103–121.

Comer, Douglas C. *Ritual Ground: Bent's Old Fort, World Formation, and the Annexation of the American Southwest.* Berkeley: University of California Press, 1996.

Connelley, William E., ed. "A Journal of the Santa Fe Trail." *Mississippi Valley Historical Review* 12 (June–September 1925): 72–98, 227–255.

Connelly, Donald. *John M. Schofield and the Politics of Generalship.* Chapel Hill: University of North Carolina Press, 2006.

Connor, John. *The Australian Frontier Wars, 1788–1838.* Sydney: University of New South Wales Press, 2002.

Conover, Cheryl, ed. "A Kentuckian in 'King Andrew's' Court: The Letters of John Waller Barry, Washington, D.C., 1831–1835." *Register of the Kentucky Historical Society* 81 (Spring 1983): 168–198.

———. "'To Please Papa': The Letters of John Waller Barry, West Point Cadet, 1826–1830." *Register of the Kentucky Historical Society* 80 (Spring 1982): 183–212.

Conser, Walter H., Jr. "John Ross and the Cherokee Resistance Campaign, 1833–1838." *Journal of Southern History* 44 (May 1978): 191–212.

Conway, Thomas G. "Potawatomi Politics." *Journal of the Illinois State Historical Society* 65 (Winter 1972): 395–418.

Cook, Hugh. *The Sikh Wars: The British Army in the Punjab, 1845–1849*. London: Leo Cooper, 1975.

Cooke, Philip St. George. *Scenes and Adventures in the Army, or, the Romance of Military Life*. Philadelphia: Lindsay and Blakiston, 1857.

Corey, Albert. *The Crisis of 1830–1842 in Canadian-American Relations*. New Haven, Conn.: Yale University Press, 1941.

Corrigan, Philip, and Derek Sayer. *The Great Arch: English State Formation as Cultural Revolution*. Oxford: Basil Blackwell, 1985.

Covington, James W. *The Seminoles of Florida*. Gainesville: University Press of Florida, 1993.

Cox, J. Wendel. "A World Together, a World Apart: The United States and the Arikaras, 1803–1851." Ph.D. diss., University of Minnesota, 1998.

Cozzens, Peter, ed. *Eyewitnesses to the Indian Wars, 1865–1890*. Vol. 5. *The Army and the Indian*. Mechanicsburg, Pa.: Stackpole Books, 2005.

Craig, Gordon A. *The Politics of the Prussian Army, 1640–1945*. New York: Oxford University Press, 1955.

Croffut, W. A., ed. *Fifty Years in Camp and Field: The Diary of Major-General Ethan Allen Hitchcock, U.S.A.* New York: G. P. Putnam's Sons, 1909.

Crowder, Michael, ed. *West African Resistance: The Military Response to Colonial Occupation*. London: Hutchinson, 1971.

Cullum, George W., comp. *Biographical Register of the Officers and Graduates of the U.S. Military Academy*. 2 vols. New York: D. Van Nostrand, 1868.

Cunliffe, Marcus. *Soldiers and Civilians: The Martial Spirit in America, 1776–1865*. 2nd ed. New York: Free Press, 1973.

Curtis, James C. *The Fox at Bay: Martin Van Buren and the Presidency, 1837–1841*. Lexington: University Press of Kentucky, 1970.

Curtiss, John Shelton. *The Russian Army under Nicholas I, 1825–1855*. Durham, N.C.: Duke University Press, 1965.

Dale, Elizabeth. *Criminal Justice in the United States, 1789–1939*. Cambridge: Cambridge University Press, 2011.

Dandeker, Christopher. *Surveillance, Power, and Modernity: Bureaucracy and Discipline from 1700 to the Present Day*. New York: St. Martin's Press, 1990.

Daniel, Donald C. F., Patricia Taft, and Sharon Wiharta, eds. *Peace Operations: Trends, Progress, and Prospects*. Washington, D.C.: Georgetown University Press, 2008.

Danziger, Raphael. *Abd al-Qadir and the Algerians: Resistance to the French and Internal Consolidation*. New York: Holmes and Meier, 1977.

Darwin, John. "Imperialism and the Victorians: The Dynamics of Territorial Expansion." *English Historical Review* 112 (June 1997): 634–640.

Dawson, Graham. *Soldier Heroes: British Adventure, Empire, and the Imagining of Masculinities*. London: Routledge, 1994.

Dawson, Joseph G., III. *Army Generals and Reconstruction: Louisiana, 1862–1877*. Baton Rouge: Louisiana State University Press, 1982.

Debo, Angie. *The Rise and Fall of the Choctaw Republic.* Norman: University of Oklahoma Press, 1934.
———. *The Road to Disappearance.* Norman: University of Oklahoma Press, 1941.
DeLay, Brian. "Independent Indians and the U.S.-Mexican War." *American Historical Review* 112 (February 2007): 35–68.
———. *War of a Thousand Deserts: Indian Raids and the U.S.-Mexican War.* New Haven, Conn.: Yale University Press, 2008.
D'Elia, Donald J. "The Argument over Civilian or Military Indian Control, 1865–1880." *Historian* 24 (February 1962): 207–225.
Deloria, Philip J. *Playing Indian.* New Haven, Conn.: Yale University Press, 1998.
deMoor, J. A., and H. L. Wesseling, eds. *Imperialism and War: Essays on Colonial Wars in Asia and Africa.* Leiden, Netherlands: Brill, 1989.
Denham, James M. "'Some Prefer the Seminoles': Violence and Disorder among Soldiers and Settlers in the Second Seminole War, 1835–1842." *Florida Historical Quarterly* 70 (July 1991): 38–54.
DePalo, William A., Jr. *The Mexican National Army, 1822–1852.* College Station: Texas A&M University Press, 1997.
DeRosier, Arthur H., Jr. *The Removal of the Choctaw Indians.* Knoxville: University of Tennessee Press, 1970.
Dippie, Brian W. *The Vanishing American: White Attitudes and U.S. Indian Policy.* Middletown, Conn.: Wesleyan University Press, 1982.
Doherty, Herbert J. *Richard Keith Call, Southern Unionist.* Gainesville: University Presses of Florida, 1961.
Doubleday, Rhoda van Bibber Tanner, ed. *Journals of the Late Brevet Major Philip Norbourne Barbour and His Wife Martha Isabella Hopkins Barbour Written during the War with Mexico—1846.* New York: G. P. Putnam's Sons, 1936.
Douglas, R. Alan. *Uppermost Canada: The Western District and the Detroit Frontier, 1800–1850.* Detroit: Wayne State University Press, 2001.
Drecker, Peter R. *"The Utes Must Go!" American Expansion and the Removal of a People.* Golden, Colo.: Fulcrum, 2004.
Drinnon, Richard. *Facing West: The Metaphysics of Indian-Hating and Empire Building.* Minneapolis: University of Minnesota Press, 1980.
Duffy, Christopher. *The Military Experience in the Age of Reason.* New York: Atheneum, 1988.
Duffy, John J., and H. Nicholas Muller. *An Anxious Democracy: Aspects of the 1830s.* Westport, Conn.: Praeger, 1982.
Durkheim, Emile. *Professional Ethics and Civic Morals.* Trans. Cornelia Brookfield. London: Routledge and Kegan Paul, 1957.
Du Val, Kathleen. *The Native Ground: Indians and Colonists in the Heart of the Continent.* Philadelphia: University of Pennsylvania Press, 2006.
Dyer, Brainerd. *Zachary Taylor.* Baton Rouge: Louisiana State University Press, 1946.

Earle, Carville, and Changyong Cao. "Frontier Closure and the Involution of American Society, 1840–1890." *Journal of the Early Republic* 13 (Summer 1993): 163–179.

Eblen, Jack Ericson. *The First and Second United States Empires: Governors and Territorial Government, 1784–1912.* Pittsburgh: University of Pittsburgh Press, 1968.

Edmunds, R. David. *The Potawatomis: Keepers of the Fire.* Norman: University of Oklahoma Press, 1978.

Elias, Norbert. *The Civilizing Process. Part I: The History of Manners.* Trans. Edmund Jephcott. 1939. Reprint, New York: Urizen Books, 1978.

———. *The Civilizing Process. Part II: Power and Civility.* Trans. Edmund Jephcott. 1939. Reprint, New York: Pantheon, 1982.

———. *The Court Society.* Trans. Edmund Jephcott. 1969. Reprint, Oxford: Basil Blackwell, 1983.

Elliott, Charles Winslow. *Winfield Scott: The Soldier and the Man.* New York: Macmillan, 1937.

Elliott, Philip. *The Sociology of the Professions.* New York: Herder and Herder, 1972.

Ellis, Richard N. *General Pope and U.S. Indian Policy.* Albuquerque: University of New Mexico Press, 1970.

Ellis, Steven G. *Tudor Frontiers and Noble Power: The Making of the British State.* Oxford: Clarendon Press, 1995.

Ellisor, John T. *The Second Creek War: Interethnic Conflict and Collusion on a Collapsing Frontier.* Lincoln: University of Nebraska Press, 2010.

Emmons, David M. "Constructed Province: History and the Making of the Last American West." *Western Historical Quarterly* 25 (Winter 1994): 437–459.

Escott, Paul D. *Military Necessity: Civil-Military Relations in the Confederacy.* Westport, Conn.: Praeger Security International, 2006.

Ewers, John C. *The Blackfeet: Raiders on the Northwestern Plains.* Norman: University of Oklahoma Press, 1958.

Farwell, Byron. *Eminent Victorian Soldiers: Seekers of Glory.* New York: W. W. Norton, 1985.

Feaver, Peter D. *Armed Servants: Agency, Oversight, and Civil-Military Relations.* Cambridge, Mass.: Harvard University Press, 2003.

———. "The Civil-Military Problematique: Huntington, Janowitz, and the Question of Civilian Control." *Armed Forces and Society* 23 (Winter 1996): 149–178.

Feld, Maury D. *The Structure of Violence: Armed Forces as Social Systems.* Preface by Charles C. Moskos. Beverly Hills, Calif.: Sage, 1977.

Feller, Daniel. *The Jacksonian Promise: America, 1815–1840.* Baltimore: Johns Hopkins University Press, 1995.

———. "Politics and Society: Toward a Jacksonian Synthesis." *Journal of the Early Republic* 10 (Summer 1990): 135–161.

———. *The Public Lands in Jacksonian Politics.* Madison: University of Wisconsin Press, 1984.

Ferguson, R. Brian, and Neil L. Whitehead, eds. *War in the Tribal Zone: Expanding*

States and Indigenous Warfare. Santa Fe, N.M.: School of American Research Press, 1992.

Ferrell, Robert H., ed. *Monterrey Is Ours! The Mexican War Letters of Lieutenant Dana, 1845–1847*. Lexington: University Press of Kentucky, 1990.

Fessler, W. Julian, ed. "Captain Nathan Boone's Journal." *Chronicles of Oklahoma* 7 (March 1929): 58–105.

Fielding, A. G., and D. Portwood. "Professions and the State: Towards a Typology of Bureaucratic Professions." *Sociological Review* 28 (February 1980): 23–54.

Finer, Samuel E. *The Man on Horseback: The Role of the Military in Politics*. 1964. Rev. ed. Boulder, Colo.: Westview Press, 1988.

Fitzgerald, Michael S. "Europe and the United States Defense Establishment: American Military Policy and Strategy, 1815–1821." Ph.D. diss., Purdue University, 1990.

Ford, Lisa. *Settler Sovereignty: Jurisdiction and Indigenous People in America and Australia, 1788–1836*. Cambridge, Mass.: Harvard University Press, 2010.

Foreman, Carolyn T. "Colonel James B. Many, Commandant at Fort Gibson, Fort Towson, and Fort Smith." *Chronicles of Oklahoma* 19 (June 1941): 119–128.

———. "General Bennet Riley, Commandant at Fort Gibson and Governor of California." *Chronicles of Oklahoma* 19 (September 1941): 225–244.

Foreman, Grant. *Advancing the Frontier, 1830–1860*. Norman: University of Oklahoma Press, 1933.

———. *Indian Removal: The Emigration of the Five Civilized Tribes of Indians*. Norman: University of Oklahoma Press, 1932.

———. *Indians and Pioneers: The Story of the American Southwest before 1830*. New Haven, Conn.: Yale University Press, 1930.

———. *The Last Trek of the Indians*. Chicago: University of Chicago Press, 1946.

———, ed. *A Traveler in Indian Territory: The Journal of Ethan Allen Hitchcock*. With a foreword by Michael D. Green. Norman: University of Oklahoma Press, 1996.

Formisano, Ronald P. "Deferential-Participant Politics: The Early Republic's Political Culture, 1789–1840." *American Political Science Review* 68 (June 1974): 473–487.

Forry, Samuel. "Letters of Samuel Forry, Surgeon, U.S. Army, 1837–1838." *Florida Historical Quarterly* 6 (January 1928): 133–148; (April 1928): 206–219; 7 (July 1928): 88–105.

"Forum on the American State." *Polity* 40 (July 2008).

Fredrikson, John C. *Shield of Republic, Sword of Empire: A Bibliography of United States Military Affairs, 1783–1846*. Westport, Conn.: Greenwood Press, 1990.

Freedom, Gary S. "The Role of the Military and the Spread of Settlement in the Northern Great Plains, 1866–1891." *Midwest Review* 9 (Spring 1987): 1–11.

Fryer, Mary Beacock. *Volunteers, Redcoats, Rebels, and Raiders: A Military History of the Rebellions in Upper Canada*. Toronto: Dundurn Press, 1987.

Galbraith, John S. "The 'Turbulent Frontier' as a Factor in British Expansion." *Comparative Studies in Society and History* 2 (January 1960): 150–168.

Gallant, Thomas W. "Brigandage, Piracy, Capitalism, and State Formation: Transnational Crime from a Historical World-Systems Perspective." In *States and Illegal Practices*, ed. Josiah McC. Heyman. Oxford: Berg, 1999.

Gardner, Charles K., comp. *A Dictionary of the Officers of the Army of the United States*. New York: G. P. Putnam, 1860.

Gardner, Hamilton. "Captain Philip St. George Cooke and the March of the 1st Dragoons to the Rocky Mountains in 1845." *Colorado Magazine* 30 (October 1953): 246–269.

Garrison, Tim Alan. *The Legal Ideology of Removal: The Southern Judiciary and the Sovereignty of Native American Nations*. Athens: University of Georgia Press, 2002.

Garver, John B., Jr. "Practical Military Geographers and Mappers of the Trans-Missouri West, 1820–1860." In *Mapping the North American Plains: Essays in the History of Cartography*, ed. Frederick C. Luebke, Francis W. Kaye, and Gary Moulton. Norman: University of Oklahoma Press, 1987.

———. "The Role of the United States Army in the Colonization of the Trans-Missouri West: Kansas, 1804–1861." Ph.D. diss., Syracuse University, 1981.

Gates, John M. "The Alleged Isolation of the U.S. Army Officers in the Late Nineteenth Century." *Parameters* 10 (Spring 1980): 32–45.

———. "Indians and Insurrectos: The U.S. Army's Experience with Insurgency." *Parameters* 13 (March 1983): 59–68.

Gerth, Hans, and C. Wright Mills. *Character and Social Structure: The Psychology of Social Institutions*. New York: Harcourt, Brace, 1953.

Gibson, Arrell M. *The Chickasaws*. Norman: University of Oklahoma Press, 1971.

———. *The Kickapoos: Lords of the Middle Border*. Norman: University of Oklahoma Press, 1963.

Giddens, Anthony. *The Nation-State and Violence: Volume Two of a Contemporary Critique of Historical Materialism*. Berkeley: University of California Press, 1985.

Gitlin, Jay. "Private Diplomacy to Private Property: States, Tribes, and Nations in the Early National Period." *Diplomatic History* 22 (Winter 1998): 85–99.

Goetzmann, William H. *Army Exploration in the American West, 1803–1863*. New Haven. Conn.: Yale University Press, 1959.

———. *When the Eagle Screamed: The Romantic Horizon in American Diplomacy, 1800–1860*. New York: John Wiley and Sons, 1966.

Goldberg, David Theo. *The Racial State*. Oxford: Blackwell, 2002.

Gordon, William A., comp. *A Compilation of Registers of the Army of the United States, from 1815 to 1837*. Washington, D.C.: James C. Dunn, 1837.

Gough, Terrence J. "Isolation and Professionalization of the Army Officer Corps: A Post-Revisionist View of *The Soldier and the State*." *Social Science Quarterly* 73 (June 1992): 420–436.

Gould, Eliga H. "The Making of an Atlantic State System: Britain and the United States, 1795–1825." In *Britain and America Go to War: The Impact of War and Warfare in Anglo-America, 1754–1815*, ed. Julie Flavell and Stephen Conway. Gainesville: University Press of Florida, 2004.

Grandstaff, Mark R. "Preserving the 'Habits and Usages of War': William Tecumseh Sherman, Professional Reform, and the U.S. Army Officer Corps, 1865–1881, Revisited." *Journal of Military History* 62 (July 1998): 521–545.

Graves, Donald E. *Guns across the River: The Battle of the Windmill, 1838*. Toronto: Robin Brass, 2001.

Graybill, Andrew R. *Policing the Great Plains: Rangers, Mounties, and the North American Frontier, 1875–1910*. Lincoln: University of Nebraska Press, 2007.

Green, Michael D. *The Politics of Indian Removal: Creek Government and Society in Crisis*. Lincoln: University of Nebraska Press, 1982.

Greenberg, Amy S. *Manifest Manhood and the Antebellum American Empire*. Cambridge: Cambridge University Press, 2005.

Greengrass, Mark, ed. *Conquest and Coalescence: The Shaping of the State in Early Modern Europe*. London: Edward Arnold, 1991.

Grenier, John. *The First Way of War: American War Making on the Frontier, 1607–1814*. Cambridge: Cambridge University Press, 2005.

Griess, Thomas E. "Dennis Hart Mahan: West Point Professor and Advocate of Military Professionalism, 1830–1871." Ph.D. diss., Duke University, 1968.

Griffith, Benjamin W., Jr. *McIntosh and Weatherford: Creek Indian Leaders*. Tuscaloosa: University of Alabama Press, 1988.

Grimsley, Mark. "'Rebels' and 'Redskins': U.S. Military Conduct toward White Southerners and Native Americans in Comparative Perspective." In *Civilians in the Path of War*, ed. Mark Grimsley and Clifford J. Rogers. Lincoln: University of Nebraska Press, 2002.

Grippaldi, Richard N. "The Politics of Appointment in the Jacksonian Army: The (Non)Transfer of Ethan Allen Hitchcock to the Regiment of Dragoons, 1833." *Army History* 70 (Winter 2009): 26–35.

Guice, John D. W., and Thomas D. Clark. *Frontiers in Conflict: The Old Southwest, 1795–1830*. Albuquerque: University of New Mexico Press, 1989.

Gump, James O. *The Dust Rose Like Smoke: The Subjugation of the Zulu and the Sioux*. Lincoln: University of Nebraska Press, 1994.

Gunn, L. Ray. *The Decline of Authority: Public Economic Policy and Political Development in New York, 1800–1860*. Ithaca, N.Y.: Cornell University Press, 1988.

Gyarmati, Gabriel. "Ideologies, Roles, and Aspirations: The Doctrine of the Professions—The Basis of a Power Structure." *International Social Science Journal* 27 (November 1975): 629–654.

Haber, Samuel. *The Quest for Authority and Honor in the American Professions, 1750–1900*. Chicago: University of Chicago Press, 1991.

Hagan, William T. *The Sac and Fox Indians*. Norman: University of Oklahoma Press, 1958.

Hall, John W. *Uncommon Defense: Indian Allies in the Black Hawk War*. Cambridge, Mass.: Harvard University Press, 2009.

Hämäläinen, Pekka. *The Comanche Empire*. New Haven, Conn.: Yale University Press, 2008.

———. "The Politics of Grass: European Expansion, Ecological Change, and Indigenous Power in the Southwest Borderlands." *William and Mary Quarterly*, 3rd ser., 67 (April 2010): 173–208.

Hamersly, Thomas H. S., comp. *Complete Regular Army Register of the United States, for One Hundred Years (1779 to 1879)*. Washington, D.C.: T. H. S. Hamersly, 1880.

Hammond, M. C. M. *An Oration on the Duties and the Requirements of an American Officer, Delivered before the Dialectic Society of the United States Military Academy at West Point*. New York: Baker, Godwin, 1852.

Hannah, Matthew G. *Governmentality and the Mastery of Territory in Nineteenth-Century America*. Cambridge: Cambridge University Press, 2000.

Hansen, Marcus L. *Old Fort Snelling, 1819–1858*. Minneapolis: Ross and Haines, 1958.

Hardin, J. Fair. "Fort Jesup, Fort Selden, Camp Sabine, Camp Salubrity: Four Forgotten Frontier Posts of Western Louisiana." *Louisiana Historical Quarterly* 16 (1933): 5–26, 278–292, 441–453, 670–680; 17 (January 1934): 139–168.

Hargreaves, Mary W. M. *The Presidency of John Quincy Adams*. Lawrence: University Press of Kansas, 1985.

Harmon, Alexandra. *Rich Indians: Native People and the Problem of Wealth in American History*. Chapel Hill: University of North Carolina Press, 2010.

Harper, Elizabeth Ann. "The Taovayas Indians in Frontier Trade and Diplomacy, 1779–1835." *Panhandle-Plains Historical Review* 26 (1953): 1–32.

Hartley, Janet. *Russia, 1762–1825: Military Power, the State, and the People*. Westport, Conn.: Praeger, 2008.

Haskin, William L. *The History of the First Regiment of Artillery: From Its Organization in 1821, to January 1st, 1876*. Portland, Me.: B. Thurston, 1879.

Hatch, Nathan O., ed. *The Professions in American History*. Notre Dame, Ind.: University of Notre Dame Press, 1988.

Hauptman, Laurence M. "General John E. Wool in Cherokee Country, 1836–1837: A Reinterpretation." *Georgia Historical Quarterly* 85 (Spring 2001): 1–26.

———. *Tribes & Tribulations: Misconceptions about American Indians and Their Histories*. Albuquerque: University of New Mexico Press, 1995.

Haynes, Sam W. *Unfinished Revolution: The Early American Republic in a British World*. Charlottesville: University Press of Virginia, 2011.

Headrick, Daniel R. *The Tools of Empire: Technology and European Imperialism in the Nineteenth Century*. New York: Oxford University Press, 1981.

———. *When Information Came of Age: Technologies of Knowledge in the Age of Reason and Revolution, 1700–1850*. New York: Oxford University Press, 2000.

Hechter, Michael. *Internal Colonialism: The Celtic Fringe in British National Development, 1536–1966*. Berkeley: University of California Press, 1975.

Heidler, Jeanne T. "The Military Career of David E. Twiggs." Ph.D. diss., Auburn University, 1988.

Heitman, Francis B., comp. *Historical Registry and Dictionary of the United States*

Army, from Its Organization, September 29, 1789 to March 2, 1903. 2 vols. Washington, D.C.: Government Printing Office, 1903.

Hendrickson, David C. *Union, Nation, or Empire: The American Debate over International Relations, 1789–1941.* Lawrence: University Press of Kansas, 2009.

Herman, Daniel J. "Romance on the Middle Ground." *Journal of the Early Republic* 19 (Summer 1999): 279–291.

Hernon, Ian. *Britain's Forgotten Wars: Colonial Campaigns of the 19th Century.* London: Sutton Publishing, 2003.

Hershberger, Mary. "Mobilizing Women, Anticipating Abolition: The Struggle against Indian Removal in the 1830s." *Journal of American History* 86 (June 1999): 15–40.

Hietala, Thomas R. *Manifest Design: Anxious Aggrandizement in Late Jacksonian America.* Ithaca, N.Y.: Cornell University Press, 1985.

Higham, John. *From Boundlessness to Consolidation: The Transformation of American Culture, 1848–1860.* Ann Arbor. Mich.: William L. Clements Library, 1969.

Hill, Daniel H. "The Army in Texas." *Southern Quarterly Review* 9 (April 1846): 434–457; 14 (July 1848): 183–197.

Hill, Edward E. *The Office of Indian Affairs, 1824–1880: Historical Sketches.* New York: Clearwater Publishing, 1974.

Hill, Sarah H. "'To Overawe the Indians and Give Confidence to the Whites': Preparations for the Removal of the Cherokee Nation from Georgia." *Georgia Historical Quarterly* 95 (Winter 2011): 465–497.

Hinton, Harwood P. "The Military Career of John Ellis Wool, 1812–1863." Ph.D. diss., University of Wisconsin, 1960.

Hoffman, Paul E. *Florida's Frontiers.* Bloomington: Indiana University Press, 2002.

Hoig, Stanley W. *The Cherokees and Their Chiefs in the Wake of Empire.* Fayetteville: University of Arkansas Press, 1998.

———. *White Man's Paper Trail: Grand Councils and Treaty-Making on the Central Plains.* Boulder: University of Colorado Press, 2006.

Holden, Robert H. *Armies without Nations: Public Violence and State Formation in Central America, 1821–1960.* New York: Oxford University Press, 2004.

Horsman, Reginald. "The Dimensions of an 'Empire for Liberty': Expansion and Republicanism, 1775–1825." *Journal of the Early Republic* 9 (Spring 1989): 1–20.

———. *Expansion and American Indian Policy, 1783–1812.* East Lansing: Michigan State University Press, 1967.

———. *The Origins of Indian Removal, 1815–1824.* Lansing: Michigan State University Press, 1970.

———. *Race and Manifest Destiny: The Origins of American Racial Anglo-Saxonism.* Cambridge, Mass.: Harvard University Press, 1981.

Howe, Daniel Walker. *The Political Culture of the American Whigs.* Chicago: University of Chicago Press, 1979.

———. *What Hath God Wrought? The Transformation of America, 1815–1848.* New York: Oxford University Press, 2007.

Hoxie, Frederick E. *Parading through History: The Making of the Crow Nation in America, 1805–1935*. Cambridge: Cambridge University Press, 1995.

Hruby, Dale E. "The Civilian Careers of West Point Graduates, Classes of 1802 through 1833." M.A. thesis, Columbia University, 1965.

Hryniewicki, Richard J. "The Creek Treaty of Washington, 1826." *Georgia Historical Quarterly* 48 (December 1964): 425–441.

Hudson, Angela Pulley. *Creek Paths and Federal Roads: Indians, Settlers, and Slaves and the Making of the American South*. Chapel Hill: University of North Carolina Press, 2010.

Hughes, Willis B. "The Heatherly Incident of 1836." *Bulletin of the Missouri Historical Society* 13 (January 1957): 161–180.

Hunt, Edward B. "Army Attack and National Defense." *American Whig Review* 4 (August 1846): 146–160.

Huntington, Samuel P. *Political Order in Changing Societies*. New Haven, Conn.: Yale University Press, 1968.

———. *The Soldier and the State: The Theory and Practice of Civil-Military Relations*. Cambridge, Mass.: Harvard University Press, 1957.

Hurt, R. Douglas. *The Indian Frontier, 1763–1846*. Albuquerque: University of New Mexico Press, 2002.

———. *Nathan Boone and the American Frontier*. Columbia: University of Missouri Press, 1998.

Hutchins, James S., ed. "'Dear Hook': Letters from Bennet Riley, Alphonso Wetmore, and Reuben Holmes, 1822–1833." *Bulletin of the Missouri Historical Society* 36 (1980): 203–220.

Huttenback, Robert A. *British Relations with the Sind, 1799–1843: An Anatomy of Imperialism*. Berkeley: University of California Press, 1962.

Hutton, Paul A. "'Fort Desolation': The Military Establishment, the Railroad, and Settlement on the Northern Plains." *North Dakota History* 56 (Spring 1989): 21–30.

———. *Phil Sheridan and His Army*. Lincoln: University of Nebraska Press, 1985.

Hyam, Ronald. *Britain's Imperial Century, 1815–1914: A Study of Empire and Expansion*. New York: Palgrave Macmillan, 2002.

Hyde, George E. *The Pawnee Indians*. Denver: University of Denver Press, 1951.

Ikegami, Eiko. *The Taming of the Samurai: Honorific Individualism and the Making of Modern Japan*. Cambridge, Mass.: Harvard University Press, 1995.

Ivy, Richard F. *The Distinguished Light of Abraham Eustis: A Biography of an 1800 Artillery General*. Yorktown, Va.: Citizen Publications, 1993.

Jackson, Donald. *Custer's Gold: The United States Cavalry Expedition of 1874*. Lincoln: University of Nebraska Press, 1966.

Jackson, Robert H. *Quasi-States: Sovereignty, International Relations, and the Third World*. Cambridge: Cambridge University Press, 1990.

Jacobs, James Ripley. *Tarnished Warrior: Major-General James Wilkinson*. New York: Macmillan, 1938.

Janowitz, Morris. *The Military in the Political Development of New Nations: An Essay in Comparative Analysis.* Chicago: University of Chicago Press, 1964.

———. *The Professional Soldier: A Social and Political Portrait.* New York: Free Press, 1960.

Jensen, Richard E. "The Wright-Beauchamp Investigation and the Pawnee Threat of 1829." *Nebraska History* 79 (Fall 1998): 133–143.

John, Richard R. "Governmental Institutions as Agents of Change: Rethinking American Political Development in the Early Republic, 1787–1835." *Studies in American Political Development* 11 (Fall 1997): 347–380.

———. *Spreading the News: The American Postal System from Franklin to Morse.* Cambridge, Mass.: Harvard University Press, 1995.

Johnson, Donald D., with Gary Dean Best. *The United States in the Pacific: Private Interests and Public Policies, 1784–1899.* Westport, Conn.: Praeger, 1995.

Johnson, John J. *A Hemisphere Apart: The Foundations of United States Policy toward Latin America.* Baltimore: Johns Hopkins University Press, 1990.

Johnson, Terence P. *Professions and Power.* London: Macmillan, 1972.

———. "The Professions in the Class Structure." In *Industrial Society: Class, Cleavage, and Control*, ed. R. Scase. London: Allen and Unwin, 1977.

Johnson, Timothy D. *A Gallant Little Army: The Mexico City Campaign.* Lawrence: University Press of Kansas, 2007.

———. *Winfield Scott: The Quest for Military Glory.* Lawrence: University Press of Kansas, 1998.

Jones, Evan. *Citadel in the Wilderness: The Story of Fort Snelling and the Northwest Frontier.* New York: Coward-McCann, 1966.

Jones, Howard. *To the Webster-Ashburton Treaty: A Study in Anglo-American Relations, 1783–1843.* Chapel Hill: University of North Carolina Press, 1977.

Jones, Howard, and Donald A. Rakestraw. *Prologue to Manifest Destiny: Anglo-American Relations in the 1840s.* Wilmington, Del.: Scholarly Resources, 1997.

Jones, Wilbur D. *The American Problem in British Diplomacy, 1841–1861.* Athens: University of Georgia Press, 1974.

Jung, Patrick J. *The Black Hawk War of 1832.* Norman: University of Oklahoma Press, 2007.

———. "Forge, Destroy, and Preserve the Bonds of Empire: Euro-Americans, Native Americans, and Métis on the Wisconsin Frontier, 1634–1856." Ph.D. diss., Marquette University, 1997.

Kagan, Frederick W. *The Military Reforms of Nicholas I: The Origins of the Modern Russian Army.* New York: St. Martin's, 1999.

Kanya-Forstner, A. S. *The Conquest of the Western Sudan: A Study in French Military Imperialism.* Cambridge: Cambridge University Press, 1969.

Kappler, Charles J., comp. *Indian Affairs: Laws and Treaties.* 4 vols. Washington, D.C.: Government Printing Office, 1903–1929.

Karsten, Peter. "Armed Progressives: The Military Reorganizes for the American Century." In *Building the Organizational Society: Essays on Associational Activities in*

Modern America, ed. Jerry Israel, with an introduction by Samuel P. Hays. New York: Free Press, 1972.

Katznelson, Ira, and Martin Shefter, eds. *Shaped by War and Trade: International Influences in American Political Development.* Princeton, N.J.: Princeton University Press, 2002.

Kaufman, Scott, and John A. Soares Jr. "'Sagacious beyond Praise'? Winfield Scott and Anglo-American-Canadian Border Diplomacy, 1837–1860." *Diplomatic History* 30 (January 2006): 57–82.

Kavanaugh, Thomas W. *The Comanches: A History, 1706–1875.* Lincoln: University of Nebraska Press, 1996.

[Kearny, Stephen W.] "A Group of Kearny Letters." *New Mexico Historical Review* 5 (January 1930): 17–37.

Keep, John L. H. *Soldiers of the Tsar: Army and Society in Russia, 1462–1874.* Oxford: Clarendon Press, 1985.

Kennedy, Charles S. *The American Consul: A History of the United States Consular Service, 1776–1914.* Westport, Conn.: Greenwood Press, 1990.

Keyes, Erasmus D. *Fifty Years Observation of Men and Events, Civil and Military.* New York: Scribner's, 1884.

Khodarkovsky, Michael. *Russia's Steppe Frontier: The Making of a Colonial Empire, 1500–1800.* Bloomington: Indiana University Press, 2002.

———. *Where Two Worlds Meet: The Russian State and the Kalmyk Nomads, 1600–1771.* Ithaca, N.Y.: Cornell University Press, 1992.

Khoury, Philip S., and Joseph Kostiner, eds. *Tribes and State Formation in the Middle East.* Berkeley: University of California Press, 1990.

Kieffer, Chester L. *Maligned General: The Biography of Thomas Sidney Jesup.* San Rafael, Calif.: Presidio Press, 1979.

Kiernan, V. G. *Colonial Empires and Armies, 1815–1960.* Phoenix Mill, U.K.: Sutton Publishing, 1998.

Killingray, David, and David Omissi, eds. *Guardians of Empire: The Armed Forces of the Colonial Powers, c. 1700–1964.* Manchester: Manchester University Press, 1999.

Kimmel, Matthew W. "The Cherokee, Choctaw, and Creek Lighthorse Police: Bridging Tribal and Anglo Laws." M.A. thesis, University of Arkansas, 1996.

King, Desmond, and Robert C. Lieberman. "Finding the American State: Transcending the 'Statelessness' Account." *Polity* 40 (July 2008): 368–378.

King, Duane H., and E. R. Evans. "Tsali: The Man behind the Legend." *Journal of Cherokee Studies* 4 (Fall 1979): 194–239.

Knetsch, Joe. *Florida's Seminole Wars, 1817–1858.* Charleston, S.C.: Arcadia Books, 2003.

Knupfer, Peter B. *The Union as It Is: Constitutional Unionism and Sectional Compromise, 1787–1861.* Chapel Hill: University of North Carolina Press, 1991.

Kohl, Lawrence Frederick. *The Politics of Individualism: Parties and the American Character in the Jacksonian Era.* New York: Oxford University Press, 1989.

Kollbaum, Marc E. *Gateway to the West: The History of Jefferson Barracks from 1826–1894.* St. Louis: Friends of Jefferson Barracks, 2002.

Krasner, Stephen D. "Approaches to the State: Alternative Conceptions and Historical Dynamics." *Comparative Politics* 16 (January 1984): 223–246.

Kroeker, Marvin E. *Great Plains Command: William B. Hazen in the Frontier West.* Norman: University of Oklahoma Press, 1976.

Kutsche, Paul. "The Tsali Legend: Culture Heroes and Historiography." *Ethnohistory* 10 (Autumn 1963): 329–357.

Lamar, Howard, and Leonard Thompson, eds. *The Frontier in History: North America and Southern Africa Compared.* New Haven, Conn.: Yale University Press, 1981.

Lambrick, H. T. *Sir Charles Napier and Sind.* Oxford: Clarendon Press, 1982.

Lang, Daniel G. *Foreign Policy in the Early Republic: The Law of Nations and the Balance of Power.* Baton Rouge: Louisiana State University Press, 1985.

Langley, Lester D. *The Struggle for the American Mediterranean: United States–European Rivalry in the Gulf-Caribbean, 1776–1904.* Athens: University of Georgia Press, 1976.

Langston, Thomas S. *Uneasy Balance: Civil-Military Relations in Peacetime America since 1783.* Baltimore: Johns Hopkins University Press, 2003.

Larson, John L. *Internal Improvement: National Public Works and the Promise of Popular Government in the Early United States.* Chapel Hill: University of North Carolina Press, 2001.

———. *The Market Revolution: Liberty, Ambition, and the Eclipse of the Public Good.* Cambridge: Cambridge University Press, 2010.

Larson, Magali Sarfatti. *The Rise of Professionalism: A Sociological Inquiry.* Berkeley: University of California Press, 1977.

LaVere, David. *Contrary Neighbors: Southern Plains and Removed Indians in Indian Territory.* Norman: University of Oklahoma Press, 2000.

Lawson, Kenneth E. *For Christ and Country: A Biography of Brigadier General Gustavus Loomis.* Greenville, S.C.: Ambassador International, 2011.

Layton, Susan. *Russian Literature and Empire: Conquest of the Caucasus from Pushkin to Tolstoy.* Cambridge: Cambridge University Press, 1994.

Lea, Lt. Albert. "Notes on Wisconsin Territory [1836]." *Annals of Iowa* 6 (April 1913): 114–167.

Leach, Hamish A. "A Politico-Military Study of the Detroit River Boundary Defense during the December 1837–March 1838 Emergency." Ph.D. diss., University of Ottawa, 1963.

Le Donne, John P. *The Russian Empire and the World, 1700–1917: The Geopolitics of Expansion and Containment.* New York: Oxford University Press, 1997.

Leonard, Thomas C. "Red, White, and Army Blue: Empathy and Anger in the American West." *American Quarterly* 26 (May 1974): 176–190.

Lewis, James E., Jr. *The American Union and the Problem of Neighborhood: The United*

States and the Collapse of the Spanish Empire, 1783–1829. Chapel Hill: University of North Carolina Press, 1998.
Lieven, Dominic. *Empire: The Russian Empire and Its Rivals, from the Sixteenth Century to the Present*. London: Pimlico, 2003.
Limerick, Patricia Nelson. *The Legacy of Conquest: The Unbroken Past of the American West*. New York: W. W. Norton, 1987.
———. "Turnerians All." *American Historical Review* 100 (June 1995): 697–716.
Lincoln, W. Bruce. *The Conquest of a Continent: Siberia and the Russians*. New York: Random House, 1994.
Linn, Brian M. *The Echo of Battle: The Army's Way of War*. Cambridge, Mass.: Harvard University Press, 2007.
———. *Guardians of Empire: The U.S. Army and the Pacific, 1902–1940*. Chapel Hill: University of North Carolina Press, 1997.
———. "The Long Twilight of the Frontier Army." *Western Historical Quarterly* 27 (Summer 1996): 141–167.
Little, J. L. *Loyalties in Conflict: A Canadian Borderland in War and Rebellion, 1812–1840*. Toronto: University of Toronto Press, 2008.
Long, David F. *Gold Braid and Foreign Relations: Diplomatic Activities of U.S. Naval Officers, 1798–1883*. Annapolis. Md.: Naval Institute Press, 1988.
López-Alves, Fernando. *State Formation and Democracy in Latin America, 1810–1900*. Durham, N.C.: Duke University Press, 2000.
Loveman, Brian. *No Higher Law: American Foreign Policy and the Western Hemisphere since 1776*. Chapel Hill: University of North Carolina Press, 2010.
Lumpkin, Wilson. *The Removal of the Cherokee Indians from Georgia*. New York: Dodd, Mead, 1907.
Mackenzie, David. *The Lion of Tashkent: The Career of General M. G. Cherniaev*. Athens: University of Georgia Press, 1974.
———. "Russian Expansion in Central Asia: St. Petersburg versus the Turkestan Generals." *Canadian Slavic Studies* 3 (1969): 286–311.
Mahan, Bruce E. *Old Fort Crawford and the Frontier*. Iowa City: State Historical Society of Iowa, 1926.
Mahon, John K. *History of the Second Seminole War, 1835–1842*. Gainesville: University of Florida Press, 1967.
Mahoney, Timothy R. *Provincial Lives: Middle-Class Experience in the Antebellum Middle West*. Cambridge: Cambridge University Press, 1999.
Malone, Lawrence J. *Opening the West: Federal Internal Improvements before 1860*. Westport, Conn.: Greenwood Press, 1998.
Mamedov, Mikail. "'Going Native' in the Caucasus: Problems of Russian Identity, 1801–64." *Russian Review* 67 (April 2008): 275–295.
Mann, Michael. "The Autonomous Power of the State: Its Origins, Mechanisms, and Results." *European Journal of Sociology* 26 (1985): 185–213.
———. *The Sources of Social Power: The Rise of Classes and Nation-States, 1760–1914*. Cambridge: Cambridge University Press, 1993.

---. *States, War, and Capitalism: Studies in Political Sociology*. Oxford: Basil Blackwell, 1988.
May, Robert E. *Manifest Destiny's Underworld: Filibustering in Antebellum America*. Chapel Hill: University of North Carolina Press, 2002.
---. "Young American Males and Filibustering in the Age of Manifest Destiny: The United States Army as a Cultural Mirror." *Journal of American History* 78 (December 1991): 857–886.
McCaffrey, James M. *Army of Manifest Destiny: The American Soldier in the Mexican War, 1846–1848*. New York: New York University Press, 1992.
McCall, George A. *Letters from the Frontiers, Written during a Period of Thirty Years Service in the Army of the United States*. 1868. Reprinted with an introduction by John K. Mahon. Gainesville: University Press of Florida, 1974.
McCormick, Richard L. *The Party Period and Public Policy: American Politics from the Age of Jackson to the Progressive Era*. New York: Oxford University Press, 1986.
McCoy, Drew R. *The Elusive Republic: Political Economy in Jeffersonian America*. New York: W. W. Norton, 1980.
McCrady, David G. *Living with Strangers: The Nineteenth-Century Sioux and the Canadian-American Borderlands*. Lincoln: University of Nebraska Press, 2006.
McDonald, Forrest. *States' Rights and the Union: Imperium in Imperio, 1776–1876*. Lawrence: University Press of Kansas, 2000.
McGinnis, Anthony R. *Counting Coup and Cutting Horses: Intertribal Warfare on the Northern Plains, 1738–1889*. Lincoln: University of Nebraska Press, 1990.
McLoughlin, William G. *After the Trail of Tears: The Cherokees' Struggle for Sovereignty, 1839–1880*. Chapel Hill: University of North Carolina Press, 1993.
---. *Cherokee Renascence in the New Republic*. Princeton, N.J.: Princeton University Press, 1986.
McReynolds, Edwin C. *The Seminoles*. Norman: University of Oklahoma Press, 1957.
Meade, George Gordon, ed. *The Life and Letters of George Gordon Meade, Major-General United States Army*. Vol. 1. New York: Scribner's, 1913.
Meinig, D. W. *The Shaping of America: A Geographical Perspective on 500 Years of History*. Vol. 2. *Continental America, 1800–1867*. New Haven, Conn.: Yale University Press, 1993.
Meriwether, Robert L., and W. Edwin Hemphill, eds. *The Papers of John C. Calhoun*. Vols. 2–9. Columbia: University of South Carolina Press, 1963–1976.
Merk, Frederick, and Lois Bannister Merk. *Manifest Destiny and American Mission in American History: A Reinterpretation*. New York: Alfred A. Knopf, 1963.
---. *The Monroe Doctrine and American Expansionism, 1843–1849*. New York: Alfred A. Knopf, 1966.
Metcalf, P. Richard. "Who Should Rule at Home? Native American Politics and Indian-White Relations." *Journal of American History* 61 (December 1974): 651–665.
Meyer, Jean. "States, Roads, Armies, and the Organization of Space." In *War and Competition between States*, ed. Philippe Contamine. Oxford: Clarendon Press, for the European Science Foundation, 2000.

Meyers, Marvin. *The Jacksonian Persuasion: Politics and Belief.* New York: Vintage, 1957.

Meyerson, Harvey. *Nature's Army: When Soldiers Fought for Yosemite.* Lawrence: University Press of Kansas, 2001.

"The Middle Ground Revisited." *William and Mary Quarterly*, 3rd ser., 63 (January 2006): 3–96.

Middleton, Harry F., Jr. "Frontier Outpost: A History of Fort Jesup, Louisiana, 1822–1846." M.A. thesis, Louisiana State University, 1973.

Migdal, Joel S. *State in Society: Studying How States and Societies Transform and Constitute One Another.* Cambridge: Cambridge University Press, 2001.

———. *Strong Societies and Weak States: State-Society Relations and State Capability in the Third World.* Princeton, N.J.: Princeton University Press, 1988.

Migdal, Joel S., Atul Kohli, and Vivienne Shue, eds. *State Power and Social Forces: Domination and Transformation in the Third World.* Cambridge: Cambridge University Press, 1994.

Miller, Douglas T. *The Birth of Modern America, 1820–1850.* Indianapolis: Bobbs-Merrill, 1970.

Miller, Perry. *The Life of the Mind in America: From the Revolution to the Civil War.* New York: Harcourt, Brace, and World, 1966.

Millett, Allan R. *Military Professionalism and Officership in America.* Briefing paper. Columbus, Ohio: Mershon Center, 1977.

Missall, John, and Mary Lou Missall, eds. *This Miserable Pride of a Soldier: The Letters and Journals of Col. William S. Foster in the Second Seminole War.* Tampa, Fla.: University of Tampa Press for the Seminole Wars Historic Foundation, 2005.

Mitchell, Timothy. "The Limits of the State: Beyond Statist Approaches and Their Critics." *American Political Science Review* 85 (March 1991): 77–96.

Mkutu, Kennedy Agade. *Guns & Governance in the Rift Valley: Pastoralist Conflict & Small Arms.* Bloomington: Indiana University Press, 2008.

Moore, William H. *Chiefs, Agents, and Soldiers: Conflict on the Navajo Frontier, 1868–1882.* Albuquerque: University of New Mexico Press, 1994.

Morris, John D. *Sword of the Border: Major General Jacob Jennings Brown, 1775–1828.* Kent, Ohio: Kent State University Press, 2000.

Morrison, James L., Jr. *"The Best School in the World": West Point in the Pre–Civil War Years, 1833–1866.* Kent, Ohio: Kent State University Press, 1986.

Morrison, Michael A. "Martin Van Buren, the Democracy, and the Partisan Politics of Texas Annexation." *Journal of Southern History* 61 (November 1995): 695–724.

———. "The Westward Curse of Empire: Texas Annexation and the American Whig Party." *Journal of the Early Republic* 10 (Summer 1990): 221–249.

Morton, Desmond. "Cavalry or Police: Keeping the Peace on Two Adjacent Frontiers, 1870–1900." *Journal of Canadian Studies* 12 (Spring 1977): 27–37.

Moser, Harold D., et al., eds. *The Papers of Andrew Jackson.* 7 vols. to date. Knoxville: University of Tennessee Press, 1980–.

Moulton, Gary E. *John Ross, Cherokee Chief.* Athens: University of Georgia Press, 1978.

Muir, William Ker, Jr. *Police: Streetcorner Politicians.* Chicago: University of Chicago Press, 1977.
Mullis, Tony R. *Peacekeeping on the Plains: Army Operations in Bleeding Kansas.* Columbia: University of Missouri Press, 2004.
Murphy, Lucy Eldersveld. *A Gathering of Rivers: Indians, Métis, and Mining in the Western Great Lakes, 1737–1832.* Lincoln: University of Nebraska Press, 2000.
Myerly, Scott Hughes. *British Military Spectacle: From the Napoleonic Wars through the Crimea.* Cambridge, Mass.: Harvard University Press, 1996.
Myers, Harry C., ed. "From 'The Crack Post of the Frontier': Letters of Thomas and Charlotte Swords." *Kansas History* 5 (Autumn 1982): 184–213.
Nettl, J. P. "The State as a Conceptual Variable." *World Politics* 20 (July 1968): 559–592.
Newbury, Colin. *Patrons, Clients, and Empire: Chieftancy and Over-rule in Asia, Africa, and the Pacific.* Oxford: Clarendon University Press, 2003.
———. "Patrons, Clients, and Empire: The Subordination of Indigenous Hierarchies in Asia and Africa." *Journal of World History* 11 (Fall 2000): 227–263.
Nichols, David A. "Land, Republicanism, and Indians: Power and Policy in Early National Georgia, 1780–1825." *Georgia Historical Quarterly* 85 (Summer 2001): 199–226.
———. *Red Gentlemen & White Savages: Indians, Federalists, and the Search for Order on the American Frontier.* Charlottesville: University Press of Virginia, 2008.
Nichols, Roger L. "The Army and Early Perceptions of the Plains." *Nebraska History* 56 (Spring 1975): 121–135.
———. "The Army and the Indians, 1800–1830—A Reappraisal: The Missouri Valley Example." *Pacific Historical Review* 41 (May 1972): 151–168.
———. *General Henry Atkinson: A Western Military Career.* Norman: University of Oklahoma Press, 1965.
Nordlinger, Eric A. *On the Autonomy of the Democratic State.* Cambridge, Mass.: Harvard University Press, 1981.
Novak, William J. "The Myth of the 'Weak' American State." *American Historical Review* 113 (June 2008): 752–772.
———. *The People's Welfare: Law and Regulation in Nineteenth-Century America.* Chapel Hill: University of North Carolina Press, 1996.
Noyes, Stanley. *Los Comanches: The Horse People, 1751–1845.* Albuquerque: University of New Mexico Press, 1993.
Olson, Greg. *The Ioway in Missouri.* Columbia: University of Missouri Press, 2008.
Onuf, Peter. "Liberty, Development, and Union: Visions of the West in the 1780s." *William and Mary Quarterly*, 3rd ser., 43 (April 1986): 179–213.
Ostler, Jeffrey. "Conquest and the State: Why the United States Employed Massive Military Force to Suppress the Lakota Ghost Dance." *Pacific Historical Review* 65 (May 1996): 217–248.
———. *The Plains Sioux and U.S. Colonialism from Lewis and Clark to Wounded Knee.* Cambridge: Cambridge University Press, 2004.

Owsley, Frank L., Jr., and Gene A. Smith. *Filibusters and Expansionists: Jeffersonian Manifest Destiny, 1800–1821.* Tuscaloosa: University of Alabama Press, 1997.

Paige, Amanda L., Fuller L. Bumpers, and Daniel F. Littlefield Jr. *Chickasaw Removal.* Ada, Okla.: Chickasaw Press, 2010.

Parsons, Lynn Hudson. "'A Perpetual Harrow upon My Feelings': John Quincy Adams and the American Indian." *New England Quarterly* 46 (September 1973): 339–379.

Patrick, Rembert W. *Aristocrat in Uniform: General Duncan L. Clinch.* Gainesville: University of Florida Press, 1963.

Pearce, Roy Harvey. *Savagism and Civilization: A Study of the Indian and the American Mind.* 2nd ed. Berkeley: University of California Press, 1988.

Peers, Douglas M. *Between Mars and Mammon: Colonial Armies and the Garrison State in Early Nineteenth-Century India.* London: I. B. Tauris, 1995.

Pelzer, Louis. *Marches of the Dragoons in the Mississippi Valley.* Iowa City: State Historical Society of Iowa, 1917.

———, ed. "Captain Ford's Journal of an Expedition to the Rocky Mountains." *Mississippi Valley Historical Review* 12 (March 1926): 556–568.

———. "A Journal of Marches by the First United States Dragoons, 1834–1835." *Iowa Journal of History and Politics* 7 (July 1909): 331–378.

Perdue, Theda, and Michael D. Green. *The Cherokee Nation and the Trail of Tears.* New York: Viking, 2007.

Perkins, Kenneth J. *Qaids, Captains, and Colons: French Military Administration in the Colonial Mahgrib, 1844–1934.* New York: Africana Publishing, 1981.

Perry, Lewis. *Boats against the Current: American Culture between Revolution and Modernity, 1820–1860.* New York: Oxford University Press, 1993.

Perry, Richard J. *From Time Immemorial: Indigenous Peoples and State Systems.* Austin: University of Texas Press, 1996.

Peskin, Allan. *Winfield Scott and the Profession of Arms.* Kent, Ohio: Kent State University Press, 2003.

Pessen, Edward. *Jacksonian America: Society, Personality, and Politics.* Rev. ed. Homewood, Ill.: Dorsey Press, 1978.

Peters, Virginia B. *The Florida Wars.* Hamden, Conn.: Archon Books, 1979.

[Phelps, John W.] "Letters of Lieutenant John W. Phelps, U.S.A., 1837–1838." *Florida Historical Quarterly* 6 (October 1927): 67–84.

Pinheiro, John C. *Manifest Ambition: James K. Polk and Civil-Military Relations during the Mexican War.* Westport, Conn.: Praeger Security International, 2007.

Pletcher, David M. *The Diplomacy of Annexation: Texas, Oregon, and the Mexican War.* Columbia: University of Missouri Press, 1973.

Ponko, Vincent. "The Military Explorers of the American West, 1838–1860." In *North American Exploration.* Vol. 3. *A Continent Comprehended,* ed. John Allen Logan. Lincoln: University of Nebraska Press, 1997.

Porch, Douglas. *The Conquest of the Sahara.* New York: Alfred A. Knopf, 1984.

———. *Wars of Empire.* London: Cassell, 2000.

Porter, Andrew, ed. *Oxford History of the British Empire*. Vol. 3. *The Nineteenth Century*. London: Oxford University Press, 1999.

Porter, Kenneth Wiggins. *The Black Seminoles: History of a Freedom-Seeking People*. Rev. ed., ed. Alcione M. Amos and Thomas P. Sutter. Gainesville: University Press of Florida, 1996.

Porter, Valentine M., ed. "Journal of Stephen Watts Kearny. Part I: The Council Bluffs–St. Peter's Expedition, 1820." *Collections of the Missouri Historical Society* 3 (January 1908): 8–29.

Powell, William H. *A History of the Organization and Movements of the Fourth Regiment of Infantry, etc.* Washington, D.C.: M'Gill and Witherow, 1871.

Price, Catherine. "Lakotas and Euroamericans: Contrasted Concepts of 'Chieftainship' and Decision-making Authority." *Ethnohistory* 41 (Summer 1994): 447–463.

Priest, Dana. *The Mission: Waging War and Keeping Peace with America's Military*. New York: W. W. Norton, 2003.

Prucha, Francis Paul. *American Indian Policy in the Formative Years: The Indian Trade and Intercourse Acts, 1790–1834*. Cambridge, Mass.: Harvard University Press, 1962.

———. *Broadax and Bayonet: The Role of the Army in the Development of the Northwest, 1815–1860*. Madison: State Historical Society of Wisconsin, 1953.

———. *The Great Father: The U.S. Government and the American Indians*. 2 vols. Lincoln: University of Nebraska Press, 1984.

———. *A Guide to the Military Posts of the United States, 1789–1895*. Madison: State Historical Society of Wisconsin, 1964.

———. *The Sword of the Republic: The United States Army on the Frontier, 1783–1846*. New York: Macmillan, 1969.

———, ed. "Reports of General Brady on the Patriot War." *Canadian Historical Review* 31 (March 1950): 56–68.

Pugh, David G. *Sons of Liberty: The Masculine Mind in Nineteenth-Century America*. Westport, Conn.: Greenwood Press, 1983.

Ralston, David B. *Importing the European Army: The Introduction of European Military Techniques and Institutions into the Extra-European World, 1600–1914*. Chicago: University of Chicago Press, 1990.

Ravenal, Earl C. "Ignorant Armies: The State, the Public, and the Making of Foreign Policy." *Critical Review* 14, 2–3 (2000): 327–374.

Reese, Calvin. "The United States Army and the Indian: Low Plains Area, 1815–1854." Ph.D. diss., University of Southern California, 1963.

Reinhard, Wolfgang, ed. *Power Elites and State Building*. Oxford: Clarendon Press, for the European Science Foundation, 1996.

Remini, Robert V. *Andrew Jackson and His Indian Wars*. New York: Viking, 2001.

Reséndez, Andrés. *Changing National Identities at the Frontier: Texas and New Mexico, 1800–1850*. Cambridge: Cambridge University Press, 2005.

Richter, William L. *The Army in Texas during Reconstruction, 1865–1870*. College Station: Texas A&M University Press, 1987.

Robbins, William G. *Colony and Empire: The Capitalist Transformation of the American West.* Lawrence: University Press of Kansas, 1994.

Roberts, Alasdair. *America's First Great Depression: Economic Crisis and Political Disorder after the Panic of 1837.* Ithaca, N.Y.: Cornell University Press, 2012.

Robinson, R. E., and J. A. Gallagher. *Africa and the Victorians: The Official Mind of Imperialism.* London: Macmillan, 1961.

Rockwell, Stephen J. *Indian Affairs and the Administration State in the Nineteenth Century.* Cambridge: Cambridge University Press, 2010.

Rogin, Michael Paul. *Fathers and Children: Andrew Jackson and the Subjugation of the American Indian.* New York: Alfred A. Knopf, 1975.

Rohrbough, Malcolm J. *The Land Office Business: The Settlement and Administration of American Public Lands, 1789–1837.* New York: Oxford University Press, 1968.

———. *The Trans-Appalachian Frontier: People, Societies, and Institutions, 1775–1850.* New York: Oxford University Press, 1978.

Rolater, Fred S. "The American Indian and the Origin of the Second American Party System." *Wisconsin Magazine of History* 76 (Spring 1993): 180–201.

Rollings, Willard H. *The Osage: An Ethnohistorical Study of Hegemony on the Prairie-Plains.* Columbia: University of Missouri Press, 1992.

Ronda, James P. *Beyond Lewis and Clark: The Army Explores the West.* Tacoma: Washington State Historical Society, 2003.

Rosen, Deborah A. *American Indians and State Law: Sovereignty, Race, and Citizenship, 1790–1880.* Lincoln: University of Nebraska Press, 2007.

Rosen, Stephen Peter. "Alexander Hamilton and the Domestic Uses of International Law." *Diplomatic History* 5 (Summer 1981): 183–198.

Rotundo, E. Anthony. *American Manhood: Transformations in Masculinity from the Revolutionary Era to the Present.* New York: Basic Books, 1993.

"Roundtable on American Colonial, Postcolonial, and National Histories." *William and Mary Quarterly*, 3rd ser., 64 (April 2007): 235–286.

Rowe, Mary Ellen. *Bulwark of the Republic: The American Militia in the Antebellum West.* Westport, Conn.: Praeger, 2003.

Royster, Charles. *A Revolutionary People at War: The Continental Army and American Character, 1775–1783.* Chapel Hill: University of North Carolina Press, 1979.

Rubinstein, Jonathan. *City Police.* New York: Farrar, Straus, and Giroux, 1973.

Sadosky, Leonard J. *Revolutionary Negotiations: Indians, Empires, and Diplomats in the Founding of America.* Charlottesville: University Press of Virginia, 2009.

Sahlins, Peter. *Boundaries: The Making of France and Spain in the Pyrenees.* Berkeley: University of California Press, 1989.

Said, Edward W. *Orientalism.* New York: Pantheon Books, 1978.

Santoni, Pedro. *Mexicans at Arms: Puro Federalists and the Politics of War, 1845–1848.* Fort Worth: Texas Christian University Press, 1996.

Satz, Ronald N. *American Indian Policy in the Jacksonian Era.* Lincoln: University of Nebraska Press, 1974.

Schlicke, Carl P. *General George Wright, 1803–1865: Guardian of the Pacific Northwest.* Norman: University of Oklahoma Press, 1988.
Schmidt, Hans. *Maverick Marine: Smedley Butler and the Contradictions of American Military History.* Lexington: University Press of Kentucky, 1987.
Schroeder, John H. *Shaping a Maritime Empire: The Commercial and Diplomatic Role of the American Navy, 1829–1861.* Westport, Conn.: Greenwood Press, 1985.
Schubert, Frank N. *Vanguard of Expansion: Army Engineers in the Trans-Mississippi West, 1819–1879.* Office of the Chief of Engineers. Washington, D.C.: Government Printing Office, 1980.
Scott, Robert Garth, ed. *Forgotten Valor: The Memoirs, Journals, & Civil War Letters of Orlando B. Willcox.* Kent, Ohio: Kent State University Press, 1999.
Scott, Stuart D. "The Patriot Game: New Yorkers and the Canadian Rebellion of 1837–1838." *New York History* 78 (July 1987): 281–295.
Scott, Winfield. *Memoirs of Lieut.-Gen. Winfield Scott, L.L.D., Written by Himself.* 2 vols. New York: Sheldon, 1864.
Sefton, James E. *The United States Army and Reconstruction, 1865–1877.* Baton Rouge: Louisiana State University Press, 1967.
Sellers, Charles. *The Market Revolution: Jacksonian America, 1815–1846.* New York: Oxford University Press, 1991.
Shaw, Frederick B. *One Hundred and Forty Years of Service in Peace and War: History of the Second Infantry, United States Army.* Detroit: Strathmore Press, 1930.
Sheehan, Bernard W. *Seeds of Extinction: Jeffersonian Philanthropy and the American Indian.* New York: W. W. Norton, 1974.
Shoemaker, Nancy. *A Strange Likeness: Becoming Red and White in Eighteenth-Century North America.* New York: Oxford University Press, 2004.
Short, John Rennie. *Representing the Republic: Mapping the United States, 1600–1900.* London: Reaktion Books, 2001.
Silberman, Bernard S. *Cages of Reason: The Rise of the Rational State in France, Japan, the United States, and Great Britain.* Chicago: University of Chicago Press, 1993.
Silver, James W. "A Counter-proposal to the Indian Removal Policy of Andrew Jackson." *Journal of Mississippi History* 4 (October 1942): 207–215.
———. *Edmund Pendleton Gaines: Frontier General.* Baton Rouge: Louisiana State University Press, 1949.
Silverstone, Scott A. *Divided Union: The Politics of War in the Early American Republic.* Ithaca, N.Y.: Cornell University Press, 2004.
Skelton, William B. *An American Profession of Arms: The Army Officer Corps, 1784–1861.* Lawrence: University Press of Kansas, 1992.
———. "The Army Officer as Organization Man." In *Soldiers and Civilians: The U.S. Army and the American People*, ed. Garry D. Ryan and Timothy K. Nenninger. Washington, D.C.: National Archives and Records Administration, 1987.
———. "Army Officers' Attitudes towards Indians, 1830–1860." *Pacific Northwest Quarterly* 67 (July 1976): 113–124.

———. "The Commanding Generals and the Question of Civilian Control in the Antebellum U.S. Army." *American Nineteenth-Century History* 7 (June 2006): 153–172.

———. "Officers and Politicians: The Origins of Army Politics in the United States before the Civil War." *Armed Forces and Society* 6 (Fall 1979): 22–48.

———. "Professionalization in the U.S. Army Officer Corps during the Age of Jackson." *Armed Forces and Society* 1 (Summer 1975): 443–471.

———. "Samuel P. Huntington and the American Military Tradition." *Journal of Military History* 60 (April 1996): 325–338.

———. "The United States Army, 1821–1837: An Institutional History." Ph.D. diss., Northwestern University, 1968.

———. "West Point and Officer Professionalism, 1817–1877." In *West Point: Two Centuries and Beyond*, ed. Lance A. Betros. Abilene, Tex.: McWhiney Foundation Press, 2004.

Skowronek, Stephen. *Building a New American State: The Expansion of National Administrative Capacities, 1877–1920*. Cambridge: Cambridge University Press, 1982.

Slezkine, Yuri. *Arctic Mirrors: Russia and the Small Peoples of the North*. Ithaca, N.Y.: Cornell University Press, 1994.

Slotkin, Richard. *Regeneration through Violence: The Mythology of the American Frontier, 1600–1860*. Middletown, Conn.: Wesleyan University Press, 1973.

Smith, Carlton B. "The United States War Department, 1815–1842." Ph.D. diss., University of Virginia, 1967.

Smith, Daniel Blake. *An American Betrayal: Cherokee Patriots and the Trail of Tears*. New York: Henry Holt, 2011.

Smith, F. Todd. *The Caddo Indians: Tribes at the Convergence of Empires, 1542–1854*. College Station: Texas A&M University Press, 1995.

———. *From Dominance to Disappearance: The Indians of Texas and the Near Southwest, 1786–1859*. Lincoln: University of Nebraska Press, 2005.

Smith, Joseph R. "Letters from the Second Seminole War." Ed. John K. Mahon. *Florida Historical Quarterly* 36 (April 1958): 331–352.

Smith, Mark A. *Engineering Security: The Corps of Engineers and Third System Defense Policy, 1815–1861*. Tuscaloosa: University of Alabama Press, 2009.

Smith, Ralph A. "Indians in American-Mexican Relations before the War of 1846." *Hispanic American Historical Review* 43 (February 1963): 34–64.

Smith, Sherry L. "Lost Soldiers: Re-Searching the Army in the American West." *Western Historical Quarterly* 29 (Summer 1998): 149–163.

———. *The View from Officers' Row: Army Perceptions of Western Indians*. Tucson: University of Arizona Press, 1990.

Southerland, Harry DeLeon, Jr., and Jerry Elijah Brown. *The Federal Road through Georgia, the Creek Nation, and Alabama, 1806–1836*. Tuscaloosa: University of Alabama Press, 1989.

Sprague, John T. *The Origin, Progress, and Conclusion of the Florida War*. 1848.

Reprinted with an introduction by John K. Mahon. Gainesville: University of Florida Press, 1964.

Spurr, David. *The Rhetoric of Empire: Colonial Discourses in Journalism, Travel Writing, and Imperial Administration.* Durham, N.C.: Duke University Press, 1993.

Stacey, C. P., ed. "A Private Report of General Winfield Scott on the Border Situation in 1839." *Canadian Historical Review* 21 (December 1940): 407–414.

"State Autonomy." Special double issue. *Critical Review* 14 (Spring–Summer 2000).

Steinhauer, Dale R. "'Sogers': Enlisted Men in the U.S. Army, 1815–1860." Ph.D. diss., University of North Carolina, 1992.

Stephan, John J. *The Russian Far East: A History.* Stanford, Calif.: Stanford University Press, 1994.

Stephanson, Anders. *Manifest Destiny: American Expansion and the Empire of Right.* New York: Hill and Wang, 1995.

Stevens, Kenneth R. *Border Diplomacy: The Caroline and McLeod Affairs in Anglo-American-Canadian Relations, 1837–1842.* Tuscaloosa: University of Alabama Press, 1989.

Stewart, Gordon. *The American Response to Canada since 1776.* East Lansing: Michigan State University Press, 1992.

Stowe, Steven M. *Intimacy and Power in the Old South: Ritual in the Lives of the Planters.* Baltimore: Johns Hopkins University Press, 1987.

Strachan, Hew. "The Early Victorian Army and the Nineteenth-Century Revolution in Government." *English Historical Review* 95 (July 1980): 782–809.

———. *The Politics of the British Army.* Oxford: Clarendon Press, 1997.

Stuart, Reginald C. *United States Expansionism and British North America, 1775–1871.* Chapel Hill: University of North Carolina Press, 1988.

Sullivan, Anthony Thrall. *Thomas-Robert Bugeaud, France, and Algeria, 1784–1849: Politics, Power, and the Good Society.* Hamden, Conn.: Archon Books, 1983.

Sunderland, Willard. *Taming the Wild Field: Colonization and Empire on the Russian Steppe.* Ithaca, N.Y.: Cornell University Press, 2004.

Sweninger, Joseph M. "'A Lingering War Must Be Avoided': The Defense of the Northern Frontier, 1812–1871." Ph.D. diss., Ohio State University, 1998.

Tagliacozzo, Eric. *Secret Trades, Porous Borders: Smuggling and States along a Southeast Asian Frontier, 1865–1915.* New Haven, Conn.: Yale University Press, 2005.

Takaki, Ronald T. *Iron Cages: Race and Culture in Nineteenth-Century America.* New York: Alfred A. Knopf, 1979.

Tate, Michael L. *The Frontier Army in the Settlement of the West.* Norman: University of Oklahoma Press, 1999.

———. "The Multi-purpose Army on the Frontier: A Call for Further Research." In *The American West: Essays in Honor of W. Eugene Hollon*, ed. Ronald Lora. Toledo, Ohio: University of Toledo Press, 1980.

Taylor, Alan. *William Cooper's Town: Power and Persuasion on the Frontier of the Early American Republic.* New York: Alfred A. Knopf, 1995.

Taylor, Brian D. *Politics and the Russian Army: Civil-Military Relations, 1689–2000.* Cambridge: Cambridge University Press, 2003.

Thomson, Janice E. *Mercenaries, Pirates, & Sovereigns: State-Building and Extraterritorial Violence in Early Modern Europe.* Princeton, N.J.: Princeton University Press, 1994.

Tilly, Charles. *Big Structures, Large Processes, Huge Comparisons.* New York: Russell Sage Foundation, 1984.

———, ed. *The Formation of National States in Western Europe.* Princeton, N.J.: Princeton University Press, 1975.

Tobias, John L. "Canada's Subjugation of the Plains Cree, 1879–1885." *Canadian Historical Review* 64 (December 1983): 519–548.

Tooker, Elisabeth, ed. *The Development of Political Organization in Native North America.* Washington, D.C.: American Ethnological Society, 1983.

Townshend, Charles. "Martial Law: Legal and Administrative Problems of Civil Emergency in Britain and the Empire, 1800–1940." *Historical Journal* 25 (March 1982): 167–195.

Unrau, William E. "The Civilian as Indian Agent: Villain or Victim?" *Western Historical Quarterly* 3 (October 1972): 405–420.

Utley, Robert M. *Frontier Regulars: The United States Army and the Indian, 1866–1891.* New York: Macmillan, 1973.

———. *Frontiersmen in Blue: The United States Army and the Indian, 1848–1865.* New York: Macmillan, 1967.

———. *Indian Frontier of the American West, 1846–1890.* Albuquerque: University of New Mexico Press, 1984.

———. *The Last Days of the Sioux Nation.* New Haven, Conn.: Yale University Press, 1963.

Van Alstyne, Richard W. "Empire in Mid-Passage, 1845–1867." In *From Colony to Empire: Essays in the History of American Foreign Relations*, ed. William Appleman Williams. New York: J. Wiley, 1972.

Van Arsdol, Ted, ed. *Frontier Soldier: The Letters of Maj. John S. Hatheway, 1833–1853.* Vancouver, Wash.: Vancouver National Historic Reserve Trust, 1999.

Vandervort, Bruce. *Indian Wars of Mexico, Canada, and the United States, 1812–1900.* London: Routledge, 2006.

———. *Wars of Imperial Conquest in Africa, 1830–1914.* Bloomington: Indiana University Press, 1998.

Viola, Herman J. *Thomas L. McKenney: Architect of America's Early Indian Policy, 1816–1830.* Chicago: University of Chicago Press, 1974.

Vipperman, Carl J. "The Bungled Treaty of New Echota: The Failure of Cherokee Removal, 1836–1838." *Georgia Historical Quarterly* 73 (Fall 1989): 540–558.

Volpe, Vernon L. "The Origins of the Frémont Expeditions: John J. Abert and the Scientific Exploration of the Trans-Mississippi West." *Historian* 62 (Winter 2000): 244–263.

Wade, Arthur P. "Roads to the Top—An Analysis of General-Officer Selection in the United States Army, 1789–1898." *Military Affairs* 40 (December 1976): 157–163.

Wagner, Michael D. "'A Few Days Late in Coming': Major General Winfield Scott's Role in the Aroostook War." *Maine History* 34 (Winter/Spring 1995): 162–177.

Wallace, Edward S. *General William Jenkins Worth: Monterey's Forgotten Hero*. Dallas: Southern Methodist University Press, 1953.

Wallerstein, Immanuel. *The Modern World-System III: The Second Era of Great Expansion of the Capitalist World-Economy, 1730s–1840s*. San Diego, Calif.: Academic Press, 1989.

Walraven, Bill, and Marjorie K. Walraven. "The 'Sabine Chute': The U.S. Army and the Texas Revolution." *Southwestern Historical Quarterly* 107 (April 2004): 573–601.

Ward, Alan. "Law and Law Enforcement on the New Zealand Frontier, 1840–1893." *New Zealand Journal of History* 5 (October 1971): 128–149.

Warren, Stephen. *The Shawnees and Their Neighbors, 1795–1870*. Urbana: University of Illinois Press, 2005.

Warshauer, Matthew. *Andrew Jackson and the Politics of Martial Law: Nationalism, Civil Liberties and Partisanship*. Knoxville: University of Tennessee Press, 2006.

Watson, Harry L. *Liberty and Power: The Politics of Jacksonian America*. New York: Hill and Wang, 1990.

Watson, Samuel J. "Continuity in Civil-Military Relations and Expertise: The U.S. Army during the Decade before the Civil War." *Journal of Military History* 75 (January 2011): 221–250.

———. "Developing 'Republican Machines': West Point and the Struggle to Render the Officer Corps Safe for America." In *Thomas Jefferson's Military Academy: Founding West Point*, ed. Robert M. S. McDonald. Charlottesville: University Press of Virginia, 2004.

———. "Flexible Gender Roles in the Era of the Market Revolution: Family, Friendship, Marriage, and Masculinity among U.S. Army Officers, 1815–1846." *Journal of Social History* 29 (Fall 1995): 81–106.

———. "The Growth of the Professional Army, 1815–1860." In *The Oxford Atlas of American Military History*, ed. James C. Bradford. New York: Oxford University Press, 2003.

———. "How the Army Became Accepted: West Point Socialization, Military Accountability, and the Nation-State during the Jacksonian Era." *American Nineteenth-Century History* 7 (June 2006): 217–249.

———. *Jackson's Sword: The Army Officer Corps on the American Frontier, 1810–1821*. Lawrence: University Press of Kansas, 2012.

———. "Knowledge, Interest, and the Limits of Military Professionalism: The Discourse on American Coastal Defense, 1815–1860." *War in History* 5 (Fall 1998): 280–307.

———. "Manifest Destiny and Military Professionalism: A New Perspective on Junior

U.S. Army Officers' Attitudes toward War With Mexico, 1844–1846." *Southwestern Historical Quarterly* 99 (April 1996): 466–498.

———. "Professionalism, Social Attitudes, and Civil-Military Accountability in the U.S. Army Officer Corps, 1815–1846." 2 vols. Ph.D. diss., Rice University, 1996.

———. "Resisting Removal: Seminole Strategy, 1812–1842." In *America's Hundred Years' War: U.S. Expansion to the Gulf Coast and the Fate of the Seminole, 1763–1858*, ed. William S. Belko. Gainesville: University Press of Florida, 2010.

———. Review of John C. Pinheiro, *Manifest Ambition: James K. Polk and Civil-Military Relations during the Mexican War. Journal of Military History* 71 (October 2007): 1237–1239.

———. "'This Thankless . . . Unholy War': Army Officers and Civil-Military Relations in the Second Seminole War." In *The Southern Albatross: Race and Ethnicity in the South*, ed. David Dillard and Randal Hall. Macon, Ga.: Mercer University Press, 1999.

———. "Thomas Sidney Jesup: Soldier, Bureaucrat, Gentleman Democrat." In *The Human Tradition in the Early Republic*, ed. Michael A. Morrison. Wilmington, Del.: Scholarly Resources, 2000.

———. "The Uncertain Road to Manifest Destiny: Army Officers and the Course of American Territorial Expansionism, 1815–1846." In *Manifest Destiny and Empire: Essays on Antebellum American Expansionism*, ed. Christopher Morris and Sam W. Haynes. College Station: Texas A&M University Press, 1997.

———. "U.S. Army Officers Fight the 'Patriot War': Responses to Filibustering on the Canadian Border, 1837–1839." *Journal of the Early Republic* 18 (Fall 1998): 487–521.

———. "The U.S. Army to 1900." In *The Blackwell Companion to American Military History*, ed. James C. Bradford. Oxford: Wiley-Blackwell, 2009.

———. "What Do We Mean by Partisan? Army Officers and Politics during the Evolution of the Second Party System." Unpublished paper presented to the Southwestern Historical Association, 1999.

Webb, Stephen Saunders. *The Governors-General: The English Army and the Definition of Empire, 1569–1681*. Chapel Hill: University of North Carolina Press, 1979.

Weber, David J. "American Westward Expansion and the Breakdown of Relations between *Pobladores* and '*Indios Bárbaros*' on Mexico's Far Northern Frontier, 1821–1846." *New Mexico Historical Review* 56 (July 1981): 221–238.

Weeks, William Earl. "American Nationalism, American Imperialism: An Interpretation of United States Political Economy, 1789–1861." *Journal of the Early Republic* 14 (Winter 1994): 485–495.

———. *Building the Continental Empire: American Expansionism from the Revolution to the Civil War*. Chicago: Ivan R. Dee, 1996.

———. "New Directions in the Study of Early American Foreign Relations." *Diplomatic History* 17 (Winter 1993): 73–95.

Weigley, Russell F. *History of the United States Army*. New York: Macmillan, 1967.

Weinberg, Albert K. *Manifest Destiny: A Study of Nationalist Expansionism in American History*. Baltimore: Johns Hopkins Press, 1935.

Welter, Rush. "The Frontier West as an Image of American Society: Conservative Attitudes before the Civil War." *Mississippi Valley Historical Review* 46 (March 1960): 593–614.

———. *The Mind of America, 1820–1860*. New York: Columbia University Press, 1975.

Wesley, Edgar B. *Guarding the Frontier: A Study of Frontier Defense from 1815 to 1825*. Minneapolis: University of Minnesota Press, 1925.

Wettemann, Robert P., Jr. "A Part or Apart: The Alleged Isolation of Antebellum U.S. Army Officers." *American Nineteenth-Century History* 7 (June 2006): 193–217.

———. *Privilege vs. Equality: Civil-Military Relations in the Jacksonian Era, 1815–1845*. Westport, Conn.: Praeger Security International, 2009.

Wharton, Clifton. "The Expedition of Major Clifton Wharton in 1844." *Collections of the Kansas State Historical Society* 16 (1925): 272–305.

White, Frank F., Jr., ed. "A Journal of Lt. Robert C. Buchanan during the Seminole War." *Florida Historical Quarterly* 29 (October 1950): 132–151.

———. "Macomb's Mission to the Seminoles: John T. Sprague's Journal Kept during April and May, 1839." *Florida Historical Quarterly* 35 (October 1956): 130–193.

White, Richard. *The Middle Ground: Indians, Empires, and Republics in the Great Lakes Region, 1650–1815*. Cambridge: Cambridge University Press, 1991.

———. "The Winning of the West: The Expansion of the Western Sioux in the Eighteenth and Nineteenth Centuries." *Journal of American History* 65 (September 1978): 319–343.

Whittaker, William E., ed. *Frontier Forts of Iowa: Indians, Traders, and Soldiers, 1682–1862*. Iowa City: Iowa University Press, 2009.

Wiebe, Robert H. *The Opening of American Society: From the Adoption of the Constitution to the Eve of Disunion*. New York: Alfred A. Knopf, 1984.

———. *The Segmented Society: An Introduction to the Meaning of America*. New York: Oxford University Press, 1975.

Wik, Reynold M., ed. "Captain Nathaniel Wyche Hunter and the Florida Indian Campaigns, 1837–1841." *Florida Historical Quarterly* 39 (July 1960): 62–75.

Wilhelm, Thomas. *History of the Eighth U.S. Infantry, from Its Organization, in 1838*. 2nd ed. N. p.: Eighth Infantry Regiment, 1873.

Williams, David. *The Georgia Gold Rush: Twenty-niners, Cherokees, and Gold Fever*. Columbia: University of South Carolina Press, 1993.

Williams, Robert A., Jr. *Linking Arms Together: American Indian Treaty Visions of Law and Peace, 1600–1800*. London: Routledge, 1999.

Williams, William Appleman. *The Roots of the Modern American Empire: A Study of the Growth and Shaping of Social Consciousness in a Marketplace Society*. New York: Vintage Books, 1969.

———, ed. *From Colony to Empire: Essays in the History of American Foreign Relations*. New York: J. Wiley, 1972.

Wilson, James Q. *The Varieties of Police Behavior*. Cambridge, Mass.: Harvard University Press, 1968.

Wilson, Major L. *The Presidency of Martin Van Buren.* Lawrence: University Press of Kansas, 1984.

———. "Republicanism and the Idea of Party in the Jacksonian Period." *Journal of the Early Republic* 8 (Winter 1988): 419–432.

Wilson, Mark R. *The Business of Civil War: Military Mobilization and the State, 1861–1865.* Baltimore: Johns Hopkins University Press, 2006.

Winders, Richard Bruce. *Mr. Polk's Army: The American Military Experience in the Mexican War.* College Station: Texas A&M University Press, 1997.

Wolf, Eric R. *Europe and the People Without History.* Berkeley: University of California Press, 1982.

Woolworth, Nancy L. "Captain Edwin V. Sumner's Expedition to Devil's Lake in the Summer of 1845." *North Dakota History* 28 (April 1961): 79–98.

Wooster, Robert. *The American Military Frontiers: The United States Army in the West, 1783–1900.* Albuquerque: University of New Mexico Press, 2009.

———. "The Army and the Politics of Expansion: Texas and the Southwestern Borderlands, 1870–1886." *Southwestern Historical Quarterly* 93 (October 1989): 151–167.

———. *The Military and United States Indian Policy, 1865–1903.* New Haven, Conn.: Yale University Press, 1988.

———. "Military Strategy in the American West, 1815–1860." M.A. thesis, Lamar University, 1979.

———. *Nelson A. Miles and the Twilight of the Frontier Army.* Lincoln: University of Nebraska Press, 1993.

Wright, J. Leitch, Jr. *Creeks and Seminoles: Destruction and Regeneration of the Muscogulge People.* Lincoln: University of Nebraska Press, 1986.

Wyman, Mark. *The Wisconsin Frontier.* Bloomington: Indiana University Press, 1998.

Yapp, Malcolm. *Strategies of British India: Britain, Iran, and Afghanistan, 1798–1850.* Oxford: Clarendon Press, 1980.

Young, Mary. "The Exercise of Sovereignty in Cherokee Georgia." *Journal of the Early Republic* 10 (Spring 1990): 43–63.

Young, Mary E. *Redskins, Ruffleshirts, and Rednecks: Indian Allotments in Alabama and Mississippi, 1830–1860.* Norman: University of Oklahoma Press, 1961.

Young, Otis E. *The West of Philip St. George Cooke, 1809–1895.* Glendale, Calif.: Arthur H. Clark, 1955.

———, ed. *The First Military Escort on the Santa Fe Trail, 1829, from the Journal and Reports of Major Bennet Riley and Lieutenant Philip St. George Cooke.* Glendale, Calif.: Arthur H. Clark, 1952.

Young, Tommy R., II. "The United States Army in the South, 1789–1835." Ph.D. diss., Louisiana State University, 1973.

INDEX

Abert, James W., 30
Abert, John J., 29, 119, 139
accountability, U.S. Army officer corps, 2, 214, 225, 274, 277, 409
   fiscal, 93, 130, 133–135, 137, 253, 432
   legal, 82, 108, 111, 119, 242, 275, 300, 414
   local civil authorities and, 297, 300
   nation-state and, 240, 247, 250, 287, 389–390, 421
   politics and, 227, 236, 252, 290, 340, 386, 407, 412, 415, 433–435
   professional, 95, 159, 180, 235, 238, 240–241, 258, 282, 378, 386–387
   socialization and, 132, 194, 437
   subordination and, 35, 113, 127, 194, 244, 412, 438 (*see also* U.S. Army, civilian control of)
Adams, John Quincy, 54, 78
   Georgia Indian lands and, 89–93, 96–102
   Indian policy and, 79, 105, 124–125
Alden, Bradford, 229
Allen, James, 74–75
Allen, Robert, 383, 391
alternative polities, 10, 22, 38, 49, 241, 323, 418
Alvarez, Manuel, 359
Alvord, Benjamin, 231, 393
American Civil War, 3, 8, 12, 14, 21–22, 25, 408, 424–425, 437, 440
American Fur Company, 4, 43
Ampudia, Pedro de, 404

Anderson, Robert, 166, 188–189, 208, 228–229
   Canadian border crisis and, 266–269, 280, 311–312
Andrews, Timothy, 91–94
Apache Indians, 12–13, 237, 369, 425, 427–429
Arbuckle, Matthew, 86, 99, 217, 219
   peacekeeping and, 345, 351, 353
   Texas and, 335, 337–339, 341–344
Arkansas Territory, 324–325
Armistead, Walker, 115, 208, 211, 224
Armstrong, Francis W., 133, 136
Army, U. S.
   adaptation and, 219–223, 422
   civilian control of, 1, 30, 47, 204, 236, 297, 377, 385, 388, 408
   coastal defense and, 246, 248–250, 252, 256–257, 259, 261
   Corps of Topographical Engineers, 29
   expeditions and, 22, 74–75, 350–352, 365–367
   force structure of, 20–21, 59, 186, 189
   Fortifications Board and, 246, 249–250
   international security role of, 14
   law enforcement operations (*see* law enforcement operations, U.S. Army)
   logistical operations and, 131–135, 375, 424
   personnel policies and, 189–190
   preparedness and, 385–386, 394
   press relations and, 153

619

Army, U. S. (*continued*)
    projection of power and, 20, 22, 24, 351, 356, 365–367, 423, 425
    rules of engagement and, 169
    tactics and, 20–21, 219–223, 422–425, 487n43
    See also enlisted soldiers, U.S. Army; officer corps, U.S. Army; peacekeeping, U.S. Army
Army and Navy Chronicle, 70, 356, 385
    Second Seminole War and, 188, 193, 198–201, 206, 211–212, 214, 220–221, 225, 228–231
Arikara War, 422
Arthur, George, 274
Ash Hollow, battle of, 8
Atkinson, Henry, 41, 44, 51, 72
    Big Neck War and, 64
    Black Hawk War and, 58–61
    diplomacy of, 65–70, 347
    Winnebago War and, 53–54
atrocities, 169, 471n13
    citizen-soldiers and, 7–8, 20–21
    genocide, 8, 21, 182, 225
    Indians and, 56
    military and, 3, 8–9
    militia and, 84–85
    settlers and, 427
authoritarianism, U.S. Army officer corps, 1, 3, 40, 331, 389, 421
    civil affairs and, 14, 86, 108
    diplomacy and, 321
    nationalist, 111, 240
autonomy, U.S. Army officer corps, 17, 30, 79, 113, 118, 258, 306, 439–440
    citizen soldiers and, 241, 247
    operational, 161, 287, 390, 421
    politics and, 16, 32, 43, 110–111, 126, 160, 236–237, 242, 259, 280, 378, 435, 438
    removal process and, 133–134, 137, 176
    slavery and, 214, 219

Bad Axe, battle of, 8, 58
Bancroft, George, 369
Bankhead, James, 301
Bannock Indians, 425
Barbour, James, 92–93, 98
Barbour, Philip, 392, 397–398, 403, 406
Barry, John W., 139–140
Barry, William, 379
Bean, Peter Ellis, 335
Bear River Massacre, 7
Beauregard, P. G. T., 383
Belknap, William, 341
Bell, John, 85
Belton, Francis, 139, 222
Benton, Nathaniel, 292–293
Benton, Thomas Hart, 29, 31–32, 198, 372
Bernard, Simon, 249
Birch, George, 86
Black Hawk, 57–59, 62, 427
Black Hawk War, 8, 58–63
Black Hills, 13, 426
Bliss, W. W. S., 381
Bonnell, Joseph, 298, 336
Bonneville, Benjamin L. E., 27–29
Boone, Nathan, 67, 357, 366
Bradford, William, 353
Brady, Francis W., 107–108, 110–111
Brady, Hugh, 59, 61, 70, 302, 382
    Canadian border crisis and, 260, 264, 267, 277–279, 281, 284, 289, 305
    militia and, 293, 295
Brearley, David, 100, 110
Britain, 256–257, 383
    Anglophobia and, 257–258, 312–316, 379–382, 392
    Canadian border crisis. *See* Canadian border crisis
    Texas annexation and, 383
British Band, 57–58
Brooke, George Mercer, 306
Brooks, Horace, 304
Brooks, Jehiel, 329
Brown, Major Jacob, 405
Brown, Jacob J., 41, 52, 90, 101–103, 377, 382
    Canadian border crisis and, 254
Bureau of Indian Affairs, 17, 46

Burgwin, John, 363–364
Butler, Benjamin, 153, 155
Butler, Edward G. W., 95, 98

Caddo Indians, 15, 43, 323–324, 327, 329, 336–337, 341–343
Cadle, Joseph, 332
Cadwalader, Thomas, 92
Calhoun, John C., 77, 86–87, 127, 190, 324–325
Call, Richard K., 84, 195, 197–200
Camp Holmes, treaty of, 351
Canadian border crisis, 249–250, 530n27
  American attitudes toward, 257, 289–290
  Aroostook crisis, 265–266, 274, 281, 306–309
  Britain, American attitudes toward, and, 311–316
  British commercial competition and, 250
  deserter exchanges and, 286–287, 537n29
  federal-local conflict and, 290–293
  filibusters (*see* filibusters)
  Hunters' Lodges and, 292
  martial law and, 276–277, 297, 299, 301–302
  McLeod crisis and, 303–304
  military manpower and, 279–281
  military relations, Anglo-American, and, 253–255, 258–260, 262–269, 306
  neutrality policy and, 275–277, 282, 288, 297, 299
  officer reactions to, 274–275
  Patriot movement (*see* Patriot movement)
  peacekeeping and, 274–277, 281–285
  rule of law and, 275–276
  Windmill Point incursion and, 274, 283–285
Cannon, Newton, 146, 338–339
Carleton, James H., 355
Carroll, William, 153–154, 162

Cass, Lewis, 27, 44, 114, 117–118, 120
  Cherokee removal and, 146
  Second Seminole War and, 197
  Texas and, 335, 337, 373
  Winnebago War and, 53
Chambers, Talbot, 43
Chapman, William Warren, 203, 227–228
Charter Party, 252
Chase, William H., 251
Chehaw massacre, 84–85
Cherokee Indians, 13, 47, 77, 123–124, 423
  alcohol and debt and, 148–149, 155, 167
  diplomacy and, 49, 144, 348, 350–351
  domestic dependent status and, 79, 124
  factionalism and, 319, 345, 356
  Georgia land and, 87, 91, 97, 426
  gold fields and, 106–110
  Indian Territory and, 353–356
  land allotments and, 149
  nationalism of, 124
  North Carolina land and, 115
  Osage conflict and, 319–320, 324, 347, 353
  Qualla incident and, 169–174
  removal of 1838 and, 73, 123–124, 163, 165–174, 176–177
  resistance of, 106, 138, 144, 150, 162, 169–170
  squatter removal and, 83–84, 87, 106–110, 115
  Texas border and, 326, 329, 336, 343
  Trail of Tears and, 141
  Treaty of New Echota (*see* New Echota, Treaty of)
Cheyenne Indians, 12–13, 348, 351, 367, 422
Chickasaw Indians, 83, 353–357
  removal and, 73, 124, 138
  resistance and, 106, 141
Childs, Thomas, 208
Choctaw Indians, 106, 324
  corruption and, 136–138

Choctaw Indians (*continued*)
  diplomacy and, 348, 350, 355
  Indian Territory and, 353–355
  removal and, 73, 123–124, 129, 131–138, 141
  squatter removal and, 83, 135
Churchill, Sylvester, 169, 172–173, 213, 289, 300
citizen-soldiers, 6–9, 374, 422–423, 428, 434
  atrocities and, 8, 20–21, 60, 143, 237
  Canadian border crisis and, 294
  discipline of, 12–13, 59, 146, 237, 424–425, 440
  effectiveness of, 13, 197–198, 237, 434, 440
  expense of, 7, 130, 237
  mobilization of, 12, 422
  officer attitudes toward, 60, 198, 200, 295, 413
  Second Seminole War and, 198–202
  (*see also* militias; volunteers)
civil-military relations, 1–4, 9–10, 38, 47, 177, 234, 433, 436
  Black Hawk War and, 59–60
  Canadian border crisis and, 254, 295, 305–306, 315
  Cherokee removal and, 161, 166–167
  Creek removal and, 92
  Indian Territory and, 353
  mounted mobility and, 20
  removal policies and, 79, 86, 109, 126, 134, 180
  Second Seminole War and, 182–183, 193, 232
  southwestern frontier and, 323, 335, 373
  squatters and, 108
Clark, John B., 134–135, 187, 193
Clark, Michael, 187
Clarke, Newman, 265, 281, 290
Clinch, Duncan, 159–160
  Second Seminole War and, 185–186, 192–193, 195–200, 211–212, 233
Collinsworth, John T., 332
Colquohoun, William S., 136–137, 327

Comanche Indians, 12, 24, 65, 398
  diplomacy and, 348–351
  military attitudes toward, 321
  Santa Fe Trail and, 349–350
  Southwestern border raids and, 317, 320–321, 350–351, 362, 427
Compact of 1802, 90
Congress, 22, 24, 40, 80, 111, 242, 264
  appropriations and, 7, 17, 29, 43, 186, 189–190, 198–199, 307, 349
  Army Act of 1838 and, 280
  criticism of Army by, 407–408
  eminent domain and, 123
  expropriation and, 81, 126
  Indian debt and, 148
  lead tariffs and, 52
  Mexican American War and, 398, 406
  neutrality law and, 271, 275–276
  oversight and, 1, 129, 198
  preemption legislation and, 57, 105, 121–122
  Removal Act of 1830 and, 106
  Santa Fe Trail and, 20, 552n2
  squatters and, 16–17, 37
  Texas annexation and, 368, 389
  Trade and Intercourse Acts and, 16, 80, 358
  United States Military Academy and, 134, 191, 230, 237, 253
Constitution, U. S., 79–80
  abuse of power and, 125
  separation of powers and, 38, 81, 148, 240, 439
  treaties and, 159
  violation of, 113
Cooke, Philip St. George, 60–61, 319, 357–365
Crane, Ichabod, 197, 261, 280, 305
Crawford, William, 83, 100
Creek Indians, 124, 320, 354, 366
  Alabama land and, 109–112, 114–115, 144, 426
  allotments and, 114–115, 119, 138
  Chehaw massacre and, 84–85, 130
  diplomacy and, 348, 350, 355
  Georgia land and, 89–102, 106, 124
  Indian Territory and, 353–355

removal of, 109, 124–125, 138–141, 143, 165
resistance of, 121, 128, 131, 138, 144–145, 147, 149–150, 156, 427
Second Seminole War and, 214, 219, 225
slavery and, 214, 219, 355
squatter removal and, 83–84, 86, 118, 115–118, 138
Crook, George, 8
Crosman, George, 347
Crowell, John, 91–93, 99–101, 105–106
Cummings, Alexander, 325–326, 347
Currey, Benjamin, 153–154
Custer, George Armstrong, 426

Dana, Napoleon Tecumseh, 390, 392, 395–397, 399–401
Dancing Rabbit Creek, Treaty of, 134
Davenport, William, 195, 200
Davis, Jefferson, 58
DeHart, William C., 389
Delaware Indians, 320, 348, 350, 353, 355, 357
Denny, St. Clair, 280
diplomacy
  coercive, 3, 10, 57, 106, 149, 151–152, 208, 256, 258, 356, 372, 493n15
  federal-state, 89–93, 96–101, 105
  international, 258–259, 275, 283–286
direction of armed force, U.S. Army officer corps, 2, 211, 225, 237, 242, 372, 440
  Cherokee country and, 146
  citizen-soldiers and, 20–21, 202, 376
  dissent and, 229, 232
  filibusters and, 413, 331
  nation-state and, 16, 247, 418, 429
disease
  Army and, 59, 181, 187–189, 350, 370
  Indians and, 6, 63, 75, 141, 348, 545n6
Dodge, Henry, 54, 59, 64, 69, 233, 348–349

Donelson, Andrew Jackson, 369, 404
Dorr Rebellion, 252
Duncan, James, 292, 379, 403
Dunklin, Daniel, 66
Dunlap, R. G., 147
Dutton, William, 391, 396
Duval, William, 87

Early, Jubal Anderson, 330–331
Eaton, John, 109, 110, 131, 133, 211
encroachment on Indian lands, 6, 64, 122
  Cherokee Indians and, 87, 108, 146, 158
  Creek Indians and, 109, 112
  federal policy toward, 80, 83, 106
  Ho-Chunk Indians and, 54
  state sovereignty and, 82, 84–85, 87, 96
  white, 16, 23, 49, 51–52, 56–57, 73, 82, 324
  See also squatters
enlisted soldiers, U.S. Army, 229, 287, 296
  brutality against, 40–41, 521–522n23
  civilian hostilities and, 162, 193
  desertion and, 319, 337–338, 397, 532n39, 537n29, 550–551n37
  discipline of, 9, 40–41, 46–47, 202, 297, 327
  ethnicity of, 7, 393
  filibusters and, 274, 331
  officer attitudes toward, 36, 225, 234, 298, 306, 396–397
  Second Seminole War and, 188–190, 224, 232
  squatters and, 109, 111
Erie Canal, 257
ethnic cleansing, 10, 19, 81, 128, 140, 173, 176, 343
ethnocentrism, 35, 47–48, 313, 385
European officer corps and armies, 5, 14, 16, 40
Eustis, Abraham, 86–87, 207, 213
  Canadian border crisis and, 264, 279–280, 286, 293, 300, 308–311
Ewell, Richard Stoddard, 47, 392

624   Index

expansion, territorial, 29, 126–127, 252, 315, 333
  Congress and, 7
  cost of, 7, 64, 72, 425, 430
  Democratic view of, 17, 29
  economics and, 411
  funding of, 7, 10
  Indian resistance to, 21
  international, 239–240
  Jacksonian, 7, 64, 425
  Jeffersonian, 91
  military attitudes toward, 1–4, 10, 14, 19, 25, 29–30, 36–37, 64, 240, 242, 245, 312–316, 340, 412–414
  military strategy and, 25
  pace of, 23–25, 100
  process of, 2
  products of, 241
  revolution and, 238
  sectionalism and, 412
  southern, 100
expropriation, Indian, 7, 10, 57, 65, 77, 87, 123
  Black Hawk and, 58
  Choctaw Indians and, 131–138
  corruption and, 126, 129, 137–138
  cost of execution and, 79–82, 129–131
  Creek Indians and, 109, 124–125
  fraud and, 131, 133–134, 136–137
  Ho-Chunk Indians and, 72
  John Quincy Adams and, 98–99
  justification for, 148
  logistics of, 131–137
  Mississippi Valley Indians and, 63
  oversight and, 129–132
  pace of, 87, 92, 133, 138
  policy and, 57, 87, 99, 123, 128
  political opposition to, 79, 82, 106, 125, 134
  political parties and, 79–81, 126–127
  Potawatomi Indians and, 69–70
  process of, 123, 128
  Removal Act of 1830 and, 106
  resource scarcity and, 75 (*see also* individual tribes)

Fairfield, John, 306–308
federalism, 1, 3, 15, 119, 137, 299–300, 430, 436
  compromise and, 110
  Constitutional restraints and, 81
  failure of, 323
  nation-state and, 417
  political authority and, 204
  reaction against, 83
  state sovereignty and, 77
federal sovereignty, 79–80, 85–87, 121–122, 126, 413
  Alabama and, 110, 119
  Canadian border crisis and, 243, 315
  Georgia and, 90, 96
  Indian Territory and, 355
Field, George, 282
filibusters, 23, 37
  Canadian border crisis and, 241, 243, 245, 247–248, 256–259, 21, 265, 267–269
  desertion and, 532n39
  foreign policy and, 412–413
  law enforcement and, 290, 292–293
  Plains Indians and, 347
  pursuit of, 273–275, 277–278
  Texas and, 331–332
foreign policy, 248, 262–263, 419
  economic relations and, 250, 256–257
  filibusters and, 412, 243
  military attitudes toward, 38, 240–241, 244–252, 384, 392, 412, 415
  republican internationalism and, 246, 249, 251, 380
  Texas and, 329–330
  See also Canadian border crisis
Forsyth, John, 274, 307
Fort Jackson, Treaty of, 83, 123, 125
Fort Laramie, Treaty of (1851), 71
Fort Mitchell, Treaty of, 101
Forts
  Alabama, 222
  Armstrong, 53, 60
  Atkinson, 73–74
  Brady, 48, 259
  Brooke, 194, 222

Claiborne, 324
Coffee, 351
Crawford, 51–54, 56, 58, 74
Croghan, 73, 356
Dearborn, 54, 58, 115
Des Moines, 73–74
development of, 22–23, 26–27, 72–74, 476n30
Fairfield, 308
Gibson, 26, 324–325, 336, 342, 349–350, 353–355, 357
Hancock Barracks, 259, 307–309
Howard, 53, 74, 305
Jefferson Barracks, 53, 64, 357, 368
Jesup, 324, 328, 368
Kent, 308–309
Leavenworth, 64, 353, 357, 365
Mitchell, 109, 111, 115, 118
Monroe, 58–59
Niagara, 255, 261, 282
Sanford, 73, 356
Scott, 355–356
Selden, 324
Smith, 26, 86, 324, 343, 353
Snelling, 51–53, 75–76
Taylor, 324
Texas, 403, 405
Towson, 26, 324–329, 336, 347, 353, 356
Washita, 74
Wayne, 356
Wilkins, 74, 305–306
Winnebago, 54, 58, 74
Foster, William, 168, 170–172, 199
Fox, Henry, 261, 301, 307
Fox-Forsyth agreement, 307
Fox Indians, 8, 49, 51–52, 54, 68
British Band and, 57–58
ceded lands and, 71, 73–74, 427
diplomacy and, 51, 53, 58, 348
Prairie du Chien massacre and, 56
squatter removal and, 56, 115
Fredonian Rebellion, 326–327
Frémont, John C., 29–32, 366
frontier, description of, 15, 17, 34fig
frontiersmen
belligerence of, 3–5, 113

crimes against, 43
greed and, 36, 43, 114, 116, 182, 192, 202–203, 267, 427
legal harassment by, 43, 194–195, 204, 325
racism of, 18
restraint of, 41, 82, 107, 431–432
settler societies and, 11
Texas and, 357–358
violence of, 66–67
fur trade, 24, 27–28

Gaines, Edmund, 69, 128
British Band and, 57
court of inquiry and, 197, 338, 373, 375–377
empathy for Indians of, 18, 41–42
federal-state conflict and, 119, 121
foreign policy and, 251
Georgia peacekeeping and, 91–92, 94–98, 101
Indian agents and, 46
Santa Fe Trail and, 362–363
slavery and, 217
Texas and, 245, 325–330, 333–340, 368, 373–376
Winnebago War and, 53
Gaines, George S., 133
Garrow, H. N., 292
General Survey Act of 1824, 133
gentility, U.S. Army officer corps, 86, 107, 421
Anglophilia and, 313
biases of, 431
brutality and, 223
citizen soldiers and, 199
commitment to, 224
emphasis on, 2
social concepts of, 393
socialization and, 19, 179, 439
social status and, 190, 225
tensions and, 238, 246
Ghent, Treaty of, 255
Gibson, George, 132–137
Gilded Age, 420, 438
Gilmer, George, 107–108, 111
gold mining, 106–110

626   Index

Graham, James D., 32
Grant, Ulysses S., 388
Gray, George, 327–328
Great Lakes, 49
Greenville, Treaty of, 83, 123
Gwynne, Thomas, 290

Halleck, Henry, 385
Harmar, Josiah, 423
Harney, William, 9, 206, 222–224, 226
Harris, C. A., 45, 149–151, 153, 155, 161
Harrison, William Henry, 206, 339
Harvey, Sir John, 307
Hatch, John Porter, 393, 398–400
Hatheway, John, 223, 309
Heatherly War, 64, 66
Heintzelman, Samuel P., 204
Heiskell, Henry, 267–269, 283
Henderson, Thomas, 198, 201
Henry, William S., 342, 390
Hernandez, Joseph, 197, 515n34
Hitchcock, Ethan Allen, 45, 137
  Second Seminole War and, 196, 203, 205, 208
  Texas and, 330–333, 357, 369, 388, 402–403
Ho-Chunk Indians (Winnebago), 49–54, 57–59, 69–73, 75
Holmes, Reuben, 60
honor, professional, U.S. Army officer corps, 205, 216, 227, 282, 296, 410
  desire for, 41
  dissent and, 212
  integrity and, 35–36, 135, 281
  obligation and, 292–293
  popular pressure and, 113, 126–127
  reputation and, 80, 82, 129, 405
  rule of law and, 243
  socialization and, 225, 235
  subordination and, 173
  war and, 381
Houston, Samuel, 330, 342, 336, 368–369, 393
Howe, Marshall, 521–522n23
Hudson's Bay Company, 28

Humphreys, Andrew A., 196
Humphreys, Gad, 86
Hunt, Edward, 388
Hunt, Henry, 380
Hunter, Nathaniel Wyche, 188–189, 204–206, 210, 224, 228–229, 233
Hyde, Russell, 327

Indian agents, 5, 53, 69, 85, 355, 482n17
  Cherokee removal and, 124
  Choctaw removal and, 130, 132–137
  Indian rations and, 69, 75, 132–134, 136
  officer attitudes toward, 44–47, 319, 327, 342
  partisan patronage and, 44–45, 130
  Second Seminole War and, 203
  southwestern border and, 319, 321, 327–328
  squatters and, 54
Indian removal. *See* expropriation, Indian
Indian Removal Act of 1830, 80, 122, 125–126, 134
Indians. *See* Native Americans
Indian Springs, Treaty of, 89–90, 95–96, 98, 100
Indian Territory
  civil-military relations and, 353–356
  immigration and, 324, 328
  inter-tribal relations and, 324, 329, 353–356
  squatter removal and, 323–324, 327
  Texas Revolution and, 336
insulation, U.S. Army officer corps, 212, 219, 280, 371, 435–436, 438–440
  autonomy and, 111, 306
  bureaucracy and, 412
  commissioning and, 130
  honor and, 126
  legal, 16
  logistical efficiency and, 135
  mission effectiveness and, 237
  nationalism and, 236, 242
  peacekeeping and, 258–259

internationalism, 246, 249, 251, 380
Ioway Indians, 51, 55, 63–64, 66, 69, 348

Jackson, Andrew, 40, 44, 104, 433
  Cherokee removal and, 149–153
  Creek removal and, 96–99
  foreign policy and, 249
  goldfields and, 111
  Indian policy and, 77, 110–111, 125, 128, 131, 148
  Indian removal and, 83, 125
  military autonomy and, 159–161
  military courts of inquiry and, 158
  Nullification Crisis and, 122
  squatter removal and, 83–85, 324
  Texas and, 330, 337–340
Jefferson, Thomas, 36, 83, 125, 249
Jesup, Thomas, 69, 127, 138, 143, 158
  Cherokee removal and, 145, 147
  foreign policy and, 262
  Second Seminole War and, 186–188, 193–195, 198, 200, 205–208, 210, 212–213, 222–223, 225–227
  slavery and, 214–217, 219
  Texas Revolution and, 334
  War of 1812 and, 382
Johnston, Abraham, 368, 522n23
Johnston, Albert Sidney, 331
Jones, Evan, 149
Jones, James, 521–522n23
Jones, Roger, 66, 145
Jones, Thomas Catesby, 373

Kansa Indians, 27, 63, 348, 552n2
Kearny, Philip, 311
Kearny, Stephen W., 33, 59, 311–312, 363
  expedition of 1845 and, 367–368
  fort development and, 73, 328
  martial law and, 44
  Mexican American War and, 406
  peacekeeping and, 65–70
Kemble, Gouverneur, 260, 266
Key, Francis Scott, 117
Keyes, Erasmus, 173
Kiamachi River, 26, 323–324

Kickapoo Indians, 49, 58, 324, 348, 355
King, Benjamin, 268
Kingsbury, Gaines P., 353
Kinsley, Zebina, 260
Kiowa Indians, 349–351, 353, 355
Kirby, Reynolds, 168

land lotteries, 143
Larnard, Charles, 168
law enforcement operations, U.S. Army, 2, 38, 179, 244, 365, 435
  Canadian border crisis and, 254–255, 260, 263, 290, 298, 306, 308, 435
  Cherokee removal and, 170
  Creek removal and, 140
  squatter removal and, 107, 115, 118
  Texas border and, 321, 325–328
Lawson, Thomas, 206
lead mining, 51–54, 56
Leavenworth, Henry, 49, 55, 64, 382
  dragoon expedition of 1834 and, 350
  southwestern frontier and, 328–329
  lead district and, 52–54
Lewis and Clark Expedition, 25
liberalism, 242, 249, 253, 362, 420, 431–432, 439
Lindsay, William, 157–158, 162–163
Linn, Lewis, 29, 198, 211, 372
Long, James, 319
Long, Stephen H., 26–27, 32
Louisiana, 205, 319, 325, 333
  Caddo Indians and, 15, 328–329, 335–337, 342, 344
  smuggling and, 255, 328, 330
Louisiana Purchase, 329–330, 419
Lumpkin, Wilson, 147, 151–155, 166
Lundy's Lane, battle of, 170, 188, 262, 264, 281, 313, 324, 372, 381–382, 403
Lyon, Thomas, 158

Macomb, Alexander, 27, 64, 127
  Canadian border crisis and, 253–255, 261, 263, 278
  Cherokee gold fields and, 108
  Indian agents, view of, 45
  Indian relations and, 39, 41

628   Index

Macomb, Alexander (*continued*)
  Indian removal and, 69, 71
  Second Seminole War and, 197, 208, 212–213
  Plains expeditions and, 347–350
  southwestern frontier and, 328–330, 336, 341
  squatter removal and, 112, 115, 119
Madison, James, 242, 421, 432
Malden, battle of, 265
Manifest Destiny, 244, 313, 356, 390, 429
  civilian expansionists and, 244
  officers' view of, 37, 180, 238, 252, 382, 386, 393, 412–414
Manning, David, 117
Mansfield, J. K. F., 204, 212
Many, James, 326–329, 335, 342–344, 349–350
Marcy, William, 291, 369–370, 375, 375
Marias Massacre, 8
Market Revolution, 25, 133, 137, 390, 411, 420, 437
Marshall, John, 79, 159, 433
Marshals, U. S., 194
  arms seizures and, 292
  filibusters and, 305
  Indian removal and, 130
  lottery lands and, 100–101
  negligence of, 297
  partisan patronage and, 44
  squatters and, 76, 80, 110, 115–116
  use of force and, 108, 115–116, 118
martial law, 44, 60, 182, 207, 276, 319, 367, 534n8
  Canadian border crisis and, 276–277, 297, 299, 301–302
Mason, James, 252
Mason, Richard B., 351
McCall, George, 63, 173
  Second Seminole War and, 186–188, 199–200, 203, 208
McClellan, George, 396
McClintock, William, 208, 213–214
McIntosh, James S., 115–119, 121
McIntosh, Roley, 99, 355

McIntosh, William, 89–90
McKenney, Thomas, 53, 98
McLeod, Alexander, 303–304
McLeod, Hugh, 332
McNeil, John, 54, 381–382
McWhorter, George, 285–286, 298
Meade, George, 383, 388, 391, 395, 400–402, 404
Meigs, Return, 87
Mejia, Francisco, 404
Menominee Indians, 49, 51, 56, 58
métis, 75
Mexican American War, 373
  officers' attitudes toward, 384–389, 391–392, 394–397, 405–406
  Palo Alto, battle of, 387, 405
  Resaca de la Palma, battle of, 406
Mier Expedition, 357
Miles, Nelson, 8
militia, 53, 58–61, 63–64, 122, 241, 247, 197–200
  atrocities and, 6–8, 12, 20, 58, 65, 84–85
  Canadian border crisis and, 256, 259, 274, 279, 292–295, 301, 306
  Creek removal and, 89–90, 92, 99–101, 144
  discipline of, 6–7, 13, 57, 130, 424, 427
  effectiveness of, 21, 197, 373–374, 423–425
  expense of, 72, 347, 374
  mobilization of, 64, 68–70, 87, 90, 99, 196, 374
  operational control of, 237
  restraint of, 69
  Second Seminole war and, 196–197, 199–201
  slave rebellions and, 214
  Texas border and, 327, 336, 342 (*see also* citizen-soldiers; volunteers)
Miller, John, 63
Miller, Morris Smith, 189, 220, 273
Mississippi Valley Indians, 63
Missouri Indians, 56, 63
Mitchell, David B., 85, 110
Modoc Indians, 12, 425, 428

Monroe, Captain James, 304
Monroe, James, 89
Monroe Doctrine, 244, 249
Montgomery, William, 283
Moore, Benjamin, 355
Morgan, Willoughby, 43, 52, 56
Motte, Jacob Rhett, 209
Mounted Rangers, Battalion of, 21, 59, 71, 350

Napier, Charles, 373
National Intelligencer, 210, 359
nationalism, 108, 236, 312, 436, 438–439
   Cherokee and, 124
   Europe and, 248
   Jacksonian, 108
   Mexican, 395
   officer corps and, 236–237, 240, 243, 294, 309, 315, 382, 385, 390, 392
   United States Military Academy socialization and, 19, 179, 304
national sovereignty, 19–20, 23, 79, 356, 417, 419, 431–432, 434
   Canadian border crisis and, 241, 243, 255, 259–260, 274–275, 287, 290, 293, 300, 312
   Constitutional law and, 121
   Indian relations and, 42, 71, 126
   international relations and, 165
   officer corps and, 2, 14, 37, 80, 119, 357, 413–414
   Texas border and, 319, 328
   Trade and Intercourse laws and, 155
nation-state, 2, 236, 248, 409–410, 417–418, 429, 436, 438
   accountability to, 231, 237, 250, 252–253, 390, 414, 421
   authority of, 36, 362, 365
   autonomy of, 79, 428
   citizen representation and, 24, 417
   popular pressure and, 81, 299
   rule of law and, 3, 16, 242
   sovereignty of, 245, 247, 269, 274, 283, 285, 287, 290, 416
   subordination to, 18–19, 43, 47, 63, 91, 111, 384, 389, 411

Native Americans
   alcohol and debt problems and, 47, 73, 123, 139, 143, 148, 155
   auxiliaries and, 425
   combat effectiveness of, 12
   crimes against, 42
   domestic dependent nation status of, 79
   economic systems, incompatibility of, 353
   Indian sovereignty and, 40
   inter-tribal relations, 45–49
   inter-tribal violence and, 6, 21, 46, 51, 56
   legal systems and, 22
   military view of, 3–5
   pacification of, 21–22, 46
   removal of (*see* expropriation, Indian)
   resources and, 12–13, 73, 75, 319–321, 423, 427
   tactical skill and, 423
   See also individual tribes
Nauman, George, 265
Navajo Indians, 12, 13, 425, 427
Navy Island, 256, 273, 277, 280, 303
Neutral Ground, 56, 73–74
Neutrality Act, 271, 275–276, 291, 304
neutrality policy, 319, 327, 336
Newcomb, F. D., 110
New Echota, Treaty of, 138, 143, 146, 149, 151, 153–154, 157, 163, 165
Nez Perce Indians, 12, 15, 425
Nicollet, Joseph, 30
nonpartisanship, U.S. Army officer corps, 19, 165, 389–390, 433–435
   accountability and, 227, 236, 314
   bureaucracy and, 18, 410–412
   socialization and, 234, 409
   Texas and, 44, 111, 127, 386–387
non-state actors, 11, 13, 24, 241, 270
Nullification Crisis, 64, 105, 109, 115–117, 119, 435

objectivity, U.S. Army officer corps, 93, 137, 236, 408–415, 435, 439
   Canadian border crisis and, 258–259
   Indian relations and, 4, 45, 70
   slavery and, 215

630   *Index*

officer corps, U.S. Army
  accountability and (*see* accountability, U.S. Army officer corps)
  atrocities and, 9, 223–224
  authoritarianism of (*see* authoritarianism, U.S. Army officer corps)
  autonomy of (*see* autonomy, U.S. Army officer corps)
  brevet rank and, 402–403
  Britain, attitudes toward, 379–383
  careerism and, 409–412
  commissions and, 190–191 (*see also* United States Military Academy)
  cultural inversion and, 219–222, 224
  culture of, 14, 16
  deployment hardships and, 400–402
  direction of armed force and (*see* direction of armed force, U.S. Army officer corps)
  dissent of, 229–233, 250 (see also *Army and Navy Chronicle*)
  filibustering and, 547–548n24
  foreign policy and, 412–415
  frontiersmen, view of, 3–5, 118, 123, 180, 182, 344
  gentility of (*see* gentility, U.S. Army officer corps)
  honor of (*see* honor, professional, U.S. Army officer corps)
  Indian agents and, 46, 85
  Indian relations and, 36–39, 45
  Indian removal, attitudes toward, 79, 91–92, 109, 126–130, 137, 179–181
  insulation of (*see* insulation, U.S. Army officer corps)
  international diplomacy and, 258–259, 283–286
  legal jurisdiction over, 116–118
  legal training of, 17
  Mexico, attitudes toward, 379–381, 383, 391–398
  nativism and, 393, 565n22
  nonpartisanship of (*see* nonpartisanship, U.S. Army officer corps)
  objectivity of (*see* objectivity, U.S. Army officer corps)
  paternalism of, 36, 41–42, 45, 63, 129, 284, 323
  personnel policies and, 231, 497n9
  political views of, 127
  professionalization of (*see* professionalization, U.S. Army officer corps)
  promotion of (*see* promotions, U.S. Army officer corps)
  reductions in force and, 32, 233, 245, 248, 407, 409, 433–444
  resignations (*see* resignations, U.S. Army officer corps)
  rule of law (*see* rule of law)
  rules of engagement and, 113, 276
  socialization of (*see* socialization, U.S. Army officer corps)
  squatter removal, attitudes toward, 80–83, 86
  subordination of, 16–17, 30, 38, 47, 85, 107
  tactical adaptation and, 219–223
  Texas annexation, attitudes toward, 330–334
  values of, 2–4, 9–10, 19, 35–37, 113, 212, 235
  wartime opportunities and, 398–399
  Whiggishness of, 9, 18, 127, 251, 266, 269, 314, 331, 380
Ojibwa Indians, 51, 53–54, 75–76, 430
  inter-tribal conflict and, 27, 48–49, 56, 71, 73
Okeechobee, battle of, 198, 201, 207, 209
Omaha Indians, 55–56, 63–64, 351
Ordnance Bureau, 52
Oregon, 379–383
Oregon Trail, 367
Osage Indians, 67, 325, 348, 552n2
  Cherokee conflict and, 49, 319–320, 324, 345, 347, 353
  Indian Territory and, 350–351, 353–356
Osceola, 184, 203, 215, 220, 222–223, 225

Oto Indians, 55–56, 63, 348, 351, 365
  Kearny expedition of 1839 and, 67, 70
Ottawa Indians, 54
Owens, Hardeman, 116–118

pacification, 4
Page, John, 139, 166
Paiute Indians, 12, 425, 428
Palmerston, Lord, 303, 306–307
Palo Alto, battle of, 387, 405
Panic of 1819, 87
Panic of 1837, 232–233, 256–259, 269, 532n39
Paredes, Mariano, 395–396, 404
Patriot movement, 256, 258, 261, 263, 266–269
  law enforcement and, 273–279, 290, 292–293
  military recruitment and, 280
  sympathy for, 289–290
Pawnee Indians, 63, 67, 365–367
  inter-tribal conflict and, 71, 319–320, 345, 348, 351
  Santa Fe Trail and, 347–350
Payne, Matthew, 157, 166
Payne's Landing, Treaty of, 138
peacekeeping, U.S. Army, 6–7, 14, 73, 193, 237, 356, 435
  Canadian border crisis and, 161, 256, 258, 261, 269, 276–277, 290, 301, 306, 309
  dilemmas of, 39, 107, 285
  encroachment on Indian land and, 64, 67, 109
  inter-tribal conflict and, 71–72, 345
  southwestern frontier and, 319, 323, 327, 374
Pecan Point, 323–324, 326–327
Peck, John J., 401–402, 405–406
Pegram, George, 188–189, 213
Phelps, John W., 198, 203–205, 224
Pierce, Benjamin, 299
Pike, Zebulon Montgomery, 25–26
Pillow, Gideon, 403

Pinckney's Treaty, 419
Plains frontier
  diplomacy and, 348–351, 355
  dragoon expeditions and, 350–352, 365–367
  engineer expeditions and, 26–27
  inter-tribal conflicts and, 345, 347–349, 353
  martial law and, 367
Platt, James, 294
Platte Country, 69
Plympton, John, 75
Poinsett, Joel, 150, 156–157, 165–166
  Canadian border crisis and, 259, 261–263, 268, 275, 277, 279, 291–292, 294, 300
  Indian Territory and, 355
  Second Seminole War and, 198, 208, 215
  Texas and, 339, 341–342
Point Isabel, 405
politics
  expropriation and, 77
  partisan patronage and, 407–408, 499n30
  political parties and, 79–81, 106, 126–127, 252, 407–408, 433–435
  popular pressure and, 81, 87, 150 (*see also* liberalism; populism; republicanism)
Polk, James K., 31–32, 340
  Mexican American War and, 375–377, 404, 560–561n10
  Texas and, 369–373, 377, 388, 406
Ponca Indians, 63
populism, 1–2, 36, 43, 102, 109, 115, 121, 419
  disregard for law and, 326
  frontier, 334
  Jacksonian, 1, 36, 43, 121, 246, 252, 299, 338
  officer corps and, 331
  standing armies and, 373, 411
Porter, Giles, 277, 286, 293

632   Index

Potawatomi Indians, 7, 46, 51, 58, 64, 68, 115
  ceded lands and, 54, 69–71, 427
  inter-tribal conflict and, 49, 53, 57, 73, 356
Prairie du Chien, 56. *See also* Fort Crawford
Preemption Act, 121
professionalization, U.S. Army officer corps, 221, 235, 249–251, 407, 420, 437–440
  accountability and, 180–183, 185, 189–191, 227, 238, 277, 282, 387–390, 409–410, 417, 421, 432
  autonomy and, 287, 306, 421, 428
  careerism and, 409–412, 416, 419, 431
  citizen-soldiers, 198, 201, 224–225, 436
  desirability of war and, 244–245, 309, 384–385, 398–399, 435
  direction of armed force and, 241, 247, 418
  dissent and, 214, 219, 229–233
  filibusters and, 248, 258–259, 269, 312
  international affairs and, 252, 255, 419
  nonpartisanship and, 234–237, 433
  preparedness and, 246–247, 250
Progressive Era, 420, 438
promotions, U.S. Army officer corps, 3, 29, 175, 236, 253, 281
  expansion of army and, 382, 386
  junior officers and, 245, 252, 315, 331–332, 379–380, 387
  pace of, 198, 233–234, 238, 250, 313, 331, 390
  partisan influence and, 130, 300, 408
  resignations and, 400, 408
  seniority and, 16, 28–29, 111, 230, 399
  war and, 243, 245, 315, 386, 395, 398–399, 410

racism, 6, 8, 10–11, 18, 100, 140
  Jacksonian policy and, 182
  Second Seminole War and, 209, 214, 225
  See also slavery

railroads, 428–429
Rains, Gabriel, 135–136
Raymond, Samuel, 391
Read, Leigh, 199
Rector, Wharton, 327
Red River, 323–324, 328, 330, 350, 353–355
Regiment, U.S. Army
  Eighth Infantry, 264–265, 280–281, 301, 306
  Fifth Infantry, 49
  First Dragoon, 21, 59, 72, 350
  First Infantry, 56
  Fourth Infantry, 70, 162, 169, 171, 185, 368
  Second Dragoons, 162, 368, 521n23
  Second Infantry, 57, 70
  Seventh Infantry, 27–28, 86, 99, 337, 339, 350–351
  Third Infantry, 368
Removal Act of 1830, 105, 328
republicanism, 127, 240, 242, 265–266, 420, 430–432, 437–439
  international, 239, 248–249
  Monroe Doctrine and, 244
  officer accountability and, 236
  officer corps and, 380–381, 390
Resaca de la Palma, battle of, 406
resignations, U.S. Army, 331–332
  Second Seminole War and, 180, 183, 185, 189–190, 192, 200, 227, 232, 510n5
  Texas and, 373, 386–387, 400–403, 405, 408
Reynolds, J. G., 140
Reynolds, John, 71–72, 162
Riddle, David, 43
Riley, Bennet, 64, 337, 349
Rio Grande River, 348, 369–371, 376–377, 387, 389–390, 394–395, 398–399, 402–406
Ripley, Eleazar, 319
Rogers, A. W., 291–292
Ross, John, 143–144, 146, 149, 163, 176–177

rule of law
   Andrew Jackson, contempt for, 36, 79–80
   Army officers, adherence to, 1, 3, 36, 242, 258, 260, 290, 413–414, 439
   nation-state and, 417
Rush-Bagot Agreement, 261
Rusk, Thomas, 343

Sabine, Camp, 341–342
Sabine River, 324
St. Clair, Arthur, 423
Saint Lawrence River, 257
Sand Creek Massacre, 7–8
Sandom, Williams, 285
Santa Anna, Antonio López de, 332–333, 336, 396
Santa Fe Trail, 63, 317, 552n2
   caravan protection and, 319, 347–349, 356–363, 366
Sauk Indians, 40, 49, 51–57, 63, 71–74, 348, 355, 427
   Bad Axe, battle of, and, 8
   Black Hawk War and, 4, 58–61
   Heatherly War and, 66
   Neutral Ground with Sioux, 56, 73–74
Schoolcraft, Henry, 27
Schureman, James Wall, 304, 391, 401
Scott, Winfield, 58, 97, 101–102, 117, 127, 252, 289
   Canadian border crisis and, 243–245, 263–268, 270, 273–274, 280, 282, 290–295, 304, 307–308, 311–313
   Cherokee removal and, 165–171, 173
   courts of inquiry and, 157–158
   Mexican American War and, 403, 406
   Second Seminole War and, 185, 192–193, 197, 199, 201–202
   squatter removal and, 122, 328–329
   Texas and, 334, 339–340, 394
   Vinton dispute and, 174–176
   War of 1812 and, 382
Second Great Awakening, 393
Second Party System, 127, 252, 387, 420, 435

Second Seminole War, 71, 211–212, 223
   African American maroons and, 181, 209, 214–215
   Afro-Seminoles and, 181, 214–217, 219
   atrocities and, 8–9, 224–225
   blacks, disposition of, 216–217, 219
   casualty statistics and, 185, 198, 202, 510–511n7
   civil-military relations and, 193–198
   Dade Massacre and, 185, 192, 197, 231
   disease and, 187–189
   flags of truce and, 222–226
   officer cultural inversion and, 219–222, 224
   officer discontent and, 180–183, 185–192, 204–213, 232, 234
   slavery and, 181, 198, 209, 214–217, 219
sectionalism, 23, 106, 121–122, 137, 433, 436
   federal sovereignty and, 315
   officer autonomy from, 17, 109, 111, 126
   slavery and, 215
Seminole Indians, 373
   military relations and, 219–221
   officers' view of, 202–203
   resistance of, 183, 202, 207
settlers. *See* frontiersmen
Seward, William, 303–304
Shawnee Indians, 63, 327
Sherman, William Tecumseh, 176, 206, 228, 383, 389–390, 428
Shoshone Indians, 12
Simonton, Isaac, 135–136
Sioux Indians, 13, 64, 76, 224, 237, 427, 430, 470n7
   alliances, 49
   British Band and, 58
   Canadian border and, 15
   combat effectiveness of, 12, 422
   depredations by, 71, 75
   Fox massacre and, 56
   hunting grounds and, 51, 55

634   Index

Sioux Indians (*continued*)
  inter-tribal conflict and, 27, 49, 64, 70–72, 347–348, 356, 366
  Neutral Ground with Sauk and, 56, 73–74
  southwestern border and, 320–321
  Treaty of Fort Laramie and, 71
  slavery, 340, 355, 389–390, 437
  Second Seminole War and, 181, 198, 209, 214–217, 219
Sloan, T. T., 140
Smith, Ephraim Kirby, 383, 396–399, 405
Smith, Joseph, 40, 189, 213
Smith, Samuel, 100
Smith, Thomas A., 26
Snelling, Josiah, 45, 51, 56
Snively, Jacob, 357–359
socialization, U.S. Army officer corps, 181, 191, 205, 225, 407, 437
  nationalism and, 304, 315, 382, 392, 438–439
  values and, 235, 237 (*see also* United States Military Academy)
Somervell Expedition, 357
Spencer, John Canfield, 208
Sprague, John T., 139–140, 220
squatters, 75–76
  Alabama and, 115–119
  Cherokee land and, 84
  Fox land and, 56
  Ho-Chunk land and, 54
  Ioway land and, 64
  removal policy and, 80–84
  statutory sanction of, 122
  Sauk land and, 73 (*see also* encroachment on Indian lands)
State Department, U.S., 17, 101, 130, 307, 355, 358
state sovereignty, 82, 121, 123–125
  Andrew Jackson and, 105, 117
  assertion of, 77, 91
  Cherokee removal and, 87, 108, 124, 147, 155
  Creek removal and, 89, 91, 96, 100–102, 110
  extension of, 105

Indian relations and, 125, 130
Indian resistance to, 102, 121
squatter removal and, 108, 110, 114, 116–117
Stillman's Run, battle of, 58, 60, 63
Stillwell, William Shaler, 332
Stuart, John, 351
subordination, U.S. Army officer corps, 30, 59, 107, 316
  civilian authority and, 11, 250, 258, 277, 433, 435
  democracy and, 11–12, 426, 438–439
  discretion and, 16–17, 45, 72, 79, 83, 108, 110, 119, 134, 440
  removal policy and, 135, 137, 173, 176, 183 (*see also* Army, U.S., civilian control; accountability, U.S. Army officer corps)
Sully, Alfred, 208
Sumner, Edward Vose, 67, 74–75
Supreme Court, U. S., 91, 123–125
Swartwout, Henry, 335
Swearingen, Joseph Van, 333–334
Swords, Thomas, 366, 368

Tallmadge, Nathaniel, 154–155
Taylor, Zachary, 18, 43–44, 70, 249
  Black Hawk War and, 59–61
  Mexican American War and, 373, 377, 403–406
  peacekeeping and, 345, 355–357
  Second Seminole War and, 187–188, 194–196, 198, 200, 205, 208
  slavery and, 217, 219
  Texas and, 357, 368–376
Terrett, B. A., 361
Texas
  annexation of, 330–334, 368–371, 388–391, 395–396, 400
  Armies of Observation and Occupation and, 357, 368–376, 379, 384–385, 387–388, 396–397, 399, 401, 404–406
  civil-military relations and, 325–328
  Cordova Rebellion and, 343
  filibusters and, 326–327, 331, 335
  Indian threat and, 337–338, 342–344

Index   635

law enforcement and, 325–330
occupation of, 384–392, 400–402
racism and, 323
Revolution and, 330, 332–333, 335–337, 340
Santa Fe Trail and, 357–363
slavery and, 340, 389–390
Texas Rangers, 7, 23
Thayer, Sylvanus, 333, 381
Third Seminole War, 422
Thomas, George H., 228
Thomas, Martin, 52
Thornton, Seth, 406
Totten, Joseph, 249, 259
Trade and Intercourse, 4, 6, 16, 42–44, 47, 122, 470n7
    enforcement of, 79–81, 86, 110, 125, 155, 193, 277, 345
    state sovereignty and, 159
    Texas and, 358
Trail of Tears, 176, 482–483n17
Transcontinental Treaty, 317, 330
Trans-Mississippi West, 25–26
Treasury Department, U. S., 16, 44, 83, 93, 292, 326
    filibusters and, 285, 290, 305
    land allotments and, 114
    land values and, 83
    legal costs and, 43, 118
    militia expense and, 92, 196
    removal process and, 130, 134, 137, 147
    smuggling and, 255, 355
Troup, George, 88–93, 95–97, 100–101
Tsali, Charley, 169, 171–173
Turner, Henry, 366–369, 380
Tustenugee, Halleck, 208
Twiggs, David, 119, 207, 402–403, 406
Tyler, John, 187, 339, 358, 368–369, 375–376

United States Exploring Expedition, 29–30
United States Lead Mining District, 51–52, 54

United States Military Academy, 18–19, 28, 30, 93, 130, 133–134, 137
    criticism of, 183, 192, 220, 230
    officer commissions and, 190–191, 407, 409, 434
    officer socialization and, 28, 30, 132, 191, 194, 224, 237, 253, 304, 390
    Texas Revolution and, 332
Upper Mississippi Valley
    expansion and, 21, 76, 425
    reconnaissance of, 26–27, 74
Upper Missouri Valley, 76, 321, 426

Van Buren, Martin, 138, 145, 162, 165–166
    Canadian border crisis and, 256–257, 259, 303, 307
    Cherokee removal and, 161, 163, 169
    Second Seminole War and, 186
    Texas and, 341–342
Vandeventer, Christopher, 85
Van Rensselaer, Rensselaer, 273
Van Vliet, Stewart, 228
Vega, Romolo de la, 404
Vinton, John, 100–102, 174–176
volunteers, 12, 418, 515n34
    atrocities and, 8
    Black Hawk War and, 57, 59, 61
    Canadian border crisis and, 278–279, 283, 295–296, 307
    Cherokee removal and, 144, 146–147, 149, 155–156, 162–163, 173
    cost of, 7, 131, 347, 373, 425
    Creek removal and, 144
    discipline of, 7, 9, 196, 374
    effectiveness of, 12, 20–21, 59, 423–425
    Georgia Guard, 107
    Indian Territory and, 336
    Mexican American War and, 405
    mobilization of, 337–338, 341
    Second Seminole War and, 196–202, 213, 215
    slave rebellions and, 214
    Texas and, 336–337, 340–342, 373–377
    (*see also* citizen-soldiers; militia)
Vose, Josiah, 195–196, 335, 343, 402

Wager, Philip, 109–114, 118–119, 121
Wahoo Swamp, battle of, 198
Wainwright, Robert A., 193, 213
Wall, William, 205, 213
War Department, U.S., 3–4, 7, 111, 130, 136, 223, 304
  Alabama land allotments and, 119
  brevet rank and, 176
  Canadian border and, 309
  Cherokee removal and, 144, 153
  Choctaw removal and, 134, 136
  court of inquiry and, 365
  directives, vagueness of, 107, 111
  fort development and, 22, 73
  gold mining region and, 108
  lottery lands and, 100
  Mexican American War and, 405
  military personnel policy and, 111, 305
  militia and, 69
  Pawnee aggression and, 347–348
  planning and, 21
  removal logistics and, 136
  Santa Fe Trail and, 350, 357–358, 363
  Sioux and, 13
  slavery and, 216–217
  smugglers and, 328
  squatter removal and, 115
  Texas and, 368
Warfield, Charles, 357, 360
War of 1812, 49, 57, 131, 201, 330
  officer experience in, 18, 372, 379, 381, 408 (*see also* Battle of Lundy's Lane)
Washington, Treaty of, 96, 99, 100–101
Washita River, battle of, 8
Wayne, Anthony, 423
Webb, Richard, 283
Webster, Lucien, 168–169, 173, 308–309
Webster-Ashburton Treaty, 308

West Point. *See* United States Military Academy
Wharton, Clifton, 365–366
Whistler, William, 47, 53, 337–339, 354, 402
White, Hugh Lawson, 150
Whiting, Henry, 267
Wichita Indians, 347, 349–351, 355
Williams, William, 167
Windsor, battle of, 284
Winnebago Indians. *See* Ho-Chunk Indians
Winnebago War of 1827, 51–54
Wisconsin Heights, battle of, 61
Wisconsin territory, 75
Wool, John, 69, 75–76, 97, 127, 142, 252
  Canadian border crisis and, 263–264, 268, 276–278, 280, 289, 292–295, 300, 304, 308
  Cherokee removal and, 144–160
  court of inquiry and, 157, 161–162, 177
  insubordination of, 154–155, 157
  Mexican American War and, 371, 406
  Texas Revolution and, 334
  War of 1812 and, 381–382
Worth, William, 72, 166, 288–289, 382
  Canadian border crisis and, 256, 261, 264–268, 271, 273–286, 290–299, 313
  Mexican American War and, 371, 387, 404, 406
  Second Seminole War and, 186–187, 194, 208, 217, 219, 224
  Texas and, 402–404
Wounded Knee Massacre, 8
Wright, George, 194, 279, 347

Young, Nathaniel, 283–284
Young America, 37, 252, 386